RELIGIOUS THOUGHT IN THE VICTORIAN AGE
A Survey from Coleridge to Gore

RELIGIOUS THOUGHT IN THE VICTORIAN AGE

A Survey from Coleridge to Gore

Second edition

Bernard M. G. Reardon

Longman
London and New York

LONGMAN GROUP LIMITED,
Longman House, Burnt Mill,
Harlow, Essex CM20 2JE, England
and Associated Companies throughout the world.

Published in the United States of America
by Longman Publishing, New York

© Longman Group Limited 1971, 1980, 1995

First published under the title *From Coleridge to Gore*, 1971
First published in paperback as *Religious Thought in the Victorian Age:*
A Survey from Coleridge to Gore, with corrections, 1980
Second edition, 1995.

ISBN 0 582 26514 2 CSD
ISBN 0 582 26516 9 PPR

British Library Cataloguing-in-Publication Data

A catalogue record for this book is
available from the British Library

Library of Congress Cataloging-in-Publication Data

Reardon, Bernard M. G.
    Religious thought in the Victorian age : a survey from Coleridge
to Gore / Bernard M. G. Reardon. -- 2nd ed.
        p.   cm.
    Includes bibliographical references and index.
    ISBN 0-582-26514-2 (hard). -- ISBN 0-582-26516-9 (pbk.)
    1. Religious thought--Great Britain. 2. Religious thought--19th
century.   I. Title.
BR759.R4   1995
230'.0941'09034--dc20   95-15347
                                                          CIP

Set 7A in Monotype 9½ on 12 Times
Produced by Longman Singapore Publishers (Pte) Ltd
Printed in Singapore

CONTENTS

Preface   ix

Preface to the 1980 paperback edition   xi

Preface to the second edition, 1995   xii

Introduction   1

1 The early decades   16
   The Evangelicals   16
   Some High Churchmen   22
   Liberal opinion   29
   Thomas Arnold   35

2 Coleridge   43
   The philosopher   43
   Reason and understanding   45
   Christian belief   52
   The Bible   58
   Church and State   61

3 The Oxford Movement   65
   The inwardness of religion   65
   The Catholicity of the English Church   67
   Orthodoxy and holiness   75
   Justification and sanctification   84

4 John Henry Newman   88
   The Tractarian leaders   88
   Newman's personality   91
   The nature of belief   94
   The '*Grammar of Assent*'   98
   The development of doctrine   105
   W. G. Ward and J. B. Mozley   111

5 F. D. Maurice (1) The Kingdom of Christ   115
   The Coleridgean influence: J. C. Hare   115
   The theologian's vocation   118

Contents

The Kingdom of Christ   123
The marks of the Church   128

6 F. D. Maurice (2) Theology and Life   136
   Theological essays   136
   Church, State and society   142
   Christian socialism   148
   Last years   156

7 The limits of religious knowledge   159
   The Maurician spirit: Frederic Myers and F. W. Robertson   159
   H. L. Mansel   164
   The meaning of revelation   175
   Broad Church tendencies: Milman, Stanley and Mark Pattison   179

8 The erosion of belief   184
   An epoch of change   184
   Freethinkers   185
   George Eliot and others   188
   John Stuart Mill   198
   Note: The influence of Spinoza   208

9 Religion, science and philosophy   210
   The Bible and geology   210
   The theory of evolution   213
   Herbert Spencer   220
   The neo-Hegelians   223
   Personal idealism   230

10 Liberal theology and the biblical question   237
    Essays and reviews   237
    Benjamin Jowett   245
    Further controversy: Colenso on the Pentateuch   251
    Biblical study at the universities   255

11 Literature and dogma   266
    The poets   266
    The hero as prophet: Thomas Carlyle   276
    The critic as theologian: Matthew Arnold   282

12 Scottish developments   293
    Thomas Erskine of Linlathen   293
    Traditionalism breached: McLeod Campbell and
        Robertson Smith   299
    Renewal and reaction   307

Contents

13 Critical orthodoxy   318
     The *Lux Mundi* group   318
     Charles Gore   328
     Liberalism, Anglican and Free Church   337
     Note: Church and Society   348

Appendix I: The Gorham Judgment   351
Appendix II: Liberal Catholicism   354
Appendix III: Gladstone on Church and State   362

Select bibliography   366

Index   370

In Memoriam S.G.R.

PREFACE

It is a sound principle that an author should have in mind as clearly as may be the public for whom he is writing. My aim in this book has been to meet the needs of students of religious thought in nineteenth-century Britain. In the past these were well served, at any rate for the first sixty years of the period, by V.F. Storr's *The Development of English Theology in the Nineteenth Century*, published as far back as 1913; but the volume has been long out of print and in any case its point of view, as well as its interests and emphases, would today call for some readjustment. L. E. Elliott Binns's *English Thought 1860–1900: The Theological Aspect*, which took up the story where Storr left off, is also, although of more recent date, not now available. And the same has to be said for C. C. J. Webb's admirable *A Study of Religious Thought in England from 1850*. Thus the number of works which can be used with profit as an introduction to this subject has become seriously diminished, a fact of which, as a university teacher, I have been repeatedly reminded by my own pupils. To fill the gap, therefore, is what the present volume attempts to do.

I offer it, however, in all modesty. I have not sought to be original, in the sense of providing either fresh facts or unusual judgments. The scope of my book is too limited to admit the former, had they indeed come to light; and as to the latter, although I have not gone out of my way to conceal my personal views, I consider that from a textbook the student has a right to expect unbiased guidance. My intention has simply been to supply as much detail as space allowed in as objective a way as possible, so enabling the reader to arrive at tentative conclusions of his own. There are aspects of my subject to which I would have liked to pay more attention, but to have done so would have been to make the book even bigger than it is and hence more costly.

My material has had, in fact, to be very selectively treated. I have concentrated on what seems to me to have been of real significance as marking new concerns and pointing to farther horizons. What especially is evident during this period is the awakening consciousness that religious belief poses problems not only as to the truth or otherwise of specific doctrines but in regard to its essential nature, evolution and social utility. Accordingly I have not tried to take account of what may be called the literature of popular religious edification. This in the Victorian age gave satisfaction to a very numerous public, but consideration of it was not to my purpose.

My title, I may add, was suggested by the Archbishop of Canterbury's *From Gore to Temple*, published in 1960, and my own book was in the first instance planned as a kind of forerunner to Dr Ramsey's. But I soon realized that to confine myself to Anglican teaching, for all its domination of the theological scene, would have proved a hampering restriction in view of what I felt to be wanted.

The task I have assigned myself has been one purely of historical survey. As the century passed the issues which were to confront theology in our own time came more and more closely into sight, but the temptation to discuss them in their wider bearing had to be resisted. The historian of thought may permit himself to comment, but he should avoid using historiography as a platform for canvassing his own opinions, a mistake which Storr himself sometimes made. The period with which I have dealt witnessed a general relaxation of the ties of orthodoxy and tradition and a growing appreciation of the variety, complexity and ultimate importance of human interests and values. This, religiously speaking, may have been desirable as well as inevitable. I personally think it was. But I believe also that liberal attitudes in religion have resulted in a loss of that sense of the divine rule and governance in life which through much of the nineteenth century was almost instinctive with a vast number of people in this country, of whatever class of society. The difference between the Victorian era and ours is in this respect greater perhaps than in any other. If to us our grandparents' and greatgrandparents' habitual manner of expression often seems tiresomely religiose and doubtfully sincere it may only be because we fail to understand the force of a conviction which we in this age are unable to share with them.

In selecting a period of history for special study one is always confronted with the problem of limits. To avoid arbitrariness is scarcely possible: the continuum of time has to be broken at some point or other. Coleridge's *Aids to Reflection* was published in 1825, but he was then turned fifty and his contemporaries included Wilberforce and the Evangelical philanthropists, High Churchmen such as van Mildert and Joshua Watson, and liberals like the 'Noetics' of the Oriel Senior Common Room. It is therefore with these that I have appropriately begun my study. To fix a *terminus ad quem*, however, has been more difficult. I have balanced the name of Coleridge with that of Charles Gore, another great Anglican. But the greater part of Gore's career—as a bishop indeed all of it—belongs to this century. Yet as editor of and contributor to *Lux Mundi* he is a very significant figure of the last. I have therefore considered his work as far as his *Dissertations*, beyond which I did not feel justified in going. I have alluded, I admit, to men and books of later date; but this has been only where omission of them would in my view have been a fault. To have made the turn of the century an insurmountable barrier would have been pedantic. Nevertheless the year 1901 marks the start of a new epoch and the close of my inquiry.

BERNARD M. G. REARDON

The University of Newcastle upon Tyne

PREFACE TO THE 1980 PAPERBACK EDITION

In bringing out this paperback edition of *From Coleridge to Gore* I have agreed with my publishers to change the title to *Religious Thought in the Victorian Age*. This unfortunately may lead to some little confusion, but my excuse for the alteration is a practical one, namely, that I think the new title more likely to convey to the prospective reader what my book is mainly about. Certainly Coleridge, and a number of other authors of whom I treat in my opening chapters, antedate the Victorian scene by a good many years, but the rest belong essentially to it, even when, as with Bishop Gore himself, they actually outrun it in life-span. Historical periods are, in fact, rarely contained within clearly defined chronological limits. Also I have taken the opportunity of a new printing to correct a number of errors that have come to my notice. If others still lie undetected I shall be glad to be apprised of them.

A more difficult matter is the inclusion, or otherwise, of a general bibliography. This problem indeed I had to face when preparing the first edition, despite the presence of numerous bibliographical references in the footnotes to the text itself. The truth is that a really comprehensive bibliography for all the writers dealt with would be very long—so long as to render doubtful the possibility of a new edition containing it without adding to the bulk, and therefore to the cost, of the volume as a whole. I have therefore decided, if with some reluctance, to attempt nothing of the kind. The serious student who wishes to pursue his researches further will have recourse to the relevant sections of *The Cambridge Bibliography of English Literature*. However, for the benefit of the general reader (as he is vaguely termed) I append a list of works which he is likely to find both instructive and entertaining. Some of course will appeal to him more readily than others, but all, I judge, will repay the time and attention he bestows upon them.

BERNARD M. G. REARDON

Newcastle upon Tyne

PREFACE TO THE SECOND EDITION, 1995

In bringing out this new edition of *Religious Thought in the Victorian Age* I have been able to correct some errors which escaped my attention in its predecessor as well as to introduce a small amount of additional material in the text and footnotes which seemed to me desirable. I have also, here and there, modified the expression of a personal opinion. Otherwise the book remains unaltered. As I said in my preface to the paperback edition, the reference in the then new title to 'the Victorian age' may appear a little misleading. But to repeat what I stated at the time, my excuse for the change was a practical one, namely, to convey to the prospective reader what the volume is mainly about. Historical periods are, in fact, rarely if ever contained within clearly defined limits. Nevertheless the focus of my interest is the Victorian period precisely. Again, I have not attempted to draw up a comprehensive bibliography, which would have turned out to be unwieldy for my purpose. I simply wish, by providing one of smaller compass, to encourage the engaged reader to pursue the subject further—an enterprise I am confident he or she will enjoy—by indicating books which will be found to be more or less accessible. Accordingly I have extended my former list to include publications that have appeared during the past decade or so—evidence, as I believe they are, of the continuing attraction, perhaps slightly nostalgic, which the Victorian cultural scene has for an age so very different from that of John Henry Newman and Frederick Denison Maurice. Again, committed students wishing to pursue their researches further may have recourse to the relevant sections of *The Cambridge Bibliography of English Literature*.

BERNARD M. G. REARDON

Newcastle upon Tyne

INTRODUCTION

The world we know today, with all its turbulence and ceaseless change, had its birth in the nineteenth century, an age which, viewed now in the lengthening perspective of time, seems to have combined progress with order, experimentation with moral certainty, in a measure unique in history. The recollection of it indeed, as one beholds our troubled contemporary scene, can easily arouse feelings of nostalgia. At heart we long for the same sense of security and confidence. And of no sphere of life is this more deeply so than the religious. The Victorian Church had every appearance of advantage. It boasted distinguished bishops, natural leaders of men; it had learned divines and conscientious parish clergymen; its public voice was heeded, in whatever degree, by all but the utterly heedless or grossly ignorant; its influence on society was a pervasive force for moral good. Nor was Protestant dissent a negligible quantity; on the contrary, its numbers, over the century, grew steadily and its stern conscience was always respected and sometimes feared. Likewise the old religion of Rome, from being at the beginning of our period an all but forgotten sect, increased rapidly as the decades passed, despite prejudice, suspicion and even active hostility, until at the end it had won for itself high prestige and an acknowledged place in the nation's life. From the viewpoint of institutional Christianity the Victorian age was outstanding. For most men, at least among the educated classes, were convinced that religion is a matter of serious concern and that its social recognition is a prime responsibility among a people still claiming the Christian name.

Yet to heighten the contrast beteeen that epoch and our own, tempting though it is, would be a mistake. To whatever century, taking the longest vista, historians may wish to assign the origins of the modern world, the modernity that we all readily identify as such made its *début* then, for the last century was an age not merely of innovation but of revolution. [1] When it began, although the portentous political and social upheaval in France was already more than a decade old, it was still scarely to be distinguished, in almost any regard, from a period which today can be evoked only by an effort of the imagination working on knowledge studiously garnered. When it ended, the world war of 1914 to 1918 and its immediate product, the Russian Revolution, were, so to say, but a stone's throw off, and Western technology was bestriding the entire globe. In the interval man's

---

1. Thus A.R. Vidler entitles his history of Christianity from 1789 to the present day *The Church in an Age of Revolution* (1961). K.S. Latourette parallels this with his *Christianity in a Revolutionary Age* (1959–63).

knowledge of himself and of his physical environment had immeasurably increased, whereas his faith in another and better world beyond, of which his ancestral religion yet spoke, was far less secure. Moreover, such a world, to a growing multitude of men, seemed not only not very real but not very relevant either. Life here had become so varied and complex, and its potential so much greater, that concern for a hereafter whose blessings looked shadowy beside more proximate and solid goods hardly justified the mental and moral discipline involved.

Our task in the chapters that follow will be to consider a single aspect of the nineteenth century cultural revolution in Britain; that, namely, of informed thought about the Christian religion, its aims and its truth. The epithet is necessary in order to bring the enterprise within manageable limits. What is offered, that is, is not a sociological study. It certainly does not attempt to deal with its subject in *depth*, if by depth is meant the 'grass roots' of popular belief—the religious aspirations and hopes of those who constitute the great majority of the members of any denomination in any age. What it undertakes, rather, is a survey of the manner in which many believers for whom religion was of serious intellectual as well as practical concern sought to understand it in the light of increasing—and unsettling—secular knowledge. This means that little attention will be paid to publications which simply reiterated traditional Christian doctrine, Catholic or Protestant, in the traditional way, although for a large number of people—as it goes without stating—such works, whether intended for a wider or a narrower public, provided all that they asked. Interest will be concentrated instead on what was new, searching and tentative; on what, it may be claimed, was characteristic of the age itself. Hence the room allowed for writings of a broadly apologetic nature, designed to explain and defend the accepted creed in its relation to history, science and philosophy; for it was in the nineteenth century that the studies known as the history, science and philosophy of religion had their beginnings and fruitful development. More and more was it apparent that even those who, despite inevitable questionings and recurrent doubt, continued to hold to their Christian profession, were finding it natural to stand aside, as it were, from faith itself and to view it with at least a degree of detachment and in a critical spirit. That such an attitude was now judged both possible and proper emerges clearly from the work of two great Anglicans, Coleridge in the early decades of the century and Charles Gore in the last. How far new intellectual approaches to old orthodoxies were to succeed in vindicating them is not, however, to our purpose to estimate. What we shall be investigating are simply, in a particular field, the phenomena of continuity within change, marking as we go what maintains itself in being and what perforce disappears with the years.

At the commencement of the century religious thinking in Britain was in a state of torpor. The Hanoverian Church, after its forays against deism, had succumbed to a quiet worldliness, well content to be untroubled by either overmuch intellectual speculation or 'enthusiastic' piety. Its one great name had been that of Joseph Butler, whose celebrated apology for revealed religion was to be a bastion of orthodoxy for generations to come; for although John Wesley remained to the end of his long life a clergyman of the establishment, strongly repudiating separatism, the Church could claim no credit for the movement he led and little exoneration for the breach which eventually occurred. The leading divines of the period 1790 to 1810—Paley, Watson, Horsley, Porteus—were all men whose attitudes had been formed in the previous age and none disclosed the slightest awareness of the new outlook already evident on the European continent. William Paley, archdeacon of Carlisle, [2] who died in 1805, had won fame with his *Elements of Moral and Political Philosophy* (1785), in which virtue is defined as 'doing good to mankind in obedience to the will of God and for the sake of everlasting happiness', and still more so with *Evidences of Christianity*, which appeared in 1794, and the treatise on *Natural Theology* eight years later. These all in their day were acclaimed as masterly presentations of the theistic case. To us their arguments are as frigid and unpersuasive as are the author's utilitarian ethics. Leslie Stephen concedes Paley's ability but finds his theology 'frozen': 'His writing is as clear and cold as ice'. The focal point of the *Evidences* is the testimony of miracle, from which the divine origin of Christianity draws its conclusive proof. Whether the miraculous is a possible conception is a question not asked: presumably the celestial Watchmaker does as he pleases with his handiwork. Richard Watson, bishop of Llandaff from 1782 until his death in 1816 (although he preferred to reside on his Westmorland estates), was mainly interested in church reform, for the most part equated with anti-popery, revision of the liturgy in accordance with latitudinarian principles and a loosening of the bonds of subscription. Samuel Horsley (d.1806), bishop successively of St David's, Rochester and St Asaph, was a noted scholar and preacher, but a stickler for dogmatic rectitude, his detestation of heretics being matched only by his antipathy to Methodists and sectaries generally. Let the establishment clergy but do their duty faithfully, he urged, and the 'moralizing Unitarian would be left to read his dull lectures to the walls of a deserted conventicle, and the field preacher would bellow to the wilderness'. On the other hand, Beilby Porteus, bishop of London from 1787 to 1809, was both a practical reformist and a warm sympathizer with evangelicalism within and without the Church. But he was no theologian.

Nor, it seems, was theology of much concern to Dissenters either. The Baptists, in the main still loyal to their Calvinist past, were preoccupied with domestic affairs. Robert Hall, their most eloquent preacher, was in his younger days an admirer of the French Revolution and retained a more liberal outlook than was usual among his brethren. The Independents—or Congregationalists, as they later came to be called—were also conservative in their theological tenets, apart from the unitarian fringe attacked by John Pye Smith, a tutor at the Homerton Academy and a man of learning and influence, in his *Letters to Belsham*. Thomas Belsham, himself a former Independent, had founded the Unitarian Society in 1791 and became, with Joseph Priestley, the sect's acknowledged leader. He was the author of a book on Christian evidences, but merely reiterated the arguments of Paley.[3] Christ he

---

2. His other preferments included prebendal stalls at St. Paul's and Lincoln cathedrals, and the rich benefice of Bishop Wearmouth in Co. Durham. See Leslie Stephen in *D.N.B.* 'Paley' (1895). *History of English Thought in the Eighteenth Century* (1876), vol. 1, p. 372.
3. *A Summary View of the Evidences and Practical Importance of the Christian Revelation* (1807).

regarded as a divinely guided teacher of heavenly truths, especially that of a future life with its appropriate rewards and punishments. The gospel miracles he accepted, on what he believed to be the reliable testimony of inspired witnesses. On the Old Testament, however, he felt less assured, questioning in particular the inspiration of Genesis on the ground that it is only a compilation of ancient documents and not the unitary work of Moses. The English Presbyterians, professing a wide degree of tolerance in doctrinal matters, also had strong leanings to unitarianism, whether in an Arian or a Socinian form. But the Wesleyans were rigorously orthodox, although their one scholar of eminence, Adam Clarke, was himself generally considered unsound. Suspected of Pelagian tendencies, he certainly denied the traditional doctrine of the Sonship of Christ, holding that the very phrase 'Eternal Son' is self-contradictory.

It needs little knowledge of these now remote figures to realize how isolated, and in its isolation how jejune, English religious thought then was. It was not until the third decade of the century that new intellectual pressures began to make themselves felt: physical science—although in this field British effort was well forward; a deeper understanding of the significance of history and of the nature of historical change; the Romantic ethos in literature and the arts; and, in due course, the philosophical idealism of Kant and his successors. To these forces must be added that of political democracy and the democratic spirit. Yet even after 1830 positive theological reaction was tardy enough. For long religion had been devoid of intellectual stimulus and was satisfied to rest on accepted beliefs, a naive biblicism and the social prop of the state connection. But the French Revolution and the ensuing wars spelt the end of an epoch in this as in other things and the consequent sense of once more 'living in history', to borrow Arnold Toynbee's phrase, meant that the time sequence itself, as measured in terms of political, social and cultural advance, now entered as a dominant factor into men's estimate of reality. Reason, that is, could no longer stand above the flux of events; life had to be historically viewed. Thus the past, acquiring a new significance, demanded more sophisticated methods of study, methods of which, in Germany, Lessing and Herder had been the pioneers. In fact the nineteenth century may be characterized as the century of History even more than of Science, immense as the latter's progress was to be. At all events the key concept of the whole era, the principle of evolution, was applied by Hegel and the German idealists to human history long before Darwin made signal use of it in biology.

Scientific history was the outcome of the attempt to see the past in its once living movement. Historical facts were henceforth to be presented not in mere fragmentary separation but as parts of an interconnected whole; a whole, moreover, organically related to the present as parent to offspring. The age of rationalism had, of course, not viewed it so, its own procedure being selective and abstract and content with surface impressions. Of any true sentiment for the past or of understanding sympathy with those aspects of it which most conspicuously differ from the present, it had little if any. History might be called on for useful lessons or exposed as a salutary warning, but its intrinsic character was not of interest and was unappreciated. Towards the end of the century, however, a sense of the past as the past and as having an appeal and a significance of its own was already awakened.

4

The ensuing years were to show how the feeling could produce systematic knowledge. Thus the great age of German historical scholarship began, although at first no doubt too much blinkered by metaphysical presuppositions which, for all their apparent usefulness as explanatory categories, hindered rather than helped genuine scientific headway. It was inevitable also that the efforts to recover the past in its true semblance and with the aim of comprehending the laws of historical change should before long be made to include the biblical history and in particular the origins of Christianity, the primary documents of which furnished capital material for the scientific investigator. Here especially, perhaps, was progress impeded by the notion that historiography is really a branch of philosophy and can best yield results when guided by preconceived ideas. This speculative treatment of history was very evident in the work of D. F. Strauss, as too in that of F. C. Baur and other scholars of the Protestant school of Tübingen. Indeed its outcome, in the eyes of the British reading public, only succeeded in giving the 'higher criticism' a bad name, thus retarding its influence. But when historians were able at last to divest themselves of the philosopher's mantle research was at liberty to adopt more profitable methods. The upshot was the development of biblical study on properly scientific lines. This, in the field of Old Testament criticism, was the achievement of such men as Eichhorn, De Wette, Gesenius, Vatke and Ewald, as later of Kuenen, Graf and Wellhausen. But Baur's pre-eminence as a student of the New Testament and the early Church was incontestable, whatever subsequent modifications, often drastic, had to be made in regard to his actual conclusions.

The application of the historical method to Christianity's title-deeds was, however, of more than academic consequence. It had theological implications of far-reaching scope. If the Scriptures were to be examined like any other *corpus* of ancient writings and submitted, as to the circumstances of their composition, to the judgment of investigators whose procedures seemed to require them to lay aside their religious convictions, then what room might be left for the concepts of revelation and inspiration, or what meaning attached to the claim that the Bible possesses unique authority? Further, since the method was genetic, the growth of doctrine and dogma, no less than that of ecclesiastical organization and ritual, would be subject to the same type of scrutiny and the same subtle process of devaluation. Any clear cut distinction between natural and supernatural might well disappear and in the end Christianity itself be seen as no more than a phase in the long course of human civilization. Such risks had none the less to be run. That the researches of the historian would continue, in this realm as in others, was plain, and to ignore them was scarcely more possible than to inhibit them. But the change of attitude to traditional religion which this entailed was something the true nature of which was to be increasingly apparent as time went by. The earlier generation was to blame, we may think, for its timidity in welcoming what it so little understood, but can we say today that its fears were entirely groundless?

The difficulty which historical criticism presented to orthodox faith was its evident refusal to look beyond natural causation to explain events, even those of 'sacred' history. But the scientific historian could not, without abandoning a fundamental postulate of his discipline, attribute any occurrence simply to direct divine intervention. On the contrary, he could not rightly introduce theological categories at all. He might indeed have a philosophical interest, even to the point of attributing history's whole movement to a single operative principle. But such, were it capable of being indentified, was necessarily to be understood as inherent in the process itself. Of any transcendental teleology he could as a historian know nothing. Providence and miracle belong to the context of faith, not of science. The result was a division between religion and history such as the theologians of an older day had never contemplated. For them sacred and secular history had been interwoven, and the pattern of the whole, secular as well as sacred, was divinely ordered. But historical criticism could admit faith, if at all, only at a quite different level of interpretation from its own. Certain events might be allowed a 'transcendent' meaning, but in their purely material and temporal aspect they had to be shown to belong to the natural sequence of things. This it was, more than anything else, which gave rise to the immanentism increasingly characteristic of the religious philosophy of the period. It was a tendency to which the nature-mysticism of the early Wordsworth and later on the influence of the German idealism afforded corroborative expression.

But the historical method was not only genetic; it was comparative as well. Christian theology was being studied as history, but it had to be seen in relation to other religious traditions too, they likewise being taken not merely as true or false but as aspects of man's spiritual consciousness in all its diverse manifestation. Hence the emergence of what has come to be known, perhaps not altogether happily, as comparative religion. Its beginnings in Britain were amateurish enough. Carlyle, in May 1840, delivered the lecture on Mohammed which appeared in *Heroes and Hero-worship*, whilst one of F. D. Maurice's few works to gain a popular readership was his volume of Boyle lectures, *The Religions of the World*, published in 1846. But the very attempt to describe non-Christian religions objectively betokened a significant change from the attitude of mind which abruptly dismissed them as mere human superstition. The subject was one that aroused public interest, the more so as information about these religions increased. For here was an altogether fresh province of knowledge—in Frazer's words, 'the faith and the practice, the hopes and the ideals, not of two highly gifted races only, but of all mankind'. It was one also, as Jowett sagely predicted, which was to have an immense influence on Christian theology itself.[4] With the work of E. B. Tylor; Robertson Smith—notably his *Religion of the Semites* (1889); Frazer himself, the first edition of whose *Golden Bough* came out in 1890; of the orientalist, Max Müller, editor of a series of translations, 'The Sacred Books of the East'—'the real history of man', he suggested, 'is the history of religion' of Edward Caird; F. B. Jevons and Andrew Lang, the whole vast field of research at last came under exploration. But in the light of the new knowledge and with a widened intellectual sympathy resulting from it the accepted view of the absolute uniqueness of Christianity needed qualification. At any rate, even when its distinctiveness and special claims were insisted upon its apparent affinities with other faiths and cults had the almost inevitable effect of causing its authority to be questioned as a wholly God-given revelation of truth.

4. See *The Epistles of St Paul* (1855), ii,p. 186.

That a heightened sentiment for the past was a leading feature of the Romantic movement is a commonplace. Yet it was one element only in a complex phenomenon. Romanticism, in literature, music and the visual arts, as likewise in philosophy and theology, defies precise characterization. But in English thought, as compared with German and French, it was, again, a less potent impulse; the national insularity tempered it. Nevertheless the age of Wordsworth, of Coleridge and of Byron—the last-named, in many eyes, the very embodiment of the Romantic spirit—could not but be aware of a changing intellectual climate. Reason was quickened, sometimes indeed superseded, by imagination. Coleridge defined it now as 'the power of universal and necessary convictions, the source and substance of truths above sense, and having their evidence in themselves'. The knowledge of truth, for the Romantic mind, was a visionary experience, an intuition or immediate beholding. But vision, intuition, is of its very nature subjective. External proof is irrelevant, even alien to it. 'All the subtleties of metaphysics', wrote Rousseau, 'would not lead me to doubt for a moment the immortality of my soul or a spiritual Providence; I feel it, I believe it, I desire it, I hope for it and will defend it to my last breath'. To this frame of mind a mere calculation of probabilities on the basis of adducible evidence could effect nothing of importance. As Schleiermacher put it: 'The feelings, the feelings alone, provide the elements of religion', an utterance paralleled by Keats's 'I am certain of nothing but the holiness of the Heart's affections and the truth of the Imagination'. Not argument but experience became the foundation of faith, an experience personal, individual and in its ultimate essence incommunicable. Coleridge insisted that what justifies Christianity is a man's own felt need of it. Maurice believed all men to be religious and have only to be made conscious of the fact. The whole trend of nineteenth-century thought was thus a retreat from the view, self-evident to the age of reason, that religion is a body of propositional truths requiring demonstration and that what cannot be so demonstrated may be discarded. No abstract verification of religion but its practical utility was the pertinent criterion. Even in Catholic France it was religion's social function that particularly impressed the more original minds. Chateaubriand's *Le Génie du Christianisme*, published in the spring of 1802, on the eve of Napoleon's concordat with the Vatican, marked the beginning of a new style in apologetics. Philosophically null, it disclosed all the same an emotional thirst for religion which only the living imagination could satisfy.[5] But it was also, in the words of Sainte-Beuve, 'as the rainbow, a brilliant token of reconciliation and alliance between religion and French society'.

In the intellectual approach to Christianity a parting of the ways was signified by the critical philosophy of Immanuel Kant, the counterpart in the sphere of thought to the French Revolution in politics. Old-style rationalism in religion was demolished, although it was the Scotsman Hume who first brought home to the

5. The appeal was frankly aesthetic: 'Le christianisme sera-t-il moins vrai quand il paraîtra plus beau? . . . Sublime par l'antiquité de ses souvenirs, qui remontent au berceau du monde, ineffable dans ses mystères, adorable dans ses sacrements, intéressant dans son histoire, céleste dans sa morale, riche et charmant dans ses pompes, il réclame toutes les sortes de tableaux' (*Le Génie du Christianisme*, pt. I ch. i). Sainte-Beuve saw in Chateaubriand little more than 'a sceptic with a Catholic imagination'.

German master that the work needed doing. Things–in–themselves, the *noumena* that lie beyond *phenomena*, we do not and cannot know, says Kant, because they are outside human experience. At least, when the mind strays beyond its province it at once involves itself in contradictions—in *antinomies*. Freedom and necessity, for example, are each demonstrable, but yet are mutually inconsistent. Hence any so-called proof reaching out to the supernatural realm is bound to fail. Of the classical arguments for divine existence not only does the ontological harbour a fallacy but the cosmological also, which itself turns upon the ontological; whilst the teleological, despite its obvious appeal, is unable to show that the Creator's attributes are infinite. Yet for Kant these criticisms do not end in pure scepticism. His aim, in his own words, was to abolish knowledge in order to make room for faith, which alone is religion's proper basis. And faith springs from man's moral nature, which testifies certain fundamental truths. That God exists and that man possesses freedom and immortality are to be accepted, that is, as postulates—not theoretical dogmata but presuppositions of an essentially practical import. Although, in other words, morality does not *prove* God's existence the fact that to us moral criteria are inescapable makes such existence a necessary assumption on our part, if the highest good known to man is to be fulfilled. Hence if God is to be discovered at all he must be sought in man's own inner life as a moral being, which is the only real sphere of human freedom. Salvation accordingly consists in that ethical self-realization which is open to every rational creature. It implies no external restraint or arbitrary change in human nature, since in obeying the moral law we but submit to an imperative the reason and justice of which is wholly in accord with our own best judgment. And what universal morality thus dictates religion will interpret as the command of God, the community of all who so recognize it—the 'ethical commonwealth', in Kant's term—providing the requisite environment for the promotion of individual virtue and happiness.

This ethical commonwealth was easily identifiable with what Christian faith understands as the Kingdom of God, or the Church Invisible. Kant's own attitude towards Christianity was determined by his philosophy. He approved it for its approximation, closer than that of any other religion, to the ideal of a purely ethical theology. Christian doctrine presented the deepest moral insights under symbolic form; but the symbolism, to continue to remain acceptable, had to be interpreted in harmony with morality. The idea of heaven, for example, is profoundly inspiring, but duty must be pursued for its own sake and not from hopes of a celestial reward. The Christ of the gospels Kant saw as an embodied ideal of moral goodness; not, however, in an absolute sense, since moral man himself, who has the shaping of all moral idealism, is still in course of development. The real significance of Jesus stands in the immense influence his example has exerted upon man's own moral progress, a truth obscured by preoccupation with metaphysical accounts of his person.

In these respects Kant's impress upon nineteenth-century religious thought was to prove indelible. Its outcome is to be seen, in Germany mainly, but also to some extent in France and the United States of America, in the teaching of Albrecht Ritschl and the Liberal Protestant school which he inaugurated. But any direct influence Kantian philosophy might have had on English theology, apart from

Coleridge, was not extensive, and Ritschlianism certainly had no impact here until near the end of the century.[6] The influence which did make itself felt, after 1870, was that rather of Kant's idealist successors, at first as mediated by T.H. Green, although the Caird brothers certainly went back to the original fount of the doctrine, to Hegel himself. The attraction of idealism was in the means of exit it afforded from the *impasse* of mechanistic naturalism. In a modified form it 'claimed supreme worth for self-conscious personality as the only possible subject for the spiritual activities, knowledge, love and goodness, on which we set the highest value, and as therefore the only adequate revelation of the ultimate reality which we call God'.[7] Green's epistemology led him to posit an 'intellectual principle', a 'self-distinguishing consciousness', an 'eternal intelligence' as the organizing principle of the universe, even if he failed to make clear any final distinction between the universe, and the personality which informs it. But in an age when the prestige of science (conjoined as it often was with a positivistic philosophy ostensibly based on it) was steadily rising any reasoned assurance that the essential nature of the universe is spiritual was as music in Christian ears, and the theologians who contributed to *Lux Mundi* were glad to make all the use they could of the idealist metaphysic. Moreover, idealism gave to the historical process a full valuation. Kant's thought, progressive in other respects, had been typical of its century in its non-historical character. But Hegel and his school had identified spirit by its historical manifestations. Hence, therefore, the importance they attached to historiography. But the historical processs was interpreted also as evolutionary or developmental, an idea which concurred (as it seemed) with Darwinism. Spiritual philosophy and physical science thus might go hand in hand.

For the shadow of physical science alone undoubtedly brought a chill to the hopes and sentiments of orthodox religion. The area of life of which the sciences could now claim to provide exact knowledge was immense and continually growing. Would it in the end assert a dominion over the whole of man's reason and understanding? If so, what would have become of the very different world view described or implied by traditional Christianity? The latter still professed to give sufficient account of man and the universe in terms of divine purpose. But the God hypothesis, as was becoming ever plainer, was one with which science, intent only upon so-called secondary causes, could very properly dispense. Theological or metaphysical control of its conclusions was therefore precluded. Facts must be sought and correlated for their own sake, in the interest of truth itself. Further, autonomy of procedure was clearly leading to unity of view. Nature was seen to be at all levels subject to the operation of the same inherent forces and to be capable of description as a unitary system of law. A clash between religious beliefs and scientific theory was thus inevitable: first, on the question of the Genesis story of the creation, then on Darwinism, especially as propounded by T. H. Huxley, whose respect for the susceptibilities of theologians was minimal, and finally on the doctrine of materialism generally, a philosophy destructive of all spiritual values.

6. Ritschl's principal work, *Justification and Reconciliation*, appeared in an English translation (by H.R. Mackintosh and A.B. Macauley) in 1900 (2nd edn. 1902). See the present author's *Liberal Protestantism* (1968).
7. C.C.J. Webb, *Religious Thought in England from 1850* (1933), p. 112.

The issue of science *versus* religion was most prominent from about 1860 to 1880, when both sides were in the mood for conflict, the theologians from an authoritarian confidence whetted by fear, the scientists (or their publicists) from an exhilaration born of achievement. The struggle was carried on with much bitterness, particularly since the combatants on either hand were making larger assumptions than a cool concern for truth would have warranted. A truce was possible only when it was recognized that the spheres of both were limited. Philosophy contributed not a little to the settlement; in the case of science by pointing out where its bounds might be said to lie, namely in the selectivity and abstractness of its methods; and in that of religion by enhancing its understanding of what the spiritual dimension of life does and does not include. Moreover, as remarked above, the principle of evolution provided a useful area of conceptual common ground. At least, as the century drew to its close, theologians and scientists were no longer merely shouting at one another from opposite sides of a brick wall. Charles Gore even went so far as to claim that if the Darwinian theory had been formulated in the intellectual atmosphere of early Greek Christianity—the Fathers being accustomed to interpret the opening chapters of Genesis allegorically—it would have presented no difficulty for faith[8].

The aid and succour which idealist philosophy brought to orthodox theology in its confrontation with science was, however, paid for at a price. This, we have noted, was the acceptance, in varying degree, of the idea of the divine immanence. Naturalism could be rejected as inadequate to explain human experience as a whole, or indeed science itself; but the philosophers' conception of nature was such also as to lead them to seek its determining spiritual principle *within* rather than outside nature's own observable processes. On this view the historic doctrines of Christianity demanded reinterpretation as symbolic representations of the inner significance of man's life, in all ages and under all conditions, rather than as factual statements of unique and miraculous events directly expressive of a transcendent divine will. The implication was clear that 'super-naturalism', in the old sense of the word, was now incapable of acceptable restatement, and values whose source had hitherto been located in a world 'other' than this must henceforth be sought within the structures of the here and now. Orthodoxy, in truth, was not prepared to admit the conclusion outright, and its own vigorous revival towards the end of the century was in large part actuated by the genuine conviction that a *super*natural faith could yet be successfully adapted to the spiritual needs of the age. The assurance was one for which Gore contended all his life, despite a philosophical atmosphere increasingly inhospitable to Christianity's basic postulates. But there could be no disguising the fact that religious belief was under heavy pressure from a cultural environment no longer disposed to derive its valuations from or pin its hopes to an order of things for which the phenomenal world is but a temporary screen.

However, the forces making for change in religious outlook were not only intellectual; they were also political and social. To some, as to Charles James Fox,

8. *Belief in God* (1921), p.10. He was not at all sure that even Paley and Darwin were wholly irreconcilable . See *The Incarnation of the Son of God* (1891), p. 31.

10

or the poet William Wordsworth, the French Revolution had come as a new vision of hope for mankind:

> Bliss was it in that dawn to be alive,
> But to be young was very heaven.

With the setting up of the Terror, on the other hand, and the European war which followed, the movement's appeal waned, even for these enthusiasts. Revolutionary ideals now appeared subversive of all order in society. In particular, the French innovators had shown slender regard for ecclesiastical authority or even for religion itself. Had not the Goddess Reason, in the person of a woman of the Paris streets, been enthroned in the cathedral of Notre Dame? Furthermore, behind the Revolution lay not only deist modes of thought but, in the philosophy of men like Holbach and Cabanis, sheer godless materialism. Thus to sober opinion in England the dreaded name of Jacobin was usually synonymous with atheism. The immediate result was a reawakened concern for the safety of the Church and the maintenance in the nation of a sound Christian profession. Certainly among the rapidly growing industrial population respect for the Church and its clergy was scant enough, to the point of overt hostility. But dislike of the ecclesiastical inheritance was for the most part an expression of a more widely diffused resentment against class-privilege in general than of any real rejection of religion as such. Accordingly in the early decades of the century the Church actually stood higher in public esteem than it had done for a generation or more previously. In its turn the Church, despite its notorious antagonism to reform—the solid opposition of the bishops to the great Reform Bill of 1832 has always been cited as the palmary instance of clerical intransigence—felt the necessity of making some demonstrable response to the needs of the age, and a time of unwonted activity began. Abuses, all too numerous, in the ecclesiastical system were removed; the Ecclesiastical Commission was established in 1835, new churches were built in districts hitherto unprovided for, and Christian responsibility in the matter of popular education was freely recognized. At the outset of Queen Victoria's reign the national Church was astir with a new sense of its obligations and mission, of which the Oxford Movement, in principle anti-liberal though it was, appeared as the timely and challenging utterance.

Yet all this was but a phase, a reaction to an existing situation. Of more permanent significance was the growth over the century of democratic feeling and aspiration. The traditional structure of society, once fear of Jacobinism and revolutionary subversion had begun to abate, became an open question. Distinctions of social class and wealth no longer seemed pre-ordained and unalterable. The liberty on which Englishmen were wont to pride themselves also entailed freedom from the iron restraints of poverty; nor could liberty be fully realized unless equality accompanied it. The prophets and doctrinaires of the new democracy were the Philosophical Radicals—Jeremy Bentham and his disciples, who proceeded on the assumption that it was both possible and necessary to apply disinterested intelligence to social problems. Their principle of the greatest happiness of the greatest number, warmed by the sentiment of a common humanity, was in intention plainly altruistic. The result was the gradual permeation of the public mind with a feeling of social responsibility. Men, it was now realized, possess a natural solidarity, of which the body politic, incorporating and articulating the community's reason and conscience, is alike the expression and ultimate safeguard.

Such ideas could not but have their effect upon religious opinion. The day of individualism, rationalistic or pietistic, was passing, making possible a recovery of the idea of the Church as a collective entity. Indeed, for F.D. Maurice all humanity was one in Christ its Head. Further, even the individual, when seen in the due perspectives of history, was manifestly the product of the social conditions under which his life was lived; conditions not immune therefore to a moral judgment rendered all the more imperative in view of the economic and social problems thrown up by the rapid growth of industrialism. Christian thinkers, that is, felt increasingly obliged to consider man not only as a soul on pilgrimage to heaven but as he is at present, in his determining social and economic relations. It was no fit discipline of the spirit that the body should be arbitrarily deprived of its elementary needs. But the lesson was not easily learned and it took the Church the best part of the century to comprehend on the social plane the full ethical implications of its own gospel. The so–called Christian Socialist movement at the turn of the half-century was an early and single instance of this concern, even if by socialism its promoters meant not an economic doctrine but an ethical ideal: 'the science of partnership among men'.[9]

The main lines of development in religious thought in Britain during the century can be summarily indicated. At the outset, as we already have seen, intellectual interest was at a discount. Influences from the European continent had not yet begun to make themselves felt, and the stagnation of the closing decades of the preceding century continued. In any event men's minds were preoccupied with national affairs. After 1820, however, new trends were clearly discernible. First we have the liberal or 'Noetic' school at Oxford, associated with the Oriel senior common room: rationalizing—hostile observers complained that the place 'stank of logic'—and well aware that increasing historical knowledge would mean the end of some long-cherished illusions, yet sharing also in the narrowness and insularity of their time and place. Next to be noted is the teaching of their Scottish contemporary, Thomas Erskine of Linlathen, which, as against mere 'evidence' theology, made a direct appeal to spiritual experience and the inward testimony of the feelings—a man whose writings Maurice judged to mark 'a crisis in the theological movement of this time'. Thirdly, there was the phenomenon of Coleridge, a genius of astonishing gifts whose achievement, although falling short of promise, was to prove, through his religious philosophy, one of the most potent spiritual influences of the century and who, already in advance of the Oxford Movement, declared it his 'fixed principle' that a 'Christianity without a Church exercising spiritual authority is vanity and dissolution'. The decade 1830 to 1840 saw that Movement's rise, with its call to the national Church to a renewed

9. On the later phases of the Christian Social movement see below, pp. 148ff. and the appended Note to Ch. 13.

understanding of its true status and vocation. Yet for all Tractarianism's *réclame* and apparent novelty its impulse was reactionary and in intellectual terms produced less than what the talents and scholarship of its adherents would seem to have augured. Its strength lay rather in its practical effect on Church life and worship. As a revival of faith within the university of Oxford itself its force was spent by the time of the defection in 1845 of its leader and dominant personality, J.H. Newman. After 1845 changes in the intellectual climate there were unmistakable. Mark Pattison, a Tractarian disillusioned, might subsequently rejoice that the spell of ecclesiasticism had been broken and the university at last set free to go about its proper business—a large measure of reform in the ancient universities was introduced in the 'fifties[10]—but a period was beginning of intellectual questioning and unsettlement: science was confronting devout churchmen with some awkward problems; the Bible, under the searching light of historical criticism, seemed to be losing its authority—to be the work, of God perhaps, but also, more and more patently if the critics were to be believed, of fallible men. Inquiry into the literary history of the Old Testament was disturbing enough, but the publication in 1835 of Strauss's *Leben Jesu*, as still more the English version of it by George Eliot a few years later—W.G. Ward remarked at the time that it was selling more than any other book that had appeared on the market—presented the supreme issue of the New Testament in the shape of an alternative before which traditional belief could not but tremble. Yet it was at this time that Maurice, a conservative by instinct and a theologian in every facet of his thought, stood forth as the unflinching upholder of Christian idealism, even if to many of his contemporaries the obscurity of his utterance also attenuated the relevance of its message. But his influence was to persist and bear fruit later.

In the second half of the century the Christian churches found themselves living in an obviously changed environment. The inescapable presence of physical science, intent on pursuing knowledge by its own tried methods, had to be reckoned with. Criticism of the Scriptures, although it might still appear impious to the majority of churchmen, could not now be disregarded and some attempt to meet it constructively was imperative. *The Origin of Species* was significantly followed, a year later, by *Essays and Reviews*, whilst the controversy which the latter provoked was soon to be further enflamed by Bishop Colenso's idiosyncratic study of the Pentateuch and Joshua. But by the 1870s Christian opinion, or at least its better informed sections, was beginning to accept the facts of the situation. The theory of evolution had to be assimilated, and divines whose loyalty to the creed could not be doubted were learning to approach the Bible in a state of mind less inhibited by dogmatic presuppositions. Meanwhile a new and sophisticated attempt to defend the whole concept of revelation from philosophical attack had been undertaken by a Bampton lecturer, H.L. Mansel, on the seemingly paradoxical basis of complete metaphysical agnosticism, in a way indeed foreshadowing theological trends

10. The Oxford University Act was passed in 1854, that affecting Cambridge two years later. By the abolition of religious tests at matriculation dissenters were able to be admitted as undergraduates. Such tests were also abolished for most degrees. Owen Chadwick, *The Victorian Church*, vol. 2 (1970), pp. 439-462.

characteristic of our own day. Nor, in the course of the long theological debate, were the imaginative writers silent. Tennyson voiced both the misgivings of his era and its determination to cling to 'the larger hope'. Browning, fundamentally optimistic, was nevertheless under no illusions as to the gravity of the trial to which religious belief was being subjected. George Eliot, among the *avant-garde* thinkers of the time, was, however, no iconoclast and to the end remained deeply sensitive to the appeal of a faith she had herself early on felt compelled to abandon. In her fashion she was typical of the intellectual dilemma of the age.

The three final decades of the century are marked by an effort to imbue the old orthodoxy with new confidence. The great Cambridge triumvirate, Westcott, Lightfoot and Hort, were the first on the scene, and with their work biblical study in this country was able at last to face comparison with what had been done in Germany. For the most part they were conservatives, Westcott especially so; but their conservatism was one of considered principle, not of lethargy or fear. With the appearance of *Lux Mundi* in 1889 a group of the younger High Churchmen made it clear that the heirs of Tractarianism also were set upon modifying its traditionalism and even giving up positions once judged to be vital. Evolution was made a leading *motif* in their philosophy and the doctrine of biblical inerrancy was frankly jettisoned. By the close of the century the dogmatic stance of the Thirty-nine Articles was widely felt to be an anachronism.[11] Adjustments had to be effected and concessions made at many points. The question now was not whether such a course was permissible but where precisely it could be halted. Gore, the outstanding English theologian of the day, was himself scarcely in two minds. The Scriptures, he held, must be seen to have been in their outward form products of their time and circumstances, and thus with inevitable human limitations attaching to them. But the content of the creed remained and must remain the residuum of faith apart from which Christianity ceases to be orthodox in form or even recognizable in substance. The Broad Church party, moreover, so far from having been 'extinguished by popular clamour', as had been claimed some years earlier, had very arguably succeeded, in the words of a then rising young liberal, Hastings Rashdall, 'in leavening the tone of theological thought and theological temper among the clergy and religious world at large'.[12] By the beginning of the new century Broad Churchmen had become definitely liberal or 'modernist', to use a term then coming into vogue,[13] and was attracting adherents from Evangelicalism, hitherto still solidly conservative.

11. Already by the terms of the Clerical Subscription Act of 1865, a detailed subscription 'willingly and *ex animo*' to the Articles had been changed to a 'general assent'. A clergyman was now required simply to declare his belief in 'the doctrine of the [United] Church of England [and Ireland], as therein set forth, to be agreeable to the Word of God'. The new form also necessitated an alteration in Canon 36 of the Canons Ecclesiastical. The disestablishment of the Irish Church was carried out by Gladstone in 1869.

12. P.E. Matheson, *The Life of Hastings Rashdall* (1928) p. 45.

13. Cf. H.D.A. Major, *English Modernism* (1927), ch. iii, where the author distinguishes between Broad Church, Liberal and Modernist. But the last of these terms was used more precisely of a movement of thought in the Roman Catholic Church, and many Anglican liberals objected to its adoption on that account.

Outside the established Church the demands of modernity were similarly gaining recogition. The Baptist and Methodist bodies continued to hold the new views in suspicion, but Congregationalism, always more intellectually alert, showed no such hesitation in welcoming them, and men like Fairbairn and, a little later, Forsyth were easily among the best theological minds of the period. In Scotland the century was largely one of movement away from the more or less strict Calvinism of the past, a movement in which the most prominent figure was John McLeod Campbell, who preached an unlimited atonement, as the only possible ground for man's assurance of God's absolute love. In the field of biblical study the path of criticism was opened up by William Robertson Smith. Both men paid for their independence by loss of office, ministerial or academic. But by 1900 the intellectual outlook of the Scottish Churches, established and free, had greatly changed, and as in England the old orthodoxy was being either restated or in certain points dropped altogether.

The era of religious thought which we are to survey in the ensuing chapters was thus one of adjustment, slow and at times painful, to intellectual and social conditions of a kind increasingly to render the religious interpretation of life difficult in a way that it had never been before. Religion was no longer conceived as a set of ideas and aspirations which society, or at any rate its more responsible section, was bound to maintain as a matter of conscience. The attitude of faith had now to be defended—explained and if possible justified in terms which to the less sophisticated were bound to seem remote. Indeed the moral prestige of faith passed to science itself, whose primary virtue was intellectual integrity and respect for evidence. 'Agnosticism', it has fairly been said, 'had the temper of the age on its side',[14] especially when retreating credulity, in its last-ditch struggles, appeared to care for nothing beyond its own self-preservation. Yet at times also one kind of dogmatism became the excuse for another: the cocksureness of some representatives, or partisans, of science likewise was uninviting. The impression left on the student of the history of ideas is that at the close of the period the received Christian teaching was finding it necessary to concede so much to its critics as evidently to have undergone a complete transformation. The divine, it could be said, had now to be sought much less in a transcendent Creator, Lawgiver and Judge than in an immanent Power, progressively manifesting itself in the course of the universal progress, including man's own advance in cultural self-realization. Theologians and philosophers who were anxious for their responsibility to historic Christianity might endeavour to resist the tendency, and assuredly before the present century was many years old a reaction against it had set in. But the intellectual comprehension of religion and its place in life was profoundly altered, with the consequence that in our own day the former clear-cut alignments and antagonisms, Catholic and Protestant, High Church and Evangelical, Anglican and Nonconformist, appear less and less consistent or even intelligible. It is a development whose implications are perhaps not wholly reassuring.

14. G.M. Young, *Victorian England* (1936), p. 109.

Chapter 1

THE EARLY DECADES

The Evangelicals

'The deepest and most fervid religion in England during the first three decades of this century', wrote Henry Parry Liddon, 'was that of the Evangelicals. The world to come, with the boundless issues of life and death, the infinite value of the one Atonement, the regenerating, purifying, guiding action of God the Holy Spirit in respect of the Christian soul, were preached to our grandfathers with a force and earnestness which are beyond controversy.'[1] As a party within the Church of England the Evangelicals, although the heirs of the religious revival of the preceding century the outcome of which had been the Methodist schism, were loyal adherents of the establishment and the Prayer Book. No doubt, too, they were 'Low' Churchmen, but at the same time they were clearly distinguishable from the Whig Latitudinarians who commonly bore the designation. Always dedicated to charitable causes, they, like the Methodists, nevertheless cultivated the inner life as the spititual substance of all true religion. In the impression they made on the public mind of their day they were unique, combining as they did an energy for good works with an evangelistic zeal and a personal moral discipline which provoked both admiration and dislike, but rendered indifference impossible. Criticism they certainly encountered: the party, although influential, was not popular. The majority of the clergy resented or distrusted them; not entirely without reason, for the tone of evangelical piety was sometimes distasteful even to men of goodwill.

Preferment, in the early days, eluded them. Henry Ryder, appointed to the see of Gloucester in 1815, was the first to be raised to the episcopate. The bishop of London, Beilby Porteus, was markedly sympathetic, but as a rule his brethren on the bench were chary of ordaining men with known evangelical leanings, whilst the universities, as the experience of Charles Simeon at Cambridge well illustrates, were *milieux* of a kind which no evangelical clergyman was likely to find very congenial. As late even as 1810 the subscription lists of the Church Missionary Society did not include the name of a bishop or peer, and it was difficult for any clerical member of the Society to gain access to a pulpit. The Evangelicals' rise to power—for later the party became very powerful in the Church, to remain so until quite recent years—was gradual. The current of opinion began to flow in their favour chiefly as a result of frank recognition of evangelical virtues and

---

1. *The Life of Edward Bouverie Pusey*, ed. Johnston and Wilson (1893–4), i, p. 255.

achievements, but also, in the fourth decade of the century, from a reaction to the supposedly Romanizing aims of Tractarianism. For the evangelical teaching was uncompromisingly Protestant and its puritan moral temper fully in accord with a growing seriousness of outlook in the nation at large.

The older generation of Evangelicals, typified by such men as John Newton and Richard Cecil, scarcely survived the age of Wesley himself. The new generation was associated mainly with Clapham, then an outlying London suburb, and with Cambridge, where Simeon, a fellow of King's, was vicar of Holy Trinity. The 'Clapham Sect'—and Sidney Smith's label at once stuck to them—comprised a group of high-principled and energetic men, friends and neighbours united by a shared religious faith and a common philanthropic purpose. A natural leader was the banker, Henry Thornton, member of parliament for Southwark and a tireless promoter of good causes. His nearest neighbour and close friend was William Wilberforce (1759–1833), himself a rich man and a member of parliament also—he was an intimate of William Pitt's—who won renown as the protagonist in the movement for the abolition of the slave trade. Other members of the group were Granville Sharp, Zachary Macaulay—Thomas Babington Macaulay's father—likewise devoted to the anti-slavery campaign, Lord Teignmouth, a former govenor-general of India, and James Stephen, a man in Brougham's opinion of 'the strictest integrity and nicest sense of both honour and justice'. All were laymen, but they were warmly supported by John Venn, rector of Clapham from 1792 to 1813. Frequent visitors to the district included Hannah More (1743–1833), prolific author of edifying books and pamphlets and a courageous worker for the poor, insufferably condescending though her social attitudes would now be judged, and the two outstanding members of the Cambridge following, Charles Simeon (1759–1836) and Isaac Milner (1751–1820), the latter president of Queens' College and dean of Carlisle, a man of respected position in the university and the most impressive scholar in the party.

The literary organ of the Evangelicals was *The Christian Observer*, founded in 1802, which did much to publicize their opinions, but their contribution to theological study was meagre. Wilberforce's *Practical View*, first published in 1797 and repeatedly reissued, is representative and in its day had great influence.[2] But although they are chiefly remembered for their philanthropy, which their wealth made possible, they were not simply activists. None of them ever thought of his religion only in terms of moral endeavour. What moved them was a fervently held if narrow Bible Protestantism, although their contemporaries often despised them for the weakness of their theology, with its alleged lack of intellectual fibre and the conventionalism of its language. Thus Newman dismissed it as 'but an inchoate state or stage of a doctrine', whose final resolution would be in rationalism. But the charge is hardly fair. Evangelical theology was unspeculative certainly, and it had very little to offer in the way of an ecclesiology, whilst the emotive phrases of the popular evangelism in which it found expression were apt to sound glib. Yet

2. Its full title is *A Practical View or the prevailing Religious System of Professed Christians in the higher and middle classes in this country contrasted with Real Christianity*. The book was translated into several languages.

its teaching, within its limits, was clear and firm. The very point of Wilberforce's book was to impress on its readers the need of an adequate Christian belief. There was much, he feared, in the religion of people of his own social class—and his words were addressed to them—which was merely nominal and formal, yet if the basis of faith was insecurely laid the superstructure was bound to be precarious. A superficial and complacent moralism, the notion that 'if, on the whole, our lives be tolerably good, we shall escape with little or no punishment', would not do. Such an error sprang from an impoverished idea of what the fundamentals of Christianity really are. The 'fruits of holiness', contrary to the popular view, are the effects not the causes of justification and reconciliation. The intrinsic corruption of human nature—'the sense we ought to entertain of our natural misery and helplessness'—the death of Christ, accordingly, as the one satisfaction for human sin, and the converting and sanctifying influence of the Holy Spirit—these are the elemental truths necessary to a real Christian profession. They are not abstruse, and the poor and simple can grasp them often better than the sophisticated. The humblest intelligence may hold to the death of Christ as an atonement for sin and the purchase price of a believer's future happiness.

The Reformation doctrine of justification by faith lay at the root of evangelical piety. The Christian religion was a way of personal salvation, rendered urgent by the presence and power of sin in human life. In the words of John Overton's *True Churchman Ascertained* (1801), a reply to Robert Fellowes's *The Anti-Calvinist*: 'We *can* only teach that every man who is born, considered independent of the grace of God, and in respect to spiritual concerns, is wholly corrupt, utterly impotent, under the wrath of God, and liable to everlasting torments.'[3] Overton indeed, unlike most English Evangelicals of the time, was a pronounced Calvinist, taking the gravest view of man's spiritual incapacity. But even Wilberforce, himself not at all of the Calvinist conviction, followed suit in this matter, believing sincerely that humanity is 'tainted with sin, not slightly and superficially, but radically and to the very core'.[4] This impressed him as the plain teaching of the Church of England, in its Articles even more expressly than in its liturgy. Nothing in this world was so important as the salvation of individual sinners from their sin and its consequences. Good intentions, however, are unavailing; rather must one turn to 'the high mysterious doctrines' professed by 'real' Christians. Wilberforce speaks with warmth of 'the profaneness of . . . treating as matters of subordinate consideration those parts of the system of Christianity, which are so strongly impressed on our reverence by the dignity of the person to whom they relate'. Man's only hope lies in Christ crucified:

> If we would love Him as affectionately, and rejoice in Him as triumphantly, as the first Christians did, we must learn like them to repose our entire trust in Him, and to adopt the language of the Apostle, 'God forbid that I should glory, save in the cross of our Lord Jesus Christ'.

Thus the atonement is the heart of Christian truth. It was no mere example of self-giving love but a unique event in which, by the substitution of the sinless one for

3. Second edition, 1802, p. 157.
4. *A Practical View*, p. 27.

sinners, the just wrath of God was appeased and his attitude to mankind changed. Man himself contributes no more to his redemption than he did to his first creation. To God alone is the praise.

Yet neither is salvation unconditional. To accept or reject it is the sinner's own awful responsibility and he can accept it only by an act of faith beyond all consideration of personal merit. 'You build for eternity', said Isaac Milner, 'on the righteousness of Christ; you renounce for ever, as a foundation of hope, your own righteousness.'[5] A true Christian indeed is one who is moved to believe that Christ died, not to endorse some broad moral principle, but, quite literally, *for him*. It was *his* sin, along with that of all his fellows, which made that holy death necessary. To admit this, out of personal conviction, is the beginning of conversion. Once possessed, the sense of sin is overwhelming. Moral virtues are discounted and one is aware only of mercy received. To suppose therefore that the Evangelicals' works of charity were done from utilitarian motives, in expectation of a heavenly reward, is to misconceive them completely. But good works, it was believed, are rightly taken as evidence of a justified state. They show that the faith professed is a living one. For the sinner to go unrepentant, and so fail to bring forth the fruits of the Spirit, is to await eternal doom. Even a man like Simeon adhered to the doctrine of reprobation without the slightest misgivings. It was sufficient that the Bible should teach it.

The Evangelicals were agreed, then, that the aim of religion is not only to humble the sinner and exalt the Saviour but to promote personal holiness. Sanctification was as much a divine operation as conversion. The two, in fact, were continuous, since conversion, so far from being of necessity instantaneous, is only the start of a process expected to last through life. The nature of holiness was conceived on puritan but not ascetic lines. Prayer and Bible-reading were vital to it, and regular attendance at Sunday worship was its dutiful expression. Thus G. W. E. Russell recalled from his youth 'an abiding sense of religious responsibility, a self-sacrificing energy in works of mercy, an evangelistic zeal, an aloofness from the world, and a level of saintliness in daily life such as I do not expect to see realized again on earth'.[6] Such testimony may be over-idealistic, but conduct in evangelical households was carefully regulated and a benefiting tone of 'seriousness' or 'earnestness' always looked for. Yet the Thorntons and the Wilberforces and their friends—unworldly men of the world—did not eschew the solid comforts and conveniencies appropriate to their rank in society. Nor were 'innocent' amusements by any means prohibited; it was only that the question of innocence had 'not to be tried', as Wilberforce put it, 'by the loose maxims of worldly morality, but by the spirit of the injunctions of the word of God'. Believers, he said, are not gloomy. 'The Christian relaxes in the temperate use of all the gifts of Providence.' Imagination and taste and genius, and the beauties of creation and works of art, all lie open to him. No doubt the advice was honestly meant, but it cannot be claimed that the Evangelicals displayed much aesthetic sensibility or an interest in liberal culture for its own sake. It was religion that dominated their lives and

5. *Sermons* (1820), i, p. 107.
6. *The Household of Faith* (1902), p. 232.

imposed a kind of ethical stewardship 'for every hour passed and every penny spent'.

The Evangelicals of the early nineteenth century, unlike many of their predecessors in the eighteenth, were not usually Calvinists. Legh Richmond, vicar successively of Brady in the Isle of Wight and Turvey in Bedfordshire, was among those who maintained the tradition in the Church of England, if in a modified form, whilst Overton was probably its doughtiest defender. But by this time the heat had gone out of the controversy.[7] The majority of Evangelicals believed that Christ had died for all men and not simply for the elect few and that the appeal of the gospel is universal, a conviction with which their missionary zeal fully accorded. They were genuinely lovers of souls and could not contemplate that any should finally be lost, unless from his own hardness of heart.

The practical basis of evangelical religion was Bible study. Scripture was the Word of God, indeed the very words of God. It was verbally inspired in the sense that every statement in it was divinely authorized and essentially inerrant. The result was a biblicism, not to say a bibliolatry, the effect of which was intellectually benumbing. The sacred pages were treated as an oracle. Not only was critical curiosity about the facts of the Bible's historical origins non-existent; the Evangelicals produced remarkably little in the way of Scripture exegesis. Thomas Horne, who ministered at the Welbeck Chapel in London, wrote an *Introduction to the Critical Study of the Holy Scripture* (1818), but this ponderous enterprise hardly drew its inspiration from Evangelicalism. The best of the party's exegetes was Thomas Scott (1747–1821), whose commentaries were much read and admired. It was Scott of whom Newman records in the *Apologia* that he had made a deeper impression on his mind than any other writer, one 'to whom (humanly speaking) I almost owe my soul'.[8] Nothing else calls for mention.

The Evangelical view of Scripture indicates indeed where the weaknesses of Evangelicalism lay.[9] Intellectually it was constricted and naïvely reactionary. The wider problems of faith and reason did not trouble it and in philosophical theology it had no interest. Such matters, in evangelical eyes, did nothing to advance real religion. Christianity meant the gospel, and the gospel the converting of sinners. It

7. *A Refutation of Calvinism*, by George Tomline, bishop of Winchester, published in 1811, was a somewhat belated though vociferous contribution to the debate. Tomline detested the Calvinist tenets, but he overstates his case when he declares that 'there is not in any part of our Book of Common Prayer, or in our Articles, a single expression, which can fairly be interpreted as asserting or recognizing any one of the peculiar doctrines of Calvinism'. A more judicious examination of the Calvinism of the Articles was made by Richard Laurence, archbishop of Cashel, in his Bampton lectures of 1804.

8. Scott, who in 1781 succeeded John Newton as curate of Olney was converted by the latter from Arminianism to Calvinism. His chief work, *The Holy Bible with ... Notes*, was published in four volumes between 1788 and 1792. Newman himself was brought up in an evangelical household.

9. Not that the Evangelicals were unique in their exaggerated biblicism. Bishop van Mildert of Durham, for instance—one of the most thoughtful and scholarly churchmen of his time—considered it 'impossible even to imagine a failure, either in judgment or in integrity in the Bible' (*An Inquiry into the General Principles of Scripture Interpretation* (1804), 3rd ed, p. 158.

was to be taught and believed to this end and no other. Philosophy, science and the arts were things intrinsically of this world, and of no consequence for eternity.

> To be happy in another life [wrote Isaac Milner], to square all our conduct by that object steadily and primarily kept in view; to attend to the things of this life only as necessary, not as objects of choice . . . these are the grand objects in the religion of Jesus.[10]

In any case the practical Christian, faced by the spiritual and moral condition of the mass of his fellow-men, would have little time to spare for pursuits that gave no lasting satisfaction and easily became the occasion for sinful pride. All the same, it is slight wonder that the evangelical influence, which in time permeated Victorian society, encouraged philistinism and sometimes hypocrisy. Popular Protestantism, fundamentalist and illiberal, identified the Christian ethical ideal with the moral inhibitions of the middle classes. A reaction therefore was bound to come about, of which, in their differing ways, Arnold and Pater and William Morris were to be the mouth-pieces. 'Nothing', observed Walter Bagehot, 'is more unpleasant than a virtuous person with a mean mind. A highly developed moral nature, joined to an undeveloped intellectual nature, an undeveloped artistic nature, is of necessity repulsive'—severe criticism, and as regards the best of the Evangelicals hardly applicable. Wilberforce's certainly was not a mean mind, but the limitations of the evangelical attitude were very evident even to contemporaries. Moreover, in the field of social morality it maintained a certain obtuseness which posterity has been unable to overlook.

Theologically likewise Evangelicalism had its faults, especially of omission. Of religion as a historical and cultural phenomenon, to be studied as such, it, needless to say, had no conception. Even the history of Christianity as a major phase in the education of the human race did not interest it, whilst the idea of religious development would have appeared irrelevant, if not false. Further, although themselves loyal members of the Church of England, the Evangelicals ignored much that was best in the Anglican inheritance. The importance of conversion was insisted upon, but little guidance was offered for subsequent spiritual training.[11] All, it was assumed, that the convert needed was the open Bible. The result was an excessive individualism; the corporate character of the religious life, except as it might find expression in common effort for special ends, was unappreciated. Of the Church as a visible institution having a historic experience continuous ultimately with that of the apostolic age itself the Evangelicals had no real sense: as Gladstone wrote, 'I had been brought up with no notion of the Church as the Church or body of Christ'.[12] The 'Catholic Church' acknowledged in the creed was barely more indeed than an abstract term, and episcopacy merely the accepted form of ecclesiastical government, involving no theological principle. Fellowship in all essentials with Dissenters they did not question, since provided a man was in right relation with God and believed the true gospel it mattered little to what sect or denomination

10. *Sermons*, ii, p. 260.
11. Cp. *Remains of Alexander Knox*, ed. Hornby (2nd edn, 1836), i, p. 72.
12. W. E. Gladstone (ed. D. C. Lathbury), *Letters on Church and Religion* (1908), i, p. 8.

he belonged. The genuinely faithful—Wilberforce's 'real' as distinct from 'nominal' Christians—would spontaneously associate for the promotion of good causes. Thus voluntary societies became typical of evangelical life.[13] The party did not by any means disregard the sacraments, but it cannot be said that its characteristic piety was centred upon them. Baptism and the Lord's Supper were taught as no more than symbolic and commemorative acts, enjoined by Holy Writ. The sober among them might deplore 'enthusiastic' excesses, but they were far from ever adopting High Church positions.[14] Clergymen were simply ministers of the congregation, not the stewards of the mysteries of God. For the Evangelical personal religion, grounded in an intensely held faith in the atonement, was all-important; the Church was but the assembly, for prayer and praise and the hearing of the word of God, of those who possessed it. That they lacked a clearly defined ecclesiology was perhaps the Evangelicals' most signal deficiency. Because of it they gave a ready weapon to the Tractarians.

Some High Churchmen

The evangelical 'Clapham Sect' was to some extent paralleled by a contemporary group of High Churchmen known as the 'Hackney Phalanx', from the district of London where they resided and from which their influence radiated. The designation High Church was at this time somewhat vague. It was commonly used of such as were not 'Low Churchmen'—Latitudinarians, that is—or Evangelicals, and included not only the exponents of 'high' sacramental views but, more generally, the 'high-and-dry' Church-and-State men: orthodox, anti-Roman, hostile to Dissent, severely critical of 'enthusiasm' and Tory in politics. With these latter, and their numbers were considerable, we are not here concerned, since to the positive thinking of their age they contributed virtually nothing. As Alexander Knox said of them, they were for the most part 'men of the world, if not of yesterday', and 'worn out'. The evangelical revival had conspicuously not touched them. The Hackney group, however, were spiritually awake and socially active. The extent of their influence was, furthermore, out of all proportion to the relative modesty of their social rank. In temper and outlook they and the type of High Churchmen of whom they were representative harked back to the ecclesiastical ideals of the Nonjurors and the Carolines. Politically of the Tory party, they valued but did not especially stress the State connection and stood rather for the Church's independence as essentially a spiritual and not merely a political entity. They were the immediate forerunners of the Tractarians, whose doctrines and attitudes they anticipated at almost every point; but unlike the Oxford High Churchmen of the

13. Of these there were very many. Suffice it to mention the Religious Tract Society (1799), the Church Missionary Society (1799), the British and Foreign Bible Society (1804), the British and Foreign School Society (1807), and the London Society for Promoting Christianity among the Jews (1809).
14. To suppose otherwise is the error of Ford K. Brown in *The Fathers of the Victorians. The Age of Wilberforce* (1961), pp. 498–506. Cp. David Newsome, 'Father and Sons', in *The Historical Journal*, vi. 2 (1963), pp. 295–310.

'thirties they were not propagandists. They adhered to their beliefs with a reasoned assurance and would gladly have had others share them, but they wanted zest for bold policies, judging that sound opinions require cautious procedures as well. They were polemical only when forced to defend their convictions against opponents, whether Latitudinarian, Nonconformist or Roman Catholic. But they respected theological learning whilst distrusting speculation. Eccentricity and eclecticism seemed to them likely only to lead to error. At the same time a man should have an understanding faith, knowing why and on what authority he believes as he does. Their defensiveness and fear of change may have indicated a defect of spiritual vitality; Knox, a shrewd observer, himself thought so. Yet, as the Hackney men prove, they were not indifferent to practical religion and philanthropy. In their quieter and less obtrusive way they were as forward in this regard as were the Evangelicals.

It was the advance of liberalism, both political and theological, which in the fourth decade of the century led High Churchmen to assume a more aggressive tone. The events of 1833 may well be looked on therefore as marking the turning-point in the party's destiny. Yet the novelty of the Tractarian teaching should not be overstated. The Oxford divines did not set out to innovate, as they themselves insisted. But in appealing to the example of their seventeenth-century predecessors they were prone to undervalue the clear and consistent church teaching of the generation immediately behind their own. The great difference between them and the older men was that they had come to see the past in a more dramatic light. It was not enough simply to accept traditional doctrines as things always taught; rather their truth was to be *felt*, to be taken to the heart. Hence the younger churchmen could be spoken of, in a way that their elders could not, as (in R. W. Church's phrase) 'the movement party', showing as they did all the self-propagating energy of a genuine spiritual revival. On their lips the term 'catholic' acquired a fresh, almost a revolutionary, significance. The doctrine of the apostolic succession reappeared as a principle to be striven for and with full recognition of its practical implications. What in short the Oxford leaders did for the old High Church theology was to make it into a *cause*, so that endorsement of their opinions became the equivalent of loyalty to the Church itself.

The 'orthodox' party of pre-Tractarian days was not numerous, but it included some prominent men. Its bishops—notably William van Mildert of Durham (1765–1836), Charles Lloyd of Oxford (1784–1820) and Herbert Marsh of Peterborough (1757–1839)—were among the most distinguished on the bench. But, conscientious and learned though they were, their influence was restricted. They offered no challenge to a lax public opinion. Conservation rather than propagation was their watchword, and their teaching, strict in principle, was in presentation unimaginative. Traditionalist by nature, the real trends of the time they scarcely saw.

Apart from the bishops—and the archbishop of Canterbury himself, Manners Sutton, might perhaps be classed with them—the leading members of the party comprised the scholarly Thomas Middleton (1769–1822), who became bishop of Calcutta; the archdeacons Charles Daubeny (1744–1827), a hard-hitting controversialist, and George Cambridge, and John James Watson, the rector of

Hackney; Watson's brother-in-law, Henry Handley Norris, also a Hackney incumbent, a man of both means and energy; Norris's gifted father-in-law, Thomas Sikes of Guilsborough, Northants; Hugh James Rose (1795–1838), rector of Hadleigh; and Christopher Wordsworth, brother of the poet and Master of Trinity College, Cambridge. Two stalwarts of the Hackney Phalanx (or 'Clapton Sect', as it was also sometimes called) were, however, laymen—Joshua Watson the rector of Hackney's brother, and William Stevens, both of them retired London merchants and staunch churchmen.[15] A layman, too, was Alexander Knox (1757–1831), a member of the Church of Ireland and the intimate friend and tireless correspondent of Bishop Jebb of Limerick, who himself strongly sympathized with Knox's views. The High Church periodical was *The Christian Remembrancer*, which began publication in 1819.

Distinctive of High Church teaching was the importance it attached to church polity and the sacraments. On these matters Archdeacon Daubeny, whose celebrated *Guide to the Church* came out in 1789, was as rigid as any Anglo-Catholic of a later day. His style of writing, however, may be judged from the statement that 'as the time of our Saviour's departure from the world drew near, the future establishment of His Church appears to have constituted the most interesting subject of His thoughts'.[16] On the apostolical succession he was firm: the Church must have a duly commissioned ministry deriving its authority in direct line from the apostles. Without episcopal government a 'true and lawful Church' indeed does not exist. The priesthood is a divine institution, since 'Christ was in all that the Apostles did'. Sacraments are the 'seals of the divine covenant',[17] but those of Dissenters, who lack a properly constituted ministry, are mere human ordinances, without effect. 'There is a holiness of *office* independent of the holiness of the minister; the former being essential to the validity of the ministerial act.' For the eucharist to be a sacrifice and for the presence therein of Christ to be real it must be celebrated by a priest. Schism in any case is indefensible, unity in the Church's membership being a Christian obligation. The civil toleration of dissent is no more than a political expedient, in principle inadmissible. In religion external authority must have the final voice; private judgment is unwarranted, for no man has a right to think otherwise than as God has ordained. The supreme duty of conscience is to recognize divine law as made known by revelation and taught and safeguarded by the Church.

Harsh towards Protestant nonconformity, Daubeny reserved a milder censure for Rome, since she and Canterbury (he claimed) are agreed on essentials. Thus he chides 'indiscriminating' Christians who are 'frightened with the words cross, altar, sacrifice or priest, words peculiarly characteristic of the Christian Church'.[18] But it is the Calvinists who really provoke his anger. Overton's reply, in *The True*

---

15. Watson's activities on behalf of Christian missions and popular education—he and Norris were co-founders in 1811 of the National Society—place him in this respect with the keenest of the Evangelicals.
16. *Guide to the Church* (ed. 1829), p. 6.
17. *Ibid.*, p. 180.
18. *Ibid.*, p. 220.

Churchman Ascertained, to anti-Calvinist polemic has already been mentioned, but it did not silence the archdeacon, who in *Vindiciae Ecclesiae Anglicanae* (1803) answered both it and Wilberforce's *Practical View*.

Another divine of whom it was said that 'orthodoxy oozed out of his pores, and that he would talk it in his dreams' was, of course, van Mildert, who before his elevation to the episcopate, of which at the time he was the most learned member, had been Regius Professor of divinity at Oxford and both Boyle and Bampton lecturer.[19] He was as emphatic as Daubeny that episcopacy is of the essence of the Church. Sacraments and priesthood are, he held, 'interwoven into the very substance of Christianity and inseparable from its general design'. Dissenters accordingly are outside the Church. Bishop Marsh of Peterborough maintained a similar view, as, too, had the highly respected Horsley of Rochester, who denounced Methodists and 'gloried' in the name of High Churchman.

Thomas Sikes (1767–1834), although he never won preferment and spent his life as a country parson, was a man of strong personality whose opinions were greatly valued—he was known locally as 'the Pope'—and advice widely sought. He is especially remembered as a prophet of the Oxford Movement. What in general the churchmen of his day lacked, he judged, was any real understanding of the doctrine of the *Church* itself, which as an article of the creed was scarcely at all considered. Certain words of his uttered in 1833 and recalled long afterwards by Edward Bouverie Pusey in a letter to the archbishop of Canterbury, William Howley, have often been cited but are worth repeating here in full, in view of their remarkable prescience.

> I seem [he said] to think I can tell you something which you who are young may probably live to see. Wherever I go about the country I see amongst the clergy a number of very amiable and estimable men, many of them much in earnest and wishing to do good. But I have observed one universal want in their teaching: the uniform suppression of one great truth. There is no account given anywhere, so far as I can see, of the one Holy Catholic Church. I think that the causes of this suppression have been mainly two. The Church has been kept out of sight, partly in consequence of the civil establishment of the branch of it which is in this country, and partly out of false charity to Dissent. Now this great truth is an article of the Creed; and if so, to teach the rest of the Creed to its exclusion must be to destroy the 'analogy or proportion of the faith'. This cannot be done without the most serious consequences. The doctrine is of the last importance, and the principles it involves of immense power; and some day, not far distant, it will judicially have its reprisals. And whereas the other articles of the Creed seem now to have thrown it into the shade, it will seem, when it is brought forward, to swallow up the rest. We now hear not a breath about the Church; by and by those who live to see it will hear of nothing else; and just in proportion perhaps to its present suppression, will be its future development. Our confusion nowadays is chiefly owing to the want of it; and there will be even more confusion attending its revival. The effect of it I even dread to contemplate, especially if it come suddenly. And woe betide those, whoever they are, who shall, in the course of Providence, have to bring it forward. It ought especially of all others to be a matter

---

19. In 1802–5 (*An Historical View of the Rise and Progress of Infidelity*) and 1814 (*An Inquiry into the General Principles of Scripture Interpretation*) respectively.

of catechetical teaching and training. The doctrines of the Church Catholic and the privileges of Church membership cannot be explained from pulpits; and those who will have to explain it will hardly know where they are, or which way they are to turn themselves. They will be endlessly misrepresented and misunderstood. There will be one great outcry of Popery from one end of the country to the other. It will be thrust upon minds unprepared, and an uncatechised Church. Some will take it up and admire it as a beautiful picture, others will be frightened and run away and reject it; and all will want a guidance which one hardly knows where they shall find.[20]

It may be that Sikes's statement was somewhat coloured in Pusey's memory from his knowledge of subsequent events, but its substantial accuracy as he records it need not be doubted, even though it would appear to have been hardly fair to much current High Church teaching. The expression, 'an uncatechized Church', conveys precisely the Tractarians' own complaint: churchmen were largely ignorant of and indifferent to their doctrinal heritage. A new religious revival must appeal not to mere sentiment, nor to the primacy of a single article of belief, as did the Evangelicals to the doctrine of the atonement, but to a body of theological principles which the Church of England had in the final resort received from the undivided Church of antiquity.

It remains to speak of Knox, a lay theologian—in those days a rare enough phenomenon in itself—of a singular insight and breadth of sympathy. The ecclesiastically-minded layman is prone to be more, not less, rigid than the cleric. It was not so, however, with this surprising Irishman, Lord Castlereagh's onetime private secretary. A freelance among orthodox churchmen, he was both sure of his principles and consistent in applying them, yet wholly devoid of a spirit of exclusiveness or the controversialist's desire to use truth mainly in order to impale error. High Churchman though he was, he had a profound admiration for John Wesley, with whom he had from time to time corresponded, and was fully in accord with the spiritual ideals of Methodism, if not with its express theology. What his own party needed, he was convinced, was an infusion of the Methodists' fervour. Newman spoke of him as a remarkable instance of 'a man searching for and striking out the truth by himself'. Could we, he added, 'see the scheme of things as angels see it, I fancy we should find he has his place in the growth and restoration (so be it) of Church principles'.[21] Pusey too had a great respect for him, although there is little evidence that the Tractarians in general acknowledged any special debt to him, partly because he and they alike looked back for inspiration to the 'Anglo-Catholic' divines of the seventeenth century, but partly also because there is in Knox's outlook a broad, almost Coleridgean, quality less to their liking.[22] Knox himself did not live to witness the Oxford Movement, but had he done so his reactions would have been interesting. Archdeacon Daubeny—'a strange kind

20. H. P. Liddon, *The Life of Edward Bouverie Pusey*, i, p. 257.
21. *Letters and Correspondence of John Henry Newman*, ed. Anne Mozley (1891), ii, p. 93.
22. Thus Newman's good opinion had definite qualifications. 'He seems to say dangerous things . . . I should be unwilling to think him more than an eclectic, though that is bad enough. Froude did not like him. I think his works on the Eucharist have done much good' (from a letter to Robert Wilberforce, dated 9 June 1838. See D. Newsome, *op. cit.* p. 197).

of clergyman at Bath'—was evidently not a man after his own heart. The fact is that Knox, like F. D. Maurice later, was an individualist, fitting exactly into no party. A reclusive scholar, he preferred, for all his deep regard for the traditions of the Church Catholic, to think for himself.

The fruits of his thought are contained in the four volumes of his *Remains*,[23] and the two further volumes of his correspondence with Bishop Jebb.[24] It is in a letter of the year 1816 on 'The Situation and Prospects of the Established Church' that he criticizes the High Churchmen of his day for their lack of religious feeling and of what he calls 'interior learning'—that instinctive understanding of the needs of the human heart which Wesley and the Evangelicals, despite their defective theology, unquestionably possessed. The High Church critics of Evangelicalism all too often failed, he thought, to appreciate where its strength really lay. The grounds of its personal appeal they should have studied rather than derided. The coldness of their own teaching, characteristic though it was of the times in which they lived, was an impediment to the gospel message and to the extension of the Church's influence on the popular mind. Orthodox doctrine is greatly to be desired, but of itself is no substitute for that 'spiritual view of religion which implies an habitual devotedness to God' such as could be found in Methodism. What Knox judged most likely to arouse the national Church from its prevailing torpor was the growth of liberalism and the spread of an anti-ecclesiastical spirit among the common people. The old-fashioned 'high-and-dry' churchmanship was utterly insufficient for the nation's needs in an age of change and disintegration. Its principles were sound, but the teaching of them lacked all conviction. The party wanted revitalizing, and for this even persecution might not come amiss. What in particular was required was a genuine sentiment for the Church, a lively interest in its history and the continuity of its witness, in its corporate being and in its 'unsurpassed liturgy'. Preaching had sunk to the level of mere routine moralizing: there was 'intellectual pumping' but no 'gushing of the spring.'[25]

A further reason for the all but universal failure among Englishmen to weigh the significance of the word 'catholic' and therefore to attach any substantial meaning to the idea of the Catholic Church was, he considered, the inveterate suspicion of Rome. Rome doubtless was in error in many respects, but she also had preserved vastly more that was true. The answer to the dogma of transubstantiation was not to turn the eucharist into a bare memorial ceremony any more than was the claim to infallibility to be met by every man deciding his own creed.[26] Scripture certainly is the ultimate source of authority in matters of faith, but catholicity rests upon the additional principle of 'the concurrent judgment or tradition of the Church', the *consensus omnium*, the *quod ubique quod semper quod ab omnibus*, which next to Scripture is 'our surest guide'. Knox for his part looks back to the Church of the first centuries for the solid content of Catholic

23. 1834–37.
24. *Thirty Years' Correspondence between Bishop Jebb and Alexander Knox*, ed. Forster (1836).
25. *Correspondence*, i, p. 14.
26. *Remains*, i, p. 58.

teaching and to the early seventeenth century for that special presentation of it characteristic of the reformed branch of the Catholic Church established in England. At the Reformation the English Church, whilst asserting its right to decide in controversies of faith, also acknowledged its allegiance to an older and wider inheritance, an allegiance 'which reduces all that was done about articles and homilies to such a municipal rank, as to make it, of necessity, but subordinately and conditionally obligatory, even on subscribers.'[27] Thus to call the national Church Protestant is to make do with a very inadequate description. Her body indeed, thanks to the circumstances of her history, may be Lutheran, but her soul is Catholic.

Knox was devoted to the Book of Common Prayer, the spirit and language of which he found entirely congenial because unquestionably Catholic. The viability of the Church of England had lain in its identity of organization and mental character with the Church of former ages, the one secured by our 'unbroken episcopacy',[28] the other exemplified by the liturgy—the latter being a standard of doctrine as well as of devotion. He had no quarrel with the Thirty-Nine Articles as such, but denied that they bore the same intrinsic authority as the prayer book. Whereas the former were 'very much human' the latter 'fell little short of divine'.[29] As for the establishment, he esteemed it well enough for its actual, or potential, influence on the life of the nation, but more, he thought, should be understood by the term than the mere state connection, however beneficial. The Church's real strength was in its interior organization. 'An Hierarchical Church has the nature of an Establishment whether it is, or is not, allied with the State.' To this inherent structure state support added little.

Consonant with Knox's hierarchial conception of the Church was his strong sacramentalism. His view of baptism indeed is qualified. He believes that the sacrament may be said to effect regeneration, but in the sense only of contracting indelible relations between God and man, relations which may either be realized or nullified on man's part, to his spiritual loss or gain. In the case of infant baptism the grace bestowed is unconditional: 'Nothing less can be concluded than that a vital germ of all virtuous dispositions and pious affections is implanted in the mind of the baptized infant.' Nevertheless the germ will not grow up of itself, and it does not follow that because a man has been baptized he is in fact regenerate.[30] On the doctrine of the eucharist, however, Knox is remarkably firm. His argument is directed expressly against the eighteenth-century divine, Daniel Waterland, for whom the bread and wine were no more than 'the signs or pledges of concomitant blessing'. But Knox holds that the consecrated symbols are properly to be regarded as themselves vehicles of saving grace and hence as the 'permanent representatives of [Christ's] incarnate Person'.[31] By them God works invisibly in us, even though we cannot explain how. Knox is satisfied that he finds this teaching not only in

27. *Correspondence*, ii, p. 502.
28. On Knox's opinions in the matter of the apostolical succession see I. Brillioth, *The Anglican Revival* (1925), pp. 46–55.
29. *Remains*, i, p. 425.
30. *Ibid.*, i, pp. 488–510.
31. *Ibid.*, ii, p. 155.

the Fathers of the early Church but in St Paul himself, and deems it the natural interpretation of Christ's own words.

> Of this supernatural influence I consider the Lord's Supper the divinely constructed conduit: it is the connecting link between earth and heaven, the point where our Redeemer is vitally accessible, 'the same yesterday, today, and for ever'; and when He said, 'This is my body' and 'This is my blood', He made the sacrament, the simple elements (which, wherever thus used, receive the same divine touch and the same efficacious sublimation), to be for ever the vehicle, to all capable receivers, of all that is vitalizing, sanative, purificatory, confirmative, in Himself—in His life, or in His death, His exquisite humanity, or His adorable divinity.

In receiving the sacraments devotional feeling is not necessary. The only impediment to true communication is incapacity:

> The co-operation of mind on the part of the receiver, which in all the common means of edification must be deemed indispensable, was, in the Eucharist, peculiarly and mysteriously superseded; and *capacity* the requisite for the reception of the heavenly blessing.[32]

For the truth is that 'we cannot co-operate in the divine act, because it is so purely divine as to exclude even subordinate co-agency.'

Regarding the inspiration of Scripture Knox avoids any rigid or exclusive theory. Inspiration is given in degree and is not confined to a single age, nor is it entirely lacking even to the heathen. The commonly accepted view, he complains, 'has kept very many back from exercising their judgments on its structure and composition'.[33] Altogether Knox's was an independent and forward-looking intelligence. Not only did he presage Tractarianism, Maurice, too, had in him a worthy forerunner. His influence would assuredly have been greater but for the modesty, or personal disinclination, which inhibited him from making his voice heard in the world by publishing more than he did.

Liberal opinion

The liberal theologians of these early decades also compose a group, although from the very nature of liberalism a less clearly defined one. They at any rate did not constitute an ecclesiastical party. At the beginning of the century liberal opinions were generally not much in evidence among churchmen. Conservatism, militant or lethargic, was the mark of the age. Men like Paley and Bishop Watson of Llandaff favoured prayer book revision and the abolition of subscription; otherwise latitudinarianism was in decline. One rather solitary, not to say eccentric, figure is, however, worth noticing, namely Robert Fellowes (1771–1847), a cleric of deistical views. The earlier of his two books, called *Religion without Cant* (1811), is intended to be a defence of the established Church against the objections of Dissenters, but much church doctrine also comes under fire. Original sin, for example, is dismissed

32. *Ibid.*, ii, p. 280.
33. *Correspondence*, i, p. 41.

as a falsehood for which the Bible itself is not responsible. Man is not by nature depraved and the story of the Fall is no more than an allegory. The Trinity, again, is a mystery beyond human comprehension. The later volume, *The Religion of the Universe*, published in 1836, is pure deism and prefers science to Christianity as a basis for the moral life. True religion is essentially a matter of the rational understanding, of which science is now the ripest fruit. Knowledge of nature in fact is knowledge of God. Miracles, disallowed by science, can have no place in religion. Even prayer rests on a misconception of God's perfection. As for creeds and dogmas, what are they but priestly contrivances fostering superstition? Yet for all its crudity Fellowes's book is of some interest on account of its grasp of the principle of evolution, though the word itself is not mentioned. Geology is right in what it tells us of the immense age of the earth, and the first organisms must have been extremely simple. It is doubtful, moreover, whether man himself represents a special act of creation; although even as a part of nature and the product of secondary causation alone he still is a manifestation of 'divine agency' and the climax of a long providential development. Immortality, finally, is a reasonable belief in view of man's inherent capacities.

Fellowes, as a clergyman of his time, was doubtless an oddity. He was a man of intelligence, but essentially (in biological language) a 'sport'. On the other hand, the nearest thing to a liberal *school* is to be found in the group of Oxford teachers associated with Oriel College and known in their day as 'Noetics', a nickname which, like most such, was not intended to be flattering. To the traditionalists they appeared self-opinionated and brash. Their common disposition was to examine and criticize received beliefs in the light of history and reason. A provost of the college, Edward Copleston (1776–1849), may be said to have been the originator of the group, although his predecessor, Eveleigh, had already shown—what then was rare—a reforming spirit in university affairs. Copleston himself was a man after Eveleigh's own stamp. 'August and commanding', he was a keen judge of intellectual ability, as his appointments to college fellowships proved, and he made a principle of taking the liberal line in most matters. His pupils included some of the best minds of the following generation—Whately, Hampden and Baden-Powell among them. Yet he was not at all an original thinker, or in any sense a theological adventurer, and could fairly be classed as a High Churchman. Although he found no support among the sixteenth-century Reformers for a rigid theory of episcopacy, he believed the Church as a visible institution to be of divine foundation and to possess an inherent authority secured by a ministry having historical continuity with that of apostolic times. What he could not sanction was the view that this continuity ensures the transmission of a special power or virtue, or that ordination confers on the individual minister any distinctly sacerdotal character. His attitude to Tractarianism—'that folly', he dubbed it—was accordingly unsympathetic.

Edward Hawkins (1789—1882), Copleston's successor at Oriel, was no less critical of the new High Church divinity, dismissing the doctrine of the apostolical succession, which he regarded as central to it, as devoid of adequate basis in known historical fact. Episcopacy as the traditional form of church government was one thing; exclusive claims built upon it quite another. Yet his depriving of three such brilliant college tutors as Newman, Hurrell Froude and Robert Wilberforce of their office was prompted, we may suspect, as much by personal jealousy as by conscientious difference of view. In any case Hawkins had little of his predecessor's force of character and was not himself in any marked degree a liberal. 'The Church to teach, the Bible to prove' was a maxim he shared with the Tractarians.

The real inheritor of the liberal tradition was Richard Whately (1787–1863), who joined the Oriel common room in 1811. With his hard-headed trust in the all-sufficiency of reason he was the very type of a 'Noetic', and proud of the influence he believed himself to exert. Religion, he was confident, needed a stiff infusion of the critical spirit. Party bias especially was an obstacle to truth.[34] But although a born questioner, even if rather cocksure of his own answers, Whately was no rationalist in the sense of refusing to recognize the limits of reason when faced with the mysteries of faith. The fault of too much religious philosophy was, he considered, its glib assumption that the meaning of such words as 'cause', 'time' and 'eternity' is self-evident. Religion pertains to a realm of thought demanding the temper of the scientific investigator more than of the dogmatist. The prime necessity, however, was a renewed study of the Bible, a task the nature and scope of which he sought to indicate in his own *Essay on Some Difficulties in the Writings of St Paul* (1828). In this he takes another look at a vocabulary long familiar in theological debate. What, he asks, is the real significance of terms like 'election', 'law', 'grace', 'justification' and 'imputed righteousness', as distinct from the meanings which centuries of misuse had forced upon them? Let the modern theologian rid himself of his preoccupation and return with an open mind to the text of Scripture itself. A book of the Bible should be read as a whole and with its general character and content in view, not merely picked over for isolated 'texts'. Scripture is not a manual of theology, and definitions and consistency in the use of words are absent. Nor is it of equal revelational value throughout, since much of it has slight bearing on the practical religious life. Certainly revelation has no function to instruct us in the natural sciences. All the same, Whately had little taste for German negations: the errors of one extreme do not validate those of another. Conventional ideas call for re-examination in the light of new knowledge and superstitions have to be dispelled. But the religious spirit will always employ judgment with reverence.

The *Essays* served their turn at a time when biblical studies in this country were in poor shape, but their author, who was never much more than an ecclesiastical publicist, left behind him no book of lasting interest. As a writer he could hit hard, but the sort of thing he was best at is of its nature ephemeral. To Tractarian ideas he was implacably opposed, particularly disliking a reactionary exaltation of the principle of authority. For Newman and his friends the one source of truth was in the past as he saw it, in church tradition. Reason was distrusted or disparaged, a docile and unquestioning faith extolled. Such a state of mind could lead in the end only to scepticism, or at best to that mere 'reason of the heart', or the paradox of an argued irrationalism, which Coleridge seemed to be proclaiming. For Whately an internal disposition was no substitute for external evidences open to examination

34. The subject of his 1822 Bampton lectures was *The Use and Abuse of Party Feeling in Matters of Religion*.

by any reasonable inquirer. In some respects, and despite his swashbuckling manner, his own standpoint was very much that of his orthodox contemporaries. He did not reject the dogmatic principle, or institutionalism in religion. His anonymous *Letters on the Church: By an Episcopalian* (1826)[35] describe the Church as 'a body corporate, of divine institution' and even entertain the doctrine of the apostolical succession in so far as it implies a delegated authority and a rightly exercised discipline. The author also disapproves the state establishment: Christ's kingdom is not of this world, and to fulfil its spiritual vocation it must enjoy a freedom with which such political and legal bondage, whatever seeming privileges it may confer, is incompatible. Disestablishment, though without the inconvenience of disendowment, ought not to be delayed. Later, however, these opinions underwent modification.[36] One now looks in vain in the Bible for instruction as to the formal constitution of the Church. How actual Christian societies should organize themselves is a matter for historical circumstances to determine, in the light of Christian principles. The Church indeed, like the human race itself, is 'undoubtedly one', but not as a society. Visible unity will be realized only 'in its future existence': hence the designation 'the Universal Church' is a phrase only; there is no corresponding reality having a recognizable cohesion or focus of authority, and no existing Christian body justly claims so comprehensive a title. The Jews no doubt did so, and rightly, since they already were one people; but Christians are not in a like situation. Unity is not, at any rate, constituted by the episcopate, as the Tractarians argued, for episcopacy has no credentials as the sole legitimate form of ecclesiastical government. Criteria such as this were not laid down by Christ or his apostles, but are simply men's 'unauthorized conjectures'. The truth of the Church's teaching is substantiated only by Scripture. Tradition adds nothing, inasmuch as its own witness depends on Scripture.

Newman, in spite of their mutual estrangement, always admired Whately, who, he said, 'opened my mind, and taught me to think and to use my reason'.[37] But of Whately's close friend, Dr Hampden, he was bitingly critical. Renn Dickson Hampden (1793–1868) principal of St Mary Hall and professor of moral philosophy, was, no doubt, a very controversial figure in the Oxford of the 'thirties. A dull sort of man, yet he was a scholar whose distinction only sheer prejudice could have denied. Newman and his followers, however, both denigrated his scholarship and ridiculed the man. That he lacked personal attraction is evident. But the campaign

35. Whately never admitted, but he also never denied, authorship of the pamphlet. That it came from his pen was generally understood. With the years Whately's attitude to the Oxford Movement, and Newman particularly, became increasingly critical. See Jane Whately, *The Life and Correspondence of Richard Whately, D.D., late Archbishop of Dublin* (1866).
36. See *Essays on Some of the Dangers to Christian Faith which may arise from the Teaching or the Conduct of its Professors* (1839), especially Note A to Essay III.
37. *Apologia pro Vita Sua*, ed. Svaglic (1967), p. 23. Newman adds: 'What he did for me in point of religious opinion, was, first, to teach me the existence of the Church, as a substantive body or corporation; next, to fix in me those anti-Erastian views of Church polity, which were one of the most prominent features of the Tractarian movement' (*op. cit.* p. 24).

mounted against him in 1836, when Lord Melbourne (on Whately's persuasion) nominated him Regius professor of divinity at Oxford, is an event lying beyond our purview here, fascinating though its details are to the connoisseur of ecclesiastical and academic *causes célèbres*.[38] Hampden, not only then but since, has frequently been underrated,[39] and in any case there is no question of his being a strongly original or influential theologian, nor as a writer does he always succeed in making his meaning clear. But he had considerable insight and a prescient sense, far beyond that of most of his critics, of where the religious thinking of the future would tend. A Tory in politics and in his way a firm churchman, he was both astonished and grieved at the animus his opponents displayed against him, not only in 1836 but years later, when he was appointed to the see of Hereford. He assuredly was not by intention the heresiarch he was accused of being, and as a bishop he came to be regarded as a moderate High Churchman, his supposedly heretical opinions having by then been forgotten. He himself, in his old age, denounced the heterodoxy of Bishop Colenso.

Hampden, like the rest of the Oriel liberals, believed that in religion as elsewhere critical reason has its rights. The paramount authority of Scripture he never doubted. His Bampton lectures of 1832, which dealt with *The Scholastic Philosophy considered in its Relation to Christian Theology*, were described by him modestly enough as an inquiry into the nature of theological terms.[40] The essential truth of Christianity, he held, is to be distinguished from the particular forms in which history has clothed it and which have been largely moulded by Greek philosophy. The source of dogmas is the Bible, whose content alone is to be received as divine revelation. Theology is necessary for the definition and defence of the faith, but is itself secondary and mutable, a human discipline serving heavenly truth but no integral part of it. The fault of scholasticism had been its infatuation with abstractions and deductive logic, its absorption in mere *reasoning*. The result had been the creation of a vast theological superstructure wrongly identified with the fundamentals of revelation itself. The Church in resisting one kind of rationalism had adopted another, and schemes of doctrine took the place of the living truths they were intended to clarify and safeguard. A return to the Scriptures was the only way out of the speculative mazes into which theology had been led. For Scripture gives us not theories but facts. To the question, however, of what exactly these facts amount to Hampden accords no very clear answer. Does the Bible not teach doctrines, or, as he seems to imply, are the doctrines themselves the 'facts'? If he means only that the doctrinal statements in Scripture are not formal or systematic, that they are presented imaginatively and for practical ends, few would disagree with him. In any case it is a just *caveat* that the Bible should not be read

38. For the particulars see W. O. Chadwick, *The Victorian Church*, i (1966), pp. 112–26.
39. Thus A. O. J. Cockshut, *Religious Controversies of the Nineteenth Century* (1966); p. 102, is satisfied that as a theologian Hampden was 'comparatively unimportant' and in the wake of R. W. Church calls him 'a muddled and inconsistent thinker'.
40. Earlier publications of his included *An Essay on the Philosophical Evidence of Christianity* (1827) and an article on 'Thomas Aquinas and the Scholastic Philosophy' contributed to the *Encyclopedia Metropolitana*.

with mistaken presuppositions. Hampden's point was that while Scripture contains the germs of the developed doctrines the development itself, in its historical course, has drawn upon material which is not scriptural. This is not necessarily an illegitimate procedure, but the instructed believer must distinguish the kernel from the husk.

Such general considerations, Hampden maintains, help us to assess the true function and purpose of dogmatic theology, which primarily are negative: its first aim is to exclude error. The Christian religion, by a natural process, 'has been acted on by the force of the human intellect', but the outcome may be distortion as well as clarification. Theology's task is to keep the original deposit intact whilst excluding interpretations which would transform its essential character. But dogma has also a positive role as a bond of social union. Beliefs, to be shared, depend on effective communication, and the institutionalizing of faith is a necessity if the social and cultural environment is not to prove a solvent. Conciliar definitions and their accompanying anathemas are the price to be paid for a requisite service.

Hampden's thesis was not strikingly new, views similar to his were often voiced during the previous century and the lectures provoked no especially hostile criticism until the occasion of his nomination to the divinity professorship, although his pamphlet on *Religious Dissent*, 'with particular reference to the use of religious tests in the University', which appeared in 1834, did give some offence. Here he had argued that Christianity is basically a disposition of will and feeling, not a body of doctrinal formulae, and that purely intellectual criteria ought not therefore to be made a condition of unity among Christians. In view, however, of the Crown's choice of Hampden for high academic office his published opinions could not be overlooked. But Newman's criticisms of them, under the title 'Elucidations of Dr Hampden's Theological Sentiments', was a work of more skill than scruple. Pusey, too, had a good deal to say,[41] noting how heretics invariably quote Scripture in preference to the definitions of the Church. Hampden, although aggrieved and distressed at the way in which he felt himself to have been misrepresented, stood firm.

> It is one thing [he wrote in a letter to Lord John Russell] to endeavour to unfold the theories on which a particular phraseology is employed in the systematic statement of divine truth, and adapted to its purpose, and quite another thing to state that the truths themselves, which that phraseology expresses, are mere theories, or mere opinions, or probable conclusions having no certainty in them. The latter misconstruction belongs to those who have taken it up, it is not mine.

In his inaugural lecture as Regius professor, as well as in the preface to a new edition of the Bamptons, he tried to explain the nature and drift of his opinions. The foundation of all his teaching, he protested, was Jesus Christ. Trinitarian doctrine he received in the full sense, as the Church had declared it. The authority of the Scriptures uncontestably was final, but he did not deny that of the Church also: it was simply that ecclesiastical authority cannot challenge biblical. In any

41. *Dr Hampden's Theological Statements and the Thirty-nine Articles: By a resident member of Convocation.*

event the ultimate criterion of truth is bound to be the reason. On the particular point of the 'facts' of Scripture it was his undoubted intention, he explained, to include also its *doctrines*.

The agitation against Hampden is usually quoted as a prime example of Tractarian bigotry; nevertheless in the eyes of the new Oxford High Churchmen his position was a threat to true belief. The importance he attached to Church tradition and authority seemed to them insufficient. His explanations of his meaning were so far acceptable, but ambiguity was not wholly removed, whilst Pusey scored a hit by showing that the new professor had failed to distinguish between the scholastic theology and that of the early Church fathers. Yet Hampden's book had merit and is to be praised for its grasp of the principle of organic development in Christian doctrine in response to changes in the cultural environment. This the Tractarians, with their static conceptions, did not understand. Newman himself omitted to face the problem until the need to defend post-Tridentine Catholicism compelled him to devise a theory of his own. Again, Hampden's appeal to simplicity in belief and his refusal to identify faith with theology was a plea for religious feeling. He also realized that traditional Christianity would in the light of historical science inevitably come to assume a new aspect. But of its basic truth he declared he had as firm a conviction as had his critics. It was only that in his view a living theology was likely to be a theology awake to its own limitations.

Hampden's *University Sermons* (1848), always forthright and lucid, are a sustained critique of Tractarian ideas, which he saw as Romanism in a fresh guise. Was ecclesiastical tradition really to enjoy an authority parallel with the Bible? The new Oxford divinity, in allowing it the sole right to determine the sense of Scripture in fact accorded it precedence, whereas the witness of the apostolic writers is unique and whatever comes after it must be tested by it. Thought and experience may confirm the scriptural message, but they can neither add to nor alter it. Of itself tradition has no evidential value. Moreover, there is doubt as to where its authentic voice is to be heard. In general councils? In the papacy? There was no more reason, in Hampden's judgment, for believing in the infallibility of the one than of the other. Patristic exegesis has its value, but it, too, has no charisma of inerrancy. The use of theological terms varies from age to age and affords no unquestionable assurance of truth. Newman's doctrine of development also comes in for severe handling: the whole idea of an *unfolding* of religious truth is subject to the necessary proviso that the Church has actually possessed it from the beginning. And this only the Scriptures can demonstrate.

Thomas Arnold

The last of the Oriel liberals to be considered here, a figure of greater interest than any of the others, is Thomas Arnold (1795–1842). Educated at Winchester and Corpus Christi College, Oxford, he was elected to an Oriel fellowship in 1815. At the age of thirty-three he became Master of Rugby School, a post his tenure of which was to mark him out as one of the greatest of English educationists. The caricature drawn by Lytton Strachey can at once be dismissed. Maliciously amusing, it is essentially false. But with Arnold the schoolmaster we are not now concerned.[42] As a religious thinker he is most impressive when expounding Scripture, of which he had a penetrative understanding not common in his day. Arnold's devotion to the Bible sprang from his own deep moral seriousness, coupled with an inherited reverence for what all Englishmen then regarded as the word of God. At root it was personal and rather naïve. Arnold did not approach the Bible as a theologian, for theologian he was not, and the philosophical theology then in the ascendant in Germany made no appeal to him: probably he knew little about it. Nor was he interested in the details, or even the methods, of scientific biblical criticism as this, too, was being developed in the German universities. Yet his great respect for the work of Neander, whom he knew personally, sharpened his appreciation of the importance of the critical attitude in biblical study. He is thus to be placed among the earliest of British divines to take account of the new historical perspectives. Nevertheless his primary concern was with exegesis, and was motivated by his unfailing sense of mission as a preacher and teacher. Criticism, he realized, could not leave the traditional theology unaffected, and its influence, unless disciplined by religious faith, might be disastrous. Secure in his own beliefs, he felt it his duty to show how the results of criticism fortified rather than weakened the Bible as a witness to divine truth. His published *Sermons* (1829–34) can still be rated an impressive attempt to uphold the Scriptures in an age in which the fear was already growing that the biblical foundations of Christianity were no longer safe.

The proper task of theology, as Arnold judged it, lay in biblical exposition; but how was it to be performed? The customary method had involved a culling of isolated texts, as though the several books had 'all been composed at one time, and addressed to persons similarly situated'. Obscurities, contradictions and moral stumbling-blocks hence remained unexplained. What now was required was a historical view, enlarged by the wider context of other religious and literary traditions, showing revelation to have been progressive. This necessary discipline did not imply, however, only a cold detachment, although some there were for whom, truly enough, 'the Bible has presented itself to their minds more frequently in connexion with their studies than with their practice'. But as a book with a history it called for such aids as historical science could provide; its difference from all other books was that it contained the words of eternal life. The theologian's responsibility was its sound interpretation, bringing out the spiritual meaning as distinct from the merely literal or historical. The fault of the allegorical method had been to separate them altogether, in failing to realize that the historical form is the necessary vehicle for the spiritual truth. Behind the history, that is, stand certain 'general principles'. With these prophecy 'is busy', and inasmuch as the particular nations, persons and events represent the principles 'up to a point, so far is it concerned also with them'. But their mixed character, as it embraces and qualifies the judgment of the historian, must 'necessarily lower and qualify the promises and threatenings of the prophet'. A Messianic prophecy (say) will thus, from the historian's standpoint, refer to particular historical circumstances, fairly

42. See D. Newsome, *Godliness and Good Learning* (1961), ch. i.

clearly determinable. But beneath the surface play of far-distant events there lies a deep and permanent truth, addressing itself to men's abiding spiritual wants, 'an answer given by God to the earnest questionings of their nature'. When we perceive the real significance of the prophetic utterance, Arnold contends, we realize that it is not simply predictive, a precise forecast of what is to come. The prophet's teaching is, rather, both a message for his contemporaries, in their own situation, and a truth effective for the future; the latter meaning, however, being latent and possibly unconscious. In so far as a prediction may be fulfilled it will be in substance, not in detail.

The influence of Coleridge upon Arnold's opinions seems here beyond doubt. In January 1835 Arnold wrote to Coleridge's nephew, Mr Justice Coleridge, asking whether he had seen his uncle's 'Letters on Inspiration' and noting their likely bearing on a matter which 'involves so great a shock to existing notions',[43] although he expresses also his own confidence that 'in spite of the fears and clamours of the weak and bigoted' the outcome will be 'the higher exalting and more sure establishing of Christian truth'. Indeed Coleridge's posthumously published *Confessions of an Inquiring Spirit*[44] is anticipated by Arnold in his own 'Essay on the Right Interpretation and Understanding of the Scriptures', which appeared in 1832, in the second volume of his *Sermons*. What Arnold has to say would today, of course, be considered trite, but it must be taken in the context of its time. Revelation, he argues, is progressive, accommodated to men's capacity to receive it. Christ himself 'must often have spoken as a man who possessed no greater knowledge than the men of that time and country'. Further, once it is understood that revelation is adapted to the circumstances of the recipient some at least of the moral problems presented by the Old Testament can be satisfactorily explained. Inspiration is not a guarantee of inerrancy nor does it displace the writer's own personality.

> Inspiration does not raise a man above his own time, nor make him even in respect to that which he utters when inspired, perfect in goodness and wisdom; but it so overrules his language that it shall contain a meaning more than his own mind was conscious of and this gives it a character of divinity, and a power of perpetual application.

But criticism, in dealing with the Bible's literary history, is not attempting to settle 'questions of religion' and does not disprove revelation.

Arnold believed that the best critical aid to the study of Scripture is a thorough general education, in particular a knowledge of history, and regretted that on this score the clergy were so often deficient. Arnold was not himself a very erudite man, but he had a breadth of mind which set him above most of his contemporaries.[45] More, he was a deeply convinced Christian who saw all life and experience as

43. A. P. Stanley, *The Life and Correspondence of Thomas Arnold D.D.* (ed. 1898), ii, p.69.
44. See below, Ch. 2.
45. A letter of his son, Matthew, dated 20 February 1869 (addressed to his mother), speaks of his father's 'immense superiority', 'mainly because, owing to his historic sense he was so wonderfully, for his nation, time, and profession, European . . .' See *Letters of Matthew Arnold*, ed. G. W. E. Russell (1895), ii, p. 5.

ideally related to Christian truth and morality. Thus he believed that society as such ought to be recognizably Christian; that, in the words of his biographer, 'the region of political and national questions, war and peace, oaths and punishments, economy and education, so long considered by good and bad alike as worldly and profane, should be looked upon as the very sphere in which Christian principles are the most applicable'.[46] Such an end, however, could be attained only if Christians themselves were visibly united. The sectarian or party spirit in religion Arnold detested. The historical divisions among Christians were a major source of weakness, especially when they rested on no really basic differences and could be regarded only as matters of opinion. He declared that he himself had one great principle: 'To insist strongly on the differences between Christian and non-Christian, and to sink into nothing the differences between Christian and Christian'.[47] The Church of the future would have to be truly comprehensive, although uncompromising on fundamentals. Dogmatic uniformity, in the nature of the case, is an impossible goal and to insist upon it as a condition of unity will only render division permanent. The mark of a Christian, Arnold believed, is a readiness to worship Christ and all who do so may be reckoned members of a genuinely national church. Unitarians present an obvious difficulty, but as long as they are willing in principle to render such worship no pressure need be put on them to define their understanding of Christ's divinity. A formulary like the Thirty-nine Articles should be used positively, to secure agreement, not 'to serve as a test of latent error'.

   Arnold in fact had little use for abstract theology. The Athanasian creed presumed to do what cannot be done and ought not to be attempted. The one test of any religion is its efficacy for moral good. God's self-revelation to man has a practical not a theoretical end, and Christian doctrine must be understood accordingly. 'There can be no more fatal error,' he wrote, 'none certainly more at variance with the Scripture model, than to acquaint the mind with the truths of religion in a theoretical form, leaving the application of them to be made afterwards.'[48] The method of Scripture is pragmatic, 'as producing a certain particular moral impression on our minds—not as declaring some positive truth in the nature of things',[49] a statement foreshadowing the argument elaborated many years later by his son in *Literature and Dogma*. The soul draws its nourishment from history more than from doctrines, and theology can easily become faith's enemy. Yet Arnold denied that his views were rationalistic or latitudinarian, and so far from minimizing the importance of church teaching he wished only to give it greater consistency and relevance. But it should be essential teaching, the gospel

46.   A. P. Stanley, *op. cit.*, i, p. 126. A projected work of Arnold's on Christian politics was never carried out.
47.   *Ibid.*, p. 223.
48.   *Fragments on Church and State* in *Miscellaneous Works* (1845), Appendix II, p. 34.
49.   Thus God's moral attributes 'are of the last importance, because such as we suppose Him to be morally, such we strive to become ourselves; but opinions as to His nature metaphysically may be wholly unimportant, because they are often of such a kind as to be wholly inoperative upon our spiritual state: they neither advance us in goodness; nor obstruct our progress in it' ('Principles of Church Reform', in *Miscellaneous Works*, p. 325).

of truth itself. Subscription to formulae, when necessary, should be taken always in the broadest sense, 'except on points where they were especially interested to be stringent, and to express the opposite of some suspected opinion'. The Articles, subject to this proviso, are to be assumed to exclude 'Romish' doctrines, but they might at a pinch cover tender consciences. What mattered was sympathy with the Church 'in its main faith and feelings'.[50]

It was a cardinal point in Arnold's creed that Church and State have the same essential function and would ideally merge with one another.

> Civil society aims at the highest happiness of man according to the measure of its knowledge. Religious society aims at it truly and really because it has obtained a complete knowledge of it. Impart then to civil society the knowledge of religious society, and the objects of both will be not only in intention but in fact the same. In other words, religious society is only civil society fully enlightened; the State in its highest perfection becomes the Church.

This was the old Hookerian principle in more modern guise: the Church is (or should be) the State in its religious aspect. Indeed, Arnold thinks that the State's officers actually perform a Christian service and are even in their way Christian ministers, no less than the accredited ministers of the Church. In case of necessity they should be empowered to discharge the latter's duties, including the administration of the sacraments. The Church's organization should be more democratic and rely less on a rigid and arbitrary distinction between clergy and laity.

Arnold had no objection to episcopacy as such, but the great obstacle to the united Church of his dreams was the doctrine of the episcopate as *jure divino* and the only legitimate system of ecclesiastical government, a doctrine which in principle unchurched an immense number of sincere followers of Christ. A just policy would encourage dissenters to return to the fold of a church at last become truly national. That such a Church should also be established was an advantage to society itself, not least in securing the presence throughout the country, in the persons of its territorial clergy, of a body of well-educated men 'whose sole business is to do good of the highest kind'—another echo of Coleridge.

Arnold's views, as set out in his *Principles of Church Reform* (1833), were widely condemned, especially by the clergy. That they should have been is scarcely surprising. His defence was that the times were critical and the situation urgent.

> I cannot [he wrote] get over my sense of the fearful state of public affairs; is it clean hopeless that the Church will come forward and crave to be allowed to reform itself? ... I can have no confidence in what would be in men like—but a death-bed repentance. It can only be done effectually by those who have not, through many a year of fair weather, turned a deep ear to the voice of reform, and will not be thought only to obey it because they cannot help it.[51]

His despair of the established Church in its existing condition left him no comfort: no human power, he thought, could save it. To a friend about to leave for India

50. Stanley, *op. cit.*, ii, p. 173.
51. Stanley, *op. cit.*, i, p. 176.

as a missionary he declared: 'You are going from what bids fair, I fear, to deserve the name of a City of Destruction.' The tone of Arnold's utterances, it has to be said, is apt to be overstrained, and to the great majority of churchmen, not necessarily the complacent, his words gave offence.[52] Moreover, his proposed remedies, extremist and quite evidently impractical, afforded no reassurance. Opposition came mainly from the Tractarians. Newman even feigned a wonder whether Arnold was a Christian.[53] But to Arnold in turn Tractarian doctrines were no less repugnant. The doctrine of the apostolic succession he dismissed as a sacerdotalist superstition. 'Bishops confer a *legal* qualification for the ministry, not a real one, whether natural or supernatural.'[54] Were the national Church to succumb to the new Oxford doctrines its essential character, as rooted in Protestantism, would be lost. Newman and his associates he pointed out, made much of the witness of antiquity, but the evidence to which they appealed was that of the fourth century, not the first. Nor did they stand in the authentic tradition of Anglican divinity, and men like Hooker or Bull or Pearson would not have countenanced their teachings. But Arnold's bitterest attack came in his notorious *Edinburgh Review* article of 1836, written in defence of Hampden, entitled 'The Oxford Malignants'.[55] In this he overreached himself, his tone verging on the hysterical. Were, he proclaimed, 'the pitiful objects' of High Church fanaticism—'the fanaticism of mere foolery'—to be gained, 'they would make no man the wiser or better,—they would lead to no good, intellectual, moral, or spiritual—to no effect, social or religious, except to the changing of sense into silliness, and holiness of heart and life into formality and hypocrisy.' For this outburst Newman never forgave him.

Arnold was not a very profound thinker nor, theologically, a very influential one. The real significance of the Oxford Movement he did not appreciate, whilst his liberalism was of the latitudinarian pattern then going out of date. Yet he left a mark on his times by the sheer force of personal character. His ideal of a national Church 'to Christianize the nation, and introduce the principles of Christianity into men's social and civil relations' was noble. A man of real faith, he was the embodiment of his own declared conviction that Christianity is primarily a way of life, not a creed or confession or speculative system. When he died at the early age of forty-seven his fellow-countrymen knew that a man of the finest moral grain had passed from their midst.

52. Yet the hardheaded Whately was almost as alarmist. 'Whatever turn things take', he wrote, 'I can see nothing that bodes well to the church establishment; I fear its days are numbered' (E. J. Whately, *The Life and Correspondence of Richard Whately* (1866), i, p. 159).

53. See *Apologia* (ed. M. Svaglic), p. 42. Also A. Whitridge, *Dr. Arnold of Rugby* (1928), p. 170 n. Newman thought the contents of Arnold's pamphlet 'atrocious' (*Letters*, i, p. 332).

54. *Principles of Church Reform*, in *Miscellaneous Works*, p. 329.

55. The actual title was the editor's, not his own. His views on Tractarianism are more carefully stated in the Introduction to the collection of sermons, *Christian Life, its Course, its Hindrances, and its Helps* (1841), and in his discussion of Priesthood in the Appendix to Sermon xi of the third volume of the *Sermons*.

In concluding this chapter there is one more name to list, that of Connop Thirlwall (1797–1874), bishop of St David's for thirty-four years. He was not one of the Oriel group, having taken his degree (in law) at Trinity College, Dublin, but he was closely akin to them in temper and outlook. His lifelong concern was that Christian teaching should take positive account of the changing spirit of the times and the immense advances in human knowledge. Firmly convinced that the critical intelligence cannot be debarred from the religious sphere, he was far from being a narrow rationalist and possessed a rare capacity for seeing both sides of a question. But a keen judgment joined with considerable learning made him a formidable figure among nineteenth-century liberal churchmen. His episcopal charges in particular afford an invaluable commentary on some of the chief intellectual issues of the mid-century, as a clearsighted Christian viewed them. His legal training also stood him in good stead, for he was never misled by irrelevancies or rhetoric. His earliest published work, dating from 1825, when he was still a layman, was his translation of Schleiermacher's *Essay on St Luke*. The great German theologian was then little known in England, although his name provoked fear. Thirlwall prefaced the book with an introduction of his own, in which he observed that 'it would almost seem as if at Oxford the knowledge of German subjected a divine to the same suspicion of heterodoxy which we know was attached some centuries back to a knowledge of Greek'.[56] His personal opinions, like his choice of author, displayed some courage. Thirlwall was among the few in England who through proficiency in the German language were familiar with contemporary German thought. His interest in biblical studies was stimulated by acquaintance with the German scholar diplomat, Baron Bunsen, and by his friendship with Julius Hare (a disciple of Coleridge), with whom he collaborated in a translation of Niebuhr's *History of Rome*. He did not, however, succumb to the fascination of Hegel, then at the height of his fame and influence. On the contrary, his reaction was one of complete antipathy, and the foremost philosopher in Europe he dismissed as an impudent literary quack. Whether this failure in appreciation is to be attributed to unusual insight or simply to an intellectual 'blind spot' opinions will differ.

The bishop's views on the controverted subject of Tractarianism were temperate. Whether the Oxford teachings were or were not compatible with the doctrine of the Church of England was, in the light of history, a matter not easily to be settled. The national Church had from the start aimed at comprehension and hence had tolerated more than one theological tradition. At the time also of the *Essays and Reviews* uproar in the 'sixties Thirlwall struck a balanced attitude. Liberal though he was he felt that the contributors had gone too far and that their book was a potential danger. Yet he had no doubt that the policy of hushing up the more disconcerting implications of biblical criticism was a mistaken one and that when free inquiry was permitted views like theirs were to be expected. They could properly be met only on their own terrain, candidly and with a sufficiency of knowledge. On the point of biblical inspiration he maintained that a critical judgment does not preclude belief that the Scriptures are truly inspired and that their authors had been secured from material error. But 'verbalist' theories were to be rejected, the

56. *Translation, with Introduction, of Schleiermacher's Critical Essay on St Luke*, p. ix.

limits of inspiration not being exactly definable. The pious reader can be sure only that where needed it had been given and may assume that what fell within the writer's own experience or had been related by him on the testimony of inspired witnesses required no special charisma.

It should be evident even from such a relatively brief survey as we have undertaken that English theology during the first three decades of the last century was not nearly as moribund as has sometimes been said. For the Evangelicals, narrowly channelled though their thinking was, religious belief was still a vital force. High Church doctrine too had exponents personally committed to the principles for which they stood; whilst liberal churchmen were already prescient of issues which the future was to render increasingly important. What, on the other hand, was lacking among all parties and groups was a new intellectual and imaginative stimulus. Attitudes were conventional and determined for the most part by traditional alignments. This was true even of the Noetics, who owed more to the eighteenth century than they seem to have realized. Happily new impulses were soon to make themselves felt. Evangelicalism, it is true, was to continue for a good many years yet in an intellectual doldrums, but High Church orthodoxy, without in any way modifying its basic positions, was, under the subtly compulsive leadership of Newman, to acquire a wholly fresh vigour. But for Anglicanism generally another factor had emerged, the effects of which were quickly to become apparent, leaving no party untouched by it. This was the mind of Samuel Taylor Coleridge, to whom we now must turn.

Chapter 2
COLERIDGE

The philosopher

It was John Stuart Mill, a man of a totally different disposition and outlook, who, in often-quoted words, described Coleridge as one of 'the two great seminal minds of England of their age', the second, of course, being Jeremy Bentham.[1] 'By Bentham beyond all others', he judged, 'men have been led to ask themselves in regard to any ancient or received opinion, Is it true? and by Coleridge, What is the meaning of it?'[2] The contrast thus noted indicates at once the bias and the strength of both men. Bentham, a rationalist impatient of humbug, was typically a child of the eighteenth century. Coleridge, on the other hand, a poet as well as a critic and philosopher, proclaimed the ideals of a new age of visionary romanticism. That Mill appreciated his genius as perceptively and as generously as he did is no little testimony to the breadth of his own mind. His pithy account of the romantic revolution could hardly, in fact, be bettered. 'The Germano-Coleridgean doctrine', he suggested, expressed the revolt of the human mind against the philosophy of the preceding century: it was 'ontological' because that was 'experimental'; conservative and religious, because that was 'innovative' and infidel; concrete and historical, because that was abstract and metaphysical. The old had been prosaic, the new was poetical.[3] Mill's genuine admiration for Coleridge is beyond doubt: no one of his time, he considered, had 'contributed more to shape the opinions of those among its younger men, who can be said to have opinions at all'. Yet in his personal philosophy he reveals nothing of Coleridge's influence, and so far as his *Essays on Religion* are concerned the author of *Aids to Reflection* might never have uttered a word on the subject.

The singular originality of Coleridge's genius has its witness in all who studied him closely enough to admit some reflexion of it. One of the earliest of these was Thomas Arnold, who acknowledged Coleridge as 'a very great man indeed, whose equal I know not where to find in England'. Newman, though critical and guarded in his language, was also impressed.[4] Julius Hare, an avowed Coleridgean, recalled

1. *Dissertations and Discussions* (1867), i, p. 330.
2. *Ibid.*, p. 394.
3. *Ibid.*, p. 403.
4. In an article on 'The Prospects of the Anglican Church' published in 1838, he wrote: 'And while history in prose and verse was thus made the instrument of Church feelings and opinions (i.e. by Sir Walter Scott), a philosophical basis for the same was under formation in England by a very original thinker (i.e. Coleridge) who, while he indulged

in 1848 how twenty years before it was beginning to be said by not a few that the poet-philosopher was 'the true sovereign of modern English thought'.[5] F. D. Maurice, who more, probably, than any other is reckoned an apostle of the Coleridgean teachings, confessed his great debt to Coleridge in the preparation of his own book, *The Kingdom of Christ*, declaring that it was mainly from him that contemporary theology had learned how 'the highest truths are those which are beyond the limits of Experience' and that 'the essential principles of the Reason are those which cannot be proved by syllogisms'.[6] 'The power of perceiving', he added, 'that by the very law of the Reason the Knowledge of God must be *given* to it; 'that the moment it attempts to create its Maker, it denies itself ... I must acknowledge that I received from him.'

Always an omnivorous reader, Coleridge possessed a capacity for assimilating ideas which has rarely been equalled. Yet whatever ideas were borrowed they acquired from him a new life and character. A highly idiosyncratic thinker, his opinions show his personality at every turn. What unhappily he lacked was the capacity to organize his thinking, or at any rate the literary expression of it, on an extended scale. His writings in consequence are bewilderingly unsystematic. He jumps from point to point, from theme to theme, as the mood, or some inward and personal logic, impels him. But for all his idiosyncrasy and defect of system Coleridge is by no means a confused thinker. The pattern of his doctrine, we may be sure, was clear enough in his own head. What emerged in print, or was scribbled down in his notebooks, is often tantalizingly haphazard and ambiguous, and inconsistencies remain, however patiently the underlying unity may be sought. But to suppose that, in the words of one hostile critic, Coleridge was 'a slothful, pusillanimous dreamer, in whom sincerity, if it ever existed, had been destroyed by the use of laudanum', would be the grossest of errors.[7] Despite the vices which so disorganized his personal life as to render necessary the protective care bestowed upon him over his last years by the admirable Dr Gilman, his intellectual keenness, his acute spiritual sensitivity and his moral integrity are now unquestionable. For all his weaknesses and failures Coleridge was a soul *naturaliter christiana*.

---

a liberty of speculation which no Christian can tolerate, and advanced conclusions which were often heathen rather than Christian, yet after all instilled a higher philosophy into inquiring minds, than they had hitherto been accustomed to accept' (*Essays Critical and Historical*, ed. 1897, p. 268). See also p. 97 below.

5. See his edition of Sterling's *Essays and Tales*, p. xiv. Hare's own *The Mission of the Comforter* (1846) is dedicated 'To the honoured memory of Samuel Taylor Coleridge, the Christian Philosopher.'

6. *The Kingdom of Christ* (ed. 1842), p. xxv.

7. A. W. Benn, *The History of English Rationalism in the Nineteenth Century* (1906), i, p. 262f. On the other hand a very favourable critic also admits that Coleridge's 'system'—if it may be so called—'was really a strategy for reconciling conflicting oppositions in his own mind, and it is perfectly obvious that some of his manœuvres were less successful than others'. What matters, however, is 'the rich variety of complex philosophical and religious opinions which filtered through the mind of this genius' (James D. Boulger, *Coleridge as Religious Thinker* (1961), p. 219).

To separate the many interwoven threads of his philosophy is, then, a task far from easy. He must be read sympathetically and always with the closest attention. At times he is baffling. Often he is tortuous and obscure. Truth comes to him by intermittent flashes of insight. He will pursue an idea for the fascinating prospect that suddenly opens up before him, and then as suddenly abandon it for some other equally alluring. Such is his way, but the reader must take him for what he is and for what he so liberally gives. And the gifts, as in recent years we have come more and more to appreciate, are superlatively rich. Indeed, satisfaction with the much that he did accomplish is qualified only by regret for being without the more which, with a greater self-discipline, he might have accomplished. But a man's nature is not a matter of option. Coleridge is both an astonishing and a disappointing genius. Had his talents been more prosaic his luminous insight might have been less bright. He could have been one of the greatest philosophers of modern times had he submitted his exuberant intelligence—not to mention his personal conduct—to a stricter control. That he did not it is idle to deplore. As it is this country has produced few thinkers of his order, whilst his right to be considered one of the Church of England's most brilliant sons is beyond doubt.

Reason and understanding

In early manhood Coleridge's thinking had been swayed by a mechanistic philosophy. His release from this in the first years of the new century is described at length in the *Biographia Literaria*,[8] where the Hartleian school comes in for some abrasive criticism. His disillusionment with associationist doctrines, therefore, need not detain us. What had attracted him to this philosophy was the simplicity of its explanations: any idea could be reduced to the pattern of its antecedent mental vibrations and every act of will made the product of mechanical force. But by March 1801 he could no longer accept it or 'the irreligious metaphysics of modern infidels' that accompanied it. The human mind, he now saw, is not merely passive but has its own energy and creativity—it is not simply receptive of objects but can in some way be said to enter into them. Hence 'any system built on the passiveness of the mind must be false, as a system'.[9] What in fact he had come to realize was that the mind's constitutional energy is the *will*. Deny this, he thought, and the ground beneath both ethics and theology gives way. Man's fundamental conviction of volitional freedom, his capacity for originative action, are something of which abstract argument has no power to deprive him: 'It is the principle of our personality.' But Coleridge's mechanistic period was over before he had begun to reflect seriously on religious questions and it had no real influence upon his later views. What is of importance was that a heavy impediment had been cast off, once for all. And along with associationism went also the Socinianism he had imbibed from Joseph Priestley, leaving him with the orthodox Christianity in which he had

8. Chaps. 8 and 9.
9. *Letters*, ed. E. H. Coleridge (1895), i, p. 352.

been brought up. Having gone the whole hog he was able, as he afterwards put it, 'to come right round to the other side'.[10]

The fact of man's freedom is, then, the basis of a Christian philosophy; but we do not know the meaning of freedom, of a 'responsible will', apart from the law of conscience and the existence of evil: evil, that is, which is essentially such and 'not by accident of outward circumstances, nor derived from its physical consequences, nor from any cause, out of itself'.[11] The law of conscience, like the responsibility of the will, is a 'fact of consciousness', the existence of evil being a 'fact of history'. Thus Coleridge opposes both the necessitarianism of men like Hobbes, and its contrary, the deism of Shaftesbury and his followers:

> In contradiction to their splendid but delusory tenets, I profess a deep conviction that man was and is a *fallen* creature, not by accident of bodily constitution, or any other cause which *human* wisdom in a course of ages might be supposed capable of removing; but as diseased in the *will*, in that will which is the true, and only synonime of the word, I, or the intelligent Self.[12]

In these truths the Christian thinker has his starting-point. To Coleridge they were the postulate of a new type of apologetic.

Just such an apology *Aids to Reflection* was designed to be, and we fail to appreciate either its inherent importance or the nature of its author's procedure—daunting enough to the modern reader who takes up the book without previous warning of what he should expect—unless we relate it to its theological background. When it appeared in 1825 it offered an altogether fresh approach to Christianity as understood in terms of Anglican orthodoxy. Its novelty indeed was too much for its immediate contemporaries, who in the main chose to ignore it. Current religious discussion, in so far as it ventured upon philosophical problems at all, fastened on the 'evidences' of Christianity, chiefly in an attempt to refute the sceptic Hume. Coleridge's aim was to break entirely with these arid and unconvincing methods.

> I more than fear [he wrote] the prevailing taste for books of Natural Theology, Physico-Theology, Demonstrations of God from Nature, Evidences of Christianity, and the like. Evidences of Christianity! I am weary of the word. Make a man feel the want of it; rouse him, if you can, to the self-knowledge of his need of it; and you may safely trust to its own Evidence.[13]

For not only was evidence-theology useless—ineffectual for its own end; it was also false in principle. Its procedure was purely rationalistic and made no appeal to religious feeling. To the believer external evidences are unnecessary: he builds his faith on other grounds; whilst to the philosophically-minded unbeliever they rest on a mistaken premise. The reader Coleridge sought to address was the intelligent doubter, especially if he were among the young, whom the conventional arguments

10. *The Table Talk*, ed. H. N. Coleridge, 1835, p. 517, entry for June 23, 1834: 'I think Priestley must be considered the author of modern Unitarianism. I owe, under God, my return to the faith, to my having gone much further than the Unitarians, and so having come round to the other side.'
11. See *Aids to Reflection* (Bohn's Library ed.), pp. 190f.
12. *Ibid.*, p. 92.
13. *Ibid.*, p. 272.

left untouched. He himself held Christianity to be such a faith as a reasonable man could reasonably embrace, and that the objections commonly brought against it may be fully met. But not only was Christianity reasonable; it is, he was persuaded, the very 'Perfection of Human Intelligence', the sum and fulfilment of all truths. That there are many speculative difficulties to be faced he did not deny; but speculative difficulties, if no more than speculative, can be put aside, since religious truth is not discoverable by speculation merely as such. The only substantial objections would be moral,[14] and for readers sensitive to these he admits a special concern. Difficulties at the purely intellectual level, that is, do not necessarily preclude the holding of a reasonable faith, for faith is practical, not theoretical, and Christianity a life, not a philosophy.[15] To one who asks for proof Coleridge would simply reply, Try it; the truth of the Christian religion is self-testifying. 'Ideas, that derive their origin and substance from the *Moral* Being, and to the reception of which as true *objectively* (that is, as corresponding to a *reality* out of the human mind) we are determined by a *practical* interest exclusively.'[16]

The basis of faith, then, is not argument but experience, and deep thinking is attainable only by a man of deep feeling. All truth is a species of revelation; it cannot be possessed unless the heart has 'fed' upon it. Christian doctrine, to be meaningful, must be understood (as we now would say) existentially. In attacking the current evidence theology his particular target was Paley, whose smug and superficial apologetic was repugnant to him. The author of the *Evidences of Christianity* and the *Principles of Moral and Political Philosophy* was a rationalist appealing to rationalistic criteria in order to impress other rationalists. But Coleridge saw also that the rationalistic method, however misconceived, was specious and popular. Its point was obvious: the average 'intellectual' Christian, persuading himself that his own belief rested on such arguments, assumed that others were to be won over by the same means. *Aids to Reflection* was an attempt to dispel this illusion and put something real in its place. As Coleridge once wrote to Wordsworth, what was needed was a

> general revolution in the modes of developing and disciplining the human mind by the substitution of life and intelligence ... for the philosophy of mechanism, which, in everything that is most worthy of the human intellect, strikes *Death*, and cheats itself by mistaking clear images for distinct conceptions, and which idly demands conceptions where intuitions alone are possible or adequate to the majesty of the Truth.[17]

That such a mechanical philosophy as Paley's should pass, in the universities as among readers generally, for a serious Christian philosophy was a fact which irked Coleridge beyond endurance. He found himself bound 'in conscience to throw the whole force of my intellect in the way of this [Paley's] triumphal car, on which the tutelary genius of modern Idolatry is borne, even at the risk of being crushed under the wheels'.[18] No man ought to be argued into faith, even were it possible. Instead

14. *Ibid.*, p. 103.
15. *Ibid.*, p. 134.
16. *Ibid.*, p. 108.
17. *Letters*, ii, p. 649.
18. *Aids to Reflection*, p. 273.

he should be led to feel within himself the vital need of it; and a genuine philosophy of belief would help him to do so. Spiritual things must be spiritually discerned, we learn them through moral experience only.

> The Law of Conscience, and not the Canons of discursive Reasoning, must decide in such cases. At least, the latter have no validity, which the single veto of the former is not sufficient to nullify. The most pious conclusion is here the most legitimate.[19]

The authority of Christianity is to be seen not in logical demonstration, the procedures of which are inapplicable in this realm, but in its power to meet the needs of our humanity. And of this each must judge for himself.

What we must learn to realize, Coleridge teaches, is that spiritual truth is to be apprehended by man only in the fulness of his personal being. It cannot be a matter chiefly of the feelings, as many Evangelicals seemed to suppose. Reason too has its necessary part, for although the mere intellect is unable to make any certain discovery of 'a holy and intelligent cause' it nevertheless may supply a demonstration, in order that no legitimate argument may be drawn from the intellect *against* its truth. Yet the conviction is not to be resisted that religion, as both the cornerstone and the keystone of morality, must have a *moral* origin. At all events the evidence of its doctrines is not, like the truths of abstract science, independent of the will.[20] Faith, rather, is an energy relating to the whole man, 'in each and all of his constituents, faculties and tendencies'.[21]

These considerations bring us to Coleridge's primal distinction between the reason and the understanding, a parallel to the one he draws in aesthetic theory between the fancy and the imagination. Both imagination and reason are, he holds, to be stressed as against the modern mind's infection with 'the contagion of its mechanic philosophy'. Coleridge's conception of reason is peculiar. It does not signify 'reasoning', in the usual sense. The latter he would cover by the word 'understanding'. Reason, he thinks, is essentially 'the organ of the supersensuous', whereas understanding is 'the faculty of judging according to sense'. The one is 'the science of phenomena', the other 'the Power of Universal and necessary Convictions, the Source and Substance of Truths above Sense, and having their evidence in themselves'.[22] Understanding deals with means, reason with ultimate ends. Reason is the eye of the spirit, understanding the mind of the flesh. The latter remains 'commensurate with the experimental notices of the sense from which it is generalized', the former 'either predetermines experience, or avails itself of a past experience to supersede its necessity in all future time'. Reason's capacity is to affirm truths 'which no sense could perceive, nor experiment verify, nor experience confirm'. The understanding, needless to say, has a large and a perfectly legitimate use; its concern is with measurement and analysis, abstraction and classification, in short, with the method of natural science. We employ it necessarily and consistently in the affairs of daily life. With reason, however, there is

19. *Ibid.*, pp. 108f.
20. *Biographia Literaria*, ed. J. Shawcross (1907), i, pp. 134f.
21. *Aids to Reflection* ('An Essay on Faith'), p. 349.
22. *Ibid.*, p. 143.

an *Intuition* or *im*mediate Beholding, accompanied by a conviction of the necessity and universality of the truth so beholden not derived from the senses, which intuition, when it is *construed* by *pure* sense, gives birth to the Science of Mathematics, and when applied to objects supersensuous or spiritual is the organ of Theology and Philosophy.[23]

The mistake of the age was to suppose that the understanding is competent to treat of what belongs to the sphere of the reason. This confounding of one mode or order of knowledge with another had led to the 'godless revolution' which had installed utilitarianism, determinism and atheist materialism in the place of spiritual religion, or alternatively had reduced spiritual religion to mere rationalism, its mysteries 'cut and squared for the comprehension of the understanding', after the manner of eighteenth-century divinity. Coleridge's whole position is well summarized in a passage in *The Friend*, a weekly paper which he edited from 1809 to 1810.[24] 'The groundwork of all true philosophy', he there says,

is the full apprehension of the difference between the contemplation of reason, namely that intuition of things which arises when we possess ourselves *as one with the whole* ... and that which presents itself when ... we think of ourselves as separated beings, and place nature in antithesis to mind, as object to subject, thing to thought, death to life. (Italics ours.)[25]

In *The Statesman's Manual*—'a Lay Sermon', as he calls it, published in 1816—Coleridge undertakes some further explanation of what he sees the place of reason in religion to be. The two things, religion and reason, he points out, differ only as a twofold application of the same power. Reason is neither sense nor understanding nor imagination, but contains within itself all three,[26] although it cannot in strictness be described as a faculty, much less a personal property, of any human mind. Religion is 'the consideration of the particular and the individual ... as it exists and has its being in the universal'. If, in other words, in a too exclusive devotion to the specific and individual religion 'neglects to interpose the contemplation of the universal' it becomes superstition. Even so, it is never an abstract matter. It is born, not made, and thus, being a sort of organism, must grow. As the finite expression of the unity of the infinite Spirit it is 'a broad act of the soul', a life within a life.[27]

It has commonly been assumed that Coleridge owed his distinction between reason and understanding to Kant, and certainly the influence of Kant upon his English admirer's thinking was deep and lasting. Coleridge first became acquainted with the *Critique of Pure Reason* in about 1799 and was forthwith converted. But Kant's was by no means the sole influence. In any case it probably was more formal than material, and 'to have resided', as Shawcross puts it, 'rather in the scientific statement of convictions previously attained than in the acquisition of new

23. *Ibid.*, p. 155 n.
24. It originally comprised twenty-eight numbers. It was reissued in 1812 with supplementary matter; and again, with some new material, in 1818.
25. Bohn's Library ed., p. 366.
26. 1839 ed., Appendix B, p. 266.
27. *Ibid.*, p. 282.

truths'.[28] Kant, that is, enabled Coleridge to give intellectual definition to a view already emerging from his reading of the seventeenth century English Platonists and one which remained fundamentally more Platonist than Kantian in its inspiration.[29] As the poet made his way through the writings of men like John Smith, Henry More and Archbishop Leighton he was more and more delighted with a conception of reason differing entirely from the arid intellectualism still current in his day. Rationalist reason appeared to alienate faith altogether; the two principles were virtually antithetical. But as the Cambridge Platonists saw it reason and faith were essentially one; reason indeed was 'the candle of the Lord'. It was not, in Smith's words, a faculty, 'but rather a light, which we enjoy, but the source of which is not in ourselves, nor rightly by any individual to be denominated *mine*'. Reason, as an emanation of the divine, is seen here as the necessary vehicle or medium of spiritual experience at its fullest, as opposed to the merely discursive or reflective function of individual reasoning. Yet it was evident also that the Platonists had no clearly conceived epistemology. 'What they all wanted was a pre-inquisition into the mind, as part organ, part constituent of all knowledge.' They, however, had lived in an older world and did not have to face the type of problem now posed. For them any difficulty of the 'lower' reason could be solved by appeal to a 'higher'. But the work of Locke and Hume had made this expedient impossible. What was needed, Coleridge realized, was a logical propaedeutic, a systematic investigation of the human intellect as such 'which, previously to the weighting and measuring of this or that, begins by assaying the weights, measure, and scales themselves'. This task, envisaged long before by Bacon, had now been accomplished by Kant in his great *Critique*.

Coleridge imbibed Kant, we may allow, with characteristic zest, but the main attraction of Kantianism lay for him in the Transcendental Dialectic. The Aesthetic, he was confident, had shown that the 'understanding' faculty was the legitimate instrument of truth in scientific inquiry; yet the fact was that Coleridge, for all his immense curiosity, was not himself greatly interested in the grounds and scope of scientific knowledge, at least as compared with metaphysical, theological and literary questions. It was not unnatural, therefore, that he should have stressed the negative side of what Kant had said about the understanding, to the neglect of the more positive, dealt with at length in the Transcendental Analytic. What struck him most about Kant's teaching was the principle that the understanding, of its

28. *Biographia Literaria*, i, p. 198.
29. The Kantian element in Coleridge's philosophy is especially emphasized by both René Wellek (*Kant in England* 1931), and Elizabeth Winkelmann (*Coleridge und die Kantische Philosophie*, 1933). Wellek finds the combination of the critical Kantian with the mystical Platonist elements to have resulted in a basic inconsistency, and concludes that Coleridge finally 'gave up any attempts at a solution and came to take for granted the dualism of speculation and life, of the head and the heart'. 'At length', he says, 'he seduced the struggling spirit to acquiesce in immediate knowledge and faith, he lured it to enjoy a mere feeling of mystery and to give up the labor of thinking penetration into problems' (*Kant in England*, p. 134). Wellek insists on Coleridge's dependence on German idealism, to the point even of plagiarism. Winkelmann's assessment however is more balanced.

very constitution, is incapable of establishing truth in the realm of metaphysics, ethics and theology. Kant's purpose of supplying a sound philosophical basis for Euclidean geometry and Newtonian physics could well take care of itself, the possibility of scientific knowledge being beyond all doubt. But science, so the Dialectic had demonstrably shown, could not extend its territory into the metaphysical. The processes of the 'pure speculative reason', in Kantian terminology, are not 'synthetic'. Pure reason has no finally satisfying object, since on the great metaphysical issues—God, the Self, Freedom, Immortality—it arrives only at contradictory conclusions. Metaphysical knowledge is not, therefore, possible. Kant's solution of the difficulty is to distinguish between what he calls the noumenal and the phenomenal. Noumenal ideas are not scientific, but have only a *regulative* force. They are essentially practical: we must act *as if* they were true and valid, even though they cannot be grasped with the scientific understanding. Yet it was this side of Kant's doctrine which most deeply impressed the theologians and philosophers of the nineteenth century, encouraging them, moreover, in the very kind of speculation which on the principles of the critical philosophy was henceforth to be excluded. Coleridge himself was no exception.

For Kant, it seemed to him, had succeeded in delivering the really important truths—the truths of faith and religion—from the thraldom of mere logic. Hume's objections, before which the customary apologetic appeared impotent, had now been met. But was it enough that metaphysical ideas should have only a regulative function, a merely postulated validity? What Coleridge desiderated for them was the ontological reality which they possessed for the Platonists. In contrast, therefore, to the 'understanding'—Kant's pure speculative reason—Coleridge asserted the existence of a 'higher reason' for which the great truths of the spirit were truths indeed, not simply plausible assumptions.[30] Kant's 'practical reason' thus becomes something more than what he himself was content to understand by it. For Coleridge 'the Practical Reason alone is Reason in the full and substantial sense'. It is reason 'in its own sphere of perfect freedom; as the source of IDEAS, which Ideas, in their conversation to the responsible Will, become Ultimate Ends'.[31] In other words, the reason is no less valid a means of apprehending truth than is the understanding. Spiritual experience can *know* itself to have an objective ground—without presumably having to render any account of itself in terms of an inappropriate, and perhaps inconvenient, logic. Such at least is the impression that Coleridge's argument often conveys. *Le coeur a ses raisons que la raison ne connaît point.* Hence the charge that he used Kantian language as a cloak for Platonist doctrine and that his thought fails to resolve the inconsistency of a fundamental dualism.[32]

---

30. In this he received further encouragement from the German mystical writer, F. H. Jacobi, for whom reason is the 'eye' wherewith man beholds spiritual realities. Coleridge was considerably influenced by Jacobi.
31. *Aids to Reflection*, p. 277 n.
32. Cp. Boulger, *Coleridge as Religious Thinker* p. 84: '[Coleridge's] was an adventure in the meaning of faith, incomprehensible alike to those for whom it implies a retreat into fancy, and for those for whom it implies a steady objectivity. ... What he offers is an authentic example of the religious mind reporting a variety of experiences in religion to religious dogma; the validity of this experiment in the strict sense no man can judge.'

So long as we confine ourselves to Coleridge's attempt simply to define what he means by reason the conclusion would indeed seem warranted. Certainly his definitions are not free from ambiguity. A more fruitful approach is to study the *use* which he makes of his distinction when confronted with the actual data of Christian experience. For Coleridge is a religious man in the process of thinking out his faith, and although the relationship between faith and speculative thought may defy precise formulation, in the full context of a living experience the problem assumes a different aspect. Coleridge's religious philosophy is in this sense a practical one. His answers may dismay the rationalist and the dogmatist, but, like Pascal or Newman or Kierkegaard, he was a man for whom any *rationale* of faith must be made in essentially personal terms. To have tried to put it on a purely objective basis would in his view have been a misapplication of the function of the 'understanding'. As he saw it, it was something which every man must work out for himself, by resort to criteria which in the long run are peculiar to himself. Herein lies Coleridge's chief significance as a religious thinker, for after him it was impossible to omit the subjective consciousness from any serious discussion of the basic issues of religious belief. And beside him virtually all of his immediate British contemporaries seem to belong to a different intellectual world.

Christian belief[33]

Turning now to Coleridge's view of the content of religious faith, we find it dominated by his belief in God as a Being with whom man can hold communion. The gravest error of deism—a creed as cheerless as atheism itself—was its denial of an assurance without which we may have a philosophy but not a religion. So far is man from being alien to God that he himself participates in the divine nature.

> Whenever by self-subjection to this universal light, the will of the individual, the *particular* will, has become a will of reason, the man is regenerate, and reason is then the spirit of the regenerated man, whereby the person is capable of a quickening communion with the Divine Spirit.[34]

The mediator, or the effort, connecting 'the misery of the self' with the blessedness of God is *prayer*. But first the reason must be justified in its claim that God really exists as more than an impersonal Absolute. That any fully rational demonstration of this kind is possible Kant had very plausibly disallowed: divine existence is not open to speculative proof. Coleridge agrees, therefore, that faith is the prerequisite. It was in vain, he tells us, that he looked round to discover a vacant place for a *science* whose result had to be the 'knowledge and assertainment' of God. Proofs of divine existence founded either on the senses or on reasonings from them are to be discounted, along with the type of theology which appeals to them. The ever-popular argument from design Coleridge admits to being superficially impressive, but he rejects it as firmly as did Hume; not, however, merely from the consideration that it would prove the existence only of a limited deity, a demiurge, but because

33. For an attempted systematization of Coleridge's mature views on Christian doctrine see J. Robert Barth, *Coleridge and Christian Doctrine* (1969).
34. *Aids to Reflection*, p. 143.

to infer that nature's adaptations necessarily imply intelligence in the creative force behind them is to beg the whole question. The conclusion has in fact been assumed as a premise. But although the traditional arguments are too faulty to be of any real service, the exposure of their faults, Coleridge thinks, does not of itself prove that all rational argument in this regard is unavailing. Rather is it that the idea of God is something which, in Lockean phrase, 'cannot be conveyed into the mind' at all. An idea of this order can only be conjured up, or brought into consciousness, by an appropriate experience. The arguments have a certain subjective effectiveness, but the proper task of philosophy is to designate the kind of experience which does induce belief in God and to help remove the obstacles which may impede its full acceptance. Yet when all is said such belief 'could not be intellectually more evident without becoming morally less effective; without counteracting its own end by sacrificing the *life* of faith to the cold mechanism of a worthless because compulsory assent'.[35] Faith, that is, is neither a matter exclusively of the 'heart', of the 'emotions', as Schleiermacher appeared to teach, nor of the 'head', the purely intellectual judgment, but is the reasoned belief of a practical man.[36]

Coleridge, then, thought of the God of experience as living and active, and the indwelling light and life of all mankind. But since the divine light lighteth every man no sharp distinction can be drawn between natural religion and revealed. The parcel of truth in any religion is *ipso facto* revealed. That there is a pantheistic tendency here is to be conceded, and other passages in Coleridge's writings having a pantheistic tone can readily be instanced; but the claim that the whole drift of his thought inevitably carried him into pantheism cannot be sustained. He had certainly at one time been influenced by Schelling, finding in the latter's *Natur-Philosophie* and *System des Transcendentalen Idealismus* 'a general coincidence' with a good deal in his own thinking, especially Schelling's theory of the imagination, which appeared to confirm his personal aesthetic doctrines. But further consideration awakened a more critical judgment. 'The more I reflect', he wrote, 'the more I am convinced of the gross materialism which underlies the whole system'.[37] Idealistic monism could not be reconciled with Christian dualism. 'In short, Schelling's System and mine stand thus: In the latter there are God and Chaos: in the former an Absolute Somewhat, which is *alternately* both, the rapid legerdemain shifting of which constitutes the delusive appearance of Poles.'[38] The

35. *Biographia Literaria*, i, p. 136.
36. Thus J. H. Muirhead goes so far as to claim that Coleridge's philosophy is 'in a true sense metaphysical rather than mystical'. 'Coleridge was prepared ... to admit that in the end *omnia in mysteria exeunt*. But he was also prepared to maintain that it is only following our reason that we are able to discover when we come to that end, and to protect ourselves against the mistake, not to say the arrogance, of drawing the line where it happens to suit our prejudices or the desires of our indisciplined hearts' (in *Coleridge Studies by Several Hands*, ed. E. Blunden and E. L. Griggs (1936), p. 197).
37. See *Biographia Literaria*, i, p. 248 and section vi of Shawcross's Introduction.
38. Unpublished Notebook 28, ff 30v–31 (quoted Boulger, p. 108). Coleridge's manuscript notebooks, which are in the British Library, have been edited by Kathleen Coburn in 3 vols (1957–73). See also her *Experience into Thought: Perspectives on the Coleridge Notebooks* (1979). On Coleridge's alleged pantheism see T. McFarland, *Coleridge and the Pantheist Tradition* (1969).

idealist Absolute was impersonal and abstract, whereas for Coleridge personality, in man and in God, is a fact always of supreme value. Schelling's *Ich* was not the living, personal subject, but a mere logical principle, the first step in a system in which a personal deity could have no place. As soon as Coleridge realized this—and his notebooks provide copious evidence of the way his thought developed—he fell back more and more upon a metaphysic of the traditional Christian kind. God could not be the source of the indubitable reality of moral evil. The object of faith and worship is not some sort of *anima mundi*, nor can the doctrine of the divine omnipresence, whatever its difficulties, be expressed simply by the maxim *Jupiter est quodcunque vides*, since in Christian theology omnipresence means that all things are present *to* God, not that they *are* God. Unless God is truly personal the spiritual experience of man becomes unintelligible. 'To hesitate to call God a person is like hesitating to speak of the root which is antecedent to stem and branches.' The all-important thing about man himself is his personality; the reality, therefore, that is beyond sense cannot itself be less than personal. The visible universe *manifests* deity: God is to be perceived *in* it, by the eye of the spirit. Underlying both nature and the interpreting mind there is a principle of identity: that which is known is *like* that which knows it.

> The fact, therefore, that the mind of man in its primary and constituent forms represents the laws of nature, is a mystery which of itself should suffice to make us religious; for it is a problem, of which God is the only solution, the one before all, and of all, and through all.[39]

None the less there is a difference between personality as we know it in ourselves and the personality which we ascribe to God. Divine personality includes the qualities which belong to ours, but in a higher degree of perfection. Coleridge even coins a new word, 'Personeity', to mark the difference.

But he is by no means insensitive to the problem of reconciling the order of the universe disclosed by science with the idea of God demanded by the religious consciousness; an idea which requires belief in providence and renders prayer natural and meaningful. Such an idea can be sustained by faith, understood as the *fidelity* or personal adherence of the individual will to the moral reason. But the question is bound to arise of the connection of this assurance with *belief* in the sense of intellectual affirmation. Coleridge himself thinks that faith so defined does not imply belief as of necessity. It may exist without it, and even in despite of it, since faith at its root is an act of volition, a personally activated submission to that transcendent Will upon which reason itself ultimately depends. Thus prayer involves the recognition that behind all rational order there is a supreme Volition, or Purpose of God, with which human purposes must ever seek to identify themselves. Acceptance of this divine will, and therefore of the order of providence, is to secure the only conditions under which man can achieve self-fulfilment, rational as well as moral.

---

39. *The Statesman's Manual*, Appendix B, p. 273.

As a light from God directly and immediately such, was necessary in the past instance to actuate the Human Reason, and as it were, to induct and inaugurate it into its legislative capacity & offices, it follows likewise that the Human Reason began in *Faith*; that an insight into the reasonableness of obedience was anterior and antecedent to an insight into the reasonableness of the command to be obeyed; that therefore even from the beginning Man's moral Being had the primacy over the intellectual, and the Light of Reason in the conscience a far higher authority than the Light of Reason in the Understanding.[40]

But man's self-fulfilment cannot be thought of aside from his immortality. Here Coleridge parts company altogether with Kant, for whom the ethical imperative needs no such exterior support. He could not in truth conceive of a 'supreme moral Intelligence' at all unless he also could believe in his own immortality. The alternative would be to accept 'a whole system of apparent means to an end which has no existence'. Give this up, he tells himself, and virtue wants all reason. He could conceive dying a martyr's death, even knowing that death in *his* case would mean annihilation, 'if it were possible to believe that all other human beings were immortal and to be benefited by it'; but emphatically not from any benefit that would affect 'only a set of transitory animals'. 'Boldly should I say: O Nature! I should rather not have been; let that wh. is to come so soon, come now, for what is all the intermediate space, but sense and utter worthlessness?'[41] Such language reveals the force of a conviction greater surely than any ordinary affirmation of orthodox faith. The mind and will of man cannot, of their very nature, remain satisfied with the transient objects of sense, but must reach out to whatever amid ceaseless flux seems to have the character of permanence, to be one, that is, with man's own essential being. Nor can the apparently universal intimation or presentiment of a life hereafter be disregarded. For why should Nature, who normally fulfils her promises, deceive man, her noblest creation, only in this? Coleridge is even prepared to press his conviction into the shape of a logical argument:

> If we assume a graduated scale of assent from the minimum of consciousness ... up to the highest imaginable perfection of consciousness that can exist in a *Creature*, there must be some first instance, in *which* the consciousness survives the metempsychosis of the *Creature*—even as there must be a first, in *which* the consciousness becomes *individual* (i.e. proper self-consciousness). Now as this latter takes place *first* in Man, there is every reason to suppose and none to deny, Man will be the first instance of the former likewise.[42]

Whatever be thought of this argument, it at least testifies to Coleridge's belief that what we find ourselves obliged to think is unlikely to have no purchase at all on reality.

> Immortality! [he elsewhere exclaims] What is (it) but the impossibility of believing the contrary? ... The moment that the soul affirms, I Am, it asserts, I cannot cease to be.

40. From Notebook 26 (quoted Boulger, p. 226).
41. See J. H. Muirhead, *Coleridge as Philosopher* (1930), pp. 233f.
42. Notebook 26, ff 45–45ᵛ.

For the I Am owns no antecedent, *it* is an act of Absolute Spontaneity and of absolute
necessity. No cause existing why it *is*, no cause can be imagined why it should cease
to be. It is an impossible thought so long as I Am is affirmed.[43]

The nature of the belief, as Coleridge held it, thus stands revealed: the intellectual
argument is at every point underpinned by the emotional assurance; or rather, the
two together compose a single structure of reasoned, but nonetheless impelled,
self-commitment. Coleridge would have to concede, of course, that the idea of
immortality, merely as an abstract speculation, is quite undemonstrable. But he
does not allow that rightly it can be so stated. On the contrary, it is a
'preassumption' at the root of every primal hope, fear and action. When, however,
it becomes a specific article of Christian faith it acquires a further aspect: not that
simply of a life to come and a future state, 'but *what* each individual soul may
hope for itself therein; and on what grounds'. It is a state which has become 'an
object of aspiration and fervent desire, and a source of thanksgiving and exceeding
great joy', already, moreover, to be anticipated in this world, in the life of grace.

If for Coleridge religion was the highest activity of the human spirit, in
Christianity it reached its apex. The Christian religion teaches man two things: the
worthlessness of a life given over merely to the senses, and the true meaning and
vocation of human existence. Thus the two great principles or 'moments' of
Christian doctrine are original sin and redemption. Any suggestion, however, that
in embracing Christian orthodoxy Coleridge abandoned the rational quest of the
philosopher would be misleading. His mind was by native constitution an enquiring
one, ever seeking to discover, to correlate and to explain. On the one hand he could
not deny the plain facts of his experience, but on the other, his interpretation of
them always strove for expression in intellectual terms. That much would
necessarily remain mysterious he freely admitted, since the mystery is inherent in
the facts themselves. Original sin undoubtedly is mysterious, yet not so
intransigently as to defy the probings of philosophy. The notion of hereditary sin
Coleridge dismissed as 'a monstrous fiction'. The seat of moral evil is in the will;
and an evil common to all must have a ground common to all. But unless this evil
ground, unthinkably, originates in the divine will, it must be referred to the will of
man. So much Coleridge tells us in *Aids to Reflection*; but his concern there is
simply practical and religious. In his unpublished notebooks he attempts to search
the mystery by the light of his metaphysic. In the earlier work, that is, he gives us
the doctrine in terms that any man could refer back to his own experience. The
subsequent discussion, by contrast, is daringly speculative. Yet from the one position
to the other there is a smooth and natural transition, and further proof if needed
of the basic unity of Coleridge's thought, for all the fragmentaries of its
expression.

The essence of sin, he holds, resides in the subjection of the individual will to
an alien control and the repudiation of its own true law. We should not blame
Adam for it—here Coleridge finds the traditional Christian concepts uniformly
unsatisfactory—but the will that is in every one of us. For 'every man is the

43. Notebook 39, f 37ᵛ.

adequate representative of all men'. Each may be described as a 'separated finite', that which is not God nor yet with God. When the individual will is in harmony with the Absolute Will it is in positive 'potency'. Its negative potency consists in its ability to act for itself: in other words, to yield the possibility of evil.[44] Such negative potency has its maximum realization in the 'Apostasy of Satan', but partially also in the sin of mankind. Where the will *wills* its autonomy—of which, again, the devil is the supreme symbol—it falls into original sin. But with man all such self-willing, being only partial, involves an inherent contradiction, since the capacity for redemption remains, a capacity revealed in man's potentiality for good as well as evil. Hence the possibility is open to him of a restored harmony with the Absolute Will. Yet it is only too obvious that the will *per se* cannot effect this restoration: its self-contradiction always limits it to the selfish ends presented to it by its separation from the Absolute. Help therefore is needed from without, from a mediator or redeemer.

If sin is disobedience to the true law of one's being in pursuit of natural appetites, redemption, on the other hand, is achieved by a willing return to this law and the resumption of the freedom which it confers. It is a new birth in the spirit, although how so is a 'transcendent Mystery'; but its results are 'Sanctification from Sin, and liberation from the inherent and penal consequences of sin in the World to come, with all the means and processes of Sanctification by the Word and the Spirit'. The 'Agent' in redemption is the incarnate Son of God—'tempted, agonizing, crucified, submitting to death, resurgent, communicant of His Spirit, ascendant'. Yet for all this Coleridge does not appear to have been greatly interested in the problem of the historicity of the gospels. The broad facts he accepted; but rather, it seems, as marking what had come to pass by God's eternal purpose. It is hardly surprising, therefore, in view of this attitude, that he should have dwelt comparatively little upon the doctrine of the incarnation itself, central though it is in all traditional theology. He is credited indeed with the opinion that the 'law of God and the great principles of the Christian religion would have been the same had Christ never assumed humanity'.[45] Hence, too, his lack of concern over the question of miracles. In fact, as touching the human life of Christ Coleridge is persistently evasive, perhaps because the difficulties it involves appeared to him incapable of satisfactory treatment. Yet in one of his notebooks he asks, concerning Jesus's ignorance of temporal matters, whether the repugnance to such a supposition is not

---

44. Cp. Notebook 31, f 33 (quoted Boulger, pp. 153f.): 'For pure Evil what is it but Will that would manifest itself as Will, not in Being [Ετερότησ] not in Intelligence (therefore formless—not in union or Communion, the contrary therefore of Life, even eternal. ... It is the creaturely will which instead of quenching itself in the Light and the Form, to be the Warmth [of Life] and the Procession [of Love]; and so resolve itself into the Will of the One, it would quench the Light of the Form, and shrink inward, if so it might itself remain the One, by recoiling from the One—and find a centre by centrifuge—and thus in the Self-love, it becomes Hate and the lust full of Hate—and in the striving to be one (instead of striving after and toward the One) it becomes the infinite Many.'
45. *Letters, Conversations and Recollections of S. T. Coleridge*, ed. Allsop (1836).

grounded in the habit of the Christian world since the Arian controversy of directing their thoughts so exclusively to the Son of God in his character of co-eternal Deity as to lose sight of the *Son of Man*, and to forget that the Son of Mary, in whom the Word εσχηνωσεν (=tabernacled), was still *the Man*, Jesus.[46]

He even applies to the problem his distinction between reason and understanding:

> The human understanding is in each individual united with the Reason in one and the same person, and yet cannot comprehend the Reason which shines down into it; for if it did it would cease to be Understanding ...[47] Who [he goes on to ask], will dare assert that the Gospel represents *Jesus* as omniscient in his personal consciousness as Jesus? Jesus knew that the Son of God was the *true* and proper ground of his Being—which was to him what our Reason is to us ...[48]

He confessed to himself, however, that the only right thing to be done in face of the difficulties was to 'walk humbly and seek Light by Prayer'.[49]

Thus, then, does Coleridge find Christianity to be necessary. It is a necessity for the human spirit itself if it is to be saved from the destructive pressures of all 'mechanic' philosophies. But in claiming this he also conscientiously avoids the fundamentalist attitudes of contemporary orthodoxy, according to which revelation and the order of grace are miraculous divine *interpositions* upon the order of nature and reason. It is the universal and abiding need of man, in all his parts and potentialities, which religion exists to serve. From this the question of its truth is inseparable. No theology, therefore, which sees God and humanity in terms of a radical mutual 'alterity' can be satisfactory. To understand what Christianity essentially is we must view it as a growth, a becoming, a progression. It is history, and history under the form of moral freedom, in which alone its 'idea' can be realized. Hence it is not simply the Scriptures which prove the divine origin of the Christian religion, but the 'progressive and still continuing fulfilment of the assurance of a few fishermen that both their own religion and the religion of their conquerors should be superseded by the faith of a man recently and ignominiously executed'. In other words, the existence of the Church itself is the required proof, had the apostles indeed left no scriptures behind them.

The Bible

But Coleridge for all his metaphysical interest did not overlook the Scriptures, and his posthumously published *Confessions of an Inquiring Spirit*[50], designed as a supplement to *Aids to Reflection*, was among the first books to challenge public opinion in this country with a plea for a new and more perceptive approach to the

46. Notebook 35, ff 19^v–20.
47. *Ibid.*
48. Notebook 37, 19^v–20.
49. Notebook 25, ff 21–21^v.
50. The first edition, by H. N. Coleridge, appeared in 1840. A reprint of the third edition, 1853 (with J. H. Green's introduction and a note by Sara Coleridge), was issued in 1956. It is edited by H. St J. Hart.

Bible as a whole. He certainly was among the few to have any firsthand acquaintance with contemporary German investigations in this field. For during his stay in Germany from 1798 to 1799 he read Eichhorn's *Introduction to the New Testament*, and made a close study of the writings of Wilhelm Gotffried Lessing, including the latter's edition of the Wolfenbüttel Fragments of Reimarus, former professor of oriental languages at Hamburg. The operative principle of biblical criticism became clear to him from Eichhorn, but it was from Lessing, by whose ideas he was deeply impressed, that he learned to appreciate history as a developmental process. The outcome of these influences was that he achieved a more intelligent grasp of the nature and implications of the biblical problem than was possessed by any other Englishman of his time. Not that he personally acquired any special degree of technical knowledge as a biblical scholar; nor that he ever felt called upon to offer the detailed conclusions of such scholarship to the general reader. Here, too, his own role was rather that of the Christian apologist trying to meet the increasing difficulties which historical criticism raised for the received belief that the Bible is a book uniquely inspired and authoritative.

Coleridge's special purpose in the *Confessions* is to show that the customary 'literalist' theory of inspiration is unsatisfactory in itself and in any case untenable when confronted with the facts of the Bible's literary history. He argues that a broader, more historical conception of it not only will not diminish but will actually enhance its inherent spiritual value. To be rightly appreciated the Bible must be read like any other book; but the reader with his mind thus open will soon come to realize that in reality it is *not* like any other book and that its appeal is entirely its own, since more fully than any other does it meet the needs of man's spiritual being. The Bible, that is to say, like Christianity itself, is its own sufficient evidence.

> In every generation, and wheresoever the light of Revelation has shone, men of all ranks, conditions, and states of mind have found in this volume a correspondent for every movement towards the Better felt in their own hearts.[51]

The final test, as always, is that of personal experience.

> With such purposes, with such feelings, have I perused the books of the Old and New Testaments,—each book as a whole, and also as an integral part. And need I say that I have met everywhere more or less copious sources of truth, and power, and purifying impulses;—that I have found words for my inmost thoughts, songs for my joy, utterances for my hidden griefs, and pleadings for my shame and feebleness?[52]

In short, he declares, whatever *finds* me, bears witness for itself that it has proceeded from 'a Holy Spirit'. But this conviction is not merely a subjective reaction. It implies that although Scripture truly is a revelation of God from without, the knowledge it conveys has to be assimilated to that which a man has within him. To read the Bible spiritually, therefore, is a living experience of which divine word and personal faith are the constituents; for 'as much of reality, as much of objective truth, as the Scriptures communicate to the subjective experiences of the Believer, so much of present life, of living and effective import' do these experiences in turn

51. *Confessions*, ed. Hart, p. 68.
52. *Ibid.*, p. 42.

give to the letter of the Scriptures. The notion that the Bible was divinely dictated, requiring as it does the corollary that all its parts are equally inspired, really makes this impossible. This doctrine Coleridge maintains—and it was the doctrine generally held by Christians in this country at the time—simply petrifies the whole body of Holy Writ with all its harmonies and symmetrical gradations.

> This breathing organism, this *panharmonicum*, which I had seen stand on its feet as a man, and with a man's voice given to it, the Doctrine in question turns at once into a colossal Memnon's head, a hollow passage for a voice, a voice that mocks the voices of many men, and speaks in their names, and yet is but one voice, and the same;—and no man uttered it, and never in human heart was it conceived.[53]

The Bible, however, is not a unity, nor homogeneous, but a body of literature in varying stages of development, some of it primitive, some of it highly advanced; whilst inspiration properly signifies 'the actuating influence of the Holy Spirit' in quickening the writer's entire personality, thus rendering it more perceptive of spiritual truth.[54]

Coleridge saw plainly that the traditional view, when examined, throws up insuperable difficulties. It demands in effect that the Bible from cover to cover be read as a transcript of the pronouncements of an infallible intelligence. Yet Scripture itself nowhere advances such a claim. Further, once the character of infallibility is attributed to it there can be no admission of degree; it extends to all matters, physical no less than spiritual. Hence every statement, whatever its content, must be taken as unequivocally true, and the curses of the Psalmist are no less 'inspired' than the Beatitudes of the gospel. On the other hand, if you distinguish between infallible truth and its fallible expression where exactly is the dividing line to be drawn? For what is the *criterion* of infallibility? The fear that criticism will destroy the authority of the Bible can be met, Coleridge believes, by appeal to the general drift and tenor of the Scriptures. Indeed,

> the more tranquilly an inquirer takes up the Bible as he would any other body of ancient writings, the livelier and steadier will be his impressions of its superiority to all other books, till at length all other books and all other knowledge will be valuable in his eyes in proportion as they help him to a better understanding of his Bible.[55]

And he personally confesses to the reader how 'difficulty after difficulty has been overcome from the time that I began to study the Scriptures with free and unboding spirit, under the conviction that my faith in the incarnate Word and His Gospel was secure, whatever the result might be'.[56]

---

53. *Ibid.*, p. 52.
54. Thus Coleridge deplores the then current 'literal rendering of Scripture in passages, which the number and variety of images employed in different places, to express one and the same verity, plainly mark out for figurative'; as likewise 'the practice of bringing together into logical dependency detached sentences from books composed at the distance of centuries, nay, sometimes a *millenium*, from each other, under different dispensations, and for different objects' (*ibid.*, pp. 58f.).
55. *Ibid.*, p. 75.
56. *Ibid.*, p. 63.

Coleridge was ahead of the vast majority of his fellow-countrymen in his perception both of what criticism would mean for traditional attitudes towards the Bible and of how also the genuine worth and authority of Scripture are to be vindicated. His 'literary and spiritual insight placed him', it has been well said, 'upon a point of vantage from which he could overlook the nineteenth-century country in front of him, and reply in advance to all that the *Zeitgeist* thereafter would bring forward.'[57] Assuredly much of the bitter and futile controversy about the rival authorities of religion and science could have been avoided if the argument of the *Confessions* had been more deeply pondered by both the churchmen and the scientists of the generation following. The book, brief though it is, is a work of capital importance. Its appeal, as always with Coleridge, is to the spirit as against any merely mechanical adherence to the letter; only when spiritual things are spiritually judged can criticism of the letter be usefully pursued. Wisely, he bids his reader not to be 'an Infidel on the score of what other men think fit to include in their Christianity'. The Christian religion is constituted not by the Bible but by Christ and the truth revealed through him, the proof of its divine authority being its fitness to our nature and its needs; and, as Coleridge himself puts it, 'the clearness and cogency of the proof' is 'proportionate to the degree of self-knowledge in each individual hearer'. The Bible, beyond any doubt, is 'true and holy' in consideration of its declared aims and purposes, and for all who seek truth with humility of spirit a sure guide.

Church and State

One more aspect of Coleridge's far-ranging thought remains to be discussed. With his political opinions in general we are not here concerned, but his mature reflexions on the relations of church and society, set forth in his essay on *The Constitution of the Church and State*,[58] are of immediate relevance. The strands of his thought are always so tightly interwoven that seldom if ever can any one of his characteristic ideas be properly assessed apart from the others. Thus for him there could be no politics without a religious reference, and no religion without political implicates. No other writer of his day, in this country, possessed anything approaching either his philosophical detachment or the instinctive sympathy for the task he set himself in this treatise. His purpose is the basic one of examining the 'ideas' of both Church and State in respect of their essential functions. By 'idea', however, he means not an abstraction from the given historical conditions but a conception determined by a knowledge of objectives. Hence an idea may be true without its ever having had an historical embodiment. He cites in illustration the notion of the Social

57. Basil Willey, *Nineteenth Century Studies* (1949), p. 40.
58. Published in 1829. A critical edition of the text, edited by J. Colman, was published in 1976 as the tenth volume of the *Collected Works*, ed. by K. Coburn (Princeton University Press). The references given below are to the 1839 edition. Coleridge's influence is to be detected in W. E. Gladstone's early work on *The State in its Relations with the Church*, first published in 1838, in which some affinity with Maurice's views is also evident. See Appendix III below.

Contract, which was never an historical event yet is none the less valid as a symbol of that 'ever-originating social contract' apart from which society could not maintain its existence. It is, in a word, a necessary *regulative* idea, comparable, as a 'truth-power' of the reason, with such other regulative ideas as those of God, freedom, will and the values we call absolute. These life itself requires, however short the understanding may fall in its effort to provide them with a sufficient rational foundation, or indeed however little we are able to realize them in action. 'Ideas', Coleridge insists, 'correspond to substantial beings, to objects the actual subsistence of which is implied in their idea, though only by the idea revealable.' So when we turn to the idea of the State we discover that two equally requisite but evidently opposing principles or interests must be held in balance: *permanence* and *progression*. The former is represented by the landed classes, the latter by the mercantile and professional. Both are reflected in the British constitution, which secures such a balance without its ever having been expressly devised to do so.

That it was by no means a perfect balance Coleridge knew well enough. In his own day, as he points out, the landed classes enjoyed an excess of power and influence relative to the monied interests, whereas the health of the body politic as a whole demands the adequate representation of every vital and energetic element in society. But it is the failure of the 'third estate' of the realm, the Church, to counterbalance these two which seems to him the great social defect of the age. The true function of the third estate is of a National Church whose responsibility is 'to secure and improve that civilization, without which the nation could be neither permanent nor progressive'.[59] Its purpose, in fact, is nothing less than the promotion of 'the harmonious development of those qualities and faculties that characterize our humanity'. The State is concerned with citizenship, the Church with the powers and instincts which constitute the man, and 'we must be men in order to be citizens'. But by the National Church Coleridge does not mean either the Church of Christ, in the high theological sense, or the Church of England as an established institution. His view is a good deal wider, and what he wishes us to understand by it is perhaps not altogether easy to grasp. The National Church, as he envisages it, comprehends the sum of the nation's cultural and spiritual resources—'all the so-called liberal arts and sciences, the possession and application of which constitute the civilization of a country, as well as the theological'—and is composed of what he rather oddly calls 'The Clerisy', the entire body of 'clerical persons', that is, whose *raison d'être* is to safeguard, develop and disseminate the spiritual and cultural heritage as a whole. It thus will consist not only of the clergy, as the specifically ministerial order in the Church, but also of the learned of all denominations and professions, expert in their several fields. The former Coleridge views from a sociological standpoint. The Church's chief function, under this aspect, was not primarily that of teaching religion but of providing, in the parish clergyman, 'a resident guide, guardian and instructor' throughout the land. This the existing establishment fulfilled with only qualified success, but the machinery itself, and the opportunity of enlarging it, already existed.

59. *The Constitution of the Church and State* (ed. 1839), p. 4.

Coleridge's fear was that in an epoch of rapid technological advance the higher values of civilized life would be neglected or destroyed. 'We live under the dynasty of the understanding, and this is its golden age.' *Means* in plenty were being put at men's disposal—'With these the age, this favoured land, teems'; but there was a remarkable uncertainty as to ultimate *ends*. Whence, he asks, shall we seek for information concerning these? Material prosperity does not automatically bring happiness and the production of greater wealth may also cause greater poverty. Education, synonymous with instruction, would, he also foresaw, become increasingly secular:

> Knowledge being power, those attainments, which give a man the power of doing what he wishes in order to obtain what he desires, are alone to be considered knowledge, or to be admitted into the scheme of national education;[60]

whilst the Church itself, amid dissent and unbelief, would be reduced to the status of a sect.

The Christian Church in relation to the National Church was for Coleridge 'a blessed accident'—a singular phrase which he explains as meaning that 'Christianity is an aid and instrument which no State had a right to expect'. It certainly is not a kingdom of this world, nor an estate of any realm, but 'the appointed opposite to them all collectively—the sustaining, correcting, befriending opposite of the World; the compensating counter-force to the inherent and inevitable evils and defects of the State, as a State'.[61] But it is neither invisible nor secret; on the contrary, it is visible and militant. Yet it has no local centre of unity, and no visible head or sovereign. Nor in any sense ought it to be described as an institution over against and rivalling the State. It offers, that is to say, no alternative organization of human society, but only a corrective to the evils arising within it. Its 'paramount aim and object' is another world; not a world to come exclusively, but 'likewise another world' to that which now is and to the concerns of which alone the epithet 'spiritual' can be applied without a mischievous abuse of the word.[62] Finally, the Christian Church is of its nature universal. It is neither Anglican, Gallican nor Roman, neither Latin nor Greek. In England there exists a 'Catholic and Apostolic Church', which he himself would prefer to call simply the Church, or Catholic Church, of Christ *in* England. The Roman Church plainly is not national, but neither is it universal. The English Church, still standing in an authentic tradition, is the best adapted to the needs of Englishmen.

The significance of Coleridge's genius rests in its many-sidedness. As a philosophical thinker he is always stimulating and often profound, even though his place in the textbooks of modern philosophy is not prominent. Insatiable in the pursuit of truth, his mind was perhaps too eclectic. He has aptly been called 'the first of the great nineteenth century "thinkers" rather than a philosopher in the strict technical sense'.[63] His concern was with the spiritual life of man in its widest

60. *Ibid.*, p. 66.
61. *Ibid.*, pp. 124f.
62. *Ibid.*, p. 12.
63. G. Hough, 'Coleridge and the Victorians', in *The English Mind*, ed. H. S. Davies and G. Watson (1964), p. 178.

range, so that theology, philosophy, politics, social theory and aesthetics are severally viewed by him as the intellectual aspects of a single existential reality. To English theology he gave what certainly it most needed, a broader horizon and a wholly fresh inspiration, doing for it indeed, in his way, what Schleiermacher in different circumstances did for theology in Germany. Rationalism, deism, evangelicalism, high-and-dry traditionalism—all were either dead or in need of an infusion of fresh spiritual or intellectual life. Coleridge's thinking struck out new paths, which he followed with a degree of spiritual concentration, an awareness of essential problems and a personal if idiosyncratic self-dedication for which his times, in this country at least, afford no parallel. It could be said that from Coleridge it is but a step to Kierkegaard and modern existentialism. Like the Danish thinker he came to see Christianity in an entirely new perspective. Conventional Church teaching suddenly acquired the depth and urgency of life itself. Truth was something to be 'done' and not merely argued about. Religion was an expression of the nature of man himself, in all its complexity, a yearning of the soul which only the ultimate assurance of God could satisfy. As Coleridge interprets them the great dogmas of faith—the incarnation, the atonement, the trinity, original sin—are not simply theoretical propositions but regulative and practical norms of experience. As theoretical principles alone they would be inexplicable, whereas accepted in the full context of man's moral nature they are a revelation of a mystery, a form of being rather than a system of knowledge. 'Too soon', Coleridge warns his Christian readers, 'did the Doctors of the Church forget that the *heart*, the *moral* nature, was the beginning and the end; and that truth, knowledge, and insight were comprehended in its expansion.'[64] The Christian religion is not a theory or a speculation, but a life; not a philosophy of life but a process of living, proved in the act.

Coleridge's direct influence is apparent in Thomas Arnold, in Julius Hare, in F. W. Robertson, and above all in F. D. Maurice, as possibly too in Newman.[65] Yet his true rank and importance as a religious teacher was not really appreciated until more recently, and with the study of his unpublished writings. Today his frequent anticipations of the modern standpoint seem of an almost uncanny appositeness. As a purely literary figure he has, of course, received his meed of praise, perhaps even in excess when the tribute has been accompanied by expressions of regret that so fine a poetic imagination should eventually have run to waste in a desert of metaphysical ruminations. But Coleridge was not merely a poet *manqué* whose intellectual energy had therefore to cast about for some new and congenial outlet. Had he possessed a more sustained architectonic gift, a more evident ability to control and direct the flood of his often paradoxical thought, he might have been the greatest original theologian this country has ever produced, as well as one of its foremost philosophers. As it is his very failures are such that beside them other men's successes look meagre.

---

64. *Aids to Reflection*, p. 126.
65. See below, p. 97. For an interesting comparison of Coleridge and Newman see David Newsome, *Two Classes of Men: Platonism and English Romantic Thought* (1974), ch. 4.

Chapter 3

THE OXFORD MOVEMENT

The inwardness of religion

The story of the Oxford Movement has so often been told that it needs no further repetition here, the main course of events being familiar.[1] Nor is it part of our task to assess its influence on the Church's life and worship, all-pervasive though this has been. Our concern, after a brief glance at the movement's causes, will be to review the underlying principles which in the given context make up its particular contribution to the religious thought of the century. The subject is a large one and our study of it must necessarily be concentrated.[2] But first, why did the movement occur, and occur when it did?

It arose from a variety of circumstances, political as well as theological. The era was one of reform. A spirit was abroad no longer tolerant of old abuses and injustices. The Test and Corporation Acts, by then indeed an insult rather than an injury to those against whom they discriminated, had been repealed in 1828. The Roman Catholic emancipation measure, though hotly disputed, passed into law the following year. In 1832 came the great Bill for parliamentary reform, to which the national Church, not least as represented by its bishops, was in solid opposition: 'In every village', the Whigs complained, 'we had the black recruiting-sergeant against us.' Before many months had gone by clerical fears were endorsed by the government's proposal to abolish ten out of the twenty-two bishoprics of the Church of Ireland, a measure which in view of the actual situation in Ireland was neither unreasonable nor inappropriate. To High Churchmen, however, rootedly Tory and deeply apprehensive of the growing 'march-of-mind' liberalism, it seemed to portend only one result: a relaxation of the age-old bond of sympathy which held Church and State together in a Christian realm and an increasing likelihood that the former would find itself yoked with a partner whose ends and purposes might cover much that to a sound churchman would be repugnant. Parliament could now no longer be taken as voicing ecclesiastical opinion with any degree of certainty. Yet it retained, by virtue of the establishment, complete control over ecclesiastical affairs. It was the Irish Church Bill which gave John Keble the theme for the assize sermon which he preached in the university church at Oxford on 14

1. R. W. Church's classic account in *The Oxford Movement: Twelve Years 1833–1845* (1891) is still the best.
2. Of the theology of the movement Brilioth's *The Anglican Revival* (1925) is unsurpassed as a detailed study. A useful collection of extracts from Tractarian writings is included in Owen Chadwick, *The Mind of the Oxford Movement* (1960).

July 1833, and to which he accorded the alarmist title of 'National Apostasy'—an event which has usually been regarded as setting the Oxford Movement on its way.[3]

A more insidious danger, however, was felt to be liberalism in religious teaching. Not only was the old faith being questioned, the Bible was exposed to critical examination and its inspiration, in some quarters, impugned. For men like Arnold, the Church, it thus followed, was merely a human institution, to be reorganized on new lines as conditions might require. Why, it could be asked, as Arnold himself had done, should not different opinions, rites and ceremonies be brought together in a single Christian body coextensive as far as possible with the entire nation? Exclusiveness, promoted by 'the anti-Christ of priesthood', had no place in Christ's own fellowship. To Newman such views were anathema. The very spring of liberalism was the antidogmatic principle, or the notion that a man's creed was his own affair, about which others had no business to vex either themselves or him.[4] In face of this the Evangelicals' zeal was of itself impotent. At any rate as High Churchmen judged them the Evangelical party's lack of doctrinal platform meant that against such a philosophy mere emotional individualism had no foothold. The liberal menace could be met only by recourse to the historic teachings of Catholic Christianity which the Church of England, despite the Reformation, had preserved in its formularies and which the best of its divines had never sought to minimize. Hence the Oxford school of the 1830s were far from claiming to be innovators. Their business was not to invent anything but to recall men to ancient truths that had for too long been overlooked or had ceased, in an age of indifference, to stir the pulses of faith. To preach these truths became therefore a mission. An urgent work was to be done, the doing of which demanded not only learning and fixity of principle—for such, as we have seen, were by no means wanting among many churchmen—but for the personal dedication and commitment which alone would arouse merely nominal Christians from spiritual lethargy and arm them to resist the forces under which all religious belief might in the end crumble. 'I do not', declared Newman in an article written some years after the movement began, 'I do not shrink from uttering my firm conviction that it would be a gain to the country were it vastly more superstitious, more bigoted, more gloomy, more fierce in its religion than at present it shows itself.'[5]

Yet the historian today, as he looks back upon the movement over more than a century of time, can view it in a larger perspective than either the political or the theological. Seen thus it appears as an aspect of the general cultural renaissance denoted by the word romanticism. Newman himself, in the *Apologia*, spoke of 'a spirit afloat' thirty years previously. What precisely this spirit was is not easy to

3. Such was Newman's view, as stated in the *Apologia* (ed. Svaglic), p. 43 (cp. also *Letters*, i, p. 380 and *Correspondence of John Henry Newman*, edited at the Birmingham Oratory, 1917, p. 316). Others did not necessarily share it. See F. L. Cross (1933), *John Henry Newman*, Appendix iv, 'The Myth of July 14, 1833', pp. 162f.
4. *Apologia*, p. 54: 'My battle was with liberalism; by liberalism I mean the antidogmatic principle and its developments. This was the first point on which I was certain ... From the age of fifteen dogma has been the fundamental principle of my religion.'
5. 'The State of Religious Parties', in *The British Critic*, April 1839.

define. Romanticism was curiously complex in manifestation and affected many areas of thought and action: literature, scholarship, philosophy, the arts and religion all reflected it. Essentially it was a protest against rationalism and formalism, alike in art and in life. Its ideals might have very varied utterance, but always freedom and spontaneity were deemed the vital conditions of their pursuit. Self-expression in all its modes required for authenticity immediacy of feeling, originality of insight, and liberty of imagination. Truth was to be found not in prescribed formulae or in abstract argument but in the direct apprehensions of personal experience. If we are to understand the deeper significance of the Oxford Movement this latter consideration is of special importance. The teachings of the Oxford divines in their own day and since has often been superficially judged. It was absurd to see in the new High Churchmanship, as did Arnold, the 'mere foolery' of a dress, a ritual, a name, or a ceremony. It would be only a little less wrong to think that Tractarianism was no more than a reactionary insistence upon dogma and tradition for their own sake. In some respects the movement was reactionary, as in its proclaimed hostility to 'liberalism'. But always the appeal to the letter was made in the interest of the spirit. The past which these men venerated was no enshrined corpse but, however idealized their conception of it, a living and active principle, a spur to the imagination and the feelings. Religion as they saw it was not simply a matter of doctrines and rites, but of the life of prayer and worship, the sense of eternity, the discipline of the self's wayward desires. Dogma, like ritual and ascetic practice, existed solely to promote it. Experience was the necessary test. A merely 'notional' assent to religious truth could know nothing of what such truth really is, for the fundamental testimony is that of conscience. Tractarianism, whatever its shortcomings, was rightly described by the most brilliant of its leaders as 'a spiritual awakening of spiritual wants'. True to the romantic impulse, which in other regards it might deplore, it was an assertion of the claims of the creative spirit as against externalism, routine or the cold mechanism of logical reason.

The Catholicity of the English Church

Thus the Oxford Movement gave to the old High Church theology what Alexander Knox believed it so much needed: interiority and spiritual warmth. Herein lay its vital difference. Bishop van Mildert might have spoken of the apostolical succession with as clear a grasp of its principle as did Newman in the first of the *Tracts for the Times*. But with Newman the idea takes wing. The very creed becomes a banner unfurled in the wind. Traditionary institutions and orthodox principles exist only that men may find the way of sanctity and have the divine life within themselves. Not that the Tractarians did not insist on inherited forms and sound professions: on the contrary, men like Dr Pusey and William Palmer were dedicated to their maintenance. But even if its concern for orthodoxy tended to be obsessive the long-term effect of the movement was a change in the whole ethos of English religious life. Upon the theological and philosophical thought of the age it left a mark much less distinct. The fact is indicative of where the true strength of the movement lay and the grounds of any just appraisal of its achievement.

Tractarianism, then, was a genuine revival of the spirit, arousing in its adherents a sense of elation. The disciples of Newman displayed all the enthusiastic energy of new hopes and purposes. Their cause imbued them with confidence. Mere antiquarianism or the praise of things past could not have done this. The Oxford divines believed themselves to be addressing the supreme need of their times. The decorous, torpid Protestantism commonly identified with the national religion could do nothing, they believed, to stem the advancing tide of irreligion. The Church establishment in its existing condition was a deplorable compromise with worldliness. It had lost its sense of spiritual direction and failed to teach with the authority that belonged to it. If the Church was to fulfil its apostolic commission and restore to the lives of the people an awareness of the presence and claims of the invisible and eternal, then it must recover the Catholic heritage which still was its by right. But to do so would mean re-emphasizing the fact that the Church of England, although reformed, was not 'Protestant' and that if its real identity was to be disclosed traditions of faith and polity which Calvinism, Erastianism and latitudinarianism had overlaid would have once more to be put before the world. Faced with this grave vocation the party could spare no time for the outward appurtenances of religion. The immediate task was to underpin and strengthen the doctrinal foundations; and the doctrines which called for the clearest reassertion were those of the supernatural authority of the Church and of the efficacy of sacramental grace.

If the Church of England should continue to look on such teachings only as 'Romish' then plainly it had misunderstood its own nature and status; and if to stress them seemed to de-Protestantize it, then let the work of de-Protestantizing be carried out regardless of the opposition it might incur. This emphatically was Hurrell Froude's conviction. Froude, Newman's close friend and in its early days the movement's *enfant terrible*—he died in 1836, at the age of 33—declared that he had come to 'hate the Reformation and the Reformers more and more'.[6] He confessed that for nothing would he abuse the Roman Church *as a Church* 'except for excommunicating us'. 'We are', he announced, 'Catholics without Popery, and Church of England men without Protestantism.'[7] His words are the theory of the *via media* in a nutshell. The national Church was not what she was popularly supposed to be, as her wisest teachers had always made clear. In avoiding one kind of error she had not heeled over into another. She had providentially chosen a middle course, and to pursue it was her divine destiny here on earth. But if in the past mistaken emphases for which many of the sixteenth-century Reformers themselves were responsible, had obscured this truth it was up to the men of a

---

6. Froude's *Remains*, edited by Keble and Newman, were published in 1838–9. Unfortunately the book did much to swell the movement's adverse press. 'The world', as Dean Church puts it, 'was shocked by what seemed [Froude's] amazing audacity both of thought and expression about a number of things and persons which it was customary to regard as almost beyond the reach of criticism.' 'Whether', he adds, 'on general grounds [the editors] were wise in startling and vexing friends, and putting fresh weapons into the hands of opponents by their frank disclosure of so unconventional a character, is a question which may have more than one answer' (*op. cit.*, pp. 42f.).
7. *Remains*, i, pp. 389, 395, 404.

later age to readjust the balance. As Froude aphoristically put it: 'The Reformation was a limb badly set—it must be broken again in order to be righted.' The resetting might indeed be painful. The actions of those whose task it was to carry it out would be misunderstood. Not only were Catholicism and Popery synonymous in the popular mind, but some assumptions that had for generations passed unquestioned would now be challenged. 'The Bible and the Bible alone' might well be the religion of Protestants, but it was not and could not be the religion of the Church, whose own primary teaching office was an inalienable responsibility. Again, the State connexion, far from being a spiritual privilege, had rather proved to be an Egyptian bondage. The imagined 'purity' of English Protestant Christianity was only a meagre reduction or paring down of a once richer truth, as the Church's poverty in saints regrettably testified. The Reformers were not wholly at fault, but their doctrine was one-sided and sometimes false, whilst they themselves had too often been politically-minded timeservers.

Such was the polemic of Tractarianism. But its theory of the *Via Media* was capable of a more positive shape: namely, to exhibit the Church of England as a true branch of the Church Catholic, with the Churches of Rome and of Constantinople as coordinate branches—a position argued with much force by Newman in his *Prophetical Office of the Church* (1837).[8] This work appeals in support of the theory to the 'Anglo-Catholicism' of divines like Andrewes, Laud, Hammond, Butler and Wilson. Newman's three essential 'points' are dogma, the sacramental system and anti-Romanism (the maintenance, that is, of the 'Catholic' claim of the English Church against the familiar objections of Rome). In basic matters indeed the Church stands with Rome: in both systems, it is contended, the same creeds are acknowledged; both hold certain doctrines as unconditionally necessary to salvation: the trinity, the incarnation and the atonement; both believe in original sin and the need of regeneration, in the supernatural grace of the sacraments and in the apostolical succession; both teach the eternity of a future punishment. Further, if the two Churches are so far united on fundamentals they are 'also one and the same in such plain consequences as were contained in those fundamentals and in such natural observances as outwardly represented them'.[9] Newman goes on:

> It was an Anglican principle that 'the abuse of a thing doth not take away the lawful use of it'; and an Anglican Canon of 1603 had declared that the English Church had no purpose to forsake all that was held in the Churches of Italy, France, and Spain, and reverenced those ceremonies and particular points which were Apostolic. Excepting then such exceptional matters, as are implied in this avowal, whether they were many or few, all these Churches are evidently to be considered as one with the Anglican. The Catholic Church in all lands had been one from the first for many

8. The full title is: *Lectures on the Prophetical Office of the Church viewed relatively to Romanism and Popular Protestantism*. This able book is outstanding among Tractarian publications. F. L. Cross calls it 'a magnificent apology for what may be termed the Anglican ethos' (*op. cit*, p. 70). Christopher Dawson, a Roman Catholic, thinks that it 'perhaps still remains the best justification for the essential Anglican position' (*The Spirit of the Oxford Movement*, 1933, p. 102).
9. *Apologia*, ed. Svaglic, p. 72.

centuries; then, various portions had followed their own way to the injury, but not to the destruction, whether of truth or of charity. These portions or branches were mainly three:– The Greek, Latin, and Anglican. Each of these inherited the early undivided Church *in solido* as its own possession. Each was identical with that early undivided Church, and in the unity of that Church it had unity with the other branches.[10]

The three branches thus agreed together in all but their later accidental errors. The Anglican Church was one with the Church of the middle ages. 'The Church of the twelfth century was the Church of the nineteenth', and Dr Howley[11] sat in the seat of St Thomas the Martyr. Anglicans ought to be indulgent to Rome, even though Rome teaches much which they would not wish to adopt. 'By very reason of our protest, which we had made, we could agree to differ.'

The Oxford leaders—and Newman at that time not less so than the rest—were entirely convinced of the controversial strength of their position. Their views, they had no doubt, were not novel and a weighty tradition supported them. The great defect of the national Church was that so many of its members had forgotten or had chosen to disregard its true character and constitution. What had now to be upheld were, first, the Church's apostolic descent as the real ground of its authority, and secondly, the dependent principle that the sacraments, not preaching, are the covenanted sources of divine grace.

The apostolic theory was advanced by Newman in the very first of the *Tracts*, published along with others on 9 September 1833. The authority of the Church's ministry rested not, as commonly supposed, on legal status or popularity or temporal distinctions but on Christ's original commission to his apostles, who in turn had commissioned by the laying on of hands those who should succeed them. Thus by a constantly repeated rite the sacred gift had been 'handed down to our present bishops, who have appointed us as their assistants, and in some sense representatives'. Such was the meaning of the doctrine which, it was claimed, is inherent in the ordination service itself. 'Make much of it', Newman exhorted his clerical readers. 'Show your value of it. Keep it before your minds as an honourable badge, far higher than that of secular responsibility, or cultivation, or polish, or learning, or rank, which gives you a hearing with the many.'

This implied that the kind of veneration and devotion ordinarily felt by Protestants for the Scriptures was now to be extended to the Church. 'The Church Catholic is our mother'.[12] She had the right and duty to teach, appealing to Scripture in vindication of her teaching.[13] But the doctrine of the apostolic succession was vital to that of the Church. Without the succession there would have been no Church, or no true Church. The threefold ministry of bishops, priests and deacons, in lineal descent from the apostles themselves, is constitutive of a sacred order apart from which real sacraments, as distinct from merely external signs, the *simulacra* of sacraments, could not exist. As Newman put it in the fourth of the *Tracts*:

10. *Ibid.*
11. William Howley was archbishop of Canterbury from 1828 until 1848. With Newman's opinions, however, he himself had no sympathy.
12. *The Prophetical Office of the Church* (ed. 1838), p. 314.
13. J. H. Newman, *The Arians of the Fourth Century* (1833), p. 55.

70

> The Holy Feast on our Saviour's sacrifice, which all confess to be 'generally necessary for salvation', was intended by Him to be constantly conveyed through the hands of commissioned persons. Except, therefore, we can show such warrant, we cannot be sure that our hands convey the sacrifice. We cannot be sure that souls are worthily prepared … are partakers of the Body and Blood of Christ.

The reason for the English Church's authentic standing in Christendom is the fact of its possession of the unbroken historic succession. Public position and influence are of themselves insufficient. Although the life of the non-episcopal bodies may flourish by God's 'uncovenanted mercies', churches, and Catholic, in the proper sense they are not.

Yet what was it to be Catholic, in the proper sense? How far could the Church of England itself lay just claim to Catholic status? That it was a 'true' church was guaranteed by the episcopal succession. The reverence of Anglican teachers for the witness of antiquity could be demonstrated. It also could be argued that on doubtful points the Church would defer to that witness instead of to the Reformers 'as the ultimate exponent' of its meaning. Yet on the face of it the contents of the Articles called for some measure of explanation. Their Protestant character seemed obvious and as a Protestant manifesto they had always in fact been taken. In particular how did they stand to the prayer book? Is not the latter to be read in their light? To this problem Newman was later to address himself with all the resourcefulness of a supple dialectic as well as the fixed determination to defend a controversial position of the validity of which he was sincerely convinced. His solution we shall have to return to in a moment. But the Tractarian conception of the Church was itself undergoing some revision as a result of a deepening sacramentalism. Catholicity, it appeared, might be interpreted either statically, as residing essentially in a form of order, or dynamically, as an 'extension' of the incarnation, the means whereby the life of the eternal Christ is imparted to every new generation of believers. For the 'Catholic' the sacraments, and especially the eucharist, focus his faith and piety, and are the point at which Christ, in symbolic guise, comes to meet him. In Newman's eloquent words:

> Christ shines through the sacraments, as through transparent bodies, without impediment. He is the Light and Life of the Church, acting through it, dispensing of His fulness, knitting and compacting together every part of it; and these its Mysteries are not mere outward signs, but (as it were) effluences of grace developing themselves in external forms, as Angels might do when they appeared to men. He has touched them and breathed upon them; and thenceforth they have a virtue residing in them, which issues forth and encircles them round, till the eye of faith sees in them no element of matter at all.[14]

Thus the Church is the Body of Christ in no merely figurative way. It lives because he lives. It is the expression of his mind. In a real sense it 'incarnates' him here on earth. But this means that the Church, because alive with the life of its divine founder and master, can and must 'grow'. It looks forward to the future as well as back to the past. Its authority is not simply traditionary but intrinsic. As

---

14. *Parochial Sermons*, iii, p. 302.

Newman pointed out in reply to critics of Tractarian 'antiquarianism', the Fathers are not to be imitated for imitation's sake—a servility 'likely to prevent the age from developing Church principles so freely as it might otherwise do'. Nineteenth-century men had to be men of their own century, not of the fourth; nor, and the inference is plain, of the sixteenth either. Hence in the English Church's growing realization of its Catholic heritage the marks of such a temporary vicissitude as the Reformation must be judged of less account than formerly. If one inquires what doctrines are fundamental the question, Newman answers, is not what is necessary to be believed by *this particular person or that*, since none but God can decide 'what compass of faith is required by given individuals', but what doctrines the Church Catholic teaches indefectibly, or enforces as a condition of communion, or rescues from the scrutiny of private judgment—in a word, what doctrines are the foundation of the Church. To find them, to discover what that common faith is which the Church 'now holds everywhere as the original deposit', one must turn to the creed, in which all branches of the Church agree.[15]

A local confession of faith, therefore, or a mere set of 'articles of religion', can beside this universal formulary be no more than a temporary particularization of Christian truth. It was thus, Newman contended, that the famous Anglican confession of 1571, to which the clergy were obliged to make *ex animo* subscription, was to be understood. Its terms were certainly not sacrosanct, and in any case its purpose, as its ambiguous phrases disclose, was to comprehend rather than exclude. Catholicism, accordingly, it was never intended to shun. To interpret the Articles in a manner favourable to Calvinism or even latitudinarianism was usual enough; but was it not also demonstrable that they were not only not contradictory of the witness of the early Church but likewise not opposed to Catholic doctrine down the ages, being incompatible, that is, with 'the dominant errors of Rome' alone? To attempt such a demonstration was Newman's aim in the notorious *Tract 90*, published in 1841.[16] To be merely polemical was not his intention, nor was it his purpose to declare what the Articles ought to be taken to mean. Nor again was he concerned to inquire what might or might not have been in the minds of those who framed them. His sole interest was to examine how far the language of the formulary could be read in accordance with the faith of the Church Universal

15. *The Prophetical Office of the Church*, pp. 264f.
16. The enterprise was not without precedent. To show that the Articles were patient of a Catholic interpretation had been undertaken as long ago as 1634 by Christopher Davenport—known after his conversion to Roman Catholicism as Sancta Clara—in a work printed at Lyons entitled *Deus, Natura, Gratia, sive Tractatus de Praedestinatione, de Meritis, et peccatorum remissione, seu de Justificatione, et denique de Sanctorum Invocatione*. A supplement to the main treatise is described as a *Paraphrastica Expositio reliquorum Articulorum Confessionis Anglicanae*, the purpose of which is stated as: 'Articuli Confessionis Anglicanae paraphrastica exponuntur, et quantum cum veritate compossibiles reddi possunt, perlustrantur.' An English translation of this *Expositio*, by F. G. Lee, was published in 1865. Sancta Clara's arguments are ingenious but seldom plausible. Like Newman he distinguishes Roman doctrine proper from popular misconceptions of it, although unlike Newman he attributes these to Rome's critics, not to Catholics themselves. It is not clear that at the time of writing *Tract 90* Newman was familiar with Sancta Clara's work. On Davenport see G. G. Perry in *D.N.B.*

without doing violence to its grammatical and literal sense. He was himself, he considered, doing no more than had been done by adherents of other ecclesiastical parties on behalf of their own beliefs. He simply was objecting that the Articles 'need not be so closed as the received method of teaching closes them, and ought not to be for the sake of many persons'. Were their meaning to be confined to the Protestant interpretation alone the risk would be incurred of driving such persons into the Church of Rome, when on an 'open' view of the said Articles, and one historically quite justifiable, they could remain loyal members of the Church of England.[17] But this further twist to the theory of the *Via Media* was more than Anglican opinion as a whole was ready to countenance. Newman was bitterly attacked. Many even of his sympathizers voiced their misgivings. Oxford officialdom accused him of evading rather than explaining the sense of the formulary and reconciling subscription to it with the adoption of errors which it was expressly designed to prevent. 'It was a crisis', observes Church, 'in which much might have been usefully said, if there had been any one to say it … But it seemed as if the opportunity must not be lost for striking a blow.'[18] Not surprisingly the effect on the author was to cause him, in time, to reconsider the basic assumptions of the argument which he had so carefully elaborated. Was the Church of the *Via Media* after all nothing more than what at first he had thought it, a 'paper Church'? By 1842 he was, as he phrased it years later, 'on his death-bed' so far as the Church of England was concerned. The entire notion of the English establishment as a true part of 'the Church Catholic and Apostolic, set up from the beginning', revealed itself to him as an illusion. The establishment had a life of a sort, assuredly; but it was not Catholic life. It was essentially Protestant, Erastian and national. The very idea of the supernatural was alien to it. Christ's Kingdom, as Englishmen saw it, was a kingdom very much of this world, and one over which parliament exercised a plenary authority. The establishment simply kept back 'those doctrines which, to the eye of faith, give real substance to religion.

The full force of Newman's disillusionment did not, however, find vent until the publication in 1850—five years after his secession to Rome—of his lectures *On the Difficulties felt by Anglicans in Catholic Teaching*, where traces of a lingering personal resentment are not absent. Thus in allusion to the Gorham dispute he could say:

17. The exact title of *Tract 90* was: *Remarks on Certain Passages in the Thirty-Nine Articles*, the Articles discussed being 6 and 20, 11, 12 and 13, 19, 21, 22, 25, 28, 31, 32, 35, and 37. 'Our present scope', the author explained, 'is merely to show that while our Prayer Book is acknowledged on all hands to be of Catholic origin, our Articles also, the offspring of an un-Catholic age, are, through God's good providence, to say the least, not un-Catholic, and may be subscribed by those who aim at being Catholic in heart and doctrine.' He ended with the statement: 'The Protestant Confession was drawn up with the purpose of including Catholics, and Catholics now will not be excluded. What was an economy in the reformers, is a protection to us. What would have been a perplexity to us then, is a perplexity to Protestants now. We could not then have found fault with their words: they cannot now repudiate our meaning.' On the controversy in Oxford see Owen Chadwick, *The Victorian Church*, i, pp. 181–9.
18. *The Oxford Movement*, p. 291.

The Evangelical party, who in former years had the nerve to fix the charge of dishonesty on the explanations of the Thirty-nine Articles, put forward by their opponents, could all the while be cherishing in their own breasts an interpretation of the Baptismal Service, simply contrary to its most luminous declarations.[19]

Yet the memory of his Anglican days was still something he treasured, and the experience of grace which he then knew, and which countless others continued to know, might not, he realized, be gainsaid:

> Cannot I too look back on many years past, and many events, in which I myself experienced what is now your confidence? Can I forget the happy life I have led all my days, with no cares, no anxieties worth remembering; without desolateness, or fever of thought, or gloom of mind, or doubt of God's love to me, and providence over me? ... O my dear brethren, my Anglican friends, I easily give you credit for what I have experienced myself.[20]

The trouble was that although individual Christians might and undoubtedly did show the workings of God's grace within them, yet, apart from the divinely authenticated ordinances, it was not *safe*—the word is Newman's own—consciously to do so. Quality of life is not the guarantee of soundness of doctrine. Only in a Church which is unquestionably Catholic is there real assurance of salvation.

But Newman's personal rejection of Anglicanism as a true 'middle way', although influencing the rank and file among a large number of his followers, did not deter the other Oxford leaders. Dr Pusey's solid if unimaginative learning strongly upheld the idea. John Keble had no doubts at all. The High Church party rallied after Newman's defection and the doctrine that Anglicanism presents an authentically 'Catholic' form of Christianity, avoiding alike the unwarranted accretions of Rome and the manifest deficiencies of Protestantism, lived on to gain, as the years went by, ever larger acceptance with a new generation of Anglicans as the true account of their Church's historic character and claim. For although it may have been the case, in part at least, that, as Mark Pattison complained, 'the Tractarians desolated Oxford life, and suspended for an indefinite period all science, humane letters, and the first stirrings of intellectual freedom which had moved in the bosom of Oxford',[21] the Church of England became increasingly in outward appearance what the Tractarians had insisted that it is in principle. And however it may have failed to stem the tide of liberalism and the nation's growing secularization the established Church at the end of the century was in every aspect a very different thing from what it had been at the beginning. To that extent the work initiated by the Oxford divines was accomplished. Whether they would have approved the result it is idle to speculate. Events have their own logic and those who deliberately set them in train rarely foresee their course.

19. *Op. cit.*, p. 20.
20. *Ibid.*, pp. 71f.
21. *Memoirs* (1885), p. 101.

Orthodoxy and holiness

Newman, beyond question, was the movement's presiding genius and the sincerity of the compliments he paid to others as he looked back on a scene from which, after much heartsearching, he himself had chosen to withdraw do not hide the fact. Quite apart from his great personal influence in the immediate circle of his followers, he was easily the movement's leading publicist, with his unrivalled gifts as a writer. But the *Tracts* were not his work only. Out of a total of ninety he was responsible for twenty-nine. Keble wrote eight, Pusey seven, three of which (nos. 67–69), on baptism, make up a weighty volume. The rest were from various hands—Froude's, Perceval's, Isaac Williams's and J. W. Bowden's chiefly. Not all were original compositions: eighteen were reprints of the works of old authors such as Wilson, Cosin, Beveridge, Bull and Ussher. The public reception of the tracts also varied. The evangelical *Record* was generally critical. But among the parish clergy, to whom in the main they were addressed, widespread curiosity was aroused. 'They fell', says Church, 'on a time of profound and inexcusable ignorance on the subjects they discussed, and they did not spare it.'[22] Pusey records that 'the Tracts found an echo everywhere. Friends started up like armed men from the ground. I only dreaded our being too popular.'[23] On the other hand, some were in the position of Charles Kingsley, who confessed that his own heart 'strangely yearned towards them from the first', but that he soon realized that the Oxford writings contained only half-truths. Arnold, as we saw, entirely deplored them and poured scorn on the ideas they were seeking to promote. The episcopal reaction was for the most part cool. One or two bishops seem to have been genuinely puzzled by them; others, like Sumner of Winchester, were mildly appreciative. Sooner or later the charge of Romanism was inevitable. The theological knowledge was, in Church's judgment, 'wanting which would have been familiar with the broad line of difference between what is Catholic and what is especially Roman'.[24]

Were, in fact, the views expressed in them really in accord with Church doctrine, as embodied in the liturgy and articles and in the writings of representative Anglican divines? The question cannot properly be answered without regard to historical conditions. The Church's formularies might well enshrine Catholic principles, as an impressive body of earlier Anglican theology testified that they did. Hooker, the Carolines, the Non-jurors and contemporary High Churchmen like van Mildert, Joshua Watson and Alexander Knox had never looked on the national Church in a purely 'Protestant' light, Protestant though it indubitably was in regard to Rome herself. But the average Englishman saw it otherwise. For the Church of England stood for what he believed to be Bible Christianity in opposition to the errors of 'Popery', that ill-defined but always emotive word. It was this uninstructed mass opinion which the Tractarians believed it their mission ultimately to convert. The task, however, was immense. Prejudice against all 'Catholic' notions was

---

22. *The Oxford Movement*, p. 120. The tracts were at first circulated privately and the earliest of them were anonymous.
23. H. P. Liddon, *Life of E. B. Pusey*, ed. J. O. Johnson and R. F. Wilson (3rd ed. 1893–5), i, p. 259.
24 *Ibid.*, p. 121.

deep-rooted and ignorance might prove invincible. The kind of language that came so easily to their own lips—'priest', 'absolution', 'apostolic succession', the word 'Catholic' itself even—had for the great majority of churchgoers an alien and sinister sound. The new Oxford theologians could of course cite prayerbook authority for employing it and might exercise great care in explaining what it meant, but public feeling on these matters had its own assurances, which were of a contrary nature. Moreover, such feeling was increasingly to be reflected in episcopal pronouncements, notably those of John Bird Sumner, bishop of Chester and subsequently archbishop of Canterbury, who in 1838 spoke out against the 'undermining of the foundations of our Protestant Church by men who dwell within her walls'.

Tractarian belief in the Church as a divine institution had for corollary an insistence on strictness in adhering to the received doctrines. With these men orthodoxy was not only a principle but a passion, liberalism and dissent alike representing, in their different ways, grave declensions from the truth. Several of the tracts took the form of *catenae*, lengthy extracts from the Fathers or from High Church divines of the past to show how certain teachings—that on the eucharistic sacrifice, for example—are rightly to be held by loyal members of the Church of England. Similarly Keble's *The Christian Year*, the publication of which in 1827, rather than his 1833 sermon, could as plausibly be taken as marking the real start of the movement, was deliberately composed with the aim of expressing Church doctrine in verse of 'a sober standard of feeling'.[25] Their author's sermon *On the Baptismal Offices* and his later *Treatise on Eucharistic Adoration* are imbued with the same concern. Pusey, despite his early, tentative interest in German rationalism, remained a monument of orthodoxy,[26] abjuring all idea that he and his friends taught peculiar doctrines'.

In any case the purpose of the tracts was practical and popular, and as a rule technical theology was avoided. The intention of all the writers was soundness of doctrine and simplicity. Questions of ritual and ceremonial were not dealt with. Tractarian practice continued to be 'low'—Newman, for instance, always celebrated holy communion at the north end of the table, Pusey maintaining that the times were not ripe for anything more than the needful reassertion of Catholic principles and that attention paid to the externals of worship would only compromise the teaching of essentials.[27] Frederick Oakeley, who later became a Roman Catholic, seems to have been the first to interest himself in such matters. 'We are for carrying out', he wrote in an article in the movement's organ, *The British Critic*[28], 'the

---

25. Newman thought the poems 'exquisite' (*Letters*, i, p. 165). But Keble's own estimate of them was unfeignedly modest.
26. His *Historical Inquiry into the Probable Causes of the Rationalistic Character lately predominant in the Theology of Germany*, in which he displayed considerable knowledge of the contemporary intellectual scene in that country, was published in 1828.
27. He thought it 'beginning at the wrong end for ministers to deck their persons; our own plain dresses are more in keeping with the state of our Church, which is one of humiliation'. For this reason he deprecated the attempt to restore 'the richer style of vestments' used in Edward VI's reign. See Liddon, *Life of Pusey*, ii, pp. 142–5.
28. January–April 1840, p. 270.

symbolic principle in our own Church to the utmost extent which is consistent with the duty of obedience to the rubric.' If ornaments in churches should to some appear trivial, let them be reminded 'that care about minutiae is the peculiar mark of an intense and reverent affection'. There was, he thought, 'something quite revolting in the idea of dealing with the subject of External Religion as a matter of mere taste'. The subsequent growth of ritualism in the parishes was in fact an obvious practical development of the Tractarian ecclesiology and sacramental doctrine.

One tract which, rather surprisingly, aroused a good deal of adverse comment was Isaac Williams's *On Reserve in Communicating Religious Knowledge*, no. 80 in the series, described by Church as 'a protest against the coarseness and shallowness which threw the most sacred words about at random in loud and declamatory appeals'; a protest, in short, against much current evangelical preaching. The use of the term 'reserve', however, caused alarm. Did it not mean a holding back of the full truth of the saving gospel? Worse still, it suggested devious ways—priestcraft and Jesuitry. Thus innocently, for Williams was a man of a singularly modest and retiring disposition, did the unfortunate author provoke suspicion not only as to his own motives but towards the movement as a whole, a suspicion which was never to be allayed, and to which *Tract 90* appeared to supply the most devastating confirmation. But there was nothing at all of a prevaricating spirit among the tract writers. They were simply careful of their language. 'Prune thy words', wrote Newman, 'the thoughts control'

> That o'er thee swell and throng;
> That they will condense within thy soul,
> And change to purpose strong.

The Church's doctrine filled them with awe, for soundness of creed was the road to personal holiness. The Tractarians' moralism, as has been particularly stressed by modern commentators, was in some respects the most striking thing about them. 'Be ye perfect', they would have said, 'even as your Father in heaven is perfect.' The profoundest mysteries of the faith—and no doctrine was more profound or mysterious than the atonement—were not in their judgment to be exhibited indiscriminately before minds unchastened by moral discipline. The articles of the Christian creed, wrote Williams, 'contain great sacred truths of the very highest possible importance that we should know; but if we attempt to arrive at any knowledge of them by speculation, or any other mode but that of practical obedience, that knowledge is withheld, and we are punished for the attempt'.

The note the Tractarians struck in their sermons was consistently one of moral severity. A recent writer indeed detects in the work of all of them 'an undercurrent of pessimism and gloom'.[29] Thus Newman gave to one of his earliest published sermons, preached in August 1826, the title 'Holiness necessary for future blessedness', whilst in another, of June 1825, he declared that 'the whole history of redemption ... attests the necessity of holiness in order to attain salvation'. In a Whitsun address of 1831 he warned his hearers that 'our ascended Saviour, who

---

29. David Newsome, *The Parting of Friends* (1966), p. 180.

is on God's right hand, and sends down from thence God's Spirit, is to be feared greatly, even amid His gracious consolations', reminding them of the apostle's words, 'Work out your own salvation with fear and trembling.' Again, many years later, in September 1842, he speaks of the danger of attempting one aspect of the Christian character while neglecting another: 'Religion has two sides, a severe side, and a beautiful; and we shall be sure to swerve from the narrow way which leads to life, if we indulge ourselves in what is beautiful, while we put aside what is severe.'[30] Pusey likewise says that everything may, and does, minister to heaven or hell:

> We are, day by day, and hour by hour, influenced by everything around us; rising or falling, sinking or recovering, receiving impressions which are to last for ever; taking colour and mould from everything which passes around us and in us, and not less because unperceived; each touch slight, as impressed by an invisible spiritual hand, but, in itself, not the less, rather the more lasting, since what we are yielding ourselves to is, in the end, the finger of God or the touch of Satan.[31]

If, therefore, certain doctrines seem to make religion gloomy and even repulsive, it is because, in Newman's words, it 'must ever be difficult for those who neglect it'.

> All things that we have to learn are difficult at first, and our duties to God, and to man for His sake, are peculiarly difficult, because they call upon us to take up a new life, and quit the love of this world for the next. It cannot be avoided; we must fear and be in sorrow, before we can rejoice. The Gospel must be a burden before it comforts and brings us peace ... Religion is in itself at first a weariness to the worldly mind, and it requires an effort and a self-denial in everyone who honestly determines to be religious.[32]

It is the duty of a Christian to witness to God and to glorify him, to be as a light on a hill, through evil report and good report; the evil report and good report being indeed less of his own making than the natural consequence of the Christian profession itself. Such admonitions, on Tractarian lips, were far from being the stock-in-trade of conventional pulpit utterance. These men believed wholeheartedly in their message and practised it in their daily lives. For the world they cared nothing. They despised its comforts and set little or no value on its honours. They did not aim at popularity, nor seek social advancement—which most of them never in any case obtained. Newman believed that 'the Church itself is always hated and calumniated by the world', since Christians, in actually thwarting the world's pride and selfishness, are inevitably disliked by the world. This intense moral earnestness was for the Oxford divines the acid test of a genuine religious conviction. Beside it A. P. Stanley's remark, echoing Arnold, on 'the trivial elements which produced so much excitement' is itself trivial.[33]

30. *Sermons bearing on Subjects of the Day* ('Feasting in Captivity') (ed. 1918), p. 391.
31. *Parochial Sermons* (1869), iii, p. 431.
32. *Parochial Sermons* (1837–42), i, p. 26.
33. Newsome calls attention to this same note of severity in the parochial sermons of H. E. Manning, afterwards archbishop of Westminster and cardinal. In the first volume, for example, there are addresses bearing such titles as 'Salvation a Difficult Work' and

In view of this strong moral *motif* in Tractarianism it is scarcely surprising that the Evangelicals at first saw little to object to in it, apart from its doctrine of the ministry. 'Holiness rather than peace', which Newman took as motto, had been a principle of Thomas Scott, the Calvinist Bible commentator, to whom, 'humanly speaking', Newman confessed he almost owed his soul.[34] Long after, in 1851, Robert Wilberforce, a son of the great philanthropist, recalled in a charge to the clergy of his archdeaconry that

> during the first quarter of the century men were roused from slumber and wakened to earnestness; the next period gave them an external object on which to expend the zeal that had been enkindled. For it must be observed ... that these movements, though distinct, were not repugnant. On the contrary, persons who had been most influenced by the one, often entered most readily upon the other. ... So then the second movement was a sort of consequence of the first.[35]

The leaders of the Oxford Movement were, then, as intent upon moral commitment as were any of its Evangelical or Broad Church critics. In this indeed they were Englishmen typical of their age and social class. They had, moreover, assiduously read their Bishop Butler, by whom Newman in particular was profoundly influenced and in a way that reinforced the strong ethical predisposition imparted to him by his own evangelical upbringing. To all of them the ground of religion, especially of a religion whose teaching authority was the Bible, lay in the moral consciousness. The heightening of religious sensibility, a deepened understanding of religious doctrine, depended in the first instance upon obedience to the law of conscience. Not, of course, that grace was only secondary, for without grace the soul could make no progress in the saving knowledge of God. Rather, as Newman expressed it, 'the grace promised us is given, not that we may know more, but that we may do better'[36]—advance farther along the path of sanctification, in the more studied performance of our duty to God and man. It was in fact this very moralism which sharpened the Tractarians' criticism of the evangelical theology. For the Evangelicals' emphasis on soteriology led them, in the classical Protestant manner, to disparage man's inherent moral capacity, although without it the preaching of repentance itself could hardly have much meaning; as also to lose sight of the wider significance of that *incarnation* of the Son of God whence the death on Calvary necessarily drew its efficacy. Christ's assumption of humanity was, in truth, 'a higher gift than grace', being the pledge of

---

'A severe Life necessary for Christ's followers'. 'To all mankind, as fallen men,' says the preacher, 'the way of life is not more blessed than it is arduous. ... There must pass on each a deep and searching change. And this change, though it be wrought in us of God, is wrought through our striving. It is no easy task to gird up the energies of our moral nature to a perpetual struggle. ... It is a hard thing to be a Christian.' See Newsome, *op. cit*, pp. 207f.

34. *Apologia*, ed. Svaglic, p. 18.
35. R. I. Wilberforce, *A Charge to the Clergy of the East Riding, delivered at the Ordinary Visitation* (1851), pp. 10f (quoted Newsome, *ibid.*, p. 14).
36. *Parochial Sermons*, i, p. 234.

God's presence and His very self
And essence all divine.

This incarnationalist *motif* in Tractarian thought was to reveal its broader implications in the work of a subsequent generation of High Churchmen; but its immediate result was an enhanced appreciation of the sacramental means whereby the divine life is communicated to the believer and an insistence upon his gradual conformation to the moral pattern of Christ's own supreme example.

A main reason why Isaac Williams's tract *On Reserve* had offended evangelical susceptibilities was, as we have noted, its objection to any exploitation of the mystery of the atonement. 'The highest and most sacred of all Christian doctrines', he wrote, 'is to be brought before and pressed home to all persons indiscriminately, and most especially to those who are leading unchristian lives.' The only fitting approach to religion is through holiness of life; otherwise superstition is the outcome, as in the tendency of Roman Catholicism to substitute the Virgin Mary for God in ritual and devotion—a plain illustration, he thinks, of the way in which 'the natural heart lowers the object of its worship to its own frailty'. The risk of idolatry in the case of the atonement was in suggesting that acceptance by 'faith' of the merits of Christ's death is alone sufficient and that moral obedience may be dispensed with, whereas conscience is our first and always necessary guide: 'There is no one living but to whom Wisdom speaks, a voice that tells him of something better which he ought to do than what he does. ... Until he follows this voice, the higher and better wisdom is hid from him.'

Mankind's innate moral sense was for all the Tractarians the threshold of the knowledge of God. So far they recognized a divine revelation outside the Bible, a. revelation which Christian doctrine itself presupposes. Further, Christian doctrine could not properly be understood until its moral dimension had been fully realized. Thus Hurrell Froude could admit that although he assented to the damnatory clauses of the Athanasian creed as affirming no more than Scripture itself teaches, yet he did so with difficulty since it seemed to him axiomatic that no opinion *as such* can be the object of God's wrath or favour. If an opinion is condemned it is because it involves 'something moral as its effect or cause, or both'.[37] Again, the same writer, in an address significantly entitled 'The Gospel as the Completion of Natural Religion', states his belief that the only possible way of comprehending the doctrines of the trinity and incarnation and of profiting by them, 'or, indeed, by entering at all into their meaning', is by leading that sort of life which they are intended to help us in leading. Referring again to the Athanasian creed, he goes on to say:

We must ask ourselves, not 'Am I thoroughly convinced and certain that these mysterious doctrines arc true?' for that is a matter over which we can have no control; we cannot feel certain by trying to feel ever so much; and God will not require of us impossibilities. But what we must ask ourselves is this: 'Is my conduct such as it *would be* if I was thoroughly convinced of them? In the first place, do I act as if I believed God to be my Father, and my neighbour to be my brothers?' That is, 'do I believe

37. *Remains*, i, p. 117.

in earthly things ?'[38] and, secondly, 'as to heavenly things, do I endeavour with all my might and with all my soul, and with all my strength, to *follow and obey* the Lord Jesus Christ *as* my Saviour and my God?'[39]

Newman is no less explicit. In an Oxford University sermon preached in 1830 on 'The Influence of Natural and Revealed Religion Respectively' he considers the knowledge of the divine order which may be attained apart from an express revelation, and observes that:

> Such is the large and practical religious creed attainable (as it appears from the extant works of heathen writers) by a vigorous mind which rightly works upon itself under (what may be called) the Dispensation of Paganism. It may even be questioned whether there be any essential character of Scripture doctrine which is without its place in this moral revelation. For here is the belief in a principle exterior to the mind to which it is instinctively drawn, infinitely exalted, perfect, incomprehensible; here is the surmise of a judgment to come; the knowledge of an unbounded benevolence, wisdom, and power, as traced in the visible creation, and of moral laws unlimited in their operation; further, there is something of hope respecting the availableness of repentance, so far (that is) as suffices for religious thought; lastly, there is an insight into the rule of duty increasing with the earnestness with which obedience to that rule is cultivated.[40]

From this it ensues that the heathen are not in danger of perishing in so far as they follow the 'secret voice' of conscience within them. On the other hand, to arguments for natural religion based merely on the evidences of design in nature Newman was less sympathetic. To a believer in God such evidences might be beautiful and interesting, 'but where men have not already recognized God's voice within them ineffective, and this, moreover, from some unsoundness in the intellectual basis of the argument'.[41] It is the same indeed with history itself. Of God's existence Newman is as certain as he is of his own; but the world, as he looked out on it, filled him, as he afterwards confessed in one of the most memorable passages he ever wrote, with 'unspeakable distress'. It seemed to him to give the lie to a truth of which his own whole being was full.

> The effect upon me is, in consequence, as a matter of necessity, as confusing as if it denied that I am in existence myself. If I looked into a mirror, and did not see my face, I should have the sort of feeling which actually comes upon me, when I look into this busy world and see no reflection of its creator.

But this conviction was inescapable only because of the voice of conscience—that 'aboriginal Vicar of Christ', as he called it—inside him. Save for this minatory counsellor, speaking so authoritatively as it did, he might, he says, have been 'an

---

38. The reference is to John iii, 2.
39. The Tractarians, it appears, had not read Kant, but there are Kantian overtones in such a passage as that quoted. Religious doctrines are to be understood as essentially practical and moral. It is a view, moreover, which anticipates the religious pragmatism of the Catholic Modernists, especially E. Le Roy, who describes a dogma as 'une prescription d'ordre pratique, une règle de conduite pratique' (*Dogme et Critique*, 1907, p. 23).
40. *Oxford University Sermons* (1843), ed. 1892, p. 21.
41. Concerning Newman's distrust of rational proofs in religion see below, ch. 4.

atheist, or a pantheist, or a polytheist'. The spectacle of the world as it is is 'nothing else than the prophet's scroll, full of "lamentations, and mourning, and woe" '.[42]

But the Oxford Movement's profound moralism received perhaps its most insistent expression in the work of William George Ward (1812–82), a fellow of Balliol and a tutor in philosophy, who eventually, like Newman, left the Church of England for that of Rome. Ward in earlier days had been a disciple of Arnold, whose moral earnestness made a strong appeal to him. What he sought, and in Arnold (it seemed) had discovered, was a 'wholesome antidote' to all mere formalism in religion, whether as the old-fashioned Protestant cult of respectability or the new, romantic antiquarianism. Plainly Arnold was a man to be trusted, and Ward, with his natural capacity for philosophical thinking, was willing to give him his trust; but, as his son and biographer, Wilfrid Ward, relates, 'on hearing Newman preach for the first time he found in his tone and teaching all and more than all of that exalted ethical character which had won him to Dr Arnold'.

> The devotion to antique rule, the love of unreal supernatural legend, the advocacy of superstitious rites as all-important, which had in his mind been the essence of Newmanism, did not appear at all, and the idea of holiness as the one aim was the pervading spirit of the whole sermon.[43]

In comparison with the doctrines to be heard from the pulpit of St Mary's church Arnoldism clearly 'stopped short', at every turn. Intellectually it stopped short, for the principle of free critical inquiry which Arnold extolled appeared to lead to scepticism rather than faith. Practically, too, it stopped short: as a way of religion it kept the supernatural at a distance. Likewise, ethically it stopped short: 'It had no saints. It watered Christianity down to what seemed more practicable to the average Christian than Christ's own teaching.'[44] Thus the reflection passed Ward's mind, as he considered whither the consistent application of latitudinarian principles might lead, that there may yet prove to be 'some indissoluble connection between the plenitude of doctrine and the highest morality'. If so, then belief could not be simply a matter of the intellect, a rational balancing of pros and cons. Its true genesis, rather as under Newman's guidance he was coming to see more and more plainly, was in obedience to conscience. Obedience is primary, knowledge secondary. Men see God by being pure in heart; they do not become pure in heart by seeing God. 'He who learns the truth from argument or mere trust in men may lose it again by argument or by trust in men; but he who learns it by obedience can lose it only by disobedience.'[45]

This view was re-emphasized in Ward's main work, *The Ideal of a Christian Church*, published in 1844, a year before his conversion to Rome.[46] It seemed to

42. *Apologia* (ed. Svaglic), pp. 216f.
43. *W. G. Ward and the Oxford Movement* (2nd ed., 1890), p. 79.
44. *Ibid.*, p. 86.
45. *Ibid.*, p. 77.
46. The book was formally condemned, on 13 February 1845, by the university of Oxford, and its author deprived of his degrees. See Church, *The Oxford Movement*, pp. 380 ff. 'The 13th of February', Church adds, 'was not only the final defeat and conclusion of the vast stage of the movement. It was the birthday of the modern Liberalism of Oxford' (*ibid.*, p. 393).

the author that the Protestant doctrine of justification *sola fide* ignored the truth that 'careful moral discipline is the necessary foundation, whereon alone Christian faith can be reared'.[47]

> To do what is right because it is right, and from a motive of duty, is the highest and noblest of all habits ... far nobler than the doing what is right out of gratitude for free pardon.[48]

In any case the intellect should never be permitted to replace conscience as the arbiter of religious truth. The one faculty to be visited by divine grace is the sense of duty.[49]

> If conscience [he averred] be not on all moral and religious subjects paramount, then it does not really exist; if it do not exist, we have no reason whatever, nay, no power whatever to believe in God,

pointing out that Auguste Comte's atheism was grounded in his very denial that such a faculty exists. Again, in a passage cited by his biographer, remarkably reminiscent of Coleridge, Ward maintains that whereas the knowledge of phenomena is obtained by the intellect, knowledge of realities comes from the conscience; the one by inquiry, the other by obedience. The former, he thinks, 'tends to pride', the latter 'indispensably requires and infallibly increases humility'.[50] Nevertheless, if the one vitally important principle is the absolute supremacy of conscience, the other—and here we have the presiding thesis of his book—is 'the high sacredness of hereditary religion'. For conscience needs to be educated if private idiosyncrasies are not to pervert its judgment. To fulfil the role of universal moral educator a visible Church is a necessity; a merely unseen one would be 'a very sorry antagonist against so very visible a world'. As he wrote to Pusey:

> The more a person feels his deficiency in the apprehension of unseen things, the more painfully he feels the want of so consoling and impressive an image of a visible Church as even Rome displays; the more difficult he finds his contest with his old nature; the more he regrets that he has not been trained from the first in regular confession; the more he misses the practical rules of conduct in which Roman books of devotion abound, drawn from the stores, which they have retained, of traditional teaching; the more he misses the guidance of a priest carefully trained with a view to the confessional.[51]

The Ideal might and did appear to many as '*Tract* 90 writ large', and the goal towards which its author was heading was plain enough; but always it is the Church and the externals of religion as ministering to and promoting personal sanctity which is the core of his argument.

---

47. *The Ideal of a Christian Church*, p. vii.
48. *Ibid.*, p. 301.
49. *Ibid.*, p. 204.
50. Wilfrid Ward, *op. cit.*, p. 258.
51. *Ibid.*, p. 183.

Justification and sanctification

The stress on inwardness characteristic of the movement is manifest in its understanding of the doctrine of justification. Newman's lectures on this subject, published in 1838, may well be considered the most important contribution to dogmatic theology to have come from the Tractarian school. Their purport was to show that the teaching laid down in the Thirty-nine Articles is by no means irreconcilable with Catholic doctrine on the priesthood and sacraments. The lectures are not indeed among their author's most arresting works, but they make up a treatise of unquestionable learning and penetration. The true doctrine, he thinks, steers a middle course between the Lutheran and the Roman.

> Whether we say we are justified by faith or by works or by Sacraments, all these mean but this one doctrine, that we are justified by grace, given through the Sacraments, impetrated by faith, manifested in works.[52]

He then examines some of the diverse views that have from time to time been held. Of these the first asserts that we are justified directly upon the holiness and good works wrought in us *through* Christ's merits by the Spirit. This he calls the 'high Roman view'. Its opposite is the 'high Protestant', which insists that Christ's merits and righteousness, imputed to us, become the immediate cause of our justification, superseding everything else in the eye of the heavenly judge. Between these extremes fall two further views, the one holding that we are justified 'directly upon our holiness and works *under* the covenant of Christ's merits', the other 'that our faith is mercifully appointed as the substitute for perfect holiness, and thus as the interposing and acceptable principle between us and God'. Whether these doctrines really are but differing forms of what is commonly considered the High Church view among Anglicans—as Newman himself believes—is open to question. But his clear purpose is to oppose both the Roman doctrine (as he understands it), which, although maintaining that the atonement wrought on man's behalf by Christ is the only ground of good works, nevertheless denies the need of a continual imputation of Christ's merits to make good the defects of man's actual obedience, and the Protestant doctrine (again as he understands it), which, in putting all the weight on the imputation of Christ's merits as the substitute for man's failure in obedience, seems to deny the need for any subsequent effort after the maximum holiness on his part, and even to suspect the wish for such holiness as in some way casting doubt on the sufficiency of Christ's sacrifice. As between these poles more stress or less may be placed on the respective roles of faith and works, so long as we regard works as effective only because springing from a faith made possible by the grace of Christ.

What in his treatment of this subject Newman was basically concerned to establish is that to be 'justified' means for the believer an intrinsic 'newness of life', and not merely, as the Evangelicals taught, a forensic attributing of Christ's own holiness to one who is himself 'vile'. Sacramental incorporation into the mystical Body of Christ involves *gratia infusa*, an actual *impartation* of the righteousness of

---

52. *Lectures on Justification*, p. 348.

Christ. A mere imputing and not an imparting of that righteousness is but a 'joyless shadow' of the glorious reality. Not that Newman himself knew nothing directly of a conversion experience. As related in the *Apologia*, he had as a youth undergone just such an experience, of which he was still, at the time of writing (1864), 'more certain than that he had hands and feet'.[53] But by the time he delivered the lectures on justification he had embraced opinions very different from those in which he had been nurtured. Conversion experiences of the evangelical type now appeared to him to rely far too much on feelings of confidence, or, as the term was, an 'assurance' of salvation. By contrast the Tractarians were too conscious of their unworthiness and of the need for perpetual moral vigilance. As Pusey expressed it in his own book on *Justification*, published in 1853:

> It is easy to deceive ourselves as to our deeds, if we will but look into our consciences by the light of the law of God. It is easy to say 'Lord, Lord'; it is *not* easy, but of the power of the grace of God, to 'deny ourselves and take up our cross and follow Him.' ... It is *not* easy, amid the fire of passion within, the manifold force of temptation without, the delusive pleasure dancing before our eyes, the treachery of our own hearts, to be 'dead to the world, that we may live to God'.

The evangelicals, for all their talk about sin, were apt to be smug. This difference of view, however, was only one aspect of a deeper-lying difference of theological emphasis. In Christ, so the Tractarians believed, a man at once finds a new quality of life. He has become one with the Risen Christ and no longer is a mere suppliant at the cross of the Crucified. On this Newman is explicit:

> If the Resurrection be the means by which the Atonement is applied to each of us, if it be our justification, if in it are conveyed all the gifts of grace and glory which Christ has purchased for us, if it be the commencement of His giving Himself to us for a spiritual sustenance, of His feeding us with that Bread which has already been perfected on the Cross and is now a medicine of immortality,[54] it is that very doctrine which is most immediate to us, in which Christ most clearly approaches us, from which we gain life and out of which issue our hopes and duties.[55]

It is strange, reading these statements, to recall that the common charge against the Tractarians, then and later, was of 'medievalism' and preoccupation with externals. What in their sight mattered above all else was the soul's inner state, whilst in their faith in the resurrection they drew inspiration less from the cross-centred piety of the middle ages than from antiquity. Thus sanctification—the continuing growth in holiness—more than justification, at least when the latter is isolated as the supreme 'moment' in the process of the soul's regeneration, is the heart of their religious concern. Even in their eucharistic theology attention fastens upon the presence rather than the sacrifice, upon communion rather than propitiation. The 'special joy' of the eucharist to the believer, as more than a simple

---

53. He was fifteen years of age at the time, but the experience was not a predominantly emotional one. See H. Tristram, *John Henry Newman: Autobiographical Writings* (1957), pp. 79f, 172.
54. The allusion is to Ignatius' φάρμαχον ἀθαυασίας (*Ephesians*, 20).
55. *Lectures on Justification*, pp. 254f.

85

commemoration of Christ's redemptive acts or a showing forth of his death or a spiritual strengthening and refreshment, is that it is 'the Redeemer's very broken Body' and 'His Blood, which was shed for the remission of his sins'.[56] There is, of course, no question of a *transubstantiation.* What was bread remains bread, and what was wine remains wine. 'We need no carnal, earthly, visible, miracle to convince us of the Presence of the Lord Incarnate.' But 'He who is at the right hand of God, manifests himself in that Holy Sacrament as really and fully as if He were visibly there'.[57] In communion the faithful recipient of the sacramental grace becomes spiritually one with Christ himself.

A like conviction explains the importance to the Tractarians of the doctrine of baptismal regeneration. This had been a point of controversy between them and their critics from the beginning. Evangelicals did not identify baptism with conversion, by which alone, as they saw it, the sinner could be said to be regenerate. A rite administered to infants, however fitting in its way, gives no assurance as to the spiritual and moral quality of the recipient's subsequent life as an adult, and one who showed none of the influences of religion could not with propriety be described as 'born again'. Yet the Church's baptismal service seems clearly to affirm that the baptized as such are regenerate, and it was upon this evident meaning of the Prayer Book language that the Oxford school built its case.[58] They saw nothing either superstitious or mechanical in the idea that an infant child should so be described. For what is given in baptism, they held, is nothing less than the new life of the Risen Lord. This it is which makes possible a real and not merely an imputed holiness and provides the incentive as well as the means of a progressive sanctification. The baptized has more and more to become what in spiritual *status* he already is, learning to contemplate himself, so Newman explains, not as he is in himself, but as he is 'in the Eternal God'.

> Fall down in astonishment at the glories which are around thee and in thee, poured to and fro in such a wonderful way that thou art (as it were) dissolved into the Kingdom of God, and art as if thou hadst nought to do but to contemplate and feed upon that great vision.[59]

All the necessary exactness of obedience, the anxiety about failing, the pain of self-denial, the watchfulness and zeal and self-chastisement, do not interfere with this vision of faith. Moreover, the baptized does not stand alone, even though fortified by the resources of grace within him. For by the sacrament he becomes a member of the Church, Christ's Body. He is now as by right a citizen of a new realm of faith, hope and love.

This teaching is brought out with special fervour by Pusey, who has been aptly called the *doctor mysticus* of the movement. He was not indeed among its most compelling preachers—of Newman's pulpit magnetism he had nothing; but when his mind turns to the mystery of the unity of God and man wrought by the redemption his utterance becomes rapturous:

56. E. B. Pusey, *University Sermons* (1859), pp. 18f.
57. J. H. Newman, *Parochial Sermons*, iv, p. 167ff.
58. See below, Appendix I: The Gorham Judgment.
59. Newman, *op. cit.*, p. 166.

Oh the blessedness beyond all thought! Unutterable riches of the mercy of God, to be for ever not our own, but to be His, His by creation, His by redemption, His by re-creation, but His too by His indwelling, His life, His love, His glory, His light, His wisdom, His immortality within us; yea, all but His infinitely, and that the endless object of our contemplation, never cloying, never exhausted, because He is infinite. ...[60]

Yet for all the learning and the moral energy which the leaders of the movement were together able to command, its contribution to religious thought cannot, in the end, be deemed very great. Newman, of course, must be excepted, even though it appear unfair to make an exception so large—he was after all, until 1845, its leading figure. But Newman throughout his life, Catholic as well as Anglican, was deeply concerned with the basic problem of belief to a degree, to which other Tractarians—unless we exclude his disciple, Ward—were not. For that reason alone he requires separate discussion. Whilst being beyond question the movement's greatest personal force he always stood, in some manner, a little apart from it, as not wholly of it. But if the 'mind' of the movement is to be taken to mean the doctrine of the *Tracts*—and the identification is one which the tract-writers themselves would have endorsed—then it cannot be said that it denoted anything creatively new or, for the future, important. The Oxford divines were no more in the forefront of theological advance than were the Evangelicals. The doctrines which they rehabilitated, of the authority and catholicity of the Church, and the sacramentalism which accompanied these, were to have potent influence upon the life of the Church of England and her daughter churches of the Anglican communion in general, as indeed upon churches outside the Anglican world. But this influence affected the piety, the religious ethos, of the Anglican Church, more than its wider theological outlook. That Church now learned to think of itself, in no formal or nominal sense merely, as Catholic; the once complacently accepted designation of Protestant seemed more and more to be inadequate and misleading. Tractarian revivalism, however, intellectually speaking, pointed to no new horizons. Advances in scientific knowledge, in biblical criticism and in philosophical speculation were viewed with either indifference or distrust. Yet the spirit of reaction in a party which even in its early career showed promise of becoming the most vigorous and influential within the established Church could not prevail indefinitely. The men of the ensuing generations felt less need to erect bulwarks against the tide of change, anxious though they were that the treasures of an ancient and irreplaceable heritage of faith should not be lost. These were the men who, more than forty years after Newman's secession, were to explore the possibility of a Catholic theology fixed no doubt in its principles 'yet ever yielding up new meanings even from its central depths, in the light of other knowledge and human development'. The manifesto of this new phase in Anglican thought was a volume significantly entitled *Lux Mundi*. But of this it must remain to speak in a later chapter.

60. *Parochial Sermons*, iii, pp. 422f.

Chapter 4

JOHN HENRY NEWMAN

The Tractarian leaders

The Oxford Movement was not the creation of a single mind, however fertile, any more than, contrariwise, it was the planned procedure of a closely organized group. Each of its leading figures brought to it a distinctive personality and a particular aptitude and point of view. Such diversity inevitably entailed differences of emphasis and judgment or idiosyncrasies that resisted the mould of a united purpose and resolve. Keble was very unlike Hurrell Froude; the characters of Newman and Pusey stood in signal contrast to each other; between Isaac Williams and W. G. Ward there may seem almost no affinity of either aim or temper. Yet the Movement as a whole appeared to its more hostile critics as nothing less than conspiratorial alike in its designs and its methods; and even the presentday historian is at once made aware of its strong sense of an agreed purpose and a shared enthusiasm, enough to give it a still live interest, despite the remoteness of its antiquated teachings.

The special dispositions of the protagonists call at this point for some notice. John Keble (1792–1866), whom Newman looked on as the Movement's 'true and primary author', nevertheless possessed few of the characteristics usually associated with the leadership of a radical party. Mildness and modesty he had almost to a fault. Even Dean Church, who admired him greatly, admitted that there was nothing in him to foreshadow the role he was to assume in a bold and influential movement. 'He was absolutely without ambition.' He hated show and mistrusted excitement. Popularity he shunned. Even to exercise influence, at any rate consciously, he had no care. 'He had deliberately chosen the *fallentis semita vitae*, and to be what his father had been, a faithful and contented country parson, was all that he desired.' Not a man of many friends, or a party chief, he was distinguished, however, by qualities of mind and heart which won him the deep regard of those who knew him best.[1] That he had intellectual gifts of no mean order the brilliance of his youthful academic career demonstrates, and as a scholar his edition of the works of Hooker has done him lasting credit. But forcefulness, novelty, even the customary artifices of pulpit rhetoric, he avoided. Ecclesiastically he was rather narrow, 'an old-fashioned English Churchman, with great veneration for the Church and its bishops, and a great dislike of Rome, Dissent and

---

1. R. W. Church, *The Oxford Movement*, pp. 23–7. See G. Battiscombe, *John Keble: a Study in Limitations* (1963).

Methodism'.[2] Yet he was not without spirit. The subdued tone, the personal diffidence, indicated no weakness in his adherence to principles. Unquestionably he was a source of personal strength to the Movement in its early days, and it is impossible to think of it without recalling him. His positive contribution to its thought, on the other hand, is not easy to determine. Even the famous sermon on 'National Apostasy' proclaims nothing new or arresting, and is little more than a *réchauffé* of the unimaginative 'political' High Churchmanship of his father's generation. Keble, in fact, was a power in the Movement more by what he himself was, as an embodiment of its moral idealism and sober piety, than by his writings, with the single exception of *The Christian Year*. He was the pure type of the Christian gentleman and country pastor devoted to his flock. As such he stands for what the Movement essentially was, a revival of practical religion and the re-creation of the Anglican clerical ideal. An imaginative intelligence his was not. It is said that the advice he once gave a friend—could it have been Newman?—was 'Don't be original'.[3]

Nearest to Keble in character and outlook was his pupil, Isaac Williams (1802–65), although oddly enough he was the author, as we have seen, of what turned out to be one of the most controversial of the *Tracts*. He too preferred the obscurity of his rural parish. Church says of him that he caught from Keble 'two characteristic habits of mind—a strong depreciation of mere intellect compared with the less showy excellencies of faithfulness to conscience and duty; and a horror and hatred of everything that seemed like display or the desire of applause or of immediate effect'. But he notes also that 'it seemed sometimes as if in preaching or talking he aimed at being dull and clumsy'. His churchmanship was identical with Keble's. He came to know Newman well, but confessed that from the first he saw in him what he learned to look upon as the greatest of dangers—'the preponderance of intellect among the elements of character and as the guide of life'.[4]

Richard Hurrell Froude, in the early days of the Movement Newman's most intimate friend and the original link between the latter and Keble, was a man of a very different temperament. 'Froude', Newman remarks, 'was a bold rider, as on horseback, so also in his speculations.' Hugh James Rose noted that 'he did not seem to be afraid of inferences'. Church found in him 'a man of great gifts, with much that was most attractive and noble', but sensed that 'joined with this there was originally in his character a vein of perversity and mischief, always in danger of breaking out, and with which he kept up a long and painful struggle'.[5] What inspired him was a roseate vision of the middle ages. The establishment, so much revered by elder churchmen, he wholly despised. 'Let us tell the truth, and shame the devil; let us give up a *National* Church and have a *real* one'.[6] The Reformation he considered a disaster; it had introduced 'a spirit of lawlessness', of which liberalism was the latest offspring. What he longed for himself was the restoration

2. Church, *ibid.*, p. 26.
3. On Keble's thought see W.J.A.M. Beek, *John Keble's Literary and Religious Contribution to the Oxford Movement* (Nijmegen, 1959).
4. *Ibid.*, p. 72.
5. *Ibid.*, p. 36.
6. Quoted by Church, *ibid.*, p. 54.

of England's 'ancient religion', a second and better Reformation, inspired by the teachings of the age not of Cranmer but of Laud. 'Never', he declared, 'would he call the Holy Eucharist "the Lord's Supper", nor God's Priests "ministers of the word", or the Altar "the Lord's Table" '. Remarks like these were readily quoted by critics of the Movement from his *Remains*, much of the contents of which from his private journal, would have been better left unpublished. But its author was a chronically sick man. With better physical health his live and vigorous intelligence would have lent added weight to the Movement intellectually, although it is hardly to be doubted that he would have followed Newman to Rome rather than remain behind with the stolid if cautious Pusey.

For Pusey (born 1800), though never the Movement's leader in the way that Newman had been, proved to be its mainstay and guide after the latter's defection, as well as a pillar of strength to it in its beginnings. Newman deeply respected his learning, his immense diligence and above all his 'simple devotion to the cause of religion'. Pusey, he wrote in the *Apologia*, 'gave us a position and a name'.[7] The professorship of Hebrew, and the canonry of Christ Church which accompanied it and which he held from 1828 until his death in 1882, secured him a respected status in the university. He was also well-to-do, generous, and through his family connections influential. In Newman's judgment—here, surely, clouded by excess of modesty—he gave a form and personality to what without him had been 'a sort of mob'. Church more realistically describes him as the Movement's 'second head, in close sympathy with its original leader, but in many ways very different from him', providing it with a guarantee for its stability and steadfastness. 'An inflexible patience, a serene composure, a meek, resolute self-possession, was the habit of his mind, and never deserted him in the most trying days'.[8] Newman, however, was right in seeing in Pusey a man of large designs and sanguine disposition, unafraid of others and haunted by no intellectual perplexities. But he was not a theologian in an original or speculative sense. His mind was no more venturesome than Keble's, and the kind of gifts which make for great leadership he did not possess. He was pre-eminently a scholar, laborious and painstaking, but—and especially in his later years—astonishingly lacking in critical judgment. His contributions to the *Tracts* were of outstanding erudition (and sometimes bulk), but their propaganda value was less than that of the often brief but always shrewdly aimed pamphlets of Newman.

Pusey in all things was a conservative. He wished only that the soundly 'Catholic' doctrines inherited from the past should be perpetuated in or restored to the Church's current teaching. His distinctive contribution to the Movement was in the extent to which he created its spiritual tone. In addition to his translation and adaptation of foreign books of devotion and his pioneering work in the revival of the religious life in the Church of England he gave to the traditional teaching itself a new quality of spiritual fervour. That this at times is somewhat forced and the demand for personal effort overpressed has to be recognized. Pusey's nature was scrupulous to excess and he in practice attached too little weight to the joy and

7. Ed. Svaglic, p. 64.
8. Church, *op. cit.*, p. 134.

peace of believing.[9]But in this respect his attitude characterizes the Movement as a whole. Severe always in his moral judgment, his weakness lay in his shortness of intellectual vision, in his lack of understanding of his own times, his failure to see what most lesser men saw plainly, his rigidity in positions adopted once for all, his frequent credulity. His own name provided a sobriquet for the Movement whose leadership, after the departure of Newman, inevitably devolved upon him.

Newman's personality

But the dynamism of the Oxford Movement came, beyond all question, from the man who after twelve years of untiring work on its behalf found it necessary in conscience to abandon it and to leave the Church of which by now he was the most brilliant and controversial member. Yet as a thinker John Henry Newman (1801–90) is by no means easy to classify. He was not—as he himself readily acknowledged—a theologian in the narrower, professional sense, in spite of the learning displayed in the *Lectures on Justification*. He possessed a mind of great dialectical force and subtlety, and wrote much on questions of philosophical interest; but of technical philosophy he knew little and held it in no high esteem. For church history he had an abiding concern, but for all the labour bestowed on *The Arians of the Fourth Century* (1833) he was not a scholar-historian to be ranked with others of the kind, then and since. Throughout his long career a wide range of subjects caught his attention and to all of them he brought a keen and critical intelligence. As the author of *The Dream of Gerontius* (1866) and part-author of *Lyra Apostolica* (1836)[10] he could claim to be a poet, if a minor one. To the literature of educational theory he contributed, in his *The Idea of a University Defined and Illustrated* (1873),[11] what has since become a classic. As a controversialist he possessed a skill which few have ever rivalled. As a preacher he commanded an eloquence that captivated all who heard him, however dubious the doctrine of which it was the vehicle.[12] His literary output as a whole was immense;

9. After the death of his wife, Maria, in 1839 his personal austerity became so severe that Keble, his spiritual director, had to bid him to take care. Unfortunately his intellectual outlook suffered from a similar constriction. Cf. his *Collegiate and Professional Teaching and Discipline* (1854), cited in V.H.H. Green, *Religion at Oxford and Cambridge* (1964), p. 268.

10. *Verses on Religious Subjects* was published in Dublin in 1853. Most of the poems in that collection, as of the earlier book, were republished in *Verses on Various Occasions* (1868).

11. This volume contains the Dublin *Discourses on the Scope and Nature of University Education*, dated 1852. The first English edition was published in 1859 under the title *The Scope and Nature of University Education*, in which the first and second discourses were combined and the fifth omitted.

12. 'His afternoon sermons at St Mary's', wrote the Presbyterian, Principal Tulloch—to quote one witness among many—'became a spiritual power. They deserved to be so. Here he is at his best, away from the fields of history and of controversy, searching the heart with the light of his spiritual genius, or melting it to tenderness with the music of his exquisite language. All his strength and little of his weakness, his insight, his subtlety, his pathos, his love of souls, his marvellous play of dramatic as well as spiritual faculty, his fervour without excitement, his audacity without offence or sophistical

he wrote ceaselessly. Physically somewhat frail, he was endowed with an interior strength which neither external trials nor the tensions of a mind always exercised at stretch ever overcame. Although by nature or defect of training he may have lacked the specialist qualifications that confer eminence on many men far less gifted than he, his talents were raised to the plane of genius by the compelling force of his personality, one whose magnetism is evidenced not only by the indelible impression it left upon his contemporaries, but also by the fascination it continues to hold even in a world to which his ideals are now for the most part scarcely intelligible. He is, probably, the outstanding religious figure of his century, with the sole exception of Kierkegaard, a man of whom he himself had doubtless never heard. And as with Kierkegaard, it is posterity which has come to realize the full force and capacity of his genius. In his lifetime he was, save among his friends, undervalued, both in the ministry he relinquished and in that he afterwards embraced. Today, however, we are able to see him in a whiter light. Not only is the charm of his curiously elusive character still felt by us both in his writings, public and private, and in the recorded reminiscences of those who knew him in the flesh;[13] his attempted solution of those problems of religious faith to which his mind repeatedly returned, though we can discern well enough the reasons for its failure, is nevertheless such as to render the problems themselves only the more engrossing. The spiritual experience of so energetic and subtle an intelligence is striking enough in itself to make us continue to examine it for its possible underlying truth, or at the very least to study with deepened sympathy the psychological milieu of so intense a moral conviction. If in the end Newman's positive teachings leave us incredulous, the man himself still fascinates an age whose foreshadowings within his own he always feared and consistently denounced.

Newman, let us repeat, was far from being an academic thinker. Yet when we have considered his role as an ecclesiastical leader and publicist he remains, upon questions of religious belief, an authority whose opinions demand attention. For more, often, is to be learned from the process of his thinking, even when he is wrong, than from the acceptable conclusions of most others. The reason for this is that Newman's thought, like Pascal's, is the outcome and expression of great spiritual travail. It is the distillation of a living experience. Here, we recognize at once, the man and his philosophy are an indivisible unity. But his strength is also his weakness. Apart from the experience the philosophy collapses, since in the final reckoning it is not a philosophy at all but a personal apology. His preoccupation, his bias, is not with reasons valid in logic but with the actual workings of the human mind as he knows it from introspection. He is the skilled analyst of the nature of religious belief itself, not of the grounds that would make it intrinsically

---

aggression, appear in his sermons. He was a presence as other men are poets or orators' (John Tulloch, *Movements of Religious Thought in ihe Nineteenth Century*, 1885, p. 114).

13. Even Mark Pattison, whose *Memoirs* leave no doubt about their author's antipathy to Tractarianism, could write to Newman himself in old age: 'The veneration and affection wh. I felt for you at the time you left us are in no way diminished & however remote my intellectual standpoint may now be from that which I presume to be your own, I can still truly say that I have learnt more from you than from anyone else with whom I have ever been in contact.' See M. Trevor, *Newman: Light in Winter* (1962), p. 620.

acceptable. That is why, fundamentally, he is not a systematic thinker. He identifies himself, properly enough, with the Church's tradition of doctrine, but once he has stepped aside, so to speak, from this framework he attaches slight importance to system or even, it would seem, to consistency of argument.[14] Of his fellow-Catholics who criticized his *Grammar of Assent* he declared: 'Let those who think I ought to be answered ... first master the great difficulty, the great problem, and then, if they don't like my way of meeting it, find another. Syllogizing won't meet it.' Syllogizing, he felt, would never meet the profounder difficulties of religious faith. Belief arises out of life, draws its strength and its colour from life, pertains always to life. Arguments do not create it nor systems authenticate it.

It is evident that Newman's thinking lacked architectonic power. 'A more inspiring teacher', remarked F. J. A. Hort, 'it would be difficult to find, but the power of building up was not one of his gifts.'[15] In order to write easily he needed, as he himself confessed, a definite *call*. The occasion, the impulse, had to come from without; he could then respond to it—the case of Kingsley's challenge is the signal example—with all the rigour of his nature. But deliberate system-building was not in his genius. As he reflected at the close of his *Prophetical Office of the Church*, 'the thought, with which we entered on the subject, is apt to recur, when the excitement of the inquiry has subsided, and weariness has succeeded, that what has been said is but a dream, the wanton exercise, rather than the practical conclusions, of the intellect'.

> Such [he goes on] is the feeling of minds unversed in the disappointments of the world, incredulous how much it has of promise, how little of substance; what intricacy and confusion beset the most certain truths; how much must be taken on trust, in order to be possessed; how little can be realized except by an effort of the will; how great a part of enjoyment lies in resignation.

No doctrine, indeed, is quite to be separated from the man who teaches it, certainly no moral doctrine. But with Newman the truism attains to a new level of truth. Often the specially revealing phrase—'What intricacy and confusion beset the most certain truths', 'How little can be realized except by an effort of the will'—can do more to reconcile us to his viewpoint than will his set arguments, with the impression these sometimes convey of artifice and even sophistry. Newman's writings—sermon, treatise, private letter, polemical pamphlet—not only instruct or exhort or amuse; they have the added power of the work of art to create *empathy*, to move the reader to enter into the author's own frame of mind, to share his hopes and disappointments. The student of Newman's philosophy must therefore be prepared to approach it not only critically—for criticism has little difficulty in exposing its evasions and inconsistencies—but with personal understanding. *Cor ad cor loquitur.*

14. His apologetic can at times be reckless. He writes, for instance, concerning transubstantiation: 'I cannot, indeed, prove it; I cannot tell how it is; but I say, "Why should it not be? What's to hinder it? What do I know of substances or matter? Just as much as the greatest philosophers—and that is nothing at all." ... The Catholic doctrine leaves phenomena alone: ... it deals with what no one on earth knows anything about—the material substances themselves' (*Apologia*, ed. Svaglic, p. 215).
15. A. F. Hort, *The Life and Letters of F. J. A. Hort* (1896), ii, p. 424.

The nature of belief

Newman's religious convictions began to take shape in boyhood, under the influence of a Calvinistic evangelicalism, and the note of austerity in his teaching which persisted through life may in part at least be attributable to this. As a youth, he relates, he readily accepted the doctrine of final perseverance, believing that his adolescent conversion would last into the next life and that he was elected to eternal glory. He retained this Calvinist tenet until the age of twenty, when, he tells us, it gradually faded away. But he thought that it had had some influence on his opinions, notably in the direction of certain 'childish imaginations' such as the sense of isolation from surrounding objects, confirming him in his curious distrust of the reality of material phenomena and—in his own often quoted words—'making me rest in the thought of two and two only absolute and luminously self-evident beings, myself and my Creator'.[16] Another early and permanent conviction was that of the necessary place of dogma in religion. From the age of fifteen, he avers, dogma had been to him an essential principle: religion as a mere sentiment was 'a dream and a mockery'. Liberalism accordingly, as 'the anti-dogmatic principle and its developments', was real religion's most insidious foe. For without its authoritative dogmas Christianity is but a mirage. Yet the statement seems hardly to consist with what Newman himself repeatedly says about the nature of faith. If the essence of religion lies in its positive doctrines then clearly these must be held as propositions completely and accurately true; and it was in seeking an authority for the traditional Christian doctrinal system in its most articulate form that Newman eventually found refuge in the Roman Catholic Church, which alone could speak with a voice not only firm but infallible. On this showing religion and its intellectual expression were for him one. Yet his reflections on faith constantly tend away from such intellectualism. A rational faith, he says in one of his *Oxford University Sermons*, need not mean more than that belief is consonant with right reason in the abstract, *not* that it results from it in the particular case. But if the act of faith is only partially rational, and therefore on grounds of strict reason inexplicable, why should we demand of dogma an exact and sufficient rendering of the *content* of faith? The discrepancy here is a fault that runs through the whole of Newman's thinking and accounts, arguably, for its pervasive ambiguity, despite the verbal skill with which it is set forth. Newman was not, let it again be said, a philosopher attempting an objective analysis of the rationale of religious belief. His purpose, almost always, was practical and apologetic—to build up and defend the faith. What Wilfrid Ward says of the Oxford school generally is particularly true of him: namely, that it was treating, not like the liberals, of the science of evidence, but of the art of religious knowledge.[17] Furthermore, in Newman's case, at any rate after 1845, this was religious knowledge as propounded by the only body on earth that could do so with an indefeasible authority. For what his arguments present is an account both of the way of faith and of the only satisfactory goal to which, in his view, it will lead. But it is this also which vitiates it as a properly

16. *Apologia*, p. 18.
17. Wilfrid Ward, *W. G. Ward and the Oxford Movement*, i, p. 392.

rational defence of faith, since the goal is presupposed at starting. Hence faith becomes a realm of its own, to which reason has no clear right of access. It is, however, thus only, Newman would assure us, that doubt can be resolved into certitude, reason being always a devious guide. For a man of Newman's peculiar temperament such a position may prove possible, if not indeed the only resort. But for one who puts higher store by reason than did the author of *A Grammar of Assent* such a device cannot succeed and the grounds of doubt will remain.

Basically Newman's theory of belief was not changed by his conversion to Rome. He was ill at ease with the conventional Catholic apologetic, choosing in this field to follow his own path—an independence which in time brought him into some disfavour with ecclesiastical authority. The process of argument so elaborately deployed in the Roman *Grammar*—at the time of its publication in 1870 he had been a Catholic for about twenty-five years—is already to be found in the Anglican *Sermons*.[18] In considering it, therefore, and here we are at once in the mid stream of Newman's religious philosophy, we must begin with the latter. At the very outset we meet with the claim that faith is independent of reason, to the extent at least that, as an internal habit or act, it is not the consequence of a preliminary rational inquiry but has its own special basis.[19] Faith, again, does not require evidence so strong as that needed for rational conviction, since it is mainly swayed by 'antecedent considerations'—by previous notices, prepossessions and prejudices ('in a good sense of the word'—whereas reason demands direct and definite proof. Faith moreover is 'a principle of action, and action does not allow time for minute and finished investigations'. It is the reasoning of a religious mind, or of what Scripture calls a right or renewed heart, acting upon presumptions rather than evidence. In this matter there are in fact two distinct processes: the original process itself, and the secondary one of investigating such reasoning. All men reason, says Newman, for to reason is nothing more than to gain truth from truth, without the intervention of sense; but all men do not *reflect* upon their reasoning, much less reflect truly and accurately enough to do justice to their own meaning. They do so only in proportion to their abilities. 'In other words, all men have a reason, but not all men can give a reason.' Thus the distinction resolves itself into one between unconscious and conscious reasoning, or reason implicit and explicit; and too often are they confounded. 'Clearness in argument certainly is not indispensable to reasoning well. Accuracy in stating doctrine or principles is not essential to feeling and acting on them.' The actual process of reasoning is therefore something complete in itself and independent. The analysis that may follow is merely an account of it and makes neither the conclusion correct nor the inferences rational. Indeed to render sufficient account of one's implicit reasoning may be impossible, no analysis being subtle and delicate enough to represent adequately the state of

18. Newman observed in a letter of August 1870, to Aubrey de Vere: 'As to my Essay on Assent, it is on a subject which has teased me for these twenty or thirty years.' See Wilfrid Ward, *The Life of John Henry Cardinal Newman* (1912), ii, p. 245. But perhaps most readers will prefer the more tentative and exploratory approach adopted in the earlier book.
19. *Oxford University Sermons* (ed. 1892), p. 184. A new edition by D. M. Mackinnon and J. D. Holmes was published in 1970.

mind under which one believes or the subjects of belief as they are presented to one's thoughts. 'Is it not hopeless', Newman asks, 'to expect that the most diligent and anxious investigation can end in more than giving some very rude description of the living mind and its feelings, thoughts, and reasonings?'[20] In moral and religious inquiries the arguments formally stated are in truth symbols of the real grounds rather than the grounds themselves.[21] Hence the conclusion is reached that the reasoning and opinions which are involved in the act of faith are latent and implicit, and that although the reflecting mind is able to invest them with some definite and methodical form faith nevertheless is complete without this reflective faculty, which may often be more of an obstacle than an aid.

Plainly, then, if the proof of Christianity, by Scripture or any other means, is of this subtle kind it will not be exhibited to advantage in formal exposition. And the danger is that writers on Christian 'evidences' or scriptural 'proofs' will always be tempted to press their case too far or to oversystematize. Religious arguments are not like mathematical demonstrations, to be followed passively and by attending only to what is stated and admitting nothing but what is urged. On the contrary, what they really demand is a certain *disposition* in the inquirer—'an active, ready, candid, and docile mind, which can throw itself into what is said, neglect verbal difficulties, and pursue and carry out principles'. But here we are in the *personal* sphere, the world of faith, which is not simply intellectual assent but an engagement of the whole moral personality. Thus in the *Prophetical Office* Newman points out that faith differs from opinion in considering God's 'being, government, and will as a matter of personal interest and importance to us, not the degree of light or darkness in which it perceives the truth concerning them'. Like Coleridge, he is unimpressed by evidence-theology, aimed only at the logical reason. To him it is typical of the preceding century, 'a time when love was cold'. As a general rule, he thinks, religious minds embrace the gospel chiefly on 'the great antecedent probability of a Revelation' and the suitableness of that gospel to meet their needs, whilst on irreligious minds evidences are thrown away. Further, considerations which are of no practical purpose tend to divert men from the true view of religion and lead them to think that faith is largely the result of argument: 'For is not this the error, the common and fatal error, of the world, to think itself a judge of Religious Truth without preparation of the heart?' In its schools the ways to truth are looked on as open to all men, at all times, regardless of personal disposition. Truth there is to be approached 'without homage'. In religion, however, it is otherwise. Here it is antecedent probability that determines, and antecedent probability involves a personal judgment. Probability of itself may indeed prove nothing; but, equally, facts of themselves persuade no one. Probability is to fact as the soul is to the body, and although mere presumptions may have no force, mere facts have no warmth. 'A mutilated and defective evidence suffices for persuasion, where the heart is alive; but dead evidences, however perfect, can but create a dead faith.' Thus in the presence of faith reason bows and retires; or rather, in words already quoted, faith is itself *the reasoning of a religious mind*. Such a

20. *Ibid.,* pp. 267f.
21. Ibid., p. 275.

mind holds the gospel to be probable because it has a strong love for it, even when the testimony is weak. Moreover, so far from faith being the reasoning of a poorly-equipped mind, as its critics object, it is really that of a divinely enlightened one. For 'as reason with its great conclusions is confessedly a higher instrument than Sense with its secure premises, so Faith rises above Reason in its subject-matter more than it falls below it in the obscurity of its process.'[22]

If faith is a mode of thinking that is commonly dismissed as irrational and therefore despicable—'till the event confirms it'—it is because the real and substantial grounds of inference lie in the character of the individual mind itself and in its general view of things—above all in its actual impressions concerning God's will and the anticipations derived from its own inbred wishes. Hence it is of the essence of faith that it should be an *antecedent* judgment or presumption. Newman allows, of course, that some safeguard is needed which will secure it from becoming mere superstition or fanaticism; but such safeguard is not simply the reason, nor—as liberal opinion contends—is it education. The real safeguard, he insists, is 'a right state of heart', a sound moral disposition. 'It is holiness, or dutifulness, or the new creation, or the spiritual mind, however we word it, which is the quickening and illuminating principle of true faith, giving it eyes, hands, and feet.'[23] In short, it is love which forms it 'out of the rude chaos into an image of Christ', or what the scholastic theology calls *fides formata charitate*—as distinct from the Lutheran conception of a bare *fides informis*, an act or attitude of mind which in itself has no moral content.

Newman's whole idea of faith is thus of something intrinsically personal, an expression of the *totus homo*.[24] The weakness of reason, taken in the abstract, is that it is impersonal. At this point the resemblance of his thinking to Coleridge's is very apparent. For both men faith enlists the entire self, of which the individual's particular bent, aptitude, characteristics and circumstances form a necessary part. Their use of words obviously differs. Newman takes the eighteenth-century view of reason as *ratiocination*, a meaning much closer to Coleridge's *understanding*. What Coleridge himself connotes by reason, however, is more akin to Newman's *faith*, which itself includes reason as a kind of inner guiding principle—

a presumption, yet not a mere chance conjecture,—a moving forward, yet not of excitement or of passion,—a moving forward in the twilight, yet not without clue or direction,—a movement from something known to something unknown, but kept in the narrow path of truth by the Law of dutifulness which inhabits it, the Light of Heaven, which animates and guides it.[25]

22. *Ibid.*, pp. 198, 200, 203, 216.
23. *Ibid.*, pp. 218, 229, 234.
24. This is the ground of his distinction between 'notional' and 'real' assent. 'I say, then, that our most natural mode of reasoning is, not from propositions to propositions, but from things to things, from concrete to concrete, from wholes to wholes' (*An Essay in Aid of a Grammar of Assent*, 1870, p. 263). A new edition of this work, essential to an understanding of Newman's mind, was published in 1973.
25. *Ibid.*, p. 245.

It is only by faith indeed—by this essentially personal attitude and insight—that the believer comes to recognize personality in God himself. Natural religion teaches God's unity, power and majesty, and even his wisdom, goodness and moral governance, but little or nothing in regard to his personal being.[26] The philosopher, Newman says, aspires towards a divine *principle*, the Christian towards a divine *agent*.[27] The vital thing in truly religious experience is the testimony of conscience. The marks of design in creation say nothing of God to one who does not already believe in him, a fact which suggests that any attempt to prove divine existence from purely rational as distinct from moral considerations is misguided.[28] In the end it is only the spiritual mind that can judge spiritually. As Newman put it in a letter to W. G. Ward, 'the religious mind sees much which is invisible to the irreligious. They have not the same evidence before them.'[29] It is not that either the intelligence or the honesty of the sceptic's actual reasoning is in doubt; what signifies is his lack of spiritual training, preventing him from recognizing certain data, or a special aspect of things, which, had he perceived them, he would have had to take into account. That he should have failed to do this—where, it may be, a quite uneducated believer will have made no such omission—is a matter for serious reflexion, and none can lightly pass judgment on him. But to Newman the inference is plain that whatever a man believes or does not believe will depend, not only on considerations that are external and rational, but on his whole mental constitution and character—upon an antecedent disposition for which, however, he is not himself without moral responsibility.

The '*Grammar of Assent*'

We now must turn to what is probably Newman's most carefully contrived work, his *Essay in Aid of a Grammar of Assent*, a study of the psychology of belief the interest and value of which time has still not dissipated. Its insight into the processes of the human mind is extraordinarily subtle, whilst as a piece of literary exposition

26. See Sermon ii, 'The Influence of Natural and Revealed Religion Respectively', dating from April 1830. 'Conscience', Newman says, 'is the essential principle and sanction of Religion in the mind'; but even conscience, though it seems 'to point in a certain direction as a witness for the real moral locality (so to speak) of the unseen God', affords no certain argument 'for a Governor and Judge, distinct from the moral system itself', to those who dispute its informations (pp. 18, 25). Newman states, by the way, that at the time he made this observation he was not acquainted with Coleridge's writings and in particular 'a remarkable passage' in the *Biographia Literaria*, 'in which several portions of this Sermon are anticipated'. See H. F. Davis, 'Was Newman a disciple of Coleridge?', in *The Dublin Review*, October 1943.
27. *Oxford University Sermons*, p. 28.
28. *Ibid.*, p. 70. Cf Sermon x, 'Faith and Reason, contrasted as Habits of Mind': 'It is indeed a great question whether Atheism is not as philosophically consistent with the phenomena of the physical world, taken by themselves, as the doctrine of a creative and governing Power' (p. 194). Also Newsome, *Two Classes of Men*, ch. 4. See supra, p. 64.
29. Wilfrid Ward, *The Life of John Henry Cardinal Newman*, ii, p. 247.

it is the product of a master hand. Yet it is a difficult book to read, demanding close attention. Many have found it sophistical, and if its real purpose is misunderstood sophistical it undoubtedly appears. For whatever Newman himself conceived his purpose to be in writing it, his procedure throughout is directed by his own profound concern with the actual conditions under which religious faith arises. Again, his temperamental egocentricity ensures that his approach is consistently personal and individualist. The process of 'assent' is, naturally enough, given a generalized form, but the model for it, one cannot help feeling, is the author's own mind. What indeed 'right' reasoning is—how the intellect 'ought' to operate in its quest of truth—is an inquiry which he does not pursue. We must, he seems to say, take the understanding as it is, as we ourselves are introspectively familiar with it. What use the instrument of reason can be put to is determined by its native constitution. It has no 'law' beyond its own intrinsic character. This sweeping prescription of the inquirer's task once made, the only profitable thing to do is to examine *how* men—ordinary men—do reason, and in particular how they attain to religious conviction or certitude.

> That [Newman says] is to be accounted a normal operation of our nature which men in general do actually instance; that is a law of our minds, which is exemplified in action on a large scale, whether *a priori* it ought to be a law or no. Our hoping is a proof that hope, as such, is not an extravagance; and our possession of certitude is a proof that it is not a weakness or an absurdity to be certain. How it comes about that we *can* be certain is not for me to determine; for me it is sufficient that certitude is felt . . . It is unmeaning in us to find fault with our own nature, which is nothing else than we ourselves, instead of using it according to the use of which it ordinarily admits. We must appeal to man himself, as a fact, and not to any antecedent theory, in order to find what is the law of his mind as regards Inference and Belief. . . . If then, such an appeal does bear me out in deciding, as I have done, that the course of inference is ever more or less obscure, while belief is ever distinct and definite,—and yet that what is in its nature thus absolute does in fact follow upon what in outward manifestation is thus complex, indirect and recondite, what is left but to take things as they are, and resign ourselves to what we find? That is, instead of devising, what cannot be, some sufficient science of reasoning which may compel certitude in concrete conclusions, to confess that there is no ultimate test of truth besides the testimony borne to truth by the mind itself; and that this phenomenon, perplexing as we may find it, is a normal and inevitable characteristic of the mental constitution of a being like man on such a stage as the world.[30]

It is not, of course, that Newman is content merely to conclude that what a man actually does believe, because his mind happens so to 'work', is on that account true. In principle at least he distinguishes between 'reasons', or causes, of belief and the grounds that would justify it. The trouble is that in practice the distinction is blurred and an analysis of the act of faith becomes its sufficient validation. The word used in the book's title—*assent* is therefore important. For this, very plainly, is its author's real interest. What he seeks to show is how such assent may be unconditional; as amounting, that is, to a state of complete mental certitude.

30. *Grammar of Assent*, pp. 344–350.

Locke's view, that assent admits of degrees, he flatly rejects. Once an assent is made it allows of no qualification. Whatever we may or may not be certain of we at least are certain of our uncertainty. The mind cannot rest in mere probabilities; it wants not only to know but to *know* that it knows. Truth, to give the satisfaction of the truth, must be held *as such*. And undeniably men do achieve assurance of this kind, in a vast number of matters. The mark of certitude is a 'feeling of satisfaction and self-gratulation, of intellectual security arising out of a sense of success, attainment, possession, finality, as regards the matter which has been in question'. In this respect it exactly parallels conscience. As a conscientious deed is attended by a self-approval such as it alone can create, so certitude is united to 'a sentiment *sui generis* in which it lives and is manifested', although in fact the two are unrelated. It is simply that as the performance of what is right is distinguished by 'religious peace', so the attainment of what is true is attended by a sense of intellectual security.

But here an obvious question occurs: how far, namely, do confident feelings amount to anything more than subjective assurance? Does my being personally convinced that what I believe is true provide reason enough for someone else to accept it as the truth also? I may, after all, come to change my mind. Newman sees this quite clearly, and allows that certitude does not admit of an interior, immediate test sufficient to discriminate it from false assurance. But he argues that an adequate criterion of its genuineness lies in its 'indefectibility'. For a man, in other words, to lose his conviction on a given point is proof that he has not really been certain of it. 'Certitude', says Newman, 'ought to stand all trials, or it is not certitude.' Its every office is 'to cherish and maintain its object', its lot and duty 'to sustain rude shocks in maintenance of it without being damaged by them'. But again the question is: How does one know that the new conviction will prove more durable than the old? The fact that a man now holds an opinion which contradicts a former one is no guarantee of his present and final possession of the truth. Yet to this quite unsubtle objection Newman really gives no answer. For if in matters of faith and morals it is the authority of the Church which alone produces the ultimate guarantee then the entire argument is at once removed to another plane and all previous considerations cease to be relevant.

The basis, as we have seen, of Newman's whole position is that the very foundation of religion is conscience. Here he undoubtedly was powerfully influenced by Bishop Butler, of whose solemn utterance one repeatedly catches an echo in Newman's own writings. The study of the *Analogy*, he himself tells us, marked 'an era' in his religious opinions. Nevertheless this all-pervading moralism was rooted in his character. Whatever other certainties may in the end have eluded him, the conviction that in the depths of the moral consciousness he truly heard God speak was inexpugnable. 'Even philosophers, who have been antagonists on other points, agree in recognizing the inward voice of that solemn Monitor, personal, peremptory, unargumentative, irresponsible, minatory, definitive.'[31] It was this rocklike assurance of moral values which gave to Newman's own faith grounds that could never be questioned. It was not a matter to be argued for or about, but to be taken as immediate evidence of the existence and presence of a divine Person:

31. *Ibid.*, p. 123.

If, as is the case, we feel responsibility, are ashamed, are frightened, at times transgressing the voice of conscience, this implies that there is One to whom we are responsible, before whom we are ashamed, whose claims upon us we fear. If, on doing wrong, we feel the same tearful, broken-hearted sorrow which overwhelms us on our hurting a mother; if, on doing right, we enjoy the same serenity of mind, the same soothing, satisfactory delight which follows us on receiving praise from a father, we certainly have within us the image of some person, to whom our love and veneration look, in whose smile we find happiness, for whom we yearn, towards whom we direct our pleadings, in whose anger we are troubled, and waste away. These feelings in us are such as require for their exciting cause an intelligent being: . . . 'The wicked flees, where no one pursueth;' then why does he flee? whence his terror? Who is it that he sees in solitude, in darkness, in the hidden chambers of his heart? If the cause of these emotions does not belong to this visible world, the Object to which his perception is directed must be Supernatural and Divine; and this the phenomena of Conscience, as a dictate, avail to impress the imagination with the picture of a Supreme Governor, a judge, holy, just, powerful, all-seeing, retributive, and is the creative principle of religion, as the Moral Sense is the principle of ethics.[32]

The entire passage from which the foregoing is cited is intensely illuminating. As Bremond says, whereas so many other Christian thinkers require religion to be the foundation of conscience, Newman makes conscience the foundation of religion.[33] Conscience is more indeed than the foundation of mere natural religion. In his own vivid phrase, it is 'the aboriginal Vicar of Christ'. Revelation itself has its primary authentication here. Once you recognize the origin of conscience you are bound, Newman seems to say, to recognize its scope also. All Christian truth rests ultimately on conscience for its testimony and cannot be apprehended apart from it. Even 'Apostolical Order' is an ethical principle 'or it is not worth much'.[34]

This it was—but, it would appear, this only—which for Newman rendered God's existence a certainty. He repeatedly declared—and we cannot for one moment doubt his word—that it was impossible for him to believe in his own existence without believing 'in Him who lives as a personal, all-seeing, all-judging being in my conscience'. As soon, however, as he tried to put the reasons for this certainty into logical shape he ran into difficulty. When he looked outside of himself—at nature, at history—he beheld nothing that could give him convincing assurance. Without the guiding light within, the phenomena of the physical world could as

---

32. *Ibid.*, pp. 109f.
33. Henri Bremond, *The Mystery of Newman* (trans. H. C. Corrance, 1907), p. 333.
34. But Bremond is right in saying that we should avoid the error of trying to present Newman as a mystic, 'in the rigorous sense of the word'. 'He does not claim that each perception of a moral truth brings him directly into touch with the Absolute. His conscience says nothing else to him except "Do this; do not do that"; but by an inevitable association he immediately regards each of these commands or prohibitions as the infallible expression of the will of God in Three Persons, of the Incarnate Word. Thus each of the affirmations of his conscience is, if I may say so, charged with dogmas. And I know well that it does often so happen; but what is extraordinary enough is that it should never have occurred to Newman to dissociate, in thought, such distinct elements, and that this indirect experience of God should always have had for him, if not the delight, at least the certitude of an immediate experience and of a vision face to face' (*Op. cit.*, pp. 333f).

easily point to atheism as to faith; and as for the world of human society, arguments drawn from it might indeed have real force, 'but they do not warm me, or enlighten me: they do not take away the winter of my desolation, . . . or make my moral being rejoice'.[35] Back, then, to one's own inner experience, to one's fundamental spiritual instincts! Here, plainly, Newman stands with Coleridge. But Coleridge's was a speculative mind, Newman's was not. He distrusted speculation, as he distrusted the metaphysics which rested on it. Take that road and the certainties of life begin to crumble. If belief is to be justified—and the *Grammar of Assent*, as we have remarked, is a highly-wrought and sophisticated attempt at such justification—then it must be so not by objective 'proofs' which bypass conscience but by examining the subjective conditions under which belief actually arises. Behind it, of course, is the assumption that God has so constituted man's mind as to make it possible for him to attain truth. Our belief may accordingly be trusted even though we fail to render full account of it. But to most minds the assumption will seem the very point at issue.

Yet the odd thing is that although Newman's argument depends on this assumption, reason remains for him suspect and the world it essays to interpret ambiguous. Hence, therefore, the further assumption that first principles are beyond dispute; that, to cite his own words, 'the Initial truths of divine knowledge ought to be viewed as parallel to the initial truths of secular; as the latter are certain, so too are the former'.[36] In this regard human and divine knowledge resemble one another. Each of them opens out into a large field of mere opinion, but in both the primary principles, the general, fundamental or cardinal truths, are immutable. These are the principles, the truths, by which man is bound to live, in the spiritual order as in the temporal. They are not a matter of mere probability:

> It is on no probability that we are constantly receiving the information and dictates of sense and memory, of our intellectual instincts, of the moral sense, and of the logical faculty. It is on no probability that we receive the generalizations of science, and the great outlines of history. These are certain truths; and from them each of us forms his own judgments and directs his own course.[37]

Likewise with regard to the 'world invisible and future'. Of 'our Maker, His attributes, His providences, acts, works, and will', we have, claims Newman, a direct and conscious knowledge. But he also makes the striking assertion that beyond this knowledge lies 'the large domain of theology, metaphysics, and ethics, on which it is not allowed to us to advance beyond probabilities, or to attain to more than an opinion'.[38] His meaning here, it must be said, is unclear. Is not the knowledge of God and his attributes, providences, and so forth precisely the matter with which theology does affect to deal? But Newman's words seem to imply that, while we have a deep-seated intuitive or instinctive knowledge of God, any attempt to rationalize this knowledge in the style of traditional Christian metaphysics immediately brings us on uncertain ground, ground becoming more and more

35. *Apologia* (ed. Svaglic), p. 217.
36. *Grammar of Assent*, p. 237.
37. *Ibid.*, p. 239.
38. *Ibid.*, pp. 239f.

uncertain the farther we move from the initial (and unarguable) assurances. It is these last, as the immediate and spontaneous deliverances of experience, which for Newman constitute the substance of religion; and the whole long argument of the *Grammar of Assent*—moving and subtle always, if in the end question-begging—is simply a plea on behalf of the beliefs by which a man of faith lives but of which the full logical structure cannot in the nature of things be articulated. But it is best to let this author speak for himself:

> First, we know from experience that beliefs may endure without the presence of the inferential acts upon which they were originally elicited. It is plain that, as life goes on, we are not only inwardly formed and changed by the accession of habits, but we are also enriched by a great multitude of beliefs and opinions, and that on a variety of subjects. These, held, as some of them are, almost as first principles, constitute as it were the furniture and clothing of the mind. Sometimes we are fully conscious of them; sometimes they are implicit, or only now and then come directly before our reflective faculty. Still they are beliefs, and when we first admitted them we had some kind of reason, slight or strong, recognized or not, for doing so. However, whatever those reasons were, even if we ever realized them, we have long since forgotten them. Whether it was the authority of others, or our own observation, or our reading, or our reflections which became the warrant of our belief, anyhow we received the matters in question into our minds, and gave them a place there. We believed them and we still believe, though we have forgotten what the warrant was. At present they are self-sustained in our minds, and have been so for long years. They are in no sense 'conclusions', and imply no process of reasoning. Here, then, is the case where belief stands out as distinct from inference.[39]

And what is true of belief affirmed is true, too, of belief lost. Good arguments do not necessarily preserve it or restore it, any more than they create it. Probability, according to Bishop Butler, is the guide of life; but on basic things one does not live by probabilities merely:

> Life is not long enough for a religion of inferences; we shall never have done beginning if we determine to begin with proof. . . . Resolve to *believe* nothing, and you must prove your proofs and analyse your elements, sinking farther and farther, and finding 'in the lowest depth a lower deep', till you come to the broad bosom of scepticism . . .

Some assumptions doubtless are better than others. But knowledge of premises and the inferences made upon premises—this is not to *live*. 'Life is for action: to act you must assume, and that assumption is faith.'[40]

Hence the all-importance of assurance, of certitude; and the mark of certitude is the mind's spontaneous and prompt rejection of whatever appears incompatible with the truth which it believes itself to hold. 'No man is certain of a truth who can endure the thought of the fact of its contradictory existing or occurring.' Psychologically indeed this may be true; and as a piece of psychological analysis the successive chapters of the *Grammar* are, we repeat, extraordinarily acute. That process of hidden or telescoped inference which Newman calls the Illative Sense, defined as 'the personal action of the ratiocinative faculty', is unquestionably the

39. *Ibid*, p. 167.
40. *Ibid.*, pp. 94f.

mode by which men's conclusions on very many matters are actually reached.[41] As he well observes, it has its function in the beginning, middle and end of all verbal discussion and inquiry. Where, however, he surely goes wrong is in maintaining that the illative sense is *nothing else* than a personal gift or acquisition and that it supplies 'no common measure between mind and mind'. The individual, truly enough, may not be able to assign specific reasons for his beliefs, but what Newman overlooks are the logical connections between individual reasoning, subject as it quite obviously is to personal conditions, and the general reasoning of the race. If the individual cannot produce and may not be aware of the evidence on which his opinions rest, that evidence nonetheless does exist and is producible. However difficult it may be to give exact definition to this general reason or collective understanding, it altogether transcends the workings of the individual mind and furnishes it with both a guide and a corrective. I may have a complete conviction that a belief of mine is true, but if it happens to conflict with what the vast majority of men take to be the case then it behoves me to reconsider the grounds of my belief with the utmost possible care. To fail to do so is to foster ignorance and fanaticism. Newman certainly was not ignorant, nor was he a fanatic, but his preoccupation with the mental states of the individual was the outcome of an intense personal autocentrism. Again and again, one feels, when he is speaking of man in general he really is alluding to one very unusual man—himself.

But what Newman could not bring to the question, by any process of doubt, was his own spiritual instinct. He yearned for God; and his conscience gave him what seemed to be an immediate assurance of God. In face of this assurance and to meet this yearning mere reasoning offered nothing that would in any way either strengthen the one or assuage the other. On the contrary, its action was all too likely to be corrosive. For with all his own tireless reasoning, channelled into countless books and sermons and papers, Newman in ultimate matters distrusted reason. Even theological doctrines, as the artifacts of human intelligence—albeit working on the data of revelation—do not, he seems to say, take us beyond probabilities, beyond what in the last resort is mere opinion. Such can be *known* to be true only when enunciated by authority. Increasingly during his Anglican career Newman sensed the need of authority. The Church of England, with its discordant voices, evidently lacked it. Yet the assumption that, if it were the Creator's purpose to retain in the world a knowledge of himself, 'so definite and distinct as to be proof against the energy of human scepticism', he would have introduced therein a power having infallibility in religious matters, seemed wholly warrantable. The conviction thus grew in him that not only an authority but an infallible authority actually existed which would restrain men's liberty of thought, in itself one of the greatest of their natural gifts, in order to rescue it from its own suicidal excess—'a working instrument, in the course of human affairs, for smiting hard and throwing back the immense energy of the aggressive intellect'. Rome, he was becoming confident, would be found right in the end. Moreover, the Church was a great historical fact, a vast and impressive reality. Christianity was a *Revelatio*

41. *Ibid.*, p. 345. Newman further defines it as 'the reasoning faculty, as exercised by gifted, or by educated or otherwise well-prepared minds' (p. 361).

revelata, a definite message from God to man distinctly conveyed by his chosen instruments and to be received as such; hence to be positively acknowledged, embraced and maintained as true, on the grounds only of its being divine, *'not as on intrinsic grounds* nor as probably true, or partially true, but as absolutely certain knowledge, certain in a sense in which nothing else can be certain, because it comes from Him who neither can deceive nor be deceived'.[42] Thus doubt might be crushed by infallible authority and certitude made indefectible by the centuries-old witness of the Catholic Church. Only so could the ever-questioning voice of reason be silenced. But even the most sympathetic observer of the cardinal's spiritual pilgrimage is likely to feel that his certainties are something of a façade and that behind them the 'aggressive intellect' still pursued its destructive work.[43] And although he told the world so much about himself in the *Apologia* and elsewhere, there remained, the reader is moved to conclude, an inner chamber of his mind—as perhaps of his personal emotions also—whose door he never opened to others.

The development of doctrine

But what of the charge against Rome, brought by all Protestants, that she had added to the original deposit of the apostolic faith doctrines for which Scripture provides no evidence or justification? Could the Roman Church afford guarantees of truth if she herself had so manifestly defaulted in her obligation to teach truth? The objection was a grave one. Were it to be successfully sustained—and it had been urged continuously since the sixteenth century or earlier—Rome's authority would inevitably have been impaired, and at the bar of Scripture itself. The issue was one which, for a man in Newman's position, could not be evaded and to its effective resolution he devoted much care and ingenuity in a work composed by him on the very eve of his reception into the Roman Catholic Church—the *Essay on the Development of Doctrine*, published towards the end of 1845.[44] Of greater intrinsic interest than even the *Grammar of Assent*, it is no exaggeration to describe it as one of the most significant books of its century; significant, however, less for its positive arguments, which are neither very plausible nor consistent, than for its method of approach to the whole problem of Christian doctrine in its relation to the New Testament. The idea of development as applied to this sphere was, for British theology, completely novel. In Germany it was already familiar: for the Hegelian philosophy development was a master concept, whilst the growth, in the

---

42. *Ibid.*, p. 387.
43. Cp. James Martineau's remark: 'His certainties are on the surface, and his insecurities below' ('Personal influences on Present Theology', in *Essays Reviews and Addresses* (1890–1), i, p. 234).
44. Newman brought out an extensively revised edition in 1878, when he was in his late seventies. The changes, however, consist largely in the rearrangement of its contents, and this is quite drastic, although Owen Chadwick speaks of the author's 'tinkering' with the book in his old age. In the revised edition the 'tests' of a true development become 'notes'. A new edition of the 1845 text by J. M. Cameron (with an editorial introduction) was published in 1973.

German universities, of scientific historical study, far ahead of anything of the sort here, had clearly established the principle of continuous change as a means of correlating and interpreting historical phenomena. The developmental idea had even been employed, in the interpretation of Catholic doctrine, by J. A. Möhler (1796–1838), of the Catholic faculty at Tübingen, in his book on *Symbolism*, published in 1832, a work which Newman himself acknowledges in his introductory chapter.[45] Möhler's essay is indeed an anticipation of Newman's, without, however, evincing very much of the latter's originality or suggestiveness. From the date of the publication of Newman's work fifteen years were to elapse before the appearance of Darwin's treatise on *The Origin of Species*, yet the theological essay foreshadows Darwin's procedure in the biological sphere in its grasp—if, unhappily, only intermittent—of the concept of organic evolution as distinct from logical explication.[46]. Like so much of what Newman wrote it seems pregnant with ideas the broader scope and implications of which the author himself did not fully realize; ideas, moreover, of which others were destined to make more radical use later.

Newman's purpose, in the first instance at least, was overtly apologetic. He was propounding 'a hypothesis to account for a difficulty'.[47] By now he was well aware of his own leaning towards Rome, but the problem created by Rome's apparent innovations upon the teachings of the early Church, to which he hitherto had looked for authoritative guidance, was one which had to be grappled with. That

45. An English translation of Möhler's *Symbolik* came out in 1843, but there is no evidence of Newman's having used it in writing his *Essay*. From what he says it would seem that he had not even read it. Nevertheless Möhler's view, stated in an earlier book on Church unity (*Die Einheit in der Kirche*, 1825), that 'Christianity does not consist in expressions, in forms, in phrases', but is 'an interior life, a holy force', its various dogmas having validity 'only in so far as they express the substance which is presupposed', would certainly have appealed to him. (On Möhler's work generally see E. Vermeil, *Jean-Adam Möhler et l'école catholique de Tubingue, 1815–1840* and J. R. Geiselmann, *Lebendiger Glaube aus geheiligter Uberlieferung. Der Grundgedanke der Theologie J. A. Möhlers und der katholischen Tübinger Schule*, 1942.) It is also very doubtful whether Newman owed much to Dionysius Petavius (Denis Pétau) (1583–1652), the French Jesuit theologian and historian of doctrine, who long before Möhler's time had introduced the idea of development into Catholic theology. Petavius's criticism of the early Church Fathers rests less on an understanding of their theological immaturity, as judged by later standards, than on his hostility to Platonism in any shape or form. Owen Chadwick, although he allows that Newman must have studied Petavius (along with Bishop Bull's answer to his criticisms), considers that he had only 'an insignificant part in Newman's mind' (*From Bossuet to Newman* (1957), p. 59), an opinion with which the present writer agrees. A useful discussion of the development of Christian doctrine from the standpoint of the historical theologian is J. H. Walgrave, *Unfolding Revelation: the Nature of Doctrinal Development* (1972). Speaking of Newman's theory he remarks that 'it did not arise in his mind as a part or aspect of a more comprehensive religious view connected with the philosophy of the day. It is impossible to trace his insights back to definite historical influences' (pp. 293f.). See also N. Lash, *Newman on Development: the Search for an Explanation in History* (1975) and P. Hinchliff, *God and History: Aspects of British Theology (1875–1914)*, (1992), ch. 2.

46. It is noteworthy that Newman makes remarkably little use of Darwin's ideas in the 1878 edition of the *Essay*.

47. *Essay on the Development of Doctrine*, p. 27.

ancient touchstone of catholicity, the Vincentian Canon—*quod semper, quod ubique, quod ab omnibus creditum est*—plainly could not be made to countenance the more specifically Roman doctrines and practices; although to this stock Protestant objection he might, he judged, reply with a *tu quoque*: 'Whatever be historical Christianity, it is not Protestantism. If ever there was a safe truth, it is this.'[48] The appeal, then, to the universal witness of Christendom would not do, for what one age deemed orthodox had, in another, become heresy. Likewise inadmissible is the notion of a *disciplina arcani*—of truths, that is, which, although known from the beginning, have been disclosed by authority only gradually, in the interests of 'reserve' or 'economy'—for 'the variations continue beyond the time when it is conceivable that the discipline was in force'.[49] Other criteria had therefore to be adduced. The postulates of his own theory he stated thus: firstly,

The increase and expansion of the Christian creed and ritual, and the variations which have attended the process in the case of the individual writers and Churches, are the necessary attendants on any philosophy or polity which takes possession of the intellect and heart and has any wide or extended dominion;

secondly,

From the nature of the human mind, time is necessary for the full comprehension and perfection of great ideas;

and thirdly,

The highest and most wonderful truths, though communicated to the world once and for all by inspired teachers, could not be comprehended all at once by the recipients, but, as received and transmitted by minds not inspired and through media which were human, have required only the longer time and deeper thought for their full elucidation.[50]

These principles allow of and require a genuine development in the Church's doctrines, involving the emergence of truths till then unknown or at least unrecognized. Yet it can, Newman holds, be shown that these new truths, for all their apparent novelty, are intimately connected with what had gone before, represent no strange and unwarranted departure, and are no mere corruption or decadence, but are of a piece with what the Church has ever held and taught and thus serve to vindicate 'the reasonableness of every decision of Rome'.

For, it is patently the development of *Rome* that Newman is intent upon explaining and justifying. Always it is the Roman Church's massive historical presence which impresses him. It cannot then but be, he persuades himself, that what has occurred under Rome's virtually universal aegis must be right. For he is obliged to admit and to insist on her immense power of survival and revival and on the awe-inspiring coherence of her teaching. This intrusion of the sheer *fact* of Roman Catholicism is for him the really potent consideration, before which Protestant objections spend their force in vain.

48. *Ibid.*, p. 5.
49. *Ibid.*, pp. 26f.
50. *Ibid.*, p. 29.

If, Christianity being from heaven, all that is necessarily involved in it, and is evolved from it, is from heaven, and if on the other hand, large accretions actually do exist, professing to be its true and legitimate results, our first impression naturally is, that these must be the very developments which they profess to be. Moreover, the very scale on which they have been made, their high antiquity yet present promise, their gradual formation yet precision, their harmonious order, dispose the imagination most forcibly towards the belief that a teaching so consistent with itself, so well balanced, so young and so old, not obsolete after so many centuries, but vigorous and progressive still, is the very development contemplated in the Divine scheme.

The providential outcome must be accepted or rejected as a whole; attenuation will only enfeeble it—one cannot pick and choose. And such is the coherence of the scheme that to accept any single part of it entails, 'by a stern logical necessity', acceptance of the entirety.[51] Nor is this all: behind Newman's reasoning there is a further assumption. For if, he maintains, the Christian doctrine as originally taught admits of true and important developments, then that in itself is a strong argument in favour of a 'dispensation' having been supplied for putting the seal of authority on those developments. But this is nothing other than the principle of the infallibility of the Church. Nay, 'the common sense of mankind' suggests, he tells us, that the very idea of revelation implies 'a present informer and guide, and that an infallible one'.[52]

It thus becomes evident how far Newman's conclusion is predetermined by his initial assumptions. What the Roman Church is, he decides, must be what the Church of Christ in its historic evolution was divinely intended to be, inasmuch as it has been preserved from actual error by its God-given infallibility. Nevertheless he recognizes that history witnesses to other developments within Christianity and feels accordingly that both the legitimacy of the Roman and the illegitimacy of the non Roman call for demonstration by means of certain empirical tests. These, seven in number, Newman lists as: preservation of the type, continuity of principles, power of assimilation, early anticipation, logical sequence, preservative additions and chronic continuance. Christianity he sees as an 'idea', and, he points out, an idea not only modifies but is modified or at least influenced by the state of things in which it is carried out, and is dependent in various ways on the circumstances which surround it. It is this process which constitutes its development. It also is a living process because, unlike the working out of a mathematical theorem on paper, it takes place in the minds of men, using them as instruments and becoming dependent on them in doing so.

Its development proceeds quickly or slowly; the order of succession in its separate stages is irregular; it will show differently in a small sphere of action and in an extended; it may be interrupted, retarded, mutilated, distorted, by external violence; it may be enfeebled by the effort of ridding itself of domestic foes; it may be impeded and swayed or even absorbed by counter energetic ideas; it may be coloured by the received tone of thought into which it comes, or depraved by the intrusion of foreign principles, or at length shattered by the development of some original fault within it.[53]

51. *Essay*, ed. 1906, pp. 93f.
52. *Essay*, p. 125.
53. *Ibid.*, p. 38.

Yet whatever the risk of corruption from intercourse with the world around it such risk, Newman contends, must be endured if the idea is to be properly understood and fully exhibited. Indeed all that he says, in a general way, concerning the growth and development of an idea, so clearly governed as it is by organic imagery, is admirable. Contemporary critics of the *Essay* even objected to it for its supposed modernism—it was, said one, 'German infidelity communicated in the music and perfume of St Peter's ... Strauss in the garment and rope of the Franciscan.'[54] Unfortunately the progress of Newman's own insight as the argument unfolds fails to live up to promise. The point to be ascertained, he reflects, is the unity and identity of the idea with itself through all the stages of its evolution, from first to last. To guarantee this unity and identity, he says, it must be seen to be *one*, alike in type, principles and assimilative power; one also in logical consecutiveness, in the witness of its earlier phases to its later and in the protection which its later extend to its earlier, as finally in its union of vigour with continuance, in its tenacity. Thus he arrives at his seven tests. But in applying them a change occurs in the whole conception of development: the organic gives place to the logical. For example, regarding his fifth test—logical sequence—he explains that he means 'to give instances of one doctrine leading to another; so that if the former be admitted, the latter can hardly be denied, and the latter can hardly be called a corruption without reflecting on the former'.[55] Newman's difficulty, it is apparent, is that of *precluding* those developments which have not issued in modern Roman Catholicism and which, therefore, on his theory are inadmissible; and it is fairly certain that later in life he more or less assimilated his own view to the 'logical' theory approved by Roman theologians, according to which the whole corpus of dogmas had been held in substance by the Church since apostolic times, though not necessarily in the precise terms in which they were eventually promulgated.[56] In fact this conception was already present in the original *Essay*, controlling the author's use of the seven tests, since he may well have realized that in the hands of others their application might lead to very different results. But, as ever with Newman, it is not the argumentation as such which moves the reader as it often fails to cohere, but the personal motives that sustain it.

For in the end it is the man himself who rivets the attention of posterity. The ideas and ideals to which Newman dedicated himself throughout his long career, first as an Anglican and then as a Roman Catholic, were backward-looking and reactionary even in his own times. Not that he had no interest in the age or its

54. In *Fraser's Magazine*, 1846, pp. 256, 265. In response to the 'liberalizing' charge—brought by, among others, so judicious a thinker as J. B. Mozley—F. L. Cross has shown clearly what Newman's real purpose was—that, namely, of resolving a 'concrete theological dilemma'. See 'Newman and the Doctrine of Development', in *The Church Quarterly Review*, January 1933.
55. *Essay*, p. 397. It has been observed of these tests that 'it is not too much to say that it is impossible to conceive a corruption of the Gospel which could not be brought under one or other of them' (Alfred Fawkes, *Studies in Modernism*, 1913, p. 277).
56. Thus he writes that 'the holy Apostles would without words know all the truths concerning the high doctrines of theology, which controversialists after them have piously and charitably reduced to formulae, and developed through argument' (pp. 191f).

concerns, or that he did not read widely. But there is truth in Mark Pattison's comment that 'the force of his dialectic and the beauty of his rhetorical exposition were such that one's eye and ear were charmed, and one never thought of inquiring on how narrow a basis of philosophical culture his great gifts were expended'.[57] His wariness of reason led him into intellectual positions which even to his warmest sympathizers looked precarious. Gladstone remarked that 'he places Christianity on the edge of a precipice, from whence a bold and strong hand would throw it over'. Manning, in his Anglican days at least, thought the *Essay on Development* sophistical, and was 'persuaded that Bishop Butler, if he were alive, would in his quiet way tear the whole argument into shreds'.[58] Thomas Huxley suggested that 'a primer of infidelity' could be compiled from the great divine's works. Certainly as a Roman priest Newman was looked on by his ecclesiastical superiors as insufficiently conservative and lacking in the requisite spirit of intransigence. Manning noted in a letter to a correspondent in Rome that

> he has become the centre of those who hold low views about the Holy See, are anti-Roman, cold and silent—to say no more—about the Temporal Power, national, English, critical of Catholic devotions, and always on the lower side ... I see much danger of an English Catholicism, of which Newman is the highest type. It is the old, Anglican, patristic, literary, Oxford tone transplanted into the Church. It takes the line of deprecating exaggerations, foreign devotions, Ultramontanism, anti-national sympathies. In one word it is worldly Catholicism, and it will have the world on its side.[59]

But not only was his 'tone' inadequate; his meaning also was dubious: 'Newman miscet et confundit omnia', was the common Vatican opinion. Years later the leaders of the Modernist movement condemned by Pius X readily acknowledged their own debt to him. Thus Loisy, who recalls that he in 1896 was reading Newman with enthusiasm, judged him 'the most open-minded theologian the Church had had since Origen'.[60] Tyrrell thought that in his notion of an 'idea' as a spiritual force rather than an intellectual concept Newman had identified himself with the modern as contrasted with the scholastic mind. 'It is the weapon that Modernists have taken from him and turned against much of that system in whose defence he had framed it.'[61] There are indeed passages in the *Essay on Development* any one of which the Modernists might have taken as the epigraph of a collective manifesto.

---

57. *Memoirs*, p. 210.
58. See E. S. Purcell, *The Life of Cardinal Manning* (1895), i, pp. 311f.
59. *Ibid.*, ii, p. 322.
60. A. F. Loisy, *Mémoires pour servir à l'histoire religieuse de notre temps* (1930–1), i, pp. 421, 426. Loisy examined Newman's theory of development in an article in the *Revue de clergé français* of 1 December 1899, and found it superior to those of Harnack and Auguste Sabatier. He remarks: 'La théologie catholique a eu de nos jours le grand docteur dont elle avait besoin.' But 'il lui a manqué peut-être quelques disciples' (*op. cit.*, p. 20). For Loisy, however, the development of Christian doctrine is a matter strictly for historical investigation, not *a priori* theorizing. Moreover, the development as he sees it in *L'Evangile et l'Eglise* (1902) has been genuinely 'evolutionary', capable of producing new 'species' or forms.
61. *Christianity at the Cross Roads* (1910), p. 33.

Thus we may read that 'one cause of corruption in religion is the refusal to follow the course of doctrine as it moves on, and an obstinacy in the notions of the past'; or that 'a power of development is a proof of life, not only in its essay, but in its success; for a mere formula either does not expand or is shattered in expanding. A living idea becomes many, yet remains one.' That Newman himself either did not see, or seeing turned away from, the implications of his own doctrine, can in no wise be held to mitigate the significance his thought was to have for a future generation. Doubtless had he lived to read the works of some who claimed his inspiration he would have been scandalized. But for all his introspection and critical self-analysis he could never conceal, in even his most considered utterances, the Janus-image in which his mind was naturally cast.

W. G. Ward and J. B. Mozley

William George Ward, Newman's ardent follower, was himself what Newman was not, namely, a philosopher *à métier*. James Martineau, a good judge, testified to his 'singular metaphysical acuteness'[62] whilst W. H. Hutton's description is of one who might still today be regarded as the typical Oxford philosopher: 'He never seemed to see the half-lights of a question at all. There was no penumbra in his mind, or, at least, what he could not grasp clearly he treated as if he could not apprehend at all.'[63] Even Mill thought that in replying to Ward's criticisms of his own philosophy he was answering 'the best that is likely to be said by any future champion'.[64] Here then for certain were a mind and interests very different from Newman's. As Church put it, 'Mr Newman's ideas gave him material, not only for argument but for thought. The lectures and sermons at St Mary's subdued and led him captive'.[65] But Ward had felt the pull of Rome sooner and, at first, more surely than his master. As was clear from the *Ideal of a Christian Church*, he immensely admired the Roman Church's power and capacity to teach with authority, its explicit doctrine of the supernatural, its sacramentalism, and its spiritual discipline and ethos. Rome could produce saints; the Church of England could, or did, not. But what in Protestantism he especially objected to was—to quote Church again—its 'ostentatious separation of justification from morality, with all its theological refinements and fictions'.[66] It was, we have seen, Newman's own deeper moralism which drew Ward away from so earnest a moralist as Thomas Arnold. No mere antiquarian ritualism but the idea of holiness was what impressively emerged from Newman's teaching. Thus Ward himself came more and more to believe that moral discipline alone is the real foundation of faith. The notion in particular of making the intellect rather than conscience the arbiter of moral and religious truth was abhorrent to him; and repeatedly in his book one comes across

62. See Wilfrid Ward, *William George Ward and the Catholic Revival* (1893), p. 312.
63. *Ibid.*, p.304.
64. Wilfrid Ward, *William George Ward and the Oxford Movement* (1889), 2nd ed., p. 273.
65. R. W. Church, *The Oxford Movement*, p. 340.
66. *Ibid.*, p. 342.

passages in which Newman's insistence on a right state of heart receives still sharper emphasis. The sense of duty, we are told, is 'the one faculty which is visited by divine grace, and which under that grace leads us onward to salvation'.[67] It was customary, he points out, to talk as though the gospel were in some way a *reversal* of the natural law rather than—what it is—solely and exclusively its *complement*.[68] Luther's great error was in denying or disparaging this principle, although Ward concedes a certain virtue to the continental Reformers in having at least followed their consciences, whereas the motivation of their English counterparts was largely political. Later in the book he writes that:

> The priest of a country parish will endeavour to lay his foundation within the heart of his flock; he will not consider any attendance of theirs on Divine Service, even the most regular, even (if so be) daily as well as on Sunday, to be any real security for so much as the beginning of a truly Christian life. It is the feeling of *accountableness* throughout the day, the habitual thought of judgment to come, the careful regulation of thought, words, and actions, which he will impress on his flock as the one thing needful. Their presence in church may be useful as giving him the power to address them, but he will use that power for the very purpose of impressing on their mind that the true religion must have its spring from *within*.[69]

Such a passage, from a work intended to exalt as the ideal of a Christian Church one strongly resembling the actuality, so its author believed, of the Church of Rome, might well have astonished its Protestant readers. Yet it is typical of the prevailing attitude of the Oxford divines—'Holiness', in Newman's aphorism, 'rather than Peace'.

But although Ward shared with Newman a common standpoint on the relations between faith and the moral consciousness, he did not follow him in the attempt to work out a new and more amenable type of apologetic. As an Anglican Newman had been liberalism's firmest opponent, yet as a Roman Catholic he acquired, paradoxically, the reputation of being himself a liberal. This no doubt rested on a misunderstanding. In a number of respects he was less liberal than Acton or Richard Simpson, for example. But he disliked the kind of arguments with which Catholicism was wont to be defended and wished to put something in their place that would bring the non-Catholic closer to the springs of Catholic religious experience. Ward, on the other hand, was satisfied with things as they were, and was stubbornly opposed to the liberalizing trends which in some quarters were beginning to make themselves felt.[70] The Church, with the long record of its saints, had proved itself an incomparable training ground of Christian souls, and the task of reason, once the Church's authority is accepted, could only be to defend what that authority had laid down and the tradition which witnesses to it. He did indeed welcome *The Grammar of Assent*, since its basic position was after all what he had himself always been contending for. But for all his acuteness Ward was without

67. *The Ideal of a Christian Church*, p. 204.
68. *Ibid.*, p. 248.
69. *Ibid.*, p. 438.
70. On the liberal tendency in nineteenth century English Catholicism see Appendix II below.

the imaginative genius that led Newman, whether in the English Church or the Roman, towards horizons distant from and strange to either communion as it then was.

In concluding this chapter some mention is due of Newman's brother-in-law, James Bowling Mozley (1813–78), who occupied the Regius professorship of divinity at Oxford from 1871 until his death. Church considered him as, after Newman, 'the most forcible and impressive of the Oxford writers'. For some ten years he was joint editor of *The Christian Remembrancer* in close association with Newman. Yet the event of 1845 left him unshaken. The leader's step, he shortly afterwards wrote, 'was not unforeseen; but when it is come those who knew him feel the fact as a real change within them—feel as if they were entering upon a fresh stage of their own life. May that very change turn to their profit, and discipline them by its hardness!'[71] Discipline of mind was an essential part of Mozley's character and personal loyalties did not deter him from pursuing the truth as he saw it. As time went by he carried his Tractarianism with a notable difference. The Gorham judgment in particular caused him to revise some of his earlier opinions, his newer views being expressed in a series of monographs bearing the respective titles, *On the Augustinian Doctrine of Predestination* (1855), *On Primitive Doctrine of Baptismal Regeneration* (1856) and *A Review of the Baptismal Controversy* (1862).[72] All show a decidedly Augustinian bent. Mozley's best work, however, is probably his Bampton lectures of 1865, *On Miracles*. In this he is mainly interested in the basic issue of the credibility of the miraculous. That miracles are credible he argues with considerable skill, denying (after Hume) that the uniformity of nature is either a self-evident or a demonstrable truth, although for very many minds it is an irresistible belief. But in order to know it as a rational principle one would need to be completely conversant with the ultimate structure of the world. If, however, the principle of uniformity is not rational, in the rigorous sense of the word, then neither is belief in miracle irrational. In any case the dogmatism of Mill and of *Essays and Reviews* in this matter was without warrant.[73]

Of interest, too, is Mozley's treatment of what he calls 'mysterious truths', such as original sin, the atonement and the trinity. These, he says, are truths 'which agree with human reason in a large and general way',[74] and hence are recognizable as truth, although a full understanding of them is not open to us. There are things, that is, as to which we are not totally ignorant of what they affirm but of which also we have no complete or rationally adequate conception. In philosophy they include the ideas of substance, cause, mind or spirit, power and infinity. In dealing with them, therefore, we have to be circumspect, refraining from logical inferences or practical conclusions that offend the moral sense. This is (or should be) evident

71. *The Christian Remembrancer*, January 1846, p. 167 (quoted Church, *op. cit.* p. 404.)
72. See below, Appendix I.
73. R. W. Church reviewed the lectures in *The Times* for 5 June 1866 and suggested that 'the way in which the subject of Miracles has been treated, and the place which they have had in our discussions, will remain a characteristic feature of both the religious and philosophical tendencies of thought among us' (*Occasional Papers*, 1897, ii, pp. 82ff.).
74. *Lectures and Other Theological Papers* (1883), p. 102.

in the instance of such doctrines as original sin and predestination, where logic seemingly demands that vast numbers of human beings can expect only perdition. The idea behind these doctrines is a sound one, but it has to be offset by a counter-truth no less necessary. And the fact that a doctrine cannot be stated with full logical consistency does not imply that it cannot be believed. The truth we seek in religion is something essentially that 'we feel and react after rather than intellectually apprehend'.[75] We receive it by faith, an attitude of mind by no means non-rational but at the same time not amounting to intellectual certitude; for faith has often to endure paradox—the admission of apparently conflicting principles—where an attempt at a compromise acceptable to reason fails to do justice to the spiritual experience in which all theological doctrine claims to be grounded. Divine revelation, moreover, poses difficulties from the very fact that it is progressive. Thus the Old Testament sometimes commands actions which in the context of a deeper spiritual understanding would not have been done or commanded, but which in the circumstances prevailing at the time were of necessity the best. But Mozley's width of sympathy did not extend to the new Broad Church liberalism represented by *Essays and Reviews*[76] or even by A. P. Stanley. He was astonished that the latter seemed unable to recognize the immensity of the difference between a religion with miracle and one without it,[77] whilst of the ideas canvassed in the famous volume of 1860 he could foresee no consequence, in the event of their dissemination among the masses, than 'simple infidelity and indeed atheism'.[78] On the other hand his criticism, in *The Theory of Development*, dating from 1878, of Newman's treatment of the concept was little less severe. Reason here has its proper rights and obligations. Granting that a divine revelation has been vouchsafed, is it not, he asks, more reasonable to suppose that for its interpretation and application men have, after all, been left to their own power of judgment?

75. *Op. cit.*, p. 114.
76. See below, ch. 10.
77. *Letters of J. B. Mozley* ed. Anne Mozley, (1884), p. 260.
78. *Ibid.*, p. 250.

Chapter 5

F. D. MAURICE (1) THE KINGDOM OF CHRIST

The Coleridgean influence: J. C. Hare

The influence of Coleridge on the religious thought of the early Victorian age is a fact beyond all question. Yet to particularize—to indicate where precisely, and how, it proved itself—is somewhat less easy. The Tractarians certainly were not impervious to it, but were chary of acknowledging any debt. Newman admitted the force of Coleridge's insight, if he also deprecated the boldness of his speculations. One, however, who some years before the first of the *Tracts* was to make its appearance could write that 'My fixed principle is: that a Christianity without a Church exercising spiritual authority is vanity and delusion. And my belief is, that when Popery is rushing in on us like an inundation the nation will find it to be so',[1] had already pointed the way the new generation of High Churchmen was to follow. Nevertheless it is not to the Oxford school that we have to look for the Coleridgean teaching's most visible fruits. Rather is it to those who, if in a markedly different spirit, carried on the more exploratory thinking of the Noetics: notably J. C. Hare and F. D. Maurice, although A. P. Stanley, Rowland Williams, John Sterling, F. J. A. Hort and possibly even Dean Church should be counted among them. Maurice confessed how much he himself owed to the poet-philosopher in the Dedication to *The Kingdom of Christ*, even though he elsewhere prefers to adopt a more guarded tone.[2] Hare's regard for Coleridge is sufficiently explicit in the dedication prefacing a volume of his sermons, *The Mission of the Comforter*, published in 1846 'to the honoured memory of Samuel Taylor

---

1. *Aids to Reflection*, p. 295.
2. Thus in his Introduction to Hare's *Charges* (1856) he spoke of those who ultimately experienced a discontent from intercourse with Coleridge. 'They had', he said, 'felt for him the passionate devotion which earnest and generous minds always feel towards one from whom they have received great spiritual benefits; their devotion had become idolatrous, and they demanded from the idol that which it could not bestow.' But he recognized as well that there were some who 'welcomed the voice of a man who said to them, "What you are feeling after is that Father's house which the men of old-time spoke of. It was not a cunningly devised fable of theirs, that their Father and yours is seeking to bring back his children to himself: these struggles and failures of yours confirm their words." Beneath all strange mystical utterances—beneath those tetrads which might or might not be useful as scientific expositions of a truth lying beyond the senses and the intellect—they hear this practical message from, they saw that he could not have received it or proclaimed it unless the whole man within him had passed through a tremendous convulsion' (J.C. Hare, *Charges*, i, pp. xxff.).

115

Coleridge, the Christian philosopher, who through dark and winding paths of speculation was led to the light in order that others by his guidance might reach that light, without passing through the darkness', and who, in particular, had helped him, the author, 'to discern the sacred concord and unity of human and divine truth'. For what Coleridge had done for these men was to guide them into new ways of understanding Christianity, to show them indeed new approaches to the whole problem of truth in the spiritual and moral realm. In Hare and Maurice—as also in Maurice's Scottish friend and mentor, Thomas Erskine—the traditional Church teaching acquired a new philosophical depth, away from the shallows of so much current controversy and ecclesiastical partisanship.

Julius Charles Hare (1795–1855) was born in Italy and spent most of his early life there and in Germany. His knowledge of the German language was thorough and he was well versed in German literature and scholarship, an accomplishment rare among the churchmen of his day. With the aid of Connop Thirlwall he translated Niebuhr's *History of Rome*, but in philosophical interests he was more strongly drawn towards contemporary German idealism than his sceptical collaborator, who disliked it. Educated at Trinity College, Cambridge, and for a time a fellow there, he subsequently held the living of Hurstmonceux in Sussex and was appointed archdeacon of Lewes. Among his pupils at Trinity were Maurice and John Sterling, who afterwards was his assistant curate at Hurstmonceux. Both were to remain his lifelong friends, and for both he had a high admiration, especially for Maurice—'the greatest mind since Plato' was his enthusiastic verdict—although Maurice on his own admission owed much more to the older man's teaching of the classics than to his theology. In fact Maurice's characteristic doctrines are scarcely to be found in Hare's writings.[3] The latter's own published work consists of collections of sermons—notably *The Victory of Faith* (1840), as well as the already mentioned *Mission of the Comforter*—and three volumes of his archidiaconal charges (1856), in which he ranged over matters of all kinds, from controversial theology to unsightly church stoves,[4] and a series of 'Vindications' of writers whom he thought to have been often misunderstood and misrepresented. Of these last the paper on Luther is outstanding.[5]

---

3. 'When', says Maurice in his introduction to Hare's *Charges* (p. viii), 'we met again many years after, my theological convictions had already been formed by a discipline very different, I should imagine, from any to which he was subjected; they were not altered in substance, nor, so far as I know, even in colour, by any intercourse I had with him. But to his lectures on Sophocles and Plato, I can trace the most permanent effect on my character, and on all my modes of contemplating subjects, natural, human, and divine.' But Maurice did acknowledge his indebtedness to Hare for his ideas on sacrifice. See *The Life of Frederick Denison Maurice*, by Frederick Maurice (1884), ii, pp. 504–7.
4. The unsigned introductory memoir of the author is by Maurice himself.
5. In another he took up the cudgels on behalf of Dr Hampden, whose nomination to the see of Hereford aroused bitter opposition from among the clergy. A.R. Vidler finds Hare's sermons 'practically unreadable' (*F.D. Maurice and Company*, 1966, p. 228); even Stanley thought them, as pulpit discourses, 'needlessly long and provokingly inappropriate' (see *The Quarterly Review*, June 1855, p. ii), but praises the Charges—justly—for their intelligence and vigour of style.

Hare belonged to no church party, although his personal sympathies lay with the Evangelicals, from whom, however, he differed sharply both on the question of biblical inspiration and on the central evangelical doctrines of the atonement and justification by faith. Theories of satisfaction and expiation he rejected, maintaining that the Jewish sacrifices, on which they were founded, embodied the idea not of penal suffering but of the sacrifice of the carnal will. It was of this that Christ's own sacrifice on the cross provided the supreme instance. Faith too, he considered, involves more than belief in the particular merits of the Lord's atoning death: a broader attitude of trust in and gratitude for the love of God revealed in the incarnate life as a whole. But if he criticized current evangelical theology he also had little good to say of Tractarianism, in which he saw an exaggerated sacramentalism, an over-rigid conception of the ministry and in general such excessive veneration of the past as could only inhibit the appreciation of new truth. His in fact was the type of mind for which dogmatism is always uncongenial. The depths of revelation, it seemed to him, were not to be plumbed by shallow definitions. Divisions among Christians that sprang only from differences of theological interpretation were to be deplored. Truth, he felt, does not issue from mere polemic; it would too soon be 'twisted about and distorted' to suit the polemist's aims. 'It swells out to a huge bulk, and absorbs all other truths, or hides them from our view.' As Maurice said of him, 'he felt himself called to bear a continual witness against those who confound the crushing of opponents with the assertion of principles; he believed that every party triumph is an injury to the whole Church, and an especial injury to the party which wins the triumph'.[6] Ecclesiastically he was a liberal, desiring the revival of Convocation and wishing to see more powers conferred on the laity in the administration of church affairs. A man of wide reading and sane outlook, his opinions were constantly sought and always valued. Above all he had the courage of sometimes unpopular convictions and was a ready opponent of injustice in whatever quarter.[7]

Hare's conception of faith closely resembles Coleridge's, but he seems to have reached it by way of his own study of Kant and before the publication of *Aids to Reflection*. Reason, he thinks, is in its highest sense a function of the whole personality, and faith accordingly an expression of it. Thus:

> Every genuine act of Faith is the act of the whole man, not of his Understanding alone, not of his Affections alone, not of his Will alone, but of all three in their central aboriginal unity. It proceeds from the inmost depths of the soul, from beyond that firmament of consciousness, whereby the waters under the firmament are divided from the waters above the firmament. It is the act of that living principle which constitutes each man's individual, continuous, immortal personality.[8]

6. Introduction to Hare's *Charges*, p. lxi.
7. As in both his spirited defence of Hampden and his reply to an article—anonymous, but known to be from the pen of William Palmer—in *The English Review* for December 1848, entitled 'On Tendencies towards the Subversion of Faith' and attacking a number of contemporary writers, including Hare himself. The reply took the form of a lengthy 'Letter' to the editor and was published as a pamphlet of over seventy pages. Hare was especially concerned to protect the reputation of Sterling who, in his last years and in the grip of a mortal disease, had given up orthodox Christian belief.
8. *The Victory of Faith*, pp. 37f.

Religious truth must be seen in the light of human need and human experience. Hence the continuing necessity of doctrinal restatement, since fresh insights require new modes of expression. Much avoidable strife and tension within the Church had been caused by clinging to obsolete forms no longer adaptable to men's enlarging knowledge. Revelation itself has again and again been identified with a particular dogmatic system. The Bible, however, clearly shows how truth is originally conveyed to men; not, that is, as abstract doctrinal schemes but in terms of concrete example or, at least, of principles capable of more than one formulation. 'A living faith seeks unity, which implies diversity, and manifests itself therein: whereas a notional faith imposes and exacts uniformity, without which it has no ground to stand on.'[9] His own religious outlook was, moreover, essentially Christocentric. Christ is the only true fulfilment of man's spiritual longings and aspirations, and in him alone do the truths which other religions were seeking after find their real validation. But Christ must be known as a *person*, in a vital experience. He is not merely the residual fact of a methodically sceptical historical inquiry after the manner of D.F. Strauss, nor the founder of a self-justifying system of ethics. For Christianity *is* Christ; he himself is the truth which he proclaimed, truth indeed which cannot be known except as personally realized in him. He is the Truth *because* he is the Way and the Life.

The theologian's vocation

Frederick Denison Maurice (1805–72) was arguably the most original theological thinker that the nineteenth century produced in this country. His originality was, in fact, too much for the majority of his contemporaries. In October 1853 the Council of King's College, London, felt it, in view of the tenor of his teaching, 'to be their painful duty to declare that the continuance of Professor Maurice's connection with the College as one of its Professors would be seriously detrimental to its usefulness', and he was dismissed. At the other end of the spectrum, John Stuart Mill thought more intellectual power was wasted in him than in anybody else of his time. 'Few of them', he continued, 'had so much to waste.'

> Great powers of generalization, rare ingenuity and subtlety, and a wide perception of important and obvious truths, served him not for putting something better into the place of the worthless heap of received opinions on the great subjects of thought, but for proving to his own mind that the Church of England had known everything from the first, and that all the truths on the ground of which the Church and orthodoxy had been attacked (many of which he saw as clearly as anyone) are not only consistent with the Thirty-Nine Articles, but were better understood and expressed in these Articles than by anyone who rejects them.[10]

Carlyle, who knew Maurice well, while reflecting that he 'ought to esteem his way of thought at its full worth', nevertheless confessed that hitherto he had found it

9. *Ibid.*, p. 74.
10. *Autobiography* (1867), p. 153.

'mainly moonshine and *Spitzfindigkeit*';[11] J.B. Mozley considered he had not 'a clear idea in his head'.[12] Benjamin Jowett saw in him undoubtedly 'a great man and a disinterested nature', but otherwise 'misty and confused', and dismissed his writings as not worth reading.[13] Yet James Martineau, the Unitarian scholar and one of the most perceptive among observers of the contemporary intellectual scene, held that 'for consistency and completeness of thought, and precision in the use of language, it would be difficult to find his superior among living theologians'.[14] Gladstone admitted to finding him, intellectually, 'a good deal of an enigma', but he also admired him as 'a spiritual splendour'.[15]

What then did his pupils think of him? It seems, highly, if with inevitable puzzlement. In the words of a recent historian:

> His face was noble and his expression reverent. He exalted his hearers, but he could not make them understand what he said. In lecturing or preaching he visibly reached upwards towards God, pouring forth words, contorting himself and his language, passionate for truth yet believing truth to be found only in hints and shadows. His better students loved him. His worse students abandoned the exhausting effort and ragged his lectures. Whether his students were better or worse, they could make nothing of the notes they took from his lips. But a lofty purpose and a reverent mien did better for some of them than information or coherence. They could see and feel the grandeur and mystery of truth.[16]

What, at least, emerges from such diverse comment is that Maurice was the sort of man which it is impossible to classify. He fits into no clear intellectual category, even as he belonged to no ecclesiastical party. He evidently had great gifts both of mind and character, as, equally evidently, he lacked the power of effective verbal self-expression. Perhaps also there is something a trifle absurd about him, a high-principled fatuity, a defect of that worldly wisdom (not untouched by disillusionment) which adds the needed salt to inspiration; as certainly, too, a lack of self-critical humour, a quality indeed with which the Victorians generally were not over-well served. But for all the faults of Maurice's published works—and the *Life* (1884) by his son, Sir Frederick Maurice, conveys a far better picture of the man than do his own often laboured productions—his thinking has a range, prescience and depth which gives it permanent value. It can be studied today for its intrinsic and not only its period interest.

The unconventionality of Maurice's opinions, for his times, is unquestionable. He stood quite alone. He had affinities with the Evangelicals, the Broad Churchmen and the Tractarians, each in turn. Yet clearly he belongs to no school or party or following. Neither, on the other hand, is he a purveyor of mere novelties. On this

11. *New Letters of Thomas Carlyle* (1904), ed. A. Carlyle, i, p. 29. But Maurice could be equally caustic upon Carlyle's own 'silly rant about the great bosom of nature.' See *The Life of Frederick Denison Maurice,* i, pp. 282f.
12. *Letters of J.B. Mozley*, p. 222.
13. E. Abbott and L. Campbell, *The Life and Letters of Benjamin Jowett* (1899), ii, p. 45.
14. *Essays, Reviews and Addresses*, i, p. 258.
15. *Life*, ii, p. 208.
16. Owen Chadwick, *The Victorian Church*, Part i (1966), p. 349.

he was himself emphatic. 'But while', he wrote, 'I utterly disclaim *novelty* ... there is a sense in which I earnestly desire to be original.'

> An original man is not one who invents—not one who refuses to learn from others. I say, boldly, no original man ever did that. But he is one who does not take words and phrases at second hand; who asks what they signify; who does not feel that they are his, or that he has a right to use them till he knows what they signify.[17]

Maurice assuredly was one who did not take words and phrases at second hand without making them his own, interpreting them in the light of his personal thinking and experience and impressing on them the mark of his distinctive outlook. So ready was he to borrow from whatever source appeared to him fruitful that he even incurred the charge of eclecticism and of wanting any real principle of coherence in his teaching. But eclecticism, like novelty for novelty's sake, he absolutely abjured. Nothing, he thought, was so emasculating. Better far was 'the keen mountain misty air of Calvinism', or anything else, 'however biting', that would stir to action.[18]

Although, then, the eclectic standpoint was not to his liking, that of the mere system-builder was even less so. Theological systems were anathema to him. Construct one, he declared, and the very gifts and qualities which otherwise would serve the investigation of truth at once become its greatest hindrance. For in system-building, elements which not only are different but often also disparate have to be made to fit in with one another. 'Dexterity is shown, not in detecting facts, but in cutting them square.'[19] The Bible contains no system, nor for that matter do the creeds or the Prayer Book. The Bible records the history of God's acts towards men, not of men's thoughts about God.[20] The creed always has been a statement for the people, something which the 'schoolman' cannot and dares not meddle with.[21] And as for the Book of Common Prayer, it was not its merits as a literary composition which endeared it to him—'I never never called it "an excellent liturgy" in my life'—but the fact that, more than any other book after the Bible, it helped him to understand the love of God and man.[22] Yet even systems have their use and Maurice could not believe that any of them exists without serving some good.[23] Had he indeed possessed one of his own he might perhaps have succeeded in making himself more intelligible. Intellectual schemes, once grasped in their organizing principle, remain in the mind and help to give meaning to whatever data are related to them. Maurice, however, had no skill of this order. He preferred to wait for the light as it might come to him, distrusting fixed assumptions. The attainment of truth was the all-important thing, and for this a

---

17. *The Doctrine of Sacrifice deduced from the Scriptures* (1879), pp. xf.
18. *Life*, i, p. 339. See also, e.g., *The Kingdom of Christ* (ed. A.R. Vidler, on the basis of the 2nd ed., 1842), i, pp. 178–82, and ii, p. 330.
19. *Lectures on the Ecclesiastical History of the First and Second Centuries* (1854), p. 22.
20. *Ibid.*, p. 2.
21. *The Prayer Book ... and The Lord's Prayer* (1880), p. 147. This publication comprises two collections of sermons.
22. *Life*, i, 512.
23. *The Kingdom of Christ*, i, p. 68.

man had to be ready 'to be detected in error'—a virtue which resolute systematizers do not easily acquire—and to be certain that 'God's meaning is infinitely larger than ours, and that other men may perceive an aspect of it which we do not perceive'.[24] But because Maurice steered clear of theological schemes it is not to be assumed that he was without method or respect for logic. Logic could be a tyrannical mistress, but as a handmaid she is ever necessary; whilst apart from method (always to be distinguished from system) life, freedom and variety (which system opposes) cannot exist.[25]

Maurice sought always to present the truth as he himself saw it; but because truth has many aspects its consistency is not invariably evident. Hence the confusion that often arose in his readers' minds and the adverse impression he created upon the unsympathetic or impatient. Moreover, he was not helped by his literary style, which is without grace and often repetitive and rambling. His sentences become tangled, their sense obscured by a cumbersome piling up of phrases. It was his practice, especially in his later works, to dictate, with results far from happy, since the manuscripts were sent to press without adequate revision. Unquestionably his shortcomings as a writer, prolific though he was, have prevented due appreciation of his standing as a theological thinker. It was said of him that in conversation he was apt to exhaust his interlocutor, and most readers have found his books certainly no less taxing. His reputation nevertheless grew steadily, reaching its zenith in the 1890s, only to fall precipitously in the early decades of the present century. Within the last generation, however, interest in his intellectual achievement has revived, and we now see him for the remarkable, and possibly the great, theologian that he was.

For it was primarily as a theologian that Maurice saw himself and such he claimed to be. His social reformism, for which he has usually been remembered, is really an aspect of his theology and an expression of one of its fundamental principles. At the beginning of the second volume of his *Moral and Metaphysical Theology*[26] he says that it will be evident to his reader that 'I have felt as a theologian, thought as a theologian, written as a theologian'. All other subjects were in his mind connected with theology and ultimately subordinate to it. But he explains also that he uses the word in its old sense as of that which concerns the being and nature of God, pointing out that he means by it God's self revelation to men, 'not any pious or religious sentiments which men may have respecting God'.[27] Nor, be it added, did he take theology, even as thus defined, in a merely formal way. The knowledge of God, he held, comes to men in experience, is indeed their basal experience. Not only is it the coping-stone of knowledge, the presiding element in the universe of man's thought, but the one foundation on which all else stands. He even said that in his opinion the name theology would better be exchanged for that of God, in that God himself is the root from which human life and society as well as nature itself are derived.

24. *The Claims of the Bible and of Science* (1832), pp. 30f.
25. *The Kingdom of Christ*, i, p. 236.
26. Published posthumously in 1882.
27. *Op. cit.*, p. ix.

It was from this viewpoint that Maurice approached the problems of economics and politics. Society was not to be re-created 'by arrangements of ours' but regenerated, rather, 'by finding the law and ground of its order and harmony, the only secret of its existence', in God.[28] In short, to be a theologian was to be a prophet, a man *en rapport* with God and speaking directly as from God. The prophet in the Old Testament is not a systemizer of men's reflections about God, and he never speaks of his experience with detachment, *as* an experience; he does not enunciate a doctrine; he is not, in that sense, a teacher at all. He repeats what God himself utters. Similarly the theologian's role is one of witness—of witness to a Being who, moreover, is not remote from the common interests of mankind; for the world which God made and governs must by that very fact be the theologian's immediate concern, the highest theology being that most closely connected with 'the commonest practical life'. Maurice was convinced that theology would never be more than a *hortus siccus* of schoolmen until carried down into the air of nations and humanity. Worse, politics itself would be simply a ground on which 'despots and democrats, and the tools of both', play with the morality and happiness of their fellow-beings unless 'we seek again for the ground of them in the nature and purposes of the Eternal God'.[29] His views as a Christian socialist are only an attempt to apply basic Christian principles, and to regard him as in the main a social thinker is to misunderstand him. It is fairly to be claimed, of course, that his social doctrine has a particularly historical significance, and in this respect he was undoubtedly a pioneer among churchmen. He himself, however, would have given this side of his teaching, for all its importance and urgency, a subsidiary place. His own view was that the theologian can speak to men convincingly, even on non-theological matters, only when he addresses them *as* a theologian.

> If [he wrote] I consider what I say I believe, if I determine to hold that fast, I may discover that I have in theology a much broader as well as a firmer meeting-ground with men as men, with men of all kinds and professions, of all modes and habits of thought, with men who attack my convictions, with men who are indifferent about their own convictions, than any maxims of trade, of convenience, of modern civilization, of modern tolerance, can supply me with.[30]

Wise words, we may say, which theologians of any age should lay to heart. For when men hearken, as they think, to a prophet, it is the prophet's authentic message which they ought to be able to hear, not simply information they themselves could have given him. Unhappily in Maurice's own case, though his intentions were sound, the 'prophetic' character of his discourse was sometimes of a kind to darken counsel. His actual phrases can often be telling, whereas his meaning is elusive. But unlike many prophets he has been lucky in that his admirers have since done him the service of making his thoughts clearer.

28. *Life*, ii, pp. 136f.
29. *The Gospel of St John* (1885), p. 475.
30. *The Conflict of Good and Evil in Our Day* (1865), p. 182.

'The Kingdom of Christ'

It has been said that Maurice's teaching draws its inspiration as much from Plato as from the Christian Scriptures. Thus a Victorian critic, the Methodist theologian J. H. Rigg, stigmatized it as 'Platonism in gown and cassock', and argued that Maurice's doctrine of creation is emanationist—all reality exists in the mind of the Logos, so that the distinction between divine and human becomes blurred—whilst his doctrine of redemption, in minimizing the significance of Christ's actual historicity, tends to treat the Saviour as an abstraction or a merely impersonal spiritual influence.[31] Maurice said himself that he had never taken up a dialogue of Plato's without getting more from it than from any other book not in the Bible.[32] But the Platonizing charge is easily exaggerated. Maurice, like a great many other Christian teachers from the Alexandrians onwards, found in the ancient Greek thinker a major source of intellectual and spiritual stimulus. In his own instance it was the truth-seeking quality in Plato's writings that especially stirred him. To quote his own words:

> It was the necessary consequence of Plato's situation, and of the task which had been committed to him, that he was always seeking for principles. The most simple everyday facts puzzled him; nothing that human beings were interested in was beneath his attention; but then it was the meaning of these things, the truth implied in them, which he was continually inquiring after. He found the commonest word that men speak, the commonest act that men do, unintelligible, except by the light which comes from another region than that in which they are habitually dwelling.[33]

This quality he did not find in Aristotle, the collector, arranger and classifier *par excellence* of facts, the framer of definitions. What attracted him in the Platonist philosophy was its abiding sense of the eternal and unchanging behind the surface-show of everyday things, an ultimate reality in which alone man can gain satisfaction and rest. Yet it is Plato's method of inquiry which was the effective influence. Plato taught him to examine his own ideas, his own terms. And this, he claims, was also Christ's procedure.

> I find Him beginning His pilgrimage on earth as a questioner ... I find Him sanctioning that as His own sound method of detecting falsehood and laziness, and of urging men to seek truth that they may find it.[34]

Rigg's specific objections to Maurice's 'Neo-Platonism' need not detain us. He quite certainly overstates his case. Sufficient is it to say that Maurice's Platonism is to be seen in his general attitude to truth rather than in any express attempt to recast Christian doctrine in a particular philosophical mould.

His earliest theological work, *Subscription No Bondage*,[35] was a defence of the

---

31. See *Modern Anglican Theology*, published in 1859.
32. *Life*, ii, p. 37.
33. *Moral and Metaphysical Philosophy*, i, p. 180.
34. *What is Revelation?*, p. 29.
35. Published in 1835 under the pseudonym of Rusticus, it bore the subtitle: 'On the Practical Advantages afforded by the Thirty-Nine Articles on matriculation in the University of Oxford'.

obligation of subscribing to the Thirty-nine Articles on matriculation in the university of Oxford. He had himself been brought up in Unitarianism—his father was a minister of the sect—and when at Cambridge the fact that he was not a member of the Church of England was a bar to his proceeding to a degree. When later he became an Anglican and entered Exeter College, Oxford, the requirement of subscription to a detailed theological formulary did not, however, trouble him. The act he considered to be no more than a declaration of the terms on which the university professed to teach its students and they in turn agreed to learn. It was fairer, he thought, to declare those terms openly than to conceal them, and in any case the Articles were in his judgment a not unfitting introduction, *being* theological, to a general education to science both humane and physical. Further, they might contribute to the reconciling of what is positive in the teaching of all Christian sects. This was a point of view entirely congenial to the Tractarians and seemed on the face of it to place him among their friends. But strong believer in the Church though Maurice was, the Tractarian rigidity repelled him. By nature he was not a party man, however broad the party's professions, and the exclusiveness of Newman and his followers towards Dissenters repelled him. That he was not for them nor they for him soon became evident. The realization of this, so far as he was concerned, came on his reading of Pusey's tract on baptism. This sacrament, as the Movement party saw it, was an instantaneously transforming act instead of, as he himself conceived it, a witness to the abiding truth of God's communion with man, the spiritual fact of the living presence of Christ in the life of humanity. For the basic principle of Maurice's theology was his conviction of the *nearness* of God. The Almighty is not a supreme governing Power, remote and impersonal, but the loving Father of mankind. As such he has revealed himself in the past and is ever waiting to do so in the present. Christ indeed, as Christians are bound to believe, was a full and final revelation of the divine; but the imparting of that revelation to men is a continuing process. What above all they should learn from it is that they are already *in* Christ, and therefore, through him, in God. 'Except', Maurice once said, 'I could address *all kinds of people* as members of Christ and children of God, I could not address them at all.'[36] Man as such is a member of Christ and a child of God; baptism does not make him so. Maurice was emphatic that man does not by baptism or faith or any other process acquire a new character, in the sense of certain inherent qualities and properties not before possessed. If he does become a 'new creature' it is as having already been created anew by Christ, of having been grafted into him and become an inheritor of his life. Hence if baptism gives a man 'the filial name and the filial privilege' it is because Christ has first vindicated that name and privilege for all human beings, by himself assuming their flesh. But it confers no separate grace on any creature.

It can only say: 'Thou belongest to the head of thy race; thou art a member of His Body; thou dost not merely carry about with thee that divided nature which thou hast inherited from the first Adam—a nature doomed to death, with death stamped upon

36. *Life*, ii, p. 236 (italics ours).

it—thou hast the nature of the Divine Son, thou art united to Him in whom is life, and from whom the life of thee and of all creatures comes.[37]

Hence, too, although Maurice fully shared the Tractarians' belief in the Church as a divine society—as he was also at one with them in his recognition of its marks of identity—he could not endorse that aspect of their doctrine which pressed its separateness from either the Christian sects or the world without. Neither the world nor the sects *were* the Church, yet they were not without their special witness to the truth, distorted or one-sided in presentation though it might be.

Maurice, however, could not accept the common criticism of the Oxford Movement that it was preoccupied with 'forms'. On the contrary, he was convinced it was a movement not towards fanaticism but away from it.

> It arose, I believe, [he afterwards wrote] from a strong and deep feeling, that if forms exist at all they must have meaning in them, otherwise they are shams and delusions. They did exist; by the Evangelical party they were regarded as useful accessories to personal devotion, in Oxford [i.e. by old-fashioned High Churchmen] they were regarded with antiquarian and traditional homage. The acknowledgement of them, as possessing present worth, as being the witnesses of an actual connexion between man and the invisible world, of an actual fellowship between man and man, was wanting to both.

And he adds:

> To recover this conviction was to recover that which is the great principle of social faith, the principle that we exist in a permanent communion which was not created by human hands, and cannot be destroyed by them.[38]

The doctrine of the human race as itself both created and redeemed in Christ its Head and King is central to Maurice's whole teaching. Mankind, he says, stands not in Adam but in Christ,[39] and his proper constitution is his constitution in Christ.[40] All men, therefore, are God's adopted sons, a relationship which existed in Christ before all worlds and was manifested when he came in the flesh. What we have to do is to claim it, looking on ourselves as God himself sees us. For man was created in the divine image; man, that is, as a kind, and individual man only so far as he is the member of a kind;[41] though if we are to behold that image in its true likeness we must do so as it is in Christ, the Man who is God's perfect likeness.[42]

> Men are told that they are made in the image of God: how it could be they knew not. Here is His express image, not shewn in the heaven above, nor in the earth beneath, but in a man. In Him creation has subsisted, in spite of all the elements of

---

37 *Sermons preached in Lincoln's Inn Chapel* (1891), i, p. 81.
38. From an open letter, 'On Right and Wrong methods of supporting Protestantism', dated 1843, to the Evangelical leader and philanthropist, Lord Ashley, afterwards Earl of Shaftesbury.
39. *Life*, ii, p. 358.
40. *The Church a Family* (1850), p. 46.
41. *Sermons preached in Lincoln's Inn Chapel* (1891), ii, p. 51.
42. *Ibid.*, iii, p. 31.

confusion and discord within it ... In Him we find how humanity has been a holy thing, though each man felt himself to be unholy.[43]

Again:

> The principle that man was made in the image of God, is not a principle which was true for Adam and false for us. It is the principle upon which the race was constituted and can never cease to be constituted.[44]

Maurice's objection to the traditional presentation of Christian doctrine concerned what seemed to him to be its false basis. Theology, Catholic and Protestant alike, made its starting-point the Fall, so that Christ's incarnation and death, despite St Paul's language about the mystery of Christ as the ground of all things in heaven and earth, were commonly regarded only as provisions against its more or less catastrophic effects. What had always been insisted on was the fact of man's depravity. 'The Fall of Adam—not the union of the Father and the Son, nor the creation of the world in Christ—is set before men in both divisions of Christendom as practically the ground of their creed.'[45] That it was this doctrine which lent force to the evangelical preaching Maurice readily allowed, and without the evangelical rekindling of it the faith of the English people would, he thought, utterly have died. Yet as he saw it 'it made the sinful man and not the God of all Grace the foundation of Christian theology'.[46] What the Christian theologian had to decide was upon what ground humanity really rests, whether upon the fall or upon redemption. Put thus, Maurice held, there could be only one possible answer, and this the Christian conception of God itself dictates.

Not that Maurice entertained any less grave a view of sin than did Evangelicals, or for that matter High Churchmen, although he has been criticized for doing so.[47] Man, he believed, is a child of God, surely; but he is a wayward child, and his actual estate is a sad decline from his true and original one. The power of evil in human life and the horror of its consequences no just view can mitigate. Besides, Maurice was himself a man of keenly sensitive conscience. 'How hard', he exclaims, speaking of the clause 'Deliver us from evil', in the Lord's Prayer,

43. *The Epistles to the Hebrews* (1846), p. 29. This work also contains a preface in which the author discusses Newman's theory of development.
44. *The Patriarchs and Lawgivers of the Old Testament* (1890), p. 56.
45. *The Conflict of Good and Evil in Our Day*, p. 170.
46. *Theological Essays* (3rd ed., 1853), p. xvi. In this, of course, the Evangelicals were simply following the doctrine of the sixteenth century Reformers. 'In the Calvinistic bodies from the first, and in the Lutheran so far as they caught the purely Protestant complexion, the idea of the Incarnation was deposed from the place which it occupied in the older divinity of the Church. The state and constitution of humanity was determined by the fall; it was only the pure, elect body, which had concern in the *redemption*; that redemption, therefore, could only be contemplated as a means devised by God for delivering a certain portion of his creatures from the law of death, to which the race was subjected' (*The Kingdom of Christ*, i, p. 126). William Wilberforce had declared that the corruption of human nature 'lies at the very root of all true Religion', and 'is eminently the basis and groundwork of Christianity' (*A Practical View*, p. 24).
47. See R.H. Hutton, *Criticisms of Contemporary Thought and Thinkers* (1894), p. 88.

how hard, when evil is above, beneath, within, when it faces you in the world, and scares you in the closet, when you hear it saying in your heart, and saying in every one else, 'Our name is Legion', when sometimes you seem to be carrying the world's sins upon yourself ... oh how hard, most hard, to think that such a prayer as this is not another of the cheats and self-delusion in which we have worn out our existence.[48]

In fact, sin is so grievous and its effects so manifest that it is vital for man to know the truth about himself and whether it is Christ or the devil who is master. The joy of the Christian gospel is that it proclaims Christ to be men's lord. It shows us why the life of man is not vanity, in that it is drawn from the life of the Son of God himself, in whom alone is life and light. Man's existence becomes a vain show only as and when he seeks his good elsewhere than in the one source of all good, when he looks for the satisfaction of his being 'in the things which he is to rule, not in the Lord who rules him'.[49] Herein also is the essential difference between the believer and the non-believer; but it is a difference 'not about the *fact*, but precisely in the belief *on* the fact'. For the truth is—Maurice re-emphasizes it—that every man is in Christ, whereas the condemnation of every man is that he will not own the truth, will not *act* the truth. The gospel is simply the full discovery of him who is 'the Living Centre of the Universe' and the assertion that all men are related to him as member to head.

Does this then mean that there is no standing and no function for the Church as such and distinct from the whole race? It certainly is not Maurice's meaning and the answer he would have given to the question is plainly stated in the *Theological Essays*.[50] The world, he there says, contains the elements of which the Church is composed. In the Church these elements are penetrated by a uniting, reconciling power. The Church is to be thought of, therefore, as human society in its *normal* state, whereas the world is the same society in an irregular and abnormal state. 'The world is the Church without God; the Church is the world restored to its relation with God, taken back by Him into the state for which He created it.'[51] To this conception of the Church Maurice devotes what is probably his most important book and the one in which he comes closest to a systematic exposition of his views: namely, *The Kingdom of Christ; or Hints on the Principles, Ordinances, and Constitution of the Catholic Church, in letters to a member of the Society of Friends*, the first edition of which appeared in 1838.[52] In this his aim is to present a constructive doctrine by taking full account of the kind of objections to the Catholic idea which might be made by, in turn, a Quaker, an orthodox Protestant, a Unitarian and a contemporary rationalist—an enterprise he carries out with remarkable insight and understanding. He seeks to affirm the positive principle in each, freely acknowledging whatever validity it possesses, while at the same time showing how, when this positive principle is over-emphasized and made the basis

48. *The Prayer ... and The Lord's Prayer,* pp. 318f.
49. *Sermons preached in Lincoln's Inn Chapel,* iii, p. 90.
50. A new edition, by E.F. Carpenter, was published in 1957.
51. *Theological Essays,* p. 403.
52. The second and considerably revised edition of 1842 carries a dedication to Coleridge's son, Derwent. It is this edition which was republished in 1958 by A.R. Vidler, in two volumes.

of an entire system, it rapidly becomes a major error. Then, having considered a number of such systems, he looks for those signs of a 'spiritual and universal Kingdom' by which they could be transcended. That such a Kingdom exists is, he claims, beyond all doubt: it is constituted by the whole body of Christ's witnesses, of all 'who through God's mercy' have heard the gospel of Christ, confessed it to be true and assumed the privilege of belonging to his Church. The signs or marks of this society are the sacraments of baptism and the eucharist, the creeds, the liturgy or forms of worship, the episcopate and the Scriptures.

The marks of the Church

Maurice's review of opinions, the merits of which he acknowledges whilst deploring their exclusiveness, is characterized by a sympathy so large as to astonish, when the reader is mindful of the controversial clamour of the decade in which his volume saw the light. His efforts to understand may even at times seem laboured, but his criticisms, when voiced, are penetrating. The Quaker, for example, in failing to appreciate the significance of the incarnation is apt to lose sight of the distinctiveness of the sacred and so allow his vision to become secularized. Similarly the Protestant, in making a shibboleth of justification by faith, loses sight of Christ himself as the Justifier in his preoccupation with the experience of being justified.[53] The Unitarian, again, makes much of the God of love, but in denying the incarnate misses what was really the supreme manifestation of that love. In all these failures Maurice sees the consequences of system-building: distortion. Rome's great fault is its obsession with system, in both its doctrines and its practice, filling the place between the believer and Christ with, on the one hand, abstract theologizing, and on the other a mere mechanism for locating an absent Saviour.

The principle of a divine society Maurice finds in Scripture. 'Everyone who reads the Old Testament must perceive that the idea of a covenant of God with a certain people is that which presides in it.'[54] Divine election, however, was not exclusive: the choice of one people was to be for the blessing of all. Israel was the Church of God, first as a family, then as a nation in which king, priest and prophet, law, temple and sacrifice are elements of an integral whole—a way of approach to the ecclesiological doctrine in which Maurice—and again we must bear in mind the period in which he wrote—displays signal originality. For the Christian Church as it has existed in history has its essential principles already disclosed in the Bible. It is a holy nation, a people of God; and as Israel of old had the appropriate signs of its corporate life and calling so too has the Church. To present Maurice's account of these signs is in effect to expose the lineaments of his entire theology. But to him the obvious implication of the idea of the Church as the one people of God, called and redeemed in Christ, is its condemnation of sectarianism. Maurice, as we have said, detested the sectarian spirit with which religion in his day was rife. That

53. Cf. *Life*, i, p. 139: 'Are there not some people who preach Faith instead of preaching Christ?'
54. *The Kingdom of Christ*, i, p. 237.

sects come into existence on admissible pretexts and with the best of intentions he did not deny. Often enough they bear genuine witness to truth. Nevertheless, the sectarian impulse, especially since the Reformation, has more and more driven out the old faith and has led people to think 'that the Church must be either a mere world, or else a narrow, self-willed confederation; that it must either cease to be a spiritual body, or cease to be a universal one'.[55] In any case sectarianism does not necessarily imply purity: 'Every experiment to make bodies holy by cutting off the supposed unholy portions from the rest, has proved the more unsuccessful and abortive, the more consistently and perseveringly it has been pursued.'[56] Besides, it encourages bigotry: when any sect or school becomes dominant it changes too easily from a witness to Christ to a witness to itself, while the once vital convictions of its founders pass into pointless actions and unmeaning phraseology. It is largely by its opposition to other schools that it retains any energy of its own.[57] Indeed on this topic Maurice is perhaps prone to overstate. The appearance of a sect may have been a historical necessity if some aspect of the truth were not to be forgotten altogether. But in the main his protest was salutary.

Maurice's view of the basic meaning of baptism we have already noted. The rite is a declaration of what man redeemed actually is: a child of God; and it bids him live as such. It is of the baptized accordingly that the Church consists.

> Baptism asserts for each man that he is taken into union with a divine Person, and by virtue of that union is emancipated from his evil *Nature*. But this assertion rests upon another, that there is a society for mankind which is constituted and held together in that Person, and that he who enters this society is emancipated from the *world*—the society which is bound together in the acknowledgement of, and subjection to, the evil, selfish tendencies of each man's nature.[58]

But if baptism is the sign of man's redeemed state as such, the eucharist is the sign of his communion with God in the largest and fullest sense of the word. It testifies that 'a living and perpetual communion has been established between God and man; between earth and heaven; between all spiritual creatures; that the bond of this communion is that body and blood which is the Son of God and the Son of Man offered up to His Father, in fulfilment of His will, in manifestation of His love'. It is the sacrament of his continual presence with his universal family, testifying to each man his own place in that family, and his share in its blessings. It is 'the pledge and spring of a renewed life', and the assurance that that life is his own eternal life.[59] Further, it shows that by the use of material elements men's bodies are redeemed as well as their souls. Maurice speaks of the eucharist in traditional language as both sacrifice and presence, though by presence he does not mean a *descent* of Christ into the consecrated elements, but rather a taking of them into Christ's glorified body. The presence is truly 'real'—faith does not create it—for the words of institution mean what they say. But what those words referred

---

55. *The Church a Family* (1850), p. 15.
56. *Sermons preached in Lincoln's Inn Chapel*, ii, 23.
57. *Life*, ii, p. 444.
58. *The Kingdom of Christ*, i, p. 279.
59. Cf. *The Prayer Book ... and The Lord's Prayer*, pp. 230ff.

to when first uttered was the Lord's *risen and ascended* body, not that present with the disciples at the Last Supper. So, too, the sacrificial aspect of the eucharist lies in its being a celebration of the completed sacrifice of Christ.

> I have maintained [Maurice writes] that because the sacrifice had once for all accomplished the object of bringing our race, constituted and redeemed in Christ, into a state of acceptance and union with God, therefore it was most fitting that there should be an act whereby we are admitted into the blessings thus claimed and secured to us.[60]

Such an act the eucharist is. It registers the truth that without a sacrifice for sins there could be no communion between God and his creatures.

> Until One appeared who said, 'Lo! I come, in the volume of the book it is written, to do thy will, O God'—until He offered up Himself as a perfect and well-pleasing sacrifice to God, how could there be perfect contentment in the mind of a holy and loving Being, how could a perfect communion exist between Him and men?

That is why the Church teaches the necessity of a real and spiritual sacrifice to the atonement of God and his creatures, a sacrifice offered and accepted once for all for the sins of men. Further, Maurice sees in the eucharist the centre of Christian unity, a rite which 'keeps doctrines from perpetual clashing with each other, and men from being the slaves of doctrines',[61] a boldly paradoxical idea, one may think, in view of the bitter disputes to which the problem of its theological interpretation has given rise. But it is the rite itself, not men's arguments about it, for which Maurice makes his claim. For what Christ has here embodied in a living feast is 'the complete idea of the Kingdom, which we, looking at things partially, from different sides, through the prejudices and false colourings of particular times and places, are continually reducing under some name, notion, or formula of ours'.[62]

The creed Maurice connects directly with baptism, as the Christian's open acknowledgement of what he believes his spiritual status to be. 'The name into which we are adopted there, is the name we confess here.'[63] It thus is a declaration of basic faith; it is not a summary of doctrine nor a statement of theological opinion.

On this point Maurice is very explicit. In the creed, he says, 'a man is speaking'. The form of it is, *I believe*. That which is believed in is not a certain scheme of divinity, but a name: a Father who has made the heaven and the earth; his Son, our Lord, who has been conceived and born, has died and been buried and has gone down into hell, who has ascended and is now at the right hand of God, and who will come to judge the world; a Holy Spirit who has established a holy and universal Church, who fashions men into a communion of saints, who is the witness and power whereby they receive forgiveness of sins, who will quicken their mortal bodies and bring them to everlasting life. Maurice's point is that faith is directed not to a doctrine but to a *person*. The creed takes us beyond doctrinal schemes; and whereas they divide it unites. This, he maintains, is true even of the Nicene

60. *The Kingdom of Christ*, ii, p. 71.
61. *The Kingdom of Christ* (1838 ed.), i. p. 315.
62. *The Kingdom of Christ*, ii, p. 69.
63. *Ibid.*, p. 20.

creed, in spite of the circumstances of its origin. For that confession, too, is an affirmation of belief in a name rather than mere notions and it differs from the Apostles' creed only in that it unites with 'a declaration of the divine relations with men, a declaration of the relations in the Godhead'.[64] That it is a confession of the Church and not a statement for the use of theologians alone is a matter for rejoicing. Both creeds are a 'defence of the Scriptures and the poor man against the attempt of the doctors to confuse the one and to rob the other'. Without them the ordinary believer would be at the mercy of the experts.

So also with the liturgy. Forms of worship are 'one of the clear and indispensable signs of a spiritual and universal fellowship'.[65] Here continuity is of positive value and antiquity has special authority. 'The prayers written in the first ages of Christianity are in general more free, more reverent, more universal, than those which have been poured forth since.'[66] Prayer itself is a natural human activity, but there is nothing unnatural in its regulation. In any case a society needs *common* prayer, not simply prayer adapted to special temperaments and moods.

> Prayer is meant to be an expression of the wants of humanity, uttered through one Head and Lord of man; individuals, if they would pray really and spiritually, must learn to take part in the speech and music of humanity, and not to isolate themselves in phrases and discords of their own.[67]

In common worship men lose their self-enclosed individualism and take the ground which they all share of being justified and redeemed in Christ.

Maurice now turns to the Church's ministry as his next principle of catholicity. The ministry is part of the Church's necessary structure. Christ intended his Church to be bodied forth in certain permanent and universal institutions. A permanent ministry would be a means of declaring his will and dispensing his blessings to the faithful as a whole. Its essence is service, not of a minority but of mankind generally, the Church's task being 'to remould the world, not to make a world for herself'. The original ministry was of course the apostolate, as we learn from the gospels and the Acts; the former relate the apostles' call as individuals, the latter tells us how at Pentecost they became a society, not of their own founding but of Christ's. How exactly the historic ministry emerged from the apostolate Maurice admits to be unclear. But the question at issue is whether or not any office corresponding in essentials to the New Testament conception of ministry was to be continued in the Church. 'The common opinion is, that by the perpetuation of this office the Church has been perpetuated; the connection of different ages with each other realized; the wholeness and unity of the body declared.' Changes have over the centuries taken place in it, but none of them of a kind to affect either its nature or its object.[68] Certainly the main constituent of the Church's polity is the episcopate. Bishops have the direct commission of Christ, as much as did the original holders of the apostolic office. What they expressed is the universal, diffusive, cosmopolitan

64. *Ibid.*, p. 143.
65. *Ibid.*, p. 40.
66. *Ibid.*, p. 45.
67. *Ibid.*, p. 221.
68. *Ibid.*, pp. 128f.

element in the Church's constitution, which without them would lose its literally 'catholic' character. Maurice even speaks of 'the necessity for Apostolic Succession and Episcopal Ordination'; but he makes it clear that, unlike the Tractarians, he does not imply by this that Christian communions which lack them are not of the Church. Catholicity is a matter of degree; though some Churches may want its fulness they yet have it in a measure and sufficiently. A national Church, moreover, is in no way incompatible with the Catholic ideal. On the contrary, it is the Church's duty to address the nation as such. The Ten Commandments were given to the people of Israel. A national Church, accordingly, is one which exists to purify and elevate the national mind, to impress on it the grandeur of law and of the source whence it comes and to warn it that 'all false ways are ruinous ways, and that truth is the only stability of our time or of any time'. The Church of England, Maurice was convinced, is at once Catholic and national; and in its national aspect Protestant. For Protestant and Catholic are not antithetic principles: the gospel itself has both a Catholic and a Protestant side and justice cannot be done to either one of them when the other is abandoned. The lessons of both have to be learned.

Finally there are the Scriptures. And here it has to be said that Maurice was somewhat behind his own times rather than, as in most other matters, ahead of them. The critical study of the Bible, as already developed in Germany, was beginning to make an impact on opinion in this country. Strauss's *Leben Jesu*, in George Eliot's translation, made its English debut in 1846.[69] Darwin's *Origin of Species*, with its sinister implications for traditional views on biblical inspiration, the *Essays and Reviews* volume and Colenso's *Commentary* all appeared when Maurice was in mid-career and aroused immense controversy. In these matters, however, he felt himself on alien ground. His knowledge of science was negligible—he had no interest in it—while his own attitude to the Bible was markedly conservative. In any case what he sought from Scripture was *religious* truth. Of *Essays and Reviews* he confessed to feeling how hopeless it was to expect any 'theology or humanity' from it. 'One can only hope that the discussion may lead us to seek a deeper foundation than the essayists or their opponents appear to deem necessary'.[70] For himself the authority of the Bible remained absolute. Scripture was to be looked at less in its parts than as a whole, and as a whole it was of God. This did not mean simply that it was *inspired* by God, and anyhow divine inspiration was not to be taken in a narrow, verbalist sense. Every man who does the work that he is set to do may believe that he is inspired with a power to do that work. 'Inspiration is not a strange, anomalous fact; it is the proper law and order of the world.' The question, therefore, is not whether the biblical writers were divinely inspired *as* writers, but whether they were in a certain position and appointed to a certain work.[71] Thus what makes the Bible inspired is essentially the character of its contents. Its authority rests on the uniqueness of these. 'We declare that there is a book, which so far as it fulfils its idea, becomes the key by which all books may be interpreted, that which translates them into significance

69. See below, ch. 10.
70. *Life*, ii, p. 384.
71. *The Kingdom of Christ*, ii, p. 162.

and determines the value and position of each.'[72] But the unquestionable truth of its inspiration does not guarantee it against error. Nor does the Bible stand on its own, for the Church is its interpreter. Church and Bible have a mutual relationship. 'The Church exists as a fact, the Bible shows what that fact means. The Bible is a fact, the Church shows what the fact means.'[73] The written word and the living society are interdependent because the written word is subject to the living society, and *vice versa*. In Scripture 'the circumstances and relations of ordinary life are exhibited as the ladder through which God is guiding man up to a knowledge of Himself'.[74] It is concerned indeed with the transcendent, the supernatural, but through the relations of ordinary daily life. Hence Maurice's stress on the Bible as a *history* since it is the history of the establishment of God's universal Kingdom. But if this history be all-important as history then the question of its authenticity is surely insistent. And here Maurice's touch becomes less certain. The fact is that he was impatient of historical inquiries generally; they too easily tended, he thought, to the neglect of the really vital matter of the Bible's theological content. For his part he was content to be a traditionalist, although he recognizes that such difficulties as the obvious discrepancies between the four gospels do exist.[75] Criticism, no doubt had its place. It could discourse about documents, their origin and their purpose; but he himself was far more concerned with what the Scriptures teach, which in the last resort does not depend on the precise historicity of the facts stated.

> If the gospel is a Divine message to mankind it *cannot* depend for the proof of its veracity, for its influence over men, upon any theories about the composition of the books which contain it, upon any arguments about their authenticity or inspiration, upon any definitions which we can give of the words 'Authenticity' and 'Inspiration'.[76]

His own method of interpretation was similarly straightforward. The real question was what the biblical doctrine means as a whole; a mere culling of proof texts in support of a preconceived theological system was worse than useless, Scripture not being a collection of logical propositions or exactly defined articles of faith. Nor did he favour the allegorical or typological method. It is the events themselves that are significant, not the supposed analogies which a misguided ingenuity brings to them. Besides, he feared—by no means unreasonably, as much modern typological exegesis has made us aware—that the method is apt to beget a feeling that the Bible is not 'a real book containing a history of actual men'. He does not say that the Old Testament is without types of the New. On the contrary, because the

---

72. *Ibid.*, p. 167.
73. *Ibid.*, p. 178.
74. *Ibid.*, p.153.
75. Cp. *The Unity of the New Testament* (1854), p. 244: 'With respect to the times, it seems quite clear that each Evangelist is always ready to sacrifice mere chronology to that order or succession of events which most revealed his purpose. In the short period of our Lord's ministry there are certain great land-marks, such as the Temptation, the Transfiguration, the Entry into Jerusalem, which all observe. Within those land-marks they follow the bent and course of thought which the Spirit has given to each; they group events according to another than a time order.'
76. *The Kingdom of Christ*, i, p. xxxii.

patriarchs were real men, made in God's image, Maurice felt bound to regard them 'as showing forth some aspect of His life whom I recognize as the express image of God's person'. Indeed the Old and New Testaments constitute a unity. To read them in continuous order is to witness the drawing aside, as it were, of a series of veils, the final stage being one which discloses the full atonement of God and man, the complete revelation of God's name, hitherto denied or concealed by sin. Miracles, lastly, as attestations of this divine revelation, are not mere prodigies, exceptions to a divinely established rule, but manifestations of it. They were demonstrations that spiritual power is superior to mechanical, that the world is subject to God and not to chance or nature, that, in short, 'there is an order'.[77]

Before concluding our remarks on Maurice's attitude to the Bible as a constituent or mark of the Church some notice, necessarily brief, should also be taken of his other writings relating to Scripture. So far from neglecting biblical theology, as he has occasionally been accused of doing, Maurice was in fact wholly preoccupied with it. His *The Claims of the Bible and Science*, for example, is a series of letters on the Colenso controversy.[78] Maurice allows the rights of historical criticism in principle but strongly contests Colenso's view that because numerous inconsistencies and inaccuracies can be found in the biblical history it is therefore as history unreliable and properly to be used only as a source for 'religious ideas'. Religious ideas there certainly are, and they are important; but of greater importance are the events themselves, the basic authenticity of which criticism has not destroyed, any more than the deficiencies of Herodotus cast doubt on the battle of Salamis. For whatever the shortcomings of the biblical historian the event of the Exodus itself, a fact of determining significance for Israel's whole subsequent life and destiny, is unchallengeable. The really important issue is unaffected by points of detail. Even the traditional Mosaic authorship is not essential, for Moses was a fallible human figure, and upon a mere man, however inspired, divine truth ultimately does not depend. Maurice's own account of what is or is not historical does not, admittedly, make altogether reassuring reading; historical insight was not notable among his talents, nor had he the technical equipment of the critical scholar. But he firmly upholds a principle—that the Bible relates the acts of God in history—although his way of doing so is rather naïve. As has justly been said of him,

> He was, for all the clumsiness of his handling of the problem of history, putting his finger upon an important point concerning the nature of history and historical evidence. It *is* valid for a great event, that a nation's literature and religious experience took a certain shape, and that an event must be postulated such as created this shape.[79]

What in all his extensive writings on the Bible Maurice aimed at doing was to bring out the fundamental sense of Scripture as the self-disclosure of God to men. In this he is an early forerunner of that revival of concern for biblical theology as such which has been so conspicuous a feature of the theological development in

77. *Ibid.*, ii, p. 172.
78. See below, ch. 10.
79. A. M. Ramsey, *F.D. Maurice and the Conflicts of Modern Theology,* (1951) p. 89.

our own century. Of his other books in this field, *Patriarchs and Lawgivers of the Old Testament*, which did not appear until 1890, many years after his death, is probably the most satisfactory. But Maurice's work generally is replete with biblical teaching, interpreted in accordance with his characteristic standpoint. Always it is the mighty acts of God in history upon which the student of the Bible must fix his gaze. It is with these, not with 'religion', that the sacred book deals.[80] Nor for certain are they arbitrary inventions, but assertions of the divine sovereignty, proofs of the abiding reality of God's Kingdom. The particular sequence of these acts is a progressive revelation of the divine justice as it operates in and upon human affairs, the culminating event being the coming of Christ, the *Christus Consummator* in whom that Kingdom is fully and finally established. Thus Law points forward to Gospel, as Gospel in turn presupposes Law, since he who is Creator is also Redeemer, and will, at the appointed time, be likewise Judge.

80. 'Religion' Maurice thought 'a peculiarly ambiguous' word, 'and one that is likely to continue ambiguous, because we connect it habitually with the study and treatment of the Bible, though the Bible itself gives us no help in ascertaining the force of the word.' Unfortunately, 'we have been dosing our people with religion when what they want is not this but the living God'. See *What is Revelation?*, pp. 239f, and *Life*, p. 369.

Chapter 6

F. D. MAURICE (2) THEOLOGY AND LIFE

'Theological essays'

Even Maurice's warmest admirers have tended to regard his *Theological Essays* (1853) as among the least admirable of his works, and often rather tiresomely disputatious and clumsily written. R. W. Church complained of its 'tormenting indistinctness'. Professor Chadwick describes it as 'filled with literary head-scratching'.

> Maurice [he says] engaged ghostly objectors in vehement dialogue. The tone was intense, the inspiration jerky. He waded along a stream of rhetorical questions and littered the banks with parentheses, dashes, inversions, notes of exclamation. The reader is battered and fatigued by the demand to feel indignation on subjects where he did not know himself to feel anything; unable to grasp the author's meaning while seeing that this meaning is life and death to the author.[1]

The description is colourful but apt. To plough through these essays is a task which only the most dedicated or industrious student is likely to accomplish. Yet it is an important book—indeed an indispensable—for the comprehension of Maurice's views on a variety of themes. It is addressed to Unitarians, and the writer, pursuing his favourite method, goes far in the concessions he is willing to make to his readers' susceptibilities. But the section which most offended Anglicans—for there also was much else in the book which did so—was one near the end, on everlasting punishment. The Council of King's College, London, at which institution Maurice was then a professor, took great exception to it, condemned the entire volume as calculated to unsettle the minds of the students, and forthwith relieved the author of his academic duties.

The trouble was that he had trampled on an all but universal religious assumption of his day: namely, that 'eternal' meant everlasting, and in particular that eternal punishment meant dereliction and torment without end. It was not that he himself believed in universal salvation, or, still less, that the love of God could simply

---

1. Owen Chadwick. *The Victorian Church*, i, p. 545. The truth is that Maurice wrote far too much. It is estimated that his published writings extend to more than 16,300 octavo pages and comprise nearly 5 million words. 'Could I have guided Maurice's pen', observed his publisher, Alexander Macmillan, 'I would have published about three books for him instead of thirty.' See Charles Morgan, *The House of Macmillan (1843–1943)*, p. 36. Maurice's pen simply ran away with him before he had got his thoughts in order.

ignore sin. 'I have no faith', he declared, 'in man's theory of a Universal Restitution.' But to his essentially Johannine and Platonist cast of mind eternal life consisted in the knowledge of God; he could not think of it merely as an extension of personal existence into an unending future. His own conception, he explained, was founded on St John xvii, 3: 'This is life eternal, that they should know thee, the one true God, and him whom thou hast sent, even Jesus Christ.' Eternity is something 'outside of' time, an attribute of God's very being. Yet to live 'eternally' is also a possibility for human life in this world, and is the beginning of salvation. On the other hand, *not* to know God, to suffer the alienation from God which sin encompasses, is dire loss and spiritual death. But here too the idea of duration in time is an irrelevance: separation from God cannot be measured in temporal terms. The divine righteousness condemns sin—eternally; but the divine love ever struggles to overcome sin in the individual, and its efforts are not to be thought of as curtailed by the cessation of earthly existence. The return of the prodigal, in this life or any other, is always possible and always desired by the Father in heaven.

> I cannot [he confessed in a letter to F. J. A. Hort] speak of God punishing for a number of years, and then ceasing to punish, or of the wicked expiating their crimes by a certain amount of penalties. The idea of a rebel will is, to those who know themselves what it is, far too awful for such arrangements as these ... I know that we may struggle with the light, that we may choose death. But I know also that love does overcome this rebellion.[2]

Thus impenitence at death does not necessarily imply the soul's damnation and consignment to everlasting torments. That men can go on resisting the divine entreaties is not to be doubted.

> I dare not pronounce what are the possibilities of resistance in a human will to the loving will of God. There are times when they seem to me (thinking of myself more than others) almost infinite. But I know there is something which must be infinite in the abyss of love beyond the abyss of death. More than that I cannot know, but God knows—I leave myself and all to Him.[3]

Unfortunately Maurice's standpoint in this dark matter was one which was not easily appreciated even by more sophisticated minds. The theology of divine rewards and punishments was generally looked on as a necessary prop for morality. Maurice, it seemed, had denied hell, and with this potent sanction removed what might the moral consequences not be? King's College, after all, had the welfare of its pupils to consider.

The most discerning of Maurice's critics was J. B. Mozley. Mozley acknowledged Maurice's 'prophetic' bent of mind and that his strength lay in force of conviction more than skill in argument. He realized that the conception of eternity as 'pure existence' was for Maurice a vital truth; but it was one extremely difficult even for the trained intelligence to grasp, 'and our Lord was addressing not philosophers

2. *Life*, p. 15. Hort himself remarks on 'the small number of even thoughtful men at Cambridge who were able to recognize the distinction between time and eternity'. See *Life*, i, p. 266.
3. *Theological Essays*, p. 406.

but simple people when He gave his stern warnings about future reward and punishment'. That at least was a religious teaching which the plain man could understand. Moreover, the finest theological minds—and he cites St Thomas Aquinas—had defined eternal life not without reference to a temporal duration as a *conditio interminabilis*. In any case, Maurice's contention that he was interpreting the Church's formularies in their *intended* sense was mere special pleading.[4] Mozley's own conclusion was that King's had done 'a substantial duty to the Church and the nation in suppressing a teaching that immediately interferes with the very foundation of religion and morals'.[5] It is one which to the modern mind is likely to appear illiberal and absurd, but it indicates how far Christian opinion even in the last century was wedded to the idea that religious beliefs and moral conduct stand in direct relationship, and that where the former were wrong the latter could not be right.

On the extent to which Maurice's doctrine is genuinely biblical there is more room for debate. Eternity in the Bible is thought of in temporal terms, although the Johannine eschatology approximates more closely to the Hellenic conception. And it was the Johannine view, interpreted with a Platonist bias, which appealed to Maurice's own religious temper and outlook.[6]

A further aspect of Maurice's teaching sharply criticized by his contemporaries bore on the theory of the atonement, since here again it seemed to run counter to deeply entrenched beliefs. Sin, and the cross as God's remedy for sin, were the staple of Victorian preaching. To the Evangelicals in particular the atonement was the heart of the gospel, and to this doctrine a chapter in the *Theological Essays* is devoted, although Maurice's own position is more fully expounded in his *Doctrine of Sacrifice*, a volume of carefully considered sermons published in 1879. In the essay he inveighs against the manner in which this profound mystery of the faith was all too commonly presented. The death of Christ was not, he argued, penal,

4. *Essays Historical and Theological* (1878), ii, pp. 256ff.
5. *Letters* (1885), p. 298. But Maurice's views on eternal punishment were the ostensible rather than the real reason for his dismissal. The real reason was political: his connection with the Christian Socialist movement, especially in the person of Charles Kingsley. Sir Benjamin Brodie, a member of King's College Council, wrote to C. J. Hare: 'It would have been much better if [Maurice] had avoided connecting himself with the Christian Socialists, and discussing questions on which it is plain that persons having great influence in the college would be at variance with him' (*Life*, ii, p. 198f.). The Principal of King's, Dr Jelf, himself advised Maurice openly to disavow Kingsley. See *Life*, ii, 80.
6. It is nevertheless the fact that Maurice was a good deal influenced by the millenarianism of the Rev. J. A. Stephenson, rector of Lympsham, whose assistant curate he was for a time. See *Life*, i, p. 167 and pp. 147–52 (Maurice's own 'Memoir' of Stephenson). Stephenson held that the events leading to the destruction of Jerusalem in A.D. 70 'were nothing less than the actual manifestation of Christ's kingdom, the actual establishment of a communion between the two worlds, the creation of a new heaven and a new earth' (p. 150). This idea is resumed by Maurice himself in his lectures on the Apocalypse, one of his favourite books in the Bible. 'I believe the Apocalypse,' he once said, 'to be the book which will at last be found to remove most veils from this mystery [the Trinity], as well as from the meaning of all the previous Bible history, and from the course of God's government of the world from the beginning to the end' (*Life*, ii, p 354).

nor did the satisfaction Christ rendered consist only in his dying, a denial which must have appeared to commit the author to the 'exemplarist' view suggested by the words of St John's gospel (xii, 32): 'I, if I be lifted up, will draw all men unto me.' However, to repeat the teaching of Abelard was not at all Maurice's intention. In *The Kingdom of Christ* he had already expressed a conviction which no traditionalist could have quarrelled with:

> Without a sacrifice for sins [he there wrote] there could be no communion between God and His creatures. His sacrifice removes those impediments to the communion, which the blood of bulls and goats, sacrifices of mere arbitrary appointment, though precious as instruments of moral and spiritual education, could not possibly have removed. Until One appeared who said, 'Lo! I come, in the volume of the book it is written, to do thy will, O God'—until He offered up Himself as a perfect and well-pleasing sacrifice to God, how could there be perfect contentment in the mind of a holy and loving Being, how could a perfect communion exist between Him and man?

Hence the Church teaches that 'a sacrifice, a real and spiritual sacrifice', was necessary to the atonement of God and His creatures, and that it was offered up 'once and for all, and was accepted for the sins of men'.[7] On this the *Theological Essays* are no less explicit:

> Since nowhere is the contrast between infinite Love and Infinite Evil brought before us as it is there, we have the fullest right to affirm that the cross exhibits the wrath of God against sin, and the endurance of that wrath by the well-beloved Son. For wrath against that which is unlovely is not the counteracting force to love, but the attribute of it. Without it love would be a name, and not a reality.

As love Christ himself saw it, and so endured it; nor was he willing that it should end before it had effected its full loving purpose. 'The endurance of that wrath was the proof that He bore in the truest and strictest sense the sins of the world, feeling them with that anguish with which only a perfectly pure and holy Being, who is also a perfectly sympathizing and gracious Being, can feel the sins of others.' Complete suffering with and for sin is possible only in one who himself is completely free from it.

That the cross is thus an exhibition of God's wrath against sin is evidently, then, as firm a conviction of Maurice's own as of any Evangelical of his day. He even speaks of the atonement as a 'transaction'. But he also is most careful to point out that, in presenting the doctrine, the theologian or preacher must remember that whatever is good and right *is* God's will; that the Son is ever one with the Father and that his whole incarnate life was a submission to that will and thus a revelation of it; that Christ's work rescued humanity from death and the devil, not from a vengeful deity; and that the cross removes sin itself and not simply the penalties of sin. The satisfaction rendered by the offering of God's own holiness and love constituted 'the only complete sacrifice ever offered'. Was not this, Maurice asks, 'in the highest sense, Atonement'?

7. *The Kingdom of Christ* (1838 ed.), i, pp. 272f.

Nonetheless his views caused disquiet and provoked some severe comment. He had failed to stress the penal motive, and his meaning in any case was obscure. For in this as in other respects the Maurician theology tries to draw distinctions evidently of great significance to its author but a good deal less than clear to his readers. And do his objections to the prevailing theory imply that he himself saw the atonement only in a moralistic light? So at least it was inferred. But any assiduous student of Maurice is struck, rather, by his traditionalism in this matter. Christ, he believed, assuredly did bear the penalty of mankind's sin, yet not only *as* a penalty. The Saviour, in his death as in his life, was utterly obedient to the Father's will, not indeed as under constraint but in a spirit of wholly self-giving love. Hence in bearing the penalty of sin he did so not as sinful mankind's substitute but as his *representative*. His act is both Godward and manward, an accomplishment as man and for man of what man himself could not do. The theory as Maurice propounds it is no doubt insufficiently lucid, is even to some extent confused. But this, as often, was the consequence, for a man whose power of self-expression was inferior to the originality of his thinking, of an attempt to avoid extreme positions on either hand as both alike erroneous. His teaching, however, was the notable precursor of some later attempts at a more satisfactory interpretation of the doctrine within the framework of an integral orthodoxy.

The Doctrine of Sacrifice takes a wider view of the sacrificial theme, although the field is always strictly biblical. Sacrifice in the Old Testament is first dealt with: the offerings of Cain and Abel, of Noah, Abraham and Moses are considered in turn. It all makes strange enough reading today, since the author's standpoint is innocently precritical. But interest is sustained by the theological exegesis. Sacrifice is seen as a divine ordinance, not a human means for cajoling deity, and as such man offers it in thankful self-submission and self-dedication. The difference between the two attitudes is shown in the respective oblations of Cain and Abel, the one fearful and self-seeking, the other selflessly obedient. Noah's sacrifice is that of a man who feels himself to be God's instrument in furthering the divine purpose. His action assumes 'eternal right in the ruler of the universe' and that 'all caprice has come from man in his struggle to be an independent being'. Abraham's, again, is a testimony of selflessness and thankfulness, the offering of the dearest thing he possessed, for in offering his son he also offered himself. It is the same, Maurice contends, with the Passover, with the sacrifices of the Law, and with the self-offering of David, the last conspicuously so. David has nothing to render but himself in his utter humiliation, and thus is open to receive what God alone can give him, a right and a true spirit. In this way his example discloses the real as distinct from the merely legal meaning of sacrifice: that it is man's offering of *himself* and not simply of his belongings, for whereas the latter can be surrendered without ultimate cost the former is total. Only when David had made this full oblation was he in a restored state, in the state in which God intended him to be, as 'a dependent creature, a trusting creature, capable of receiving his Maker's image'.[8]

8. *The Doctrine of Sacrifice deduced from the Scriptures*, p.100.

When Maurice turns to the New Testament he finds the teaching of the Old worked out in the clearest and most explicit manner. It now is seen as a revelation of the very nature of God himself: sacrifice has its ground in the divine being, as manifested in that perfect unity of will and substance between the Son and the Father which is the only possible source of the obedience and fellowship of a new, restored humanity. Sacrifice, therefore—and the point is typically Maurician—is not simply an expedient, a device for dealing with sin, but is 'implied in the very original of the universe', in the divine obedience of the Son 'before the worlds were'. 'In the latter days', however, its particular purpose is to take away sin, sin and sacrifice now being 'the eternal opposites'.[9] How the power of sin was in fact overcome Maurice attempts to show in terms of Scripture itself. The truth he is especially concerned to stress is that he who knew not sin deliberately identified himself *with* the sinner. The meaning conveyed in this Pauline idea appeared to him much richer than the usual teaching about Christ's taking the punishment of sin in man's stead. The latter conveyed 'no impression of the sense, the taste, the anguish of sin, which St Paul would have us think of, as realized by the Son of God—a sense, a taste, an anguish which are not only compatible with the not knowing sin, but would be impossible in any one who did not know it'.[10] In Christ's sacrifice God defeated both sin and death. By it men learn that sacrifice, not selfishness, is the law or principle of their being, for through it they are transformed after his likeness.

> The giving up of His Son to take upon Him their flesh and blood, to enter their sorrows, to feel and suffer their sins; that is, '*to be made sin*'; the perfect sympathy of the Son with His loving will towards His creatures, His entire sympathy with them, and union with them; His endurance, in His inmost heart and spirit, of that evil which He abhorred; this is God's method of reconciliation; by this He speaks to the sinful will of man; by this He redeems it, raises it, restores it.[11]

Hence the presentation of the one perfect and sufficient sacrifice to the Father and its continual thanksgiving is the central act of all worship, as of all fellowship among men.

Maurice's views as set out in these addresses, as in the *Essays* before them, did not find favour. His biblical interpretations are often indeed subjective, even wilful. A more serious accusation was that he had blurred the line between the divine and the human. Christ's action in identifying himself with man seemed to be directed to the latter rather than to God, and to have been, in the final count, a process of enlightenment rather than an effective renewal of corrupted human nature. R. S. Candlish, for example, in his *Examination of Mr Maurice's Theological Essays* (1854), objected: 'If the Gospel is to tell me, not that I must and that I may become what I am not—but only that I ought to know what I already am—then there can be no occasion for any radical renovation or revolution in my moral being. All that is needed is that I shall be informed and persuaded; not that I must be converted, created anew'.[12] And he added that throughout Maurice's book there

9. *Ibid.*, p. 118.
10. *Ibid.*, p. 188.
11. *Ibid.*, p. 192.
12. *Op. cit.*, p. 27.

was 'a careful and consistent disavowal of anything being really done by God'.[13] But Maurice's correction of the popular evangelical view was necessary and timely, a reminder of the too frequently forgotten New Testament teaching that God was in Christ reconciling the *world* unto himself; whilst his elevation of the principle of self-sacrifice to a level of universal moral significance, thus uniting the theological motifs of atonement and creation, has been of profound moral consequence for modern Christian thinking. Beside it the strictures of Maurice's critics appear narrow and antiquated.

Church, State, and society

Not always, however, was it misunderstanding and criticism that Maurice encountered. With his Boyle lectures of 1846 on *The Religions of the World*, in which he deals with the relationship of Christianity to other great faiths, he gained an undoubted popular success. Here he rejects the idea that the essential truth of all religions has been found when each has been stripped of its distinctive features. Such a result, he holds, would be merely an abstraction without any real spiritual substance or appeal. Better is it to look for what is positive in them and compare this with Christianity in order to discover whether in the latter this positive element is not present in fuller measure. His contention is that in Christ is the wholeness of truth of which other faiths reveal only partial expressions. The right procedure for the overseas missionary therefore becomes clear: it is to show not that the religion of the people is false but that what is true in it is more richly exhibited in Christ. For God makes himself known, in varying ways and degrees, to all who genuinely seek him. If a man looks into his own soul he will learn there that God is love and so will understand how Christ is the supreme revelation of that love. But can such an individual and personal apprehension of truth be conveyed to another? How can the Christian's claim for Christ be proved to have universal validity? Maurice weighs these questions, yet he is convinced that fundamentally all men have the same spiritual needs, aspirations and ideals, and that these are of a kind that only the faith of Christ can meet. Christ is in fact, as some of the early Christian Fathers taught, the divine Logos in every man. 'The postulate of the Bible is that man could not be what he is, if God did not hold converse with him; that this is his distinction from other creatures; that this is the root of all that he knows, the ground of what is right and reasonable in him.'[14]

Is this, as some objected, merely the reduction of the Christian dogma to a vague Platonism or a high-minded sentimentalism? Maurice's language, admittedly, is often unguarded and effusive, but the charge is scarcely fair. Certainly he had no intention of watering down the express teaching of the creeds, the value of which he argued at length in *The Kingdom of Christ*. The creeds testify to a fact of Christian experience which cannot be gainsaid: that Christians have found in Christ, uniquely, the Way, the Truth and the Life. The religion of personal feeling,

---

13. *Ibid.*, p. 35.
14. *The Doctrine of Sacrifice*, p. 4.

'subjective religion', thus points to what is objectively real, that in Christ God himself became incarnate. All the great religious thinkers of whatever race and time carry some witness to truth; but only one of them *is* the truth, so far as it is possible for one man to embody it. It is this which is asserted in the doctrine of Christ's divinity, a doctrine that does not deny but rather affirms whatever is of God in the beliefs of the heathen. Christ is always *Consummator*. As Maurice puts it in his lectures on the Epistle to the Hebrews, published in the same year as *The Religions of the World*:

> The revelation of God ... is truly the unveiling of Himself. First, He speaks in that which is most distant from Him, the mere things He has formed; then in men whom He created to rule over these things; lastly, in Him who by the eternal law is the inheritor of all things, in whom and for whom they were created. The order of the world, the succession of the ages, spoke of the permanence of God. Here he speaks in Him by whom He framed the order of the world, the succession of times.[15]

It was this profound assurance of his that God's revelation of himself to man is a real self-disclosure, albeit 'in divers manners', that forced him into public repudiation of the ideas of Professor Mansel of Oxford.[16]

The theme which runs through all Maurice's work is that of the universality of the divine rule and sovereignty. The world, mankind, is not to be made God's; it *is* God's. He created it and he has redeemed it. As Maurice expressed it in a letter to J. M. Ludlow: 'The Kingdom of Heaven is to me the great practical existing reality which is to renew the earth and make it a habitation for blessed Spirits instead of Demons. To preach the Gospel of that Kingdom; the fact that it is among us and is not to be set up at all, is my calling and business.'[17] But as God is Lord of the whole so is he of its parts. The task of theology, as Maurice saw it, is to comprehend man in his secular endeavours no less than in his spiritual vocation. Human society in its natural constitution is divisible into the family and the nation. Of these the former is the first great bulwark which God has provided against the domination of the senses and of the purely external world, and to be the sphere in which personality, as distinct from mere individuality, is developed. It is in the family that the meaning of authority and obedience is learned. Positive law therefore presupposes the family relationships as its basis; relationships which express, in the simplest form, the necessary dependence of human beings on one another. Undervalue the family and other types of human association will certainly come to be overvalued. But next in order to the family is the nation. Here a man discovers that he is under law and has personal responsibility. Personality thus finds a still wider field for its development. Under the law of the national community 'each man is taken apart from every other. Each one is met with a "Thou". The Law is over families, but is addressed to everyone who hears it separately, without reference to his ancestors or his descendants'.[18] Of the highest

---

15. *Op. cit.*, p. 28.
16. See below, ch. 7.
17. See Cambridge University Library, Additional Manuscripts 7348, art. 8, no. 65. It is dated 24 September (1852).
18. *Social Morality*, 2nd ed, pp. 124f. These Cambridge lectures, first published in 1869, contain a well-balanced statement of Maurice's doctrine on the nature and constitution of human society.

importance in this respect is language, which is the inheritance of the national community; for language is a primary mode of communication and the means of distinguishing truth from falsehood. In short, in the life of one's nation one learns to be, in the fullest sense, a *person*.

But the bond, Maurice now proceeds to argue, which holds society together as a community of persons is no bare abstraction or impersonal scheme of law, but the will of a supreme Person. Indeed to regard the basis of human society as something impersonal and abstract is to undermine the personal relationship which subsists between all its members. In other words, the foundation of the national community is a *divine* Person; which means that the nation can never be looked on as a purely secular society. That it is so, Maurice concedes, many Christians themselves suppose. He, however, solemnly denies it.

> If by 'secular' is meant that which belongs to the fashion of a particular age—that which shuts out the acknowledgement of the permanent and the eternal—that, I grant, is hostile to Christian faith, that is the 'evil world' against which we are to fight. But one of the greatest weapons which God has given us in our conflict with this enemy—whether it invites us to worship the conceits of our own age, or of some departed age—is the assurance that the Nation has lived, lives now, and will live in Him, who was, and is, and is to come.[19]

The pattern of national life is provided, Maurice believed, by the history of the Jews. As God had dealt with them so will he deal with all other peoples.

But does not the Church of Christ obliterate national differences? By no means, Maurice thinks; on the contrary, it enables the different nations each to acquire an enhanced strength and distinctiveness of character. The Church, in the shape of a national institution, would itself participate in this distinctiveness, as it would in turn promote it. It was the misfortune of the Jews in the time of Christ to have gone far towards losing their sense of nationhood and to have become, rather, a collection of covetous individuals moved by the spirit of the sect or the faction more than by the conviction of a common origin, land and Lord. National characteristics are therefore good. It is a false universalism which would depreciate them, just as it was a vicious sectarianism or party fractiousness which would weaken them by its divisions. A nation conscious of its nationhood, so Maurice considered, thereby had its faith in God fortified.

> Let us be sure that if we would ever see a real family of nations, such as the prophets believed would one day emerge out of the chaos they saw around them, a family of nations which shall own God as their Father and Christ as their elder Brother, this must come from each nation maintaining its integrity and unity.[20]

Plainly, in so thinking, Maurice was living before the era of modern secularist nationalism, but he founded his belief, naïve as it may seem to us now, on the witness of Israel. For the fact that Israel was called by God *as a nation* is a token of the similar calling of every other nation. He therefore thought that an

19. *The Ground and Object of Hope for Mankind* (1868), p. 46.
20. *Sermons on the Sabbath Day, on the Character of the Warrior, and on the Interpretation of History* (1853), pp. 93f.

Englishman has as much right to speak of his own nation as holy as had the Hebrew prophets of theirs. It is holy 'in virtue of God's calling', and its members are unholy in so far as they deny this calling and the kind of unity it implies. Hence also the citizen of one land must respect the citizens of every other; they are in a like position with himself, as having the same advantages and obligations. Thus the spirit of an exclusive nationalism is condemned, even if 'no man has ever done good to mankind who was not a patriot'.[21]

By a nation or a state—he uses the two words as equivalents—Maurice understands 'a body connected in a particular locality, united in the acknowledgement of a certain law, which each member of this body must obey, or suffer for its isolation'; but a body also 'recognizing a supreme and invisible Being as the author and sanction of this law'. It is an essential part of the state's function to promote the moral and spiritual welfare of its citizens. Church and State are both requisite to the constitution of man; nay, 'a State is as much a witness for God one way as a Church is a witness for Him in another way'.[22] The State is in fact as much God's creation as the Church. But if this is so what is their exact relationship? Wherein do they differ? Further, what is the relation between national churches and the Church Universal? Maurice's answer is that since Church and State alike have their respective places in the divine purpose their functions are complementary and the one needs the other. This is why the State is not a merely secular institution. It even has claims on the citizen's conscience which the Church itself cannot make, and it bears a witness—in the field of justice, for example—over and above the Church's. Without the State the Church is 'necessarily a maimed and imperfect thing', not simply because it lacks material means and coercive powers, but because 'God hath ordained an eternal connection between the law, which is embodied in the State, and the religious, life-giving principle which is embodied in the Church, so that one shall always sigh and cry till it has found the other to be its mate'.[23] In sum:

> We distinguish most carefully between that which is spiritual and that which is legal, that which is ecclesiastical and that which is national, that which concerns the knowledge and cultivation of the good, and that which concerns the suppression of the evil. But we say that one of these, as much as the other, is to be referred to God.[24]

When Church and State are united, as in the nature of things they should be, law and gospel can cooperate. Both are opposed to human selfishness, the State through legal safeguards, the Church by its persuasive doctrine and example. Love and justice therefore are not, as Christians sometimes have asserted, antagonistic principles. Love needs justice as its instrument. The Kingdom of Christ finds a measure of articulation and definition in the kingdoms of men. Church and State, accordingly, have to learn from each other, in mutual accommodation. The State, that is to say, as equated with the *nation*; for Maurice considers the relation a

---

21. Cf. *The Kingdom of Christ* (1838 ed), iii, p. 377.
22. *Ibid.*, pp. 13f. For a similar view stated by W. E. Gladstone, see Appendix III below.
23. *Ibid.*, p. 106.
24. *Ibid.*, p. 389.

positive and fruitful one only in the case of the nationstate. It could not have been realized under the conditions of the Roman empire, nor of the medieval polity. These amorphous agglomerations of peoples did not and could not possess the moral 'personality' which Maurice discovers in the nation proper. Indeed he goes to extreme lengths in his personalization of the State as a society of which, so he claims, we can predicate 'spiritual conditions and spiritual emotions', and which can repent and be reformed as truly as can any individual.

Nevertheless of the virtues of populist democracy Maurice was not by any means convinced. The will of the majority seemed to him neither well informed nor, as a rule, wisely exercised, and certainly deserved no flattery. The sovereign people has no more right than an individual autocrat to do what it pleases. For the danger in the one case as in the other is love of power for its own sake, a craving to which Demos is no stranger. On this point Maurice expressed his mind forcibly to J. M. Ludlow after the assassination of Abraham Lincoln:

> As to democracy, I regard Lincoln's inauguration speech as the grandest return from the democracy of the Declaration of Independence to the theocracy of the Pilgrim Fathers that I might have seen anywhere. I always hoped that might be the effect of the war on the best Americans. I never dreamed of seeing it expressed officially in such language as that. And it was not merely the old Calvinistic theocracy—the divinity *minus* humanity. In so far as it recognized the Divine vengeance for the wrongs of the coloured race, it implied a Christ as Head of the human race. I should count it a treason to Lincoln's memory to relapse into the other kind of speech, as we must do if we call the other people to sympathize with him as a democrat. The horror of democracy which you impute to me is a horror in the interests of the people. I believe the Sovereign has been great in so far as he or she confessed a ministry—ignominious so far as they have been aristocrats or oligarchs. I apply the same maxim to the larger class. If they will accept the franchise as a ministry, be it as high as it may, as a calling, I shall rejoice. If they grasp at any power merely as a power, I believe the voice of Demos will be the devil's voice and not God's.[25]

And as for the cant phrase about 'the greatest happiness of the greatest number', he confessed that he could not understand it. What measure would one have of it? Indeed what *was* happiness, and how was its maximum distribution to be ascertained? Ask the masses what they consider happiness and the answer might well be 'something profoundly low and swinish'.[26] And not only was the democratic principle one of devaluation, it was a direct threat to freedom. Destroy a hierarchical society, having sovereign divinity as its apex, and the probability is that rule will fall into the hands of some minority despotism holding the great body of the population in servitude, moral, political, and perhaps even physical.[27] Maurice, 'socialist' though he professed himself to be, was a firm believer in monarchy and aristocracy, providing each was mindful of its obligation to minister. There was nothing amiss with the principle of either. Even the different political

25. *Life*, ii, p. 497.
26. *The Workman and the Franchise: Chapters from English History on the Representation and Education of the People* (1866), p. 202.
27. *Life*, ii, p. 129.

parties stood respectively for truths which are not *per se* antagonistic. Reconciliation was possible and desirable, for the total public good.

The responsibility of a national Church is one of witness to the law of God before all estates of the realm. It exists to purify and elevate the nation's mind, to remind those whose power and duty it is to frame and administer the laws both of the significance of law and of the ruin to which false ways must inevitably lead. Thus the Church's function in respect of the nation is one essentially of education.[28] As being itself a national institution the Church can discharge this function, whereas mere sects cannot—an argument cogent enough when the Church comprises, at any rate nominally, the vast bulk of the population, but obviously implausible where the religious loyalties of the people are divided among a number of numerically comparable denominations. That education, therefore, is a primary responsibility of the State as such Maurice had eventually to admit. But he also believed that the State can meet its task, in face of every kind of enemy to the common life, only with the active assistance of the various denominations. In any event, the fact that prevailing conditions impeded the national Church from performing the work which ideally it ought to do was no reason for its not doing what it could.

Humanly speaking the Church's call is to be 'the life-giving energy to every body in the midst of which she dwells'.[29] The Church of a single nation, however, is the token of the bond that unites the citizens of all nations: namely, their universal relationship to an invisible Person, supreme over all men. This it can do as the local embodiment, locally characterized, of the Church which is catholic, worldwide, 'the same in all countries and all ages'. For the Catholic principle to Maurice is essentially that of universality. A nation may be Protestant; it cannot be 'Catholic'. Protestantism's strength lies in its emphasis on individual responsibility and a personal relation to God; Catholicism's in the importance it attributes to society as such and the individual's role in society. Neither the one nor the other ought to be repudiated nor its truth forgotten. Indeed 'we have to learn Protestantism again as well as Catholicism'.[30] Both are indispensable to the life of a Christian society.

Hence Maurice's admiration of the Church of England. It was at once Catholic and Protestant. But by this he meant something rather different from the Tractarian apologetic. The idea of a *via media* did not appeal to him; it suggested compromise, and the Church is not a compromise between Catholicism and Protestantism. 'Compromise must always tend to the impairment of moral vigour, and to the perplexity of conscience, if it is anything else than a confession of the completeness of truth, and of the incompleteness of our apprehension of it'.[31] So far from the Church's pursuing a tenuous middle course between two clear and solidly based but antagonistic positions, it is 'most Catholic', Maurice judged, when 'most

---

28. See his early work, *Has the Church, or the State, the Power to Educate the Nation?*, published in 1839.
29. *The Kingdom of Christ*, ii, p. 254.
30. *Life*, i, p. 357.
31. *Ibid.*, ii, p. 392.

Protestant'. The argument looks like one of those paradoxes by which he was apt to confuse, if not himself, at all events his readers. His implication seems, however, to be that the Church's good is not secured by a little Catholicism here offset by a touch of Protestantism there, the inclusion of *this* necessitating the exclusion of *that*. Catholicism and Protestantism are to be combined in their fullest vitality, in their utmost concentration. The Tractarian view was not acceptable, despite the fact that Maurice repeatedly uses language having a Tractarian ring, because it was a limited and a limiting conception. He himself was content to look upon the national church as a part or branch of the true Church, but the systems advocated by the ecclesiastical parties, 'whether called Evangelical, Liberal, Catholic, or purely Anglican', were manmade, 'of the earth, earthy', although each had some particular truth in its grasp. Happily and providentially, the English reformers of the sixteenth century had avoided the system-mongering of their continental counterparts, whether or not they had fully realized what they were doing. The Church of England, as it emerged from the Reformation, was a Church more concerned with life than with precise and exigent schemes of doctrine. Accordingly 'that peculiar character which God has given us, enables us, if we do not slight the mercy, to understand the difference between a church and a system, better perhaps than any of our neighbours can'. And he adds, as though prescient of the Anglican part in the ecumenical dialogue of the century to come:

> Our position, rightly used, gives us a power of assisting them in realizing the blessings of their own. By refusing to unite with them on the ground of any of their systems, by seeking to unite with them on the grounds of the universal Church, we teach them wherein lies their strength and their weakness.[32]

Not that Maurice was in any wise blind to the defects of the establishment as it then was. He admitted its 'corruption', its 'evil condition'—thanks in no small part to its deliberate cultivation of the sectarian feeling within its own bosom. But having himself been brought up in a sect he had learned to value the *ethos* of a *church*, whatever its faults. For as a church it had a wider platform of truth than any of the dissenting bodies, and was perhaps less arrogant and intolerant. He firmly believed, however, as he wrote in *Subscription No Bondage*, that unity would bring a profounder apprehension of the truth, since truth itself suffers from the absence of unity.

Christian socialism

Until the revival, after the second world war, of interest in Maurice as a theologian he was chiefly remembered as the protagonist of Christian Socialism. This was a mistake. Maurice first and foremost was a theological thinker, an ideologue. In his own day he was thought to have had his head too much in the clouds and to have been a dreamer of intellectual dreams whose practical significance was none too evident. When, therefore, the theology came to be disregarded its author's work

32. *The Kingdom of Christ*, ii, p. 343.

as a social theorist, more readily comprehensible, retained its appeal. Nevertheless the social theory stemmed from the theology and was its natural expression. 'Christ', he insisted, 'came to establish a kingdom, not to proclaim a set of opinions. Every man entering this kingdom becomes interested in all its relations, members, circumstances; he cannot separate himself in any wise from them; he cannot establish a life or interest apart from theirs.'[33] Theology is a matter of life, not merely of contemplation, and there can be no cleavage in principle between religion and the secular order. Indeed, as we have seen, Maurice could recognize no secular order exclusively as such. It was mankind as a whole whom Christ came to redeem and whose head he now is. In consequence every aspect of man's being is related to Christ and thus falls within the Christian purview. The conviction was one which deepened the sensitivity of Maurice's naturally sensitive social conscience. And to the condition of the labouring classes in the 1840s only the totally insensitive could remain indifferent. The collapse of Chartism made the need for some kind of social action imperative, and Christian opinion, by virtue of its professed principles, was the obvious force to give stimulus and if possible to provide leadership.

Yet Maurice himself could never have been the effective leader of a political or social movement. He was a man of the strongest moral feeling, but constitutionally an 'intellectual' lacking in practical talent.[34] The issue, however, he saw in the sharpest outline: the condition of the poor was a fact to appal, but it did not lie in the unalterable nature of things; it was the outcome of wrong economic relations, a state of remediable social injustice. A false economy, with its resulting social evils, rested on the principle of competition, whereas what society desperately needed was the principle of cooperation. The Church, accordingly, was bidden to assert 'an actual living community under Christ, in which no man has a right to call anything that he has his own, but in which there is spiritual fellowship and practical cooperation'. That the task, were it to have positive effect, would be of immense difficulty he was under no illusion.

> I believe [he wrote] whoever enters on this path must lay his account with opposition, active or passive, from all quarters, must eagerly welcome and set down for fair gain all tokens of sympathy, must have no confidence in himself; must cultivate entire confidence in God and in the certainty of His purposes. It will and must be a long battle, in which many, even standard-bearers, will fall. But the issue is not to be doubted; let us work and trust for it.[35]

It was an undertaking, unfortunately, for which churchmen of whatever party were ill-prepared. The Evangelicals had behind them a great record of organized

---

33. *Ibid.*, (1838 ed), iii, 387.
34. He could never overcome his dislike of the mere machinery of social action. 'I should have to go into a long personal history', he wrote to Ludlow, 'if I undertook to explain how the dread of Societies, Clubs, Leagues, has grown up in me, how I have fought with it and often wished to overcome it, how it has returned again and again upon me with evidence which I cannot doubt, of being a divine not a diabolical inspiration' (from a MS letter of 24 November 1849 in the Cambridge University Library, Additional Manuscripts 7348, art. 8, no. 19).
35. *Life*, ii, pp. 9f.

charitable endeavour, which was continued in the unceasing efforts of Lord Shaftsbury to promote legislation for the removal of specific social evils. Intellectually, however, they were not abreast of their times, the trend of which they feared and failed to comprehend. As C. E. Raven says:

> On its intellectual side the Evangelical movement was not only hampered in the acceptance of new ideas but driven into opposition to them. ... The democratic and liberalizing tendencies in politics were naturally combined with liberal views upon literary and historical subjects, and particularly so in religion, because the dominant theory laid stress upon just those elements of Old Testament teaching, the conception of the monarchy as a thing of divine decree and the insistence upon submission to law, which the reformers were driven to dispute.[36]

Such was no less true of the Tractarians. Chartism was something altogether beyond the ken of most of their sympathizers. From the Oxford of Newman and Pusey the new industrial world was too distant and the subjects which dominated the former's thinking seemed to have no more bearing upon it than had it upon them,[37] even though it be true that the Oxford Movement, along with Coleridge and Arnold, 'stood for a reaction against individualism through their emphasis upon the organic and historical character of society'.[38] But none of them questioned the basis of class privilege or the gross disparities in economic status between different sections of society which everywhere prevailed. In any case, for the most part, as G. C. Binyon puts it, 'the super-natural character of the Church made public life, in their eyes, an alien, secular, hostile region rather than a field for Christian action'.[39] By contrast Maurice felt that as a theologian simply it was his business 'to dig, to shew that economy and politics must have a ground "beneath themselves"', that 'society'—and here he declared his opposition to the utilitarians and other secularizing reformers—'is not to be made anew by arrangements of ours, but is to be regenerated by finding the law and ground of its harmony, the only secret of its existence, in God ... All my future course must be regulated on this principle, or on no principle at all'.[40]

At heart, then, Maurice distrusted democracy and feared political action of any sort as an instrument of Christian moral idealism. The leader of a *party* of Christian Socialists he had, therefore, no wish to be; nor could he have been so, his antipathy to all 'systems' being too deeply entrenched. Certainly he desired to see socialism Christianized and Christianity 'socialized'. But how this should be done, apart from theological and moral instruction, he never indicates. As he afterwards said, 'they found that I regarded the knowledge of God the key to all other as that which connected knowledge with life. They found that I accepted the Bible as the interpretation of the history of mankind.'[41] Maurice's notion of a Christian society hence remained essentially idealistic and doctrinaire. His generalizations, as

36. *Christian Socialism, 1848–1854* (1920), pp. 13f.
37. Cp. E. L. Woodward, *The Age of Reform* (2nd ed., 1962), p. 493.
38. V. A. Demant, *Religion and the Decline of Capitalism* (1952), p. 53.
39. *The Christian Socialist Movement in England* (1931), p. 64.
40. *Life,* ii, p. 137.
41. *Ibid.,* i, p. 493.

statements of basic principle, are unexceptionable, but their practical applications are left in suspense. He boldly supported the socialist cause with his pen, and for educational ventures he had great enthusiasm, but the only practical scheme in which he joined with full consent was the Producers' Associations. Fortunately for the prospects of the social movement Maurice had friends whose talents were more pragmatic. Of these, the first easily, was John Malcolm Ludlow (1821–1911), a barrister and a man with considerable understanding of the requirements of effective political action.[42] Educated in France, he was closely associated with socialist and revolutionary groups in Paris, where he had personal acquaintance with working-class conditions. With the hopes and aspirations of the 1848 he was in warm sympathy. From Paris he wrote to Maurice at the time 'to express his conviction that Socialism was a real and very great power which had acquired an unmistakable hold not merely on the fancies but on the consciences of the Parisian workmen, and that it must be Christianized or it would shake Christianity to its foundations, precisely because it appealed to the higher and not to the lower instincts of the men'.[43] To which Maurice replied, characteristically, that 'the necessity of an English theological reformation as a means of averting an English political revolution and of bringing what is good in foreign revolutions to know itself', had been more and more pressing upon his mind. The upshot was a decision, taken along with Charles Kingsley (1819–1875), to bring out a new series of 'Tracts for the Times' in the shape of a penny journal to be called *Politics for the People*. This particular enterprise lasted for only a few months, but the views expressed were always to the point, especially when Ludlow was their author. For Ludlow was radical and clearheaded. He cared nothing for the susceptibilities of the traditional political parties, believed in a massive extension of the franchise—although he was opposed to universal suffrage—and favoured large increases in direct taxation.

Kingsley, under the *nom de plume* of 'Parson Lot', assumed the role of fire-eating journalist. His only quarrel with the Charter, he declared, was that it did not go far enough. The Bible was a book, not to keep the poor in order, but to admonish the rich; it was throughout, and not in a few places only, the true 'Reformers' Guide'.[44] The idea of religion as an opiate for the people infuriated him. Instead it should be an exhortation, a challenge, a stimulus. The Church, he wanted his readers to believe, was in support of popular aspirations.[45] But on the whole *Politics*

42. See A. D. Murray, *John Ludlow. The Autobiography of a Christian Socialist* (London, 1981), an abbreviated version of Ludlow's own long, unpublished autobiography. Ludlow could be very critical of Maurice's impracticality, but he always maintained the highest personal regard for him. Indeed he described him as 'by far the greatest man I have ever known', to be ranked with some of the greatest figures in the history of Christianity (*Autobiography*, p. 114).
43. *Life*, i, p. 458.
44. *Charles Kingsley. His Letters and Memories of his Life* (ed. by his wife) (1877), i, p. 115.
45. An example of Kingsley's journalistic style was the placard, displayed in the London streets on 12 April, 1848, which proclaimed: 'Workmen of England! You say that you are wronged. Many of you are wronged, and many besides yourselves know it. ... You have more friends than you think for. Friends who expect nothing from you, but who love you because you are their brothers, and who fear God, and therefore dare not

for the People, amateurish and somewhat inept in its editing, did not provide reading matter of a type to reach the masses. The Chartists themselves suspected the motives behind it. Yet it did some good in showing that barriers of class and education were not insurmountable.

Kingsley's position is not altogether easy to assess. His bark was loud, but did he do more than make a noise? Undoubtedly he was better informed than Maurice about the real condition of the English labourer, especially in the country. But he gives the impression of being a man chiefly of words. His many enthusiasms tended to run away with him. He lashed out in all directions indiscriminately and often inconsistently. But he had the born writer's gift for telling statement, as in his famous 'Cheap Clothes and Nasty', which he contributed to *Tracts by Christian Socialists*, a series planned by Ludlow.

It was in connection with this latter venture that Maurice, in January 1850, publicly accepted the designation 'Christian Socialist'. It committed him, he said, 'to the conflict we must engage in sooner or later with the unsocial Christians and the unchristian socialists'.[46] The same year also saw the publication of another periodical, actually called *The Christian Socialist*, the first number of which appeared in November. Ludlow was its founder and sole editor. Maurice indeed was dubious about it, so that Ludlow had a free hand. Its standpoint was serious and always consistently maintained, its aim being to present a view of society both Christian and Socialist. For Christianity, it was argued, had become too ecclesiastical, too cloistered, and needed to find its way back to the world proclaiming God's sovereignty over every sphere of man's life. The Christian gospel, in other words, must express itself in social action and organization, the appropriate form of which, for the present age, is socialism, which alone has a convincing message for the worker. The alternative to a Christian socialism was a godless one, and a godless socialism could have no permanence inasmuch as socialist organisation, to be effective, must have such a moral basis as only a religious faith can provide. But Ludlow was in no doubt that by socialism he *meant* socialism—State control of the economy. *Laissez-faire* had to be ended and the profit motive curbed; failing which low wages and unemployment would certainly continue. In his estimation a society economically free—competition being of its essence—was bound to involve a clash of interests between employer and workmen.

---

neglect you. His children … You may disbelieve them, insult them—you cannot stop them working for you. You think the Charter would make you free—would to God that it would! The Charter is not bad; if the men who use it are not bad. But will the Charter free you from slavery to ten pound bribes? Slavery to gin and beer? Slavery to every spouter who flatters your self-conceit, and stirs up bitterness and headlong rage in you? Will the Charter cure that? Friends, you want more than Acts of Parliament can give you. The Almighty God, and Jesus Christ, the Poor Man, who died for poor men, will bring it about for you, though all the Mammonites of the earth were against you. A nobler day is dawning for England, a day of freedom, science, industry. There will be no true freedom without virtue, no true science without religion, no true industry without the fear of God, and love to your fellow-citizens' (*Life*, i, 156f.).

46. *Life*, ii, p. 235.

Meanwhile the struggle between capitalism and labour could be mitigated by the creation of producers' associations or cooperatives, in which labour itself owns the capital and uses it to its own advantage. For this purpose funds had to be raised, and another member of the group, Vansittart Neale, a man of abounding goodwill and considerable practical ability, made over a large part of his personal fortune to the cause. It was the beginning, in fact, of the cooperative movement as we know it today, Ludlow being mainly responsible for the Industrial and Provident Societies Act of 1852, which gave legal protection to all cooperative societies. Moreover, these associations were to prove a school of citizenship and a means of preparing workers for the responsibility of the franchise. But socialist though he was Ludlow was by no means committed to ideas of economic and social equality. Such in his view would have meant communism.[47] In any case, what he stood for was a *Christian* society no less than a socialist, and in a Christian society the Church would have the role of leadership.

The question, however, was whether the existing religious bodies were capable of assuming it; and of this Ludlow was not confident. The established Church, unquestionably, was far too undemocratic. What he wanted was—to use his own phrase—an 'Americanized' church, self-governing and with a large element of lay control. It was only, he believed, a church of this type—strikingly different from the legally and socially hidebound institution which the Church of England then was—which could possibly win over the working masses. Ludlow was in truth a convinced radical. In himself a quiet, rather shy man, he nevertheless saw clearly what the situation demanded; whereas Maurice, who was generally regarded as the head of the movement, was uneasy when confronted with practical measures. He greatly respected Ludlow and tried to imbibe his opinions; it was simply that Ludlow's consistent practicality, which realized the need of a party organization, did not accord with Maurice's unpractical idealism, his 'Platonistic dreams about an Order, a Kingdom & a Beauty, self-realized in their own eternity'.[48] Maurice unquestionably wished to Christianize socialism, and, in a sense, to socialize Christianity; but he had no desire 'to Christian-socialize the universe'. His feelings towards the movement cooled, therefore. Further, his ejection from his King's College professorship, as we have seen, was not the consequence of his theological convictions alone; he was identified as the leader of a group whose activities were arousing sharp criticism, particularly in the influential *Quarterly* and *Edinburgh* reviews, representing Tory and Whig respectively, and the militantly evangelical *Record*. Maurice was not and could never have become a political radical. But he was considered to entertain too many notions of a potentially subversive kind for

47. The words are Ludlow's, who went on to complain that such dreams 'so put to shame all pretended earthly counterparts that it becomes labour lost to attempt anything like an earthly realization of them'. See a MS letter to Maurice of 13 September [1853] in the Cambridge University Library (Additional Manuscripts 7348. art. 17, no. 3).
48. Ludlow distrusted talk about 'the Rights of Labour' no less than about 'the Rights of Property'. He stated bluntly: 'I know of no inborn and inherent right in any man to any privilege or enjoyment whatsoever.' Talk of Duty was what was needed. See E. Norman, *The Victorian Christian Socialists* (1987), pp. 77f.

the tender minds of his students to be exposed any longer to his teaching. Kingsley's ardour also waned, following a somewhat ranting sermon on 'The Message of the Church to the Labouring Man' which he delivered in a London church in June 1851 and for which he was publicly rebuked by the vicar, the Rev. G. S. Drew. He had already poured much of his reformist enthusiasm into a novel, *Alton Locke*, published in the late summer or autumn of 1850, laying about him manfully whenever he espied (as he supposed) an enemy of social justice. But by 1855 his attitude was changing. In the prefaces to the subsequent editions of the book his tone became noticeably reserved and even apologetic. Evidently his opinions of earlier years were now embarrassing him. The faith also grew shaky of yet another prominent supporter of the movement, Thomas Hughes, of *Tom Brown's Schooldays* fame: Christians of a socialistic turn of mind worked better, he thought, as individuals than in concert. Neale, too, did not see eye to eye with Ludlow, about either the movement's economic socialism or its aggressive Christianity. Thus by 1854 it had virtually petered out. Ludlow was disappointed and not a little disillusioned, and Maurice turned to education as providing a better way.

For education was a necessary means to the promotion and dissemination of truth. The outcome—although the actual scheme was of Ludlow's devising—was the foundation of the Working Men's College in Great Ormond Street, London, followed by similar institutions in the provinces. The London college opened at the end of October 1854, with 120 students and the former King's professor as its principal, the latter assisted not only by others of the Christian Socialist group, Neale and Hughes among them, but by John Ruskin and Dante Gabriel Rossetti as well. The venture was, however, the expression of Christian Socialist zeal and with the movement's eventual demise its own fortunes declined.

The Christian Socialist enterprise had lasted for some six years. It failed for want of a clearsighted and viable policy. Ludlow could have given it this, but Maurice's concern was for the theological fundamentals, whilst Kingsley, although a publicist of talent, was too little of a thinker and in any case mistook verbosity for action. Hughes had not much more than a warm heart, and Neale was essentially a private philanthropist, neither socialist nor particularly Christian. Yet their efforts were not wholly unavailing and certainly were timely. Hitherto the Church had stood aloof from all such aims, when not actually resisting them. Maurice and his friends, besides asserting workingmen's right of association for a positive social purpose, had pricked the nation's social conscience. No longer could thoughtful Christians be content to ignore the human aspect of the Industrial Revolution. The wage-earner was seen as having social rights of his own and not simply as the helpless object of middle-class condescension and charity. From now on churchmen increasingly were to feel themselves at one with the worker in his struggle for a better place in society, both economically and politically. A discussion had been started which could not be allowed to drop. The very abuse which the Christian Socialists met with was itself a grotesque compliment to their intentions. In G. C. Binyon's judgment it was largely through Ludlow's influence that 'there has been in England, and particularly in the Anglican Church, a development, unparalleled in any other country or Church, of a theology consonant with the principles and ideals of Socialism, tending at once to infuse religion with a social purpose and fulfil social inspiration by religious faith'.[49] The tribute here paid to one in particular of the group may fairly be shared among them all.

After 1854 Christian social concern in this country took a variety of paths. One was the way of the ritualist priests in the slums, of men like Lowder and Mackonochie. (The Wellclose Square mission, in the East End of London, had received active support from the Christian Socialists, notably in the formation of a working-men's club and institute.) But they were not social theorists, only Christian humanitarians and zealots for 'Catholic' truth, bringing Tractarian ideals to the world of the urban poor. Another was that of H. C. Shuttleworth, a ritualist likewise and rector of St Nicholas Cole Abbey, besides being a professor at King's College. He perhaps had more of conscious principle behind him. 'Poverty', he declared, 'is not a mysterious dispensation of Providence, which, for some inscrutable reason, is the stern lot of the majority of our race; but an evil brought about by causes which can be remedied, an evil to be fought against and ultimately destroyed.'[50] Working with him at Cole Abbey was Thomas Hancock, whose published sermons, *The Pulpit and the Press*, sometimes bore revolutionary-sounding titles—'The Social Carcase and the anti-social Vultures', 'The Hymn of the Social Revolution' (i.e. the Magnificat), or 'Labour Day and the Red Flag'. Best remembered of them, however, was Stewart Headlam (1847–1924), founder in 1877 of the Guild of St Matthew, a society in which Maurician and Tractarian ideals were united in an alliance with principles avowedly socialist. Headlam's aim was to break down the barrier of prejudice between radical social thinkers on the one hand and the always conservative Church on the other without in any way compromising in the matter of strict High Church teaching and practice. That the Guild would welcome the introduction of state socialism was made plain in 1884. A resolution was also adopted which proclaimed that:

> Whereas the present contrast between the great body of the workers who produce much and consume little, and of those classes which produce little and consume much, is contrary to the Christian doctrines of brotherhood and justice, this meeting urges upon all churchmen the duty of supporting such measures as will tend—(*a*) To restore to the people the value which they give to the land; (*b*) To bring about a better distribution of the wealth created by labour; (*c*) To give the whole body of the people a voice in their own government; (*d*) To abolish false standards of worth and dignity.[51]

Headlam himself was a man of generous and unconventional sympathies, whose quixotic sorties in the field of social amelioration occasionally landed him in trouble with ecclesiastical authority. He had been an undergraduate at Cambridge during the years when Maurice held a professorship there, and relates that it was Maurice's theological teaching which first attracted him.

> He believed in the old term theology, and disliked any substitution for it of the word religion. It is easy to imagine what good news his teaching as to eternal life and eternal punishment was to such of us as had been terrified by the reiteration of the doctrine that half the world or more was condemned to future torment.

49. *Op. cit.*, p. 84.
50. *Vox Clamantium*, p. 39.
51. Binyon, *op. cit.*, p. 143.

And he adds that 'it was from the doctrines of the Incarnation and the Atonement that he derived what unifies his social teaching'.[52]

Last years

Maurice was throughout his life a controversial figure. He would not retreat before an issue upon which he felt strongly. This was further demonstrated by his famous but in some respects unfortunate dispute with Mansel about the nature of divine revelation, and in his impulsive intervention in the Colenso controversy a few years later. But his public reputation was by that time well established. Sir Thomas Acland had written to him:

> For more than a quarter of a century you have been helping Englishmen to see through the theories and systems which have been invented to prop up, restore, develop or narrow the ancient edifice of their national Church; and, amidst ceaseless contumely and misrepresentation levelled against yourself, you have striven to teach, as Alexander Knox and S. T. Coleridge taught before you, that the Bible and the Church of England can best bear witness for their own truth, and for God's providence, against infidelity and pantheism.[53]

52. See F. G. Bettany, *Stewart Headlam: a Biography* (1926), p. 20. On the after history of the Christian social movement see Peter d'A. Jones, *The Christian Socialist Revival, 1877–1914* (1968).

   The names of those referred to in the text as inheritors of the Christian Socialist tradition were all members of the established Church. But the Nonconformist denominations, usually associated with an intense religious individualism, were not without their own contributors to the growing public concern for what had come to be called 'the condition of England' problem. As Edward Norman says they 'produced some of the most telling propagandist literature: the Congregationalist *Bitter Cry of Outcast London* in 1883 [the author was Andrew Mearns], and William Booth's *In Darkest England* in 1890' (*The Victorian Christian Socialists*, p. 3). Booth called his proposals a 'scheme of social salvation'. The Christian Socialist League of 1894, some of whose adherents were committed to collectivist Socialism, was very largely of Nonconformist membership. Also to be mentioned are George Dawson, a former Baptist minister whose own independent chapel in Birmingham drew an influential congregation comprising many of the leaders of the city's political, civic and cultural life, and where he preached the Christian implications of civic duty. Even more important was the presence of R. W. Dale at the Congregationalist Carrs Lane Chapel in Birmingham until his death in 1895. Here the civic gospel was expounded with both fervour and thought. A firm evangelical in his theology, he was a liberal in politics. (For an account of the careers of Dawson and Dale see E. P. Hennock, *Fit and Proper Persons* (1973).) In Victorian Scotland it was the strongly evangelical Free Church which called loudest for reform, particularly of working-class housing conditions. James Begg especially—a man rigidly conservative (and virulently anti-Catholic) in his religious beliefs—proclaimed during 1866 and 1867 'our obligation to provide sanitary and social reform' on the strength of biblical principles. 'The social reformer and the Christian minister must not only combine in seeking to alleviate and remove the destruction of many generations, but they must be combined in the same individuals' (quoted C. G. Brown, *The Social History of Religion in Scotland since 1730* (1987).) For a general survey see A. D. Gilbert, *Religion and Society in Victorian England: Church, Chapel and Social Change 1740–1914* (1976).
53. *Life*, ii, p. 541.

Maurice was never a man simply to let matters take their course, to shrug his shoulders, to pass by on the other side. His role was that always of Mr Valiant-for-Truth, even if his assumption of it was sometimes as naïve as it was sincere. There certainly was nothing of the complacent optimist about him. The technological process on which his era prided itself, whilst bringing much good, might also, he feared, create new problems of human self-alienation. 'Are we to live', he asked, 'in an age in which every mechanical facility for communication between man and man is multiplied ten-thousandfold, only that the inward isolation, the separation of those who meet continually, may be increased in a far greater measure?'[54] And although he could foresee 'a terrible breaking down of notions, opinions, even of most precious beliefs, an overthrow of what we call our religion—a convulsion far greater than that of the sixteenth century—in our way to reformation and unity',[55] yet that such reformation and unity would in the end be achieved he did not permit himself to doubt, since his consistent belief in Christ's actual headship of the human race banished any lurking pessimism at the thought of mankind's terrestrial future.

Maurice's last years were spent partly in the incumbency of St Peter's, Vere Street, preaching Sunday by Sunday to a very varied congregation, partly—from 1866—as professor of moral philosophy at Cambridge. The professorship afforded him great satisfaction, and the two volumes of lectures on conscience[56] and on social morality[57] respectively are the harvest of this academic Indian summer. Perhaps his closest disciple was F. J. A. Hort. Hort had studied *The Kingdom of Christ* when still an undergraduate and had been deeply impressed by it. 'Though I proceed', he then wrote, 'very slowly indeed with it, every day seems to bring out more clearly to my mind the truth, wisdom, scripturality, and above all unity of Maurice's baptismal scheme.'[58] Later in life he readily admitted to the powerful influence Maurice's writings had had upon him and how he owed to them, as it seemed to him, 'a firm and full hold of the Christian faith'.[59] This influence is especially evident in his own Hulsean lectures of 1871 entitled *The Way, the Truth, the Life*. Hort's intimate friend and colleague B. F. Westcott, was likewise a Maurician in his sympathies, particularly in the field of social doctrine, but in his case the imprint was not received uncritically.[60] He seems to have been afraid lest Maurice's influence would impair his own originality.[61]

54. *Sermons preached in Lincoln's Inn Chapel*, v, 24.
55. *Life*, ii, p. 354.
56. *Conscience: Lectures on Casuistry delivered in the University of Cambridge* (1868).
57. *Social Morality: twenty-one lectures delivered in the University of Cambridge* (1869).
58. A. F. Hort, *The Life and Letters of Fenton John Anthony Hort*, i, p. 67.
59. *Ibid.*, i, p. 155.
60. *Ibid.*, i, p. 222.
61 Westcott, it would appear, had never read Maurice extensively. It has even been said that, for the reason suggested, he had confined his attention to only one book (see, e.g., W. Moore Ede, *The Modern Churchman* (December 1933), pp. 527 f.). That this literally was so may well be doubted. But the one book of Maurice's which affected him potently was *Social Morality*, of which he wrote in the preface to his own *Social Aspects of Christianity*: 'Few books can teach nobler lessons; and I should find it hard to say how much I owe to it directly and by suggestion' (p. xii). When in 1884 he read

Towards the end of the century interest in Maurice waned. A main reason for this was the growing preoccupation with critical biblical study. Serious attention to the problem of the Bible's literary history and authenticity, belated as it was in this country, had become a necessity, and until the problem had been squarely faced the task of theology proper, as distinct from its ancillary studies, was bound to be halted. Of the import of critical considerations Maurice appeared to have been little aware, so that his teaching, in itself none too lucid, now took on an old-fashioned look. In recent years this phase of neglect has passed and his thought has undergone a process of revaluation. It still indeed is difficult to believe that the original writings will ever themselves again attract readers beyond the circle of professed students of his period. Today the essence of the Maurician doctrine needs to be distilled. But orthodox religion, and Anglicanism in particular, has in modern times seldom been served by a body of ideas so consistently recognizable as the utterance of a mind profoundly Christian in all its convictions.

---

the two volumes of the *Life* he told Llewelyn Davies that he had never before known how deep was his sympathy with most of Maurice's characteristic thoughts. 'It is most refreshing to read such a book, such a life' (A. Westcott, *Life and Letters of Brooke Foss Westcott* (1903), ii, p. 37).

Chapter 7

THE LIMITS OF RELIGIOUS KNOWLEDGE

The Maurician spirit: Frederic Myers and F. W. Robertson

Two Anglican divines, contemporaries of Maurice, who in a number of ways shared his standpoint, were Frederic Myers (1811–51), practically the whole of whose life was spent as incumbent of a Lakeland parish—he was perpetual curate of St John's, Keswick, from 1838 until his death—and Frederick William Robertson (1816–53), who, from 1847 until his own very premature death at the age of thirty-seven, ministered at Trinity Chapel, Brighton, where in a short time he won national fame as a preacher of outstanding ability. Myers, who deliberately chose a life of seclusion amid the mountain scenery he loved so well, did not permit his *Catholic Thoughts on the Bible and Theology* to be published during his lifetime. Its four successive parts, dealing respectively with the Church, the Church of England, the Bible and Theology, were printed and circulated privately, the first in 1834 and the rest at intervals from 1841 to 1848. It did not appear as a whole until 1873, when edited by Myers's friend, Bishop Ewing. A new edition, with an introduction by the author's son, F. W. H. Myers, the classical scholar, came out ten years later.[1] But by this time its opinions had lost their novelty and it failed to make the impression it certainly would have done had it been given wider publicity a generation sooner. For its time it was a remarkable book, perceptive, lucid and independent in its judgments.

Myers united a genuinely religious disposition with a cool reason and refused to be hurried out of mind by current enthusiasms and controversies. He realised that the intellectual climate was fast changing and that immediate interests would before long be displaced by others, probably of more permanent significance. The advent of historical criticism would, he saw, inevitably alter the traditional basis of theology. The English theological tradition in particular would, he thought, suffer grave disturbance from its impact, since English theology was beyond all others 'textual, verbal, every way literal'—not, that is, as simply based on biblical principles but as essentially constructed out of biblical elements. It was rigid and it was insular. Myers himself believed that no sharp line of division could be drawn between the human and the divine. They coexist, the one implicit in the other, in

---

1. F. W. H. Myers suffered many changes in his religious outlook, his final position being antagonistic to Christianity in any form. A pioneer in the field of physical research, his *Human Personality and its Survival of Bodily Death* was published posthumously in 1903.

individual experience, in history, in Scripture itself, and it is impossible to say with absolute assurance that *this* is of God, *that* of man. Hence it is that what from one aspect is seen as man's quest of truth becomes, from another, God's revelation of it. Hence, too, the impossibility of a theory of biblical inspiration which would elevate it above human error. His own view he describes negatively as neither 'literal' nor 'rational'; but, positively, he felt that if the divine permeates human life through and through, then the ways of God, to be understood, must be sought over a far broader area than the dogmatically recognised channels of revelation alone. The divine action takes the form rather of a continuous providence than a series of miraculous interventions. Its method is progressive and its ends are not always obvious at any given point in time. The Bible, which in any case must be set against the vaster background of world history, is not itself revelation but the record of revelation, revelation indeed of a multiple kind, culminating in the person of Jesus Christ, by whose standard all that preceded must be viewed and judged. And the record, it is now apparent, is the work of fallible men.

Myers goes on to argue that theology is not in any strict sense a science. What exactly our knowledge of God and man may be, our knowledge of man himself, let alone of the transcendent God, does not allow us to affirm, in the terms of a closed system. The Bible itself is no body of schematized doctrine, any more than it furnishes the answers to all the many and various questions which perplex us today. This is not to say that systems of theology are illegitimate: Christians will naturally and rightly go on trying to construct them; but their legitimacy depends on two conditions. First, it must always be remembered that human speculations are not to be equated with the original truth of revelation, and that the former have in comparison with the latter only a relative and provisional value; and secondly, as following from this, that theology is a progressive discipline, changing with the growth in human knowledge over many fields and being ever open to revision in the light of altered circumstances and wider experience. For no sooner has a theological system been devised than it may have to be modified, perhaps drastically. 'We must make', Myers says, 'the base of our theology as broad and deep as Fact and Truth of all kinds, and build it up with materials as everlasting as the experience and necessities and aspirations of the human soul.'[2] But if theology is not revelation *simpliciter* neither is it religion. 'Religion is a spirit—Theology only a creed.' Religion continues, though theologies may come and go. The New Testament epistles come nearest to theology in explicit statement, but chiefly so where they have the special circumstances of the Jewish people in mind. Yet Christianity is not moralism only, a bare code of ethics. It is centred upon and animated by a Person. The truth of Christ which it proclaims is one therefore of underlying principle and not merely of correct dogma; its test is life more than logic. The doctrinal expression of what the Christian believes about Christ may be less or more adequate, but the real criterion is the sense of personal relationship with him.

On the customary appeal to evidences Myers is unhappy. In regard to miracles he considers their probative value to have been greatly over-estimated. It is

2. *Catholic Thoughts* (1879 ed), p. 187.

revelation which justifies them rather than they revelation. And as for prophecy its true nature has been misunderstood. It is not simply predictive, 'the form of an Image of History thrown from the Future upon the Present'; a more authentic view is that of 'a germinal principle continually reproducing itself in the Future'.[3] Regarding the Church the 'Primary Idea' is that of 'a Brotherhood of men worshipping Christ as their revelation of the Highest'. 'Equality of spiritual privilege', moreover, is so characteristic of its constitution that the existence of a priestly caste would necessarily destroy it. Later in the century such views had gained currency and hence appeared less challenging. When first set down, however, they were ahead of their time.

F. W. Robertson was akin to Myers in spirit and ideas. Essentially he was that comparatively rare phenomenon, a preacher who is also a teacher. The sermon, not the treatise, was his natural medium. Yet his pulpit style, effective as it was, bore well the transposition into cold print. He was keenly aware of the spiritual needs of his age and recognised also that the traditional Christian attitudes could no longer fully meet them. Nevertheless he was a firm believer in the traditional faith and in its power to respond to the deepest wants of men in all ages. His own position was 'broad', but like Maurice he was not a party man. Dogma was a necessity, but the presentation of religion ought not to be dogmatic, for the appeal of religion is not to the intellect alone but to the 'whole man'. In his own teaching, he said, his aim was to establish truth rather than merely to destroy error, whilst holding that truth itself is made up of opposing propositions and not to be thought of only as a *via media* between them. Again, since spiritual things are spiritually discerned, they should be taught 'suggestively'. Finally, we should learn that even in what is evil there is a 'soul of goodness'[4]. Not that Robertson would tolerate vagueness, a fault for which he critized the American theologian, Horace Bushnell, finding him 'shadowy' and objecting that he did not 'sufficiently show that dogmas express eternal verities', that they are 'what a mathematician might call approximative formulas to truth'.

> In this spirit I always ask—what does that dogma mean? Not what did it mean on the lips of those who spoke it? How, in my language, can I put into form the underlying truth, in correcter form if possible, but only in approximative form after all? In this way purgatory, absolution, Mariolatry, become to me fossils, not lies.[5]

Thus no dogmatic statement can be final: it is in principle liable to revision in the light of fresh knowledge or deeper understanding. Christian doctrine must be progressive and the Christian teacher keep an open mind. Hence the danger of

3. *Ibid.*, p. 311.
4. See Stopford Brooke, *The Life and Letters of F. W. Robertson* (1865), ii, pp. 160f; cp. also pp. 102 and 106. Faith, he stated in a sermon of 1849, is not assent to a credal formula but 'the broad principle of saving trust in God, above all misgiving', 'a living for the invisible instead of the seen' (*Sermons*, 4th ser., 1886, p. 141).
5. *Life and Letters*, ii, p. 40. Cp. what Robertson says in his confirmation class catechism: '*Q*. Why is correct faith necessary to salvation? *A*. Because what we believe becomes our character, forms part of us, and character is salvation or damnation; what we *are*, that is, our *heaven* or our *hell*. Every sin bears its own punishment' (*ibid.*, p. 295).

ecclesiastical parties and 'schools', which tend to narrowness and rigidity. 'Do not tremble [he wrote] at difficulties and shoreless expanses of truth, if you feel drifting into them. God's truth must be boundless. Tractarians and Evangelicals suppose that it is a pond which you can walk round and say, "I hold the truth" ... Dare to be alone with God.' This frame of mind meant that Robertson, like Maurice, hated systems. They constricted. Far better was it to teach doctrines—and Robertson's own sermons are full of doctrinal content—in their organic relation to life than with a view merely to their coherence in a closed scheme. Suggest, he repeatedly urges, do not dogmatize.

Robertson's theology was intensely Christocentric. But his principle here is that the mystery of Christ's person must be approached through the historic fact of his humanity. The thought of God can become meaningful to man only through the visible life of the incarnate. As the perfection of humanity Christ is the complete antidote to despair at the existing state of human nature. The note struck is distinctly Maurician:

> Christ was the Son of God. But remember in what sense He ever used this name—Son of God because Son of Man. He claims Sonship in virtue of His Humanity. Now, in the whole previous revelation through the Prophets, etc. one thing was implied—only through man can God be known; only through a perfect man, perfectly revealed. Hence He came, 'the brightness of His Father's Glory, the *express image* of His person'. Christ then must be loved as Son of Man before He can be adored as Son of God. In personal love and adoration of Christ the Christian religion consists, not in correct morality, or in correct doctrines, but in homage to the King.[6]

One main reason, Robertson thinks, why belief in Christ's divinity was waning was that they who held it had petrified it into a theological dogma without life or warmth. 'How are we then to get back this belief in the Son of God?' His answer has an almost Ritschlian sound: it can no longer be imposed by ecclesiastical authority, the day of which is over; begin, then, as the Bible begins, with Christ the Son of Man. The end will indeed be adoration. But to adore Christ is not simply to call him God, to cry 'Lord, Lord'. 'Adoration is the mightiest love the soul can give—call it by what name you will. Many a Unitarian, as Channing,[7] has adored, calling it only admiration; and many an orthodox Christian, calling Christ God with most accurate theology, has given Him only a cool intellectual homage.'[8] Hence, too, the idea of presenting Christian truth positively and not simply in the negative mode of contradicting error, which produces not 'converts to Christ, but only controversialists'. Controversy fastens on what is adventitious and temporary, hiding the real substance of truth.

It is in this positive spirit likewise that the great controversial issues between Protestantism and Rome must be broached.

---

6. *Ibid.*, p. 40.
7. The American theologian, William Ellery Channing, who died in 1847. In his day he came to be considered a Unitarian, but he believed Christ to have been at once the perfect revelation of God and the living ideal of humanity.
8. *Life and Letters*, ii, pp. 169–71.

Purgatory, Mariolatry, Absolution, Apostolical Succession, Seven Sacraments instead of two, Transubstantiation, Baptismal Regeneration, Invocation of Saints—each is based upon a truth; but crystallized into form, petrified into dogmas, they are false. Endeavour to trace the meaning contained in Romish institutions: do not meet them with anathemas. Discover what the Roman Catholic means, translate to him his longing, interpret to him what he wants. I can conceive no more blessed work than this for the man of large heart and clear, vigorous intellect.[9]

On the vexed question of the eucharistic presence Robertson again differs from both the Dissenter and the Romanist, whilst also rejecting a mere compromise.

In opposition to the Dissenting view, it *is* Christ's body and blood received; in opposition to the Romanist's view *it is not* Christ's body and blood to those who receive it unworthily. We do not go between the two. Each of these opposite statements of the Dissenter or of the Roman Catholic are truths, and we retain them. It is not merely bread and wine: it is, spiritually, Christ's body and blood: God present spiritually, not materially, to those who receive it worthily—i.e. to the faithful. It is not Christ's body and blood to those on whose feelings and conduct it does not tell.[10]

So also with the eucharistic sacrifice. The Romanist is right in principle, wrong in his application of the principle. As for the doctrine of purgatory, the 'ultra-Protestant' utterly denies it. 'But the law of the universe is progress.'

Is there no more pain for the redeemed? Is there nothing good in store for the bad? ... Here, then, we have the principle of purgatory. I have stated this hypothetically; the Roman Catholic states it as a dogma. Our fate is decided here. This is said rigorously by the ultra-Protestant. *So it is*; there is the Protestant truth. The Romanist states the opposite truth, and says, 'Our destiny is determined beyond the grave.' So long as either is a positive statement of a truth, it is right; but the moment either denies the truth of the other it becomes a falsehood.[11]

In the matter of baptism Robertson's ideas, as propounded in his two sermons on the subject, approximate closely to Maurice's. The sacrament, he holds, does not *make* men children of God, but only declares them to be so, the great truth being that all men are born into the world as children of God by right. Neither the sacramental action nor the recipient's faith (or that of his sponsors) is needed to bring this about. It is a fact, whether we believe it or not. The Tractarian doctrine of a new kind of human nature created at baptism seemed to him magical, as indeed did the evangelical, which differed from it only in confining the efficacy of the sacrament to select cases. Robertson approved the Gorham judgment not because he thought Gorham right but because it left the question open.

It is not surprising, therefore, that, again like Maurice, he should have stood apart from the ecclesiastical parties. The dogmatic positions they insisted on maintaining required the rejection of those of their opponents. The language of religion, however, is poetic rather than logical. This conviction governed his

9. *Ibid.*, p. 161.
10. *Ibid.*, p. 162.
11. *Ibid.*, p. 163.

hermeneutics: in the words of his biographer, 'he did not choose his text in order to wring a doctrine out of it, but he penetrated to its centre, and seized the principle it contained. It was the kernel, not the shell, for which he cared.'[12] Hence the breadth of Robertson's appeal as a preacher. He addressed himself to the ordinary man, ignorant or impatient of theological niceties. Yet he paid for the largeness of his views with the bitter opposition of some influential persons in Brighton. His sympathies with the working class were suspect and he was attacked in the press for sharing the socialist opinions of Maurice and Kingsley. That he actually held such views he denied. 'It seems to me', he wrote,' a great mistake to lead the working-classes to suppose that by any means independent of their own energy, moral improvement, and self-restraint, their condition can be permanently altered.' He disagreed with Kingsley's economic notions—'what he says of the accumulation of capital is vague and declamatory'—and thought that cooperation could not long replace competition without becoming competition itself, 'between bodies instead of individuals'. 'If we were all Christians in fact as well as by right, the difficulty would be at an end; but I do not think that the attempts which begin with society instead of the individual, will any of them solve the question.'[13] Yet he was most anxious that 'sympathy should be felt, or rather candour extended, towards the exaggerations of generous and unselfish men like Kingsley, whose warmth, even when wrong, is a higher thing than the correctness of cold hearts'. In any event Christianity would have to come in to balance and modify political economy.

H. L. Mansel

A contemporary theologian with whom Maurice found himself very much at odds was Henry Longueville Mansel (1820–71), of St John's College, Oxford, afterwards dean of St Paul's. Yet in the light of the present day Mansel stands out as one of the most startling religious thinkers of the century. What he taught was that the transcendent God, by virtue of his transcendence—if the word be taken seriously—must in himself be unknown and unknowable, a doctrine evidently in flat contradiction of beliefs to which Maurice adhered passionately. Mansel's views were fully and lucidly stated in his Bampton lectures for 1858, entitled *The Limits of Religious Thought Examined.* These discourses without doubt brought a wholly fresh interest to a series of lecture-sermons which over the years had as a rule sunk to the level of a verbose if well-meaning conventionalism. Mansel himself, who at the time of their delivery was Waynflete professor of moral and metaphysical philosophy at Oxford, was esteemed by the undergraduates as perhaps the best teacher in the university, and welcomed in senior common rooms as one of the liveliest and wittiest of its conversationalists. But behind the verbal brilliance was a keen and well-informed mind and an unusual point of view. The lectures attracted to the university church such a congregation as had scarcely been seen there since the days of Newman. Not that their style was in any sense popular. Mansel stuck

12. *Ibid.*, p. 165.
13. *Ibid.*, pp. 7f.

throughout to a close-textured argument with no concession to pulpit appeal. Many among his audience found him incomprehensible; others, understanding him well enough, demurred at what he had to say. One elderly don remarked that he 'most certainly never expected to live to hear atheism preached in St Mary's church', as he had done that morning. Yet Mansel's theology was undeviatingly orthodox and his intentions unimpeachable: his sole aim was to defend Christianity from the attacks of a sceptical philosophy. At a time when J. S. Mill was reputed the first philosopher in the land such a defence was widely considered urgent. The Tractarian enthusiasm had waned, at any rate in Oxford, and the party's leading figure, Dr Pusey, was looked on as a conservative among conservatives. A new apologetic was necessary, countering reason with reason. When, therefore, Mansel's lectures were published they were widely acclaimed, for all their admitted difficulty, as a brilliant and successful attempt to supply precisely this. Even the now elderly Keble praised the book as a 'treasure'. The religious press generally hailed it as a triumph and a severe blow to the opponents of Christian faith. Many readers judged its author to have given the final answer to the objections of unbelief. Yet it stung Maurice into violent reaction and thus precipitated the bitterest controversy of his life. Unfortunately his reply, *What is Revelation?*, is one of his least praiseworthy efforts and in the ensuing exchanges with the Oxford theologian he was routed almost with ignominy.

Mansel's work still merits serious attention. He himself was well read in German theology and philosophy, the trend of which, to judge from his Aristophanic lampoon, *Phrontisterion*, he heartily disliked.[14] But to understand his own position one must first consider its relation to the teachings of the Scottish philosopher, Sir William Hamilton (1788–1856), a quotation from whom appears on the title-page of the lectures as printed: 'No difficulty emerges in theology which had not previously emerged in philosophy.' Accompanying this is another, from Bishop Berkeley: 'The objections made to faith are by no means an effect of knowledge, but proceed rather from an ignorance of what knowledge is.' Hamilton, who from 1836 had been professor of logic and metaphysics at Edinburgh, was in his time one of the most prominent figures in British philosophy. Yet he wrote little for publication and his *Lectures on Metaphysics and Logic* did not appear until some years (1859–61) after his death. For a while, however, his influence was considerable. What impressed Mansel so deeply was his 'philosophy of the

14. The Teutonic theologians figure thus:

> Theologians we,
> Deep thinkers and free,
> From the land of the new Divinity;
> Where critics hunt for the sense sublime,
> Hidden in texts of the olden time,
>   Which none but the sage can see.

> Where Strauss shall teach you how Martyrs died
> For a moral idea personified,
> A myth and a symbol, which vulgar sense

conditioned', as he called it. Mental and material existence, Hamilton argues, are incompatibles; but this should not be taken to exclude their union in a common and more intimate source or ground. Disparate though mind and matter are, they nevertheless are relative to each other, a fact which establishes the connection as well as the distinction between them. Hamilton accordingly maintains that not only are the respective qualities of mind and matter relative to something which transcends them, they are known *only* in correlation, each with the other. Thus when a fact is said to be known it is so only as limited or conditioned by other facts known in conjunction with it. Knowledge, in a word, is of the *conditioned* alone. The unconditioned is unknown and unknowable. But what is conditioned necessarily implies the unconditioned as its complement or ground: at least, it implies its existence, albeit only as the negative of the relative and conditioned. Being, that is, can be known by us only *as* the conditioned; yet at the same time we cannot avoid positing unconditioned being, even though in itself unknowable or known only negatively as complementary to the conditioned.

Hamilton did not himself apply his doctrine to the basic problems of theology, but he did suggest that such application might be fruitful, citing with evident approval 'the declarations of a pious philosophy: "A God understood would be no God at all"; "To think that God is, as we can think him to be, is blasphemy" '.[15] His own philosophy, he thought, might prove 'the most useful auxiliary to

---

> Received for historic evidence.
> Where Bauer can prove that true Theology
> Is special and general Anthropology,
> And the essence of worship is only to find
> The realized God in the human mind,
> Where Feuerbach shows how religion began,
> From the deified feelings and wants of man,
> And the Deity owned by the mind reflective,
> Is Human Consciousness made objective.
> > Presbyters, bend,
> > Bishops, attend;
> The Bible's a myth from beginning to end ...

The philosophers are treated with no less gusto:

> With deep institution and mystic rite
> We worship the Absolute-Infinite,
> The Universe-Ego, the Plenary-Void,
> The Subject-Object identified,
> The great Nothing-Something, the Being-Thought,
> That mouldeth the mass of Chaotic Nought,
> Whose beginning unended and end unbegun
> Is the One that is All and the All that is One.

15. *Discussions on Philosophy, Literature and Education* (1853), p. 15n.

theology'.[16] To Mansel, whose thinking had been shaped in the Hamiltonian mould, the wider application was the obvious next step.[17] He launches his argument with the proposition that 'the primary and proper object of criticism is not Religion, natural or revealed, but the human mind in its relation to Religion'.[18] In other words, no attempt at a rational theology can be made without a prior examination of the nature and scope of the reason itself. As Mansel sees it there are two extremes between which religious philosophy oscillates; these he identifies as, respectively, rationalism and dogmatism. To all seeming they are antagonistic, indeed irreconcilable, yet they both rest upon a common assumption. For the dogmatist, like the rationalist, is the architect of a philosophical system, the materials of which, 'the pre-existing statements of Scripture', whilst said to have been given by a higher authority, are nevertheless pieced together into systematic form and provided with a philosophical basis. In so doing, however, the dogmatist places them on a new and merely human foundation. Similarly by rationalism is meant a system whose final test of truth is afforded by the direct assent of the human consciousness, whether as logical deduction, moral judgment or religious intuition. The rationalist, Mansel points out, is as such not bound to maintain that this has actually been imparted. It is only that he assigns to some superior tribunal the right of determining what is essential to religion and what is not, that tribunal being the rational human consciousness. Thus both attitudes look to the same end: dogmatism tries to force reason into conformity with revelation, rationalism revelation into agreement with reason. Either seeks to produce a coincidence between belief and thought and to eliminate mystery.

> In relation to the actual condition of religious truth, as communicated by Holy Scripture, Dogmatism and Rationalism may be considered as severally representing, the one the spirit which adds to the word of God and the other that which diminishes from it.[19]

Whether a complete system of revealed theology could have been divinely conveyed to men, one thing at least is certain in Mansel's view, that such a system is not given in the revelation which we possess. If it is to exist at all it must be constructed out of it by human interpretation; and it is in the way they set about this that dogmatism and rationalism exhibit their most striking contrasts. The one accepts the original disclosure and adds to it from various sources and by various means; the other aims at a similar coherence, 'not by filling up supposed deficiencies, but by paring down supposed excrescences'. At first sight the two systems may seem

16. *Ibid.*, p. 621. 'A world', he writes, 'of false, and pestilent, and presumptuous reasoning, by which philosophy and theology are now equally discredited, would be at once abolished, in the recognition of this rule of prudent nescience.'
17. Mansel's other philosophical writings include *Prolegomena Logica* (1851) and *The Philosophy of the Conditioned* (1866). His work on *The Gnostic Heresies* (1875, ed. J. B. Lightfoot), which even now has not entirely lost its usefulness, was the product of his interests as an ecclesiastical historian.
18. *The Limits of Religious Thought Examined*, p. 16.
19. *Ibid.*, p. 4. See K. D. Freeman, *The Role of Reason in Religion: a Study of Henry Mansel* (1969).

to represent the respective claims of faith and reason; but in fact this is not so, for faith, properly so called, is not constructive but receptive, whilst 'the disciples of the Rationalist are not necessarily the disciples of reason'. But the one, in striving to elevate reason to the point occupied by revelation, and the other in reducing revelation to the level of reason, have alike prejudged or neglected a previous and necessary inquiry, whether there are not 'definite and discernible limits to the province of reason itself', be it exercised 'for advocacy or for criticism'.[20]

Those, Mansel warns, who accept revelation should be extremely careful of the kind of assistance they seek from reason. There is doubtless a union of philosophy with religion in which each contributes to the support of the other; but there is one also which, in appearing to support them, in fact only preys upon and weakens the life of both. Thus the attempt to defend the doctrine of the incarnation on the assumptions of a philosophical realist, like Robert Wilberforce in his treatise on dogma,[21] only associates a fundamental Christian truth with a highly questionable speculation of medieval metaphysics.

> What does theology gain by this employment of a weapon which may at any moment be turned against her? Does it make one whit clearer to our understandings that mysterious twofold nature of the one Christ, very God and very Man? By no means. It was a truth above human comprehension before; and it remains a truth above human comprehension still. We believe that Christ is both God and Man; for this is revealed to us. We know not how it is so; for this is not revealed; and we can learn it in no other way. Theology gains nothing; but she is in danger of losing everything. Her most precious truths are cut from the anchor which held them firm, and cast upon the waters of philosophical speculation, to float hither and thither with the ever-shifting waves of thought.

And what in turn does philosophy gain? Nothing, says Mansel. 'The problems which she has a native right to sift to the uttermost are taken out of the field of free discussion, and fenced about with religious doctrines which it is heresy to call in question.'[22]

What, then, is the scope of human reason? Can it on its own account achieve any knowledge of God at all? If the philosophers, Mansel thinks, had been less ready to assume the possibility of a purely rational science, they would have spared themselves the illusions of both idealism and scepticism. More profitable would have been the investigation of the *subject* of religion, the human mind itself, since the mental conditions which determine the character of a philosophy of religion must be the same as those which determine that of philosophy in general. Hence the limits of philosophy in general, if limits they are, will be those of religious philosophy also. And we find, when we consider the matter, that consciousness is

20. *Ibid.*, p. 7.
21. Robert Wilberforce (1802–57), second son of the great Evangelical anti-slavery campaigner, became a Roman Catholic in 1854. In his Anglican (and Tractarian) days he published works on the doctrines of the incarnation (1848) and the eucharist (1853). See E. R. Fairweather, *The Oxford Movement* (1964), pp. 283–367; and cp. D. Newsome, *The Parting of Friends* (1966), pp. 370–383.
22. *The Limits of Religious Thought Examined*, p. 10.

subject to certain quite inescapable conditions. To be conscious we must be conscious of *something*, and this can only be known for what it is by being distinguished from what it is *not*. But distinction is, of necessity, limitation. Obviously therefore the infinite cannot as such be distinguished from the finite by the absence of any quality which the finite possesses, as this would imply limitation. Thus a consciousness of the infinite as such necessarily involves a self-contradiction. On this showing no positive conception of the infinite is possible. To the human mind it is a negative concept only, an assertion of the absence of the conditions under which thought is possible. Similarly impossible is it for us to conceive the Absolute, since a further condition of consciousness is *relationship*. There must be both a subject and an object; the destruction of either is the destruction of consciousness itself. A consciousness of the Absolute is as self-contradictory as a consciousness of the Infinite.

> To be conscious of the Absolute as such, we must know that an object, which is given in relation to our consciousness, is identical with one which exists in its own nature, out of all relation to consciousness. But to know this identity, we must be able to compare the two together; and such a comparison is itself a contradiction.[23]

Even if it were possible to know the Absolute we still could not know that it *is* the Absolute. All knowledge is perforce relative, and what a thing may be like *out of* consciousness no mode of consciousness can tell us. The Absolute, like the Infinite, is a term void of positive content. Its sole use is to deny the relationship by which thought is constituted.

A third condition of consciousness, Mansel points out, is that of succession and duration in time. Whatever succeeds something else and is distinguishable from it is necessarily apprehended as finite, on the principle already established. This applies to anything conceived of as having existence in time. No *temporal* object, accordingly, can be regarded as exhibiting or representing the true nature of an infinite being. Thus creation, in the ultimate or absolute sense, is inconceivable by us, inasmuch as time cannot in fact be thought of as limited: to conceive a first or a last moment of time would be to conceive a consciousness into which time enters, preceded or followed by one from which it is absent. Equally inconceivable, on the other hand, is an infinite succession in time, for this too could not be bounded by time and so could only be apprehended by a mind 'outside' time. 'Clogged', says Mansel, 'by these counter impossibilities of thought, two opposite speculations have in vain struggled to find articulate utterance, the one for the hypothesis of an endless duration of finite changes, the other for that of an existence prior to duration itself.'[24] Because of this theologians have adduced the idea that God exists outside time and that in him there is no distinction of either past, present or future. This indeed may be true, Mansel concedes, but if so it makes God utterly inconceivable by us, who exist only in time. To know God by transcending time

23. *Ibid.*, p. 52.
24. *Ibid.*, p. 57.

would be to become God.[25]

But these considerations will at once be seen to have an important bearing on the problem of divine personality. That God is personal Mansel holds, of course, to be vital to religion.

> The various mental attributes which we ascribe to God, Benevolence, Holiness, Justice, Wisdom, for example, can be conceived by us only as existing in a benevolent and just and wise Being, who is not identical with any of his attributes, but the common subject of them all;—in one word, in a *Person*.[26]

But personality as we conceive it is essentially a limitation and a relation. This undoubtedly is the case with our own personalities, and it is from them that all our representative notions of personality are derived. Hence to speak of an absolute and infinite Person is to use language of an object which under the conditions of human thought is simply inconceivable. Is it not then wholly inappropriate to speak of God in personal terms? Ought we not to confine our description of him to the impersonal and abstract? By no means. 'Personality, with all its limitations, though far from exhibiting the absolute nature of God as He is, is yet truer, grander, and more elevating, more religious, than those barren, vague, meaningless abstractions which men babble about nothing under the name of the Infinite.'[27] Personality is in fact the highest category known to us. It is by consciousness alone that we can assert God's existence or offer him service. It is only by conceiving Him as a Conscious Being, that we can stand in any religious relation to Him at all; that we can form such a representation of Him as is demanded by our spiritual wants, insufficient though it be to satisfy our intellectual curiosity.' But this clearly puts us in a philosophical dilemma. We are obliged both to think of God as personal and to believe that he is infinite, and the two representations are irreconcilable. The dilemma, however, is purely one for thought; it does not follow that it implies any impossibility in the absolute nature of God. The apparent contradiction, that is, is only the inevitable consequence of the attempt on the part of the human thinker to transcend the boundaries of his own consciousness. It proves that there are limits to man's power of thought, but no more. And such limitation is as true of metaphysical thinking as of religious, for although the mere expression, the 'infinite', when regarded as indicating only the negation of limitation—and hence of conceivability—is not contradictory in itself, it becomes so the moment we apply it in reasoning to any object of thought. In short, every object of consciousness is, *eo ipso*, finite, even the allegedly infinite. Thus contradiction is inescapable.

25. Mansel had already used this argument elsewhere. In a paper entitled 'Man's conception of eternity' he wrote: 'To conceive an Eternal Being, I must have experienced a consciousness out of time, i.e. a consciousness other than human in its constitution. The Term Eternity, in this sense, expresses not a conception, but the negation of a conception, the acknowledgement of the possible existence of a Being concerning whose consciousness we can only make the negative assertion that it is not like our consciousness' (*Letters, Lectures and Reviews*, 1873, p. 111).
26. *The Limits of Religious Thought Examined*, p. 59.
27. *Ibid.*, p. 61.

By no subterfuge can philosophy, Mansel argues, avoid the admission that the absolute and infinite are beyond its grasp. Hegelians may contend that the foundation for a knowledge of the infinite must be laid in a point beyond consciousness; but a system which starts from this assumption postulates its own failure at the outset. Consciousness, reason, is used as an instrument to prove that consciousness, rationality, is a delusion. The upshot must be that the terms 'absolute' and 'infinite', like 'the inconceivable' and 'the imperceptible', are merely names indicating not a possible object of thought but one that would be exempt from the conditions apart from which human thought would be impossible. Moreover, if the difficulties of faith are seen really to be difficulties in philosophy itself and inseparable from speculation of any kind, whether religious or irreligious, the Christian will do well to shun the allurements of a philosophical theology.

> Speculations which end in unbelief are often commenced in a believing spirit. It is painful, but at the same time instructive, to trace the gradual process by which an unstable disciple often tears off strip by strip the wedding garment of his faith—scarce conscious the while of his own increasing nakedness—and to mark how the language of Christian belief may remain almost untouched, when the substance and life have departed from it.[28]

Mansel now takes the argument a step forward by showing how in fact those elements in the human consciousness which form the basis of religion and from which positive religious ideas are originally derived require of their very nature belief in a personal deity. Religious thought, he says, is the outcome of two fundamental feelings: the sense of dependence and the sense of moral obligation. It is to these twin data of the inner consciousness that the two great outward acts by which religion has usually been manifested among men are to be attributed, namely prayer and expiation. Neither feeling yields a direct intuition of God, but both provide some intimation of his presence. They point towards a personal being who as a free agent hears and can answer prayer, and as a moral governor is the source and author of the moral law within us. As the immediate sources of mankind's knowledge of God they cannot, so Mansel claims, be set aside by the mere negative abstractions of the so-called philosophy of the unconditioned. But because consciousness of a personal deity is not in itself an institution of the absolute and infinite we are led to the conviction that behind this positive conception of God as *personal* there nevertheless remains a mystery which in our present state of knowledge we cannot penetrate. Once more are we thrown back on the distinction already established between a belief in the *fact* and a conception of its *manner*; as also upon the paradox that it is our rational duty to believe in that which we are unable to understand.

But how is the difficulty to be resolved if religious belief is not to be dismissed out of hand as an impossible attempt to comprehend the incomprehensible? Mansel replies that although we cannot contemplate God in his absolute nature we at least can view him in the perspective of his own self-revelation. If, that is, we cannot for the reasons noted have a *speculative* knowledge of God, revelation does furnish

28. *Ibid.*, pp. 70f.

us with *regulative* ideas of the divine sufficient to direct our practice although not to satisfy our intellect. 'Guided by this, the only true philosophy of Religion, man is content to practise where he is unable to speculate. He acts, as one who must give account of his conduct: he prays, believing that his prayer will be answered.' Mansel, it should be observed, is careful to define his terms. By a speculative concept is meant, he explains, a conception derived from

> an immediate perception or other intuition of the object conceived, as when I form a notion of human seeing or hearing, or of human anger or pity, from my actual experience of these modes of consciousness in myself; and a speculative truth is a truth expressed by means of such conceptions. A regulative conception, on the other hand, is a conception derived, not from the immediate perception or intuition of the object itself, but from that of something else, supposed more or less nearly to resemble it; and a *regulative truth* is a truth expressed by means of such conceptions.[29]

Thus the language we use of God, as when we speak of his hearing or seeing, or feeling anger or pity, is analogical only, borrowed from that of human consciousness and indicative of divine attributes of which we have no immediate apprehension in themselves. But in this again, Mansel contends, the theologian is in no different case from the philosopher, for whom, as already shown, the attempt to arrive at absolutely first and unconditional principles involves him in apparent contradictions, with the result that he is bound to acquiesce in ideas which he practically assumes and acts upon as true without his being able to conceive how in principle they are true, ideas which necessarily imply the existence of a mysterious and inconceivable reality beyond themselves. (How, for instance, are we to solve the age-old problems of liberty and necessity, or of unity and plurality, or of the nature of space and time?) And when we turn from natural theology to revealed we discover that precisely the same considerations hold good.

> In no respect is the Theology of the Bible, as contrasted with the mythologies of human invention, more remarkable than in the manner in which it recognizes and adapts itself to that complex and self-limiting constitution of the human mind, which man's wisdom finds so difficult to acknowledge.[30]

Take for example, says Mansel, the dogma of the person of Christ. To philosophical theologians this has been a major stumbling-block. Despising the historical and particular they have sought refuge, like Hegel, in the empty abstractions of an impersonal idea. But the result has been a 'metaphysical caricature' of the Christian doctrine.

> It is for this philosophical idea, so superior to all history and fact—this necessary process of the unconscious and impersonal Infinite—that we are to sacrifice that blessed miracle of Divine Love and Mercy, by which the Son of God, of His own free act and will, took man's nature upon Him for man's redemption.[31]

29. *Ibid.*, pp. xivf.
30. *Ibid.*, p. 106.
31. *Ibid.*, pp. 114f. Mansel concedes that Strauss at least was consistent in his rejection of the gospel's historicity.

Let philosophy say what she will, Mansel exclaims, it is the consciousness of the deep wants of our nature which really turns us to religion. 'It is by adapting His Revelation to those wants that God graciously condescends to satisfy them.' Salvation comes not through man's speculation but from God's revelation. And revelation takes the form of what man is able to understand and appropriate to his uses.

Accordingly it is to the idea of revelation that Mansel now turns his attention, and in particular to those features of it which have been attacked as contrary to reason, whether speculative or moral. But, he contends, the weapon which assails exhibits its own weakness in the act of assailing. 'If there is error or imperfection in the essential forms of human thought it must adhere to the thought criticizing, no less than to the thought criticized.' The alternatives facing us therefore are either total scepticism, 'which destroys itself in believing that nothing is to be believed', or else the simple recognition that reason, in thus criticizing, has transcended its legitimate province. In the latter case inquiry must be shifted to another field and belief determined partly by the internal character of the doctrines themselves, partly by the evidence producible in favour of their asserted origin as a fact. Talk of the so-called contradictions between reason and revelation is thus out of place, since to know if two ideas really are contradictory it is necessary to have a positive and distinct conception of both as they are in themselves; whereas in fact we have no such conceptions of the divine *per se*, only an imperfect representation through its analogy to the finite. The question to be answered—and it is fundamental—is that of the value of the conceptions we form of the divine in their highest development. Are they exact representations of divinity, yielding conclusions of scientific certainty, comparable with those of mathematics or the physical sciences, or are they merely approximate representations, leading only to probabilities such as may be balanced and modified by counter-probabilities of another kind? To Mansel it is evident that they are the latter, not the former. Theology is not a science inasmuch as we can have no properly rational knowledge of its object. Religious knowledge rests only on analogical reasoning, which furnishes nothing more than probabilities varying, it may be, from slight presumptions up to moral certainties, but whose weight in any given case can be determined only by comparison with other evidences. Hence the whole elaborate structure of metaphysical reasoning about ultimate reality stands revealed for the empty shell it is.

> Let religion begin where it will, it must begin with that which is above Reason. What then do we gain by that parsimony of belief which strives to deal out the Infinite in infinitesimal fragments, and to erect the largest possible superstructure of deduction upon the smallest possible foundation of faith? We gain just this: that we forsake an incomprehensible doctrine, which rests upon the word of God, for one equally incomprehensible which rests upon the word of man. Religion, to be a relation between God and man at all, must rest on belief in the Infinite, and also on a belief in the Finite; for if we deny the first, there is no God; and if we deny the second, there is no Man. But the coexistence of the Infinite and the Finite, in any manner whatever, is inconceivable by reason; and the only ground that can be taken for accepting one representation of it, rather than another, is that one is revealed, and another is not revealed.[32]

32. *Ibid.*, pp. 128f.

In a word, the knowledge of God depends exclusively on revelation. A 'religion within the limits of pure reason' is a figment. Mansel allows, however, that reason, although fallible, is not worthless in this realm. Where no revelation has been given it is man's only guide; and where one exists—real or supposed—it still may sift the evidences on which it rests, its role being to expose the pretences of a false revelation and aid in the interpretation of a true one. But a revelation attested by sufficient evidence is always superior to reason and is entitled to correct the errors to which reason is liable.

The forms, Mansel thinks, in which a revelation may be conveyed are of two kinds, 'presentative' and 'representative'. The one implies that man has the capacity to receive it and the capability of constructing a *science* of the divine, which he in fact has not. A 'representative' revelation, on the other hand, imparts knowledge through symbols relating to human experience. That it should be more or less anthropomorphic in character does not trouble him. On the contrary, he boldly defends anthropomorphism and derides the 'morbid horror' which the philosophers have of it. 'Fools, to dream that man can escape from himself, that human reason can draw aught but a human portrait of God! They do but substitute a marred and mutilated humanity for one exalted and entire.'[33]

When, however, he comes to discuss the actual content of revelation Mansel's radicalism is suddenly transformed into the strictest conservatism. Revealed truth is in the Bible and nowhere else. And the truth of the Bible is accepted by us on external evidences. The 'crying evil' of the present day in religious controversy is the neglect or contempt of these, and the first step towards the establishment of a sound religious philosophy would be their restoration to a fitting place in the theological system.[34] Evidences of a merely internal kind, though not without value of a sort, are, as regards the divine origin of the Christian religion, purely negative. They may in certain instances indicate that a religion has *not* come from God, but in no case are they sufficient to prove that it has. 'Where the doctrine is beyond the power of human reason to discover, it can be accepted only as resting on the authority of the teacher who proclaimed it; and that authority must then be guaranteed by the external evidence of superhuman mission.'[35] The external evidences in question are of course the usual ones of prophecy and miracle, to which may be added the fact of the rise and progress of Christianity in history. In face of them the only question to be decided is whether one is or is not prepared to affirm that Jesus of Nazareth was an impostor, an enthusiast or merely a mythical invention. Indeed, Mansel insists that there can be no compromise or qualification here. The choice is all or nothing; the Christian religion cannot be taken up piecemeal. Admit a single objection and the whole is discredited, since an objection which proves anything proves everything.

> If the teaching of Christ is in any one thing not the teaching of God, it is in all things the teaching of men: its doctrines are subject to all the imperfections inseparable from

33. *Ibid.*, p. 12.
34. *Ibid.*, p. 165.
35. *Ibid.*, p. 155.

man's sinfulness and ignorance: its effects must be such as can fully be accounted for as the result of man's wisdom, with all its weakness and error.

To criticize Christ's teaching in any particular, therefore, is both impious and futile. Even those features of the Old Testament revelation which many Christians have found morally objectionable must be accepted. A revelation, no doubt, which men do consider of questionable morality may not in fact be of divine origin at all, but the moral difficulty does not in itself disprove it, for human morality is a relative not an absolute valuation. In any case he who imposed the moral law—as man understands it—may also suspend it. Here once more religious knowledge must recognize its limits. In his moral attributes no less than in the rest of his infinite being God's judgments are unsearchable and his ways past finding out. All faith can do is confront this truth and submit humbly and gratefully to the authority whence alone the knowledge of salvation is to be had.

The meaning of revelation

There is no denying the brilliance of Mansel's venture. To many it seemed the final answer to all rationalist attacks on Christianity. Moreover, to reread the book today is to encounter a remarkable anticipation of some recent developments in theological thought. Here already is the denial of metaphysics and metaphysical theology on the ground that what lies outside human experience cannot be humanly described; the contention, accordingly, that religious language is and must be anthropomorphic in expression and symbolic in function; the assertion that there is no knowledge of God apart from the exclusive revelation which he himself has vouchsafed to man in Christ; the claim that Scripture is beyond criticism in terms of merely human philosophy. It is an argument that draws its force from its very extremism. Christianity is all or it is nothing. It is wholly true or else wholly false. It must be accepted or rejected *in toto*.[36] Further, the argument at least appears to reduce the knowledge of God to a series of propositions, instructive, useful, indeed true and necessary for their practical purpose, but in themselves incapable of drawing aside the veil which must ever hide the divine from human sight. Again, although the sticklers for orthodoxy may have rejoiced over them, are not the Manselian principles really a solvent of all theology, as Herbert Spencer maintained? The Cambridge theologian, F. J. A. Hort, certainly saw no reason for rejoicing. Mansel, he wrote,

> holds the doctrine of universal nescience more consciously and clearly than I suppose any other Englishman; a just Nemesis on Butler's probabilities! ... (What a very

---

36. W. R. Matthews recalls a sentence in Hobbes's *Leviathan* (ch. 32) which says the same thing in words characteristically homely and blunt: 'It is with the mysteries of our religion as with some wholesome pills for the sick, which, swallowed whole, have the virtue to cure, but chewed are for the most part cast up again without effect.' See *The Religious Philosophy of Dean Mansel* (1956), p. 18.

juiceless and indigestible morsel it must be to its orthodox admirers. It is clear, vigorous, and not often unfair; only a big lie from beginning to end.)[37]

It was, however, Maurice to whom Mansel's arguments gave greatest provocation.[38] His indignation overflowed. Mansel, it seemed to him, had substituted religion and even mere theology for God. On the Bampton lecturer's showing the believer could never know God as a reality; he could only know *about* him, in the shape of such limited, 'regulative' truths as have been providentially disclosed. God himself is unknown, and virtually unknowable. Thus faith is to be sited only on the void of agnosticism. It was to this effect that he replied, with such confused vehemence, in *What is Revelation?* (1859). Confused indeed the book is. Never skilful in purely literary artifice, Maurice here let his anger get the better of his judgment. The very form of the work—a collection of sermons on the Epiphany (in themselves quite admirable), *plus*, for the larger part of it, a series of involved and tedious 'Letters to a student of Theology'—presented a depressing contrast to the shapeliness and elegance of Mansel's treatise. The tone of it is often clumsily sarcastic, whilst the device of representing himself, a professional theologian after all, as only a plain man 'roughing it in the world' and confronting as best he can—like the supposititious neophyte whom he addresses—the subtle equivocations of this Oxford schoolman was a controversial trick of dubious honesty. Even Maurice's staunchest defenders are driven to admit that *What is Revelation?* could scarcely have offered a worse account of its author's case. For Maurice assuredly had a case. Mansel's thesis not only ran clean contrary to some of his deepest convictions; it appeared superficial, sophistical and lacking in the spirit of genuine religion. For divine revelation was not a matter of propositions or forms of words merely, but of the unveiling, as it were, of a *person*—'and that Person the ground and Archetype of men, the source of all Life and goodness in men—not to the eye but to the very man himself, to the Conscience, Heart, Will, Reason, which God has created to know Him, and be like Him'. Maurice goes on:

> Now if this idea of Revelation has been changed for another that is wholly unlike it—if by Revelation *we* understand certain communications made to us by God, and which we cannot dispense with, because the very constitution which he has given us makes us incapable of knowing Him as He is, because by no possibility can there be an unveiling or disclosure of His own nature, or character, or purposes to us, the whole subject must be contemplated by us, and must be presented to others, in an aspect which it never assumes in St Paul's writings and discourses, or in any part of the Old and New Testament. So that we are in the strange predicament of men fighting with prodigious zeal and prowess on behalf of the authority of books which, the moment we take them from their shelves and examine their contents, are found to set at nought the hypothesis upon which we have rested our apology for them. In

---

37. A. F. Hort, *The Life and Letters of F. J. A. Hort*, i, pp. 398 and 402.
38. J. S. Mill also was somewhat scandalized by Mansel's a-moral biblicism, which drew from him, in his *Examination of Sir William Hamilton's Philosophy*, the famous comment: 'I will call no being good who is not what *I* mean when I apply that epithet to my fellow-creatures, and if such a being can sentence me to hell for not so calling him, to hell I will go.'

establishing the necessity for a Revelation, we have done what we can to confute the Revelation of which these books testify.[39]

Maurice's position is that if Mansel is right then the Bible is a deception; for the latter speaks in terms of persons not propositions, living examples, not regulative principles. Take, says Mansel, the doctrine of the incarnation, which is absolutely central to Christianity. 'We believe that Christ is both God and Man, for that is revealed to us. We know not how He is so, for this is not revealed, and we can learn it in no other way.' Maurice's comment is that no attempt is made by the lecturer to present the doctrine as an interpretation of Christ in his *impact upon men*. Rather is it 'an additional, a hard, an insoluble difficulty, which we must receive in addition to all other difficulties, because God commands us in His book to receive it. We are left by this amazing revelation—that He who was the express Image of the Father, was made man and dwelt among us—just where we were before'.[40] Mansel drew, moreover, the conventional distinction between natural and revealed religion, Christianity, the revealed religion, being as it were superimposed upon the former. Maurice could not allow this. Natural reason and revelation are not, he held, two diverse ways of acquiring knowledge of God. On the contrary, all that men can possibly know of God comes from him and thus must be thought of as revealed. Scripture, he contended, assumes it to be the normal condition of man that he should receive communications from God. Indeed according to biblical teaching man could not be what he is if God did not hold converse with him—a fact which distinguishes him from all other creatures. St Paul certainly did not say that whereas the Jews had received a revelation the Gentiles were without one, for he expressly maintains that God did reveal his own righteousness in the conscience of the Gentile and that the sin of those who worshipped the creature more than the Creator consisted in their 'not *liking* to retain God in their knowledge'.[41] Maurice—although he does not use the terms—does distinguish between general and particular modes of revelation. The divine is revealed through nature, through the life of man and through the incarnation. But revelation under whatever mode points always to the centre. First, God speaks in what is most distant from him, in the mere things that he has formed; then in the human beings created by him to rule over these things; and finally, in him 'who by the eternal law is the inheritor of all things, in whom and for whom they were created'. Always it is the disclosure of the inmost personality of God which has constituted the goal of the whole process. To represent revelation therefore as only an imparting of propositions that can be used but never really understood is to travesty the divine action. Mansel was concerned with a system of theology, whereas Maurice detested all such systems, regarding them as a barrier not a bridge between man and God. The Bampton lecturer was meeting rationalism with rationalism and denying the inherent possibilities of faith. The theologian's proper task is not to construct a watertight intellectual scheme but to proclaim God's self-manifestation in Christ.

39. *What is Revelation?*, pp. 54f.
40. *Ibid.*, pp. 220f.
41. *Sermons preached in Lincoln's Inn Chapel*, i, p. 125.

He comes with this Gospel to mankind. So far as he is asserting, he is a dogmatist. But he does not rest his assertion upon his own judgment or upon the judgment of ages; he addresses it to the conscience, heart, reason of mankind. He leaves God to justify it in His own way, by the sorrows, needs, sins, contradictions of men. He desires only that the news should go forth with no force but its own. He can trust who had promised His Spirit of Truth to guide us into all Truth. Dogmatism and Rationalism cannot be reconciled in words; the verbal middle between them is feebler than either, destructive of what is good in both. Here is the living, real, uniting Mean between them … God declaring Himself to His creatures in a Man, that the creature may rise to a full knowledge of Him.[42]

Mansel countered Maurice's strictures in a characteristically skilful *Examination* of them, to which Maurice in turn retorted in a *Sequel to the Inquiry, What is Revelation?* This restates his position in a more moderate way, but without showing any clearer understanding of what Mansel was about. For the trouble with *What is Revelation?*, quite apart from its misjudged form and ill-tempered expression, is its evident incomprehension of the problem which *The Limits of Religious Thought Examined* was trying to tackle. Maurice had all the prophet's sense of the 'immediacy' of the divine in human life. God, he was convinced, *can* be known, because all life testifies to the fact. The whole idea of a *Deus absconditus*, concealed rather than revealed by a set of theological propositions which man has to adapt as best he may to the purposes of living—for such basically was Maurice's reading of Mansel's book—was one which seemed to him to evacuate religion of any real significance. For religion concerns facts, not doctrines. Thus he writes:

If the doctrine of the Atonement was not false as a doctrine, as an opinion, there must have been an actual Reconciliation between God and His creatures in the person of His Son. If the doctrine of the Incarnation was not false as a doctrine, the Eternal Son must have actually come forth from the Eternal Father, and have taken human flesh, and have dwelt among men; the nature and glory of the Eternal God must have come forth in the man, so that He could say, '*He that hath seen me hath seen the Father*'. You and I had to determine whether, *in this sense*, we could receive the Incarnation and Atonement—whether, *in this sense*, we could proclaim them to men. For if we called on any human being to receive them as doctrines, and yet did not set them forth as facts, it seemed that we were committing a huge injustice to our fellows, deceiving our own selves, violating the trust we had received from God.[43]

Mansel himself was strongly opposed to the idea of theology as a purely speculative system, but felt it necessary to examine the question of religious knowledge viewed simply as such. This was an inquiry which did not at all interest Maurice and for which he saw no need. It was an instance of the plain man's impatience with the philosopher, when the latter deliberately raises doubts about what the former supposes is self-evidently true. But because the Bible does not envisage any philosophical question as to *how* God can be known or what kind of propositions, logically speaking, they are in which man's thought about God is cast, it does not follow that the inquiry is misguided and useless. Maurice did not

42. *What is Revelation?*, pp. 232f.
43. *Ibid.*, p. 235.

get to grips with Mansel's arguments in that he did not understand the principles on which they were advanced. Failing this, he could only trounce their author for his culpable wrong-headedness. As has been amusingly said: 'The controversy resembles what one might imagine to have taken place had a discussion ever happened between Aristotle and one of the Minor Prophets.'[44] But the issue between them remains perhaps the most important that the theologian has to face and in our own day has become the centre of debate.

Broad Church tendencies: Milman, Stanley and Mark Pattison

A distinguished contemporary of Maurice's, who also belonged to no party or school but whose scholarship was among the best the Church of England produced in his generation, was Henry Hunt Milman, dean of St Paul's from 1849 until his death in 1868, when he was succeeded there by Mansel.[45] Chronologically—he was born in 1791—as in outlook, he could be classed with the Oriel Noetics. Yet he was not connected with them and neither Whately nor Hampden was a man after his own heart. His interest was in history, to the study of which he brought a critical spirit and a signal literary gift. His Bampton lectures of 1827, on *The Character and Conduct of the Apostles considered as Evidence of Christianity*, were conventional enough and drew no special comment, but his *History of the Jews*, published a couple of years later in three small volumes in 'The Family Library' series, was quite a bombshell. *The Dictionary of National Biography* even calls it 'epoch-making', although denying it any 'extraordinary merit'. Milman, of course, was no great historian by German standards and his work cannot in learning and scientific thoroughness be compared with that of Ewald. But unlike most English clergymen of the time he was well aware of what the German scholars were doing and his own book had, in the circumstances, the virtue of novelty. His approach to his subject was detached, with no overt design either to edify his readers or to defend traditional views. The Hebrews are regarded as one among the many ancient peoples and hence to be studied by the same methods of research as they. Certainly no Old Testament history was to be exempt from the principles of criticism, which could be shown to yield results in this field as justifiable as in any other. But what afterwards was to become commonplace to all students of the biblical records was looked on in those early days almost as a profanity. To the vast majority of churchmen the Old Testament carried supernatural credentials which placed it beyond criticism. Milman, however, was dubious of much biblical supernaturalism and entertained the possibility of naturalistic explanations, for instance the pestilential wind which he suggested as the cause of the destruction of Sennacherib's army, or the inflammable bituminous soil which could have burned Sodom and

---

44. Matthews, *op. cit.*, p. 18.
45. Tulloch went so far as as to say that 'in combination of pure genius with learning, of sweep of thought with picturesque and powerful variety of literary culture and expression, he has always seemed to me by far the first of modern English churchmen' (*op. cit.*, p. 80).

Gomorrah. Hardly less offensive to traditional sentiment was his use of expressions like 'Eastern sheik' or 'Emir' in reference to Abraham, or his 'frank' characterizations of other Hebrew worthies. Archbishop Ussher's chronology was entirely discarded. 'All kinds of numbers are uncertain in ancient MSS, and have been subject to much greater corruption than any other part of the text.'[46] A good deal of the biblical language—the story in Joshua of the sun standing still was cited in point—is poetical, not literally factual.

The History of the Jews was a pioneer work in this country and its aim was popular. But it was bitterly attacked as rationalistic and 'German' and likely to undermine the authority of Scripture. The publishers took fright and suspended further issue of the book. Milman hit back, but he had no zest for controversy and (it is said) came in the end to wish that the Jews were with the Egyptians at the bottom of the Red Sea.[47] He insisted that he was saying nothing which had not been said before by persons whose views were considered unimpeachable. 'If', he declared, 'I am driven to it I will show them'—his critics—'whence I have derived my notion of the miracles, but where precisely the same explanations are to be found—in Bishop Mant and Dr D'Oyley's *Bible*—and if I am forced I will print them in parallel columns.'[48]

The value of Milman's history lies in its imaginative feeling for its subject. He sought to depict the figures of the Old Testament as true flesh and blood and in authentic life-situations. But contemporary piety was not prepared for such an exercise in realism. Milman was not at all a rationalist. He was simply protesting against lifeless conventionalism in dealing with the scriptures, together with the habit of treating them as a mere repository of sacred 'texts'; and he judged that the historian was well equipped to help distinguish what is essential in religion from what is no more than local and temporary. His best work, however, came later: first, an edition of Gibbon's *Decline and Fall* (1838–39), and then a *Life* of the master-historian which indicated the direction the author's own studies were taking. A *History of Christianity from the Birth of Christ to the Abolition of Paganism in the Roman Empire* followed in 1840. Here Milman was on safer ground. Protestant susceptibilities were not hurt by disclosure of the sometimes all too human instruments by which ancient Christendom had been built up. At least only Tractarians took umbrage. But the crowning achievement of his career was his *History of Latin Christianity* (1854–55), his most ambitious undertaking and one in which the influence of Gibbon is apparent. Yet Milman's work, although treating of the same great theme, is entirely different from the older historian's. His concern is not with the decline of a secular empire but with the rise of a spiritual one; whilst it scarcely needs remarking that for all his talent as a writer he was manifestly not a second Gibbon. Yet the fact that a comparison of the nineteenth-century history with that bequeathed by the eighteenth is by no means inappropriate is itself testimony to what Milman achieved. It is not too much to say that in this book

46. See the Preface to the edition of 1863.
47. Quoted in Smiles's *Memoirs of John Murray*, ii, p. 301.
48. *Ibid.*, p. 300. Mant was bishop of Killaloe and a Bampton lecturer (1812). Both he and Archdeacon D'Oyley were High Churchmen.

historical scholarship in the Church of England proved its maturity.

But the typical Broad Churchman of the period is Arthur Penrhyn Stanley (1815–81), for many years dean of Westminster and still perhaps the most notable in the succession of occupants of that office. His purpose, like that of Thomas Arnold, whose pupil and biographer he was—his *Life* of Arnold appeared in 1844—was 'the enlargement of the Church', a phrase used at his installation at Westminster in 1864. The establishment he valued as the foundation of a national Christianity, and he sought to make of the Abbey church itself a symbol of the comprehensiveness he desired. Among those invited by him to speak there were Max Müller, a layman, and Principals Caird and Tulloch, both of them ministers of the Church of Scotland. Keble, Pusey and Liddon were also asked, but the latter alone could bring himself to accept, and then only after considerable hesitation. In Convocation Stanley opposed the continued public use of the Athanasian Creed, favoured a relaxation of the terms of clerical subscription, and hurried to the defence of *Essays and Reviews*, and even of Bishop Colenso. But he also spoke up on behalf of ritualist clergymen who were either being prosecuted at law or having their church services broken up by protesting mobs. He conspicuously had the courage of his broad convictions, whatever criticism their expression might bring down on him, as when he invited a Unitarian, Dr Vance Smith, to holy communion in the Abbey. That he was in any way a theologian of depth or penetration can hardly, however, be claimed and his high-minded innocency sometimes verged on the naïve. But like Milman he possessed a lively historical imagination, even if accuracy was apt to elude him. His *Commentary on St Paul's Epistles to the Corinthians*, published in 1855, is readable enough, but even in its own day was scarcely a handbook for the serious student. He was better at popular history, as in his lectures on the history of the Eastern Church (1861)—still worth perusal—or on that of the Jewish Church (1863–65), or historical travelogues such as *Sinai and Palestine* (1856). All these books have a certain charm, 'period' though it now is. Their chief fault is an excess of colour, a too florid eloquence.

Stanley's most permanently valuable literary enterprise remains the *Life* of Arnold, upon which he spent two years of unremitting toil. Happily Arnold was no more complex a character than his biographer; had he been the latter might well have found the task beyond him. But with the revered headmaster of Rugby he was on ground he knew: Arnold's opinions and interests were very largely his own also. And he avoided—what the biographer of Dr Pusey flagrantly did not—a superfluity of detail.

One last figure stands to be noticed here, a man of very different character from the large-hearted dean, namely Mark Pattison (1813–84), rector of Lincoln College, Oxford, from 1861 until his death. Oxford, or England, had at the time few men of equal learning. Indeed so absorbed in learning was he that in the event he published little. To know everything that could be known, *totum scibile*, seems to have been his ruling passion, a kind of mystical experience.[49] But apart from his

49. See J. Sparrow, *Mark Pattison and the Idea of a University* (1967). On Pattison's rectorship at Lincoln College, Oxford, see V. H. H. Green, *Oxford Common Room* (1957), pp. 203–216.

eccentricity of temperament—at the age of thirty-eight, when disappointed at not gaining the headship of his college, he turned himself into a misanthropic recluse ('A blank, dumb despair filled me; a chronic heartache took possession of me, perceptible even through sleep')—he is best remembered for his work on Isaac Casaubon (1875), in which his knowledge of Renaissance humanism had full display. His single but remarkable contribution to theological debate—he was essentially a scholar and critic, not a theologian—was his paper in *Essays and Reviews* entitled 'Tendencies of religious thought in England, 1688–1750', outstanding among the chapters in that volume.[50] As an inquiry into the nature of deism—the causes which led to its rise, as afterwards to its decay—it remains as good as anything that has ever been written on the subject. Upon the truth of the issues under discussion the author himself evinces no opinion; he is wholly detached and dispassionate. His role is that of a historian of ideas, in which field of study he was a pioneer. Had he been a more prolific as well as fastidious writer he would have been among the pre-eminent in this type of scholarship. He treats of his chosen period—his essay has little to do with the matters generally dealt with in the volume—with insight and candour. 'We have not yet learned, in this country', he declared, 'to write our ecclesiastical history on any better footing than that of praising up the party, in or out of the Church, to which we happen to belong.'[51] From being in his earlier years a warm sympathizer with Tractarianism he had become its bitter critic, looking on it as the incarnation of sectarian partisanship.[52] The principle of continuity had to be recognized: the present is what the past has made it. The whole process must be seen as a living thing, and when the history of theology is so studied it will cease to be 'an unmeaning frostwork of dogma, out of all relation to the actual history of man'. Let the Church of England, then, beware and avoid the petrifaction that has overtaken Rome. Mere defensiveness, moreover, will not suffice.[53] Advocacy belongs to the law court and should be rigorously eschewed by the theologian. 'If theological argument forgets the judge and assumes the advocate, or betrays the least bias to one side, the conclusion is valueless, the principle of free inquiry has been violated.' The eighteenth century marked the beginning of a period of theological reconstruction, and its appeal to reason was altogether needful and salutary. Its defect 'was not in having too much good sense, but in having nothing besides'. Yet it did try to relate theology to life. 'The endeavour of the moralists and divines of the period to rationalize religion was in fact an effort to preserve the practical principles of moral and religious conduct for society.' Pattison's judgment upon the age of reason is ambiguous. He

50. See below, ch. 10.
51. *Essays and Reviews*, p. 308.
52. Pattison describes himself as having been 'a declared Puseyite, and ultra-Puseyite', but as we have seen (p. 74 above), he came to regard the whole Tractarian movement as a disastrous episode in the intellectual life of the university of which its leaders were all prominent members. 'For so long it had been given over to discussions unprofitable in themselves, and which had entirely diverted our thoughts from the true business of the place. ... From that moment dates the regeneration of the University' (*Memoir*, pp. 263ff). But his personal admiration of Newman never waned.
53. 'Theological study is still the study of topics of defence' (p. 364).

182

at once praises and blames; the century did its best to stay the rot of belief by the methods which it understood, yet theology, in the true sense of the word, 'had almost died out when it received a new impulse and a new direction from Coleridge'. The 'evidence-makers' ceased from their futile labours all at once, and Englishmen heard with as much surprise as if the doctrine were new that the Christian faith is 'the perfection of human intelligence'; whereas the eighteenth-century divines and their contemporary opponents alike assumed that 'a man's religious belief is a result which issues at the end of an intellectual process'.

The moral for his own age, Mark Pattison would have inferred, was to learn the method of a new apologetic, certainly needed, from the failures of the previous century. What the principles of this new apologetic should be are left vague, and his observations, acute as they often are, remain largely negative. In this the essay is characteristic of its author, who, although he continued to perform clerical duties, had by middle age become virtually an agnostic. Besides, tart criticism and detraction were temperamentally congenial to him, as is obvious from the *Memoir* published in 1884. Thus he pronounces the Victorian clergy to be in general 'professional quacks trading in beliefs they do not share'. That his true place is with the 'honest doubters' of his age might nevertheless be difficult to maintain in view of his own retention of the clerical office long after he had given up any positive faith. Stricter honesty and rather less care for status and emoluments would surely have led him to follow the course of men like Leslie Stephen and Henry Sidgwick. George Eliot's alleged portrait of him in *Middlemarch* is a refinement of cruelty which he himself, strangely enough for one so morbidly sensitive, appears not to have felt. But, unattractive as he may have been as a man, he had courage and foresight enough to urge, at a time when university reform had become a public cause, that the real purpose of a university is to provide neither professional qualifications nor social advantage, but to train men in the knowledge of themselves and of the world.

Chapter 8

THE EROSION OF BELIEF

An epoch of change

Those aspects of nineteenth-century religious thought which we have considered so far all lay within the bounds of Christian orthodoxy. The liberal-minded may have pleaded for a less mechanical and rigid doctrine of biblical inspiration, deplored a too close insistence on traditional formularies or the niceties of dogma, and wished for the most part to put an end to the strife of ecclesiastical parties. But on the fundamentals of belief and the authority of both Scripture and Church they were staunch, however short they may have come of the more exacting standards required by Tractarians and old-style Evangelicals alike. Yet although English Christianity during the first half of the century was still largely immune from continental influences and showed little capacity of its own to strike out on new intellectual paths, it none the less was beginning to feel the mounting pressure of criticism from more than one quarter and along more than one line. No doubt educated public opinion still remained solidly Christian and predominantly Anglican, but voices were to be heard challenging the long-cherished assumptions with more and more assurance.

Scornful and openly defiant was, of course, the Utilitarian school of Bentham and James Mill. Critical too, though with some measure of sympathy, which indeed ripened with the years, was Mill's son, John Stuart. But there was another group—although the use of the word must not suggest cohesion or even a general agreement in outlook—consisting of a number of 'free-thinking' Christians, as well as sceptics and agnostics: Charles and Sara Hennell, and Hennell's brother-in-law, Charles Bray; R. W. Mackay, author of *The Progress of the Intellect*; Mary Ann Evans—the novelist George Eliot, as she afterwards called herself—and G. H. Lewes; John Henry Newman's brother, Francis; J. A. Froude, a one-time Tractarian; and A. H. Clough, the poet. At a somewhat later date—his *First Principles* appeared in 1862—Herbert Spencer could be listed among them also. Consideration of Spencer, an important figure in his day, even if posterity has long since deprived his reputation of its former gravity, we must defer to a subsequent chapter, but some notice of the rest, a rather motley company, will be in place here, preliminary to a discussion of John Stuart Mill and the Utilitarians. But first we must endeavour to take account of the chief reasons which from 1840 onwards led to a bolder and more persistent questioning of official religion as represented by both the established Church and the dissenting bodies.

What, perhaps, more than anything else contributed to a growing uneasiness about the tenability of Christian belief was an awareness that the Bible, fount and monument of 'saving truth', might no longer possess the authority once unhesitatingly conceded to it. Precise knowledge of the methods and results of biblical criticism was uncommon enough in this country at the time, even among theologians; but it was becoming more widely realized that the customary view of inspiration, according to which every statement in Scripture is divinely guaranteed truth, could not be maintained in face of enlarging knowledge, both scientific and historical. But if the Bible were at fault on a few ascertainable points, might it not be wrong on many others? Could it be relied upon at all? Such questions were the more disconcerting in that English Christianity since the Reformation had been absolutely explicit in its appeal to Scripture as the sole authority in matters of faith. Some there were—Coleridge had been among the earliest—who were convinced that the authority of Holy Writ is not impaired so long as the nature of the inspiration rightly attributed to it is properly understood. More saw the only alternatives as lying either in retention of the old idea regardless of the objections brought against it, or else in rejection of the Bible altogether if the reason for accepting it has to be sought in a doctrine now manifestly incredible. Some, it might be, allowed to Scripture a relative degree of inspiration, but denied it as the ground of a specific system of revealed doctrine. A particular difficulty was the problem of miracles. Christianity was supposed to be based on their truth, but if they could no longer be believed in religion became a purely natural phenomenon the expansion and development of which could be explained in terms of ordinary historical processes. This had been the argument of David Friedrich Strauss, whose *Leben Jesu* (1835–36) appeared in George Eliot's English version in 1846. The question that had moved Strauss to take up his task was whether the gospel history is 'true and reliable as a whole, and in its details', or not so. His conclusion was that historically the evangelical records are not reliable, although he himself insisted that the essence of Christian faith is independent of historical criticism, however negative. Strauss's book was avidly read in this country, but public opinion was very little prepared for what it contained. Its effect was to astonish and disturb.

Even apart from the biblical issue unsophisticated belief was bound to be shaken by new knowledge in science. What this involved we shall have to look at more closely later. It is sufficient to remark here that a secular account of the world and the life of humanity within it was now juxtaposed to the immemorial teachings of a religion disputed hitherto only by the impious. The early nineteenth century, so placid-seeming to us today, was in fact an era of far-reaching change, intellectual as well as social and industrial. Such indeed was its momentum that the accustomed certainties, even for those who held on to them—still the great majority—had plainly ceased to be above the tidemark of doubt. The large-scale erosion of belief had begun.

Freethinkers

Charles Hennell (1809–50), whose book, *An Inquiry concerning the Origin of Christianity*, was published in 1838, was a Unitarian. He and his sister Sara, herself the author of a volume of *Thoughts in Aid of Faith*,[1] their brother-in-law Charles Bray, who had been brought up as a Methodist, and his wife, formed a little group of earnest and open-minded seekers after truth whose ideas and personal friendship strongly influenced the always impressionable George Eliot, undermining her allegiance to the orthodox Protestantism in which she had been nurtured. Hennell's *Inquiry* had no large circulation in England, but it was translated into German and gained the warm approval of Strauss himself, who contributed a preface for the German edition and whose own position has its analogue in Hennell's pages.[2] Hennell was by no means anti-Christian and even claimed that his work would promote a truer understanding of what Christianity really is. Thus in his preface he wrote that the Christian religion,

> regarded as a system of elevated thought and feeling will not be injured by being freed from those fables, and those views of local or temporary interest, which hung about its origin. It will, on the contrary, be placed on a surer basis; for it need no longer appeal for its support to the uncertain evidence of events which happened nearly two thousand years ago, a species of evidence necessarily attainable only by long and laborious research, impracticable to most men, and unsatisfactory and harassing even to those who have most means of pursuing it; but it will rest its claim on an evidence clearer, simpler, and always at hand—the thoughts and feelings of the human mind itself. Thus, whatever in it is really true and excellent, will meet with a ready attestation in every breast, and, in the improvement of the human mind, find an ever-increasing evidence.[3]

But Hennell's outlook is purely humanist and naturalistic, as becomes still plainer in his later work on *Christian Theism*. His philosophy entirely precludes miracle, and as a historian he sees in Jesus—of whom he speaks with much reverence—only a man whose actual personality and work were for the most part translated into legend by his followers and the generation that succeeded them.

> A true account [he says] of the life of Jesus Christ, and the spread of his religion, would be found to contain no deviation from the known laws of nature, nor to require, for their explanation, more than the operation of human motives and feelings, acted upon by the peculiar circumstances of the age and country whence the religion originated.

What is of particular interest today in view of recent discussion is the importance he attaches to Essenism as the immediate source of primitive Christianity. The book is the work of a mere amateur in its field, but in its grasp of the purpose and methods of criticism it is a landmark in the history of biblical study in this country.

Bray's *The Philosophy of Necessity* came out in 1845.[4] It was ambitiously

---

1. Mary Ann Evans was lavish in her praise of it, finding it 'quite unparalleled in the largeness and insight with which it estimates Christianity as an organized experience' (J. W. Cross, *The Life of George Eliot* (1884), ii, p. 258).
2 Hennell had not read Strauss, and knew very little about the progress of German biblical scholarship, a fact which makes the originality of his own book all the more striking.
3. *An Inquiry concerning the Origin of Christianity*, p. viii.
4. Its two volumes are subtitled 'The Law of Consequences as applicable to Mental, Moral, and Social Science'. A second, much revised, edition was published in 1861.

conceived as a *magnum opus*, a definitive statement of the views to which his reading and thinking over the years had inevitably led him. He relates in his autobiography how he had arrived at 'one Truth about which I was certain, viz., that no part of the Creation had been left to chance, or what is called freewill; that the laws of mind were equally fixed or determined with those of matter, and that all instinct in beasts, and calculation in man, required that they should be so fixed'. He had therefore set himself to build up a system of ethics 'in harmony with the established fact, that everything acted in accordance with its own nature, and that there was no freedom of choice beyond this'. The reading-matter which helped to shape his ideas almost certainly included Bentham's *Deontology*, James Mill's *Analysis of the Human Mind* and George Combe's *System of Phrenology*, with its notion that the whole of a man's potential character could be deduced from the conformation of his head. As the title of Bray's book implies, nature and human life are alike the expression of a universal necessity. A cause is simply an antecedent condition. God exists only as 'the all-pervading influence which maintains the connection between all antecedents and all consequents'. Moral responsibility hence becomes a figment. What, the author had asked himself, was virtue? 'Not that which is free, spontaneous, or uncaused, but that which does the greatest amount of good, or produces most happiness.' Conduct, however, should be governed by prudence; although how this rather than fecklessness can be pursued according to his system is left unexplained, man being only a mechanism.

A work of greater interest is *The Creed of Christendom: its Foundation and Superstructure*, by another Unitarian, William Rathbone Greg (1809–81), a philanthropist and a keen if somewhat detached student of current political and social problems. Published in 1851, it is a significant addition to what John Morley called the 'dissolvent literature' of the time. Here, as in Hennell's book, we have an attempt to account for the origin and growth of Christianity in terms more or less naturalistic. To start with, no theory of the verbal inspiration of Scripture can possibly hold; nor does Scripture provide the materials for a dogmatic system. It is in vain even to look to it for a special divine revelation. How indeed can the human mind compass what it does not itself conceive, or by what means distinguish a divine idea from a human? Jesus was certainly not unique in the sense the churches claim him to have been, but he was a great prophet, and the lamentable thing is that Christendom has been more intent on worshipping his person than in heeding his words. 'It has made his life barren, that his essence might be called divine.'[5] Miracle, of course, is inadmissible; in any case it could not authenticate doctrine and a religion based upon it must collapse. A further and serious difficulty for the modern mind is that of recovering the historic truth about Jesus. The gospels being in large part legend have little value as a record of events, while the apostles understood him only imperfectly and transmitted his teachings inaccurately. Had his original doctrine been in fact better preserved the Church would have spread more slowly than it did, since the very corruption of his teaching aided its reception. Apart then from Jesus's moral example—still shining, despite the inadequacies of tradition—what has Christianity to offer? Prayer, although it is the expression of

5. *The Creed of Christendom*, p.241.

a natural impulse, cannot alter God's will. A future life is something we may hope for but cannot prove, and our sense of freedom must be set against the background of universal law. The tone of Greg's work is consistently reverent, but its conclusions, as orthodox belief would have judged them, are entirely negative.

Another attack on 'miraculous' religion had been delivered the year previously by Robert William MacKay (1803–82), a man of considerable scholarship, in a lengthy publication entitled *The Progress of the Intellect as Exemplified in the Religious Development of the Greeks and Hebrews* (1850). For the ancient mind miracles were possible and even commonplace, in that it knew nothing of the order of nature as disclosed by modern science. Toward any rational conception of life the Hebrews made little progress, and their religious outlook must be appraised accordingly. But if the world we know is an embodiment of law why should we expect the unknown to be capricious and inexplicable? God today is revealed through the regular rather than the irregular, the predictable rather than the unpredictable. Miracle therefore has ceased to have any evidential value. But this is not mere loss. The progress of the intellect in matters of religion is away from superstition and towards a reasoned faith. This may and will exceed knowledge, but should always be subject to its control. MacKay's effort was not without use in its day as a contribution to the historical study of religious phenomena. It showed how the beliefs and practices of different religions often resemble one another and in course of time take on new forms. But the author's overall position could best be described as a Christian humanism in which the idea of God is scarcely more than the symbol of an ethical ideal; and as such George Eliot welcomed it in *The Westminster Review* of January 1851. A later book of MacKay's—it appeared in 1863[6]—was *The Tübingen School and its Antecedents: a Review of the History and Present Condition of Modern Theology*, in which he sought to acquaint a public much agitated by the *Essays and Reviews* controversy with the history and principles of scientific biblical criticism. It is well-informed and discerning in its assessment of the then recent developments in Germany, but offered no reassurance to the many who saw in criticism only an insidious move against the foundations of faith.

George Eliot and others

All these writers are today figures but dimly descried. George Eliot, by contrast, occupies a commanding place in Victorian literature and as a novelist enjoys now perhaps a greater prestige than any of her contemporaries. But her work in fiction is not our present concern. Her interest in religion, as in scientific questions, was lifelong, but she soon passed from the narrow Evangelicalism of her youth, through a phase of 'radical' Christianity, to agnosticism and positivism. At the age of twenty-three, and to her father's grief, she gave up church attendance as incompatible with her changed beliefs. The influence of the Hennells and Brays

---

6. *The Progress of the Intellect* had been followed in 1854 by *A Sketch of the Rise and Progress of Christianity*. In his personal philosophical outlook MacKay was a Kantian; but he was also a devoted student of Plato.

upon her was important, though she had also been a good deal affected by Isaac Taylor's *Ancient Christianity* (1839–40).[7] In 1844 she took over from a friend, Miss Brabant, the task of translating Strauss, a laborious business which kept her occupied for three years. But by the spring of 1846 the work was finished and in the following June published. She also applied herself to the study of Spinoza, a philosopher then still little known in England. Later, on moving to London, she became assistant to Johan Chapman as editor of *The Westminster*, and it was through Chapman that she met the positivist thinker, Herbert Spencer, with whom she formed a close friendship. Spencer it was who, in turn, introduced her to G. H. Lewes, her partner in life from 1854, when she accompanied him to Weimar, until his death twenty-four years later. In 1853 she gave up her editorial work and the year after brought out a translation of Feuerbach's *The Essence of Christianity*, the only book, as it happened, that she ever published under her own name. Her first venture in prose fiction, *Amos Barton*, was written in 1856 and published two years later, along with *Mr Gilfil's Love Story* and *Janet's Repentance*, as *Scenes of Clerical Life*, under the pen-name by which history knows her. Thereafter novel-writing became her life's work. But although she had by now completely abandoned Christianity her deep sympathy with and understanding of the religious sentiment remained. Years before she had written to Sara Hennell that

> agreement between intellects seems unattainable, and we turn to the *truth of feeling* as the only universal bond of union. We find that the intellectual errors which we once fancied were a mere incrustation, have grown into the living body, and we cannot in the majority of cases wrench them away without destroying vitality ...[8]

For with George Eliot head and heart, intellectual conviction and instinctive feeling, were divided. By intellectual conviction she realized that orthodox Christianity was a myth which in the modern world had been exploded. God was inconceivable, immortality incredible. Duty, however, was peremptory and absolute, and consisted in one's obligations to one's fellow-men.[9] 'I begin', she wrote to the Brays in January 1853, 'to feel for other people's wants and sorrows a little more than I used to do. Heaven help us! said the old religion; the new one, from its very lack of that faith, will teach us all the more to help one another'.[10] Humanity, not deity, was now the object of her conscientious devotion, faith giving way to love of the brethren, from whom no man was excluded. The supernatural had no place beside, still less above, the natural. The 'highest calling and election' was '*to do without opium, and*

---

7. Taylor had found the ascetic tendencies of early Christianity especially objectionable. Such 'artificial purity'—and here, he warned, the history of Romanism was eloquent witness—could only lead to 'a violent reaction, ending, as might have been foreseen, and as every convulsive moral struggle must, in a correspondent corruption as well of manners as of principles'.
8. Cross, *op. cit.*, i, p. 121.
9. See the well-known passage in F.W.H. Myer's *Essays—Modern* (1883), pp. 268f, describing a conversation the author had with the novelist in the Fellows' Garden at Trinity College, Cambridge. It was for him an unforgettable occasion. 'Never, perhaps,' he remarks, 'have sterner accents affirmed the sovereignty of impersonal and unrecompensing law.'
10. Cross, *op. cit.*, i, p. 302.

live through all our pain with conscious, clear-eyed endurance'.[11] Breadth of view, tolerance, intellectual integrity, with—of necessity—moral stoicism added, were the virtues of the life of modern man. 'I have faith in the working out of higher possibilities than the Catholic or any other Church has presented, and those who have strength to wait and endure are bound to accept no formula which their whole souls—their intellect as well as their emotions—do not embrace with entire reverence.'

Strauss, Feuerbach and latterly Auguste Comte had left indelible marks on George Eliot's mind. Yet she had no time for brash rationalism; not only were her affections too warm, even the eye of reason could not fail to discern the grounds for a more passionate assessment of the human condition than professed humanism was prone to allow for. Hence the emotional and indeed moral value of a faith which the informed intellect, for its part, could only disown.

> Pray don't ever ask me again [she wrote to a correspondent in 1862] to rob a man of his religious belief, as if you thought my mind tended to such robbery. I have too profound a conviction of the efficacy that lies in all sincere faith, and the spiritual blight that comes with no faith, to have any negative propagandism in me.
>
> In fact [she continued] I have very little sympathy with Freethinkers as a class, and have lost all interest in mere antagonism to religious doctrines. I care only to know, if possible, the lasting meaning that lies in all religious doctrine from the beginning till now.[12]

The significance of religion in the life of mankind could not be underrated, nor did the practice of religion, for all its superstitions, call for denunciation. Christianity was essentially a great moral idea, however tenuous its claim to historical authenticity. Thus she wrote of Renan's *Vie de Jésus* that it seemed to her that

> the soul of Christianity lies not at all in the facts of an individual life, but in the ideas of which that life was the meeting-point and the new starting-point. We can never have a satisfactory basis for the history of the man Jesus, but that negation does not affect the Idea of the Christ in its historical influence or its great symbolic meanings.[13]

George Henry Lewes (1817–78), the man with whom she spent her life in a morally dedicated union unacknowledged by church or law, was in temperament very different from herself. His self-confidence was boundless, his optimism unassailable. He exercised his versatile talent now as philosopher, biographer and man of science, now as dramatic critic, novelist and even actor. Pursuits so multiple suggest superficiality, possibly even charlatanism. That he was much less adept at some than at others is, however, in no way a denial of his signal abilities. His interest for us here arises from his role as a popularizer of Comtism, since he was one of the first in this country to master the positivist system. Comte's *Cours de philosophie positive* was completed in 1842, and Lewes, in his biographical history of philosophy (1845–46)—a still quite readable book—shows him as a convinced

11. *Ibid.*, ii, p. 283.
12. *Ibid.*, p. 343.
13. *Ibid.*, pp. 359f.

disciple and warm advocate of the new doctrines. His view of metaphysics is based on Comte's own *loi des trois états*, according to which human thought has passed through three stages of development: a theological or mythological; a metaphysical, in which spiritual entities are replaced as causal forces by abstract ideas; and a positive or scientific, in which the test of truth is empirical. 'For the first time in history', Lewes enthused, 'an explanation of the World, Society and Man is presented which is thoroughly in accordance with accurate knowledge.' Indeed 'a new era' had dawned, in which all knowledge would be formed into a homogeneous body of doctrine, 'capable of supplying a Faith and consequently a Polity'. Lewes stayed faithful to positivist principles all his life, and in *Comte's Philosophy of the Sciences* (1853) he gave himself single-mindedly to explaining the whole system. The last philosophical work published during his lifetime, *Problems of Life and Mind* (1874–79), revealed his ardour to be as fresh as ever. Even among his own countrymen the French thinker has never had a more dedicated follower.

To many minds the attraction of Comtism lay in its author's claim to have presented the world with 'a sound Philosophy, capable of supplying the foundation of a true Religion'. Not many of the Victorians were ready to dispense with religion altogether, even if they could not believe in it. Orthodoxy might be impossible, but a cold and calculating rationalism was no food for the sentiments. In the Religion of Humanity, on the other hand, the balance between intellect and feeling was redressed. The latter—the 'heart'—must, of course, have pride of place, but the former is its necessary coadjutor and an authority with rights of its own and an irremovable position in the scheme of things. It is noteworthy, therefore, that of Comte's apostles in England two of the most prominent were women. For next to George Eliot in this role was Harriet Martineau (1802–76), author of *The Positive Philosophy of Auguste Comte*, published in the same year, 1853, as Lewes's book. Sister of the well-known Unitarian leader, James Martineau, she was even more explicit in her admiration of the positivist doctrine than the great novelist herself. Her brother retained his loyalty to Christianity, but Harriet, recognizing, in her own choice phrases, 'the monstrous superstition in its true character of a great fact in the history of the human race', found herself at last 'a free rover on the broad, bright, breezy common of the universe'.[14] Miss Martineau was not, all the same, the pure intellect she liked to fancy herself, and her critical capacity—W.R. Greg described her as 'dogmatic', 'hasty' and 'imperious'—sometimes evaporated before one or other of the varying objects of her esteem. She was a prolific writer in many kinds—fiction, politics, economics and history, both ancient and contemporary. Perhaps the best of her efforts, apart from the industrious exposition of Comte, was her *Illustrations of Political Economy* (1832–34), tales depicting the main principles of the science as then understood. Earnest, sentimentalizing, intellectually muddled, she is in many respects a type-figure of her period, a casualty—not too serious, however—of the persistent mid-nineteenth century war of head and heart.

Another such personage, but one also who in historical retrospect is apt to gain stature, is Francis William Newman (1805–97), a brother of the cardinal and for many years professor of Latin at University College, London. Reared as a child

14. *Autobiography* (1877), i, p. 116.

in an atmosphere of evangelical piety, he, like John, moved away from it, but in an opposite direction. High Churchism never attracted him, and when his evangelical fervour abated—he was at one time powerfully influenced by J. N. Darby, the founder of the Plymouth Brethren—he turned, *via* Thomas Arnold, to a thoroughgoing liberalism. A description of his spiritual odyssey is contained in an apologia, *Phases of Faith*, published in 1850, long before his brother's celebrated work. He began by jettisoning outright the Calvinist doctrines of his youth, especially those of the fall, total depravity and eternal reprobation, as manifestly unscriptural. But could even the authority of Scripture be maintained once reason has started to press its objections? The Bible as traditionally read presented grave difficulties, and in the light of advancing knowledge the infallibilist claim had to be dismissed. 'It had', for example, 'become notorious to the public, that Geologists rejected the idea of a universal deluge as physically impossible.'[15] Arnold's advice was that such questions are not material to religious faith, but Newman was still too much of a biblicist himself to accept this very easily. The truth had though to be faced that the problems posed by the Bible were not only of a factual kind. More serious were the moral ones, and these were not confined entirely to the Old Testament. Could ethical values be substantiated by physical miracles like those which the New Testament alleges? Seemingly not; yet in Scripture morality and miracles go hand in hand. Once a doubt of the oracular authority of the Bible had made entry its further intrusion, it seemed, was not to be halted.

The conclusions, therefore, to which Newman found himself impelled were, first, that the moral and intellectual powers of man must be acknowledged as having a right and a duty to criticize the contents of Scripture; secondly, that when so exerted they condemn certain parts of the Bible as erroneous and immoral; and thirdly, that 'the essential infallibility of the entire Scripture is a proved falsity, not merely as to physiology and other scientific matters, but also as to morals'. The problem accordingly was how to discriminate the trustworthy from the untrustworthy within the limits of Scripture itself.[16] In his perplexity he turned to the German scholars, to Michaelis, de Wette and Neander, and discovered them fruitful. His way forward he now saw more clearly.[17] A vast amount of traditional Christianity might have to be shed, but he would still continue to think of himself as a Christian, critical indeed but in intention sincere. 'Those who believed that the apostles might err in human science, need not the less revere their moral and spiritual wisdom.'[18] The solution of the miracle problem, which he viewed as basically a moral not a scientific one, could also now be broached. Miracles, so-called, cannot be the prop of faith

---

15. *Phases of Faith*, p. 122.
16. *Ibid.*, pp. 110f.
17. In 1847 Newman published an Old Testament study, *A History of the Hebrew Monarchy*, in which he acknowledged his debt to de Wette, especially for his conception of the growth and development of the Hebrew religion; for once allow that there is progress in men's ideas about God then the moral difficulties which the more primitive parts of Scripture are bound to raise can be discounted by a higher understanding. The trouble which many faced in interpreting the Old Testament sprang from the dogmatic approach, required by assent to formularies like the Thirty-nine Articles.
18. *Phases of Faith*, p. 121.

and might well prove its destruction. God's goodness and veracity are not in any case to be demonstrated thus. In short, religion in its spiritual essence can and must be distinguished from its incredible or obsolete accompaniments. As soon as the principle of liberalism in Christianity is admitted, with reason and conscience supplying the criteria, all unnecessary burdens placed upon belief can be discarded. Considerations of history and literary composition are not of final relevance. A Christian who understands his faith loves it for its *inner truth* alone, his creed resting where 'new discoveries in geology and in ancient inscriptions' and 'improved criticism of texts and of history' will not overturn it.

For Francis Newman was a man of a genuinely religious temper, and it is this side of him—to call it devout is not to use too strong a word—which stands out impressively in his *The Soul, its Sorrows and Aspirations*, published in 1849.[19] The true religion, he tells us, is a religion of the spirit, not of forms and institutions. Its guiding light is personal intuition, not dogmas and definitions. By 'Soul' Newman evidently means something like Coleridge's 'Reason', the faculty for the discernment of spiritual truth. It is 'that side of human nature, upon which we are in contact with the Infinite, and God, the Infinite Personality: in the soul alone is it possible to know God'.[20] Its operation is direct, its apprehension immediate. 'Evidences', and the sort of inference based upon them, have nothing to do with it. History and literary criticism, like logic and metaphysics, no doubt have their place, for the understanding needs to be critical; but these things are not religion and no part of its fabric. Religion, first and last, is spiritual perception, not erudition or intellectual acumen.

> Those truths, and those only, are properly to be called Spiritual, the nature of which admits of their being directly discerned in the Soul, just as Moral truths in the Moral Sense: and *he* is a spiritual man, not who believes these at second-hand (which is a historical and dead faith), but who sees internally, and knows directly.[21]

It is through the Soul that we may know with certainty that God exists, that there is in the universe 'Mind', 'acting on some stupendous scale', though of course imperfectly understood by us. But our knowledge cannot be intellectually projected in any very satisfactory way because the language of religion is not and cannot be that of science. 'A system of Theology, constructed like a treatise on Mechanics, by fine-drawn reasoning from a few primitive axioms or experimental laws, is likely to be nothing but a sham science.'[22]

Although religious language is figurative or metaphorical not literal, this does not mean that it cannot convey truth. On the contrary, 'jealously to resist metaphor, does not testify to depth of insight'.[23] The difficulty with religious belief, the reason why in fact it has lost so much of its potency, is that it has made such inordinate

19. Subtitled 'An Essay towards the Natural History of the Soul as the True Basis of Theology'.
20. Preface to the first edition, p. v.
21. *Ibid*. The distinction is one which immediately recalls his brother's between a merely 'notional' and a 'real' assent.
22. *The Soul, its Sorrows and Aspirations*, p. 90.
23. *Ibid*., p. 94.

demands at the purely intellectual level, requiring assent to a mass of propositions that can neither be proved nor properly grasped. But the same goes, too, for the modern theologian, intent upon his ancient languages, his texts and his historical inquiries. 'Our misery has been that the men of thought have no religious enthusiasm, and the enthusiastically religious shrink from continuous searching thought.' Where, however, the writ of science runs faith may not encroach, although the truths of science and the truths of the soul are not in conflict. The great danger for English Christianity was bibliolatry, which 'does not consist in reverence to the Bible, however great, as long as Conscience is too dull to rise above the Bible'.[24] Such 'depressing' of conscience and the treating of 'inspired' words as 'premises for syllogisms', as 'ready-made weapons against heretics', as 'barriers against free-thought and feeling' were all too familiar. In any case three centuries of Protestantism had demonstrated that the letter would never of itself put an end to controversy nor bring enlarged wisdom or the recognition of goodness.

On the question of a future life Newman points out that all attempts at a rational proof of immortality have failed, from Plato onwards. But here again the mistake has been in confusing religion with science. The life hereafter is a religious belief, a conviction of the soul that its union with God will never be sundered, even by death. Christ's resurrection—which Newman himself, needless to say, does not believe in as a historical event—establishes nothing. It is an 'exceptional phenomenon' claimed by orthodox Christianity as a demonstration of Christ's uniqueness.

Francis Newman's position was an unusual one. He certainly was a liberal, yet to describe him as a liberal Protestant, as the expression came to be used, would be misleading. Liberal Protestantism has centred its belief on the historical figure of Jesus as the one supreme revelation of the divine. But for Newman Jesus had no special singularity. He denies his sinlessness and even accuses him of self-seeking in trying to make men believe in him regardless of their grounds for so doing,[25] whilst in his sometimes riddling answers to questions he practised a kind of deception. Jesus's teaching has, accordingly, no absolute authority, although Newman assures us that religion will not recover its 'pristine vigour' until it appeals to the soul 'as in apostolic days'. The fact that the New Testament is permeated with definite religious concepts seems not to have occurred to him. Basically his attitude was dictated by temperament. As his elder brother could not conceive a religion without forms, so he could not conceive one with them. Everything traditionary was 'earthy husk', in contrast with 'heavenly spirit', although the intellectual implications of his own type of religious affirmation he refrains from considering. Endowed with something of the sensitivity of the mystic, he was an out-and-out individualist, to the point, as his personal life shows, of eccentricity. Hence the difficulty of taking him altogether seriously. His sincerity is beyond question, but the long list of 'causes' which won his crusading zeal—women's suffrage, pacifism, penal reform, teetotalism, opposition to blood sports, anti-vivisection: he himself confessed to being 'anti-everything'—suggest the crank.

24. *Ibid.*, p. 42n.
25. *Ibid.*, p. 146.

He was also quite without humour. John all his life looked upon him distantly and disapprovingly, whereas Francis, in spite of his radical differences of temper and outlook, was by no means unappreciative of the great personal gifts of the elder brother 'with whose name all England'—the words are his own—'was resounding for praise or blame'; for even John was in his way 'struggling after truth, fighting for freedom in his own heart and mind, against Church articles and stagnancy of thought'. But if the future cardinal's attitude was cold and occasionally acidulous, Matthew Arnold's—disagreement with Newman had arisen over the right way to translate Homer[26]—was suavely contemptuous, adding to the air of absurdity from which Newman is now hardly dissociable. But this should not be allowed to obscure his real interest as a thinker.

However, the two classic instances of Victorian doubters agonizing over their doubts are James Anthony Froude (1818–94) and Arthur Hugh Clough. Froude was a younger brother of Hurrell Froude, Newman's closest friend in the early days of the Oxford Movement, and was always himself fascinated by the Tractarian leader's personality. His two novels, *Shadows of the Clouds* (1847) and *The Nemesis of Faith* (1849), feeble enough as fiction, are significant as documents of their age, the second especially so. *Shadows of the Clouds* is plainly autobiographical. Its hero, Edward Fowler, is Froude thinly disguised. Indoctrinated as a boy with the conventional orthodoxy of the day, maturity brings insistent questioning of all received beliefs and a period of spiritual desolation ensues. In the end, by much stoical self-discipline, Fowler is able to reconstruct his life on the two fundamental articles of God's providence and man's duty. If these are abandoned existence has no moral meaning. Conduct indeed is the one test of religious belief; but a multiplication of beliefs is an obstacle rather than a help to morality. The working out of the novel's plot is implausibly melodramatic, and much of the writing, particularly when the author—very obviously under the influence of Carlyle— projects his own sentiments, is turgid. *The Nemesis of Faith* is a better book, though here again the theme of a clergyman whose faith disintegrates has too many melodramatic accompaniments. Markham Sutherland is actually driven to the verge of suicide, but is persuaded by a Roman Catholic priest, identifiable as John Henry Newman, to enter the Church. The haven of an authoritarian religion, however, is only temporary: reason will out. Sutherland-Froude—for here also the autobiographical element is scarcely concealed—seems to have equated religion very largely with the instruction and practices of childhood and adolescence. Not unnaturally he found it wanting when challenged by experience. But the only apparent alternative to this limited creed is scepticism elevated by Carlylean prophecy. He who had first been impressed with the irrationality of religion when writing a life of St Neot for Newman's *Lives of the English Saints* thus came round in the end—after studying Spinoza[27]—to a deterministic philosophy for which moral failures were errors, not crimes, and an assurance that reason must always prevail over religious authority, be it Church or Bible. On its publication *The*

26. See Arnold's *On Translating Homer* (1861), and *On Translating Homer: Last Words* (1862), lectures which he delivered as professor of poetry at Oxford.
27. See the appended Note to this chapter.

Nemesis of Faith created something of a scandal and brought Froude's Oxford career to an abrupt close. Yet what exactly the 'nemesis' of faith is does not emerge with certainty. It could be the retribution which overtakes 'the unlucky man who as a child is taught even as a portion of his creed what his grown reason must forswear'.[28] Some, on the other hand, saw in it an indictment of freethought for its regrettable moral consequences. Froude's ambiguity on the point seems to have resulted from a division of his mind between nostalgic affection for the religious certainties of youth and loyalty to the rationalizing liberalism which now rendered these impossible. He was but one of many during the middle decades of the century who found themselves in a like predicament. He was more at home with his historical studies, in which he showed himself a doughty champion of the Reformation as against its High Church detractors. In this realm the antagonism of head and heart could be more easily mitigated.

Arthur Hugh Clough (1819-61) came under Tractarian influence at Oxford, confessing later that for two years he had been 'like a straw drawn up the draught of a chimney'.[29] W.G. Ward had been among his more intimate friends. Religious difficulties began to trouble him, however, and in 1848 he resigned his Oriel fellowship. He offered no public explanation of his scruples, but 'pure reverence for the inner light of the spirit' was a genuine element in his character. He might indeed be said to have carried scrupulosity to excess. His self-distrust was almost morbid.

> Even in like manner [he wrote], my own personal experience is most limited, perhaps even most delusive: what have I seen, what do I know? Nor is my personal judgment a thing which I feel any great satisfaction in trusting. My reasoning powers are weak; my memory doubtful and confused; my conscience, it may be, callous and vitiated.[30]

The supposedly solid ground of religious authority was manifestly not open to him. Yet what satisfaction could the relentless pursuit of mere reason give? To authenticate Christianity by appeals to its historical origins was too problematic. Intellectual perplexity caused Clough distress because, although a sceptic, he had in him a strong vein of religious feeling. Faith he could not arrive at, but dogmatic unbelief was an alternative he shrank from. Suspense of judgment might have to be the answer:

> 'Old things need not be therefore true,'
> O brother men, nor yet the new;
> Ah! still awhile the old thought retain,
> And yet consider it again!
>
> The souls of now two thousand years
> Have laid up here their toils and fears,
> And all the earnings of their pain,
> Ah, yet consider it again!

28. *The Nemesis of Faith*, p. 316.
29. *Poems and Prose Remains* (1869), i, p. 14.
30. *Ibid.*, i, p. 421.

> We! what do we see? each a space
> Of some few yards before his face;
> Does that the whole wide plain explain?
> Ah, yet consider it again!
>
> Alas! the great world goes its way,
> And takes its truth from each new day;
> They do not quit, nor can retain,
> Far less consider it again.

The age-old tradition of religion, widely interpreted—this at least was a fact, found indeed 'everywhere; but above all in our work; in life, in action, in submission, so far as action goes, in service, in experience, in patience, and in confidence'.[31] All things good, all things noble feed the human spirit; and to recognize this is, essentially, to understand the vital spirit of Christianity and of man. One ought not to try to swim against the stream. Nevertheless, Clough's attitude to Christian doctrine was negative. The actual state of Christianity denied its claim to dogmatic truth:

> Christ is not risen, no—
> He lies and moulders low;
> Christ is not risen!

Clough's nature was sensitive and reflective and with a marked tinge of melancholy. Spiritually the times were out of joint for him and the problem of faith haunts his verse continually. But although life might remain an enigma he was not without either humour or hopefulness. His 'Say not the struggle nought availeth' is too well known to need quotation here, but it is not an isolated utterance. Others in the same strain of tempered optimism could be cited, as:

> Let us look back on life; was any change,
> Any now blest expansion, but at first
> A pang, remorse-like, shot to the inmost seats
> Of moral being.[32]

Or

> And yet, when all is thought and said,
> The heart still overrules the head;
> Still what we hope we must believe,
> And what is given us receive;
> Must still believe, for still we hope
> That in a world of larger scope,
> What here is faithfully begun
> Will be completed, not undone.
> My child, we still must think, when we
> That ampler life together see,
> Some true result will yet appear
> Of what we are, together, here.[33]

31. *Ibid.*, p. 424.
32. *Dipsychus.*
33. *Through a Glass Darkly.*

197

This mood of mingled doubt and hope, of dejection and determination to put the best face on things pervades much Victorian poetry. Its most poignant expression is in Tennyson and Matthew Arnold; but Clough, far inferior as a poet to the one and less clear-headed as a thinker than the other, is perhaps more characteristic than either of the dilemma of their age.

John Stuart Mill

The intellectual standpoint most obviously antagonistic to the Christian tradition was, however, that of the Utilitarians, or Philosophical Radicals, as they have sometimes been called, and of whom John Stuart Mill (1806–72) was the most brilliant if not the most typical representative. There was in fact too much humanity in Mill for him ever to have been quite the embodiment of those rationalist principles of which professedly he was always the dedicated servant. The founder of the Utilitarian school had been Jeremy Bentham, whose ideas continued to be a guiding light for all its members. But although Bentham died in 1832 he was essentially a figure of the preceding century, and this same 'period' air pervades the work of his disciples, John Stuart Mill not excepted. In his lifetime his chief adherent and interpreter was Mill's dour father, James Mill (1773–1836), a man of powerful though rigid intellect, who in person was almost a caricature of the southerner's notion of the hardheaded Scot. Although at one time a minister of the Scottish Kirk, James Mill had developed for religion nothing but contempt and hostility, and saw to it that his son was brought up according to an educative regime from which religious influences were completely barred. 'I am', the latter wrote in his *Autobiography*, 'one of the very few examples in this country of one who has not thrown off religious belief, but never had it. I grew up in a negative state in regard to it.' The father's mind was not only prejudiced in the matter; on his own unwitting disclosure it was thoroughly ill-informed. All ages, he considered, have 'represented their gods as wicked in a constantly increasing progression', doing so, 'till they have reached the most perfect conception of wickedness which the human mind can desire, and have called this God, and prostrated themselves before it'. It was under the strict tutelage of a man holding such an opinion—the product in all likelihood merely of a jaundiced reaction from Calvinism—that the immensely impressionable John Stuart was nurtured and trained. Presumably his mother had no part in the process, for of her we never hear from him. The father's views, as such, need not detain us; but their effect on the man who in the middle years of the century was accounted the most important British philosopher of the age cannot be written off. John Stuart Mill's own lack of understanding of the religious temper and outlook evidently persisted to the end of his life, a conclusion which his three *Essays on Religion*, despite their somewhat stiff-lipped attempt at sympathy, do not mitigate.

The anti-religious character of Utilitarianism is not difficult to explain. Bentham, in whom an absolute aversion from religion was ingrained, set the tone in this as in other respects.[34] James Mill's animus against all religious ideas was partly at least a personal bias. So too was Grote's—Grote was Mill's pupil—if a little less overtly so. All of them disclose virtually no appreciation whatever of the religious sentiment as an expression of a human need and to look to any of them for a fair account of the Christianity of their day is idle, since their notion of its teaching never rises above a crude deism. Of religious belief as the projection and symbol, however tentative or partial, of a high moral ideal they have hardly an inkling. But personal prejudice aside, the whole interest and tenor of utilitarian thinking was opposed to religious aspirations. Its main concern was social reform, which, it was believed, could be brought about only on the basis of a scientific study of social relations. Knowledge in this sphere was expected to emulate, or at least to imitate, the successes of the physical sciences. The life of man could and should be examined as a matter of factual analysis. Religion, professing to deal with a transcendent world, offered nothing that could be scientifically investigated. It was therefore to be dismissed. Neither credal assertions about the unprovable nor worship directed to the unimaginable could any longer rightfully take the place of legislation and education as a means of human good, and indeed served only to impede its attainment. The Church was also resented and disliked as a nest of privilege and for the support it lent to an unjust and inefficient social order.[35] Fundamentally, however, it was the Utilitarian philosophy itself, as an anti-metaphysical empiricism, which was irreconcilable with religious belief. Without their being self-declared atheists the entire trend of the Utilitarians' thinking ran contrary to the primary assumptions of Christian theology. For although they were not materialists in the sense of the *philosophe* d'Holbach or, later, Ernst Haeckel, their values were materialistic in that their conception of human nature and knowledge left no room for what was usually termed the 'spiritual'. They at all events were deficient in imagination and mistaken in their assessment of the place of the emotions in human life, whilst their necessitarianism—'circumstances make the man'—appeared to exclude any real freedom of individual self-determination. Thus Utilitarianism was a soil in which religion could not thrive or even sprout. Nor, we might add, was it any more congenial to the arts. Its atmosphere was too desiccated, too narrowly rationalist. From the spirit of Coleridge, or of

34. Bentham was the author of a number of works—*Church-of-Englandism and its Catechism Explained* (1818), *Not Paul but Jesus* (1821), *The Analysis of the Influence of Natural Religion on the Temporal Happiness of Mankind* (1822) (this last in collaboration with George Grote)—directly attacking religion, either in substance or in its traditional forms.

35. Utilitarian ideas were echoed at a socially lower and intellectually cruder level by much working-class freethinking. Its organ, *The Free Thinker*, was indeed a forum for scurrility. Less scurrilous, but no less vigorously anti-religious, was *The Oracle of Reason*, founded in 1841 by Charles Southwell. On Southwell's imprisonment for blasphemy it was edited by George Jacob Holyoake, the Chartist, who also landed himself in gaol. After this experience he modified his tone, becoming less volubly atheistic and anti-clerical, more and more like a middle-class London intellectual. See F.B. Smith, 'The atheist mission, 1840–1900', in R. Robson (ed.), *Ideas and Institutions of Victorian Britain: Essays in Honour of George Kitson Clark* (1967), pp. 205–235, and E. Royle, *Victorian Infidels: the Origins of the British Secularist Movement, 1791–1866* (1974).

romanticism generally, it was completely remote. It is a measure of John Stuart Mill's departure from strict Utilitarian orthodoxy that he was able to praise Coleridge's genius as he did, along, of course, with that fount of prudential wisdom, Bentham.

The interest of Mill for our present survey lies mainly in the fact that the doctrines he all his life professed with complete conviction do not appear wholly to have satisfied him, as they did his father and George Grote, and that he looked for some further outlet for his pent-up emotional life. But to understand Mill we must first consider what he himself has to relate in his *Autobiography*. The details of his early education need not be dwelt on: how he read Greek fluently at six years old and had got through six of Plato's Dialogues by the time he was eight, or how after the classics he went on to mathematics, history, English poetry, chemistry, logic and political economy, with philosophy in the shape of Aristotle's *Analytics* while he was scarcely in his teens. 'Anything', he wrote, 'which could be found out by thinking I was never told, until I had exhausted my efforts to find it out for myself.' Yet he denies that his abilities were abnormal. 'What I could do could assuredly be done by any boy or girl of average capacity and healthy physical constitution.' A year in France provided additional intellectual stimulus, but the climax of his education was reached with the works of Bentham, to which he was introduced by Dumont's *Traité de Législation*. This last he looked back on as an epoch in his life, the 'greatest happiness' principle bursting upon him 'with all the force of novelty'. All previous moralists he felt now to have been superseded and that with the Benthamite philosophy a new era of thought had commenced.[36] To himself he seemed even to have become 'a different being'.

> 'The principle of utility', understood as Bentham understood it, and applied in the manner in which he applied it, fell exactly into its place as the key-stone which held together the detached and fragmentary component parts of my knowledge and belief, It gave unity to my conception of things. I now had opinions; a creed, a doctrine, a philosophy in one among the best senses of the word, a religion; the inculcation and diffusion of which could be made the principal outward purpose of a life.

This was his moment of the initiate's zeal, and, as he realized, he could fairly be described as a 'reasoning machine'. But it was not long before he became aware of the defects of so straightened an outlook. He was all intellect; the heart seemed to have no room in him. His devotion to human welfare was less a spontaneous and practical attitude than a loftily detached option. What his high principles needed was their 'natural aliment, poetical culture'; the dissolvent power of mere rational analysis had been applied too far. He had started with 'a well-equipped ship and a rudder', but without 'a sail'. By the autumn of 1826 this sense of the radical deficiency in his makeup had turned into an emotional crisis which very nearly prostrated him. What the conscious issue was he afterwards stated in explicit terms:

> Suppose that all your objects in life were realized; that all the changes in institutions and options which you are looking forward to, could be completely effected at this very instant: would this be a great joy and happiness to you? And an irrepressible self-consciousness answered: 'No'.

36. See *Dissertations* (1859), i, p. 403.

So much precocious reasoning and analysing had been a worm at the root of the passions and virtues alike. Desire and pleasure had lost their savour. The breakdown continued for about a year, but restoration began with the discovery of poetry, especially Wordsworth's: 'What made Wordsworth's poems a medicine for my state of mind was that they expressed, not mere outward beauty'—this might have been too intellectual an experience—'but states of feeling, and of thought coloured by feeling, under the excitement of beauty. They seemed to be the very culture of the feelings which I was in quest of.' The outcome was not by any means a drastic qualification of the Benthamite doctrine but a realization that happiness can only be attained by not making it the direct aim of living, and that it is, rather, a byproduct of worthwhile activities, such as promote the good of mankind. Moreover the 'internal culture of the individual' was also important, as against the 'ordering of outward circumstances' alone. 'The cultivation of the feelings became one of the cardinal points in my ethical and philosophical creed.' The reading of Wordsworth was now supplemented by the study of other contemporary authors: Coleridge and his followers—Maurice for one—Goethe, Comte, Carlyle. With Carlyle he formed a close but astringent friendship, and his praise of Maurice's ability, although the theologian's views in themselves could only strike him as a kind of mental perversion, was, as we have seen, unstinting. Mill had not dismantled his earlier beliefs, but he had woken up to their limitations. His regard for the eighteenth century was unabated, but he recognized that his own age provided a needed reaction and off-set to it.

The famous *System of Logic*, Mill's first major work, was published in 1843, although completed two years previously. In it he was plainly following in his father's footsteps, as an uncompromising exponent of the empiricist philosophy. All knowledge, he holds, originates in sensation, which in turn is constructed from units of sense-impression. When the mental processes are examined it is found that they depend upon associations, a theory that James Mill had borrowed from Hartley.[37] But to reduce knowledge ultimately to sensations clearly posed difficulties. What is their organizing principle, if 'experience' is to have unity and continuity, when the 'self', as a metaphysical entity, has been excluded? 'Association', on the other hand, is not in itself an explanation. Again, if the only data of experience are sensations what exactly is it we can be said to 'know', unless we are for ever held within the circle of our own ideas? The problem obviously worried Mill, yet he would in no way qualify his dictum that 'of the outward world we know absolutely nothing, except the sensations which we experience from it'. Thus exterior reality becomes no more than the unknown and unknowable cause or occasion of our private sensations. The result would appear to be sheer individualism and subjectivism, a position which he is clearly not content with. Nevertheless, in spite of its difficulties, the *Logic* became, as Leslie Stephen said, 'the sacred Scripture of the Liberal intellectuals'.[38] More, in fact, than a technical

37. David Hartley's *Observations on Man* (1749) was an attempt—subsequent to Hume, but influenced chiefly by Locke—to explain all mental development by the association of psychic elements, on the principle that complex states may have a quite different character from that of their simple constituents.
38. *The English Utilitarians* (1900), iii, p. 76.

treatise, it was a manifesto. The author's aim was polemical: to overthrow the defences of all 'intuitionist' thinkers, whose methods, in utilitarian eyes, were sinister because *a priori*. To combat this deeply entrenched philosophy, upon which the foes of enlightenment always fell back, was the great intellectual challenge of the times. No concessions could be made; even the certainties of mathematics were in the final resort empirically grounded. What we call causation is, as Hume had argued, only a matter of invariable succession. The role of the knowing mind is reduced to a minimum.

In the sixth book of the *Logic*, on 'The Logic of the Moral Sciences', Mill turns his attention to the larger, and to him the far more interesting, questions of ethics, politics and history. His concern here is whether 'human nature' is itself capable of scientific analysis; whether indeed morality, along with the principles of social organization and historical development, is also a science. For this it would have to be shown that it exhibits fixed laws capable of demonstration. But what if man is a free agent? The question was one to be faced at the very start, and Mill does not shirk it. Volitions and actions, he contends, are always the effects of causes. Given, that is, the motives which are present in the individual's mind, as too his character and disposition, then the manner in which he will act may be unerringly inferred. Mill admits that this doctrine is repugnant to the upholders of free-will, but asks what there is derogatory to human dignity in the view that volitions and actions are 'the invariable consequents of antecedent states of mind'. Rather is it in the notion of an external causality or 'necessity' constraining the individual to act in one way instead of in another. When a man acts he 'chooses' in accordance with the motives by which he himself is inwardly moved. Our characters are not formed *for us*—'a great error', Mill judges—but *by* us. The power to alter character is thus 'to a certain extent' ours.[39] Though effects are to be traced to causes a man yet can permit himself to be determined by one cause more than by another. The cause–effect sequence, however, is strong enough for a science of human nature to be worked out. It will not be an exact science, but it can be constituted of approximate truths on the basis of general laws. What states of mind and 'associations' really are we are unable, of course, to say; at any rate we have no right, with Comte, to label them simply as physiological. It is sufficient for a *science* that it is a body of knowledge expressed in terms of law. Finally, the science of human nature—'ethology', as Mill calls it—is of paramount importance to the one to which all others lead.

Mill's ethical theory is elaborated in *Utilitarianism* (1863). Again it is the Benthamite position which is his starting-point, and as before the author is not quite comfortable in maintaining it. He is determined to adhere, that is, to the basic utilitarian principle, but at the same time be wants it to serve a higher end. Actions, he continues to suppose, are right in proportion as they tend to promote

39. 'Its being, in the ultimate resort, formed for him, is not inconsistent with its being, in part, formed *by* him as one of the intermediate agents' (*A System of Logic*, Bk vi, sect. 2). What, Mill thinks, is sound in the doctrine of free-will is its insistence on a truth which the necessitarian neglects, namely 'the power of the mind to cooperate in the formation of its own character.'

happiness, wrong as they fail to do so; but he concedes that the pleasure principle appears to many people unworthy as a *moral* criterion, and indeed so far allows the objection as to introduce a qualitative difference between sorts of pleasure: some—those of the intellect, conspicuously—are more valuable and to be desired than others. In short, the mere quantity of pleasure, on a true reckoning, is of less importance than its quality. 'It is better to be a human being dissatisfied than a pig satisfied; better to be Socrates dissatisfied than a fool satisfied.'[40] And the quality of a pleasure is to be estimated only by those best able to do so. All the same a pleasure is a pleasure and if the quest of the pleasurable is made the standard of action then self-interest will provide the motive force, be the nature of the pleasure noble or ignoble. Once more Mill feels the point of the objection and endeavours to turn it by presenting the highest pleasure as the promotion of that of others. Thus, he believes, selfishness can be transformed into altruism. But what if one's own and the general happiness do not so easily coincide? Is one not, in that case, to pursue the latter *without* reference to the former? Mill, however, will not permit himself to stray so far from his original position and insists that in advancing other people's happiness we also create our own. Such at least is the theory. But he knew enough about human nature to realize that sustained altruism needs some more potent stimulus than a disinterested concern for one's neighbour's welfare, that it demands of it a conviction more akin to religious faith. Only the religion of altruism must be a humanistic not a supernatural one, a creed based on education and sound opinion, not on a supposed divine revelation. Man has to learn to acquire a feeling of unity with his fellow-creatures, making it an integral element of conscience, as spontaneous as 'the horror of crime to an ordinarily well brought up young person'. Hence virtue becomes a habit and deliberate thought of pleasure does not arise—an admirable sentiment, to be sure, but scarcely in line with the simple, hard-headed doctrine of Mill's master. The neo-utilitarian has here in truth approached the threshold of Christianity, and it is to his carefully stated views on the religious issue that we must now turn.

These are set forth in the posthumous volume of *Essays on Religion*,[41] the first essay dealing with 'Nature', the second with 'The Utility of Religion' and the third with 'Theism'. Their intrinsic value is still substantial, but to the student of Mill himself they are of special interest. For here is a man plainly struggling to admit to himself the importance of a fact which, on the showing of a doctrine he had spent his life in propagating, had no importance at all. Yet he treats the subject throughout in a spirit of frigid detachment, entirely in the manner of the eighteenth century. Of religion as experienced by the believer he appears to sense nothing. The ethos of worship and prayer, the enthusiasm of a conviction that does not derive from logic, the impulse which sustains faith despite lack of evidence or even in face of contrary evidence, of these things Mill seems unaware or

40. *Utilitarianism* (Everyman edn), p. 9.
41. Published in 1874, with an introductory note by Mill's step-daughter, Helen Taylor. The first two, she tells us, were written between the years 1850 and 1858, the third—'the last considerable work which he completed', summing up 'the deliberations of a life-time'—many years later, between 1868 and 1870.

uncomprehending. Religion for him is a matter only of statements, propositions, true or false, capable or incapable of verification. These he reviews and considers and judges as though feeling and the needs of action had no bearing on them whatever. Faith is dissected on the study table and found to be unscientific, gravely wanting in the veridity that belongs to rational demonstration. A Schleiermacher or indeed a Coleridge might never, so far as he is concerned, have written a word. Yet Mill cannot simply write off religion, as did Bentham, or his own father. Something about it holds him and worries him, as though he suspected, deep in his mind, that there might possibly be some realm of truth which his philosophy has failed to map out.

The first of the *Essays*, that on 'Nature', scrutinizes the ancient principle of *naturam sequi*, which in modern times had been extolled by Rousseau, the *laissez-faire* economists and the poet Wordsworth. In one sense, Mill notes, it means 'all the powers existing in either the outer or the inner world and everything which takes place by means of those powers'. In another it signifies, not everything which happens but only what takes place 'without the agency, voluntary and intentional, or otherwise, of man'.[42] With these connotations the term refers merely to nature as a matter of fact, but its employment in ethics seems to invoke a third, by which nature stands not just for what is but for what ought to be. However, those who use the expression do not intend these differing senses to be exclusive; on the contrary, they think that nature does afford some external criterion of what we should do. For them what *is* constitutes the rule and standard of what *ought* to be. Yet this is precisely the question that needs explaining, for nature, on any candid view, seems anything but a model for men to adopt in determining their own actions. She is altogether mighty and wonderful, but does she evoke feelings of moral approval? For the truth is, alas, that 'next to the greatness of these cosmic forces, the quality which most forcibly strikes every one who does not avert his eyes from it is their perfect and absolute recklessness. They go straight to their end, without regarding what or whom they crush on the road'. Nearly all the things, says Mill, which men are hanged or imprisoned for doing to one another are nature's everyday performances. Natural phenomena are simply non-moral in every respect. But he does not leave his indictment there. Even nature's much-vaunted 'order' is an illusion. 'All which people are accustomed to deprecate as "disorder" and its consequences, is precisely a counterpart of Nature's ways. Anarchy and the Reign of Terror are overmatched in injustice, ruin and death, by a hurricane and a pestilence.'[43]

The theme is one certainly on which Mill can let his temperamental pessimism have its head; but the conclusion to be drawn is that on no account can it be religious or moral—as has so often been claimed—'to guide our actions by the analogy of the course of nature'. Not even our natural instincts are a safe conductor, for 'naturally' men are dirty, selfish and dishonest. 'There is hardly a single point of excellence belonging to human character, which is not decidedly

42. *Essays on Religion*, p. 8.
43. *Ibid.*, p. 31.

repugnant to the untutored feelings of human nature.'[44] The theological inference, if one be made, is obvious, therefore: God, as the author of nature, cannot be both omnipotent and benevolent. 'If the maker of the world *can* all that he will, he wills misery.'[45] Where men have maintained a faith in divine benevolence the divine omnipotence has in fact gone by the board. Accordingly,

> whatsoever, in nature, gives indication of beneficent design proves this beneficence to be armed only with limited power; and the duty of man is to co-operate with the beneficent powers, not by imitating but by perpetually striving to amend the course of nature, and bringing that part of it over which we can exert control, more nearly into conformity with a high standard of justice and goodness.[46]

The possible implications of the fact that man, who can thus pass moral judgment on nature, is himself part of nature Mill does not ponder.

In the second essay the author raises the question of the utility of religion. If religion is true there can be no doubt of its usefulness, which indeed had no need to be asserted until the truth-claims of religion had largely ceased to convince. But the present is 'an age of weak beliefs': men are more determined by their wish to believe than by any logical assessment of the evidence. Wishful thinking is not necessarily selfish, be it said; yet whether 'all this straining to prop up beliefs which require so great an expense of intellectual toil and ingenuity to keep them standing, yields any sufficient return in human well being' is something the honest mind is bound to cogitate. That religion may be morally useful without being 'intellectually sustainable' is evident; but does this moral value depend directly upon dogmas? That it does do so is something repeatedly urged, but it is clear also that morality is powerfully inculcated by other means as well—by authority, education and public opinion. Among the ancient Greeks, for example, social morality was quite independent of religion. If the latter has been a prop to morals this was for circumstantial rather than intrinsic reasons, and Mill points out how religious writers and preachers have never tired of complaining of what little effect religious motives have on men's lives and conduct.[47] The truth of morality remains, however, even though the supernatural authority for it becomes increasingly dubious. Are not moral truths, he asks, strong enough in their own evidence for mankind to believe in them, although without any higher origin than 'wise and noble hearts'?

What then is there in human nature that prompts the need for religion? Mill does not think fear to be the answer. Much more is it the sense of *mystery*, in which the imagination plays a commanding part. Poetry is one expression of this, religion another. But religion, as distinguished from poetry, comes of the craving to know whether the products of the imagination have some corresponding reality in another world. The satisfaction of human longing can, however, be had without going beyond the boundaries of this present world. Man's lot here can be indefinitely bettered, and although the effort may tax us, 'the idea that Socrates, or Howard, or Washington, or Antoninus, or Christ, would have sympathized with

44. *Ibid.*, p. 46.
45. *Ibid.*, p. 37.
46. *Ibid.*, p. 65.
47. *Ibid.*, p. 90.

us' should be a great encouragement. But if we understand the essence of religion as 'the strong and earnest direction of the emotions and desires toward an ideal object, recognized as of the highest excellence, and as rightfully paramount over all selfish objects of desire', we ought also to ask ourselves whether this condition is not fulfilled by the 'Religion of Humanity' as eminently as by the supernatural faiths, 'even in their best manifestations, and far more so than in any of the others'.[48] But that humanism, as we today would call it, is a superior religion to the traditional ones Mill finds it impossible to deny. In the first place, it is disinterested: it does not look for future rewards in a way that can only promote selfishness,[49] whilst secondly, it does not depend on the intellectual contortions involved in ascribing absolute perfection to the author and ruler of 'so clumsily made and capriciously governed a creation as this planet and the life of its inhabitants'. The author of the Sermon on the Mount is certainly a much more benignant being than the Author of Nature, but unfortunately the believer in the Christian revelation is obliged to see in the same being the author of both. Again, it is free of the moral as well as the intellectual difficulties which religion constantly poses: how God could make a hell, or why so precious a gift as salvation should have been withheld from so many. Finally, as to the religious promise of a future life, improvement in the conditions of earthly existence will render the expectation less alluring: 'When mankind cease to need a future existence as a consolation for the sufferings of the present, it will have lost its chief value for them.'[50]

The essay on 'Theism' is the weightiest of all. Mill's attitude, needless to say, is consistently detached and argumentative. He is concerned with religious doctrines simply as 'scientific theorems', and asks what evidence they appeal to which science could recognize as such. The initial inquiry accordingly relates to the existence and attributes of God and raises the issue of the classic proofs. The argument to a First Cause does not impress him. Experience does not support it: the principle of causation is not applicable to the material universe as a whole but only to its changeable phenomena.

> No cause is needed for the existence of that which has no beginning; and both Matter and Force (whatever metaphysical theory we may give of the one or the other) have had, so far as our experience can teach us, no beginning—which cannot be said of Mind.[51]

But if there is nothing in the nature of mind which in itself implies a creator then the demand for '*a priori* Intelligence' becomes unnecessary. Similar arguments from the 'general consent' of mankind and 'consciousness' do not afford any real basis for belief in God. 'It is not legitimate to assume that in the order of the Universe, whatever is desirable is true.' It is only when Mill reaches the argument from 'marks of design in nature' that he detects firmer ground. Here, he suggests, is something

48. *Ibid.*, p.109.
49. 'Even the Christ of the Gospels holds out the direct promise of reward from heaven as a primary inducement to the noble and beautiful beneficence towards our fellow creatures which he so impressively inculcates' (*ibid.*, p. III).
50. *Ibid.*, p. 119.
51. *Ibid.*, p. 153.

genuinely scientific in that it relies for its force on data of observation. 'Certain qualities it is alleged, are found to be characteristic of such things as are made by an intelligent mind for a purpose. The order of Nature, or some considerable parts of it, exhibit these qualities in a remarkable degree.' Does this then justify the conclusion of a designing Intelligence? Mill's reply is a tentative Yes: 'In the present state of our knowledge, the adaptations afford a large balance of probability in favour of' the idea.[52] Thus in spite of what he earlier has said about nature's 'disorder' he still finds enough order—sufficient evidence, in fact, of the most remarkable contrivance of means to ends—to make him feel that purposive design in the universe is *not* excluded. Since writing the essay on 'Nature', however, Mill had read Darwin, whose speculations he at once realized were not to be ignored. The Darwinian theory, 'if admitted', he observes, 'would be in no way whatever inconsistent with Creation'. But it must be acknowledged that it would greatly attenuate the evidence for it.

All things considered, therefore, Mill can allow the existence of God as creator and designer, but not with the attribute of omnipotence. The deity's power, although great, is limited, and 'any idea of God more captivating than this comes only from human wishes, or from the teaching of either real or imaginary Revelation.'[53] Whether a revelation is real depends, again, on evidences, commonly distinguished as either external or internal. Internal evidences cover such indications as the revelation itself may be thought to supply concerning its divine origin—the excellency of its precepts, for example, or its adaptability to human needs. These, Mill concedes, are important, but in the main only negatively so: they give us grounds for rejecting a revelation as divine, but not for its acceptance. As for the external evidences—miracles, in a word—Hume's objections are cogent. Mill discusses this problem at length, but in the end dismisses miracles both as having no claim to the character of historical fact and as wholly invalid when adduced in support of an alleged divine self-disclosure.

Of Christianity itself Mill speaks with a grudging praise. Even through its darkest and most corrupt periods, he recalls, it has maintained, in the image of one person, a standard of the highest human excellence; 'for it is Christ, rather than God, whom Christianity has held up to believers as the pattern of perfection for humanity'. Whatever else may be taken away from us by rational criticism, Christ, a unique figure, is still left.

> About the life and sayings of Jesus there is a stamp of personal originality combined with profundity of insight, which if we abandon the idle expectation of finding scientific precision where something very different was aimed at, must place the Prophet of Nazareth, even in the estimation of those who have no belief in his inspiration, in the very front rank of the men of sublime genius of whom our species can boast.[54]

Mill goes even further, entertaining the possibility that Christ actually was what he supposed himself to be—not God indeed, for this he made no claim at all to

52. *Ibid.*, p. 174.
53. *Ibid.*, pp. 194f.
54. *Ibid.*, p. 254.

be—but 'a man charged with a special, express and unique commission from God to lead mankind to truth and virtue'.

That Mill's conclusions on religion, at the end of a life dedicated to the service of reason, should amount to no more than a barely tenable theism, along with an unfeigned admiration for the moral doctrine and example of Jesus Christ, will strike the orthodox Christian as a meagre alternative to the traditional faith. Yet for Mill, considering his upbringing and the intellectual principles to which he was committed from his youth onwards, the concession is far from negligible. Through the many pages of dry analysis and argument there is discernible a nostalgic gleam, a half-wish that it *might* be true, in spite of the cumulative criticism which renders religion in its customary shape quite incredible. Mill, we may say, is also to be ranked among that impressive body of Victorians for whom the erosion of belief by reason, by science and by the pressure of changing social circumstances left them with a sense of deprivation and loss. The age of secularism had dawned; facts destructive of the old securities had to be faced and accepted. But the ties of the past, for all the promise of the future, were still strong enough for their breaking to be painful.

Note
The Influence of Spinoza

To the freethinkers of the age the discovery of Spinoza brought a veritable inspiration. Thus Coleridge, describing in Chapter 10 of the *Biographia Literaria* his state of mind at Nether Stowey and the growth of his mature opinions, tells us that although 'his whole heart remained with Paul and John', 'his head was with Spinoza'. It was the great seventeenth-century thinker also who helped to free the young George Eliot from the 'Procrustean bed of dogma' and to realize that 'nothing but gloomy and sad superstition forbids enjoyment', and that 'blessedness is not the reward of virtue, but is virtue itself'. In the spring of 1846 she even embarked on a translation of the *Tractatus Logico-Politicus*, finding it 'such a rest for her mind' after her labours on Strauss. George Eliot was among the pioneers of Spinozistic studies in this country, since at that time Spinoza's writings were still very little known here. (Three years previously G. H. Lewes had written an essay on Spinoza for *The Westminster Review*, claiming it, with justice, as the first attempt to vindicate this often misjudged philosopher before the English public.) George Eliot gave up the translation after her father's death in 1849, explaining to Charles Bray her feeling that what was wanted in English was not a translation of Spinoza's actual works but a true estimate of his life and system. 'After one has rendered the Latin faithfully into English, one feels that there is another yet more difficult process of translation for the reader to effect, and that the only mode of making Spinoza accessible to a large number of readers is to study his books, then shut them up and give an analysis' (Cross, *Life of George Eliot*, i, p. 238). The *Ethics*, an English version of which was also undertaken by her, was in 1856 abandoned; at least it was never published, presumably for the same reason. Froude was drawn to the rationalist philosopher by the splendour—especially in its contrast with the puerilities of popular mediaeval hagiography—of the *amor intellectualis Dei*. His article on Spinoza in *The Cambridge and Oxford Review* for October, 1857 represents him not only as the committed foe of all religious bigotry and superstition but as both the source of the 'purest and loftiest religious philosophy' of modern times and an example of the human mind in its highest development. The Spinozistic creed was in fact religion in its true essence: 'The love of God is the extinction of all other loves and all other desires. To know God, as far as man can know him, is power, self-government, and peace.' It was virtue and blessedness. (See *Studies on Great Subjects*, i, pp. 386f.) Another devotee was William Hale White (1831–1913)—'Mark Rutherford'—who published a standard translation of the *Ethics* in 1883. White's feeling, under Spinoza's guidance, that he was not a mere transient, outside interpreter of the universe, but had 'a relationship with infinity'—nay, was truly 'a part of the infinite intellect of God'—gave massive consolation for the loss of more traditional religious convictions. (See White's *Pages from a Journal* (1900), pp. 32–58.)

Chapter 9

RELIGION, SCIENCE AND PHILOSOPHY

The Bible and geology

The seventeenth and eighteenth centuries had been an era of scientific advance and consolidation. By 1700 natural philosophy, as it was then called, had reached a stage which made the Newtonian synthesis possible. Thereafter science enjoyed growing prestige as a body of truths about the physical universe which were beyond sectarian dispute and could be taken for granted by all men of good sense. Moreover, that these truths might in any important way conflict with sound religion was scarcely considered. On the contrary, throughout the eighteenth century it was the generally accepted view that science had established a realm of facts which religion may gladly accept as illustrative of the ways of God. Nature was to be read as a book of divine authorship. In the words of Addison's well-known hymn:

> The spacious firmament on high,
> With all the blue ethereal sky,
> And spangl'd heavens, a shining frame,
> Their great Original proclaim.

Thus religion and science were in mutual support. And such continued to be the prevalent view in the opening years of the nineteenth century, when the writings of William Paley in this country were at the height of their popularity. But as the decades passed a change of outlook was becoming evident. Not only was scientific knowledge itself rapidly increasing, it was determining the very ethos of civilization to a degree hitherto unparalleled. The scientific spirit now permeated thought in all its ranges. Poetry and imaginative prose responded to it. Ruskin judged that he might himself have become the best geologist of his day and chided Wordsworth for failing to understand 'that to break a rock with a hammer in search of crystal may sometimes be an act not disgraceful to human nature, and that to dissect a flower may sometimes be as proper as to dream over it'.[1] It was impossible that in the circumstances religion should be oblivious of science's presence or not become apprehensive of what its expanding influence and authority might portend for beliefs long rooted in holy Scripture. Could Genesis come to terms with the new geology? Were miracles compatible with the reign of natural law? In the past, no doubt, there had been scientists who despised religious creeds, as there had been theists who denied them. Laplace had assured the Emperor Napoleon that for his

---

1. *Modern Painters* (1843–60), iii, p. 7.

calculations there was no need for the hypothesis of God. But such men and such attitudes were exceptional. The great Newton had been a devout Christian, for whom the providence of God was as certain as the principles of natural philosophy. Cuvier, foremost among the biologists of his time, and Owen, whose fame as an anatomist was surpassed by none, maintained the fixity of animal species in the manner the Bible seemed plainly to teach. But with the development of a conception of the natural order as autonomous, continuous and uniform, the acts of God, whether in originally creating or in providentially governing, became harder to discern. Hence the appeal to natural phenomena in evidence of the divine existence and attributes began to lose its former cogency.

The issue between religion and science was first clearly posed by geology. Between 1800 and 1834 four different series of Bampton lectures had dealt with the subject, and three of them, Faber's *Horae Mosaicae* (1800), Nares's *A View of the Evidences of Christianity at the close of the Pretended Age of Reason* (1805) and Bidlake's *The Truth and Consistency of Divine Revelation, with some Remarks on the contrary extremes of Infidelity and Enthusiasm* (1811), were strongly critical of the claims being made for geological study, either rejecting outright the facts alleged or else contending that they demanded another interpretation—for example, the presence of marine deposits on mountain-tops could be explained by the Deluge. But always the clinching argument was that to question the accuracy of Scripture in any matter is to impugn divine revelation itself. Frederick Nolan in 1833—writing, that is, after the appearance of Lyell's *Principles of Geology*—was less intransigent; he allowed that the aim of the biblical authors was to teach religion not science, but had sufficient confidence in Moses's personal inspiration to believe that no serious discrepancy could arise between what the prophet was moved to write and what science long after might discover.[2] The apparent implications of geologically important advances continued, however, to exercise the minds of educated Christians. In 1829 the Earl of Bridgewater, an eccentric cleric, bequeathed the sum of £8,000 to the President of the Royal Society for the sponsoring of a number of apologetic treatises. These were duly produced between the years 1833 and 1840, the best of them being William Whewell's *Astronomy and General Physics considered with reference to Natural Theology*, and William Buckland's *Geology and Mineralogy*, although the latter was felt to have made some dangerous concessions to the scientific position. Buckland, a clergyman who later became dean of Westminster, was at the time professor of mineralogy at Oxford and a man of some ability.[3] But most of these *Bridgewater Treatises*, as they were called—there were eight of them in all—were in content thin enough. Four of the authors were physicians seeking to prove intelligent purpose in nature from physiological data; the rest were divines, and included the famous Scottish church leader, Thomas Chalmers. Doctors and divines alike approached their task with outdated presuppositions, having nothing better to offer than the physico-theology of the preceding century, with its deistic notion of an external, 'watch-maker' God.

2. See *The Anatomy of Revelation and Science Established* (1833).
3. His opposite number at Cambridge was Adam Sedgwick, a bitter opponent of evolutionary views.

The difficulty in these years was to square the statements of Genesis, till then regarded as inerrant, with the time scale required by the geologists; for whereas Scripture spoke of the mere 'days' of creation the new geology reckoned in terms of millions of years. Must not one or other of them be wrong? Or could it be that the 'days' of Genesis would have to be understood figuratively? There also was the problem of the Flood. When did it occur and how far was it universal? To the mind of an age that took the verbal inspiration of the Bible for granted such questions seemed to touch the very heart of faith. Philip Gosse, himself a scientist as well as a member of the Plymouth Brethren, believed that the Almighty had created the rocks with the fossils already in them, presumably as a trial of men's belief.[4] Much nonsense indeed was talked and written on these matters and attempts to arrive at a more reasonable conclusion were met with denunciation and abuse, not always from clergymen and pious layfolk. Buckland especially came in for opprobrious treatment by the press and in a stream of hostile pamphlets. The dean of York, William Cockburn, was his unrelenting opponent in this war of words. The latter as late as 1844 was still hammering away at the unfortunate Oxford professor, deploring that the ancient seat of learning and orthodoxy should continue to house a man who in spite of his clerical office worked only to promote infidelity.

The details of these disputes are both amusing and lamentable, but it would be pointless to dwell on them. Traditional religion had run up against new knowledge in the secular sphere and many of its cherished ideas had received a painful knock. British Protestantism was inveterately biblicist and took it as matter of course that the statements of holy writ could not be false. There seemed thus to be a head-on collision, and in the situation the theologians,—as too some scientists—still wearing the intellectual blinkers of an older time, could for the most part see nothing to avert disaster except a downright denial that what science was now saying could possibly be true.

Unfortunately for them the new findings were not to be disposed of by clamorous negations. Solid work had been done and signal discoveries made: the names in particular of Werner, Hutton and William Smith are still honourably remembered. Pre-eminent, however, was the achievement of Sir Charles Lyell, by whom the science of geology had been placed at last on a systematic basis. The importance of Lyell's work, on the long view, is that second only to Darwin's it effectually brought the whole realm of nature under the conception of developmental law. It was in a genuine sense epochal, for biological evolution is really no more, in essence, than the extension to the organic world of principles which Lyell held to be dominant in the inorganic. Lyell himself, we may note, was somewhat slow to concede this; which explains his equivocal attitude to Lamarck, whose speculations he found at once fascinating and repellent. But he was reluctant to contemplate the possibility that man himself was descended from lower forms of life. When

4. Other questions that troubled Gosse were whether Adam had been created with a navel—he gave the title *Omphalos* to a book he published 1857—or whether the trees in the Garden of Eden, when cut down, showed the usual signs of growth. But Gosse's speculations were widely regarded as foolish in his own day.

more than thirty years after the first appearance of the *Principles* he published his second major work, *Geological Evidences of the Antiquity of Man* (1863), Darwin's statement of the evolutionary theory had already caused a *furore* and the influence of the younger man's ideas was traceable in it. Nevertheless Lyell's fear of the implications of the theory—and he saw them plainly enough—disappointed Darwin, whose regard for Lyell's judgment was of the highest.

The theory of evolution

Long before *The Origin of Species*, however, a curious and much-talked of book of anonymous authorship had called attention to the evolutionary principle in the natural order. This was *Vestiges of the Natural History of Creation*, which appeared in 1844. The seal of its anonymity was not finally broken until 1884, when the fact that the writer was a certain Robert Chambers (1802–71) became publicly known. Chambers was a Scottish journalist and a man of eclectic interests, who with his brother William founded the publishing house of W. and R. Chambers, also giving his name to *Chambers's Encyclopaedia*. A prolific author, he was in no way a professional scientist and much of the biological information conveyed in the book, the sales of which were enormous—four editions were printed in six months—was wildly and even ludicrously inaccurate. Competent biologists were embarrassed at it. Thomas Huxley was incensed at 'the prodigious ignorance and thoroughiy unscientific habit of mind manifested by the writer'.[5] Darwin praised it from the literary angle, but dismissed its content as worthless. Richard Owen, on the other hand, took a more sympathetic view of it, perhaps not surprisingly. Yet a success the book undoubtedly was, in so far as it aroused great popular interest. Its merit was its readability, which eased the impact of its basic concept that once it be admitted that the system of the universe is subject to natural law it follows that the introduction of new species into the world 'must have been brought about in the manner of law also'. The idea, of course, was not new. Erasmus Darwin—Charles's grandfather—and Lamarck had both raised the hypothesis of a general modification of species by natural causes, but their suggestions had gained little public notice. Chambers's *Vestiges*, for all its shortcomings, deserves credit for having stated a principle of great scientific importance in an arresting and interesting way. It only remained for an abler intelligence and more thorough research to restate it with the support of the requisite factual evidence.

The belief that the 'Almighty Author' of nature made the progenitors of all existing species by 'some sort of personal or immediate creation' Chambers rejected as absurd. God truly is creative—'the Eternal One' had 'arranged for everything beforehand'—but he afterwards had entrusted the process of the whole to laws of his own appointing. Chambers buttressed his evolutionism with arguments not at the time familiar, such as the survival of rudimentary structures, the known development of the individual embryo, the geographical distribution of organisms and the unity of structural type among species; and he himself was prepared to

5. F. Darwin, *The Life of Charles Darwin* (1887), ii, p. 188.

believe that the organic was developed from the inorganic without special divine intervention. He thought it possible, however, that nature sometimes moves forward not by single steps only but by a leap, an opinion which orthodox Darwinism subsequently discountenanced. In any case there was nothing in the evolutionary idea as he saw it which was inimical to theism; on the contrary, it supported the argument from design in a form altogether superior to Paley's.

As a serious contribution to science *The Vestiges of the Natural History of Creation* did not bear examination; yet in the history of ideas it is in its way something of a landmark, even though dwarfed by the great literary event of 1859—the publication, after years of careful preparation, of *The Origin of Species*.[6] Nevertheless, when the reader turns to the later work its jejune forerunner is soon forgotten. Indeed it is given to few works in any field of study to have the revolutionary effect of Charles Darwin's book. Its immediate consequence, from our point of view, was that the tension between science and religious belief was to enter a new and acute phase. The power of the book lay not only in the intrinsic significance of its presiding idea, which, as we have noted, had already been anticipated, but in the mass of recorded data by which the thesis was sustained. At the time of its appearance the author was fifty and had devoted a full twenty years of his life to its gestation. The enterprise was a triumph of constructive thinking, the implications of which were to affect the entire outlook of the civilized world. But it had its critical and destructive side also. Whatever objections biologists of an older school might bring against it—and many of them, like Owen, did object to it on purely scientific grounds: all species, it was argued, were permanent[7]—its rudest challenge was felt to be to the accepted doctrines of religion. Genesis says that the world was created in six days and evidently means that the various kinds of living things as known today were produced in exactly that space of time. Darwin, on the other hand, when he observed how gardeners and pigeon-fanciers could produce new varieties by cross-breeding, had lighted on the idea that a process of purely natural selection might well be the explanation of all varieties whatsoever. Prolonged research had both confirmed him in the principle and provided him with the needed evidence. Thus the evolution of nature could be thought of as an immanent development requiring no impulsion or control from without. In the struggle for existence it was some physical capacity like strength or speed or protective colouring which ensured survival. Such creatures as had it continued and multiplied, those that had it not perished and the species died out. In a word, it was the *fittest* which survived. Special creativity by an 'external' purposive intelligence seemed no longer to be a necessary postulate.

6. There is a draft plan of the book dating from as early as July 1842. This is of interest as showing both that evolution by natural selection had already occurred to Darwin as a principle needing a factual basis and that he also was concerned to prove intelligent design in nature, were such possible.
7. John Morley remarked how 'one group of scientific men fought another group over the origin of species' (*Recollections* (1917), i, p. 13), while in 1860 Thomas Huxley, Darwin's must committed partisan, conceded that supporters of the Darwinian views were 'numerically extremely insignificant' (Francis Darwin, *op. cit.*, ii, p. 186). See C. E. Raven, *Science, Religion and the Future* (1943), pp. 35ff.

The book was denounced in pulpits up and down the land as an impious absurdity. Current journals were filled with articles and correspondence about it, most of them condemning it as irreligious. Darwin himself was certainly not a religious man: his spiritual sensitivity seems in fact to have become atrophied over the years; but he was no self-declared atheist. It was simply that he doubted 'the right of the human mind to draw so tremendous a conclusion' as that of divine existence. In any event his book was not intended as a criticism of belief, this being quite outside his purview. *The Origin of Species* is even prefixed with a quotation from Bishop Butler, and its closing words invoke the language of theism:

> Authors of the highest eminence seem to be fully satisfied with the view that each species has been independently created. To my mind it accords better with what we know of the laws imposed on matter by the Creator, that the production and extinction of the past and present inhabitants of the world should have been due to secondary causes, like those determining the birth and death of the individual. ... There is grandeur in this view of life, with its several powers having been originally breathed by the Creator into a few forms, or even one.[8]

He himself regarded 'the impossibility of conceiving that this great and wondrous universe arose through chance' as one of the chief arguments for the existence of God.

Darwin's personal opinions, however, did nothing to assuage his critics' anger. For what the theory indicated, if consistently adopted, was the pithecoid origin of the human race. Lyell, as we have seen, shrank from this prospect, and even Alfred Russel Wallace, a keen supporter of Darwinism whose own essay *On the Tendency of Varieties to depart indefinitely from the Original Type* follows an identical line of reasoning, held that the problem of human kind demands special treatment. In 1871, with the publication of *The Descent of Man*, Darwin explicitly drew the reprobated inference. Yet he did so with something also of apology to theological susceptibilities.

> I am aware [he wrote] that the conclusions arrived at in this book will be denounced by some as irreligious. But he who denounces them is bound to show why it is more irreligious to explain the origin of man as a distinct species by descent from some lower form, than to explain the birth of an individual through the law of ordinary reproduction.[9]

Moreover, by the time this second most important of Darwin's works saw the light, public opinion had gone far towards assimilating the evolutionary concept. Vituperation and abuse had proved futile, and the theory had now become part of the changed intellectual landscape.

But in the early 'sixties, when the idea first struck the public mind, 'Darwinism' to many was practically a synonym for unbelief. More offensive even than its overt questioning of a Bible truth was its seeming humiliation of man himself, whose origins were now to be sought among the beasts of the field. Further, though species themselves may persist, their individual members were 'to be envisaged rather as

---

8. When asked by Tennyson whether his theory told against Christianity Darwin replied: 'No, certainly not' (Hallam Tennyson, *Alfred Lord Tennyson: a Memoir*, ii, p. 57).
9. *The Descent of Man* (1901 ed), p. 937.

transitory embodiments of relatively abiding types than as the supremely important realities for the sake of which the whole process exists';[10] and this presumably applied also to humanity. The disgust and contempt with which a theory having such implications was widely received among churchmen is illustrated by the well-known story of the passage of arms between Bishop Samuel Wilberforce and Thomas Huxley at the 1860 meeting of the British Association at Oxford, the bishop having already subjected Darwin's book to virulent attack in an article in *The Quarterly Review*. What exactly was said on that famous occasion is not altogether clear, since accounts of it vary. But Wilberforce, it is related, after again trouncing the theory, turned to Huxley and 'with smiling insolence begged to know whether it was through his grandfather or his grandmother that he claimed to be descended from a monkey'. On this Huxley whispered to his neighbour, 'The Lord hath delivered him into my hands', and then, rising to his feet, answered the bishop—according to J. R. Green's version—with the words:

> I asserted—and I repeat—that a man has no reason to be ashamed of having an ape for his grandfather. If there were an ancestor whom I should feel shame in recalling it would rather be a *man*—a man of restless and versatile intellect—who, not content with an equivocal success in his own sphere of activity, plunges into scientific questions with which he has no real acquaintance, only to obscure them by an aimless rhetoric, and distract the attention of his hearers from the real point at issue by eloquent digressions and skilled appeals to religious prejudice.[11]

Yet just as some biologists opposed Darwinism from the start so a number of distinguished churchmen did not follow the Bishop of Oxford's suit. F. J. A. Hort, for example, intellectually one of the most keen-sighted men of his day, welcomed the theory. In March, 1860 he wrote to B. F. Westcott: 'Have you read Darwin? How I should like a talk with you about it! In spite of difficulties, I am inclined to think it unanswerable. In any case it is a treat to read such a book.'[12] Frederick Temple, a contributor to *Essays and Reviews* who was later to become Archbishop of Canterbury, saw a place for Darwin's teaching in a progressive theology as making the creation more wonderful than ever, in that he showed 'not a number of isolated creations, but all creation knit together into a complete whole.'[13] It was a great improvement, he judged, on Paley.

> To the many partial designs which Paley's *Natural Theology* points out, and which still remain what they were, the doctrine of Evolution adds the design of a perpetual progress. ... [It] leaves the argument for an intelligent Creator and Governor of the earth stronger than it was before.[14]

10. C. C. J. Webb, *Religious Thought in England since 1850* (1933), p. 13.
11. L. Huxley, *The Life and Letters of T. H. Huxley* (1900), i, p. 185. Huxley himself, who in later years was fond of peddling the story, which doubtless lost nothing in the telling, denied using the word 'equivocal'. Wilberforce, it should be said, had consulted Professor Owen beforehand and doubtless would have felt entirely justified in relying on so eminent an authority. Cp. Owen Chadwick, *The Victorian Church*, Part ii (1970), pp. 9–11.
12. F. A. Hort, *The Life and Letters of F. J. A. Hort*, i, p. 414.
13. See F. G. Sandford, *Frederick Temple: an Appreciation* (1907), p. 301.
14. *The Relations of Religion and Science* (1884), pp. 117, 122.

Dean Church, Tractarian as he was, realized nevertheless that it was useless and mistaken merely to condemn the Darwinian theory.

> I owe [he wrote] my first interest in the subject to the once famous *Vestiges*,[15] and I remember thinking at the time it came out, that the line taken against it was unphilosophical and unsatisfactory. ... Mr Darwin's book is *the* book of science which has produced most impression here of any which has appeared for many years. ... One wishes such a book to be more explicit. But it is wonderful 'shortness of thought' to treat the theory itself as incompatible with ideas of a higher and spiritual order.[16]

A fortnight later he added:

> The more I think of it, the more I feel persuaded of the 'shortness of thought' which would make out of what is in itself a purely physical hypothesis in the mode of creation or origination (in which it seems to me very difficult at present to imagine our *knowing* anything), to be incompatible with moral and religious ideas of a very different order. But I am afraid that this is the present way of thinking among our religious people: and so the theory does not get fair discussion, either for or against, because there is on both sides an irresistible tacit reference to other interests in the minds of the disputants.[17]

In 1863 Charles Kingsley told Maurice that 'Darwin is conquering everywhere ... by the mere force of truth and fact'.[18] Even H. P. Liddon, for all his profound conservatism, was not prepared quite to turn his back on the theory, which although (as he thought) by no means proven, was still 'not inconsistent with belief in the original act of creation which is essential to Theism'. Evolution, he conceded, was from a theistic point of view 'merely one way of describing what we can observe of God's continuous action upon the physical world'.[19]

Meantime Darwin's ideas were being aggressively propagated by some fellow-biologists. Of these Thomas Henry Huxley (1825–95) was the most formidable. Although lacking Darwin's great originality of insight, he was a man of letters as well as of science. His role, which he discharged with surpassing competence, was that of a disciple and popularizer, writing always clearly and forcefully and often with a scathing wit. His declared aim was 'to smite all humbugs, however big; to give a nobler tone to science; to set an example of abstinence from petty personal controversies, and of toleration for everything but lying'.[20] Not surprisingly, his career was spattered with controversies, since he was naturally pugnacious. Theologians like Dean Wace, for example, suffered much at his hands. Gladstone, too, came off decidedly the worse in one of these verbal contests, concerning the ethics of a gospel miracle.

15. Church had reviewed it in *The Guardian*.
16. M. C. Church, *The Life and Letters of Dean Church* (1895), p. 153.
17. *Ibid.*, p. 157. Church's correspondent was the noted American biologist, Dr Asa Gray, himself a convinced Christian.
18. Mrs C. Kingsley, *Charles Kingsley, his Letters and Memories of his Life* (1877), ii, p. 155.
19. *Some Elements of Religion* (1872), p. 56. On the impact of the evolutionary theory on the churches see Chadwick, *op. cit.*, pp. 23–35.
20. L. Huxley, *op. cit.*, i, p. 151.

Huxley described his own position as agnostic, a word of his own invention. He did not, that is, categorically deny divine existence; he simply did not know it to be a fact. It was the same with personal immortality, that very special article of Victorian religious faith: he could neither affirm nor deny it. 'I see no reason', he wrote to Kingsley, 'for believing in it, but, on the other hand, I have no means of disproving it. Pray understand that I have no *a priori* objections to the doctrine. Give me such evidence as would justify me in believing anything else, and I will believe that.'[21] On a subsequent occasion he confessed to the same correspondent that he had 'never had the least sympathy with the *a priori* reasons against orthodoxy', and that he had 'by nature and disposition the greatest possible antipathy to all the atheistic and infidel school'.[22] Kingsley happened to be a personal friend of Huxley's, to whom the latter would doubtless wish, in this matter, to show his most amenable side. Yet in an essay on 'Agnosticism' he stated that 'greatly to the surprise of many of my friends, I have always advocated the reading of the Bible, and the diffusion of the study of that most remarkable collection of books among the people'. He dilated, however, on the superiority of the Bible's teaching to that of the sects, whether ancient or modern, as on the fact 'that the Bible contains within itself the refutation of nine-tenths of the mixture of sophistical metaphysics and old-world superstition which has been piled round it by the so-called Christians of later times'. Nevertheless his own professed standard of truth was always that of science, the trouble with religion—which he was apt to identify only with its formal doctrines—being that it could not be verified. Nor could he appreciate its language, the personalism of which offended him.

> Whether astronomy or geology [he again is writing to Kingsley] can or cannot be made to agree with the statements as to matters of fact laid down in Genesis—whether the Gospels are historically true or not—are matters of comparatively small moment in the face of the impassable gulf between the anthropomorphism (however refined) of theology and the passionless impersonality of the unknown and unknowable which science shows everywhere underlying the thin veil of phenomena.[23]

Yet Huxley was not a secularist in the modern sense. Not only was the problem of religion and science of unflagging concern to him, he was by no means himself without a certain religious feeling, shaped though this was by the Protestant prejudices of his time and social milieu. In another and very remarkable letter to Charles Kingsley, written at the time of the death of his own eldest child, he declared:

> I have the firmest belief that the Divine Government (if we may use such a phrase) is wholly just. The absolute justice of the system of things is as clear to me as any scientific fact. The ledger of the Almighty is strictly kept, and every one of us has the balance of his operations paid over to him at every moment of his existence.[24]

21. *Ibid.*, i, p. 217.
22. *Ibid.*, i, p. 241.
23. *Ibid.*, i, p. 239.
24. *Ibid.*, i, 219. Huxley all too readily fell into a homiletic manner of speaking and writing: ' "Bishop" Huxley' he was sometimes called in mockery. But for him science was virtually a faith. He was, however, markedly anti-clerical, resenting the influence of

On the other hand, in his famous Romanes lecture of 1893, he pressed the view that ethical progress and natural evolution do not go hand in hand and that nature is, as the poet had said, 'red in tooth and claw'. But the dark view of the natural order which he there takes he did not, it seems, quite consistently hold. 'One thing', he once confessed, 'which weighs with me against pessimism and tells for a benevolent author of the universe is my enjoyment of scenery and music. I do not see how they can have helped in the struggle for existence. They are gratuitous gifts.'

Another ardent Darwinian was John Tyndall, whose own position was quite frankly materialist. He was unable to believe in anything of which a model could not be made. Matter itself, he was satisfied, contained the promise and potency of all terrestrial life, of whatever form or quality. Consciousness was only its byproduct. Yet religion could be entertained so long as it was not permitted 'to intrude on the region of objective *knowledge*, over which it holds no command', since it was 'capable of adding, in the region of *poetry* and *emotion*, inward completeness and dignity to man'.[25] W. K. Clifford, professor of applied mathematics at University College, London, who in his youth had been a devout High Churchman, was less compromising even than this. Nature, including man, is a pure mechanism, and talk of the will influencing matter he thought sheer nonsense. The emergence of life itself is in all probability attributable to a series of coincidences and thus a thing of chance. There is no such entity as the soul and morality is a social development originating from a 'tribal conscience'. Human progress is and always has been dependent on the advance of scientific knowledge and in a world dominated by such knowledge religion is an anachronism. Yet another of Darwin's converts was G. J. Romanes, whose own early religion had been evangelical. A correspondence between Darwin and himself seems to have been the turning-point and by 1875 Romanes was convinced that Darwinism had disproved Christianity. The upshot was the appearance in 1878 of *A Candid Examination of Theism*, in which he argued that belief in God is unwarrantable, as having no scientific ground. But to do so went against the grain of his personal feelings and he confessed that with the virtual negation of the divine the universe for him had 'lost its soul of loveliness'.

> When at times I think, as think at times I must, of the appalling contrast between the hallowed glory of that creed which once was mine, and the lonely mystery of existence as now I find it—at such times I shall ever feel it impossible to avoid the sharpest pang of which my nature is susceptible.[26]

---

clergymen in setting the tone of 'right' thinking, especially in scientific matters. Science, he held, should be left to professional scientists, ministers (presumably) of a 'Church Scientific'. He liked to talk about a 'New Reformation' in this respect. See R. Barton, 'Evolution: the Whitworth Gun in Huxley's war for the liberation of science from theology', in D. Oldroyd and I. Langham (eds), *The Wider Domain of Evolutionary Thought* (Dordrecht, 1983).

25. *Fragments of Science* (1879 ed.), ii, p. 198.
26. *A Candid Examination of Theism*, p. 114.

The words are eloquent of the anguished disillusionment which many a Victorian, bred to the view that Christianity provides the one sure basis of moral living, must have endured when confronted by what reason declared to be the inescapable truth. For many in these years science appeared as religion's foe, and a foe bound to win. In Romanes's own instance, however, negation was not the end of the road and at the time of his premature death in 1894 he left notes for another book qualifying his previous conclusions. These were published in the following year in an edition, entitled *Thoughts on Religion*, by Charles Gore, to whom his widow had consigned them.

Herbert Spencer

But it was in Herbert Spencer (1820–1903) that evolution had its boldest theorist, a thinker who took over the principle as the key to an all-embracing system of philosophy. Meagrely though posterity may now estimate this ambitious enterprise, of its author's intellectual courage, hardihood and expansiveness of vision there can be no question. In early life a railway engineer, Spencer might have been expected to show a mainly practical bent, but it was to speculative thought that he came to dedicate his entire energy. Although from 1848 to 1853 he was sub-editor of the *Economist*, and for some years after a regular contributor to *The Westminster Review*, philosophical study occupied more and more of his time until by 1860 the scheme of the Synthetic Philosophy had been fully devised. The rest of his long life was to witness its gradual realization. It had been preceded by a number of preliminary studies such as the books on *Social Statics* (1851) and *Over-legislation* (1854). His *Principles of Psychology*, which first appeared in 1855, was itself, in the revised edition of 1870–72, to form an integral part of the completed system, the other components being *First Principles* (1862), *Principles of Biology* (1864–67), *Principles of Sociology* (1876–96) and *Principles of Ethics* (1892–93). Yet despite this formidable output he remained always more or less of an amateur. Max Müller, for example, described him as 'a writer without any background—I say on almost every page, "There he has discovered London again".'[27] Henry Sidgwick, the Cambridge philosopher, who as a young man had been attracted to Spencer's position, was afterwards 'appalled by the grotesque and chaotic confusion' of his metaphysics and dismissed his ethical doctrine as 'crude and superficial'.[28] These deficiencies, far from proving a hindrance to Spencer's popularity, may very well have stimulated it. He was nothing if not a plain man's philosopher, offering a vast range of plausible opinions to an age in search of a world view based on the idea which Darwin had so impressively demonstrated. Spencer's writings had all the appearance of being scientific, and the extension of the evolutionary method to the study of politics and society appealed strongly to the type of progressive thinker whose idealism demands the prop of seemingly hard fact. Yet Spencer also was a dogmatist, and although for a time this in itself told in his favour, it later

27. Mrs Max Müller, *The Life and Letters of Max Müller* (1902), ii, p. 188.
28. A. Sidgwick, *Henry Sidgwick: a Memoir* (1906), pp. 277, 344.

destroyed his intellectual credit beyond recovery. Today he is unread and all but forgotten.

The basis of Spencer's philosophy is his much-criticized division between the Knowable and the Unknowable, a distinction taken directly from Mansel's Bampton lectures and thus ultimately from Hamilton's philosophy of the conditioned. But according to Spencer the unconditioned must be conceived as positive, not negative. To prove the relativity of knowledge is at the same time to postulate the existence of something beyond the relative; and because all existence, as such, is positive, all consciousness is necessarily a positive consciousness of existence. What therefore is conceived as existing beyond knowledge cannot be thought of only as negative of the knowable. Although it eludes any distinct consciousness it at least is something more and other than the limited or conditioned; something, accordingly, of which we have 'a positive though vague consciousness'. In other words, the very relativity of knowledge involves the indefinite consciousness of that which transcends definite knowledge. For the definite is such only because of its origin in the indefinite, which persists throughout the variations of definite thought: all definition implies something which falls to be defined, and which, while still undefined, nevertheless is real. Hence Spencer's conclusion is that:

> Our consciousness of the unconditioned being literally the unconditioned consciousness, or raw material of thought to which in thinking we give definite forms, it follows that an ever-present sense of real existence is the very basis of our intelligence. As we can in successive mental acts get rid of all particular conditions and replace them by others, but cannot get rid of that undifferentiated substance of consciousness which is conditioned anew in every thought; there ever remains with us a sense of that which exists persistently and independently of conditions.[29]

The latent contradiction here is readily detectable, for if we can affirm of a thing that it exists then it is not completely unknown. Not only have we, as Spencer maintains, an indefinite consciousness of reality as the ground and guarantee, so to speak, of whatever is definitely known, but reality itself is precisely that which our knowledge progressively defines. In his view the idea that we have an indefinite consciousness of reality *in addition* to the definite consciousness which constitutes knowledge is the one safeguard against scepticism. But if scepticism is thus avoided it is only at the price of complete agnosticism. Either existence, although unknown, is yet capable of being known, or else, if it truly is unknowable, nothing whatsoever can be said about it. The result in that case will be nescience, an intellectual vacuum—a strange basis indeed for the grand design of a 'synthetic philosophy'. The fact is that Spencer's unknowable is neither unknowable nor wholly unknown, but merely serves as the postulated substratum of phenomena. His failure to see this is typical of the logical blind spots which occur throughout his writings.

The *First Principles* discloses the guidelines of all Spencer's subsequent theorizing, but the metaphysical foundation is laid for the sake only of what is to be built later, and is otherwise of little importance to him. His real concern is to follow the

---

29. *First Principles*, sect. 26.

workings of the principle of evolution from the simplest to the most complex forms, thus progressing from biology to psychology, sociology and ethics. This design is vastly more ambitious than anything Darwin ever envisaged. The latter's interest was confined to the origin of species; of the origin of life itself he had nothing to say. Spencer, on the other hand, believed that he could explain all things by the single law of the persistence of force or the conservation of energy, which he posited both as the ultimate presupposition of science and as implicated in each and all of the most general forms and antitheses of consciousness. Evolution, that is, is simply 'the law of the continuous redistribution of matter and motion'. To this principle he accordingly looks for the proof of all lesser or subordinate principles that claim acceptance as expressing duly ascertained knowledge. 'The persistence of force ... being the basis of experience, must be the basis of any scientific organization of experience. To this an ultimate analysis brings us down; and on this a rational synthesis must be built up.'[30] But Spencer significantly adds that 'by persistence of force, we really mean the persistence of some cause which transcends our knowledge and conception'. In other words, the foundation of knowledge again is nescience. A single principle is made the pivot for sustaining a grandiose scheme of scientific knowledge compassing the whole of reality. Yet surprisingly the step from the inorganic to the organic is left unaccounted for. Spencer excused himself on the grounds that what comes after is the more urgent consideration. Nevertheless, for one so confident of the omnicompetence of his method the omission is glaring.

The application of the evolutionary principle to human psychology shows, in Spencer's judgment, that the development of mental functions parallels that of organic. Ideas which appear to be innate or intuitive are, like certain types of mental reaction, to be traced to heredity. Society likewise is an organism and social institutions are to be seen as the outcome of a process embodying two opposing tendencies: the state and the individual. Capacity for initiative, Spencer holds, lies with the individual, whose aggressive instincts must be curbed. Conduct, on a properly naturalistic assessment, simply means the adjustment of the organism to its environing conditions. That which secures the most nearly perfect adjustment is at once the most acceptable to society and—at least in the long run—the most satisfactory to the individual. Moral concepts arise from the experience of the race, conscience (as we call it) originating in social custom, whether restrictive or permissive. A hedonistic element—'pleasure promotes function'—has to be recognized; but the law of evolution ensures that actions which are found to be pleasurable will also be such as to possess survival value. A perfect balance of egoism and altruism, achieved when moral conduct becomes a purely 'natural' functioning and the sense of duty as such disappears, will, of course, be realized only in some future and utopian stage of social development.[31] Finally, the world's religions also take their place within the evolutionary scheme and are interpretable as expressions of man's efforts to transcend the ordinary bounds of experience. Spencer himself combined an intellectual agnosticism with feelings of mystery and

30. *Ibid.*, sect. 62.
31. See *The Data of Ethics*, published separately in 1879 but later used to form part one of the first volume of *The Principles of Ethics*.

awe at the thought of the Unknowable, an attitude which he regards as the true essence of religion. For the Unknowable, inscrutable though it is, will be apprehended by the thinking man as the ultimate source of all things.

In his day Spencer's name was one to conjure with, and the fact that his Synthetic Philosophy has long since ceased to arouse interest should not blind us to the importance it had for very many of his contemporaries. His attempt to synthesize the entire field of knowledge, although doomed to failure, was as audacious as Auguste Comte's.[32] His sociology gave impetus to that study in its earlier phases, but with increased knowledge, especially in the field of social anthropology, it inevitably came to be superseded. His attempt to effect a reconciliation between science and religion on the proposition that both have a common underlying faith in the existence of some ultimate cause of phenomena, some profound mystery which lies at the heart of the universe and from which all things proceed, was imaginative enough. His contemporary success, however, was the measure of his eventual eclipse. As a thinker he was wholly of his age and without the originality or the vision that could out-top it. When his age passed away and new intellectual forces took the ascendant his system fell into abeyance. At any rate all that is left of it is his naturalistic ethics.

The neo-Hegelians

For Spencer was confident that the ethical life of man could be sufficiently explained by the principle of evolutionary naturalism. The synthetic philosophy is not expressly atheistic, but theism has no place in it: the ultimate is unknown and unknowable. His contemporary, Henry Sidgwick (1838–1900), on the other hand, although he himself gave up orthodox Christianity as intellectually untenable—his change of convictions being marked by his resignation in 1869 of his fellowship at

---

32. Spencer, like Comte, who also took all knowledge for his province, was a positivist. Philosophy he sees as nothing other than the system of the sciences, or knowledge taken as a coherent whole, the function of science being to organize and unify by analysis and synthesis. 'Knowledge of the lowest kind is *un-unified* knowledge; science is *partially-unified* knowledge; philosophy is *completely-unified* knowledge' (*First Principles*, sect 37). The principle on which he attempts to schematize the sciences is that of their relative degree of abstractness or concreteness. A science is concrete in proportion as it deals with a thing in respect of the full actuality of its being, abstract in proportion as it disengages the properties and relations of things and treats of them in isolation. The concrete, abstract-concrete or abstract Spencer does not indeed follow Comte in arranging in a hierarchy or serial order, but he does emphasize their mutual dependence and influence, and the farther they advance the more evident does their interdependence become. Their means of coordination is that of increasing generalization, the most general principle of all—i.e. the persistence of force—being used to reinterpret the conclusions reached by each science separately. The sciences thus diverge and reunite. 'They inosculate; they severally send off and receive connecting growths; and their intercommunion has been becoming more frequent, more intricate, more wildly ramified. ... There has all along been higher specialization, that there might be a larger generalization; and a deeper analysis, that there might be a better synthesis' (*The Genesis of Science*, p. 29).

Trinity[33]—was persuaded none the less that a naturalistic ethics is inadequate to human needs. Spencer's doctrines had appealed to him as a young man, but, as we have seen, he was later repelled by their manifest defects, when viewed from the standpoint of either metaphysics or morals. His own most considerable work was *The Methods of Ethics*, first published in 1874, in which he takes up the argument on behalf of intuitionism, one of the three 'methods' he chooses to examine, the others being egoism and utilitarianism. Egoism, Sidgwick points out, seeks to justify an action from its contribution to the greatest happiness of the agent himself, utilitarianism from its contribution to the greatest happiness of all who are affected by it. Intuitionism, on the other hand, in whatever form, recognizes ultimate ends beyond mere felicity and ethical rules other than those which enjoin the maximization of the happiness of the greatest number. Ordinary men, quite plainly, accept ends or rules 'as desirable apart from the happiness they promote'—namely, the disinterested pursuit of virtue or knowledge or beauty. Yet it has also to be recognized, Sidgwick holds, that the injunctions of common sense are apt to be vague and indefinite, at times conflicting and often allowing of exceptions. They do not supply, therefore, a sufficient basis for rational conduct, even though they do tend to further the general happiness. Sidgwick admits a measure of psychological hedonism, believing that any action can to some extent be justified by showing that it promotes the agent's personal happiness; yet the egoistic principle, if consistently followed, seems repugnant to the moral sentiment. Utilitarianism, that is, can certainly offer a rationally coherent account of the moral consciousness; but the question remains whether the reasonableness of self-love can really explain what is felt to be the special character of moral obligation. Moreover, what proof is there that the general happiness and the individual's own are in fact coincident? Sidgwick concludes that only belief in God will render such a coincidence possible and give to human conduct an effective principle of unity.

Although a searching critic of naturalism, Sidgwick did not himself produce a completed system of philosophy.[34] This was more rigorously attempted by his contemporary, Thomas Hill Green (1836–82), a fellow of Balliol College, Oxford, and Whyte's professor of moral philosophy in the university from 1878 until his death. Green's doctrine was worked out in strong opposition to the empiricism, naturalism and agnosticism of his day. 'He it was', said Scott Holland, 'who shook us all free from the bondage of cramping philosophies and sent us out once again on the high pilgrimage towards Ideal Truth'.[35] Lord Bryce, who also had been Green's contemporary at Oxford, regarded him as 'the most powerful ethical and

---

33. Sidgwick retained his lectureship in moral philosophy and in 1883 was appointed Knightbridge professor in that subject. With the eventual removal of religious tests at the university his college re-elected him to a fellowship on the foundation.
34. See D. G. James, *Henry Sidgwick: Science and Faith in Victorian England* (1970).
35. *A Bundle of Memories* (1915), p. 145. Cp. the same author's *Lombard Street in Lent* (rev. ed.), Introduction: 'Philosophically the change in Oxford thought and temper came about mainly through the overpowering influence of T. H. Green. He broke for us the sway of individualistic Sensationalism. He released us from the sphere of agnostic mechanism. He gave us back the language of self-sacrifice, and taught us how we belonged to one another in the one life of high idealism.'

most stimulating intellectual influence upon the minds of the ablest youth of the university', not least upon the more religiously inclined, in spite of his own wide departure from orthodox Christianity.[36] Green was, of course, a convinced exponent of the idealist philosophy, yet he was not a mere camp-follower of Hegel, whose name appears a good deal less frequently in his pages than does that of Kant. He was, moreover, considerably affected by the 'personal idealism' of Hermann Lotze of Göttingen, whose fame and influence were now reaching out beyond his native Germany.[37] Although among the foremost British thinkers of the century, Green's ultimate influence was somewhat diminished by the clumsiness of his literary style and by the fact that the relative shortness of his life prevented his achieving a really full and mature expression of his ideas. His *Prolegomena to Ethics*, published in 1883, is the most important of his writings.

Green's approach to philosophical problems was epistemological. Experience and reality, he held, were one, experience being possible only because both knowledge and its object have a common principle or nature. Any postulated existence which could be distinguished from and opposed to knowledge would *eo ipso* have been so far qualified as necessarily to fall within its sphere. Thus even were it admitted that consciousness is conditional upon material being—matter and motion, that is—in the sense that, as known objects of consciousness, they are required to explain particular mental facts or functions, nevertheless consciousness cannot itself originate from them as though they had a reality prior to it and apart from it. Matter and motion, as known, express relations between constituent elements of experience and are insufficient therefore, in themselves, to explain the possibility of experience as a consequence of reality.[38] Any separation of the process of experience from the facts experienced is thus untenable.

> It renders knowledge, as of fact or reality, inexplicable. It leaves us without an answer to the question, how the order of relations, which the mind sets up, comes to produce those relations of the material world which are assumed to be of a wholly different origin and nature.[39]
>
> It is not that first there is nature, and then there comes to be an experience and knowledge of it. Intelligence, experience, knowledge, are no more a result of nature than nature of them. If it is true that there could be no intelligence without nature, it is equally true that there could be no nature without intelligence.[40]

But although Green's reassertion of the Kantian principle of the synthesizing activity of the mind itself may lead in the end to the Hegelian concept of infinite

---

36. *Studies in Contemporary Biography* (1903), p. 99.
37. See R. L. Nettleship, *Thomas Hill Green: A Memoir*, p. 192. And cp. p. 196*n*. Green had studied Lotze's works in their original tongue, but it was not until the appearance in 1887 of an English translation of *Mikrokosmos* that the German thinker's views became at all well known. The subsequent 'personal idealist' phase in English philosophy owed much to him, Hastings Rashdall—a notable representative—praising him as 'the one philosopher of our time who is at once a thinker of the highest rank and wholly and unexceptionably Christian in his thoughts' (*Contentio Veritatis*, 1902, p. 43).
38. *Prolegomena to Ethics*, sect. 9.
39. *Ibid.*, sect. 34.
40. *Ibid.*, sect. 36.

Spirit, his interest in religion deterred him from equating this with the sum total of finite spirits. Green disliked the way in which the traditional theism contrasts God's being with that of the world and finite spirits, and preferred himself to think of man's spiritual life as a *participation* in the divine. But neither would he identify God with humanity in its spiritual development or with the idea of human knowledge as a completed whole. At any rate the human spirit could be said to be *identical* with God only 'in the sense that He *is* all which the human spirit is capable of becoming'. God should rather be thought of as infinite and eternal Subject whose own perfect knowledge 'reproduces itself' progressively in finite subjects under the necessary modification imposed by the constitution of the human organism. As to why God, the all-perfect, should have made this imperfect world has never been answered, and in Green's view never would be.

> We know not why the world should be; we only know that there it is. In like manner we know not why the eternal subject of that world, as the spirit of mankind, or as the particular self of this or that man in whom the spirit of mankind operates. We can only say that, upon the best analysis we can make of our experience, it seems that so it does.[41]

Green was typically a Victorian in his concern for belief in the immortality of the soul, defending the idea on the grounds that the destructability of thought is a contradiction in terms, destruction having no meaning except in relation to thought.[42] How indeed the continuance of personal life after death might be maintained he did not claim to understand, but he believed such a faith to be in no way incongruous with the basic principles of his philosophy. There may be reason, he thought, for holding that 'there are capacities of the human spirit not realizable in persons under the conditions of any society that we know or can possibly conceive, or that may be capable of existing on earth'. Hence the probably justifiable supposition that the personal life, which in history or on earth is inevitably subject to conditions that thwart its development, is hereafter to be continued in a society which, although unattainable through the senses, nonetheless shares in and advances any measure of perfection attainable by man under known conditions. In any case the negative conviction must remain 'that a capacity which is working except as personal, cannot be realized in any impersonal modes of being'.[43]

There is little doubt that Green's teaching proved the most stimulating philosophical influence in this country during the latter half of the nineteenth century, especially through its critique of the presuppositions of scientific naturalism. Man, he assured his generation, is not an isolated creature in an alien universe, and the merely physical aspect of his being cannot be cited as the true cause of his actions. Green's arguments, however, are not always well stated and his language is frequently ambiguous, faults which afterwards were to reduce his standing with professional philosophers. Had he been less anxious to avoid

41. *Ibid.*, sect. 100.
42. *The Works of T. H. Green*, ed. R. L. Nettleship (1885–88), iii, p. 159.
43. *Op. cit.*, iii. p. 195.

controversy, for he had no taste for polemics, he might have given his ideas clearer shape. He was particularly scrupulous in avoiding religious controversy, although unable himself to accept traditional Christian doctrine, being content to believe that God is the sum of all perfections and the essence of religion as a consistent faith in the ideal. But orthodoxy was undoubtedly heartened by his example at a time when its very foundations seemed threatened. Anglican theology in the last quarter of the century probably owed more to him than to any other thinker since Maurice.

The impact upon British philosophy of Green's contemporary and friend, Edward Caird (1835–1908), occurred somewhat later, his revised and expanded study of Kant appearing only in 1889. Less original than Green, he was much his superior as a teacher and writer, possessing a brilliant gift for exposition. But as with the former the real weight of his achievement has to be reckoned in personal rather than in literary terms, first—and perhaps mainly—as professor of moral philosophy at Glasgow, and subsequently as master of Balliol. The idealist philosophy—and his own profound debt to Hegel he readily acknowledged[44]—was, he too believed, the necessary because only effective counterbalance to the growing pressure of naturalism and materialism. If the gulf between religion and science was not to widen further—and the naïve common sense of the Scottish school (already undermined by Hume) plainly could not bridge it—then reflection must seek a synthesis in which the opposing forces could be reconciled at a higher level. Hegel, Caird judged, had rightly perceived that the world of intelligence and freedom could not fundamentally be other than that of nature and necessity; on the contrary, it was 'only the same world seen in a new light, or subjected to a further interpretation'.[45] The spiritual world must therefore be looked for *within* the natural and not simply, as with the traditional supernaturalism, beyond it.

To the attainment of this higher view Kant, in Caird's estimation, had made an invaluable contribution, although in precisely what respect had not always been understood. The misunderstanding originated with Kant himself, in his unresolved dualism of phenomena and noumena. For what these represent are really no more than different stages in the progress of knowledge itself, the unknown and unknowable *Ding an sich* being a mere irrational residuum of which a truly critical philosophy would strive to rid itself. Dismiss the 'thing-in-itself' and it becomes evident that 'objectivity' exists only for a self-conscious subject and that between subject and object there is an intrinsic relationship, a subsisting unity-in-difference. No doubt life as we usually think of it moves back and forth between these two terms, regarded as essentially distinct and even mutually opposed. Nevertheless 'we are forced to seek the secret of their being in a higher principle, of whose unity they in their action and reaction are the manifestations, which they presuppose as their beginning and to which they point as their end'.[46] Science, of course, is held to be exclusively concerned with the object, yet in its task of discovering and

44. See the present writer's chapter on 'T. H. Green as a Theologian' in *The Philosophy of T. H. Green* (ed. A. Vincent) (1986), pp. 36–47.
45. *Hegel* (Blackwood's Philosophical Classics), (1883), p. 125.
46. *The Evolution of Religion* (1893), i, pp. 65, 67.

correlating universal laws it implicitly acknowledges the existence of an intelligible order which cannot be detached from the thought that comprehends it.

The reality which is 'at once the source of being to all things that are, and of knowing to all things that know' is what Caird understands by God. As such, however, not all men are aware of it. Religion has passed through a long process of evolution, the main phases of which admit of fairly clear distinction. The first is that of 'objective religion', in which man's thinking about the divine is conditioned entirely by experience of his external environment. Man at first looks outward, not inward, and can form no idea of anything to which he cannot give 'a local habitation and a name.' The gods, like himself, must have being in time and space. The second phase, that of 'subjective religion', is one in which God is conceived as a 'subject', and as such is 'brought under the limitations ... of a human understanding'.[47] God now is thought of as a spiritual being of a different order from both the world and man and as revealing himself above all in conscience. In the final stage, that of 'absolute religion', subject and object are recognized as essentially related and as standing in an ultimate unity. They are grounded, that is, in a Being 'who is at once the source, the sustaining power, and the end of our spiritual lives',[48] and who is disclosed to us alike in nature and in human history.

Caird's view of Christianity is illuminated by a paper he read on 22 October 1896 to the Oxford Society for Historical Theology entitled 'Christianity and the Historical Christ'.[49] It is a critique—detectably Hegelian in its bias—of the then current Liberal Protestant idea that the authentic nature of Christianity is to be found in the 'historical Jesus' as presented, in essentials, in the synoptic gospels, and that subsequent developments in the Church's intellectual and institutional life have been at best, an irrelevant increment. The highest, if also impossible, goal of such criticism, he wrote, 'would be to annihilate space and time, and to enable us to live over again the life of the disciples who enjoyed the personal communion of the Lord'. Such a hope, however, is illusory. Not only is the recovery of an 'authentic' picture a vain quest,[50] it is also in principle a misconceived one: the essence of religion is, rather, to be sought in the whole process of its historical evolution. Christ is properly to be interpreted 'by that which sprang from him, by the whole impression which he made upon his own and the immediately succeeding generation'. Fact and interpretation are conjoined: the one without the other would prove elusive. 'There are some writers', Caird observes, 'who are so zealous against the idea of a Christianity without Christ, that they are in danger of preaching a Christ without Christianity'.[51] The same point was to be made soon, and more thoroughly, by the Catholic Modernist, Loisy, in *L'Evangile et l'Eglise*, a work which Caird himself, Presbyterian though he was, read with approval.[52]

47. *Ibid.*, i, p. 193.
48. *Ibid.*, i, p. 195.
49. It was printed in the *Abstracts* of the Society's *Proceedings*.
50. As, a few years later (1906) was to be cogently argued by A. Schweitzer in *Von Reimarus zu Wrede* (Eng. trans. as *The Quest of the Historical Jesus* (1910)).
51. *Abstract*, p. 19.
52. Cf. Loisy, *Mémoires*, ii, p. 179.

With the later developments of British absolute idealism, in the work of Francis Herbert Bradley (1846–1924) and Bernard Bosanquet (1848–1923) it is hardly to our present purpose to deal. Both were academic philosophers whose writings either fall outside our period or had virtually no significant influence on contemporary theological thought.[53] Both, however, discuss religion at some length, holding it, at least on their own interpretation, in high regard. Where they parted company with anything resembling Christian conceptions was in their denial that, metaphysically speaking, personality can be judged as ultimately real. Bradley, in *Appearance and Reality*, argued that the very idea of a 'self' is so shot through with contradictions as to provide no acceptable clue to the nature of the ultimate reality, the sole criterion of which must be non-contradiction. If God were conceived as personal in the usual sense of personality he could not possibly be the ultimate. The Absolute, in other words, is not and cannot be God.[54] Reality therefore must be 'suprapersonal'.[55] A view such as this inevitably determines Bradley's account of religion itself, since if religion, as its apologists claim, is a practical attitude or feeling then plainly it is bound to have an object, and between this object and the person thus confronting it there must be a relationship. But religion, like God himself,—paradoxically, in view of the meaning of the word—is *above* relatedness, for 'short of the Absolute God cannot rest, and having reached that goal, he is lost and religion with him'[56] Alternatively religion could be seen as 'the attempt to express the complete reality of goodness through every aspect of our being. And, so far as this goes, it is at once something more, and something higher, than philosophy'.[57] In any case metaphysics cannot be used as a prop for Christianity, although in *Essays on Truth and Reality* Bradley concedes that a religious belief might be founded otherwise than on metaphysics, 'and metaphysics is able in some sense to justify that creed'. In fact in this later book he shows himself by no means unappreciative of the merely partial and imperfect truths of religion, holding that 'the demand for a theoretical consistency which mutilates the substance of religion, starts from error in principle and leads in the result to practical discord or sterility'.[58] Evidently upon this subject Bradley was not wholly sure of his position or was diffident of stating it openly. God may have to be thought of as 'appearance', but still he possesses a higher degree of reality than

---

53. Bradley was appointed to a fellowship at Merton College, Oxford, in 1870 and retained it to the end of his life, which was virtually that of a recluse. *Appearance and Reality* was published in 1893 (2nd ed., 1902) and *Essays on Truth and Reality* in 1914. He was awarded the Order of Merit in 1914. Bosanquet, who had been much influenced by Green and Nettleship, was a fellow of University College, Oxford. From 1903 to 1908 he occupied the chair of moral philosophy at St Andrews. The best known of his numerous writings are the two series of Gifford lectures, *The Principle of Individuality and Value* (1912) and *The Value and Destiny of the Individual* (1913). His express views on religion are contained in his essay *What Religion Is* (1920).
54. *Appearance and Reality*, p. 335.
55. *Ibid.*, p. 531.
56. *Ibid.*, p. 447.
57. *Ibid.*, p. 453.
58. *Essays on Truth and Reality*, p. 432.

anything else we know. 'There is nothing', Bradley is even ready to say, 'more real than what comes to us in religion'.[59]

With Bradley's ideas Bosanquet's are very largely in line, but there are differences also, probably attributable to the two men's diversity of temperament. Bosanquet believed that as between the philosophy of the Absolute and the Christian religion, particularly in the matter of the doctrine of a future life, there is a sufficient affinity to allow them to draw sustenance from one another.[60] Religion indeed, like other activities of the spirit, is necessary if man is to transcend the constricting and impoverishing limits of the individual self. Yet, as C. C. J. Webb puts it, Bosanquet's philosophy 'wears an air of almost inhuman serenity while dismissing much that has been precious to many generations of our spiritual forefathers, and is still precious to multitudes of men', whereas in Bradley's, on the other hand, we find 'a very human melancholy, as of one who, with all his devotion to his chosen task of following the argument withersoever it may lead him, is yet profoundly convinced that there are inexorable limits set to Philosophy's power of satisfying the human spirit, and acutely sensible of the discontent which must thus remain to her votaries when she has done all that she can do to reward their faithful services'.[61]

Personal idealism

The distinguished Unitarian teacher James Martineau (1805–1900), whose long life spanned nearly the whole century, is not to be classed along with the neo-Hegelians, but in the task he set himself of explaining the world and mankind in spiritual terms he is fairly to be considered in idealist company. For while he neither adopted absolutist philosophical principles nor pursued its method he was at one with the Hegelians in his strong opposition to scientific agnosticism. His most important publications, *Types of Ethical Theory* (1885), *A Study of Religion* (1888) and *The Seat of Authority in Religion* (1890), were the product of his old age, but they embody teaching which he had been imparting for many years before, both orally and in magazine articles, chiefly in the *Prospective, National* and *Westminster* reviews.[62] His main targets were the doctrines of Spencer and Tyndall, whose monism and naturalism were inadequate to meet the full facts of human existence. As against the theory of the 'atomists' he held that

---

59. *Appearance and Reality*, p. 449. Cp. *Essays on Truth and Reality*, p. 449: 'If I am forced to take reality as having ... only one sense ... nothing to me in this sense is real except the Universe as a whole: for I cannot take God as including or as equivalent to the whole Universe.... But if ... I am allowed to hold degrees in reality ... God to me is now so much more real than you or myself that to compare God's reality with ours would be ridiculous.'
60. See his 'Are we Agnostics?', in *The Civilization of Christendom* (1893), p. 141.
61. *Divine Personality and Human Life* (1920), p. 253.
62. His collected *Essays, Reviews and Addresses* were issued in a four-volume edition dated 1890–91.

to suppose that by pulverizing the world into its least particles, and contemplating its components where they are next to nothing, we shall hit on something ultimate beyond which there is no problem, is the strangest of illusions. [The atomist] must, in spite of his contempt for final causes, himself proceed upon a preconceived world-plan, and guide his own intellect, as step by step, he fits it to the universe by the very process which he declares to be absent from the universe itself.[63]

In the preface to *Types of Ethical Theory* he affords by contrast a brief sketch of his own intellectual development. He began his study of philosophy only after having first been trained as a civil engineer. 'I had', he says, 'nothing to take with me into logical and ethical problems but the maxims and postulates of physical knowledge', and so found himself 'shut up in the habit of interpreting the human phenomena by the analogy of external nature'. Thus 'steeped in the "empirical" and "necessarian" mode of thought' he served out 'successive terms of willing captivity to Locke and Hartley, to Collins, Edwards, and Priestly, to Bentham and James Mill'. A change of mind, however, began to show itself in 1834, in a review of Bentham's *Deontology*.[64] The familiar utilitarian arguments were now losing their cogency for him, thanks less to any intellectual persuasion from without than to reflection on his own inner life.

> It was the irresistible pleading of the moral consciousness which first drove me to rebel against the limits of the merely scientific conception. It became incredible to me that nothing was possible except the actual; and the naturalistic uniformity could no longer escape some breach in its closed barrier to make room for the ethical alternative … This involved the surrender of determinism and a revision of the doctrine of causation.[65]

Thenceforward his task was to be to elucidate the full meaning of the ideas of will and conscience. The former he saw as the type *par excellence* of causality, in man and in God; the latter, whose authoritative judgments are a voice divine, as the testimony of man's freedom, the evidence that personality is not wholly enmeshed in the causal nexus, necessary as this is to the maintenance of nature's order. For natural causation must also itself be referred to the divine will as its ground, the only true causes in the universe being God and rational entities: 'force' in the scientific sense—'will *minus* purpose'—is merely an abstraction and does not really exist. Martineau's religious philosophy revives in fact the teleological conceptions of an older theology, though in a more immanental way. Science, he believes, illustrates the presence of rational ends in nature, just as the moral consciousness indicates the presence within us of a moral order which in turn discloses the transcendent holiness of God. Thus a sound philosophy will postulate an adequate

63. *The Contemporary Review*, February 1876, pp. 340, 345.
64. See J. Estlin Carpenter, *James Martineau* (1905), p. 148. 'Sum up', Bentham had said, 'the values of all the *pleasures* on the one side, and those of all the pains on the other. The balance, if it be on the side of pleasure, will give the *good* tendency of the act upon the whole...; if on the side of pain, the *bad* tendency of it upon the whole' (*Introduction to the Principles of Morals and Legislation*, repr. 1907, p. 31).
65. *Types of Ethical Theory*, pp. xxiif.

spiritual cause for both the cosmos and the ethical experience of conscience, so linking the religion of nature with that of the moral personality.[66]

The working-out of Martineau's metaphysical theory was greatly facilitated by a period of study in Germany from 1848 to 1849, mainly under the direction of Trendelenburg and in the field of ancient Greek philosophy. The effect of this he describes as 'a new intellectual birth'. 'The metaphysic of the world had come home to me, and never again could I say that phenomena, in their clusters and claims, were all, or find myself in a universe with no categories but the like and the unlike, the synchronous and the successive'.[67] Its eventual outcome, in the long series of occasional essays as well as the books of his final years, was a restatement of ethical theism in terms which took full account of the antitheistic assumptions of contemporary science and the new philosophies based on it. Despite the author's liberal Unitarianism, Christian opinion of whatever denominational colour gladly applauded him as a formidable champion of the basic affirmations of the common faith.

In his theology Martineau remained loyal to the traditional teaching of his sect until about 1832. With the publication in 1836 of his first book, *The Rationale of Religious Inquiry*, his shift of position became evident. Reason was to be his guiding principle, and 'no seeming inspiration' could establish anything contrary to it. 'The last appeal in all research into religious truth must be the judgments of the human mind.'[68] Even so he still held belief in the gospel miracles to be a test of Christian conviction, a view he later rescinded. As the years passed he became more radical in outlook. The advances in New Testament criticism made by the German scholars impressed him deeply, and before long he came to accept the principal positions of the Tübingen school.[69] But his adoption of a liberal standpoint meant also a discarding of the old intellectualism and notably the determinism he had inherited from Joseph Priestly. Will and emotion were taken to play a larger part in the shaping of faith as an act and disposition of the whole personality. But this in turn necessitated a change in the conception of divine revelation and therefore of the seat of authority in religion. No longer was he content to think of revelation as a supernatural communication of specific truths, of which Scripture is the infallible record; nor of prophecy and miracle as an external guarantee of its veracity. Rather, if personality is the highest value known to man it is to be expected that revelation will be made through personal media and that the real criterion of divine truth is provided by the heart and conscience. In short, if a man would know the will and

66. In all ethical judgments Martineau discerns a preference: one chooses the higher rather than the lower, and it is conscience which decides, regardless of prudential consequences. For conscience, as distinct from prudence, 'is concerned with quite another order of differences; differences of inherent excellence and authority, which by their very nature must be cognisable *prior* to action, and accordingly not learned by experiment, but read off by *insight*, presenting themselves to consciousness as premonitions, not as the sequel of conduct' (*op. cit.*, p. 186).
67. *Ibid.*, p. xiv.
68. *The Rationale of Religious Inquiry*, p. 125.
69. Cp. 'The creed and heresies of early Christianity', published in *The Westminster Review*, 1853.

purpose of God let him first search the depths of his own nature. The primal authority in religion is experience itself, the inner witness of moral feeling and perception. In Jesus Christ, the supreme revelation, the character of God is disclosed under human conditions such as all men can understand.

Thus Martineau became convinced, in the light of his own religious development, that a theology tending more and more to be critical and even sceptical in tone might well mean not a weakening but a positive reinforcement of inward assurance, and he points out in a letter of 1840 to the American theologian, W. E. Channing, how 'there is a simultaneous increase, in the very same class of minds, of theological doubt and of devotional affection; there is far less *belief* yet more *faith*, than there was twenty years ago'.[70] The kind of apologetic the age needed was one which largely abandoned the old and now tenuous appeal to extrinsic 'evidences' in order to rely on that 'profounder sense of the intrinsically divine character of Christianity' which the more thoughtful among younger men were beginning to feel. It was an apologetic Martineau himself consistently aimed at and no English theologian of his age had a deeper apprehension of what the changing intellectual climate demanded or was more far-sighted in his attempt to meet it.

The case against materialism and naturalism was further elaborated, however, in the works of the 'personal idealist' school at the close of the century, which principally included Arthur James Balfour (1848–1930), the statesman—afterwards Earl Balfour—James Ward (1843–1925), naturalist, psychologist and philosopher, who was professor of logic and mental philosophy at Cambridge from 1897 until his death, and Hastings Rashdall (1858–1924), a fellow of New College, Oxford, and later dean of Carlisle. The first named, in his *The Foundations of Belief* (1895) and Gifford lectures on *Theism and Humanism* (1914), stressed the importance of the non-rational causes as well as the rational *grounds* of belief. In the formation of men's beliefs, he argued, the general psychological 'climate' inevitably counts for much and tends in fact to condition the attitude of scientists no less than of religious believers. The problem as he saw it is how non-intelligent nature can possibly be held to have produced an evaluating intelligence unless, behind and controlling it, there is an ultimate 'purpose' which itself is intelligent. All philosophies which deny such a purpose are 'intrinsically incoherent'. 'In the order of causation they base reason upon unreason. In the order of logic they involve conclusions which discredit their own premises.'[71] Nor does the Darwinian theory bring us nearer to an explanation.

> Why should faculties designed only to help primitive man or his animal progenitors successfully to breed and feed, be fitted to solve philosophical problems so useless and so remote? Why, indeed, do such problems occur to us? Why do we long for their solution?

Reflective agnosticism cannot be combined with scientific naturalism, since it is itself the product of a process which naturalism discredits.[72] More, naturalism fails to account even for the valid pursuit of natural science.

70. Quoted by J. Estlin Carpenter, *op. cit.*, pp. 183–8.
71. *Theism and Humanism*, pp. 257ff.
72. *Ibid.*, p. 259.

Here, if anywhere, we might suppose ourselves independent of theology. Here, if anywhere, we might expect to be able to acquiesce without embarrassment in the negations of naturalism. But when once we have realized the scientific truth that at the roots of every rational process there lies an irrational one; that reason, from a scientific point of view, is itself a natural product; and that the whole material on which it works is due to causes, physical, physiological and social, which it neither creates nor controls, we shall ... be driven in mere self-defence to hold that, behind these non-rational forces, and above them, guiding them by slow degrees, and, as it were, with difficulty, to a rational issue, stands the Supreme Reason in whom we most believe, if we are to believe anything.[73]

Ward, a professional philosopher as compared with Balfour, dealt with the same problem, but on more systematic lines and in a way which clearly shows the influence of the 'personal' idealism of Hermann Lotze. In the first series of his Gifford lectures, published in 1899 under the title *Naturalism and Agnosticism*, he insists on a distinction being drawn between natural science proper and naturalism as a philosophy. Mechanics, for example, deals only with the quantitative aspects of physical phenomena, whereas a mechanistic theory of nature aspires 'to resolve the actual world into an actual mechanism'.[74] The scientist *qua* scientist must be content to regard the laws of mechanics as resting on an abstract and selective methodology, valid within their limits though these laws are; what he is not entitled to assume is that of themselves they provide a sufficient account of reality as it is. But if materialistic monism is unwarranted so too is a bare mind–matter dualism: the object of knowledge can stand in relation to the knowing subject only because it is not itself heterogeneous to the subject. Indeed in Ward's view all entities are in some sense spiritual and the philosophy he himself propounds, more especially in the second series of Gifford lectures, *The Realm of Ends*, dating from 1911, is a spiritualist pluralism. It is a philosophy, he claims, founded on experience.

> The world is taken simply as we find it, as a plurality of active individuals unified only in and through their mutual interactions. These interactions again are interpreted throughout on the analogy of social transactions, as a *mutuum commercium*; that is to say, as based on cognition and conation.[75]

Ward admits that it would be possible to look no further than this plurality of finite centres of experience, particularly as the so-called proofs of divine existence are open to damaging criticism. Nevertheless the concept of God supplies a principle of unity which pluralism must otherwise lack; whilst those of creation and conservation help also to explain the existence of a multiplicity of beings.

> Without the idea of a Supreme and Ultimate Being, least inadequately conceived as personal, transcending the world, as the ground of its being, and yet immanent in it, as it is his idea—the world may well remain for ever that *rerum concordia discors*, which at present we find it.[76]

73. *The Foundations of Belief*, pp. 322f.
74. *Naturalism and Agnosticism*, i, viii (ed. 1906, p. x).
75. *The Realm of Ends*, p. 225.
76. *Ibid.*, p. 421.

Hastings Rashdall, along with G. F. Stout and F. C. S. Schiller, was a contributor in 1902 to a volume of essays expressly entitled *Personal Idealism*,[77] his own dealing with the subject, 'Personality in God and Man'. Subsequent statements of his views on the philosophical grounds of belief included the essay on 'The basis of theism' in *Contentio Veritatis*[78] and a series of Cambridge University lectures delivered in 1908 and printed the year after as *Philosophy and Religion*. Rashdall, who followed Ward closely, denied that materialism is a possible doctrine, in that all that we know of matter implies mind. On the other hand, matter does not exist solely as an object for man's transitory and incomplete knowledge. But if it cannot exist apart from mind then inferentially there must be a universal Mind in which and for which all things exist. As for naturalism it has to be said that in our experience of external nature what we encounter is not causality but, as Hume had pointed out, only succession, the uniformity of nature being a postulate of physical science, not a necessity of thought. The idea of causality really derives from our consciousness of volition, but events not caused by human volition indicate the operation of a will or wills other than human, although the systematic unity of nature suggests a single will. Further, 'if the ultimate Reality be thought of as a rational Will, analogous to the will which each of us is conscious of himself having or being, He is no longer the Unknown or the Unknowable, but the God of Religion, who has revealed Himself in the consciousness of man, "made in the image of God" '.[79] However—and the proviso is very characteristic of Rashdall's moralism—the mutual independence of divine and human personality must be clearly maintained, despite the truth that all human persons are of God's creating. Individuals are in no sense 'lost' in God or absorbed into his being—Rashdall had no sympathy with mysticism—nor was God himself to be thought of as 'superpersonal' if the term be meant to denote some kind of existence in fact lower than that of persons, 'as a force, an unconscious substance, or merely a name for the totality of things'.[80]

Philosophical idealism, both in its absolutist and in its personalist forms, was a sustained attempt to dispel the growing fear that science had turned the universe into a soulless mechanism. In this at least it resembles the Ritschlian movement in contemporary European theology, hostile though Ritschl himself was to all such metaphysical would-be aids,[81] for Ritschlianism's basic aim was to uphold man's freedom amid the enveloping determinisms of nature. The fault of absolute idealism, from the Christian standpoint, was its conclusion that although reality is to be explained in terms of mind, personal distinctions obtain only of the world of 'appearance' and thus have no ultimate validity or even meaning. Personal

77. Ed. H. Sturt.
78. The other contributors were W. R. Inge, A. J. Carlyle, W. C. Allen and H. L. Wild.
79. *Philosphy and Religion*, p. 54.
80. *Ibid.*, p. 55.
81. Ritschl, little enough of a philosopher, relied for the philosophical grounds of his theism on Kant and Lotze, and could be described loosely as a personal idealist. His *Theologie und Metaphysik*, first published in 1881, is the most explicit account he ever rendered of his own philosophical position. But it is mainly a polemic against absolutism.

idealism, it is fair to say, stood in the main for an unequivocal theism[82] as against any sort of all-dissolving monism, but its exponents were not always very rigorous in their arguments and in retrospect their systems emerge as not much more than individual statements of faith. As philosophies they are type-products of their time and now chiefly of historical interest. Not that the issue between science and religion has been demonstrably resolved one way or the other. The truth is that scientists and philosophers alike prefer to devote their attention to specific problems sooner than advance comprehensive world views in which theology can at once recognize either an enemy or an ally. But that theology, the former queen of the sciences, should find herself alone on a deserted battlefield is far from being proof that the campaign has gone in her favour.

82. J. McT. E. McTaggart, a fellow of Trinity College, Cambridge from 1891 to 1925, combined both Hegelianism and personal idealism in a highly idiosyncratic doctrine—an atheistic spiritual pluralism. 'If all reality', he thought, 'is a harmonious system of selves, it is perhaps itself sufficiently godlike to dispense with God' (*Some Dogmas of Religion*, 1906, p. 250). In terms of his own definition of religion as 'an emotion resting on a conviction of a harmony between ourselves and the universe at large' (*op. cit.*, p. 3) McTaggart was himself an intensely religious man. Truth, however, he seemed to envisage only as a kind of dream, personal and barely communicable.

Chapter 10

LIBERAL THEOLOGY AND THE BIBLICAL QUESTION

'Essays and reviews'

The publication in February 1860 of *Essays and Reviews*, the joint undertaking of six clerics and a layman, the majority of them Oxford men, proved in the event to be a turning-point in the history of theological opinion in England. At the time it caused a sensation, although this (with the book's uninviting title) was not immediate. Spring and summer, in fact, passed by and very little attention was aroused. It was only later that the storm of controversy broke, and when at last it did, 'addresses, memorials, and remonstrances against the mischievous tendencies of the book poured in upon the Archbishops and Bishops', whilst the luckless authors were denounced as 'traitors to their sacred calling' and as 'guilty of moral dishonesty'.[1] The leader of the opposition was that most able and energetic of the occupants of the contemporary episcopal bench, Samuel Wilberforce of Oxford. Our concern here, however, is with the contents of this literary enterprise, not with its reception by the public.[2] The several contributors wrote independently of one another, and in a brief prefatory note stated that each was responsible solely for his own chosen subject. But the significance of the volume lay in its general tone and tendency, which were undoubtedly meant by all the authors to be a challenge to accepted views and especially the complacent ignorance which in many instances alone sustained them. They themselves described their work modestly enough as 'an attempt to illustrate the advantages derivable to the cause of moral and religious truth, from a free handling, in a becoming spirit, of subjects peculiarly liable to suffer by the repetition of conventional language, and from traditional methods of treatment'. Benjamin Jowett, then Regius professor of Greek at Oxford, and author of the longest and perhaps most important of the essays, gave in a letter to his friend, A. P. Stanley, a firmer hint of their common intention:

> [Our] object is to say what we think freely within the limits of the Church of England.
> ... We do not wish to do anything rash, or irritating to the public or the University,
> but we are determined not to submit to this abominable system of terrorism, which

---

1. R. E. Prothero, *The Life and Correspondence of Dean Stanley* (1893), ii, pp. 30f.
2. On this see Chadwick, *The Victorian Church*, Part ii, pp. 75–90. Also B. Willey, *More Nineteenth Century Studies* (1956; 2nd ed. 1980), ch. IV, and G. Faber, *Jowett* (1957), chs XI and XII.

prevents the statement of the plainest facts, and makes true theology or theological education impossible.[3]

The immediate promoter of the scheme was Henry Bristow Wilson, vicar of Great Staughton, Huntingdonshire, and a former Bampton lecturer, the supporting contributors being Frederick Temple, headmaster of Rugby and subsequently archbishop of Canterbury;[4] Rowland Williams, rector of Broadchalke, Wiltshire, and vice-principal and professor of Hebrew at Lampeter—classicist, orientalist and theologian; Baden Powell, Savilian professor of geometry at Oxford; Charles Wycliffe Goodwin, an Egyptologist and the one layman among them; Mark Pattison, tutor of Lincoln College, Oxford, a man we have already noted as a dedicated scholar, if an enigmatic personality; and lastly Jowett himself, not as yet elevated to the headship of his college, but one who for long was to be the eminent representative of a type of churchmanship whose features his contemporaries found it difficult to determine: 'He stood', said Leslie Stephen, 'at the parting of many ways, and wrote "No thoroughfare" upon them all.' In sum, this book, like the equally notorious *Tract 90* before it, staked 'a claim to hold new and dangerous opinions within the pale of the Church of England'.[5] Churchmen at large saw it as an attempt to discredit Scripture and subvert the creed; yet today it reads as no more than a collection of theological and critical commonplaces, somewhat truculently voiced.

The opening essay, 'The Education of the World', was Temple's, and had already served its turn as a university sermon: the marks of pulpit oratory are obvious, as in its overworked and in any case dubious analogy between the history of mankind and the life of the individual. The record of the human race, it is argued, discloses three stages, corresponding to childhood, youth and maturity. Childhood needs a 'Rule', youth an 'Example', adulthood 'Principles'; and these are met by, respectively, the Law, the Son of Man and the gift of the Spirit. According to this view the ancient Greeks and Romans were but 'children', whereas the modern world has reached maturity. The principles of living are to be found in Scripture; hence 'the immediate work' of our day is the study of the Bible, since it is 'utterly impossible … in the manhood of the world to imagine any other instructor of mankind'. But the Bible must be studied with the mind of a grown man.

3. E. Abbott and L. Campbell, *The Life and Letters of Benjamin Jowett* (1897), i, p. 275. Stanley himself declined to participate, not merely from a dislike of composite publications.
4. In a speech to Rugby masters in the following year Temple explained that the book owed its origin 'to some conversation between Mr Jowett and myself, as far back as eight or nine years ago, on the great amount of reticence in every class of society in regard to religious views—the melancholy unwillingness of people to state honestly their opinions on points of doctrine. We thought it might encourage free and honest discussion of biblical topics, if we were to combine with some others to publish a volume of essays … one stipulation being made, that nothing should be written which was inconsistent with the position of a minister of our Church' (E.G. Sandford, ed., *Memoirs of Archbishop Temple* (1906), ii, p. 225.
5. F. Warre Cornish, *A History of the English Church in the Nineteenth Century* (1910), ii, p. 128.

Every day makes it more and more evident that the thorough study of the Bible, the investigation of what it teaches and what it does not teach, the determination of the degree of authority to be ascribed to the different books, if any degrees are to be admitted, must take the lead of all other studies.

Were geology to prove that the first chapters of Genesis cannot be read literally, or historical investigation to show that inspiration, though protective of doctrine, did not preclude occasional inaccuracies, or criticism reveal interpolations or forgeries, the results should still be welcome. New knowledge will of itself do no harm; on the contrary, 'he is guilty of high treason against the faith, who fears the result of any investigation, whether philosophical, or scientific, or historical'.[6] The tendency of modern times has been to modify the dogmatism of ancient Christianity by substituting the spirit for the letter and practical religion for precise definitions of truth.

Temple's contribution was in substance entirely innocuous, even if so sane a critic as Connop Thirlwall, in his episcopal charge of 1863, discovered in it 'the broadest room for an assault upon the foundations of historical Christianity', deeming it to have handed all authority in religion to private judgment. The second essay, Rowland Williams's, cut more deeply. Some years before he had published a volume of sermons entitled *Rational Godliness*, in which his views on the biblical question were clearly indicated: a human element in Scripture has to be recognized; divine revelation had been progressive and by no means confined to a single race of men; prophecy was not simply predictive. The prevailing notion of inspiration had had, he thought, the unfortunate effect of removing God altogether from the sphere of daily life, so leaving religion as an alien thing without analogy in nature or parallel in history. The biblical writings are inspired, but in varying measure, and in any case the province of inspiration is that of religious not scientific truth. The problem of the miraculous is not to be settled merely on a principle; alleged miracles must be judged on their particular merits and with regard to the relevant circumstances, which include the cultural environment. Williams's contribution to *Essays and Reviews*, on 'Bunsen's Biblical Researches', dealt specifically with the work of the eminent Prussian diplomat in the field of biblical criticism.[7]

6. *Essays and Reviews*, p. 54.
7. Baron von Bunsen, who had been Prussian ambassador at the Court of St James's from 1841 to 1854, was a man of wide learning as well as deep personal piety. His book, *God in History*, was in course of publication when *Essays and Reviews* appeared. He also was the author of a 'modern' translation of the Bible and of a history of ancient Egypt.
    The Essayists were not the first to introduce German biblical scholarship. Herbert Marsh, bishop of Peterborough (he had previously been a professor of divinity at Cambridge) had himself studied in Germany under J. D. Michaelis, a translation of whose *Introduction to the New Testament* he brought out in 1793, with notes of his own. In 1801 he published a study of the first three gospels which gave rise to some controversy. In 1825 Connop Thirlwall produced a translation of Schleiermacher's *Critical Essay on the Gospel of St Luke*, at the time a bold venture in view of the German theologian's reputation for unorthodoxy.

> Bunsen's enduring glory [he wrote] is neither to have paltered with his conscience nor shrunk from the difficulties of the problem, but to have brought a vast erudition, in the light of a Christian conscience, to unroll tangled records, tracing frankly the spirit of God elsewhere, but honouring chiefly the tradition of His Hebrew Sanctuary.[8]

The essay is not, however, confined to personal encomiums. Historical study, it argues, is not to be warned off the biblical terrain.

> We cannot encourage a remorseless criticism of Gentile histories and escape its contagion when we approach Hebrew annals; nor acknowledge a Providence in theory, without owning that it may have comprehended sanctities elsewhere.

Williams's statements, considering the times, were provocative and doubtless were intended to be. The conclusions, then novel, of continental biblical scholars were detailed: the 'Books of Moses' were a compilation of only gradual growth; the 'Child' of Isaiah vii was in fact to be born in the reign of Ahaz; chapters xl to lxvi of the same book are not the work of the prophet of that name but are of anonymous authorship and of a much later date, the celebrated fifty-third chapter having probably been written by Baruch as a portrait of Jeremiah; the Book of Daniel is not authentic history and belongs not to the sixth but to the second century B.C.; the Epistle to the Hebrews is not Pauline, nor the Second Epistle of Peter genuine. In the light of criticism a new theory of inspiration had become imperative, the facts demonstrating both that the Israelites of old were not infallible and that for a right understanding of Scripture the Spirit is ever necessary. The further proposition, that 'if such a Spirit did not dwell in the Church, the Bible would not be inspired, for the Bible is, before all things, the written voice of the congregation'[9], gave great offence; as too did the opinion that the sacrosanct doctrine of justification by faith might better be taken to mean 'peace of mind or a sense of divine approval arising from trust in God' than 'a fiction of merit by transfer'. Again, much of the language of the scriptures is that of imaginative poetry rather than factual prose, and the 'dulness which turns symbol and poetry into materialism' is only to be deplored. It was for such views that Williams was afterwards condemned in the Court of Arches.

Baden Powell's, the third in order of the essays, bore the title 'On The Study of the Evidences of Christianity', but concentrated on miracles. A fellow of the Royal Society, the author had for many years been keenly interested in the relations of science and religious belief and had not long previously published a book on *The Order of Nature*, in which his ideas on the subject of the miraculous were clearly stated.[10] He was himself convinced that the orderliness of nature testifies the control of a divine intelligence, but the very fact of such order precludes those breaches of it which the allegation of miracle demands. The essay follows up this argument by seeking to show how unsatisfactory is the kind of defence which apologists for miracle usually erect. But whatever the strength of his case Powell's way of

8. *Essays and Reviews*, p. 62.
9. *Ibid.*, p. 92.
10. Some broader aspects of the matter had been discussed by him in an earlier work, *Revelation and Science*.

presenting it leaves no favourable impression. His style is opaque, his phrasing clumsy and his use of italics unsparing. Yet the gist of it is plain. Miracle implies an 'arbitrary interposition' if the phenomenon is not in principle to be explained in terms of natural law and thus lose evidential value. With the advance of science the incidence of the miraculous is certain therefore to disappear.

> The boundaries of nature exist only where our *present* knowledge places them; the discoveries of tomorrow will alter and enlarge them. The inevitable progress of research must, within a longer or shorter period, unravel all that seems most marvellous, and what is at present least understood will become as familiarly known to the science of the future as those points which a few centuries ago were involved in equal obscurity, but are now thoroughly understood.[11]

The probative force of miracles, on which in the past so much stress was laid, has to be judged by reference to the mental outlook of those to whom it is offered, and with changing times such appeals lose their cogency. Instead of buttressing faith, as formerly, miracle now needs faith to render it credible. If Christianity in an age of science is to be effectively defended its spiritual truth must be separated from physical portents. Powell summarizes his argument as follows:

> An alleged miracle can only be regarded in one of two ways:—either (1) abstractly as a physical event, and therefore to be investigated by reason and physical evidence, and referred to physical causes, possibly to *known* causes, but at all events to some higher cause or law, ... or (2) as connected with religious doctrine, regarded in a sacred light, asserted on the authority of inspiration. In this case it ceases to be capable of investigation by reason, or to own its dominion; it is accepted on religious grounds, and can appeal only to the principle and influence of faith.

His overall conclusion is that 'advancing knowledge, while it asserts the dominion of science in physical things, confirms that of faith in spiritual; we thus neither impugn the generalizations of philosophy nor allow them to invade the dominions of faith, and admit that what is not a subject for a problem may hold its place in a creed'.[12] The distinction thus made between science and religion was one which the future was to render increasingly common as the only way of securing an anchorage for faith without inhibiting the progress of knowledge. But at the same time, and in so far as his meaning was comprehended, Powell was thought to have questioned Christianity's divine credentials. On this score alone Thirlwall, for example, deemed the essay the most balefully significant in the whole book.[13] The pity is that the author did not make a better job of what he aimed to do. If his critics were unable to produce a successful refutation their ineptitude was no measure of his own skill. But for his sudden death he too would have found himself before the courts. As it was, Jowett's prosecutors at Oxford merely observed that Powell, 'after denying Miracles', had been 'removed to a higher tribunal'.

---

11. *Essays and Reviews*, p. 130.
12. *Ibid.*, p. 152.
13. Baden Powell was alone, as it happened, among the seven contributors to refer to Darwin's *Origin of Species*. He praised it for having demonstrated 'the grand principle of the self-evolving power of nature'.

The fourth paper, '*Séances historiques de Genève*: the National Church', by Wilson, provoked more hostile comment than perhaps any other. Apart from Jowett's it was the longest, and it occupied the central position. Its purpose was to state what in the writer's view the Church of England, as the national Church, ought properly to be. The *séances* referred to had been an evangelical Christian conference lately held at Geneva, but the essay had very little to do with it, save in borrowing the term *multitudinisme*, used by one of the speakers there. This Wilson applied to his concept of the nature and function of a national ecclesiastical establishment, which in his view ought certainly to be 'multitudinist'. The idea had already been explored in the essayist's own Bampton lectures of 1851 on *The Communion of Saints*, in which he had contended both for the provisional character of dogmatic statements in theology and for a substantial broadening of the Church's comprehensiveness. On the first point he claimed that 'all dogmatic statements must be held to be modalized by greater or less probability'.[14] Fixity in such statements is not to be expected and is dangerous when insisted upon. Dogma cannot be made to supply any effective basis for unity among Christians; formularies may be and are varyingly interpreted and none can be taken as legally binding. The true bond of union is a moral one. As to the second point, it is evident that by the time he wrote his *Essays and Reviews* paper Wilson had changed his opinion on the matter of clerical subscription since the day, nearly twenty years previously, when he had been one of the four college tutors to protest against *Tract 90*. He now urged its abolition on the ground that there should not be a dual standard of belief, one for the clergy and another for the laity. Only with complete doctrinal freedom would the Church be able to move with the times and so fulfil its service to the nation. At present, 'while the civil side of the nation is fluid, the ecclesiastical side of it is fixed'; on which Thirlwall's comment was that 'a Church, without any basis of a common faith, is not only an experiment new in practice and of doubtful success, but an idea new in theory, and not easy to conceive'.[15]

On the subject of biblical inspiration Wilson refused to identify the Word of God with the Bible simply as such. The letter of Scripture contains the Word, but is not to be equated with it. He pointed out that the sixth of the Thirty-nine Articles itself gives no definition of inspiration nor even speaks of Scripture as supernaturally inspired. Instead it permits us to accept 'literally, or allegorically, or as a parable, or poetry, or legend, the story of the serpent tempter, of an ass speaking with a man's voice, or an arresting of the earth's motion, of waters standing in a solid heap, of witches, and a variety of apparitions'. There are differing kinds of truth, of which myth or legend may quite fittingly be the vehicle. 'We do not apply the term "untrue" to parable, fable, or proverb, although their words correspond with ideas, not with natural facts; as little should we do so, when narratives have been the spontaneous product of true ideas, and are capable of reproducing them.' What matters in the sacred narrative is its spiritual meaning,

---

14. The precise expression is from the same writer's essay, 'Schemes of Christian Comprehension', which he contributed to a collection of *Oxford Essays* in 1857.
15. From his episcopal Charge of 1863. See *Remains, Literary and Theological* (1877–8), ii, pp. 46f.

beside which questions of precise historicity are secondary. And the same holds true of the rest of the symbolism of religion, the sacraments included. The forms are human, the content divine; and both aspects are to be recognized. There was no need then to be exigent in particulars. 'Jesus Christ has not revealed His religion as a theology of the intellect, nor as an historical faith; and it is a stifling of the true Christian life, both in the individual and in the Church, to require of many men a unanimity of speculative doctrine, which can never exist.'

C. W. Goodwin's dissertation on the Mosaic cosmogony argues that the creation stories in the Bible have nothing in common with modern scientific hypotheses, and the efforts of such apologists as Dr Buckland, Archdeacon Pratt and Hugh Miller, author of the popular *Testimony of the Rocks*, to 'harmonize' Genesis and geology were merely misguided. 'It would have been well', says the writer, 'if theologians had made up their minds to accept frankly the principle that those things for the discovery of which man had faculties specially provided are not fit objects of divine revelation.'[16] Physical science continued to pursue its own paths unconcernedly, whereas theology, the science whose object is the dealings of God with man as a moral being, maintained 'but a shivering existence, shouldered and jostled by the sturdy growths of modern thought' and lamenting the hostility it encountered.

> Why should this be, unless because theologians persist in clinging to theories of God's procedure towards man, which have long been seen to be untenable? If, relinquishing theories, they should be content to enquire from the history of man what this procedure has actually been, the so–called difficulties of theology would, for the most part, vanish of themselves.

The essay of Mark Pattison, unobtrusively entitled 'Tendencies of Religious Thought in England 1688–1750', is the best in the book, excepting Jowett's. It is not ostensibly polemical and in form is simply a review of the religious ideas characteristic of a selected period of recent history; though as such it is of significance as the work of a pioneer in this type of study.[17] Pattison admits that the period in question had usually been written off as a time of decay in religion, licentiousness in morals, public corruption and profaneness of language—'an age whose poetry was without romance, whose philosopby was without insight, and whose public men were without character'. History, however, is not to be treated in this way; an age should be critically studied, not summarily judged. 'We have not yet learned, in this country, to write our ecclesiastical history on any better footing than that of praising up the party, in or out of the Church, to which we happen to belong'.[18] But the historian is aware of continuities and if the position of the Church today is to be understood then what has gone before, over preceding

16. *Essays and Reiews*, pp. 251f.
17. Pattison was a fastidious scholar and the bulk of his published work is not large. His study of Isaac Casaubon appeared in 1875 and the volume on Milton, in the 'English Men of Letters' series, in 1879. What was to be his most important undertaking, a life of Scaliger, remained a fragment only (see *Essays*, ed. H. Nettleship, 1889. i).
18. *Essays and Reviews*, p. 308.

generations, must be duly appreciated. In the previous century interest in Christianity seemed to turn only on its provability, and what use to make of it when proved was little considered. Similarly the only quality of Scripture dwelt upon was its credibility. Yet evidences, as they were called, 'stir no feeling' and the mind preoccupied with them 'knows nothing of the spiritual intuition, of which it renounces at once the difficulties and the consolations'. Even so, serious inquiry into the nature of the authority by which these evidences are furnished was entirely neglected. Indeed, anything like a genuine theology, as distinct from defensive argumentation, had all but died out 'when it received a new impulse and a new direction from Coleridge'; thereafter 'the evidence–makers ceased from their futile labours all at once'. Englishmen had heard 'with as much surprise as if the doctrine was new' that the Christian faith was 'the perfection of human intelligence'. Taught by Coleridge, the present age was coming to realize that faith is not the end product of a process of abstract reasoning, but rather a 'devout condition of the entire inner man', although Pattison observes that 'theological study is still the study of topics of defence'.[19]

The appeal to reason has of course its proper use and function, in theology as in other disciplines, but reason is more than 'the rational consent of the sensible and unprejudiced'. The Deists and their opponents alike had made this mistake. In fact, 'the defect of the eighteenth century theology was not in having too much good sense, but in having nothing besides'. Its aim, allowably, had been practical—to maintain the principles of moral and religious conduct for society—and so far it had merited praise. But its conceptions were too narrow. The nineteenth century must learn from its predecessor's errors, for what is needed now is the impartiality of science, not the bias of mere special pleading. 'If theological argument forgets the judge and assumes the advocate, or betrays the least bias to one side, the conclusion is valueless, the principle of free enquiry has been violated.'[20]

Pursuit of the historical method alone, Pattison thinks, will induce such impartiality and prevent theology from becoming for the Church of England what it already is for the Roman, 'an unmeaning frostwork of dogma, out of all relation to the actual history of man.' The truth was that even the existing situation afforded little encouragement for a critical observer.

> Whoever would take the religious literature of the present day as a whole, and endeavour to make out clearly on what basis Revelation is supposed by it to rest, whether on Authority, on the Inward Light, Reason, self–evidencing Scripture, or on the combination of the four, or some of them, and in what proportions, would probably find that he had undertaken a perplexing but not altogether profitless enquiry.

The implication of Pattison's dry comments was not lost on contemporary opinion: their tone was negative. His work, accordingly, for all its apparent detachment, was lumped with the rest as unconstructive and essentially inimical to orthodox

19. *Ibid.*, p. 364.
20. *Ibid.*, pp. 365f.

faith. The author remarked long afterwards that his attempt to present the English public with a philosophical monograph on a special phase of English thought was 'singularly unsuccessful. To judge from the reviews, it never occurred to any of our public instructors that such a conception was possible'.[21]

> So wholly extinct [he concluded] is scientific theology in the Church of England that the English public could not recognize such a thing as a neutral and philosophic enquiry into the causes of the form of thought existing at any period. Our clergy know only of pamphlets which must be for or against one of the parties in the Church.

The concluding essay was Jowett's. But this calls to be considered within the wider context of the writer's standing and influence as a theologian and biblical exegete.

Benjamin Jowett

The facts of Jowett's career are soon recounted. One of the outstanding classical scholars of the century, he was born in London in 1817 and educated at St Paul's School and Balliol College, Oxford, of which he became a fellow in 1838 and tutor in 1840. Two years later he was ordained. Disappointed of the headship of the college in 1854, he was elected in the following year to the Regius professorship of Greek in the university. Master of Balliol at last in 1870, on the death of the man (Robert Scott) who had received the preferment sixteen years earlier, he shortly afterwards brought out his translation in four volumes of the *Dialogues of Plato*, which, despite the somewhat carping criticism to which it has often been subjected, is the literary achievement whereon his fame as a scholar largely rests. Versions of Thucydides and the *Politics* of Aristotle appeared in 1881 and 1885 respectively, but neither will bear comparison with his work on Plato. A great educator as well as a distinguished scholar, Jowett will be remembered as one of the makers of modern Oxford. He died in 1893.

Long before the publication of *Essays and Reviews* Jowett had been known for the exceeding broadness of his theological opinions. German influence had contributed to this: he was fairly well versed, for an Englishman of his time, in Kant and Hegel, although he never himself became a Hegelian to the extent of accepting the complete idealist system. But along with T. H. Green he was mainly responsible for 'that naturalization of Hegelian thought in England which was so marked a feature of the close of the nineteenth century'.[22] Indeed, he was Green's precursor in this regard.[23] He was, moreover, familiar with the work of Schleiermacher and F. C. Baur. The latter on St Paul particularly impressed him. 'Baur's', he told A. P. Stanley, 'appears to me the ablest book I ever read on St Paul's Epistles: a remarkable combination of Philological and Metaphysical power, without the intrusion of Modern Philosophy.'[24] Whatever one thinks of the justice

---

21. *Memoirs*, p. 314.
22. A. E. Taylor, in *D.N.B. 1922–1930*, p. 102.
23. Jowett was also, it should be recalled, Edward Caird's tutor. See the article on Caird in *D.N.B.*, Second Supplement, pp. 291–5.
24. Faber, *Jowett*, p. 212.

of this last observation, it is clear that Jowett realized how much contemporary biblical criticism, as developed in Germany and especially at Tübingen, had to teach thc English student, hitherto insulated from such influences by the blind veneration in which, in this country, the very letter of Scripture was usually held. Jowett's own theological position—at least in his own mind; it never perhaps was very plain to others—was becoming more clearly defined between 1846 and 1848, and in the former year he again wrote to Stanley about an enterprise which the two of them had long contemplated: a series of commentaries on the New Testament.

> I propose [he said] to divide it into two portions: (a) the Gospels, and (b) the Acts and Epistles, to be preceded respectively by two long prefaces, the first containing the hypothesis of the Gospels, and a theory of inspiration to be deduced from it; the second to contain the 'subjective mind' of the Apostolic Age, *historischpsychologisch dargestellt*. I think it should also contain essays. ...[25]

In the event, Stanley undertook the commentary on Corinthians, completing the task by 1849, while Jowett tackled Thessalonians, Galatians and Romans, writing, however, much more slowly than his partner, the superficiality of whose own contribution is obvious. But after much interruption caused by the university reform issue, the work was at length finished and in the summer of 1855 published. Jowett's part in the collaboration is easily the weightier. Stanley's treatment is historical, after the 'picturesque' manner for which he had a *flair*—'critical notes', he admitted, 'were not his vocation'.[26] Besides, in addition to the actual commentary, Jowett had in a second volume included a number of *Essays and Dissertations*, dealing with the larger, doctrinal aspect of his subject, a supplement which retains some value even today. But although these chapters are a stage in the advance of liberal theology in England, to the reading public at the time of their appearance they were far from welcome and did more than anything else in the entire three volumes to provoke that 'storm of acrimonious controversy' described by Stanley's biographer.

It was the essay 'On Atonement and Satisfaction' which occasioned most displeasure. A true exegesis, the author maintains, must be determined by the given passage's original meaning, so far as this can be ascertained. As a rule it has been obscured by layers of subsequent theologizing, so that the task of the modern exegete has become as difficult as it is necessary. And no doctrine has suffered more from wrong-headed and even morally repulsive explanations than that of Christ's atoning sacrifice.

> God is represented as angry with us for what we never did; He is ready to inflict disproportionate punishment on us for what we are; He is satisfied by the sufferings of His Son in our stead.

The imperfection of human law is transferred to the divine, and the death of Christ explained by analogy of the ancient rite of sacrifice, 'a victim laid upon the altar

---

25. E. Abbott and L. Campbell, *op. cit.*, i, pp. 100f.
26. R. E. Prothero, *op. cit.*, i, p. 474.

to appease the wrath of God'. What was needed was a return to the simplicity of the Bible itself.

> I shall endeavour [Jowett wrote] to show: 1, that these conceptions of the work of Christ have no foundation in Scripture; 2, that their growth may be traced in ecclesiastical history; 3, that the only sacrifice, atonement, or satisfaction, with which Christ has to do, is a moral and spiritual one; not the pouring out of blood upon the earth, but the living sacrifice 'to do thy will, O God'; in which the believer has part as well as his Lord; and about the meaning of which there can be no more question in our day, than there was in the first ages.

In view of the place which the doctrine of the atonement still held in Victorian Protestantism and the manner in which it was generally interpreted, it is little wonder that Jowett's comments struck his readers as a betrayal of the gospel. His language on this subject had in fact an unwonted vehemence. 'No slave's mind', he declared, 'was ever reduced so low as to justify the most disproportionate severity inflicted on himself; neither has God so made His creatures that they will lie down and die, even beneath the hand of Him who gave them life.' Further, he was well aware that the doctrine in its familiar forms was no recent excrescence of belief, but 'the growth of above a thousand years; rooted in language, disguised in figures of speech, fortified by logic', and thus had come to seem a part of the human mind itself. 'One cannot but fear whether it be still possible so to teach Christ as not to cast a shadow on the holiness and truth of God.' A restatement of the doctrine would necessarily place Christ's death within the context of his life. Too precise a definition ought in any case to be avoided: 'In theology the less we define the better'; and the reality of the atonement is something greater far than the theories invented to explain it. Nothing should be done to divest the doctrine of its essentially moral meaning.

The essay on 'The Imputation of the Sin of Adam' dealt briefly but hardly less trenchantly with another of orthodoxy's basic tenets, original sin. On this belief whole systems of theology had been erected. But what in truth was its own foundation? When looked at critically its New Testament grounds—a couple of not unobscure passages in St Paul[27]—would be seen to be insufficient to bear the immense doctrinal superstructure built upon them. The apostle was simply employing modes of expression native to his own age and religious tradition but not to be used as intellectual currency good for any time and place. Instead of merely reproducing his words a serious attempt should be made to fathom his meaning. When Paul uses a figure of speech 'a figure of speech it remains still', an allegory appropriate to the circumstances, though with a signification that can be determined. 'It means that "God hath made of one blood all the nations of the earth"; and that "he hath concluded all under sin, that he may have mercy upon all".' We are one in a common evil nature, which, if not actually derived from Adam's sin, exists as really as if it were. 'It means that we shall be made one in Christ, by the grace of God, in a measure here, more fully and perfectly in another world. It means that Christ is the natural head of the human race, the author of

27. Romans v, 12–21; I Corinthians XV, 21, 22, 45–49.

its spiritual life.'[28] In short, Jowett tries to see the apostle Paul not as a mere storehouse of theological builder's materials but as a man of his period whose teaching, when stripped of its adventitious elements, nevertheless has spiritual import for all periods.

The only other dissertation that calls for notice here is that on 'Natural Religion', a discussion prompted by St Paul's condemnation of the heathen. It is characteristic of the 'large' outlook that had been forming in the author's mind over the years. His feeling is that no sharp distinction between nature and supernature, between natural religion and revealed, can be drawn. Man's apprehension of God from the light of nature is the presupposition of any accepted revelation, and the traditional division between the two is the result only of an abstract conceptualizing which has outlasted any usefulness it had. Nowhere has God left himself without witness and his self-disclosure is not to be confined to a single historic channel. Jowett's implication clearly is that Judaism and Christianity are themselves historical phenomena, subject to the forces which shape all such phenomena. He does not, however, wish to imply that because the Jewish–Christian tradition can be seen by the critical historian to belong to a specific context and to have incorporated elements originating elsewhere that this tradition has no special and even unique significance and value. Quite the contrary; but the question at issue—inescapable in the modern world—is one of approach, of intellectual attitude. Religion is the expression of a people's mind and character, and to study Christianity comparatively is the only fruitful way to comprehend it. Other religions, therefore, are not to be dismissed as heathen darkness, since even in their crudest forms they somewhere evidence the divine activity. In one aspect the religious impulse and the forms it assumes are natural; but in another supernatural. Nature and history—all history—are the spheres in which God works. Christians today cannot in this matter judge as uncompromisingly as did the authors of Scripture.

It is hardly surprising that Jowett's orthodox critics should have accused him of denying to the Bible, or at least to the Old Testament, any special inspiration. Of the latter he had said:

> It is not natural, nor perhaps possible, to us to cease to use the figures in which 'holy men of old' spoke of that which belonged to their peace. But it is well that we should sometimes remind ourselves, that 'all these things are a shadow, but the body is of Christ'.[29]

He had himself learned Hebrew, but seems to have made no great progress in the language, and with the Hebrew Scriptures his sympathies, Hellenist that he was, were less than perfect.

His general attitude to the Bible was set forth at length—it is a composition of some one hundred pages—in the *Essays and Reviews* chapter 'On the Interpretation of Scripture'. This had been designed to take its place in the *Commentary*, but was finished too late for inclusion. In its new setting it became 'the book's centre of

28. *Commentary on Thessalonians, Galations, and Romans, with Essays and Dissertations*, ii, pp. 315f.
29. *Ibid.*, p. 307.

gravity',[30] and is the one contribution, excepting only Pattison's, which would bear reprinting today. The writer's meaning is always transparently clear, his tone cool and candid.

> As the time has come [he states] when it is no longer possible to ignore the results of criticism, it is of importance that Christianity should be seen to be in harmony with them. That objections to some received views should be valid, and yet that they should be always held up as the objections of infidels, is a mischief to the Christian cause ... It would be a strange and incredible thing that the Gospel, which at first made war only on the vices of mankind, should now be opposed to one of the highest and rarest of human virtues—the love of truth.

The Christian religion was in a false position when all the tendencies of knowledge were opposed to it; a position, therefore, which could not be maintained for much longer and could only end in the withdrawal of the educated classes from the influences of religion, a state of things which Jowett dreaded the more because he felt it to be approaching. Might it not come to pass 'that in Protestant countries reconciliation is as hopeless as Protestants commonly believe to be the case in Catholic'? But theological reconstruction will have to be founded in a proper knowledge and understanding of the Scriptures, and this means adopting the historical perspective, with all that it entails. The would-be interpreter must set himself to rediscover the original meaning; no easy task, admittedly, but a necessary one if varying interpretations are not to proliferate. This demands historical sympathy, the ability to transfer oneself to another age, 'to imagine that he is a disciple of Christ or Paul' and 'to disengage himself from all that follows'.[31] He should especially be aware of invoking the assumptions and imposing the standards of a later age. Critical procedures must be employed to establish points of date and authorship, and figurative language be taken for what it is and not as if it were that of logical statement. To a presentday reader such stipulations are merely trite, but it should be remembered that in 1860 they certainly were not so. The canon that historical science must work in freedom had first to be secured. What Jowett in particular objected to was the narrowing and hardening of the idea of inspiration into a settled dogma. The word, 'from being used in a general way to express what may be called the prophetic spirit of Scripture, has passed within the last two centuries into a sort of technical term'. What inspiration really connotes can be discovered only within the Bible itself, and a valid theory will have to meet the requirements of the historical understanding, the broad principle of which is *Interpret the Scripture like any other book* even though there are many respects in which Scripture is unlike any other book, as a sound interpretation will readily show.

> No other science of Hermeneutics is possible but an inductive one ... based on the language and thought and narrations of the sacred writers. Fundamentally it is a matter of common sense, and the method creates itself as we proceed. But it has to be borne in mind that the Bible is the only book in the world written in different

30. Basil Willey, *More Nineteenth Century Studies*, p. 154.
31. *Essays and Reviews*, p. 408

styles and at many different times, which is in the hands of persons of all degrees of knowledge and education.

Once the general method of serious biblical study has been indicated secondary considerations fall into line. Great tact and insight are required in the interpreter, the most formidable difficulty of all perhaps being to enter into the meaning of the words of Christ himself, 'so gentle, so human, so divine, neither adding to them nor marrying their simplicity'. But any attempt, in the allegorical or typological manner, to unearth hidden and mysterious meanings is misguided. We have no business, under the guise of reverence, to make the Bible mean just what we please. Finally, the interpreter of Scripture will feel as he proceeds 'that the continuous growth of revelation which he traces in the Old and New Testament is a part of a larger whole extending over the earth and reaching to another world.' The outcome of applying the new principles of study will thus inevitably be seen in theology, in which the sort of distinctions made on the basis of the old interpretations must fade away. Not only will doctrines be differently stated and defended, there will be more caution, more reserve than formerly in dealing with doctrinal issues at all.

The whole essay was typical of its author—moderate, critical, but with a deep underlying religious sentiment. 'Much depends on the manner in which things are said—There is an aspect of truth which may always be put forward so as to find a way to the hearts of men.' Jowett was himself confident that Christianity could be reconciled with the intellectual demands of a scientific age; but it would be a Christianity a good deal lightened of its theological obesity. The paper nevertheless was his last publication in the theological field. As the years went by he had other more pressing or more congenial concerns to occupy him. But it is probable also that the uproar which the book caused disillusioned him as to at any rate the more immediate prospects of theological liberalism in the established Church. His own belief rested in an 'essential' Christianity, consisting chiefly in the Christian life itself. This, however, could be further qualified as 'the re–enactment within the soul of the life and death of Christ', meaning thereby death to the world and sin and rebirth in a union with God such as Christ himself had known. There exists, besides, an 'absolute' morality to which Plato and the gospel alike bear witness. On the other hand, the soul's immortality may in the end signify no more than a present consciousness of God, whilst even the divine personality could resolve itself simply into an 'idea'. Miracles and metaphysical dogmas will become things of the past. A faith, in any case, built on historical events of untrustworthy report cannot subsist, for 'holiness has its sources elsewhere than in history'. So spoke the older Jowett, though in private; and it is evident that his mind had moved far beyond the acknowledged positions of 1860.[32]

What then of *Essays and Reviews* as a whole? Challenging to conventional religious ideas it was designed to be, but the outcome surpassed even its author's expectations. Dean Church, ever judicious, thought it 'a reckless book' but with 'many good and true things in it'.[33] Time, it has to be said, has entirely vindicated

32.   See generally P. Hinchliff, *Benjamin Jowett and the Christian Religion* (1987).
33.   M. C. Church, *The Life of R. W. Church*, p. 155.

its overall standpoint. The essayists were right in sensing that the difficulties in which orthodox belief seemed likely to founder were in large measure the result of an untenable theory of biblical inspiration. The question of scriptural authority, its nature and its force, had to be faced and to this end the science of historical criticism, applied in the manner already familiar in the German universities, was the necessary instrument. Yet these writers, in some instances, had themselves only imperfectly assimilated the historical spirit and seemed more iconoclastic than they really were. But the book, whatever its faults, was opportune. What it said needed saying. The prevailing theological outlook in Britain, sustained by reactionary influences both High Church and Low, would in Germany have been old-fashioned a generation earlier. But the tendencies of the time were irreversible and had to be met with something more than a cry of dismay. *Essays and Reviews* gave liberalism a place in English theology from which it could not in future be dislodged and might extend a continuously widening influence. This achievement was in the main Jowett's. Lacking his contribution the volume, though little less sensational, would have been also less impressive. Yet behind the seven writers is discernible, too, the broad figure of Coleridge, interpreting dogma in terms of moral and spiritual reality. Williams, Baden Powell—who quotes the famous saying on 'Evidences'—Wilson, Pattison and Jowett himself all reflect the gleams of his luminous intelligence.

Further controversy: Colenso on the Pentateuch

Essays and Reviews attracted public notice only after the appearance of an article relating to it in the October issue of the rather *avant-garde Westminster Review* by one Frederick Harrison, a youngish man of twenty-nine and an agnostic.[34] It was headed 'Neo-Christianity' and its aim was to mock. What, the writer asked, had happened to traditional faith when clergymen in responsible positions could reject most of its basic articles, leaving only (as he put it) 'a revised Atonement, a transcendental Fall, a practical Salvation, and an idealized Damnation'? Such a reduced creed might suffice for learned divines but not for the ordinary man who could never accept that the Bible is 'a medley of late compilers', full of errors and untruths, 'and yet remains withal the Book of Life'. Orthodoxy had been sold from within, a group of eminent 'believers' having given clear proof of their unbelief. Yet these singular apologists, in words addressed to the public at large, presumed to assert that Christian dogma still possessed authority. Harrison's squib had a greater effect than probably he himself expected. The evangelical *Record* took up the cry and denounced the seven writers as 'Septem contra Christum'. The bishop of Oxford, with characteristic verve and self-assurance, responded in *The Quarterly Review* of January 1861. 'It is the doctrine', he pronounced, 'of Tract 90 carried into a new region and development, and goes far beyond it in intellectual eccentricity.[35]

34. He died in 1923, at the age of ninety–one.
35. Ironically H. B. Wilson had been one of the four Oxford tutors who twenty years previously had protested against the liberty of interpretation which the author of that notorious document had in their view so plainly abused.

251

The essayists' attempt to combine the advocacy of doctrines so negative with the status and emoluments of Church of England clergymen he repudiated as 'moral dishonesty'. But one telling quip he did get in: 'They believe too much not to believe more, and they disbelieve too much not to disbelieve everything.' Other writers in other periodicals reinforced the bishop's strain. Powell's viewpoint especially, according to a commentator in *The Guardian*, was 'for all practical purposes ... indistinguishable from atheism'. But not all the discussion was hostile. Stanley, in *The Edinburgh Review* for April 1861, came out manfully against the clamour. The writers, mistakenly or not, had sought to place Christianity 'beyond the reach of accidents', whether of science or of criticism and to rest its claims on 'those moral and spiritual truths which, after all, are what have really won an entrance for it into the heart'. Of his friend Jowett in particular he observed that he stood 'confessedly master of the situation in the eyes of the rising generation of English students and theologians'.

The archbishop of Canterbury was pressed by Samuel Wilberforce to issue a pastoral letter (which he himself had considerably drafted) expressing the disapproval of the entire episcopate. Then Convocation, awake again and vigorous after its one hundred and thirty-five years' quiescence, was also urged to take action, the Upper House witnessing the strange alliance of Wilberforce and the *quondam* 'heretic' Hampden in support of threatened faith. Although no immediate censure was adopted, several bishops insisted on carrying matters further, and at length, in June 1864, the bishop of Oxford moved to invite the Lower House to concur with the Upper in the judgment:

> That this Synod, having appointed Committees of the Upper and Lower House to examine and report upon the volume entitled *Essays and Reviews* ... doth hereby synodically condemn the said volume as containing teaching contrary to the doctrine received by the United Church of England and Ireland, in common with the whole Catholic Church of Christ.

The motion was carried, in a by no means full house, with only two dissentients—Tait, who had concurred in the Privy Council judgment, and Jackson of Lincoln. Thirlwall absented himself.[36] Meanwhile legal action had been taken against two of the contributors, Wilson and Williams, who were indicted for heresy in the Court of Arches, the adverse judgments of which were subsequently reversed, however, by the Judicial Committee of the Privy Council, to the dismay of all conservative churchmen.[37] In giving judgment the Lord Chancellor, Westbury, declared that in matters on which the Church had prescribed no rule 'there is so far freedom of opinion that they may be discussed without penal consequences'; nor did he and his colleagues feel at liberty 'to ascribe to the Church any rule or teaching which we do not find expressly and distinctly stated, or which is not plainly involved in or to be collected from that which is written'.[38] Powell would almost

36. The voting in the Lower House, with a total membership of 145, was 39 to 16.
37. The two archbishops, Longley of Canterbury and Thompson of York, and the bishop of London sat as assessors.
38. High Churchmen and Low Churchmen alike, under the joint leadership—*mirabile dictu*—of Dr Pusey and Lord Shaftesbury, united to protest against it 'for the love of God', an address to the archbishops to that effect being signed by 11,000 clergymen.

certainly have been prosecuted but for his untimely death. Jowett, at first served with a monition to appear before the vice–chancellor of his university, suffered in the event the more material indignity of being denied a long overdue increase in his professorial salary.[39] Mark Pattison, for his part, did not again fail of his college rectorship, although even his own supporters had serious reservations about his election.[40] But the disappointment of 1851 had done much to poison a nature always prone to feed on its own disillusionment. Eventually the storm passed and Temple—such ever have been the vagaries of preferment in the established Church—lived to become Primate of All England, though not without a lasting sense of embarrassment for his indiscretion in 1860.

Attempts to answer *Essays and Reviews* more constructively than by mere denunciation and legal process were numerous. But the quantity of such apologetic was no guarantee of its effectiveness. The bulk of it was feeble, the two most noteworthy of these publications being composite volumes, the one, edited by William Thompson, then bishop of Gloucester, called *Aids to Faith*, the other, edited by Samuel Wilberforce, simply *Replies to Essays and Reviews*. The former, which contained papers on 'Inspiration' (by Harold Browne, Norrisian professor of divinity at Cambridge) and on 'The Study of the Evidences of Christianity' (by W. L. Fitzgerald, bishop of Cork, Cloyne and Ross)—both of them putting up reasoned arguments on behalf of orthodox positions—was much the better. For the *Replies* was only a poorish effort; the essay by C. A. Heurtley, Lady Margaret professor of divinity at Oxford, defending miracle against Baden Powell's assault, is the strongest in the book; whereas the editor's preface reveals the astonishing fact that the writer had never even read the volume he was so vociferously criticizing. But what is most likely to surprise any modern student of the period who may happen to light upon these long-forgotten apologies, representative as they are of the official, not to say popular, religious outlook of the time, is the all but total failure of the contributors—men eminent in their day—to measure or even recognize the intellectual forces by which the old-fashioned orthodoxy would so soon be shattered. In particular the attitude to the Bible is throughout purely literalist and for these defenders of the faith the advances already achieved in scientific biblical study in Germany might never have been made.[41] The intellectual isolation of English theology at that date could not have been more signally demonstrated.

39. The chair of Greek was worth no more than its traditional £40 per annum until the dean and chapter of Christ Church, in September 1865, at last saw fit to raise it to £500.
40. See V. H. H. Green, *Oxford Common Room*, p. 201. A candid friend wrote to inform Pattison that he could not guess what his (Pattison's) religion was.
41. According to Bishop Lee of Manchester 'the very foundations of our faith, the very basis of our hopes, the very nearest and dearest of our consolations are taken from us when one line in that Sacred Volume on which we base everything is declared to be unfaithful or untrustworthy' (See *The Guardian*, 1863, pp. 302, 323). Bishop Christopher Wordsworth, in his contribution to the *Replies*, stated categorically that inspiration means that 'the Bible must be interpreted as a book written by a Being to whom all things are present, and who contemplates all things at once in the panoramic view of his own Omniscience' (p. 456).

But even the *Essays and Reviews* affair, coming so soon upon the wonder and dismay occasioned by *The Origin of Species*, did not monopolize the attention of offended orthodoxy during this unhappy decade. Further alarm was caused by the appearance in 1862–63 of the first two parts of a work entitled *The Pentateuch and Book of Joshua Critically Examined,* by John William Colenso, a Cornishman who since 1853 had been bishop of Natal.[42] A former second wrangler at Cambridge, he had taught mathematics at St John's College and afterwards at Harrow School, when Dr Longley, later archbishop of Canterbury, was headmaster. His *magnum opus* on the Old Testament had been preceded a year earlier by a *Commentary on the Epistle to the Romans*, the unsoundness of which upon the doctrines both of the atonement and of eternal punishment had already seriously disturbed Colenso's metropolitan, Bishop Gray of Cape Town. Colenso, however, was a man of courage reinforced by obstinacy and of honesty unmollified by tact. His views on the Pentateuch, to which contemporary German scholarship lent substance, were quite unprecedented for an English bishop of that time. Indeed it was the abruptness of their presentation which really upset clerical opinion, more even than their positive content, objectionable though this was. He argued that little if any of the Pentateuch as it has come down to us could be assigned to the Mosaic age, that Moses himself was a figure of dubious historicity and that Joshua must be relegated to the realm of legend. He observed, too, that Genesis contains duplicate and incompatible accounts of the creation, deluge and other events, contended that much of the so-called 'Law of Moses' was the work of priests not earlier than the Captivity, whilst the Book of Deuteronomy belonged in fact to the reign of Manasseh in the seventh century B.C., and dismissed Chronicles as a late and tendentious compilation unreliable as history. As for the actual composition of the Pentateuch, the reader was told that Samuel, whom Colenso regards as one of its principal authors, 'appears to have adopted the form of history, based upon the floating legends and traditions of the time, filling up the narrative—as we may believe—perhaps to a large extent out of his own imagination, when those traditions failed him.' Moreover, Colenso had applied his mathematical talent to introduce elaborate arithmetical calculations concerning such things as the measurements of the tabernacle and the camp in the wilderness, the size of armies and the growth of population. The sacred writers' accuracy in these matters was proof, in the bishop's forthright opinion, that the sphere of inspiration is not that of scientific history. Yet neither did he doubt that although the Bible itself, as a literary compilation, is 'not God's Word', that Word could be 'heard in the Bible, by all who will humbly and devoutly listen for it'.

The religious press condemned these utterances with prompt unanimity as impugning the truth of Holy Writ, always the most sensitive spot in an Englishman's religion. Colenso's own brother-in-law, Bishop M'Dougall of Labuan, read them as an 'attack' upon the Pentateuch and a denial of its inspiration. 'He says, in short, that he can believe in a miracle, but cannot believe

---

42. The book was not finally completed until 1879. For an account of Colenso's chequered career the reader is referred to P. Hinchliff, *John William Colenso* (1964) and H. L. Farrer, *The Life of Bishop Gray* (ed. C. N. Gray, 1883).

in a bad sum and false arithmetical statements; and so he falls foul of the Book of Numbers especially.'[43] The upshot of this new assault upon traditional ideas was, first, the despatch of a letter to Colenso, dated 9 February 1863 and signed by all forty-one English bishops (Thirlwall alone dissenting), advising Colenso to resign his office. His refusal to do so resulted in his being tried by Bishop Gray, a strong Tractarian, in the November of the same year, a process which ended in a sentence of deposition a few weeks later. Having ignored the summons to attend the court, Colenso himself appealed to the Privy Council, whose Judicial Committee, again under Lord Westbury, found that the Bishop of Cape Town had for certain technical reasons no coercive jurisdiction and that the judgment of deposition was therefore null and void in law. Thus despite the sentence of excommunication passed upon him by his metropolitan in December 1865 and the all but total opposition of the clergy of his province and diocese, the bishop of Natal was able to retain the temporalities of his see until his death in 1883, although in the meantime a bishop of Maritzburg had been consecrated by Gray—without the queen's mandate—to succour the needs of a flock which now declined its legal pastor's spiritual ministrations.

Colenso's excursion into biblical criticism had been prompted by the human conditions of the mission-field itself; to the naïve question of Zulu lads, 'Is all that true?' his heart had answered, he said, 'in the words of the Prophet, Shall a man speak lies in the name of the Lord?'; and although it left something to be desired in the way of scholarly finesse it had served a purpose in compelling churchmen to take a more realistic view of the Bible as a historical document. In Jowett's words, set down long after the events of 1865: 'He has made an epoch in criticism by his straightforwardness. No one now talks of verbal inspiration. He was attacked bitterly, but the recollection of the attacks has passed away; the effect of his writings, though they are no longer read, is permanent.'[44]

Biblical study at the universities

The initial reaction of public opinion in this country to critical biblical study—the 'higher criticism', as it came to be called—was thus far from favourable. The upshot had been controversy, denunciation by authority and legal prosecution. But the progress of scholarship could not be halted indefinitely. When indignation and fear at last subsided reason resumed its sway. By 1884 Mandell Creighton, in his inaugural address as Dixie professor of ecclesiastical history at Cambridge, could state it virtually as a truism that the traditions of theological learning had been thoroughly leavened by the historical spirit: 'Theology has become historical, and it does not demand that history should become theological.'[45] But the credit for this change of view rests mainly with the small group of scholars sometimes known as the Cambridge school, of whom it has been said that they raised English

---

43. R. T. Davidson and W. Benham, *The Life of Archibald Campbell Tait* (1891), i, pp 334f.
44. Abbott and Campbell, *op. cit.*, ii, p. 65.
45. *Historical Lectures and Addresses*, p. 2.

theology, and particularly English New Testament scholarship, from a condition of intellectual nullity up to the level of the best German work, while they infused into it a characteristic English spirit of caution and sobriety.[46] The three leading figures were those of Brooke Foss Westcott (1825–1901), James Barber Lightfoot (1829–89), and Fenton John Anthony Hort (1828–92). The first two had been at school together at Birmingham under Prince Lee, later bishop of Manchester, the last at Rugby under Tait. Wescott was Regius professor of divinity at Cambridge from 1870 to 1890; Lightfoot held professorships there from 1861 until 1879, when he became bishop of Durham, an office in which Westcott himself was to succeed him; whilst Hort likewise held senior posts in the same university from 1878 till his death. All three had experienced the fecund influence of F. D. Maurice, with his qualities of moderation and depth and his belief in the power of words. None of them aimed at popular appeal, and Westcott had more than a little of the Maurician obscurity. All of them, Hort especially, maintained the strictest standards of scholarly integrity, as they understood it.

In this triumvirate Lightfoot's pre-eminence is that of a historian, a pupil of his, H. C. G. Moule, who too became bishop of Durham, testifying in particular to his 'unfailing thoroughness of knowledge and unsurpassable clearness of exposition and instruction'.[47] As a biblical scholar he ranks with the first of his age, but in dogmatic or speculative theology he had slight interest. Indeed Hort considered him 'not speculative enough to be a leader of thought'.[48] His approach was always historical, and even in his New Testament commentaries—*Galatians* appeared in 1865, *Philippians* three years later, and *Colossians* in 1875—he is less reliable when he leaves the terrain of textual and historical criticism for that of exegesis.[49] These books were originally planned as part of a series of New Testament studies in which, in addition to Lightfoot's own work on St Paul, Westcott would deal with the Johannine writings, and Hort with the Synoptic gospels, Acts and the epistles of James, Peter and Jude, although the scheme was not fully carried out owing to the extremely slow rate of production to which Hort's stringent requirements reduced him.[50] The Galatians commentary did more perhaps than anything else to overthrow the theory of F. C. Baur and the Tübingen school, which had assigned most of the New Testament writings to the second century, Lightfoot's procedure resting on a learning no less massive than the Germans' and a caution they had too often disdained. To the Philippians commentary he had appended a long essay

46. Hastings Rashdall, *Principles and Precepts*, ed. H. D. A. Major and P. L. Cross (1927), p. 164.
47. J. B. Harford and F. C. Macdonald, *Handley C. G. Moule, Bishop of Durham* (1922), p. 19.
48. A. F. Hort, *Life and Letters of F. J. A. Hort*, ii, 89.
49. Lightfoot had the prescience of the great scholar. 'If', he wrote, 'we could only recover letters that ordinary people wrote to each other without any thought of being literary, we should have the greatest possible help to the understanding of the New Testament generally' (quoted in G. Milligan, *Selections from the Greek Papyri*, p. xx). The truth of this view has been fully confirmed by discoveries since Lightfoot's day.
50. The Apocalypse was edited by E. W. Benson, later archbishop of Canterbury and a lifelong friend of both Westcott and Lightfoot, with whom he had been at school at Birmingham.

on the primitive Christian ministry, in which he expounded the view that the three orders of bishops, priests and deacons emerged only gradually 'as the Church assumed a more settled form, and the higher but temporary offices, such as the apostolate, fell away'; supposing also that it was the diaconate which was first established, followed by the presbyterate (on the model of the Jewish elders), whose members, in the gentile Churches, bore the alternative designation of 'bishops'. The subsequent exaltation of a single bishop in each *ekklesia* he thought to have been necessitated by practical requirements. But Lightfoot's principal achievement was his edition of *The Apostolic Fathers*,[51] a veritable landmark in the history of patristic study. His work on the Ignatian question, in which, after subjecting the whole controversy to a judicious investigation, he pronounced in favour of the seven letters referred to by Eusebius, constitutes his most important contribution to early Church history. But mention is due also of his authoritative article on Eusebius himself in Smith's *Dictionary of Christian Biography*. Five volumes of essays, sermons and notes were published after his death.[52]

Lightfoot's acceptance of the bishopric of Durham—he had some years previously declined that of Lichfield—was probably a mistake; his true place was the university and had he stayed at Cambridge scholarship would almost certainly have been enriched by further products of his learning.[53] But of his personal dedication to the new and very different work imposed on him by his northern industrial diocese there was never any doubt.

Hort was a scholar in whom great erudition informed a keenly critical intelligence. His own criteria were even more exacting than those of his two colleagues. But the result was a paucity of output that can only be regretted. The work by which he is remembered is, of course, his edition of the New Testament in the original Greek, in which he collaborated with Westcott.[54] The two scholars were able to make use of the immense accumulation of new knowledge which the precursors in this field had by then rendered available, thousands of Greek New Testament manuscripts as well as versions in numerous languages having already been examined, dated and grouped in 'families'. The outcome of their own investigations had led them to set aside, first, the bulk of the readings of later manuscripts as deriving only from a fourth century Syrian revision and hence

51. Part I: *Clement of Rome*, 1890 (this two-volume edition superseded the single volume edition of 1877); Part II: *Ignatius*, 1885 (3 vols).
52. Lightfoot also replied, in a series of articles first published in *The Contemporary Review* and later reprinted in book form, to an imposing-seeming work in three volumes and of anonymous authorship which completed publication in 1874 under the title *Supernatural Religion*. He did so less, however, with the intent of refuting its arguments than of exposing its inaccuracies. The writer (subsequently identified as W. R. Cassels) defended a non-miraculous Christianity based on the teaching of Jesus *minus* its Pauline interpretations. He was particularly critical of the rationale of miracle put forward in the Bampton lectures of J. B. Mozley and H. L. Mansel.
53. As Church remarked: 'To be the foremost teacher of Christian learning at Cambridge at such a time as this is to hold a critical post, which is, in its way, alone and without its fellow, even in the highest places of the Church' (M. C. Church, *op. cit.*, p. 325).
54. They worked independently, comparing their findings afterwards. See A. F. Hort, *op. cit.*, ii, pp. 243ff.

worthless for the reconstruction of the true text; secondly, a number of mainly 'Western' readings found chiefly in Codex Bezae (D) and the Old Latin and other versions, which they regarded as early but in general to be attributed to a corruption of the original; and thirdly, an 'Alexandrian' type of text—one, that is, supported largely by authors and manuscripts associated with Alexandria—suspected of over-corruption by scribes in the course of its transmission, in favour of a 'neutral' text which, although not actually preserved in any surviving Greek manuscript or version in its original purity, found its nearest embodiment in the great Vatican uncial (B) of the fourth century, supported by the Sinai codex (ℵ), then at St Petersburg. The Introduction to the work was from Hort's pen and remains a masterly accomplishment, whatever the progress in New Testament textual study since his day. The translators of the *Revised Standard Version* of 1946, although adopting a more eclectic principle in determining the text they themselves intended to employ, nevertheless thought it 'really extraordinary' how frequently they concurred in following in the wake of the earlier scholars.

Hort's range of interests was wide, his intellectual training having included both classics and natural science. Indeed he examined in the natural sciences tripos at Cambridge the same year (1871–72) in which he delivered the Hulsean lectures, *The Way, the Truth, the Life.*[55] The only work of his to appear during his lifetime, apart from the Greek New Testament, was his *Two Dissertations* on the Nicene creed, in which he showed that the symbol bearing this name was in fact the ancient creed of Jerusalem as revised by St Cyril, *c.* 360. His other posthumous volume comprised a series of lectures delivered in 1888–89 under the title *The Christian Ecclesia* (1897). Himself a High Churchman of sorts, he is concerned here to examine the meaning of the word *ekklesia* in the light of Scripture.[56] The Christian Church originated with the apostolic band as constituted after St Peter's confession, and Hort believes the idea of a universal Ecclesia underlay the application of the term to the local communities, though it was not to be identified with that of the Kingdom of God as such. In any case the 'unit' of the Church is the individual. 'The one Ecclesia includes all members of all partial Ecclesiae; but its relations to them all are direct, not mediate.'[57]

55. Published posthumously in 1908. At one time Hort even thought of replying to Darwin's *Origin of Species*, not with any aim of rebutting its thesis—as he told Westcott, he was inclined to think it unanswerable, for all its difficulties—but in order to criticize it on particulars and to supply further illustrations. The scientific question he deemed 'a very complicated one—far more complicated than Darwin seems to have any idea' (A. F. Hort, *op. cit.*, i, pp. 415, 433). His project was not realized, but that he should seriously have entertained it indicates the scope of his learning.

56. 'I have', he confessed, 'a deeply rooted agreement with High Churchmen as to the Church, ministry and Sacraments' (A. F. Hort, *op. cit.*, i, p. 400). All three scholars had begun their careers as Evangelicals. But Westcott became critical of Evangelicalism, and Hort, who considered its characteristic doctrines 'perverted rather than untrue', liked to speak of himself as 'a staunch sacerdotalist', in contrast with Lightfoot (*ibid.*, ii, p. 86).

57. *The Christian Ecclesia*, p. 168.

Infinitely painstaking though Hort was, the minutiae of scholarship did not absorb his whole attention, the 'attainment of truth in matters of historical or linguistic fact' being, he held, 'always not an end but a means'.[58] Caution, however, was of his very nature. He declined an invitation to contribute to *Essays and Reviews* on the grounds that

> at present very many orthodox but rational men are being unawares acted on by influences which will assuredly bear fruit in due time, if the process is allowed to go quietly; but I cannot help feeling that a premature crisis would frighten many back into the merest traditionalism. And as a mere matter of prudence, it seems to me questionable to set up a broad conspicuous target for the Philistines to shoot at, unless there is some very decided advantage to be gained.

All the same, when the volume was published he judged its authors 'to believe very much more of truth than their (so-called) orthodox opponents, and to be incomparably greater lovers of truth'; and he wholly deplored 'the violent and indiscriminate agitation' directed against it and of any resultant official policy that might 'deter men of thought and learning from entering the ministry of the Church' or 'impel generous minds into antagonism to the Christian faith'.[59] For his part he averred to having 'a strong sense of the Divine purpose, guiding all the parts of the New Testament', but could not see 'how the exact limits of such guidance can be ascertained except by unbiased *a posteriori* criticism'.[60]

Hort contributed largely to the making of the Revised Version of the Bible. He attended meetings of the Revisers' committee regularly over ten years and was an unfailing source of exact and detailed information. For the New Testament, however, the committee did not adopt the Westcott–Hort text outright, paying greater regard to the *textus receptus* than the two Cambridge scholars would themselves have wished. Even so the result, published in May 1881,[61] was not pleasing to the conservative, as was shown by Dean Burgon's attack on it in *The Quarterly Review*. Although the Revisers' aim had been to produce a version which would be 'alike literal and idiomatic, faithful to each thought of the original, and yet in the expression of it harmonious and free', it was criticized, perhaps inevitably when compared with the Authorized Version of 1611, on grounds of style. But in accuracy it was much the superior, the marginal readings being especially valuable, and it served its purpose well until at length displaced by the *Revised Standard Version*, based as that is on wider knowledge.[62]

The mention of Westcott's name brings us to the member of the Cambridge group who was most in touch with the general public and able thus to exercise a

---

58. A. F. Hort, *op. cit.*, ii, pp. 53f.
59. *Ibid.*, i, pp 400, 428f.
60. *Ibid.*, i, p. 420.
61. The Old Testament translation did not appear until May 1885, and that of the Apocrypha not until 1896.
62. It is arguable that the whole undertaking was at the time premature. Armitage Robinson considered it to have been made a generation too soon. See G. R. Eden and F. C. Macdonald (eds.), *Lightfoot of Durham* (1932), p. 126, and cp. A. F. Hort, *op. cit.*, ii, p. 128.

broader influence, although purely as a scholar he is less impressive than the others. His work in the field of primitive Christianity lacks the qualities which have perpetuated Lightfoot's, and he had not Hurt's critical acumen. Immensely conscientious, he was over-conservative and in interpreting the Greek built too much on existing knowledge, which he was apt to consider final. And he was without the truly great scholar's foresight of future possibilities. But as a theologian he had depth and imaginative force, if not always clarity.[63] As a preacher he was among the most powerful of his day,[64] whilst his activities in the sphere of social and industrial problems won him national fame.[65] He was essentially a religious leader, with a strong mystical bent, if the word be taken in its popular sense, although he personally disliked it.[66] His principal theological writings, apart from his commentaries on the fourth gospel (1881) and the Johannine epistles (1883) and on Hebrews (1889) and Ephesians (1906), are the three volumes: *Religious Thought in the West* (1891), a collection of essays which includes two of special note, 'Origen and the Beginnings of Religious Philosophy' and 'Benjamin Whichcote'—the latter, a study of the Cambridge Platonist, being particularly characteristic; *The Gospel of Life* (1892), an outline of Christian doctrine and his nearest attempt at a systematic theology; and the Westminster Abbey sermons of 1885–86 which make up *Christus Consummator: Some Aspects of the Work and Person of Christ in Relation to Modern Thought* (1886). His concern for social questions is shown in *Social Aspects of Christianity* (1887) and *The Incarnation and the Common Life* (1893).

Religious faith Westcott saw as ultimately a matter of insight, a 'mystical' apprehension of those 'eternal realities which lie beneath and beyond the changeful shows of life'.[67] Certainly 'if we try to establish by argument the existence of a spiritual Being whom we may reverence and love, our intellectual proofs break down'. On the contrary, 'the Being to which they guide us is less than the Being for whom we look and in whom we trust'.[68] Science and history are lavish sources of purely human knowledge, but only revelation will add 'that element of infinity' which gives 'characteristic permanence to every work and thought',[69] although it is knowledge which supplies the material that faith uses. 'If we go back to the three fundamental conceptions, self, the world, God, we shall notice one feature that is

---

63. E. W. Benson found his manner 'at once bewildering and fatiguing' (A. C. Benson, *The Leaves of the Tree*, p. 125). Westcott said himself that 'to some I am a cloud; and I do not see how to help it' (A. Westcott, *The Life and Letters of Brooke Foss Westcott* (1903), ii, p. 24).
64. But not the most illuminating. Rather, it has been said, 'his words moved you strangely, because they moved him' (G. R. Eden, *Great Christians*, ed. R. S. Forman (1933), p. 578. Cp. H. Scott Holland, *Personal Studies* (1905), p. 132).
65. See appended Note to Chapter 13 below.
66. 'I don't think', he once wrote, 'I have ever used the word "mystics"; it is so hopelessly vague, and it suggests an esoteric teaching which is wholly foreign to the Christian. But from Cambridge days I have read the writings of many who are called mystics with much profit' (A. Westcott, *op. cit.*, ii, p. 309).
67. *Christian Aspects of Life* (1897), p. 201.
68. *The Gospel of Life*, p. 34.
69. *Ibid.*, p. 89.

common to them. In fashioning each we enter the future and the unseen, and act without hesitation on the conclusions which we have formed.' Hence experience itself compels us to look beyond experience. When Westcott quotes Whichcote, that 'reason is not laid aside nor discharged, much less is it confounded by any of the materials of religion, but awakened, excited, employed, directed, and improved by it; for the understanding is that faculty whereby man is made capable of God and apprehensive of Him',[70] he is stating a presiding truth of his own mind.

In his theological sympathies Westcott, like Maurice and unlike the Tractarians, was much more a Greek than a Latin, as is clearly brought out in the essays on Origen and Dionysius the Areopagite.[71] Origen, in contrast with Augustine, stood 'in the meeting-place of struggling thoughts' and knew that 'he had that to speak which could harmonize and satisfy every spiritual aspiration of man: an answer to the despair of the West, which saw in man's good an unattainable ideal; an answer to the despair of the East, which saw in man's way a vain delusion'. Augustine, on the other hand, faced with the barbarian invasions, 'was called upon to pronounce sentence on the old world, and to vindicate Christianity from the charge of social disintegration. One was the interpreter of a universal hope; the other was the interpreter of a secular overthrow'.[72] It was not too much indeed to say that a work remained for Greek divinity in the nineteenth century hardly less pregnant with results than that wrought by the Greek classics in the fifteenth.

Revelation Westcott held to be in its essence absolute but in its human apprehension relative.[73] That it should thus be both might appear inconsistent; but the answer to the problem lies in the special nature of the incarnation, which has the resurrection for its culmination. 'Since we have to consider a final revelation given to man ... such a revelation must come through a true human life.' But the Son of man was also Son of God. 'The Incarnation and the Resurrection reconcile the two characteristics of our faith—they establish the right of Christianity to be called historical, they establish its right to be called absolute.' These twin mysteries furnish the basis for a spiritual religion which is also intensely human, one which 'at every moment introduces the infinite and the unseen into a vital connection with the things of earth'. This last phrase is significant. Westcott's 'incarnationalist' theology, like Charles Gore's later, provided, if not the immediate stimulus, at least the ultimate rationale of his Christian socialism. 'The Incarnation', he wrote, 'binds all action, all experience, all creation to God; and supplies at once the motive and the power of service.'[74]

---

70. *Sermons*, iii, pp. 17f. See *Religious Thought in the West*, p. 383.
71. *Religious Thought in the West*, pp. 142–252. Tractarian theology carried a markedly Augustinian strain, while its doctrine of the Church was Cyprianic. Hort observed that 'the total absence of any specific influence of Greek theology upon the Oxford Movement, notwithstanding the extensive reading in the Fathers possessed by its more learned chiefs, is a very striking fact' (A. F. Hort, *op. cit.*, ii, p. 38). See D. Newsome, *Bishop Westcott and the Platonic Tradition* (Bishop Westcott Memorial Lecture, 1968).
72. *Religious Thought in the West*, p. 249.
73. *The Gospel of Life*, p. xxiii.
74. *Ibid.*, p. xxi.

As with Maurice so with Westcott, the gospel proclaims the unity—actual, not merely potential—of the whole of humanity in Christ; and the consequent solidarity of man and man entails a mutual obligation. Somewhat surprisingly, it was this aspect of Auguste Comte's system which led him to regard positivism with a measure of sympathy.[75] At all events it brought to notice features of Christian truth more or less hidden since the eclipse of Greek theology by Latin, and in its way was itself a testimony to Christianity. The great difference of course was that the latter 'does not pause where Positivism pauses, in the visible order'.[76] Westcott was also deeply impressed by Maurice's *Social Morality*, as he acknowledged in the preface to his own *Social Aspects of Christianity*.[77] His view of socialism, moreover, was, like Maurice's, ethical rather than political: socialism was the antidote to individualism, the principle of self-interest. 'Individualism regards humanity as made up of disconnected or warring atoms; Socialism regards it as an organic whole, a vital unity formed by the combination of contributory members mutually interdependent'.[78] But anything in the nature of a revolutionary ideology, or even political radicalism, was totally at variance with his cautious, aloof and fundamentally conservative nature.[79]

The new critical approach to the understanding of early Christianity, especially in relation to its pagan environment, was well exemplified in the work of a scholar who seems never to have won quite the recognition, at least in England, which his merits warranted: Edwin Hatch (1835–89), reader in ecclesiastical history and fellow of Pembroke College, Oxford. A man of very independent views, whom Sanday considered to be 'bolder and more disinterested than even the great Cambridge trio', he was probably too much of a liberal for most churchmen of his time. He wrote a good deal, his most permanent achievement being a *Concordance to the Septuagint*, completed by H. A. Redpath after his death.[80] But the volumes which aroused the widest interest were two sets of lectures, his Bamptons on *The Organization of the Early Christian Church* (1881), which attracted attention in Germany and were translated into German by Harnack in 1883, and the still more

---

75. See the articles by Westcott in *The Contemporary Review*, December 1967 and July 1868. The second of these was re-published as an appendix to *The Gospel of the Resurrection* (7th ed, pp. 249–76).

76. *The Gospel of the Resurrection* (1866), p. 273. 'Comte's view of Humanity as organic outweighed his agnosticism, in Westcott's mind' (C. E. Osborne, *Christian Ideas of Political History* (1929), p. 264).

77. Westcott's admiration for Maurice grew with the years, although he himself scarcely realized the degree of affinity between his own thinking and Maurice's until he read the latter's *Life*. Cp. A. Westcott, *op. cit.*, ii, p. 160. See also J. Clayton, *Bishop Westcott* (1906), with an appendix by Llewelyn Davies, and above, p. 214.

78. See his 1890 (Hull) Church Congress paper, reprinted in *The Incarnation and the Common Life*, pp. 223–47.

79. As President of the Christian Social Union, founded by Scott Holland and others in 1889, he declared: 'The Union affirms a principle, enforces an obligation, confesses a Divine Presence. It has no programme of immediate reforms' (*Christian Aspects of Life*, p. 252).

80. His *Essays in Biblical Greek* came out in 1889.

controversial Hibberts on *The Influence of Greek Ideas on Christianity* (1889).[81] The thesis of the latter is that the gospel, largely identified with the Sermon on the Mount, had been transformed under the influence of Greek speculative thought from a way of life into a body of *credenda*.

> The Nicene Creed is a statement partly of historical facts and partly of dogmatic inferences; the metaphysical terms which it contains would probably have been unintelligible to the first disciples; ethics have no place in it. The one belongs to a world of Syrian peasants, the other to a world of Greek philosophers.[82]

It was in fact precisely the argument for which Harnack supplied massive documentation in his *Dogmengeschichte*, in the preface to the English version of which he referred to the Oxford scholar's work as already giving 'the most ample proof of the conception of the early history of dogma which is set forth in the following pages'. Hatch's conclusion was that since the Hellenistic influence had introduced into Christianity Greek rhetoric, logic and metaphysics, 'a large part of what are sometimes called Christian doctrines, and many usages which have prevailed and continue to prevail in the Christian Church, are in their essence Greek still'.[83] But the fact posed a question, namely the relation of these Greek elements in Christianity to the nature of Christianity itself. Was what was absent from the religion in its primitive form non-essential, or was it the duty of each succeeding age at once to accept the developments of the past, and to do its part in bringing on the developments of the future?

After Hatch's death the pre-eminent figure in Oxford New Testament scholarship was William Sanday (1843–1920), at first Dean Ireland's professor at Oriel and then, from 1895, Lady Margaret professor at Christ Church. Over the years his view changed from conservative to moderate liberal, and he later—in 1914—was to join issue with Bishop Gore on the right of the 'Modernist' cleric to minister in the Church of England, claiming that what he called 'a sound and right Modernism' was entirely permissible: 'The Saviour of mankind extends His arms towards the cultivated modern man just as He does towards the simple believer.'[84] The bulk of Sanday's publications belongs to the early years of the present century and includes principally his article on the life of Christ in Hastings's *Dictionary of the Bible*,[85] reprinted in volume form in 1907 as *Outlines of the Life of Christ*, and the lectures which he delivered in 1904 at Union Theological Seminary, New York, and subsequently published as *The Criticism of the Fourth Gospel*. In the latter he confessed to having to part company with those younger critics, German and French, who (as he thought) approached the critical problem of the fourth gospel with a 'reduced' conception of Christianity akin to ancient Ebionism or Arianism

---

81. Edited by A. M. Fairbairn. A German edition by E. Preuschl, with additions by Harnack, was published in 1892. The original English edition by F. C. Grant, was reprinted in 1957.
82. *The Influence of Greek Ideas on Christianity*, p. i.
83. *Ibid.*, p. 350.
84. *Bishop Gore's Challenge to Criticism* (1914), pp. 30f.
85. Hastings's *Dictionary* started publication in 1898 and the whole enterprise was completed six years later. Its standpoint was a temperate conservatism.

and so automatically ruled out the gospel either as a dogmatic authority or as a record of historical events.[86] But the work which properly falls within our period and which established its author's reputation as a teacher as well as a scholar is the Bampton lectures on *Inspiration*, published in 1893. In this Sanday aims to show wherein, granting modern critical assumptions and methods, the spiritual authority of the Bible still lies. That the application of such methods has led to some negative results he admits, but the Bible's authority derives from its 'inspiration', a term, therefore, whose proper meaning it is all-important to examine. The traditional view, that Scripture as a whole and in all its parts is the Word of God, quickly leads to the notion of inspiration as 'something dead and mechanical'. Criticism, on the other hand, leaves room for an 'inductive' theory, based on an attempt to investigate the consciousness of the biblical writers themselves. Yet the measure of inspiration is eventually more than this: the isolated efforts gravitate towards a common goal and form part of a larger scheme. 'We may study the operations not only of these individual minds but of the central Mind',[87] that 'Higher Providence' the workings of which are detected, for example, in the writing down of prophetic utterances in the Old Testament or the preservation of occasional letters in the New so as to provide a basis for Christian theology. Also to be noted is the 'Law of Parsimony' by which all revelation is adjusted to the condition of its recipients. The 'All or Nothing' idea—that the Bible's inspiration is either 'verbal' or else non-existent—is a wholly false antithesis. Inspiration is real, but it has to be sought and tested by the means under which all truth is realized.

Old Testament studies in Oxford had been retarded rather than promoted by the occupant of the chair of Hebrew, Dr Pusey, who throughout his long career had maintained an unbudging traditionalism. Thus his massive commentary on *Daniel* (1863), as a serious study of its subject, is now negligible. But his successor, S. R. Driver (1846–1914), who understood and accepted the main positions adopted by the best continental scholarship, soon swept away the accumulated dust and established himself, with his *Introduction to the Literature of the Old Testament*, as the foremost authority in England in this domain. And with him must be placed T. K. Cheyne (1841–1915), a man, however, of far less critical reserve who, as his later work proves—especially his Bampton lectures of 1891 on *The Historical Origin and Religious Ideas of the Psalter* and the articles contributed by him to his own *Encyclopaedia Biblica* (1899–1903)—was prepared to travel as far as current radicalism would take him. In Cambridge Westcott had been succeeded in the Regius professorship by H. B. Swete (1835–1917), a biblical scholar of a generally conservative outlook and now remembered chiefly for his work on the text of the Septuagint and for his resourcefulness in organizing the studies of other people.[88]

Thus in the forty years that had elapsed since the publication of *Essays and Reviews* a great change had been wrought in the attitude of at any rate the theologically educated towards what had hitherto been a sacrosanct authority, the

86. *The Criticism of the Fourth Gospel* (1905), p. 29.
87. *Inspiration*, p. 402.
88. It was largely through Swete's enterprise that *The Journal of Theological Studies* was founded in 1899.

only ground and standard of true religion. Suggestions of a more discerning approach to the Bible and its problems had here and there been voiced earlier, though with little positive result, having for the most part been scouted as 'German rationalism'. But *Essays and Reviews* had thrown down a challenge that could no longer be ignored. Interpret the Scripture, Jowett had said, like any other book, and the task of doing so was henceforth gradually to be assumed, if with reluctance and caution. The outcome was a view of the Bible in its historical setting as a highly diversified collection of ancient writings from many different hands and periods. The 'Higher Criticism' did not trench directly upon dogmatic questions—its field of interest was simply that of objective historical inquiry—but its concern with the human conditions under which divine revelation has been received almost inevitably gave rise to misgivings about the extent to which the divine might on the critics' own showing turn out to be the all too human. This indeed had been precisely its effect on the French Catholic, Ernest Renan. But in English Protestantism, traditionalist though it was, compromise proved easier than in Catholicism, and by the close of the century theology had found means of coming to terms with criticism and even of welcoming it for the new light it could be claimed to have shed on the nature and course of divine revelation itself. Nor did the historical study of the Bible foreclose the question of its inspiration; it only suggested that what was inspired was not so much writings as writers. Yet the truth could hardly be hidden that the dogmatic systems inherited from the past had been built upon entirely different presuppositions from those which the modern critical scholar entertains. How far then would such systems continue to stand after their foundations had shifted? And when once it was acknowledged that the hope of salvation is in part at least a projection of human longing what further qualifications of it might not in the end prove necessary? These were questions to which varying answers were already being given. But one thing seemed plain: the old certitude was no more. The authority of the Bible itself had to be explained and defended. Theology, in becoming more liberal, was sapping the assurance of faith.[89]

89. It is sometimes said that by the end of the century biblical criticism had been largely accepted by the churches in Britain. This may be true of their more scholarly members, whether clerical or lay, but is otherwise too sweeping a generalization. The Roman Catholic church had emphatically not done so, as Leo XIII's encyclical *Providentissimus Deus* (1893) and the standpoint of the new Biblical Commission of 1902 make evident. The Free Churches, apart from a few scholars of distinction, were suspicious of it—witness the reception in some quarters of the Congregationalist R. F. Horton's *Inspiration of the Bible* (1888). So too was the Scottish Free Church. The Church of England was prepared to countenance freedom of criticism in regard to the Old Testament, but was decidedly chary of radicalism in approaching the new. The ordinary churchgoer, of whatever denomination, seems to have been largely ignorant of what the 'Higher Criticism' was about or felt it was a matter best left aside. See Chadwick, *The Victorian Church*, part ii, pp. 97–111.

Chapter 11

LITERATURE AND DOGMA

The poets

To appreciate fully the Victorians' concern over the problem of religious belief one must look beyond the theologians and philosophers to the writers of imaginative literature, to the poets and novelists of the age. In an epoch when the Christian creed is still very largely taken for granted explicit reference to it by authors whose purpose is not directly religious and didactic is rare. The literature belonging to the early part of our period is of such a kind. Dickens and Thackeray, like Fielding or Miss Austen before them, although they might lampoon certain types of demonstrative religiosity, evince no theological curiosity and to all showing accept Christianity, as to both its doctrines and its moral principles, without question. With the writers of the next generation, however, it is otherwise. In the mid-century and after, Tennyson and Browning, Matthew Arnold and Arthur Hugh Clough, George Eliot and George Meredith, as, finally, Thomas Hardy and Mrs Humphrey Ward—the latter admittedly at a much lower level of imaginative evocation—are all acutely aware that religious faith, at least in its traditional form, constitutes a grave problem. They question and they doubt, and in varying degrees worry about their doubts and questionings. At the same time an attitude of mere secular indifference is also unusual: to criticize religion is obviously not to ignore it. But the nineteenth century, far more than any preceding era, was making belief in Christianity increasingly difficult for the intellectually sensitive. To some indeed unbelief itself had become a moral necessity.

   The Victorian age saw the novel attain its maturity. Although in the main it lacked sophistication as an art form, it had the advantage over verse and even the prose drama in its capacity to depict the manifold actuality of life. But its function as a medium for the informed presentation of moral and social issues was of somewhat tardy growth and at first its role was simply to entertain, without any *arrière-pensée*. On the other hand the use of poetry for the higher ends of edification was both recognized and demanded. The poet, accordingly, was also a prophet, even if in the eyes of the orthodox he might turn out to be a false one, preaching strange doctrine. For many, throughout a great part of the century, this prophetic function was most signally discharged by Wordsworth. The Wordsworthian faith in Nature, with its assurance of a 'central peace subsisting at the heart of endless agitation' could, it was found, sustain the spirit in an 'iron time' when science and industrialism seemed to be turning the dogmas of institutional religion into a meaningless anachronism. Thus typically of those who now looked to Wordsworth for spiritual consolation, William Hale White, in *The Autobiography of Mark Rutherford*, could write that the poet's 'real God is not the God of the Church, but the God of the hills, the abstraction Nature, and to this my reverence was transferred. Instead of an object of worship which was altogether artificial, remote, never coming into genuine contact with me, I had now one which I thought to be real, one in which literally I could live and move and have my being, all actual fact present before my eyes'. Wordsworth, he continues, 'unconsciously did for me what every religious reformer has done—he recreated my Supreme Divinity; substituting a new and living spirit for the old deity, once alive but now hardened into an idol'. It was all the more embarrassing, therefore, to Wordsworth's agnostic admirers when in later life he aligned himself openly with orthodox Christianity as taught by the Church of England. Yet the poet's religious development was a slow and even tortuous process, starting in the Anglicanism of his early upbringing and passing through Godwinian rationalism—Coleridge thought him 'at least a semi-atheist' while under Godwin's spell—and the nature mysticism of his poetic prime, before returning to a sincerely confessed belief in God's 'pure word by miracle revealed'.

The question is how far, during the great period of his creativity, did Wordsworth depart from a basically orthodox creed. It is hard to believe that his return to orthodoxy followed immediately on his disillusionment with the Godwinian doctrines, and that that

> ...sense sublime
> Of something far more deeply interfused

of which he speaks so movingly in *Tintern Abbey* was only a way of describing his restored belief in Christian theism. Later indeed the charge of 'Spinosism' was apt to nettle him and he denied that there was anything 'of this kind in the *Excursion*'. But the poems of earlier date, from *Tintern Abbey* to the *Ode on Immortality*, disclose nothing that could be identified with a distinctively Christian conviction. It is not simply that they do not allude to the central dogmas of the faith, but that the whole attitude of mind expressed in them is quite different from the Christian. The medium of revelation of the spirit

> ...that impels
> All thinking things, all objects of all thought,
> And rolls through all things

is nature alone. A religious truth imparted through unique historical persons and events has no relevant place in a mysticism of this sort, resting as it does on visionary insight, when

> What we see of forms and images
> Which float along our minds, and what we feel
> Of active or recognizable thought,
> Prospectiveness, or intellect, or will,
> Not only is not worthy to be deemed
> Our being, to be prized as what we are,
> But is the very littleness of life.

Such consciousness the poet could then

> ...deem but accidents,
> Relapses from the one interior life
> That lives in all things.

By this interior life man had mystical communion, through the natural world, with the all-pervading spirit of the universe. For

> ...whether we be young or old,
> Our destiny, our being's heart and home
> Is with infinitude, and only there.

   This, then, was the faith which spoke so powerfully to the typical Victorian doubter, consoling him for the loss of his traditional convictions. Thus, when Mark Rutherford tells of the change wrought in him by his reading of the *Lyrical Ballads* as only comparable with that wrought in St Paul when confronted with 'the Divine apparition'[1] the reference is appropriately religious; although Matthew Arnold, himself a devout Wordsworthian, also warned his readers to be on their guard against 'the exhibitors and extollers of a scientific system of thought in Wordsworth, the poet's cast of mind not being scientific or even systematic. What he had to offer was a potent religious *feeling*, at odds alike with rationalism and industrialism, but unencumbered with impossible *credenda*. Eventually, however, Wordsworth himself came to look for something more in religion. The 'power of solitude' had ceased to be self-sufficing and he once again felt the need of the fellowship of believers and the traditional institutions of the historic faith. It was a change of mind which the literary critics have generally united in deploring. No doubt with reason, for his increasingly rigid conservatism in religion as in politics was attended by a commensurate decline in poetic inspiration: it was not the errant imagination but an assiduous study of church history which was the generative force behind *Ecclesiastical Sonnets*. And the 1840 revision of *The Prelude* shows a consistent attempt to expunge any trace of the regrettable 'Spinosism' of his earlier years.
   Wordsworth's successor in the laureateship was Alfred Tennyson, *In Memoriam* having appeared on the eve of his appointment to the office. The poem was the outcome of seventeen years of brooding on the death of his friend Arthur Hallam. Yet it is not only an elegy, an expression—the finest, possibly, of its kind in English—of a profound personal grief, but a philosophy of life and death in verse. To the public of the day it appealed strongly, on both counts, and is the basis of the author's claim to be regarded seriously as a thinker. Certainly he proves himself, for a layman, unusually well informed on scientific matters. Astronomy had been an early love of his, and Laplace's nebular theory had already found mention in *The Princess*:

> This world was once a fluid haze of light,
> Till toward the centre set the starry tides,
> And eddied into suns, that wheeling cast
> The planets: then the monster, then the man.

1. *Autobiography*, pp. 18–21.

More interesting, however, are the poet's anticipations of Darwin. *The Palace of Art* (1832) had once included among its later excised stanzas the following:

> 'From shape to shape at first within the womb
> The brain is moulded', she began.
> 'And thro' all phases of all thought I come
> Unto the perfect man.
> All nature widens upward. Evermore
> The simple essence lower lies,
> More complex is more perfect, owning more
> Discourse, more widely wise'.[2]

Lyell's *Principles of Geology* had been closely studied, the sound of streams, for example, suggesting to the poet how they

> Draw down Aeonian hills, and sow
> The dust of continents to be.

Other reading comprised Herschel's *Preliminary Discourse on the Study of Natural Philosophy* (1830) and the anonymous *Vestiges of the Natural History of Creation*. The latter in particular would seem to have furnished material for *In Memoriam*, although it is not unlikely that Tennyson's own grasp of the evolutionary principle in biology antedated Chambers's best-selling book.[3] Thus whereas to so many *The Origins of Species*, on its first publication, brought only astonishment and dismay, the poet was already facing the possible implications for a spiritual faith of the concept of a Nature bleakly indifferent to all human values, and for an appreciation of the arguments of *In Memoriam* the extent of Tennyson's reflections on the problems which science was more and more pressing upon the consideration of the religious believer must be recognized. The poetic form which such reflections took comprise, of course, some of the best-known stanzas in the whole work.

> Are God and Nature then at strife,
>   That Nature lends such evil dreams?
>   So careful of the type she seems,
> So careless of the single life;
>
> That I, considering everywhere
>   Her secret meaning in her deeds,
>   And finding that of fifty seeds
> She often brings but one to bear,
>
> I falter where I firmly trod,
>   And falling with my weight of cares
>   Upon the great world's altar-stairs
>   That slope thro' darkness up to God,

2. Quoted in Hallam, Lord Tennyson's *Memoir* of the poet (1899 ed.), p. 101.
3. *Ibid.*, p. 186.

I stretch lame hands of faith, and grope,
  And gather dust and chaff, and call
  To what I feel is Lord of all,
And faintly trust the larger hope.

      *   *   *

'So careful of the type?' but no.
From scarped cliff and quarried stone
She cries, 'A thousand types are gone:
I care for nothing, all shall go.

'Thou makest thine appeal to me;
  I bring to life, I bring to death:
  The spirit does but mean the breath:
I know no more.' And he, shall he,

Man, her last work, who seem'd so fair,
  Such splendid purpose in his eyes,
  Who roll'd the psalm to wintry skies,
Who built him fanes of fruitless prayer,

Who trusted God was love indeed
  And love Creation's final law—
  Tho' Nature, red in tooth and claw
With ravine, shriek'd against his creed—

Who lov'd, who suffer'd countless ills,
  Who battl'd for the True, the Just,
  Be blown about the desert dust,
Or seal'd within the iron hills?

No more? A monster, then, a dream,
  A discord. Dragons of the prime,
  That tare each other in their slime,
Were mellow music match'd with him.

O life as futile, then, as frail!
  O for thy voice to soothe and bless!
  What hope of answer, or redress?
Behind the veil, behind the veil?

In Memoriam is the utterance of a mind torn by doubt of whether life has any moral meaning whatsoever; a doubt made all the heavier by the sorrow of a desolating bereavement. Any death could raise the same question, but the death at the pathetically early age of twenty-two of a man of great promise whom Tennyson loved with a rare intensity rendered it inescapable. The poet felt himself like 'an infant crying in the night'. To his bitter personal problem there seemed no answer—none assuredly in the commonly accepted creed. Yet in the long course of his meditations he gropingly finds an answer. It is not the full Christian answer

270

by any means, despite the apparent confidence of the famous opening stanzas. For *In Memoriam*, although Tennyson's contemporaries were pleased to read it as such, is not a Christian poem and the questions which the poet wrestles with, under the crushing weight of his own near despair, are questions of basic import. The issue is not whether the Christian doctrine is true, or generally acceptable as true—the debate of the liberal theologians—but whether existence will admit of any spiritual interpretation at all, whether there is any possible assurance

> That nothing walks with aimless feet;
>   That not one life shall be destroy'd,
>   Or cast as rubbish to the void,
> When God hath made the pile complete.

In the end the poet follows the beckonings of his own heart rather than linger with the cold misgivings of reason:

> If e'er when faith had fall'n asleep,
>   I heard a voice 'Believe no more'
>   And heard an ever-breaking shore
> That tumbl'd in the godless deep;
>
> A warmth within the breast would melt
>   The freezing reason's colder part,
>   And like a man in wrath the heart
> Stood up and answer'd 'I have felt.'

But one notes how the poet clings to the truth of his experience when he adds:

> No, like a child in doubt and fear,
>   Then was I as a child that cries,
>   But crying knows his father near...

Hence the only positive conclusion, painfully reached, was that

> What I am beheld again
>   What is, and no man understands;
>   And out of darkness came the hands
> That reach thro' Nature, moulding man.

No doubt even with this expression of faith, hard won though it was, the mid-nineteenth century public was satisfied, and the poet's evident assurance gave his work a large measure of its popularity. It helped indeed to reassure his readers. Yet it is a good deal less a poem of belief than of scepticism, and in this respect was a mirror to its times. Such is brought out clearly in a letter of Henry Sidgwick to Hallam, Lord Tennyson, when the latter was preparing the *Memoir* of his father. The poem moved him, Sidgwick said, by its disclosure of a region deeper than the differences between theism and Christianity, a region where agnosticism and faith finally confront each other. With the passing of the years this great issue had become acute. The freedom of thought for which, in the 1860s, he and others had fought had not brought with it any well-reasoned confidence.

It brings us face to face with atheistic science; the faith in God and Immortality, which we had been struggling to clear from superstition, suddenly seems to be *in the air*: and in seeking for a firm basis for this faith we find ourselves in the midst of the 'fight with death' which *In Memoriam* so powerfully presents.

What the poem did for him in this struggle was to strengthen 'the ineffaceable and ineradicable conviction that *humanity* will not and cannot acquiesce in a godless world: the "man in men" will not do this, whatever individual men may do'.[4] And here surely is where the poem's value lies—apart, that is, from the beauty of its visual imagery and the music of its verse. Although there was little enough of the academic philosopher or theologian in Tennyson he was a man genuinely religious by nature, and it was the conflict within him between his longing for a viable faith and the growing doubts to which he and his age were prey that gave the work an appeal far beyond the pathos of the actual circumstances in which it originated. The doubt itself is the thing, and the well-known Prologue fails to carry conviction through its own over-assertion. Whatever in the outcome Tennyson may have found, it was nearer to the vague, uncertain 'Power in darkness whom we guess' than to the 'Strong Son of God, immortal Love' of the Christian doctrinal tradition. As R. H. Hutton observed, 'the lines of [Tennyson's] theology were in harmony with the great central lines of Christian thought; but in coming down to detail it soon passed into a region where all was wistful, and dogma disappeared in a haze of radiant twilight'.[5]

Tennyson's religious attitude is, then, one of faith riddled by doubt. Robert Browning, that other poetic idol of the Victorian reading public, was possessed of a very different temperament, extroverted and naturally sanguine.[6] He was more disposed, therefore, to trust his reason to yield positive conclusions. He was also better read than Tennyson in the general literature of the day and certainly more conversant with the theological. Too much has been made of a line in *Pippa Passes*, lifted out of its context; Browning's optimism was not so crass. But he was nonetheless confident that God *is* in his heaven and that in the final assessment all must be well with the world, a belief he retained from his nonconformist upbringing. Indeed as a young man he was 'passionately religious', according to Dowden, although his verse hardly conveys the impression of personal religious feeling. He later outgrew the narrowness of early Victorian dissent, which could scarcely have fostered sympathy with such diverse human types as he portrays in his verse. Yet his sympathies did not extend to Anglican ritualism and he rather arrogantly

4. See *Enoch Arden and In Memoriam*, ed. Hallam, Lord Tennyson (1908), pp. 200f.
5. *Aspects of Religious and Scientific Thought* (ed. E. M. Rosco, 1899), p. 408.
6. Browning enjoyed an approving readership among churchmen. His resolute optimism, his confidence in an ultimately beneficent providence and his belief in personal immortality—a matter of deep concern to the Victorian conscience—appealed to them strongly. Bishop Westcott, for example, was a dedicated admirer of the poet. He teaches, he wrote, 'that life now must be treated as a whole; that learning comes through suffering; that every failure felt to be a failure points to final achievement; that the visible present is but one scene in an illimitable growth' (*Religious Thought in the West*, p. 256). The whole essay, 'Browning's View of Life', is a remarkable tribute to the poet's essentially Christian spirituality, as a typical Victorian divine would have seen it.

dismisses Puseyism as 'a kind of child's play which unfortunately had religion for its object'.[7] His knowledge of the Bible was considerable, as *Saul* and *A Death in the Desert* testify; but as he grew older dogmatic Christianity meant less and less to him, his own religion assuming—to cite Dowden again—'the non-historical form of a Humanitarian Theism courageously accepted, not as an account of the Unknowable, but as the best provisional conception which we are competent to form'.[8] The poem most readily comparable with *In Memoriam* in its subject-matter is *La Saisiaz*, published in 1878, commemorating a friend who died suddenly while staying with the Brownings at a villa (called La Saisiaz) near Geneva. The author's direct concern here is with the questions of God, the soul and the life hereafter. The first part tells the story, the rest unfolds the argument. 'Was ending ending once and always, when you died?', he asks himself, and the reply he gives follows not church teachings but his own reasoning. The existence of God and the soul he postulates, but submits that if consciousness ends with physical death then life presents a baffling problem. Assume, however, that consciousness continues and the here and now takes on a very different aspect.

> Without the want,
> Life, now human, would be brutish: just the hope, however scant,
> Makes the actual life worth leading; take the hope therein away,
> All we have to do is surely not endure another day.
> This life has its hopes for this life, hopes that promise joy:
>
> life done—
> Out of all the hopes, how many had complete fulfilment? None.
> 'But the soul is not the body': and the breath is not the flute;
> Both together make the music: either marred and all is mute.

The point of view is a purely personal one, but it comprises the whole interest of the poem. To its author—and surprisingly for those who persisted in thinking of Browning as the ever unconquerable optimist—

> Sorrow did and joy did nowise, life well weighed— preponderate.
> By necessity ordained thus? I shall bear as best I can,
> By a cause all-good, all-wise, all-potent? No, as I am a man!

But on the supposition of a future life the present can be borne, suffering itself giving assurance of an ultimate gain. The poet then proceeds with his argument in the form of a dialogue between 'Fancy', or intuitive feeling, and 'Reason', contending that life in this world is not only best explained as a probation but that probation demands such conditions as in fact obtain here. The very uncertainty of a future existence, with rewards and punishments, brings to men's actions a moral dimension they would not otherwise have. Moreover, if the future life with its presumed higher faculties and greater happiness were not in doubt, would we not hasten its coming, to the detriment of our present responsibilities? The conclusion is one of 'hope—no more than hope—no less than hope'. As a piece of reasoning in verse *La Saisiaz* is arresting if unconvincing, although apart from its argument

---

7. E. Dowden, *The Life of Robert Browning* (1904), p. 86.
8. *Ibid.*, p. 364.

the verse is nugatory. What Browning really had to say could have been better said in prose.

Browning's humanitarianism comes out most clearly where he is most truly himself, in depicting human nature. It was 'Men and Women' who held his attention always. The dramatic mode of expression was also his most successful and his sense of absolute values has telling utterance in three of his best-known pieces, the dramatic monologues *Fra Lippo Lippi, Andrea del Sarto* and *Abt Vogler.* Thus in the last-named he can say—and it is perhaps his own confession of faith—

> The high that proved too high, the heroic for earth too hard,
> The passion that left the ground to lose itself in the sky.
> Music sent up to God by the lover and the bard;
> Enough that He heard it once: we shall hear it by and by.

If what Tennyson gives us is belief struggling to overcome doubt and Browning a hopeful activism—as G. K. Chesterton put it, 'he offered the cosmos as an adventure rather than a scheme'—Matthew Arnold is distinctively the poet of faith in retreat: that faith whose sea (like the English Channel on a moonlit night) was

> once at the full, and round earth's shore
> Lay like the folds of a bright girdle furl'd';

whereas now he hears—typical nineteenth century intellectual that he is—only

> Its melancholy, long, withdrawing roar,
> Retreating to the breath
> Of the night-wind down the vast edges drear
> And naked shingles of the world.

Arnold's considered views on the problem of Christianity we shall have to take note of, and at some length, later in this chapter. But whatever his reasoned opinions may have been his instinctive feelings are expressed in his verse. They are both negative and regretful. The poet felt himself to be

> Standing between two worlds, one dead,
> The other powerless to be born.

Some renewing power was needed to take the place of the old religious certainties, but its arrival was delayed. The age was one of criticism, necessary but disintegrating, and Arnold could not contemplate it with much of either joy or hope; hence the attraction for him of the author of *Obermann*, Senancour, who provided him with the subject-matter of two poems and of an essay published originally in *The Academy* for October 1869 and reprinted in the third series of *Essays in Criticism.*[9] For the Swiss writer also had sensed that 'ground tone of human agony' which an epoch of relentless change had thrown up. This mood of nostalgia for a vanished or a vanishing past for which neither present nor future could offer any greatly compensating substitute pervades all Arnold's verse. Such a consistent note of disappointment and disillusionment was bound to limit his

9. Boston, 1910.

statute as a poet, but it is also unquestionably the source of his special appeal and the reason why many today find him the most satisfying of all the Victorian verse-writers. Certainly he was no optimist on the score of his age's material progress, which, without the guidance of adequate spiritual values, promised only a desolate 'iron age' of vulgarized standards and diminished ideals. But where were such values to be discovered? The problem of modern civilization is intractable through its very complexity. The classical world, by contrast, was simple and the necessary distinctions could be easily drawn. But in face of modern difficulties no such enlightenment is to be had. This mood of near-defeatism, of all but paralysed action, is perfectly caught in *Empedocles on Etna*, in which through the lips of the ancient philosopher the modern poet himself speaks. Although excluded from the 1853 edition of Arnold's *Poems*—it had appeared in that of the previous year[10]—and not republished until 1867, it remained one of his favourite pieces.[11]

It is not surprising, therefore, that the elegaic strain should have been the mode in which Arnold was most successful as a poet. Others—Milton, Gray, Shelley, Tennyson—have written great elegies, but no poet is so much an elegiast by temperament as is Arnold. The subject of his verse may be a particular individual: in *Rugby Chapel* his father, in *A Southern Night* his brother, in *Westminster Abbey* and *Thyrsis*—his finest single work—his friends A. P. Stanley and A. H. Clough respectively; but the personal sorrow in each case is the occasion for a lament of wider import, a drooping reflection on human destiny. The fitting attitude, the poet believes, if one is 'to possess one's soul'—a favourite phrase of his—is resignation—a lesson which Nature herself teaches:

> Yet, Fausta, the mute turf we tread,
> The solemn hills around us spread,
> This stream which falls incessantly,
> The strange-scrawl'd rocks, the lonely sky,
> If I might lend their life a voice,
> Seem to bear rather than rejoice.

10. *Empedocles on Etna, and Other Poems.*
11. In a letter dated 12 November 1867 Arnold denied that Empedocles's musings were to be taken as expressing his (Arnold's) own thoughts. 'Empedocles', he wrote, 'was composed fifteen years ago, when I had been much studying the remains of the early Greek religious philosophers, as they are called; he greatly impressed me and I desired to gather up and draw out as a whole the hints which his remains offered. Traces of an impatience with the language and assumptions of the popular theology of the day may very likely be visible in my work, and I have now, and no doubt had still more then, a sympathy with the figure Empedocles presents to the imagination; but neither then nor now would my creed, if I wished or were able to draw it out in black and white, be by any means identical with that contained in the preachment of Empedocles.' On the other hand J. Campbell Shairp—Principal Shairp—had written to Clough in the summer of 1849: 'I saw the said Hero—Matt—the day I left London. ... He was working at an "Empedocles"—which seemed to be not much about the man who leapt in the crater—but his name & outward circumstances are used for the drapery of his own thoughts.' The two statements are not necessarily contradictory. See C. B. Tinker and H. F. Lowry, *The Poetry of Matthew Arnold* (1940), pp. 287ff.

Hence

> Be passionate hopes not ill resign'd
> For quiet, and a fearless mind.

Arnold's resignation is, however, a stoic virtue. It is not merely an escape from 'the hopeless tangle of the age' but an honest acceptance of the obligations which circumstances impose, even though in the end the individual will always know himself to be alone, beating where he must not pass, and seeking where he shall not find.

With Algernon Charles Swinburne, whose *Poems and Ballads* made their sensational debut in 1866 (*A Song before Sunrise* came five years later) not only is Christian dogma explicitly rejected—'Glory to Man in the highest!' the poet cries, 'for Man is the master of things'—but its morality as well. The temper now is one of open revolt against established institutions and indeed anything savouring of an ethic of restraint. All the same it is difficult to take Swinburne quite seriously as a thinker. A master of language himself, language too often mastered him and he was apt to fall back on mere posturing. His readers, at first at least, were scandalized. They need not have been: he was only trying to make their flesh creep. A voluminous writer, critic as well as poet, he fails through overstatement and his opinions, after their first audacious impact, seemed as facile as his rather too fluent verse.

The hero as prophet: Thomas Carlyle

At his best Swinburne is a musician in words, but the Victorians, as we have observed, expected their poets not only to sing but to prophesy. Certainly in an era of waning faith the man of letters was looked to for the spiritual and moral guidance which the times demanded; and in the century's middle years none fulfilled the role more impressively—to himself as well as to his readers—than did Thomas Carlyle (1795–1881). James Martineau spoke of his 'pentecostal power' and of his having given 'the first clear expression to the struggling heart of a desolate yet aspiring time, making a clean breast of many stifled unbeliefs and noble hatred':[12] and there is no question but that 'the best growler of the day', as Maurice bluntly called him, was a voice crying in the wilderness to very many young men of the period, distrustful as they were of the too-long canvassed verities of the Christian creed yet anxious for some new light in the gathering darkness. 'I, for one,' said J. A. Froude, 'was saved by Carlyle's writings from Positivism, or Romanticism, or Atheism, or any other of the creeds or no creeds which in those years were whirling about us in Oxford like leaves in an autumn storm.'[13] Indeed in this latter half of our own century, when few, one surmises, who are not professed students of Carlyle's epoch open his books, his former prestige may seem wellnigh unintelligible. Thus when Maurice, again, deplored 'his silly rant about the great bosom of Nature',[14] we may feel that for once at any rate he had hit the nail

---

12. *Essays, Reviews, and Addresses*, i, p. 226.
13. *Thomas Carlyle* (1882–84), *London Life*, i, p. 295.
14. F. Maurice, *op. cit.*, i, pp. 282f.

squarely on the head. Yet Maurice had a very genuine respect for Carlyle and esteemed his friendship highly, whilst Dean Hutton, always a reliable judge, records that 'for many years before his death Carlyle was to England what his great hero, Goethe, was to Germany— the aged seer whose personal judgments on men and things were eagerly sought after, and eagerly chronicled and retailed'.[15]

In his earlier days—until, that is, the publication in 1851 of his *Life of John Sterling*—Carlyle was generally regarded as a religious writer. But the sympathy he there displayed with Sterling's own doubts, and indeed the negative character of the book as a whole, made it plain that the author's personal standpoint was far removed from orthodox Christianity. In *Heroes and Hero-Worship* (1840) he had declared a man's religion to be the chief fact about him, but what Carlyle understood by religion was even then something different from the teachings of the churches, which appealed to him little. Not that he well understood them. The mere fact that religious institutions were by their nature traditional was, as John Tulloch remarks, equivalent to saying that they were dead.[16] But neither did he consider religion, even according to his own conception of it, to be all spirit and no embodiment. 'We inherit', he says, 'not only Life, but all the garniture and form of Life.' The garniture and forms of Christianity, however, in which he saw too much of 'Hebrew old-clothes', were not to his liking. The fault of Christian institutions was that they were no longer an adequate expression of the ideal which once animated them. Hence they had become superstition, and to superstition he desired only a speedy end.

> What can it profit any mortal to adopt locutions and imaginations which do *not* correspond to fact; which no sane mortal can deliberately adopt in his soul as true: which the most orthodox of mortals can only, and this after infinite essentially *impious* effort to put out the eyes of the mind, persuade himself to 'believe that he believes'.[17]

The efforts of a Coleridge, 'sublime man' though he had been, to revive such ancient forms were futile. Yet religious symbols are both inevitable and right: the world itself is a symbol of God, and duty God's call.

> Various enough have been such symbols, which we call religious, as men stood in this stage or another, and could worse or better body forth the godlike; some symbols with a transient intrinsic worth, many with only an extrinsic.

Nay, he continues:

> If thou ask to what height man has carried it in this manner, look on our divinest symbol, on Jesus of Nazareth, and his life and biography, and what followed therefrom. Higher has human thought not yet reached: this is Christianity and Christendom: a symbol of quite perennial character; whose significance will ever demand to be anew enquired into and anew made manifest.[18]

15. *Modern Guides of English Thought* (1887), p. i.
16. *Movements of Religious Thought in Britain during the Nineteenth Century*, p. 200.
17. *The Life of Sterling*, i, ch. 7.
18. *Sartor Resartus*, Bk III, ch. iii.

He could, it seems, when so minded, go further still in affirming the positive value of historic Christianity:

> Cheerfully recognizing, gratefully approving whatever Voltaire had proved, or any other man has proved, or shall prove, the Christian Religion, once here cannot pass away; that, as in Scripture, so also in the heart of man, is written 'The gates of hell shall not prevail against it.'[19]

Yet of the supernatural or miraculous he was entirely incredulous, and the Christian dogmas he scornfully repudiated. Little wonder is it that to his contemporaries the prophet's utterance, for all its profundity, remained enigmatic.

While still a young man Carlyle had become detached from the religion of his upbringing by 'grave positive doubts'. The mind of the eighteenth century, much as he might dislike it, was nevertheless a fact he could not blink. Voltaire, Diderot, Gibbon had not written in vain. But they were an essentially negative force and he looked for something that would serve him better. Wordsworth, rather strangely, did not help him as he had so many others. He was perhaps too close a figure, in place more even than time. Carlyle always needed distance for admiration. The year 1819 he records as one of deep despondency for him. But the 'Spiritual New-Birth', or 'Baphometic Fire-baptism', was not long delayed; and it came primarily through the inspiration of German literature—then little known in this country—and especially of Goethe. His first encounter was with Schiller, of whom he wrote a *Life* (1823–24); but Schiller, who lacked the prophetic qualities which Carlyle demanded, was not of sufficient magnitude to hold him. Novalis and Richter were more promising, but even as early as 1823 Goethe was to him 'the only living model of a great writer'.[20] Years later he wrote to his brother that the sage of Weimar was his 'evangelist'. 'His works, if you study them with due earnestness, are the day-spring visiting us in the dark night.'[21] Goethe possessed the required stature and spoke with the true oracular voice. Art was not enough, for 'in these days prophecy (well understood), not poetry, is the thing wanted. How can we *sing* and *paint* when we cannot yet *believe* and *see*?' On the other hand the difference between the two men, in temper and outlook, was all but total. The most striking aspect of Goethe's mind, according to Carlyle himself, was its calmness and beauty.[22] Nothing of the sort could ever have been said of his Scottish disciple, an irascible Puritan. But Carlyle had also both a keen intelligence and the sensibility of a poet; and Goethe's poetic genius was beyond all cavil, while as a thinker he had reflected deeply on the intricate problems of modern life. The great German was, in short, 'one to whom Experience had given true wisdom, and the Melodies Eternal a perfect utterance for his wisdom'. Goethe saw life steadily and whole, with such a calm version as the young Carlyle desiderated to compensate for the loss of old and impossible beliefs. For a religion of some kind was a necessity to him; a religion, as he put it in *Past and Present*, that would consist 'not in the

19. See essay on Voltaire in *Critical and Miscellaneous Essays* (1872), i, p. 409.
20. *Early Letters of T. Carlyle* (ed. C. E. Norton, 1886), ii, p. 191.
21. Froude, *op. cit., Early Life*, ii, p. 260.
22. See the essay on Goethe in *Critical and Miscellaneous Essays*, i, p. 287.

many things [a man] is in doubt of and tries to believe, but in the few he is assured of, and has no need of effort for believing'. In contrast with 'earnest Methodisms, introspections, agonizing inquiries, never so morbid'—not to mention 'spectral Puseyisms'— Goethe offered a spiritual faith shorn of outworn dogmas; a faith, that is, which a man of reason could maintain despite the negating rationalisms, utilitarianism and machine-worship of a soulless age.

But why after all had Carlyle not looked nearer home for guidance, namely to Coleridge at Hampstead, as so many were doing? For Coleridge was himself a recognized fount of German influence and had certainly found a way out of 'black materialism' and 'revolutionary deluges'. Apart, of course, from the fact that Carlyle was not a man ever to join a throng, the notorious comments on Coleridge in the *Life of Sterling* must be presumed to supply the reason. Coleridge 'had skirted the howling deserts of Infidelity' indeed, but had not the courage to press resolutely across them to firmer lands beyond; he 'preferred to create logical fatamorganas for himself on this hither side, and laboriously solace himself with these'.[23] No 'hocus-pocus' of reasoning versus understanding would avail to make the incredible credible. If Carlyle were to believe in God it would have to be a God of his own conceiving, or rather imagining, since although his thought was for ever turning on broadly philosophical issues he seldom expressed himself in technical philosophical language, which he distrusted. 'In the perfect state all Thought were but the picture and inspiring symbol of Action; Philosophy, except as Poetry and Religion, would have no Being.' Carlyle's deity is described nevertheless in suitably unanthropomorphic terms. As Sterling had once objected, under an abstract use of the name of God lay the conception only of a 'formless Infinite', a 'high inscrutable Necessity', as the 'mysterious impersonal base of all Existence', to which it was the sum of wisdom and virtue to submit. There is no doubt that in fashioning this philosophical pseudo-religion Carlyle had been largely aided by Goethe, with some contribution from Fichte also.[24] And it was through the imagination much

23. *The Life of Sterling*, i, ch. 8.
24. The influence of Fichte came not from the philosopher's earlier, technical writings but from his later and more popular, such as *Die Anweisung seligen Leben* (The Way to Blessed Life), published in 1806. Carlyle was neither by training nor by cast of mind an analytic thinker, and what he looked for in the German author was not analysis but stimulus for the imagination. His references to Fichte in *The State of German Literature*, dating from 1827 and thus one of his own earliest publications, show plainly enough whence the inspiration for his theological musings came. 'According to Fichte', he writes, 'there is a "Divine Idea" pervading the visible Universe, which visible Universe is indeed but its symbol and sensible manifestation, having in itself no meaning, or even true existence independent of it. To the mass of men this Divine Idea of the world lies hidden: yet to discern it, to seize it, and live wholly in it, is the condition of all genuine virtue, knowledge, freedom; and the end, therefore, of all spiritual effort in every age. Literary men are the appointed interpreters of this Divine Idea; a perpetual priesthood, we might say, standing forth, generation after generation, as the dispensers and living types of God's everlasting wisdom, to show it in their writings and actions, in such particular form as their own particular times require it in. For each age, by the law of its nature, is different from every other age, and demands a different representation of the Divine Idea, the essence of which is the same in all; so that the literary man of one century is only by mediation and reinterpretation applicable to the wants of another.

more than the speculative reason that Carlyle reached it. Here Goethe's poetry—such things, notably, as the song of the Earth-Spirit in *Faust* and the opening hymn of *Gott und Welt*—was a predominant influence; for Carlyle's divinity, like Goethe's, is immanent: a spirit of potency working in and through the universe, having nature as its living garment but revealing itself in full articulation only in man. It was this 'natural supernaturalism' which alone satisfied both his intellect and his deep-rooted religious sentiment, enabling him to reconcile acceptance of the irrefutable truths of science with the fear that if the world is really no more than a mechanism the profoundest longings of man's heart, the dynamic of his moral action, have no meaning.[25]

Carlyle, however, preached his vaguely pantheistic gospel with all the fervour of a Covenanting minister. It is a brew of strange ingredients: Old Testament prophecy, Norse mythology, Scotch Calvinism, German metaphysic. He had even undergone a conversion experience, described by him with characteristic sound and fury, in the second book of *Sartor Resartus:*

> There rushed like a stream of fire over my whole soul; and I shook base Fear away from me forever. I was strong, of unknown strength; a spirit, almost a god. Ever from that time the temper of my misery was changed: not Fear or whining Sorrow was it, but Indignation and grim fire-eyed Defiance. 'Thus had the EVERLASTING NO (*das Ewige Nein*) pealed authoritatively through all the recesses of my Being, of my ME; and then it was that my whole ME stood up, in native God-created majesty, and with emphasis recorded its Protest'[26]

Later in the same work and in the same vein of high-pitched expostulation he can invoke Nature as God:

> How thou fermentest and elaboratest in thy great fermenting vat and laboratory of an Atmosphere, of a World, O Nature!—Or what is Nature? Ha! why do I not name thee God? Art not thou the 'living Garment of God'? O Heavens, is it, in very deed, HE, then, that ever speaks through thee; that lives and moves in thee, that lives and moves in me?

Traditional Christian beliefs are thrown into the cauldron of the author's rhetoric, to reappear transformed:

> Reader, even Christian Reader, as thy title goes, hast thou any notion of Heaven and Hell? I rather apprehend, not. Often as the words are on our tongue, they have got a fabulous or semi-fabulous character for most of us, and pass on like a kind of transient similitude, like a sound signifying little.

But in every century, every man who labours, be it in what province he may, to teach others, must first have possessed himself of the Divine Idea, or, at least, be with his whole heart and his whole soul striving after it' (*Critical and Miscellaneous Essays*, i, pp. 68f.).

25. 'That the Supernatural differs not from the Natural is a great Truth, which the last century (especially in France) has been engaged in demonstrating. The Philosophers went far wrong, however, in this, that instead of raising the natural to the supernatural, they strove to sink the supernatural to the natural. The gist of my whole way of thought is to do not the latter but the former' (Froude, *op. cit., Early Life*, ii, p. 330).

26. *Ibid.*, Ch. vii.

Yet it is well worth while for us to know, once and always, that they are not a similitude, nor a fable nor semi-fable; that they are an everlasting highest fact! 'No Lake of Sicilian or other sulphur burns now anywhere in these ages', sayest thou? Well, and if there did not! Believe that there does not; believe if it thou wilt, nay hold by it as a real increase, a rise to higher stages, to wider horizons and empires. All this has vanished, or has not vanished; believe as thou wilt as to all this. But that an Infinite of Practical Importance, speaking with strict arithmetical exactness, an *Infinite*, has vanished or can vanish from the Life of any Man: this thou shalt not believe.[27]

What positive conceptions emerge, then, from Carlyle's turgid pages? His own age took him with a deadly seriousness. His pulpit thunder was reassuring. 'God' might well be a difficult notion when framed in the creeds, but the modern prophet's invocation of the 'Immensities' and 'Eternities' conveyed a hope-inspiring sense of the universe not as a mere cold mechanism but as life and purpose justifying the human struggle. The visible world, he taught, is the symbol of an invisible divine Power working its ends for the ultimate benefit of the human race. Thus there is an eternal moral order which mankind must reverence and obey. Not personal happiness—leastwise on some hedonistic calculation, some 'pleasure-principle'—but duty, the doing of God's will on earth, is paramount. 'Love not Pleasure; love God. This is the everlasting Yea, wherein all contradiction is solved: wherein whoso walks and works, it is well with him.' If a man find 'Blessedness' he can do without happiness; but wrong must in the long run bring retribution, for right is might, whatever temporary successes evil may win. Yet the impression persists that for Carlyle might itself is proof of right, although, to be fair to him, he states categorically that 'if the thing is unjust, thou hast not succeeded'. 'In all battles', he tells us in *Past and Present*, 'if you await the issue, each fighter has prospered according to his right. His right and his might, at the close of account, were one and the same. He has fought with all his might, and in exact proportion to all his right has he prevailed.'

It is not easy for us today to see the Cheyne Row oracle as his contemporaries saw him. His tortured prose style is an all but insuperable obstacle to any attempt to read him continuously, except as a deliberate task. The constant railing against this and that, the jibes and the jeers, the heavy irony, the vividness wrapped in vagueness have the effect in the end only of rant and the reader's attention flags. Carlyle—it is hard to resist the conclusion—was an egomaniac, a wouldbe man of action at perpetual odds with the times but by temperament as by circumstance unable to fulfil the heroic role—of a Cromwell or a Frederick—for which, in his own dream-world, he cast himself. The outcome of his frustration was self-contradiction. He must have a God and a Providence, but the creeds are incredible and the Church dead. The universe is a miracle, but miracles never happen. Nature is divine, but what does nature know of duty? Science is truth, but what has it to do with the existence of 'the eternal Unnameable'? Man himself is godlike, but his follies are unending. The toiling masses call for pity, but democracy is contemptible. Only the isolated Hero, the rare Great Man, is left to be admired; and the reader at once guesses that in this select gallery the author has already

27. *Past and Present*, Part II, ch. ii.

assigned himself a forward place. It is scarcely surprising that of all the eminent Victorians Carlyle should now be one of the least remembered; posterity is impatient of a bore.

The critic as theologian: Matthew Arnold

Matthew Arnold, of whose verse we have already spoken, was in almost every respect the antithesis of Carlyle. Yet in their religious philosophy they are in some ways akin, for Arnold's 'Eternal not ourselves which makes for righteousness' could also well describe Carlyle's divinity. So diverse are they, however, in mode of expression that at first glance they appear to have nothing in common.[28] Where they stand together, along with so many of their earnest-minded contemporaries, is in having abandoned the traditional dogmatic beliefs whilst at the same time strongly asserting a spiritual interpretation of life and the world along with those fixed moral valuations which this alone seemed to substantiate. But whereas the one fulminates and denounces, the other suavely reasons, not without occasional ironic banter. Arnold's role in prose was that of critic much more than preacher: he revered his father's memory deeply, but did not inherit his temper or outlook. Yet the son also was conscious of a mission to edify and 'improve', indeed to be a moral leader. Where he is distinctive is in the means by which he would accomplish it. He intends to be detached, candid, critical; and criticism, on Arnold's lips, was a word of large meaning. It certainly meant more than literary criticism. He defined it, rather, as 'the endeavour, in all branches of knowledge, theology, philosophy, history, art, science, to see the object as in itself it really is'.[29] So defined it becomes virtually a synonym for *culture*, itself to be understood as 'a study of perfection'—something greater far, therefore, than a mere scientific passion for knowing. Knowledge, of course, is indispensable; but knowledge is a matter not of mere fact-hunting or unmotivated curiosity but of 'getting to know, on all the matters which most concern us, the best which has been thought and said in the world, and through this knowledge, turning a stream of fresh thought upon our stock notions and habits'. Culture, in fine, rests on nothing less than belief in 'making reason and the will of God prevail'.

It is not necessary here to recall in detail the argument of *Culture and Anarchy*.[30] But it is a work in which the author plainly declares his sense of mission. The quest of perfection in all things demands detachment, or, in Professor E. K. Brown's

---

28. Much of the difference between the two men is patent in a single reference of Arnold's, in *Culture and Anarchy*, to 'Mr Carlyle' as 'a man of genius to whom we have all at one time or other been indebted for refreshment and stimulus'. Later, however, he could refer to him as a 'moral desperado' and deplore 'that regular Carlylean strain which we all know by heart and which the clear-headed among us have so utter a contempt for' (*Letters of Matthew Arnold to Arthur Hugh Clough* (1932), ed. H. F. Lowry, pp. 111 and 151).
29. See the lectures *On Translating Homer* (1861).
30. Subtitled 'An Essay in Political and Social Criticism', it was first published in 1869.

phrase, 'a strategy of disinterestedness'.[31] Understanding requires the object of contemplation to be seen 'as in itself it really is', without the bias, of one kind or of another, which falsifies perspectives and results in misjudgment. The anarchy which it is Arnold's aim to expose is the outcome of confused and uncriticized standards, a confusion pre-eminently visible in Anglo-Saxon society. But this necessary disinterestedness does not exclude commitment, moral engagement. In all his prose writings Arnold sought 'to get at' the English public—'such a public as it is and such a work as one wants to do with it'. In a word, he sought, like Carlyle, to preach; but his gospel is culture, 'sweetness and light'. On this Arnold at once enlarges:

> There is a view in which all the love of our neighbour, the impulses towards action, help, and beneficence, the desire for removing human error, clearing human confusion, and diminishing human misery, the noble aspiration to leave the world better and happier than we found it—motives eminently such as are called social—come in as part of the grounds of culture, and the main and pre-eminent part.[32]

What culture promotes is 'the harmonious perfection of our whole being', as it also reveals 'how worthy and divine a thing is the religious side of man', even though it is not the totality of man. Religion is in fact a vital constituent of culture, its culminating part; and the separation of religion from culture—the excess of 'Hebraism'—misrepresents, and hence weakens, religion itself. 'The worth of what a man thinks about God and the objects of religion depends on what a man *is*; and what a man *is* depends upon his having more or less reached the measure of a perfect and total man.'

Religion was in truth the apex of Arnold's whole edifice of thought. As to his father so to him, it mattered more than anything else, and his criticism, his political and social ideas, his work as an educationist are all orientated towards it. But if religion were thus of paramount importance, a thing necessary to the life of rational man, no less certain was it that the orthodox Christianity of the day was no longer available to a man of critical intelligence. This was Matthew Arnold's own dilemma, to the resolution of which he devoted much of his best effort in prose. Supernatural Christianity, he was convinced, would have to be discarded. On the European continent it already was well on the way to being so, in full consciousness; but the process had begun even in 'provincial' Britain, although the partisans of traditional religion were still unaware how decisively the whole force of progressive and liberal opinion in other countries had pronounced against Christianity. In his own essays on religious philosophy—and there are few such writings of the time which can be read today with a like interest and stimulus—he set out to present the public with a revised Christianity from which the incredible and the irrelevant, supernatural miracles and abstruse dogma, had been pruned away; a Christianity preserving the essential values but acceptable to the modern mind, impatient as that now was

---

31. See *Matthew Arnold. A Study in Conflict* (1948). Brown thinks the 'commitment' in Arnold negatived the 'detachment'. But this is a very questionable thesis. The abiding interest of Arnold's criticism is his success in achieving both.
32. *Culture and Anarchy* (popular edition, 1909), pp. 5f.

both of miraculous portents and of metaphysical puzzles. He assuredly did not wish to unsettle the beliefs of people who were content to hold to what they had always been taught. Let them continue, he says, in their simple faith. Nor was he concerned with the 'Liberal secularists', to whom the values of religion are in themselves of no consequence. Nor again was he interested in the merely frivolous. Those, however, whom he did seek to address were persons who,

> won to the modern spirit by habits of intellectual seriousness, cannot receive what sets these habits at nought, and will not try to force themselves to do so, but who have stood near enough to the Christian religion to feel the attraction which a thing so very great, when one stands really near to it, cannot but exercise, and who have some familiarity with the Bible and some practice in using it.[33]

He saw his enterprise as thus conservative and religious, an attempt to meet the spiritual needs of the modern man who neither wishes to abandon Christianity nor is able to swallow its formal doctrines. It is embodied in four notable volumes: *St Paul and Protestantism* (1870), *Literature and Dogma* (1873), *God and the Bible* (1875) and *Last Essays on Church and Religion* (1877). Of these the second is the most arresting, but all of them call for some remark.

St Paul and Protestantism, a part of which first appeared in *The Cornhill Magazine* in 1869, is a critique of the theology of Protestant Christianity as familiarly stated. Arnold points out that the Protestant position rests almost entirely on the teaching of St Paul, although Spinoza and latterly Coleridge had shown how erroneously have selected Pauline texts been used by it. Protestantism maintains that Paul's doctrines derive their sanction from his miraculous conversion, an occurrence which in the apostle's own judgment (so it is claimed) gave them their authority. In other words, it treats his ideas as though they constitute a coherent scheme of scientific knowledge about the relations of God and man. Yet such a system when constructed is dead. Paul himself wrote out of a living experience and his language has to be taken in the context of that experience. So to approach it is to adopt the method of 'culture', the only appropriate method. Taken thus the apostle's words no longer bear the rigorous interpretation which Protestant doctrine imposes on them and his role as, in Renan's phrase, 'the doctor of Protestantism' is accordingly ended. But the new Paul, Arnold thinks, will be a far more intelligible figure to all who care for the true values of Christianity, since a 'miraculous' conversion adds nothing to whatever force those values already possess of themselves. For what the Apostle is really concerned with is righteousness. Paul was a Hebrew and to the Hebrews the aim and end of all religion—namely, access to God—meant in practice access to the source of the *moral* order. 'It was the greatness of the Hebrew race that it felt the authority of this order, its preciousness and its beneficence, so strongly.'[34] Paul's intensely Hebraic religious sense, joined with his native power of intellect, enabled him to perceive and pursue a moral ideal, alike in thought and action, with extraordinary force and closeness. He had, of course, his mystical side and

33. *God and the Bible*, Preface, p. xxiii.
34. *St Paul and Protestantism* (1896 ed), p. 23.

'nothing is so natural to the mystic, as in rich single words, such as *faith, light, love*, to sum up and take for granted, without especially enumerating them, all good moral principles and habits'.[35] But the apostle's mysticism never for once blunts the edge of his moral sensibility or lessens his emphasis on the finer moral virtues: meekness, humbleness of mind, gentleness, unwearying forbearance, or the crowning emotion of charity, the very 'bond of perfectness'; as he also possesses a profound awareness of what a modern would call the *solidarity* of mankind, 'the joint interest ... which binds humanity together', involving 'the duty of respecting every one's part in life, and of doing justice to his efforts to fulfil that part'.

Whereas, then, the Paul which Protestantism portrays is the author of abstruse and unverifiable doctrines—a theurgy of election, justification, substitution and imputed righteousness—the figure discerned by one who approaches him with an open mind will be dealing with the verifiable facts of life and experience. By an adroit manipulation of texts Paul no doubt can be made to give his authority to such a theurgy, but to an unbiased reader it is evident that what chiefly concerns him is an ethic. Intellectually he had no option but to adopt the mental frame of reference of his time; but to maintain this was not his real interest. His basic concern was the 'voluntary, rational, and human world' of righteousness, of moral choice and moral effort. To this the mystical, divine world provided the necessary background, and he could pass naturally from the one world to the other. But righteousness remains his constant theme and his religious concepts are always made to serve it. The ideas of calling, justification and sanctification, essential to Protestant theology, are to him secondary. The primary order of ideas is expressed in such phrases as 'dying with Christ',[36] 'resurrection from the dead',[37] and 'growing into Christ'.[38] His originality as a thinker lies in his effort to find a moral significance for all aspects of the religious life, however mystical. Thus the resurrection he was striving after, for himself and for others, was a *present* resurrection to righteousness. 'And when, through identifying ourselves with Christ, we reach Christ's righteousness, then eternal life begins for us.'[39] But the metaphorical character of Paul's language, like the ethical preoccupation of his thought, popular Protestantism has never understood. Consequently it turns an imaginative literary utterance into pseudo-science.

This pseudo-science is the theology that has its starting-point in a notion of God as a 'magnified and non-natural man, appeased by a sacrifice and remitting in consideration of it his wrath against those who had offended him'. The doctrines of justification and election are placed in relation to this. Hence the classic formularies of historic Calvinism, notable indeed for their seriousness, but a seriousness 'too mixed with the alloy of mundane strife and hatred to be religious feeling':

35. *Ibid.*, p. 24.
36. Col. ii, 20.
37. Phil. iii, II.
38. Eph. iv, 15.
39. *St Paul and Protestantism*, p. 59.

Not a trace of delicacy of perception, or of philosophic thinking; the mere rigidness and contentiousness of the controversialist and political dissenter; a Calvinism exaggerated till it is simply repelling; and to complete the whole, a machinery of covenants, conditions, bargains and parties-contractors, such as could have proceeded from no one but the born Anglo-Saxon man of business.[40]

But all this is not the creation of St Paul and it is alien to his mind. Calvinism is intent, in the end, not upon the moral life but upon 'fleeing the wrath to come'; whilst Methodism, hardly less assiduous in holding to what it supposes is the teaching of the great apostle, is chiefly moved by the hope of eternal bliss. Both alike assign all activity to God and mere passivity to man, although for Paul righteousness requires effort and its achievement is possible for such as really strive after it.

The fatal weakness of Protestant theology, whether Calvinist or Methodist, is in Arnold's view its assumption that belief can be substantiated by either fear or hope. That an idea has scientific validity only experience can demonstrate. Paul is superior to his Protestant interpreters in founding his own beliefs on experience, from which he derives 'the conception of the law of *righteousness*, the very law and ground of human nature so far as this nature is moral'; for when the apostle starts by affirming the grandeur and necessity of the law of righteousness 'science has no difficulty in going along with him'. Here evidently Arnold is himself making a large assumption; for how can science affirm the *grandeur* of the moral law? Is it at all the function of science to attempt such final evaluations? But he would probably have replied that, as Lionel Trilling puts it, the definition is accurate and 'the mark of a scientific truth, like that of a moral truth, is that great teachers the most unlike are in agreement on the matter'.[41]

St Paul and Protestantism was not by any means Arnold's first venture into the field of religious philosophy. During his tenure of the chair of poetry at Oxford he had written articles on religious matters for *Macmillan's Magazine*. He was greatly interested in the Colenso controversy, for example, and had made a significant contribution to the public debate thereon. At the time he was a good deal influenced by his study of Spinoza, of whose 'positive and verifying atmosphere' he had written to Clough as far back as 1849 or 1850. In an article in *Macmillan's* for January 1863 he dealt with 'The Bishop and the Philosopher', contrasting Colenso's dry and technical treatment of the biblical question with Spinoza's, who, unlike both the bishop and the bishop's critics, knew how to distinguish religion from mere history, some of which may anyway be false. For the philosopher, Arnold points out, the centre of the religious life is where it should be, and he does not allow it to be shifted to peripheral matters. A little later, in a lecture of 1864 on 'The Function of Criticism', he again refers to the Colenso affair and the hostility which his own comments on it had evoked. He confesses to disliking religious controversy, but must maintain his own view that there is truth of science and truth of religion, and that the former does not become the latter till it is made religious. In the 1869 edition of *Essays in Criticism* direct reference to

40. *Ibid.*, p. 12.
41. *Matthew Arnold* (1939), p. 331.

Colenso is omitted, but Arnold includes a lengthy chapter on 'Spinoza and the Bible', in which his personal opinions on the fundamentals of the biblical question are plainly indicated.

The proposition that the truths of science and religion are separate and that the essence of all religion is moral are the themes of *Literature and Dogma*, one of the most persuasive of Arnold's writings and a work still eminently worth study. The problem, he says in his preface, is to find for the Bible and Christianity a basis in something verifiable instead of merely assumed. To the understanding of the former the theology of the churches and sects has become a hindrance rather than a help. Such a new basis—an experimental one—is indispensable if Scripture and the religion it teaches are to reach the people. The right procedure derives, again, from the idea of culture as 'the acquainting ourselves with the best that has been known and said in the world, and thus with the history of the human spirit'.[42] And this, in regard to the Bible, means 'getting the power, through reading, to estimate the proportion and relation in what we read'; a task never so necessary, Arnold considers, as in the England of his own day, nor perhaps so difficult. But the difficulty must be faced because the necessity is urgent. Literature is to be distinguished from dogma, the imaginative from the factual or scientific. And the Bible being literature, it is to be judged in the way that literature should be judged, 'without any turmoil of controversial reasonings'.

In the chapter on 'Religion Given' Arnold looks for the ground of Old Testament religion and finds it, not, for certain, in any enterprise of metaphysical speculation, but in the conviction that 'Righteousness tendeth to life'. This conviction is expressed in the concept of God, whose being is apprehended simply as a fact of experience. The term 'God' may be incurably ambiguous, but morality 'represents for everybody a thoroughly definite and ascertained idea'. God in the Old Testament is in fact 'the Eternal not ourselves which makes for righteousness', and any antithesis between the ethical and the religious is false.

> Ethical means *practical*, it relates to practice or conduct passing into habit or disposition. Religious also means *practical*, but practical in a still higher degree; and the right antithesis to both ethical and religious, is the same as the right antithesis to practical: namely, *theoretical*.[43]

A theology which is independent of or anterior to the ethical is, Arnold believes, wholly misconceived and has no warrant from the Bible. This, however, is not to say that religion and morality are indistinguishable. Religion as a binding and a transforming force is ethics heightened, enkindled, lit up by feeling. Hence its true equivalent is not simply morality, but 'morality touched by emotion'.[44] And for this the proper word is 'righteousness'.

The language of the Bible, in so far as it is literary and not scientific, is wholly fitted to convey this meaning; for

---

42. *Literature and Dogma* (popular ed, 1884), p. xix.
43. *Ibid.*, p. 15.
44. *Ibid.*, p. 16.

if the object be one not fully to be grasped, and one to inspire emotion, the language of figure and feeling will satisfy us better about it, will cover more of what we seek to express, than the language of literal fact and science. The language of science about it will be *below* what we feel to be the truth.[45]

Nevertheless, behind this figurative language and the consciousness which it articulates, what scientific or factual basis might there be? It is a question which inevitably forces itself upon us; but we have to be content with a very unpretending answer. For science, Arnold thinks, 'God is simply the stream of tendency by which all things seek to fulfil the law of their being.' As a definition this may, he agrees, seem meagre, but as compared with expressions such as 'a personal First Cause' or 'the moral and intelligent Governor of the universe' it stays within the orbit of the certain and verifiable, which alone is what science requires. However, the religious consciousness of Israel, in the course of its development, did not rest there and proceeded to add *Aberglaube*, 'extra-beliefs', and in particular the belief in the coming of a divinely appointed 'Messiah' who would restore Israel's political fortunes. Extra-belief no doubt displays the poetry of life and to that extent is justified. But it has its dangers; for it is taken as science, which it is not. The Messianic idea, an idea profoundly poetical and inspiring, had been taken as science in the age when Jesus Christ came; and it is the more important to mark that it was so, because similar ideas have performed the same function in popular religion since.

In 'Religion New-Given' Arnold discusses the New Testament and Christianity, and observes at once how the then current 'political' form of Messianism was not fulfilled in Jesus. What Jesus taught was something new, the true 'method' and 'secret' of righteousness. Judgment and justice themselves, as Israel in general conceived them, had, Arnold maintains, something 'exterior' in them, whereas what was wanted was more 'inwardness', more 'feeling', as it had indeed already been provided by adding mercy and humbleness to judgment and justice. Jesus's method was repentance or change of heart, 'the setting up a great unceasing inward movement of attention and verification' in matters of conduct; his secret, renunciation—the understanding that he who will save his life shall lose it, while he that will lose his life shall save it. Jesus himself was the embodiment of mildness and 'sweet reasonableness' (*epieikeia*)—qualities which, with self-renouncement, he made his followers realize to be their own 'best selves', and the attainment of them something in the highest degree requisite and natural, on which man's whole happiness depends. Because of this Jesus may appropriately be called the Son of God, as having with unique insight revealed the true character of God's righteousness. This was the *Christ* whom St Paul discovered and to whom personal devotion was the faith that justifies.

Yet even in the case of religion new-given *Aberglaube* reasserted itself. Miracles, and above all those of Jesus's own resurrection and ascension, to be followed by his second advent, were from the beginning firm elements in the disciples' faith; and legend, too, was soon added. These were the things which popular religion drew from the records of Jesus as the essentials of belief. They were expressed in

45. *Ibid.*, p. 31.

a short formulary, the Apostles' Creed, in which, says Arnold, we may be said to have 'the popular science of Christianity'. Yet even this was insufficient to satisfy the demands of ingenious questioners, who accordingly gave us the so-called Nicene Creed, which is 'the learned science of Christianity'. Finally, bring to this learned science 'a strong dash of violent and vindictive temper' and you have the Athanasian Creed. And the irony is that all three creeds, along with the whole body of orthodox theology, are founded upon words 'which Jesus in all probability never uttered'. The 'proofs' of this historic Christianity have, of course, been prophecy and miracle; but the *Zeitgeist* is now against both. The so-called prophecies of Christ, with the 'supernatural prescience' they imply, have ceased to stand; literary history and criticism have undermined them. So too with miracles.

> That miracles, when fully believed, are felt by men in general to be a source of authority, it is absurd to deny. But the belief is losing its strength. ... Whether we attack them, or whether we defend them, does not much matter. The human race, as its experience widens, is turning away from them. And for this reason: *it sees, as its experience widens, how they arise.*[46]

Our popular religion, Arnold adds, 'at present conceives the birth, ministry and death of Christ, as altogether steeped in prodigy, brimful of miracle;—*and miracles do not happen*'.[47] In *God and the Bible*, a sequel to *Literature and Dogma*, he enlarges on the same theme, by way of answering criticisms. He had in the earlier book treated it, he claims, only with 'brevity and moderation'. That there is no complete induction *against* miracles he admits; but there is an incomplete induction, enough to satisfy the mind that the evidence against them is untrustworthy and that we are really dealing with fairy-tales. Indeed he presses the point:

> That they *do not* happen—that what are called miracles are not what the believers in them fancy, but have a natural history of which we can follow the course—the slow action of experience, we say, more and more shows; and shows, too, that there is no exception to be made in favour of the Bible-miracles.

Christianity must, in fact, stand—if it is to stand—by its 'natural truth'. Miracles will have to go the way of clericalism and tradition; 'and the important thing is, not that the world should be acute enough to see this, but that a great and progressive part of the world should be capable of seeing this and yet holding fast to Christianity'.

So likewise with the idea of God. In *St Paul and Protestantism* Arnold says that the licence of affirmation about God and his proceedings in which the religious world indulges is increasingly met by the demand for verification. Calvinism talks of God 'as if he were a man in the next street', whose operations it intimately knew. But assertions in scientific language must bear the test of scientific examination. The notion of God as 'a magnified and non-natural man' will no longer suffice when critically examined. To satisfy what three-fourths of our being demands he must, rather, be the power 'which makes for righteousness'. But the

46. *Ibid.*, p. 96.
47. *Ibid.*, p. 12.

one-fourth of our being, concerned with art and science, with beauty and exact knowledge, has also to be considered.

> For the total man, therefore, the truer conception of God is as the Eternal Power, not ourselves, by which all things fulfil the law of our being as far as our being is aesthetic and intellective, as well as so far as it is moral.[48]

That a surrender of the customary 'personal' view of God will, in the minds of many ordinary people, mean that all is in fact lost in religion, Arnold admits. But his reply is simple:

> We say, that unless we can verify this, it is impossible to build religion successfully upon it; and it cannot be verified. Even if it could be shown that there is a low degree of probability for it, we say that it is a grave and fatal error to imagine that religion can be built on what has a low degree of probability. However, we do not think it can be said that there is ever a low degree of probability for the assertion that God is a person who thinks and loves, properly and naturally though we may make him such in the language of feeling; the assertion deals with what is utterly beyond us. But we maintain that, starting from what may be verified about God—that he is the Eternal which makes for righteousness—and reading the Bible with this idea to govern us, we have here the elements for a religion more serious, potent, awe-inspiring and profound, than any which the world has yet seen.[49]

It will not indeed be the religion which now prevails, the religion which has been made to stand on its apex instead of its base—righteousness on ecclesiastical dogma instead of ecclesiastical dogma on righteousness—but who can suppose that religion does not and ought not to change?

Traditional religion, then, to quote from Arnold's essay on 'The Study of Poetry', had materialized itself in the fact, or the 'supposed fact'; it had attached its emotion to the fact, which now was failing it.[50] But he at once adds that for poetry the *idea* is everything. 'Poetry attaches its emotion to the idea; the idea is the fact.' The real strength and value of religion, therefore, as Arnold himself sees it, lies not in its supposed factualness but in its unconscious poetry. Its truth is truth of imagination, not of science. If men today cannot do with Christianity as it is—and the advance of science and historical criticism prevent them from doing so, once the issue has been squarely faced—neither can they do without it. Christianity has enabled mankind to deal with personal conduct—'an immense matter, at least three-fourths of human life'; but physical science is incapable of this. The myths and legends of Christianity may, as alleged facts, be incredible, wholly unable to withstand 'the habit of increased intellectual seriousness' by which religion is inevitably being transformed. But intellectual seriousness is not alone sufficient for human life. Religion *as poetry* has a vital part to play. 'More and more mankind will discover that we have to turn to poetry to interpret life for us, to console us, to sustain us.'[51] The demands of the rational intellect, in religion as in all else, must be met:

48. *St Paul and Protestantism*, p. 230.
49. *God and the Bible*, p. 57.
50. *Essays in Criticism: Second Series* (1888), 1938 ed, p. I.
51. *Ibid.*, p. 2.

facts that are not facts will have to be exposed. Religion cannot of course dispense with science; but the scientific data of religion are the proven facts of moral experience, and moral experience is best illuminated by poetry. Accordingly dogma has its role in Christianity still, not as pseudo-science but as symbolism. 'It is a great error to think that whatever is thus perceived to be poetry ceases to be available in religion. The noblest races are those which know how to make the most serious use of poetry.'[52] Even ideas and phrases that time has rendered obsolete or unmeaning may still be reverenced as an attempt on man's part to articulate feelings towards things of which in the end no adequate account can possibly be given.

For all his inability to accept the old theology in the old way and his dislike (and bemused incomprehension) of metaphysics in religion, as well as for the haziness and ambiguity of his own language when trying to convey positively what he himself believed,[53] Matthew Arnold was a man of sincere religious feeling and concern. His critical intelligence obliged him to confront the intellectual problem which religion poses, but, poet that he was as well as critic, he was ever sensitive to the poetry of religion. Moreover, if poetry is 'a criticism of life' religion too is to be recognized as such: it is an evaluation of life as men actually live it. With secularist aims he had no sympathy. The attitude of a W. K. Clifford filled him with mocking contempt; for Clifford and his like talked about religion but did not understand it, nor in truth 'the great facts of life' out of which it grows. Arnold believed profoundly in the importance of religion and in the special virtues of Christianity. To the Church of England, that 'great national society for the promotion of goodness', he was always devoted. But his dilemma was that of many Victorian intellectuals; he was loath to contemplate, and indeed could barely conceive, a Western civilization, moulded as it has been by centuries of Christian

---

52. *Last Essays on Church and Religion* (1903 ed.), p. 27. Besides its important preface this volume comprises four magazine articles: 'Bishop Butler and the Zeit-Geist', 'The Church of England', 'A Last Word on the Burials' Bill' and 'A Psychological Parallel', all of them published in 1876 in either the *Contemporary* or *Macmillan's*.

53. Arnold's religious views were scathingly criticized by F. H. Bradley in the latter's *Ethical Studies*. Morality, Bradley pointed out, may be a characteristic of religion, but there is no concluding from this that religion and morality are one and the same. On the contrary, religion is more than morality. 'In the religious consciousness we find the belief, however vague and indistinct, in an object, a not-self; an object, further, which is real. An ideal which is not real, which is only in our heads, can not be the object of religion' (*op. cit.*, 2nd ed, 1927, p. 316). To define religion as morality 'touched by emotion' tells us nothing, since all morality, in one sense or another, is 'touched by emotion' (p. 281). Arnold's phrase is therefore a mere tautology. Equally vacuous, in Bradley's judgment, was the definition, 'the Eternal not ourselves that makes for righteousness'. One might as well term the habit of washing as 'the Eternal not ourselves that makes for cleanliness' (p. 283)! Nor could he approve Arnold's notion of verification. 'We hear the word "verifiable" from Mr Arnold pretty often. What is it to verify? Has Mr Arnold put "such a tyro's question" to himself?' (p. 283*n*). But whatever the force of Bradley's objections, Arnold, as a religious thinker, has some warm admirers still. See, e.g., R. B. Braithwaite, *An Empiricist's View of the Nature of Religious Belief* (1955).

thought and feeling, in which Christianity would no longer have any significant place.[54] Yet what he admired and reverenced and desired to see perpetuated failed nevertheless, in its publicly recognized form, to command the allegiance of his reason. Faith and culture, therefore, would have to reach mutual adjustment at a wholly new level if continuity were to be preserved. He thus in a way was attempting to do for his own generation what Coleridge had done for his father's. The God of orthodox trinitarianism would have to be translated into 'the Eternal not ourselves', of which nothing could be said but that it makes 'for righteousness', and for the proof and verification of which one must look to the moral consciousness alone. That the deliverances of conscience, however, come not from any transcendent source but are part of man's 'instinct' and habit—his latent impulses, his inherited norms of conduct—was a possibility Arnold did not face. Had he done so could he have prevented the metamorphosis of his ethical deism into an overtly secular humanism, for which the Christian tradition must in time have only a minimal relevance?

54. 'I believe, then, that the real God, the real Jesus, will continue to command allegiance ... I believe that Christianity will survive because of its natural truth. Those who fancied that they had done with it, those who had thrown it aside because what was presented to them under its name was so unreceivable, will have to return to it again, and to learn it better' (*Last Essays*, p. xxx).

Chapter 12

SCOTTISH DEVELOPMENTS

Thomas Erskine of Linlathen

The dominant event in the life of the national church of Scotland during the nineteenth century—and the religious tradition in that country has been considerably more homogeneous than in England—was the great Disruption of 1843, itself the outcome of a decade of acute controversy. No account of these occurrences need be given here. It is sufficient to recall that when the General Assembly met in that fateful year 451 ministers out of a total of 1,203 left the Establishment. The cause of the division was not doctrinal but administrative: the issue of lay patronage. The leading opponent of the system, abolished in 1690 but restored in 1712, was Scotland's pre-eminent divine, Thomas Chalmers, an Evangelical of strong convictions and abounding energy. But Chalmers was not himself a theologian of any distinction, while the party that he led was identified with an unbending Calvinist orthodoxy. Moreover, internal dissension resulting in open schism and its long aftermath of reconstitution and settlement—for the new Free Church, to begin with, had no material resources whatever: everything had to be acquired and organized from scratch—was by no means conducive to theological innovation or exploratory scholarship.[1] In times of external stress the old certainties are clung to with a determination all the greater. Yet it would be a mistake to suppose that Scottish churchmen, then or earlier, had no impulse at all to freer ways of thinking. The religious situation north of the border was not indeed what it was in England, and no revival of theological interest took place there comparable with that of the Oxford liberals or their Tractarian opponents. But intellectual concern was not entirely quiescent and three men in particular—Erskine, McLeod Campbell and Irving—are in their differing ways of special note. McLeod Campbell's work on the atonement remains a landmark in the history of Presbyterian thought.

Erskine's first book was published in 1820, but many years before this tendencies of a more speculative kind had already appeared, represented by such men—professors at Edinburgh university—as Sir John Leslie and Thomas Brown, neither of whom had much sympathy with the reigning theology and who therefore were held in suspicion by the Church, especially its evangelical wing. Thus strong opposition was aroused by Leslie's appointment in 1805 to the chair of

---

1. For the history of the period see J. R. Fleming, *A History of the Church in Scotland 1843–1874* (1927).

293

mathematics. A 'naturalistic' outlook similar to his—the view, namely, that nature rather than divine revelation is man's surest guide in living the moral life—was also associated with the contributors to the 'progressive' *Edinburgh Review*, founded in 1802. To all such free-thinking the Evangelicals in the Establishment were hostile, and their organ, *The Christian Instructor*, complained often and bitterly of the prevalence of 'modern heresies', an example of which, as the journal was at pains to make clear to its readers, were the opinions of Mr Erskine of Linlathen.

Thomas Erskine (1788-1870), a layman and laird of a country estate near Dundee inherited by him on the death of his brother, was trained for the law, but his life interest was religion, as to which he displayed a remarkable originality of mind. Not that his views themselves were novel; but in him their growth was spontaneous, since Erskine was not a particularly learned man and his knowledge of the history of Christian doctrine seems always to have been limited. That he was quite unaware of contemporary developments in German theology is pretty certain. Yet such an authority as Pfleiderer, commenting on the views of both Erskine and Campbell—the two men were close friends—considered them to have made 'the best contribution to dogmatics which British theology has produced in the present century', and this simply by 'their own absorbing study of the Bible'.[2] Moreover, Erskine seems never to have been influenced, directly at least, by Coleridge, the age's great spiritual mentor. But Erskine's own influence on Maurice, although the latter did not come to know him personally until 1847, when he paid a first visit to Linlathen, was profound. Back in 1831, soon after the appearance of Erskine's *The Brazen Serpent* (1830), he wrote to one of his sisters of how 'unspeakably comfortable' the book had been to him. 'The peculiarities of his system may be true or not, but I am certain a light has fallen through him on the Scriptures, which I hope I shall never lose, and the chief tendency I feel he has awakened in my mind is to search them more and more.'[3] Especially was he impressed by Erskine's conception of humanity redeemed and renewed in Christ as its head, and his concomitant refusal to press the dire consequences of Adam's fall as the proper basis of a theology. When their personal acquaintance had ripened Maurice spoke of him as 'the best man I think I ever knew'.[4] His own *Priests and Kings of the Old Testament* was dedicated to him.

Of Erskine's singularity many others, like Principals Shairp and Tulloch, have testified. What in particular struck Shairp was his 'entire openness of mind, his readiness to hear whatever could be urged against his own deepest convictions, the willingness with which he welcomed any difficulties felt by others, and the candour with which he answered them from his own experience and storehouse of reflections'.[5] Tulloch says that although 'religious conversation of the ordinary sort is proverbially difficult', with Erskine it was a 'natural effluence'. 'One felt the deep

2. *The Development of Theology in Germany since Kant and its Progress in Great Britain since 1825* (1890), p. 382. As a result of their work the doctrine of salvation, the author thinks, was 'converted from forensic eternality to ethical inwardness and a truth of direct religious experience'.
3. F. Maurice, *Life of F. D. Maurice*, i, p. 121.
4. *Ibid.*, i, p. 533.
5. Quoted in W. Hanna, *Letters of Thomas Erskine* (1877), ii, p. 369.

sincerity of the man', and that he himself 'had laid hold of the Divine in his own heart whether he understood it rightly or not'.[6] For the religious controversy which was so much a feature of the time he had no taste at all. Spiritual truth did not emerge from polemical exchanges, and to discuss theological questions merely in the abstract he considered futile. Argument, he would say, was too commonly the enemy of *light*. His own attitude was consistently that of the earnest student, the modest seeker after truth and understanding. With heavy-fisted theological pugilists like Dr Andrew Thomson, whose pulpit drubbings he was obliged to suffer, he had nothing in common. Nor did the ecclesiastical conflict which ended in the Disruption move him. Church causes involving party rivalry were simply not of his world. Religion to him was essentially an interior matter: a concern of the soul, a commitment of the moral will. Temperamentally he was introspective and given to meditation: the works of William Law had provided much of his spiritual nourishment. 'He reached the truth, or what he believed to be the truth, not so much by enlarging his knowledge, or by exercising any critical or argumentative powers, as by patient thoughtfulness and generalization from his own experience.'[7] Little wonder is it that he and the Dr Thomsons of the age were as the poles apart. Yet not a few who admired him as a man could not follow him as a thinker. Thus Mrs Oliphant saw him as 'the prophet of a creed which nobody could define'.[8] Others, like Bishop Ewing, were conscious of the difficulty of conveying the sense and quality of Erskine's very personal thinking. A very reliable witness speaks of him as

> one of those it is most natural to think of in the mysterious world that lies beyond the grave. He was never at home in this world, there was something in him that demanded a different atmosphere from ours. His realities lay all in the region we are tempted to consider unreal; the visible and tangible universe seemed to have no soil in which he could take root.[9]

Erskine's earliest published work bore the characteristic title *Remarks on the Internal Evidence for the Truth of Revealed Religion*. In view of its date (1820) it is of unusual interest and importance, since it preceded Coleridge's *Aids to Reflection* by a quinquennium. In youth Erskine had had his doubts; but these, as he tells us, had been overcome by 'the patient study of the Gospel narrative and of its place in the history of the world', in particular 'the perception of a light in it which entirely satisfied his reason and conscience'. These last words are a clue to his whole thought. Erskine, like Coleridge, could never endorse the assumption of those who, in accord with Dr Chalmers, maintained that once the Christian revelation is accepted on its historical evidence it is impious to scrutinize it at the bar of reason and conscience.

Religion, he felt bound to believe, must commend itself as inherently reasonable and conducive to moral living; as worthy, in fact, of the God to whom its worship

6. Tulloch, *Movements of Religious Thought*, p. 130.
7. *Ibid.*, p. 131.
8. See her *Memoir of Principal Tulloch* (1888), p. III.
9. Julia Wedgewood, *Nineteenth Century Teachers* (1909), p. 78.

is addressed. This conviction, as regards the prevailing orthodoxy, meant for him a parting of the ways. Dogma propounded simply on authority, even the authority of the Scriptures, was inadmissible, or rather unintelligible, until inwardly assimilated and transmuted into character. It is of the nature of Christian truth to persuade, to move the believer by evidence internally weighed, not to coerce by external compulsions.

> The reasonableness of a religion seems to me [he tells his readers] to consist in there being a direct and natural connection between a believing of the doctrines which it inculcates, and a being formed by these to the character it recommends. If the belief of the doctrines has no tendency to train a disciple in a more exact and willing discharge of its moral obligations, there is evidently a very strong probability against the truth of that religion . . . What is the history of another world to me, unless it have some intelligible relation to my duties and happiness?[10]

Yet he is here saying no more than what the Tractarians, and Newman particularly, were to say a few years later, namely that a belief should be real and not merely 'notional'. Doctrines, that is, if *believed* and not just assented to, must move the heart and will; which in turn implies that they must have gained the support also of reason and conscience. 'All that a man learns from the Bible without its awakening within him a living consciousness of its truth, might as well not be learned.'[11] Erskine was in no way minimizing the need or the fact of a truth which is *given*, but the use of the outward was to foster and educate the inward. Newman's adverse reaction to Erskine's views is curious, therefore. For it was specifically Erskine whom he attacked in *Tract 73* on the score of 'rationalism'. The offence in Newman's eyes, as in those of the divines of Erskine's own communion, was the seeming assumption that revelation can be judged by sinful men.[12] But Erskine's contention was simply that unless the truths of revelation can be genuinely apprehended—made one by the believer with the longings of his own heart and the searchings of his own mind—they remain only an alien quantity, never effective because never understood in any real sense.

Erskine was but stating the conditions of his own experience as a Christian. A layman, living in seclusion, he saw the institutional religion of his day from a distance, its paramount concerns scarcely troubling him. He was not steeped in School theology and knew little of doctrinal history. Faith, first and last, was a

---

10. *Remarks on the Internal Evidence of the Truth of Revealed Religion*, p. 58.
11. See H. F. Henderson, *Erskine of Linlathen* (1899), p. 23.
12. Newman, looking back in 1883 on the reception of Erskine's writings amongst the Oxford Evangelicals, wrote (in an unpublished letter): 'I knew, when young, Mr Erskine's publications well. I thought them able and persuasive; but I found the more thoughtful Evangelicals of Oxford did not quite trust them. This was about the year 1823 or 1824. A dozen years later I wrote against them or one of them in the Tracts for the Times, and certainly my impression still is that their tendency is anti-dogmatic, substituting for faith in mysteries the acceptance of a "manifestation" of devine attributes, which was level to the reason. But I speak from memory. I have always heard him spoken of with great respect as a man of earnest and original mind' (Newman MSS, Birmingham. Copied letters, 83 : I. To G. F. Edwards, January 2, 1883. The present writer is indebted fur this quotation to Dr D. G. Rowell).

deeply felt personal commitment; and as he felt so did he speak.

> I must [he insists] discern in the history itself, a light and truth which will meet the demands both of my reason and conscience. In fact, however true the history may be, it cannot be any moral or spiritual benefit to me, until I apprehend its truth and meaning. This, and nothing less than this, is what I require, not only in this great concern, but in all others.

The basis of his reasoning is thus the Christian *consciousness*. An orthodoxy which could no longer stimulate and shape this consciousness was otiose, for doctrine is to be judged only as it can serve this end. From the dogmatist's standpoint Erskine's position doubtless appeared rationalistic, for he teaches that human responsibility cannot be excluded from the knowledge of God and his ways. What Erskine most certainly is not is a rationalist of the eighteenth-century stamp, or even after the fashion of Whately. Religion as he comprehends it is not a matter of credal propositions buttressed by 'evidences' and arguments but a motion of the heart or at least of that 'reason' which mere rationalism fails to appreciate.

The characteristic of Erskine's thought is its subjectivity. Truth in the abstract is not truth in any sense that will satisfy the man who seeks faith. The doctrine of the trinity, for example, considered simply as a theory of the divine being, might very well be justified speculatively. But until it is related to redemption it signifies little and the ordinary man would be likely, when confronted with it, only to feel 'that Christianity holds out a premium for believing improbabilities'. Put it, however, within the context of the divine love and it becomes an illuminating belief, a constraining influence.

In his later books Erskine turned to some specific problems of Christian theology. Two years after the *Remarks* he published *An Essay on Faith* and in 1828 *The Unconditional Freeness of the Gospel*.[13] This last came as a clear challenge to prevailing teaching on pardon, salvation and eternal life. Against the view that pardon is offered to the sinner only on condition of faith Erskine maintains that God's forgiveness has already been declared—that it is a fact and not merely a possibility; all men actually have it and do not need to purchase it. As he states in one of his letters:

> You know that I consider the proclamation of pardon through the blood of Christ, as an act already past in favour of every human being, to be essentially the Gospel . . . When it is supposed that this pardon is not passed into an act of favour of any individual until he believes it, no one can have peace from the Gospel until he is confident he is a believer; and further, his attention is entirely or chiefly directed to that quality of belief in himself, so that his joy is not in God's character but his own.[14]

But pardon has to be distinguished from salvation. To equate salvation with justification, according to the common doctrine, is an error. To be effective for the life of the individual pardon must be accepted. Salvation is a positive state of the soul, a healing of its spiritual diseases, a renewal of its spiritual vitality. For this the believer must exert and discipline himself, a view which, as Erskine replied to

---

13. *The Brazen Serpent* appeared in 1831, *The Doctrine of Election* in 1837.
14. Hanna, *op. cit.*, i, pp. 167f.

his critics, implies the very opposite of antinomianism.[15] Similarly eternal life is not only a heavenly existence hereafter but rather the communication here and now of the life of God to the soul. Indeed the very idea of heaven as localized is a misconception. Properly it is 'the name for a state conformed to the will of God', with hell as its antithesis.[16]

But behind Erskine's salvation doctrine there lies the whole conception of the divine as a beneficent power in the lives of ordinary people.

> Our systems make God a mere bundle of doctrines, but He is the Great One, with whom we have to do in everything ... Religion is for the most part a covert atheism, and there is a general shrinking from anything like an indication that there is a real Power and a real Being at work around us.[17]

Theology, he felt, had become, instead of a pointer to the living God, a mere intellectual scheme, or, even worse, material for scholastic controversy. What concerned him was the life of faith, the abiding sense of the nearness of the presence of God, as one to be trusted and ever to be learned from. The notion of this life as a 'probation' offended him. Few religious phrases, he considered, had such a power of darkening men's minds concerning their true relation to God as this. 'We are not in a state of trial: we are in a process of education directed by that eternal purpose of love which brought us into being.' Hence every event, even death itself, becomes a manifestation of God's eternal purpose. 'On the probation system, Christ appears as the deliverer from a condemnation; on the education system, he appears as the deliverer from sin itself.'[18] The corollary was that if man is continually being taught by God theological systems have no final fixity: they must develop, progress. The essence of religious and ecclesiastical authority is educative. But the principle of infallibilism is not to be contemplated: an infallible Church, 'if it could be, would destroy all God's real purpose with man, *which is to educate him*, and to make him feel that he is being educated—to awaken perception in the man himself—a growing perception of what is true and right, which is of the very essence of all spiritual discipline'.[19]

Central to Erskine's teaching is the Maurician concept of Christ as head of the human race. The Lord had come once, manifested eighteen hundred years ago, but 'both before and since that time he has been, as it were, diffused throughout humanity, lying at the bottom of every man as the basis of his being .... Christ the Head was latent in humanity as the Head, but the Head did not come out and show itself to the senses until the personal Christ appeared in the flesh'.[20] He is 'the sustaining head, to the power of whose pervading presence through all the members of the human race the actual existence of every member of the race is

---

15. *The Unconditional Freeness of the Gospel*, p. 25.
16. 'Eternal life is living in the love of God; eternal death is living in self; so that a man may be in eternal life or in eternal death for ten minutes, as he changes from the one state to the other' (Hanna, *op. cit.*, ii, p. 240. Cp. p. 238).
17. *The Unconditional Freeness of the Gospel*, p. 142.
18. Quoted Henderson, *op. cit.*, pp. 128f.
19. See Tulloch, *op. cit.*, p. 132.
20. See Hanna, *op. cit.*, ii, p. 357.

alone to be attributed'.[21] The immediate witness to this truth is the conscience, which 'in each man is the Christ in each man'. In every one of us there is 'a continual inflowing of the Logos'. It is in virtue of Christ being in all men, that conscience is universal in man.[22]

Erskine had no intention of attacking traditional doctrine, but his viewpoint was sufficiently new at the time to antagonize church opinion. Dr Chalmers himself often expressed his admiration of Erskine's writings, but in this he was not voicing the common judgment, which unhappily was more certainly articulated in Thomson's polemic. Had Erskine been a minister he would probably have suffered the fate of his friend McLeod Campbell, or of the unfortunate Mr Thomas Wright, the parish minister of Borthwick.

Traditionalism breached: McLeod Campbell and Robertson Smith

John McLeod Campbell's is the outstanding name in Scottish theology during the last century and at once evokes the memory of a *cause célèbre* of a kind unparalleled south of the border, at least in modern times. Campbell (1800–72) was minister of Row, near Cardross on the Gareloch. A 'Moderate' by upbringing, he was of a studious disposition, disinclined to party affiliations and assiduous in his pastoral duties. As a parish minister, however, he was soon struck by the perfunctory attitude of most of his flock towards religion and attributed it to the lack of any individual sense of God's goodwill and favour. What was needed was a personal assurance of faith, a conviction of the objective fact of the divine love for all men. But how could any man be sure that God loves him unless he knew it as a truth that Christ died, not merely for an elect few, but for all? Assurance being essential for holiness, Christ's atonement must have been universal. Whether or not Campbell's preaching had made his meaning clear—and in many minds there undoubtedly was genuine confusion as to what precisely he was saying—the more rigid Calvinism of his day at once scented heresy. The objections to his teaching were, on the one hand, that it denied the possibility of a fall from grace, and, on the other, that it was antinomian. The upshot was that Campbell and some sympathizers—such as Robert Story, minister of Roseneath—were arraigned before the church courts and convicted of disseminating false doctrine. In the General Assembly of 1831 both Moderates and Evangelicals united in condemning Campbell and he was forthwith expelled from the ministry. In his defence he had pleaded that his teaching was not inconsistent with a fair and reasonable interpretation of the Westminster Confession, but that even if this were not so he still had the right of appeal to Scripture itself as the higher authority.

> If you show me [he declared] that anything I have taught is inconsistent with the Word of God, I shall give it up, and allow you to regard it as a heresy. . . . . If a Confession of Faith were something to stint or stop the Church's growth in light and knowledge, and to say, 'Thus far shalt thou go and no further', then a Confession of Faith would

21. *The Brazen Serpent*, p. 42.
22. Hanna, *op. cit.*, ii, pp. 353f.

be the greatest curse that ever befell a church. Therefore I distinctly hold that no minister treats the Confession of Faith right if he does not come with it, as a party, to the Word of God, and to acknowledge no other tribunal in matters of heresy than the Word of God. In matters of doctrine no lower authority can be recognized than that of God.[23]

Divine truth, in short, cannot be for ever fixed in formularies and those who seek it must in the end return to the original fount itself.

Not indeed that Campbell himself was free of the dogmatic spirit. He was not in favour of latitude in interpreting doctrine; his own strong conviction of being in the right prevented it. He referred disparagingly during his defence to the 'charity' which is tolerant of wide ranging opinions and regards 'speaking dogmatically as necessarily an evil'.[24] The remainder of his life—he afterwards ministered to an independent congregation in Glasgow—was devoted to theological study and reflection, the outcome of which was his famous work on *The Nature of the Atonement and its Relation to the Remission of Sins and Eternal Life*, first published in 1856.[25] Although it makes somewhat difficult reading today it must still be regarded as one of the most important contributions to dogmatic theology which its century produced. In so far as its author sought to overthrow the old legal and forensic view the tendency of the book was liberalizing. Theology, Campbell maintained, is useless unless spiritually fruitful, and for this it has to have its roots in life. The great atonement doctrine, however, had long been treated abstractly and legalistically, in virtual isolation from the other fundamentals of the Christian creed. The present need, if the religious value of the doctrine is to be conserved, is to recover the relationship between Christ's death and his incarnation.

Campbell's starting-point is the Fatherhood of God, as the sole ground of the atonement: the divine forgiveness is the presupposition of any theology of reconciliation. Were man himself able to atone for sin then fittingly enough forgiveness would follow; whereas if it is God who provides the atonement forgiveness must *precede* it, the actual atoning act being the manifestation of God's forgiving love, not its cause. This, Campbell argues, is the authentic Scriptural teaching: '*God so loved the world, that He gave His only begotten Son, that whosoever believeth on Him, should not perish, but have everlasting life.*' The attention of theologians, he points out, has been too much confined to the doctrine's retrospective aspect. It certainly is the case that having violated God's moral law men are sinners under a standing condemnation, a truth terrible to contemplate. Yet Christ's sufferings ought not to be regarded only as penal.

Let my readers endeavour to realize the thought. The sufferer suffers what he suffers just through seeing sin and sinners with God's eyes, and feeling in reference to them with God's heart. Is such a suffering a punishment? There can be but one answer. . . . I find myself shut up to the conclusion, that while Christ suffered for our sins as an

23. Quoted from Campbell's speech before the bar of the Synod of Glasgow and Ayr in Tulloch, *op. cit.*, p. 152.
24. D. Campbell, *Memorials of J. McL. Campbell* (1877), i, p. 80. See Tulloch, pp. 153f.
25. A new edition was issued in 1959.

atoning sacrifice, what He suffered was not—because from its nature it could not be—a punishment.[26]

In essence the atonement is the means by which God has bridged the gulf between man's actual condition as a sinner and what, in the fulfilment of the divine purpose, he was intended to be. Christ's suffering, therefore, was not a mere punishment but 'the living manifestation of the Son's perfect sympathy in the Father's condemnation of sin'. In other words, he revealed to mankind what sin means to an all-holy God.

> That oneness of mind with the Father, which towards man took the form of the condemnation of sin, would in the Son's dealing with the Father in relation to our sins, take the form of a perfect confession of our sins. This confession as to its own nature must have been a perfect Amen in humanity to the judgment of God on the sin of man.[27]

The suffering is itself a revelation of that divine righteousness which condemns sin and hence is not just its consequence. Its role is positive, a demonstration of God's love. Thus the atonement, so far from being the legal transaction commonly represented, has a profound moral and spiritual significance in view of the relation of all men to God as their Father.

> There is [Campbell urges] much less spiritual apprehension necessary to the faith that God punishes sin, than to the faith that our sins do truly grieve God. Therefore men more easily believe that Christ's sufferings show how God can punish sin, than that these sufferings are the divine feelings in relation to sin, made visible to us by being present in suffering flesh. Yet, however the former may terrify, the latter alone can purify.[28]

But at no time does Campbell try to attenuate the divine wrath. In his dealing with God on our behalf Christ must, he says, be thought of as dealing also with this, sin's due. But if Christ alone is able to make the perfect confession of man's sin, in that a perfect confession demands perfect holiness, then the truth of the incarnation is fundamental. Further, Christ's intercession is the complement of his confession and forms part of his sacrifice.

> In itself the intercession of Christ was the perfect expression of that forgiveness which He cherished toward those who were returning hatred for His love. But it was also the form His love must take if He would obtain redemption for us. Made under the pressure of the perfect sense of the evil of our state, that intercession was full of the Saviour's peculiar sorrow and suffering. . . : its power as an *element of atonement* we must see, if we consider that it was the voice of the divine love coming from humanity, offering for man a pure intercession for the will of God.[29]

The Lord's death, therefore, was the perfect culmination of his work; for only to the perfectly holy could death 'have its perfect meaning as the wages of sin' and

---

26. *The Nature of the Atonement* (6th ed), p. 101.
27. *Ibid.*, pp 116f.
28. *Ibid.*, p. 140.
29. *Ibid.*, pp. 127f.

the withdrawal of God's gift of life. 'Death filled with that moral and spiritual meaning in relation to God and His righteous law which it had as tasted by Christ, and passed through in the spirit of sonship, was the perfecting of the atonement.'

On the relation of the atonement to eternal life Campbell is insistent that Christ's attitude to sin must be reflected in men. Only so will his reconciling work avail for us. But Christ's righteousness is not simply *imputed*, in the manner of a legal fiction. Rather is it that in him men confront the true possibilities of their own humanity. Such righteousness as he showed 'could never have been accounted of in our favour, or be recognized as "ours", apart from our capacity of partaking in it.' What Christ's work really effects is deliverance from sin itself, for when we allow the atonement 'to inform us by its own light why we needed it, and what its true value to us is, the punishment of sin will fall into its proper place as testifying to the existence of an evil greater than itself, even *sins*, from which greater evil it is the *direct* object of the atonement to deliver us—deliverance from punishment being a secondary result'.[30] Christ indeed is the head and representative of humanity, and his own righteousness is to be transmitted to the redeemed human race. Men die with him in order to rise again to a higher life.

There is no need here to discuss Campbell's theory in detail. R. C. Moberly, whose own views as expressed half a century later in *Atonement and Personality* (1901) follow up the same line of thought, criticizes it as more successful in discerning the nature of the relation of Christ to God than of men to Christ.[31] Could Christ's relation to God in respect of human sin, he asked, be rightly described as a 'perfect confession'? What exactly was Campbell's scriptural authority for so calling it? But the point of interest to the historian is the import of the book itself. In regard to Calvinist orthodoxy the author was trying to pour new wine into old bottles, struggling to save the traditional language whilst infusing into it a new meaning. For him the heart of the atonement was its moral appeal: the spectacle of suffering willingly borne for the sake of others. Herein it was a revelation both of God's nature and of man's. But this implies, as Campbell's opponents were quick to observe, a very different principle from that embodied in the doctrine usually taught. In the Church of England, the censuring of views like Campbell's would have been unthinkable; in still Calvinist Scotland it was otherwise.

Campbell, moreover, was not the only divine at that time to give offence to orthodoxy. Two contemporaries, men of lesser intellectual calibre admittedly, were likewise deposed from office for their faulty beliefs: Edward Irving and Thomas Wright of Borthwick, near Dalkeith. In fact it was the same General Assembly, that of 1831, which expelled Campbell, that began proceedings against Irving, although the latter's actual deposition was not effected until two years later. His talents, let it at once be said, were markedly different from either Campbell's or Erskine's. A graduate of Edinburgh university, he had spent some time in teaching when Thomas Chalmers took him on as his assistant at St John's, Glasgow, a post which secured him the freedom of a well-known pulpit. However, no independent charge in Scotland came his way and when offered the ministry of the Caledonian

30. *Ibid.*, p. 261.
31. *Atonement and Personality*, p. 402.

church in London he at once took it. Though not an original thinker or a man of learning Irving was highly impressive as an orator and his preaching soon drew a large and eclectic audience. His *Orations*, published in 1823, the second year of his London ministry, displayed—to quote Tulloch—'grandeur of imagination, richness of poetical and spiritual conception, and fulness of vivid feeling, rather than any glow of higher insight, penetrating to the deeper problems of religion'.[32] As delivered, with all their author's fiery eloquence, they aroused great interest and a larger church became necessary.

It was about this time also that he made McLeod Campbell's acquaintance, having already become a warm admirer of Coleridge, to whom he dedicated one of his most arresting sermons. Both men exerted a widening influence on his mind, Campbell's views on the atonement especially attracting him. His own theology was 'incarnationalist' and he did not think of the death of Christ as a mystery to be contemplated apart from what to him was the more fundamental doctrine. But in stressing the reality of Christ's manhood—'bone of our bone and flesh of our flesh'—he used some unguarded turns of phrase. Christ, he preached, had completely identified himself with sinful humanity, not, of course, to the extent of actually sharing its sinfulness, but as having nevertheless its innate tendency to sin. If the Lord had been kept from sin it was only 'by the indwelling of the Holy Ghost'. The idea was startling enough to prompt the cry of 'Heresy', and unfortunately Irving had neither the critical acumen nor a sufficient knowledge of the history of doctrine to guide him safely along a slippery path. Further, he had become closely associated with a pentecostal religious movement that had arisen in the Gareloch district, where such signs of the Spirit as the gifts of tongues and healing were gaining a good deal of publicity, mainly adverse. Irving was so entirely caught up in the enthusiasm as to lose all sense of proportion, and under his inspiration similar phenomena—'Bedlam and Chaos' was Carlyle's description—occurred in his London church. His Scottish presbytery, however, was not disposed to tolerate his eccentricities farther and his dismissal followed. Irving, as it happened, had not much longer to live—a year only; but in that time he renewed his London ministry, under prophetic guidance, it was claimed, thus contributing to the rise of the so-called Catholic Apostolic Church, a sect at first known popularly as the 'Irvingites'.[33] That Irving lacked mental ballast is plain; his ideas were confused and he became less and less open to reasonable counsel and persuasion. But he undoubtedly was a man of intense religious imagination, with a rare power to kindle to the loyalty of disciples. Coleridge spoke of him, with truth, as 'a mighty wrestler in the cause of spiritual religion and Gospel morality'. In his way he was a portent, for although he was far from being a liberal or at all responsive to the more progressive trends of his day he clearly proved the need for

32. Tulloch, *op, cit*., p. 156.
33. The original moving spirit of the sect was the banker and landowner Henry Drummond (1786–1860), a man of aristocratic family, whom Carlyle described as 'full of fine qualities and capabilities—but well nigh cracked with an enormous conceit of himself'. On the history and teachings of the body see C. G. Flegg, *'Gathered under Apostles': a Study of the Catholic Apostolic Church* (1992).

something other and more than the desiccated orthodoxy which then prevailed.

The affair of Thomas Wright, a friend of Sir Walter Scott's, did not reach its crisis until a few years after the Campbell and Irving disputes, but once again the unhappy outcome was the deposition of the offender on a charge of heresy. Yet many of the books for which he was condemned—none of them works of technical theology but manuals of devotion—had appeared much earlier and at first without occasioning any unfavourable criticism. A private prayer book, *The Morning and Evening Sacrifice*, had secured a good circulation and was generally approved. Similar volumes, seemingly inoffensive, bore such titles as *The Last Supper, Farewell to Time* and *A Manual of Conduct*. All were published anonymously. Then a three-volume work called *The True Plan of a Living Temple* appeared in 1830. This was a rather different venture, not so much a practical aid as a compendium of highly personal religious reflections, and the impression it created was from the first dubious. As usual *The Christian Instructor* sniffed false doctrine, and whilst praising the book for its literary qualities denounced its theology as 'not only defective, but positively pernicious'. Certainly the latter pointed a new direction in religious thinking, little in accord with Calvinist standards. The author's criterion was that of moral fruits: Christianity is a means of producing good among men and overcoming vice and disorder. The fundamental gospel truth is that of the Fatherhood of God, who loves and pities all his children. Suffering there must be, as part of the divine method of dealing with men, a necessary element in 'the true plan of the living temple', but its aim is corrective, never vindictive. The whole tone of the book was in fact humanitarian, even 'secular'. Calvinism (and Calvin himself was here dubbed 'the prince of dogmatists'), fanaticism and 'enthusiasm' were not to the author's taste; reason, a personal ethic and social progress were. All the same its critics, though detecting far more of nature in it than of grace, could scarcely indite it for any specifically heretical teaching, and since the writer was shielded by his anonymity nothing was done. In time, however, his identity leaked out and the agitation against *The True Plan* was revived. Elderly and personally unobtrusive as Wright was, the Church authorities gave him short shrift. The time for enlarging theological horizons in the Scottish establishment had plainly not yet arrived.

This unfortunately was again demonstrated, a generation or so later, in the instance of William Robertson Smith (1846–94) of the Free Church, an eminent and indeed isolated biblical scholar whose views were well in advance of current teaching. An Aberdonian by birth, Smith was educated at Aberdeen university and New College, Edinburgh, where he studied under the noted Old Testament scholar, A. B. Davidson (1831–1903). He also spent some time in Germany as a pupil of Albrecht Ritschl at Göttingen. The scientific study of the Bible had long been *de rigueur* in German Protestant theological faculties and Smith's naturally inquiring mind encountered no problem whatever in adopting the critical standpoint. In 1870, having only just completed his formal theological training, he was elected to the chair of oriental languages and Old Testament exegesis at the Free Church college at Aberdeen, and in his inaugural lecture on 'What History teaches us to look for in the Bible' gave clear indication of his own position. The higher criticism, he explained, did not mean negative criticism, but simply 'the fair and honest looking at the Bible as a historical record, the attempt to reach the actual historical setting'. It was a process, he thought, which could be dangerous to faith only if begun without faith, when it was forgotten that the biblical history is 'no profane history, but the story of God's saving self-manifestation'.

A couple of years later he was back again at Göttingen, this time studying Arabic with Lagarde and making the personal acquaintance of the most eminent biblical scholar of the day, Julius Wellhausen. Then came the fateful invitation to contribute a series of articles to the forthcoming edition of the *Encyclopaedia Britannica*, a task of the difficulties of which he was by no means unaware. But retarded though the critical study of the Bible might be in Scotland, or even in England, where the *Essays and Reviews* uproar was still fresh in the public mind, in Germany, with the work of men like Kuenen, Graf and Nöldeke, it had been advancing by strides. The young Aberdonian professor was in fact one of the very few men in the country who were abreast of recent developments or had the professional equipment for pursuing them farther. The second volume of the encyclopaedia carried an entry of his under 'Angel' and the third a more considerable one under 'Bible', in which he frankly set out the conclusions relating to the origins of the Pentateuch, the authorship of the psalms, the real nature of Old Testament prophecy and the literary composition of the gospels which were then commonly accepted by critical scholars. The content of both articles drew disapproving comment, however, and in 1876 a committee of the Free Church Assembly was appointed to investigate the matter. Its report the following year was hostile. Smith, astonished at such a reception of what seemed to him no more than the commonplaces of an established science, responded by demanding a formal trial by 'libel' (i.e. indictment) for his allegedly heretical opinions. The resulting proceedings, as was to be expected, were complicated and long drawn out. Much more appeared to be at stake in the eyes of Free Church divines than issues of technical scholarship. If the Bible were truly the foundation of Christian faith then to treat it in such a manner as to impugn its inspiration and inerrant authority was a threat to religion itself. That Robertson Smith personally saw no discrepancy between his opinions as a scholar and his beliefs and responsibilities as a minister of the Church did not suffice for an answer. Many were gravely disturbed by the fact of such statements being set forth in an authoritative work of reference for the general reader.

In 1876 Smith virtually gave up teaching, but the successive volumes of the *Britannica* continued to bear articles from his pen. He also contributed, in 1879, a paper on totemism ('Animal Worship and Animal Tribes') to *The Cambridge Journal of Philology*. All alike were objected to as suggesting that the Bible is not of divine authorship and does not present a reliable statement of divine truth. The formal indictment was indeed withdrawn, but it was replaced by a vote in the Assembly of no confidence, with the result that in June 1881 he was dismissed from his chair at Aberdeen.[34]

34. For the details of the case see J. S. Black and G. Chrystal, *The Life of William Robertson Smith* (1912) and P. Carnegie Simpson, *The Life of Principal Rainy* (1909). Rainy was Smith's leading opponent in the Assembly, although himself a man of moderate and not extreme views.

Smith now removed to Edinburgh and took over much of the editorial responsibility for the *Britannica*, and it was largely through his efforts that the whole enterprise was brought to a successful outcome in 1888. Many more articles of his own were included: e.g. on 'Levites', 'Messiah', 'Prophet', 'Priest', 'Sacrifice' and 'Tithes', besides entries on particular Old Testament books. Meanwhile he continued his Semitic studies and travelled in Egypt, Syria and Palestine. In 1883 he was appointed professor of Arabic at Cambridge, which was to be his home for the rest of his life. A few years later he succeeded William Wright in the Adams chair of Arabic, at the same time bringing out his *The Religion of the Semites*: *Fundamental Institutions* (1889; 2nd ed, 1894), based on lectures he had given at Aberdeen. A second and much revised edition of a book on *The Old Testament in the Jewish Church* was published in 1892.

Smith's importance was that rather of a popularizer of new learning than an original contributor thereto. But although he sought to place the Old Testament within the wider context of Semitic religious culture generally he was far from satisfied with a purely naturalistic account of Hebrew development and condemned the views of 'those who are compelled by a false Philosophy of Revelation to see in the Old Testament nothing more than the highest point of the general tendencies of Semitic religion'.[35] As he stated in *The Prophets of Israel* (1882):

> There is a positive element in all religion, an element which we have learned from those who went before us. If what is so learned is true, we must ultimately come back to a point in history where it was new truth, acquired . . . by some particular man or circle of men who, as they did not learn it from their predecessors, must have got it by personal revelation from God himself. To deny that Christianity can ultimately be traced back to such acts of revelation . . . involves in the last resort a denial that there is a true religion at all, or that religion is anything more than a mere subjective feeling.

But he realized that new methods of presenting the truth were necessary. Theology had become backward-looking and defensive:

> Our whole theological literature, even when not apologetical in subject, is impregnated with an apologetical flavour; the most popular commentaries, the most current works of doctrine, do little or nothing to carry theology forward to new results, and direct all their energy to the refutation of attacks from without.[36]

The trial for heresy of a prominent scholar and sincere Christian teacher is to present-day ways of thinking repugnant and absurd. But Smith's case, however inconvenient to himself, was not simply a waste of time and energy. His own carefully worded statement, eloquent and logical, forced the biblical question upon public attention and gave rise to nationwide discussion. Issues had been brought to the fore which could not now be ignored or suppressed. Younger churchmen were bound to take account of them and ponder their implications. Criticism had so challenged orthodoxy as to make a complacent relapse into the old assumptions impossible. Within a few days of the vote which ended Smith's academic career in Scotland some three hundred of his friends and well-wishers together adopted a

35. J. S. Black and G. Chrystal, *op. cit.*, pp. 536f.
36. *Lectures and Essays* (1912), p. 315.

resolution declaring that 'the decision of the Assembly leaves all Free Church ministers and office-bearers free to pursue the critical questions raised by Professor W. R. Smith', and pledged themselves 'to do our best to protect any man who pursues these studies legitimately'.

All the same liberty of critical biblical scholarship in the Free Church was not immediately won. On two subsequent occasions decisions were forced upon the General Assembly. The first involved Dr Marcus Dods, who in 1889 was elected professor of New Testament studies at New College. Excellent scholar though he was, his views on biblical inspiration and inerrancy were highly distasteful to the conservatives, especially that section of them commonly known as 'the Highland host'. A like dissatisfaction was voiced—in the same quarter, needless to say—with the teaching of Dr A. B. Bruce at Glasgow. The Assembly's College committee examined the opinions attributed to both men and found them open to censure on a number of points, but not so far at fault as to justify proceedings against them. The Assembly took no action therefore, although it reaffirmed in unqualified terms the central articles of the Church's belief and deplored any attempts to undermine them. In particular the Assembly emphasized the infallible truth and divine authority of Scripture and deplored the use of language which seemed to maximize the element of human ignorance and error in the scriptural record. Bruce specifically was admonished for his statements on the inspiration of the gospels and other matters, including Jesus's own teaching. But neither professor was condemned, nor was the doctrine of verbal inerrancy expressly asserted. Churchmen might dislike the tone of the new biblical scholarship, but they were not prepared to inhibit its inquiries by a formal decision. This was made finally plain when in 1902 the Assembly declined to institute proceedings against George Adam Smith's *Modern Criticism and the Preaching of the Old Testament*.

Renewal and reaction

But if recognition of the right of the Church's ministers to apply scientific methods to the study of the Bible was in Scotland somewhat slow and thus possibly the cause, for a time, of a certain hesitation among Scottish divines to embark on the kind of biblical study which south of the border was making steady if cautious advance, the traditional Scottish flair for systematic and philosophical theology was by no means repressed. In this field the century's two outstanding names are those of the brothers John and Edward Caird, with whom the idealist reaction against empiricism, begun by T. H. Green at Oxford, assumed an expressly Christian form. John, the elder of the two, was born in 1820 and graduated at Glasgow university. His first ministerial charge, at Newton-on-Ayr, was followed by two years of work in Edinburgh, where his gifts as a preacher received the stimulus of a well-educated congregation. From 1849 until 1857 he was parish minister of Errol in Perthshire, devoting his leisure time to theological study and to mastering the German language. It was while here that he preached before the queen at Balmoral his famous sermon on 'Religion in the Common Life', a discourse which in published form sold in large numbers and won from Dean

Stanley superlative praise as 'the greatest single sermon of the century'. He returned to Glasgow in the same year (1857) to minister at the Park Church, and in 1862 was appointed professor of theology at the university, which had already conferred on him an honorary doctorate in divinity. Academic work suited him well and he was active on many sides of university life, displaying a remarkable business capacity, a keen interest in promoting higher education for women and a sincere readiness to implement the changes proposed by the universities commissions of 1876 and 1887. In 1878 he delivered the Croall lectures at Edinburgh, revising and enlarging them for publication in 1880 as *An Introduction to the Philosophy of Religion.* A book on Spinoza for Blackwood's series of 'Philosophical Classics' came later (1888), and in 1890 he was appointed Gifford lecturer at Glasgow. The first course, of twelve lectures, was supplemented a few years afterwards by a second of eight, during which, however, he was taken ill. He never made a complete recovery and died in the summer of 1898. The lectures were published in 1900, with a prefatory memoir by his brother Edward, under the title *Fundamental Principles of Christianity*, two other posthumous collections of his writings having appeared the year before: *University Sermons, 1873–1898* and *University Addresses.*

The inspiration behind the philosophy of both men was, as we have seen,[37] that of Hegel, although the Hegelian influence is less pronounced in the elder. Hegel's grand intention had been to support and defend Christianity by rationalizing it within the framework of an all-comprehending metaphysical system; though whether the sort of interpretation thus put upon it was not, religiously speaking, the kiss of death is a question that was soon to be asked. His contention was that theology depicts religious truth in the guise of a representation or figure (*Vorstellung*), whereas it is the task of speculative thought—and for Hegel speculation was the breath of life—to translate such figures and representations into philosophical concepts (*Begriffe*). But the impression which Hegel left on nineteenth-century theology varied greatly. In John Caird it is seen at its most constructive and conservative. Caird believed profoundly in the value and capacity of reason and its entire appropriateness to the knowledge of God. As his brother wrote in the memoir referred to above, 'the conviction that God can be known and is known, and that in the deepest sense all our knowledge is knowledge of Him, was the corner-stone of his theology'. Undoubtedly John Caird—more theologian than philosopher—like Edward—himself more philosopher than theologian—was instinctively drawn to Hegelianism, especially through his implicit trust in the power of the human intelligence to penetrate all mysteries. He refused to immunize religion against rational criticism by identifying it with feeling or the moral consciousness or aesthetic intuition. On the other hand, if, as his brother points out, a Hegelianized Christianity meant substituting a theory of reality for reality itself, or taking man for 'a mere modus of the divine', or regarding God as 'the poetic substantiation of an abstraction', or denying the essential truth of the ordinary Christian consciousness in favour of a metaphysical doctrine, then Caird was no Hegelian.[38] The lectures on the philosophy of religion, although evidently

37. See above, ch. 9.
38. *Fundamental Principles of Christianity*, i, pp. lxxviif.

the work of a man of strongly philosophical bent, are the utterance also of a genuine religious feeling: 'the words of Scripture and the dialectical evolution of thought' pass into each other 'without any consciousness of a break or incongruity'. Indeed, as Caird saw it, religion to the sophisticated intelligence naturally seeks philosophical articulation, so that as between philosophy and theology, faith and reason, there is no basic discrepancy. 'Christianity and idealism were the very poles of [his] thinking, and the latter seemed to him the necessary means for interpreting the former.'[39] The point of view is, of course, the antithesis of that maintained by Mansel in his Bampton lectures, or in their differing ways by Caird's great German contemporary, Ritschl, and in our time by Karl Barth.[40] If he committed an error, his brother comments, it was rather that he followed Hegel too assiduously 'in believing that the whole structure of dogma, as it has been developed by the Church, could be interpreted by philosophical reflection, without any essential change'.[41]

Nevertheless, John evinced a deeper regard for the positive doctrinal inheritance of Christianity than did his brother. While he opposes the drawing of any sharp distinction between natural and revealed religion inasmuch (he claims) as it is Christianity which explains natural religion to itself, he also is convinced that there is not a single doctrine of natural religion which, once it falls within the context of Christian experience, is not in some measure transformed by it. As a Hegelian he believes in the 'unity' of God and man and that it is in humanity that the divine is disclosed, but not to the extent of minimizing what is singular and specific in the Christian revelation.

> If in the religious history of mankind we can discover indications of a progressive development, it is not by leaving out of view what is peculiar to Christianity, those ideas which constitute its spiritual glory and excellence, and taking account only of that which we see or suppose to be common to it with the earliest and rudest nature worship, that we can discover the real meaning of that history: for it is just that in which Christianity differs from all the pre-Christian religions which realizes, for the first time, the true idea of religion. As the absolute and only perfect form of that idea, Christianity, whilst it explains the latent significance of all that was true in the imperfect religions, at the same time transcends, and in transcending, transmutes and annuls or supersedes them.[42]

Thus the distinctively Christian idea of God finds expression in the doctrine of the Trinity.[43] Again, for the Christian 'there is something unique in the Person of Christ', however true it be that he is the representative of humanity; and such a 'participation' in the being and life of God can be predicted of him as to distinguish him from all other members of the human race. His was pre-eminently a human consciousness 'possessed and suffused by the very spirit and life of the living God'.

39. *Ibid.*, p. cxli.
40. 'An agnostic apology for Christianity, in which security for the faith was sought in the incapacity of man to criticize it, seemed to my brother like calling in the devil to protect the sanctuary' (*Ibid.*, pp. liif.).
41. *Ibid.*, p. lxxvi.
42. *Ibid.*, p. 27.
43. *Ibid.*, p. 58.

Even the concept of God's moral personality requires, Caird thinks, to be underwritten by that of the Christian doctrine of the Logos or Son of God as 'a self-revealing principle or personality within the very essence of the Godhead'. The idea of God as an 'isolated, self-identical infinite, complete and self-contained in the abstract unity of His own being', a purely metaphysical Absolute, would of itself give no entry to that which we recognize as the highest element of a spiritual nature: namely, love.

In his teaching on the atonement Caird followed McLeod Campbell, upon whom, in 1868, he proposed the conferring by Glasgow university of the degree of D. D. Christ, he held, by virtue both of his embodiment of the ideal of spiritual perfection and of his loving us 'with a love so absolute as to identify Himself with us', making our good and evil his own, was possessed of such 'a capacity of shame and sorrow and anguish', such 'a possibility of bearing the burden of human guilt and wretchedness', as humanity, enfeebled by sin, could never bear of itself. And from this Caird passes to the still larger idea of the divine *possibility* itself. Not only can the sinless suffer for sin; there are, he contends, sufferings for sin which only the sinless can undergo in fullest measure. It is in the nature of things 'that a moral and spiritual evil should be expunged or cancelled by a suffering which is itself moral and spiritual'.[44] Of the historic life of Christ he maintained that the particular facts are of less account than the underlying ideas. 'A true idea is true independently of the facts and events that first suggested it.' Even if many of the details of Jesus's mission and teaching should fail to stand the test of scientific criticism, even indeed if the whole gospel record were lost, yet 'the ideas and doctrines concerning the nature of God and the hopes and destinies of humanity, which had their historic origin in that life, would be recognized as true in themselves, and as having an indestructible evidence in the reason and conscience of man'.[45] Hence—a further unmistakably Hegelian touch—the actual increase in the depth and richness of experience, of the spiritual *knowledge* of Christ, which has come to the Church over the ages, will also explain the 'apparent paradox' of ascribing higher opportunities of knowledge than his own immediate followers possessed to those in after times who never knew him in the flesh.

Edward Caird, professor of moral philosophy at Glasgow from 1866 until 1893, when he succeeded Jowett at Balliol, was, as we have remarked, much more consciously a philosopher than a theologian, and the sense of tension between the idealist metaphysic and traditional Christian theology which marks his brother's thought no longer occurs. One of the most eminent British philosophers of his century, his most important publications were the volume on *The Critical Philosophy of Immanuel Kant* and the two series of Gifford lectures, although the little book on Hegel in Blackwood's 'Philosophical Classics', dating from 1883, ranks yet as one of the best of all introductions to its subject. Caird believed intently in the necessary union of philosophy and religion, holding that Christianity was ideally constituted to express certain basic philosophical principles; which for him meant preponderantly, though not exclusively, those of the Hegelian system,

44. *Fundamental Principles of Christianity*, i, p. 223.
45. *Ibid.*, pp. 241f.

especially as touching the relations of God and the world and the concept of *Versöhnung* or reconciliation. The history of religion, as he sought to demonstrate in the first series of Giffords, *The Evolution of Religion*, displays a continuous process of development from lower to higher; a process indeed in which he is confident of finding religion's vindication. God is a spiritual principle manifested in all nature and history; and but for nature and history, regarded as a development having its ultimate goal and culminating expression in the life of man as a spiritual being, divine revelation could have no meaning.

Whilst Caird was teaching at Glasgow the 'common-sense' Scottish philosophy continued to hold its own and Hegelian idealism made headway only with difficulty. Love of controversy, however, was not in Caird's nature and he seldom if ever attacked opposing positions directly. He was content to propound his personal views, satisfied that in good time they would make their impact. Similarly, although in theology he was markedly more liberal and detached from the traditional formularies than were the great majority of his contemporaries among Scottish churchmen, he was never iconoclastic in his treatment of popular religious beliefs. But the effect of his doctrine, in academic circles at least, was undoubtedly to weaken the old dogmatism. In truth the teaching of both the Caird brothers did more to bring about a change in Scottish theological attitudes than any other single factor. For they both realized—Edward most certainly—that a new intellectual climate was forming in which Calvinist principles would no longer thrive. Christian belief itself was under threat from the new forces of scientific naturalism and materialism and had to be re-equipped to meet them. The Reformation standpoint had been right in its day, but in the vastly altered world of nineteenth-century science and of philosophies claiming to be scientific at the expense of spiritual valuations only an idealism which itself was fully abreast of the times would suffice to bring to Christian truth its needed metaphysical aid.

To defend theology on strictly rational grounds was also the great endeavour of that tough-minded thinker, Robert Flint (1838–1910), professor of divinity at Edinburgh university. Flint's confidence in reason as the pillar of faith was unshakable. In *Theism*, published in 1877, he declared that belief should not outstrip knowledge, holding that if a man has no *reason* to believe there is a God then he has no right to do so. 'Belief is inseparable from knowledge and ought to be precisely co-extensive with knowledge', a maxim at the opposite pole to Ritschlianism. For whereas Ritschl denounced natural theology as a sham in failing to express God's will for men as sinners, Flint saw in it the foundation of all other theology, in the same way that natural law is the foundation of all political and ethical science. No heathen religion or philosophy has ever been without the truths of natural religion, and to teach a faith that denigrates reason or relies blindly on authority Flint dismisses as 'a foolish procedure', incapable of justifying the ways of God to men. The conspicuous fault of the Reformers was in their ascribing to Scripture a position inconsistent with adequate recognition of either the rights of reason or the evidences of God in creation, providence or the nature of man himself.

> The evidences or proofs of God's existence are countless. They are to be found in all
> the forces, laws, and arrangements of nature—in every material object, every organism,

every intellect and heart. At the same time they concur and coalesce into a single all-comprehensive argument, which is just the sum of the indications of God given by the physical universe, the minds of men, and human history. Nothing short of that is the full proof.[46]

Yet the mind can only rise to the apprehension of God by a process which involves all the essentials of its own constitution, especially the will, from consciousness of which the very idea of causality is in fact derived. 'If we did not know ourselves as causes, we could not know God as a cause; and we know ourselves as causes only in so far as we know ourselves as wills.' But in the end the logical understanding is paramount. 'The whole duty of man as to belief is to believe and disbelieve according to evidence, and neither to believe nor disbelieve when evidence fails him.'[47]

But if Flint's view directly negatives Ritschl's as to the place of metaphysics in religion so too, on the other hand, did his estimate of mysticism. Mysticism, like anything else, may have its defects, but it has been of immense service to religion and 'no worthy theologian will deny profound obligations to the great masters of mystic theology'.[48] In the Catholic tradition mysticism has held a prominent place, possibly even too prominent, since it has been made to subserve ecclesiastical interests. But the disregard of it in Protestantism has been a fault. However, Flint's assessment of the role in Christianity of both reason and the mystical temper never lessened his concern for its biblical foundations. The critical study of the Bible he thought in no way profane or unwarranted, although the kind of rationalist assumptions which would exclude miracle could very well be dangerous. Dogmatics must be rooted in Scripture, from which alone it draws its truths and of which the central theme is that 'mediatorial principle' which reached its ultimate realization in an atoning death. Christian theology throughout is but a demonstration of Christ's mediating function, apart from which the human race could expect only that 'eternal death' in which, by nature, it already lies. Finally, in respect of the intellectual climate of the age, Darwinism had done nothing, Flint judged, to render theism less credible than formerly. Creation is the sole possible theory of the absolute origin of things: evolution must assume it or else hold that the universe is self-existent. The evolutionary theory is concerned with process only. 'Nothing can be conceived of as subject to evolution which is not of a finite and composite nature. Nothing can be evolved out of a finite and composite existence which was not previously involved in it. And what gives to anything its limits and constitution must be more perfect than itself'.[49]

A theologian of a very different stamp was Alexander Balmain Bruce (1831–99), professor of apologetics and New Testament exegesis at Free Church Hall, Glasgow, and the most pronounced liberal of his time in Scottish Presbyterianism. Bruce was without the technical equipment of a front-rank scholar, nor had he massive learning. With much in the Church's traditional doctrine he lacked

46. *Theism*, pp. 62f.
47. *Ibid.*, p. 358.
48. See especially his *On Theological, Biblical and Other Subjects* (1905).
49. *Theism*, pp. 390f.

sympathy on account of what he regarded as its legalism. Above all, he felt, the Christ of the synoptic gospels had been supplanted by the metaphysical abstractions of ecclesiastical dogma: what was needed was a recovered knowledge of the 'Son of Man' as the only authentic revelation of God. Apologetics was necessary—and Bruce himself was the author of a well-known treatise thereon[50]—but he despaired of any successful defence of traditionalist positions. The apologist's proper task is to present the Christianity of Christ himself, in the assurance that its intrinsic worth must convince any man of good will.[51] Yet Bruce was not a critical theologian, his attitude to the gospels is at times almost naïvely conservative, and his statements are not always self-consistent; although it has to be recognized that his opinions shifted over the years and that as between an early and popular book like *The Training of the Twelve* (1873) and his last work, the article on 'Jesus' which he contributed to Cheyne's *Encyclopaedia Biblica*, there is a very perceptible movement away from the orthodox standpoint. The fact is that while Bruce personally believed in Christ's divinity, which he held to be in full accord with the teaching of the gospels, he was increasingly unhappy about its classical formulation. From this dilemma he tried to extricate himself by recourse to what is virtually Ritschlianism. Thus in *Apologetics* he writes that:

All we really know of God in spirit and in very truth we know through Jesus; but only on condition that we truly know Jesus Himself as revealed to us in the pages of the evangelic history. Knowledge of the historical Jesus is the foundation at once of a sound Christian theology and of a thoroughly healthy Christian life.[52]

Against those who would minimalize the historical basis of Christianity Bruce brings a moral argument:

If the Jesus of the Gospels really lived as there described, I have a right to condemm nonconformity to His image in others, and am under obligation to aim at conformity thereto in my own conduct. What He was we ought to be, what He was we can approximately be. But if the Jesus of the Gospels be a devout imagination then the right to reform and the obligation to conform cease. The fair Son of Man belongs to the serene region of poetry.[53]

For the modern Christian consciousness, as for that of the early Church, Jesus Christ possesses 'the religious value of God', an affirmation which always eludes the precise categories of a philosophical definition. On the other hand Bruce had no doubt that a Christianity without dogma would be an impossibility and that a creed is a practical necessity for the Church's continuing existence as a social force. To describe him, therefore, as a liberal in the sense which the epithet came increasingly to acquire during the final years of the last century and the first of

50. *Apologetics; or Christianity Defensively Stated* (1893).
51. Of his own aim Bruce wrote: '[The author] regards himself as a defender of the catholic faith, not as a hired advocate or special pleader for a particular theological system. He distinguishes between religion and theology, between faith and opinion, between essential doctrines and the debatable dogmas of the schools' (*Apologetics*, 3rd ed., p. 37).
52. *Ibid.*, p. 350.
53. *Ibid.*, p. 352.

the present could be misleading. He seems never seriously to have questioned that Jesus is in some ultimate way a supernatural figure to whom even the character of omniscience is not improperly ascribed.

Clearly there were tensions in Bruce's thought which he did not fully resolve and which became more acute as he grew older. In *The Chief End of Revelation*, published in 1881, he voices his impatience with the customary appeal to miracle and prophecy as primary evidence for the truth of Christianity, although for his part he doubts neither the authenticity of the one nor the predictive significance of the other. But a distinction has to be drawn between '*doctrines* of faith and theological *dogmas*', and he desiderates a 'simplified creed' retaining only the essentials of belief. The supreme miracle in any case was that of Christ himself: the moral miracle of his perfect holiness, which it was natural should have 'physical relations and aspects'.[54] In *The Kingdom of Christ* (1889) his attitude towards both 'ecclesiasticism' and 'sacramentarianism' and rigid credal orthodoxy hardened. He has no hesitation in describing Jesus as 'the absolutely true and full manifestation of the Divine Being', if he also can speak, somewhat ambiguously, of Christ and God being 'one in spirit'. But he finds nothing in the synoptics at least which attributes to Jesus a divine sonship in any metaphysical sense that is clear and indisputable. Again, the gospel teaches 'a rudimentary, moral and religious Trinity', but not 'the developed, metaphysical, and speculative Trinity of theology'. Further, the divinity of Christ has to be understood ethically, the heart of what he revealed being God's Fatherhood and, in his own person, 'the prototype of sonship'. The Kingdom (as with Ritschl) is a moral quantity, the unobtrusive but certain growth of which is best appreciated in the light of Mark's parable of the seed growing secretly. Eschatological imagery cannot be taken at face value and the Son's declared ignorance of the day of his second coming makes it highly unlikely that he foretold an early Parousia.

In 1896 and the year following Bruce delivered the Gifford lectures at Glasgow, taking as his subjects *The Providential Order of the World* and *The Moral Order of the World*. The evolutionary theory of human origins he readily accepted and was prepared to concede that in the course of evolution mind may well have arisen from matter. The incarnation is appraised in ethical terms: the entry of God into human experience makes him 'a moral hero', a burden-bearer for his own children, a sharer in the sorrow and pain that overtakes the good because of the world's moral evil. The noble army of martyrs have the comfort of knowing that the Eternal Spirit is at their head, and Christ is the visible human embodiment of the Spirit's leadership. The second series treats of the relation of God and man, pursuing the Maurician theme that man as such stands indefeasibly in a relation of sonship to God. 'All men indiscriminately are God's sons.' Religious faith is simply the recognition of this in the light of 'the Galilean gospel'. The standpoint of the *Enyclopaedia Biblica* article is throughout detached: the author reviews the biblical data but avoids theological inferences. In Mark we see 'the real man Jesus, without the aureole of faith around his head'. 'For modern criticism the story, even in the

---

54.   See *The Miraculous Element in the Gospels* (1886).

most heroic version, is not pure truth, but truth mixed with doubtful legend.' Nevertheless Jesus's spiritual intuitions are 'pure truth valid for all ages'. The ultimate conclusion is that God, man and the moral ideal could not have been more truly or happily conceived than in Christianity. But whether the 'divinity' of Jesus signifies anything beyond the sum of his moral perfections is not said. What is said goes no further than the affirmations of Harnack or Sabatier.

Against the background of the Scottish Presbyterianism of his day Bruce appears a somewhat isolated figure, not easy to classify. At the other side of the picture stand two conservatives, colleagues together at the Free Church college in Glasgow: James Orr (1844–1913) and James Denney (1856–1917). Orr at all events was a diehard whose hostility to critical and liberal trends deepened with the years. Denney, although prominent as a biblical scholar, likewise lacked sympathy with the changes which to a growing number of churchmen now seemed inevitable. But he denied that he held the old-fashioned doctrine of verbal inspiration and was ready to allow that in a pre-scientific age the myth presented in the opening chapters of Genesis was an appropriate medium of revelation. Orr, on the other hand, in *The Problem of Old Testament Criticism*, published as late as 1906, launched an all-out attack on the main positions in Old Testament analysis as then held. A formidable controversialist and able writer, his view of the Bible, although he too disclaimed any 'mechanical' theory of inspiration, was that of a bygone generation. Yet he did recognize that in the gospel record of Jesus's sayings the end is gained if the meaning be preserved, whatever variations may occur in the actual form of the words. Orr is seen in a better light, however, as a systematic theologian. His volume on *The Progress of Dogma* (1901), as was to be expected, is very critical of Harnack, but in its positive aspect offers a clear and informative exposition of its subject. His understanding of the great historic tradition of Christian theology is, moreover, superior to Bruce's. His best work is probably his volume of Kerr lectures, *The Christian View of God and His World* (1893), on any showing a worthy addition to the modern literature of dogmatic theology. Orr shared Flint's trust in reason—God's existence, if a truth, must challenge rational comprehension— endorsed the role of metaphysics in religion and was appreciative of mysticism. Natural theology, with its long-established place in Christian thought, is, he judged, both possible and necessary and the believer has no reason to regret that theism can be demonstrated apart from revelation. Further, man as a creature is undoubtedly a child of God, whose image sin has not wholly defaced. Thus between the human spirit and the divine mind there is an essential kinship. In accord with this conviction Orr believed the incarnation to possess a wider significance than that purely of a remedy for sin. Its ultimate end was the 'perfecting' of humanity. Regarding the atonement he will not separate fact from theory: if the fact be a fact it can be understood. Orr's refusal to accept the evolutionary account of human origins stemmed from his fears as to its consequences for Christian belief as a whole. But he was optimistic that as between the best-attested results of science and the familiar biblical story no irreconcilable antagonism need subsist.

Denney's work as a biblical and dogmatic theologian is best seen in his books on the atonement: *The Death of Christ* (1902), its sequel, *The Atonement and the Modern Mind* (1903), and the posthumously published Cunningham lectures, *The*

Christian Doctrine of Reconciliation (1917). The basis of these studies is a close examination of the New Testament beliefs and the interpretations put upon them by Christian thinkers since. On this he rests his own restatement, convinced that precise formulation is what the doctrine still calls for. He was in full agreement with Orr, that is, on the unsatisfactoriness of merely asserting the *fact* of the atonement without any attempt at explaining it: the question what exactly it was that Christ's death effected is one which cannot rightly be evaded. And the answer he himself gives is an unhesitating reaffirmation of the classic Protestant doctrine of penal substitution: Christ, bearing in himself the condemnation of man's sin, had suffered and died in man's stead. Denney disliked the word 'representative' in this context, as implying action on the part rather of man than of God, whereas the truth is that God, out of his very love, had given Christ for man. And because sin deserves punishment such substitution was inevitably penal. In Denney's earlier writings this aspect of the atonement is especially marked; in the later it is the divine love itself which receives the prominence. Sin, as he insists, is a terrible reality, but it is not the final reality. The ultimate is 'a love which submits to all that sin can do, yet does not deny itself, but loves the sinful through it all'.

Denney's theology of the incarnation is clearly set out in his early *Studies in Theology* (1894), a course of lectures delivered in the United States of America. Here he follows the ancient patristic line in using the Logos doctrine as the key to the meaning of personality, in mankind generally as in the incarnate himself. Thus the Logos made flesh became the personal centre not of a life alien to man, but of one truly and essentially human. It is through personality as such that man's relatedness to God subsists. What might be considered the sheer paradox of the incarnation, the antithesis of divine and human, is accordingly diminished: 'In whatever sense personality is to be ascribed to the Word, that same personality is the centre of the life which began at Bethlehem.' But if in this book Denney identifies himself with the movement of thought which eventuated in the Definition of Chalcedon—a formulary he resolutely defends—a subsequent work, *Jesus and the Gospel*, dating from 1908, shows an unexpected change of front. The traditional Christology now appears to him less than adequate to convey the reality of Christ as presented in the gospels and he finds the Athanasian doctrine incapable of a satisfactory interpretation. At the same time he by no means commits himself to a 'liberal' view and his own thinking remains somewhat obscure. At any rate he had scant sympathy with Ritschlianism, of which the 1894 volume is sharply critical. Ritschl's rejection of natural theology he could not countenance, whilst a Christology founded on the concept of the *Werthurtheil* or value judgment only harboured a dangerous ambiguity.[55] Indeed one of the most remarkable features of the Scottish theological tradition is the way in which it has maintained its

---

55. Cp. *Studies in Theology*, p. 14: 'Though Jesus has for the Christian consciousness the religious value of God, He has for the scientific consciousness only the common real value of man. He is, in truth and reality, to the neutral consideration of science, mere man like any other; it is only the *Werthurtheil*, the subjective estimate of the pious Christian, that gives him the value of God.' Orr, too, thought Ritschlianism theologically unsound. See *The Ritschlian Theology* (1897).

conviction that the human mind has the capacity for a rational knowledge of God and his ways.

Although both Orr and Denney were pronounced conservatives at a time when conservatism was fast losing ground they were less of an anachronism in Scotland than they would have been south of the border. For the kind of 'modernism' which became influential in the Church of England during the first quarter of the present century and which is best represented by such men as Hastings Rashdall, J. F. Bethune-Baker and Percy Gardner, won little support in the Church of Scotland or the Free Church. At least the point of view indicated in W. A. Curtis's inaugural lecture at the beginning of the 1903–4 session at Aberdeen university proved to be a more or less isolated one. Orthodoxy might be critical, as in the work of H. R. Mackintosh, but its essential traditionalism was never in doubt. The Protestantism of the Westminster Confession, however, had retreated into the past. The teachers of the new era bore a different stamp. Mackintosh himself, George Galloway and John Oman, W. P. Paterson and D. S. Cairns, Donald and John Baillie—to such as these the English-speaking theological world still gladly acknowledges its debt.

Chapter 13

CRITICAL ORTHODOXY

The 'Lux Mundi' group

The publication in 1889 of *Lux Mundi,* like that of *Essays and Reviews* thirty years earlier, has been described as a landmark in the history of English theological thought.[1] At the least the volume marked 'a new era in Anglican thought'.[2] The joint production of a group of High Churchmen, it was a clear departure from the rigidly conservative Tractarianism represented until his death in 1882 by Dr Pusey and by Henry Parry Liddon (1829–90), canon of St Paul's and the indefatigable chronicler of the former's life. Liddon had held his canonry since 1870, in which year he also was given the Dean Ireland chair of exegesis at Oxford, and was famed as a preacher attracting large audiences. Earlier he had strongly opposed attempts to minimize the use of the Athanasian creed in public worship,[3] whilst in his Bampton lectures on *The Divinity of Our Lord*, published in 1867, he had sought to maintain the strictest standard of orthodoxy and without the slightest concession to the difficulties then being raised by biblical criticism. On the credal issue he saw the Church already 'on an inclined plane, leading swiftly and certainly towards Socinianism tempered by indifference'.

> Surrender in this case [he was writing to Samuel Wilberforce] opens the floodgates. It establishes, in an instance of capital importance, the principle of Prayer Book revision. It will constitute an *a fortiori* argument for revising the Baptismal, Ordination and Visitation of the Sick Services in the sense of the anti-Sacramental Puritans. This done, it will authorize the eternal elimination of all direct adoration of Christ, our Eternal God, in order to satisfy the Socinian school in our midst . . . For myself, I see no future when the first step on the road to spiritual ruin shall have been fairly taken by the English Church.[4]

'A particular intellectual presentation of Truth', he said, 'may be modified, but nothing of the kind is possible with an article of the Christian Faith.[5] To him it

1. S. C. Carpenter, *Church and People 1789–1889* (1933), p. 537.
2. A. M. Ramsey, *From Gore to Temple* (1960), p. vii.
3. The attitude of Broad Churchmen to the formulary was exactly expressed by Archbishop Tait: 'I believe that this Creed has done more to alienate the minds of intellectual men from the Church of England than all other causes' (R. T. Davidson and W. Benham, *op. cit.* ii, p. 129). Hort considered that its clauses 'substitute geometry for life' (A. F. Hort, *op. cit.*, ii, p. 140).
4. J. O. Johnson, *The Life and Letters of Henry Parry Liddon* (1904), pp. 157f.
5. *Ibid.*, p. 366.

seemed that originality, of which his own work was destitute, could only mean novelty, and novelty in turn heresy.

The appearance of *Lux Mundi* was certainly a blow to Liddon and may well have hastened his death some months later. The book's editor, Charles Gore (1853–1932), was himself highly regarded by the older man, who had been largely responsible for securing his appointment as principal of Pusey House, Oxford, an institution founded as a memorial to the great Tractarian. That Gore, therefore, should have gone so far in propagating opinions which Pusey would have judged a betrayal of the orthodox faith and Liddon himself could only deplore is proof of the new outlook which the heirs of the Tractarians believed that changing times and the advance of knowledge had made inevitable.[6] Dean Church, always the most openminded of the High Churchmen of his generation, had written to Liddon in the same year with the intent of reassuring him: 'Ever since I could think at all I have felt that these anxious and disturbing questions would one day be put to us; and that we were not quite prepared, or preparing, to meet them effectively'; adding:

> It seems to me that our apologetic and counter–criticism had let itself be too much governed by the lines of attack and that we have not adequately attempted to face things for ourselves, and in our own way, in order not merely to refute but to construct something positive on our own side.[7]

To construct something positive was the set purpose of all those in whose thinking there was a confluence of two theological streams, the Coleridgean–Maurician and the Tractarian. Their standpoint was made plain by Gore in his editorial preface: the enterprise was 'an attempt on behalf of the Christian Creed in the way of explanation'; and the authors were agreed that if the true meaning of the faith is to be made sufficiently conspicuous such explanation was needful. Whilst they had not written as mere ' "guessers at the truth", but as servants of the Catholic Creed and Church, aiming only at interpreting the faith they had received', they shared the conviction that

> the epoch in which we live is one of profound transformation, intellectual and social, abounding in new needs, new points of view, new questions; and certain therefore to involve great changes in the outlying departments of theology, where it is linked on to other sciences, and to necessitate some general restatement of its claim and meaning.

What the current conditions demanded was a new development in theological thinking. This should be neither an innovation or heresy, nor 'the hardening and

---

6.   What distressed Liddon was the book's 'rationalizing and pelagianizing tone'. He was not alone in so thinking. An attack on *Lux Mundi* in Convocation was led by that last-ditch defender of traditionalism, Archdeacon Denison, but with little success. The theological atmosphere had changed much since the condemnation of *Essays and Reviews*. The new volume was not a sell-out to infidelity, although it did signify a fresh approach to the problems of religious belief and one for which precedents, it was pointed out, could be found in the thought of the Cambridge Platonists, certain of the Laudian divines, St Bonaventura and the medieval Franciscans and ultimately Origen and Clement of Alexandria.

7.   M. Church, *op. cit.*, p. 341.

narrowing process of further defining or multiplying dogmas'. The whole collection of essays was very deliberately the work of writers with common presuppositions and a common goal and thus avoided the somewhat haphazard character which had marred the *Essays and Reviews* enterprise. As a group of Oxford teachers—Arthur Lyttleton, master of Selwyn, was the only Cambridge man among them and even he had for a time been a tutor at Keble—they had had many occasions over the preceding years not only to meet and discuss[8] but to confer upon specific means of 'commending the faith to the acceptance of others' and of trying to put it 'into its right relation to modern intellectual and moral problems'—a phrase which, in seeming to reverse the right order of procedure, was to give offence to some readers. It is noteworthy that in the book's contents table the authorship of the several essays is not specified, the list of contributors being inserted before the preface and each paper taking its due place in a sequence of numbered chapters.

Lux Mundi is subtitled 'A series of studies in the Religion of the Incarnation', and this declared interest was in keeping with the already settled trend of English theology, associated alike with the Tractarian teaching and with Coleridge, Maurice and the Cambridge theologians, towards readjusting the balance between the incarnation and the atonement as the focal points in a scheme of Christian doctrine. What in general the authors were concerned to emphasize was both the intrinsic importance and the ramifying implications of the claim that in Christ the Son of God had assumed human nature. The tendency of Evangelicalism had been to isolate the atonement from other aspects of Christian belief. Thus Lyttelton in his own essay on the atonement especially stresses the close connection between Christ's death and his resurrection and ascension. It had been

> the fault of much popular theology to think only of our deliverance from wrath by the sacrificial death of Christ, and to neglect the infinitely important continuation of the process thus begun. The Gospel is a religion of life, the call to a life of communion with God by means of the grace which flows from the mediation of the risen and ascended Saviour.[9]

The sixth chapter, by R. C. Moberly (1845–1903), headed 'The Incarnation as the Basis of Dogma', and the fifth, by J. R. Illingworth (1848–1915), 'The Incarnation in relation to Development', were particularly interested in connecting the dogma with the modern principle of evolution.[10] Henry Scott Holland (1847–1918), a colleague of Liddon's at St Paul's, wrote on 'Faith'; Aubrey Moore (1848–90), very strikingly, on 'The Christian Doctrine of God'; Illingworth again on 'The Problem of Pain', in its bearing on faith; E. S. Talbot (1844–1934), warden of Keble, later

8. The book was planned at Longworth rectory, near Oxford, the home of one of the contributors, J. R. Illingworth, which for some years had been the meeting-place of Gore's 'Holy Party'—i.e. the *Lux Mundi* group. It was here, too, that the essays were read and criticized before publication.
9. *Lux Mundi*, p. 301.
10. Of the actual content of the dogma the authors had little indeed to say. As A. M. Fairbairn remarked: 'Curiously the Incarnation is the very thing the book does not, in any more than the most nominal sense, either discuss or construe' (*The Place of Christ in Modern Theology*, 1893, p. 451n).

bishop of Winchester, on 'The Preparation in History for Christ'; Walter Lock (1846–1933), afterwards warden of Keble, on 'The Church'; Francis Paget (1851–1911), Regius professor of pastoral theology and a canon of Christ Church, on 'Sacraments'; W. J. H. Campion on 'Christianity and Politics'; and R. L. Ottley (1856–1933) on 'Christian Ethics'. The editor himself wrote on 'The Holy Spirit and Inspiration', an essay which provoked more comment than any other. Gore also contributed a lengthy preface to the book's tenth edition, which appeared—for such was its circulation—in the following year. In this he sought to meet objections and underline the authors' united purpose of succouring 'a distressed faith'. What was needed was not compromise but readjustment, 'a reconciliation which shall at once set the scientific and critical movement, so far as it is simply scientific and critical, free from the peril of irreligion, and the religious movement free from the imputation of hostility to new knowledge'.[11]

The unity of standpoint among all the contributors was enhanced by the pervasive philosophical influence of T. H. Green, whose pupils some of them had been. Mark Pattison indeed had noted how the philosopher's honey had been carried off to the Tractarian hive, evidently considering that they had no right to it.[12] But the fact that the younger generation of High Churchmen could thus turn for intellectual guidance to one who, although at the time the *dernier cri* in philosophy, was himself by no means an orthodox believer indicates how ready they were to seek new aids for the communication of the old faith.[13] Moreover, neo–idealism seemed to accord well with the Alexandrian type of theology which they also found attractive. Scott Holland's regard for Green, strengthened by ties of close personal friendship, was especially high. But the positive influence of idealist theories was, as we shall observe, most evident in Illingworth, particularly in his later writings.

The opening essay was Scott Holland's on 'Faith' and is a work of considerable originality, anticipating the 'personalism' which was soon to become familiar in religious philosophy. Holland sees faith as an 'elemental energy of the soul' encompassing the entire body of man's activities. Hence the difficulty of examining and defining it in isolation, since 'the deepest and most radical elements of man's being are the hardest to unearth'. It grounds itself, solely and wholly, on an inner and vital relation of the soul to its source. Faith verifies itself only in actions and can best be described as 'a struggling and fluctuating effort in man to win for himself a valid hold upon things that exist under the conditions of eternity'. Religion is simply its articulate utterance:

> The Christian Creed only lifts into clear daylight, and endows with perfect expression, this elemental and universal verity, when it asserts that at the very core of each man's being lies, and lives, and moves, and works, the creative energy of the Divine Will.

11. *Lux Mundi*, p. xii.
12. *Memoirs*, p. 167.
13. Green's own concept of God was of 'a Being in whom we exist, with whom we are in principle one: with whom the human spirit is identical, in the sense that He *is* all which the human spirit is capable of becoming' (*Prolegomena to Ethics*, sect. 187).

Nevertheless the life of faith precedes any conscious expression of itself in religion, and the secular life can continue as if faith were unnecessary to it: 'Its own practical activity is complete and free, whether it discovers its hidden principle or not.' What faith does in religion is to confess life, all life, as holy: 'God-given, God-inspired, God-directed.' Accordingly faith is not opposed to reason; it is only that it exists at a deeper level than any of the capacities of which it makes use. Reason is one of faith's essential components, though not, of course, its entire essence. 'When, therefore, the self puts out its primitive power, it will do actions which satisfy reason, indeed, but which reason cannot exhaustively analyse, or interpret, since the entire force of reason, if it were all brought into action, would still be only a partial contribution to the effect.'

But although faith is identified as 'a simple adhesion of the soul to God' it has, in its objective expression, a history of its own. The record of this is in the Bible and the dogmatic creeds, both of which derive their significance from belief in Christ; for faith, first and last, is 'a spiritual cohesion of person with person'. The formularies, for all their difficulties and complications, are the product of faith: 'The creeds only record that certain questions have, as a fact, been asked. Could our world be what it is, and not have asked them?' The articulation of faith has been shaped, that is, by the needs and complexities of man's actual existence. Yet it is always to the personal life that dogmas relate, which is why they differ from scientific generalizations. To claim that the Christian dogma is final is really no more than to assert the finality of Christianity itself. 'If we are in a position to have any faith in Jesus Christ, then we must suppose that we have arrived at this one centre to all possible experiences, the one focus under which all insights fall.'

Holland's contribution to *Lux Mundi* remained one of the best of his works. His other publications consisted of collections of sermons, *Logic and Life* (1882), *Creed and Character* (1887) and *On Behalf of Belief* (1888) being perhaps the most noteworthy.[14] His theological position as a whole was conservative. For all his sympathy, in certain regards, with Roman Catholic Modernism—he always spoke of Tyrrell's writings with profound admiration—he could follow it in neither its historical scepticism nor its philosophical pragmatism. The Christian experience, he believed, has its solid basis in historical fact; but he also was insistent that the facts can properly be known only in terms of spiritual and moral experience. The fourth gospel appealed to him as pre-eminently the gospel of fact *and* experience. It was this same belief in the mutual dependence of fact and experience, faith and life, which led him to Christian socialism, an important and characteristic side of his thought and career.[15]

The second essay in *Lux Mundi* was that of Aubrey Moore, a theologian who had also read widely in both philosophy and natural science and whose death at

14. Mention should be made of his acticle on Justin Martyr in *The Dictionary of Christian Biography* (1882); the Romanes lecture on 'The Optimism of Butler's "Analogy" ' (1908); and the posthumous *The Philosophy of Faith and the Fourth Gospel*, ed. W. Richmond, (1920). A selection of his writings is contained in the present author's *Henry Scott Holland* (1962).

15. See the appended Note to this chapter.

the age of forty–two was a loss to Oxford and to the Church of England. On the subject of the Christian doctrine of God he sought to show how far modern philosophy and science might enrich as well as modify the traditional theism. The religious and the philosophical conceptions of deity differ, but are mutually necessary. 'Religion demands as the very condition of its existence a God who transcends the universe; philosophy as imperatively requires His immanence in nature.' Christian trinitarianism makes possible the satisfaction of each requirement. The one absolutely impossible conception to the modern mind, for which evolution has become a basic category, is the deist notion of an occasional celestial visitor.

> Science had pushed the deist's God farther and farther away, and at the moment when it seemed as if He would be thrust out altogether, Darwin appeared, and under the guise of a foe did the work of a friend. It has conferred upon philosophy and religion an inestimable benefit, by shewing us that we must choose between two alternatives. Either God is everywhere present, or He is nowhere. He cannot be here and not there.[16]

The immanence of God in all things is the great spiritual lesson which science now teaches; and it wholly fits the ancient doctrines of the Logos and the Trinity. The author optimistically concludes that

> all and more than all that philosophy and science can demand, as to the immanence of reason in the universe, and the rational coherence of all its parts, is included in the Christian teaching: nothing which religion requires as to God's separateness from the world which He has made, is left unsatisfied.

Moore's argument that the 'higher pantheism' and the religion of Christ are not wholly incompatible is resumed by John Illingworth in the essay on 'The Incarnation and Development'. A key idea in contemporary thought is the principle of evolution; the question to be asked by the theologian, therefore, is its bearing on the central doctrine of Christianity, since great scientific discoveries are not merely new facts to be assimilated but involve new perspectives. Here the Fathers of the early Church are of assistance, having seen in the incarnation the climax and keystone of the whole visible creation, an idea also shared by the medieval schoolmen: the incarnation, says Aquinas, is the exaltation of human nature and the consummation of the universe. It is true that the modern scientific view of the origins and progress of life appears at first to be inimical to final causes; but at a deeper level evolution seems rather to underwrite the teleological principle and to give to the evidence of design in nature a firmer basis. 'Under scientific guidance, we have acquired a more real, as distinct ftom a merely notional apprehension of the manifold adaptations of structure to function, which the universe presents'.[17] This more thoroughgoing conception of teleology is in perfect harmony with the Christian creed. In addition it teaches the further doctrine of the indwelling presence of the eternal Reason in all things of his creation. For science has a religious as well as a theological importance, constituting as it does the element of truth in that

16. *Lux Mundi*, p. 99.
17. *Ibid.*, p. 191.

higher pantheism which the modern mind finds so amenable. No good, however, is to be had from attempts to limit the sphere of scientific advance. 'If the remaining barriers between reason and unreason, or between lifelessness and life should one day vanish, we shall need to readjust the focus of our spiritual eye to the enlarged vision, but nothing more.' Yet man himself has a unique power of initiation. Always dissatisfied with his actual achievement he presses forward to something new. Modern philosophy has helped us to grasp more fully the significance of individuality, originality and personality in man, whose capacity for self–adaptation means that the human species is virtually permanent. Hence as touching the personality of Christ it may be said that the incarnation has introduced a new species into the world, 'a Divine man transcending past humanity, as humanity transcended the rest of the animal creation, and communicating His vital energy by a spiritual process to subsequent generations of men'.[18] To the objection that the incarnation traverses experience by importing an alien factor, the miraculous, the answer is that Christianity does not rest its claim solely on its miracles. These, to many minds, are comforting; but the real basis and true verification of Christianity is in present experience. It is in fact the only power which has regenerated personal life, 'and that beyond the circle even of its professed adherents, the light of it far outshining the lamp which has held its flame'.

Illingworth's philosophical position, as expressed in his book on *Divine Immanence* (1898), was a moderate idealism. Matter and spirit, he says, are known only in combination, with the result that neither can be known completely. Yet they represent distinct and distinguishable phases of experience. As we encounter it the spirit is, of course, always embodied; but it uses matter for its purposes and must be judged to have a certain primacy. Among such uses one of the most striking has been the religious. Primitive religion always finds divinity in nature, and even where mythology is outgrown the religious influence of the external world remains as strong as ever. A survey of religious ideas, Christian and non-Christian, leads to the conclusion that basically man's religious consciousness is one and points to a spiritual reality behind all things. Herein indeed is that 'natural' religion which Christianity presupposes. If we ask how the divine Spirit is related to matter the answer, Illingworth replies, can at once be anticipated by considering our own reality as personal beings. Man's consciousness transcends the material being with which it is associated, but also is in some way immanent in it. Similarly with God: 'The divine presence which we recognize in nature will be the presence of a Spirit, which infinitely transcends the material order, yet sustains and indwells it the while'.[19] To the question whether the universe is God's body or his work different answers may no doubt be given; but the Christian is entitled to urge that the trinitarian conception—to Christian faith a primary truth of revelation—is intellectually the most satisfactory since it embraces an immanence of both kinds

---

18. *Ibid.*, p. 207.
19. *Divine Immanence*, p. 72. In his last volume, *Divine Transcendence* (1911), Illingworth sought to modify the immanentist tendency of his earlier work. God, he points out, cannot be immanent in a world he does not transcend, nor transcendent over the world unless he is immanent within it.

and so 'harmonizes with the entire analogy of our personal experience'. For according to this doctrine the Logos, the second Person of the Trinity, is the essential, adequate and eternal manifestation of the first, as, in the case of man himself, is the body to personality. He is also immanent, in a secondary sense, in his whole creation, as are we in our works; only with the obvious difference that we as finite and transient beings are there only 'impersonally' present, 'whereas He must be conceived as ever present to sustain and animate the universe, which thus becomes a living manifestation of Himself'. Whether personality as humanly understood can in all strictness be referred to God Illingworth regards as a debatable question. He would not himself object to speaking of divine personality as *supra*personal, so long as this includes 'the essential attributes of personality',[20] although he is also disposed to consider human personality as imperfect, a replica—no more—in the finite of the divine archetypal personality,[21] the psychological elements of thought, desire and will in man being a reflection of the triune personality in God. Illingworth, we may add, realized well enough that a radical immanentism would impair the uniqueness of the incarnation, a course very far from his own intentions. He was convinced of the truth of the historical revelation on which he believed all Christian doctrine must be founded (in matters of criticism he was decidedly conservative), and he resolutely defended miracles inasmuch as the incarnation—*ex hypothesi* a unique event—was not miraculous in any sense to which objection could fairly be taken: 'If the Incarnation was a fact, and Jesus Christ was what He claimed to be, His miracles, so far from being improbable, will appear as the most natural things in the world.'[22]

Moberly's chapter on the incarnation as the basis of dogma opens with a plea for dogmatic truth. The principle of dogma is not to be attacked or defended on *a priori* grounds, the only real question being the truth of what is affirmed, which is a matter of evidence. Acceptance of dogma is in itself entirely reasonable, since its claims to authority and finality are in the case of Christianity the necessary outcome of the facts accepted in it. The facts themselves are all–important and the truth they convey has a completeness which scientific theory cannot parallel.

> The Christian Creed does not simply enunciate so many abstract principles of natural or supernatural life or governance. It introduces us straight to a supreme Person, Himself the beginning and the end, the author and upholder of all. Such a doctrine may be false, but it cannot be a fragment.[23]

For the believer every aspect of experience endorses his belief. 'There is no part or element of life which does not to him perpetually elucidate and confirm the knowledge which has been given him.' In the evidence for the incarnation—'either a fact or a fiction'—the vital datum is the resurrection, a historical event that is

---

20. *Op. cit.,* p. 158. The whole problem of personality in man and God he discusses at length in his Bampton lectures, *Personality, Human and Divine* (1894), where he develops the argument that God, as trinitarian theology describes him, is in fact the perfection of human personality.
21. *Personality, Human and Divine*, 216.
22. *Divine Immanence*, p. 88. See A. M. Ramsey, *From Gore to Temple*, p. 20.
23. *Op. cit.,* p. 228.

not a mere happening but 'an eternal counsel and infinite act of God'. The dogma of the incarnation is the Church's answer to the question, inevitable in the light of its primal experience, 'What think ye of Christ?'. The decisions of the early councils represent no more than a growth in intellectual precision through encounter with error, the creed in its whole substance being the direct outcome of the fact of the incarnation. Further, dogma is to be distinguished from theological speculation. The theology of one age may be discredited and superseded in another. It may develop and it may err. Indeed so far as language is concerned even the creeds are obviously human. The so-called damnatory clauses of the Athanasian are no doubt open to misunderstanding, but nevertheless are justifiable. The formulary is addressed not to outsiders but to believers, to encourage and to warn. For thought and life are not to be separated, and Christian dogmatism is but devotion to truth for truth's sake.

The essay clearly stood for the integrity of the received faith, and the author's later work is no less firmly rooted in the Catholic tradition. Thus *Ministerial Priesthood* (1897), without presuming to challenge Lightfoot's competence as a historian, does question the Cambridge scholar's implied doctrine of the Christian ministry in his famous essay,[24] a view resting, in Moberly's judgment, on some very disputable assumptions. Lightfoot, he wrote,

> insists, truly in the main, upon the Church's essential existence as spiritual. But he uses this truth to deny the reality of her proper existence as bodily; and then, being forced to deal with her existence as bodily, he treats it, not . . . as the living, proper method and utterance of Spirit, but as a lower, politic, condescending, accidental necessity.[25]

Lightfoot further assumes, he thinks, that the words 'sacrifice' and 'priesthood' legitimately carry only the meaning put upon them in the Old Testament, and takes it for granted—confusing 'representative' with 'delegate'—that the representative character of the ministry requires that any and every member of the Church implicitly possesses the right to minister. His own theory of the priesthood, unlike (he claims) either the Roman or the Protestant conceptions, is that it is essentially a function of the Church, which itself derives from that of the exalted Christ ('If Christ is a priest, the Church is priestly'),[26] specialized and personified in certain representative instruments.

> From this representative leadership in all external enactment of worship and sacrament . . . . it follows also, on the inward and spiritual side, that those who outwardly represent the priesthood of the Church must no less specially represent its true inwardness. The priest is not a priest in the act of divine worship only. His personal relation to the priestliness of the Church is something which has been conferred on him once for all, and which dominates everything that he does, or is.[27]

Ministerial Priesthood was followed in 1901 by *Atonement and Personality*, a

24. See above, pp. 256f.
25. *Ministerial Priesthood* 2nd ed., p. 43.
26. *Ibid.*, p. 251.
27. *Ibid.*, pp. 259f.

work still to be accounted a major product of Anglican divinity: 'a study in systematic theology such as had not been produced for many years within the Church of England'.[28] Here again Moberly's standpoint is that of tradition, whilst differing from the teaching of the Congregationalist R. W. Dale's well-known book published in 1875. Dale, he thought, had made the common evangelical mistake of failing to relate Christ's death to the work of the Holy Spirit and the life of the Church. He was also critical of Dale's idea of the cross as involving penal suffering, with Christ's having submitted to the 'actual penalty of sin.' His own thesis is virtually McLeod Campbell's, that of the 'perfect penitent'. Its statement, more elaborate than Campbell's, is prefaced by an examination of the terms 'punishment', 'penitence' and 'forgiveness'. Punishment denotes retribution, but it issues in penitence. Complete penitence, however, is impossible for a sinner, since 'the reality of sin in the self blunts the self's power of utter antithesis to sin'.[29] Yet complete penitence is inherently necessary. In other words, 'penitence, in the perfectness of its full meaning, is not even conceivably possible, except it be to be personally sinless'.[30] Such sinlessness is found only in the humanity of Christ, 'identically God', 'inclusively man'. 'Only He, who knew in Himself the measure of the holiness of God, could realize also, in the human nature He had made His own, the full depth of the alienation of sin from God, the real character of the penal averting of God's face.' What Christ offered the Father was not an expiatory sacrifice but humanity perfectly penitent and righteous, wholly in accord with and responsive to 'the essential character of Deity'.[31] By the cross atonement was wrought as an eternal, objective, historical fact, consummated adequately and once for all. But since forgiveness is 'inchoate' until the one forgiven becomes righteous, the objective reality must in turn be subjectively apprehended. This the Holy Spirit makes possible, the result being a 'transfiguring' in which at last, for the first time, self becomes fully self and the meaning of human personality is consummated and realized.[32]

Moberly's treatment of his great theme is a masterly expression of Christian sentiment, yet it met with a good deal of criticism, especially in regard to his view of penitence and forgiveness and his alleged confusion of the doctrine's objective and subjective aspects.[33] Lyttelton's account of the atonement also adopts the *motif* of representation rather than (although not to the exclusion of) propitiation. Sin gives rise to that sense of alienation from God which the ritual of sacrifice endeavours to overcome, and the most complete and typical form of the sacrificial idea was embodied in the Mosaic system. Yet even this was only a partial expedient, something external and provisional. The death of the sinless Christ alone answers to the demands of the conviction of sin and of the desire for forgiveness. That

28. J. K. Mozley, *Some Tendencies in British Theology* (1951), p. 25.
29. *Atonement and Personality*, p. 42.
30. *Ibid.*, p. 117.
31. *Ibid.*, p. 404.
32. *Ibid.*, p. 153.
33. See, e.g., Hastings Rashdall's observations in *The Journal of Theological Studies*, iii (1901), pp. 178–211. Moberly's argument was in essence repeated by his son, W. H. Moberly, in an essay in *Foundations*, ed. B. H. Streeter, published in 1912.

death, in the perspective of the New Testament, was a propitiatory sacrifice. Man could offer nothing acceptable; the offering had to be made by Christ, whom it behoved to die, the punishment being willingly accepted by him as an acknowledgement of the due reward of sin. But propitiation is not the only element; on the manward side Christ acted as humanity's representative by virtue of his assumption of complete human nature. Thus there was 'nothing artificial in His sin-bearing, for His human nature was so real and so perfect that He was involved, so to speak, in all the consequences of sin'. Hence 'only as His brethren, because He has united us to Him, are we enabled to plead the sacrifice which He has offered'. In its attempt to combine two distinct ideas the essay is not, however, altogether a success. The author, anxious to omit nothing upon which traditional faith and piety have fastened, whilst at the same time correcting the errors by which atonement theology has so often been marred, fails to shape his own views into a consistent whole. But he at least tried to render a more comprehensive account of the doctrine, and one more satisfying ethically.

To return, however, to *Lux Mundi*. Upon the remaining essays, other than Gore's, we need not dwell. In 'The Preparation of Christianity for Christ' Talbot sought to do what Temple had attempted in *Essays and Reviews*. Modern historical study, he thinks, has served less to diminish than to emphasize 'the wonder of an apparently unique convergence of lines of preparation' in the Hebrew and the Greek traditions respectively. Lock's paper on the Church approaches its subject empirically, seeing in it the final satisfaction of the social need of cooperation for life, knowledge and worship, a need which the complexity of modern civilization has served only to accentuate. Paget on the sacraments urges the prominence of the sacramental principle in the gospels and its immense subsequent importance for Christian thought and piety, pointing out, at the experiential level, the correspondence between the ministry of the sacraments and the diverse elements which compose the nature of man himself. Campion, on Christianity and politics, describes the Christian role in society as at once consecrating and purifying. The Christian view of political order rests on a conception of man and his destiny: family, State and Church are each and all places of training for a 'perfected common life in the City of God'. It is this heavenly City, moreover, which 'judges and corrects the splendour of earthly States'. Ottley's essay on Christian ethics, concluding the volume, aims within its compass at providing something of a formal treatise, in view of 'the absence of books of a genuine English growth'. In an appendix the writer expressed his belief that 'every transaction between man and man is to be regarded as *personal*, and therefore *ethical*. . . . To reason rightly on social problems we must ever have regard to *personality*. . . . Our problem is how to supersede the technical and legal relation by the personal'—one that remains no less pressing or difficult today, nearly a century later.

Charles Gore

The contribution which aroused most interest, as also, in some minds, the most disquiet, was the editor's own, on 'The Holy Spirit and Inspiration'. Gore's was the task of confronting the issue, by then inescapable, of the implications of biblical criticism for the historic faith. The array of patristic learning was on the face of it reassuring, however. The writer's opening theme is the life-giving work of the Holy Spirit: in nature (the 'body' of which the Spirit is the 'breath'), in man (created for divine sonship, 'for the life of the spirit'), in man's recovery from the sin into which he had fallen (the Spirit is at work in the righteous 'remnant' of God's chosen), in Christ (the perfect realization of man's destiny), and in the Church, the special and covenanted sphere of the Spirit's regular and uniform operation, 'the home where, in spite of sin and imperfection, is kept alive the picture of what the Christian life is'. Of the work of the Holy Spirit within the Church four characteristics are to be noted. It is social, for man cannot realize himself in isolation; but at the same time it nourishes individuality, the very idea of the Spirit's gift being that of an intenser because more individualized life. The Spirit is also to be understood as consecrating the whole of nature, material existence as well as spiritual; whilst his way of procedure is always gradual: 'He lifts man little by little, He condescends to man's infirmity.' In the Church the Spirit is personally present and continuously active.

The second section of the essay deals with the theology of the Holy Spirit, of whose being and action we have through revelation a real if limited knowledge. As simply stating the orthodox doctrine it calls for no special comment. The third and last section discloses the author's main purpose: to discuss the meaning and scope of the term inspiration when applied to Scripture. Gore begins by pointing out the danger of not consistently relating the idea to the rest of the Spirit's work in the Church. Indeed, 'it is becoming more difficult to believe in the Bible without believing in the Church'. When a man believes in Christ 'he will find himself in a position where alike the authority of his Master and the *communis sensus* of the society he belongs to, give into his hand certain documents and declare them inspired'. But the doctrine of inspiration is an article of the faith, not one of its bases, although as such an *article* it has a necessary place. The difficulties occur when one asks what exactly is meant by it. The question can be answered only by actual study of the Scriptures. These in the case of the Jews are 'a national literature marked by an unparalleled unity of purpose and character, a spiritual fabric which in its result we cannot but recognize as the action of the Divine Spirit'; and in the case of the Christian Church a uniquely authoritative interpretation of Christ to the world. Practically, 'to believe in the inspiration of the Holy Scriptures is to put ourselves to school with every part of the Old Testament, as of the New', despite evident imperfections and limitations. The problem, however, is in determining how far these latter—the human factor—may detract from the Bible's divine authority. Revelation, we claim, is conveyed in a historical process, but is a certain idealization or heightened dramatization of that process, as recorded, compatible with the aims of imparting truth? Can the concept of inspiration allow for the presence even of primitive myths? In reply Gore points out that the Church is not restrained by not having committed itself to a dogmatic definition of inspiration, a fact which he regards as fortunate and even providential.

A serious obstacle to the acceptance of modern criticism might, on the other hand, be made of Christ's own evident belief in the traditional Jewish view of the authorship of Scripture: his assumption, for example, that David was the author of Psalm 110 or that Jonah really had lived and been swallowed by a great fish. The difficulty can be met, Gore thinks, on the supposition that the Son of God, in becoming incarnate, 'emptied himself' of, or temporarily laid aside, certain of his divine attributes, among them his omniscience, thus submitting to the intellectual limitations of the time and circumstances in which he had chosen to manifest himself. In Gore's own words: 'He willed so to restrain the beams of His Deity as to observe the limits of the science of His age, and He puts Himself in the same relation to its historical knowledge.'[34] Here, almost in an aside, was that speculative doctrine of the *kenosis* which he was to elaborate in subsequent works, notably the Bampton lectures of 1891, *The Incarnation of the Son of God*, and the *Dissertations on Subjects connected with the Incarnation*, published in 1895; and to it we must return in a moment.[35] Meantime we are to remark Gore's general conclusion in the essay that although it is impossible to maintain the historicity of the Old Testament at all points, and although Jesus himself spoke as a Jew of his century, yet to represent the New Testament history as 'idealized' (and hence to some extent falsified) cannot be admitted 'without results disastrous to the Christian Creed'. There the absolute coincidence of idea and fact was vital. The Church must then insist that although the New Testament may contain errors of detail the history, in a general sense, is nevertheless entirely trustworthy. Upon this Gore was to remain adamant to the end.[36]

The Bampton lectures show their author at his best.[37] Their ground theme is that nature and grace are not antithetic, and the view that the supernatural is the unnatural is wholly mistaken. 'In whatever sense men believe in God, they believe that nature is God's ordinance, and nature's laws, and the knowledge of nature as far as it goes, the knowledge of God'.[38] Christ, therefore, who according to the Church's faith and doctrine is a supernatural person, is yet himself completely in harmony with nature and is in truth its fulfilment. Redemption does not repudiate

34. *Lux Mundi*, p. 360.
35. So called from the Greek word *kenoō*, used in Phil. ii, 7 (*heauton ekenōsen*, lit. 'he emptied himself'). Kenotic theories of the incarnation have been designed to explain what actually was involved in the Son of God's becoming man. The expression seems to have first been used by Ernst Sartorius in 1832, the idea denoted by it rapidly gaining favour among Lutheran theologians, who taught that the Son, in order to assume humanity, relinquished such attributes of deity as omnipotence and omniscience and with them his exercise of cosmic sovereignty. Thus G. Thomasius (*Beiträge z. kirchlichen Christologie*, 1845) held that the Logos laid aside the fulness of his divine nature in all respects touching his self-manifestation to men. See also the same author's *Christi Person und Werke*, 1853; and F. Loofs, in *Realencyclopädie f. protestantische Theologie und Kirche* (3. Aufl.), x, pp. 246-63.
36. Thus in 1929 he wrote: 'As far as historical evidence, strictly considered, goes, the Gospels supply us with the firm foundation for the belief in Jesus which appears in the Epistles and in the Creeds of the Church' (W. R. Matthews (ed.), *Dogma*, p. 80).
37. The Gifford lectures, *The Philosophy of the Good Life*, published in 1930, have by some been ranked as his finest work, and as the final statement of their author's own deepest convictions they may well be judged so. But the prevailing intellectual climate had changed greatly in the interval and the later book was less opportune and perhaps less forceful than the earlier.
38. *The Incarnation of the Son of God*, p. 29.

creation. 'Nature as a whole, moral and physical, demands Him to accomplish its yearnings and to restore its order.'[39] This had been the assurance of the ancient Greek Fathers, who insisted that the incarnation was on the lines of God's inherence in nature and that in Christ God's presence was only intensified. So in speaking of the incarnation as 'the crown of natural development in the universe' one would not be resorting to novel language. The God who reveals himself in nature, in the advance from inorganic to organic and from animal life to rational, offers his culminating self-disclosure in Christ, to whom all that precedes leads up. Seen thus he is no affront to reason: 'The first volume of the divine author in fact postulates a second.' It appears indeed as perfectly intelligible that God should take man's nature as the medium of his own self-revelation, without either annihilating manhood or compromising the Godhead. The claim, moreover, that Christ is supernatural is relative to what is considered natural, each new stage of life appearing supernatural from the point of view below it. Moral life is supernatural from the standpoint of the physical; and similarly Christ is supernatural as seen by man. But there is also discontinuity as well as continuity; for Christ not only is the consummation of nature, he is its restoration as well, after the ravages of sin.

Yet even here there is a manifest 'order' in things. Sin is essentially lawlessness, a violation of man's true nature, and must be seen as such if the 'naturalness' of Christ is to be appreciated. Approached in this way miracle loses its arbitrariness and alleged unnaturalness. It appears not as a contradiction of nature but as a vindication of its 'true, divine orderliness', previously obscured by sin. For a miracle is 'an event in physical nature which makes unmistakably plain the presence and direct action of God working for a moral end'. The incarnate Son of God could not therefore have been otherwise than miraculous. Science itself teaches that there is emergence, novelty, in nature; and on the Christian hypothesis Christ is a new creature whose coming must be expected to have exhibited new phenomena. God violates nature's superficial uniformity in the interests of a deeper law, of a profounder understanding of what nature itself really is.

This section of Gore's book points, in fact, the direction Anglican thought on the incarnation was to take for some years to come.[40] The evolutionary principle clearly provides a leading motive and what Gore here has to say, were it taken by itself, would appear entirely in line with the current immanentist idealism. But so to take it would be to misrepresent him seriously. Gore was not by any means uninfluenced by T. H. Green, but he was at no time strongly drawn to idealism, in this differing markedly from his friend Illingworth.[41] The prophetic, sin-conscious, sin-denouncing strain in his thinking was too potent to allow him to assimilate Christ to the natural order as commonly conceived by philosophers. But here his purpose is not so much to stress the singularity of Christ and his

39. *Ibid.*, p. 39.
40. See A. M. Ramsey, *op. cit.*, p. 18.
41. Only at one place in his published work did Gore acknowledge a debt to Green, in *Belief in God* (1921), p. viii. Green's influence on Gore, in the present writer's view, lay in the field of social ethics, although it is evident that virtually all Anglican theology during the years 1890 to 1920 took up a broadly idealist position.

discontinuity with the natural, as the apologetic one of showing that in the perspective of the Christian dogma 'the Word made flesh', although unique, does not represent a mere heteronomy which the reason cannot assimilate. He is unique indeed even on the humanitarian plane; but in his uniqueness he is not isolated, having set in motion 'a new development, which is the movement of the redeemed humanity'. And of this last Christ is the centre, 'the Head with the body, the Bridegroom with the bride'.[42]

It was Gore's aside, in the *Lux Mundi* essay, on the problem of Christ's human knowledge which especially distressed Liddon, for whom the gospel history implied without a doubt that 'The knowledge infused into the human soul of Jesus was ordinarily and practically equivalent to omniscience'.[43] This, however, was an idea which Gore found objectionable. Since Christ was God in manhood it is certain that he at all times *possessed* the divine as well as the human consciousness and nature. But Gore also considered that the self-sacrifice of the incarnation lay particularly in Christ's refraining to exercise what he possessed in order that he might live under the conditions of a true manhood. There were genuinely things which on earth he did not know.[44] That the concept of the 'self-emptying' of deity involved theoretical problems Gore realized. To the question, for example, of the Son's cosmic functions he felt he could give only 'a very hesitating and partial answer'. On the one hand, as the Christian theological tradition had consistently maintained, the work of the Son could in no way have been interrupted by the incarnation; on the other, the Son in becoming incarnate, must reasonably be held to have accepted the limitations of humanity as an essential element in his self-sacrifice.

In the Bamptons these matters are dealt with only briefly, in an appended note. Gore's developed theory of the *kenosis* is set out with fulness in the *Dissertations*. He was himself well aware—much more so than any of the older school of High Churchmen—that New Testament criticism had raised the whole issue of the gospel's historicity and that a modern theologian is bound to view Christ's manhood in a historical perspective. In this regard 'much of the patristic and all of the medieval theology' was inadequate.[45] From the pen of so adept a patristic scholar such words carried weight and in conservative quarters gave offence. Gore's use of the kenotic idea had indeed been immediately anticipated by at least two Anglican theologians—in standpoint far apart from each other—T. K. Cheyne and A. J. Mason.[46] But it was he who unquestionably gave it currency and, we may say, considering his personal standing in the Church of England, respectability. Gore was a High Churchman, an 'Anglo-Catholic', yet one also who held that the Church, whilst preserving continuity in doctrine, should be free to 're-express its theological mind, as it has so often already done, in view of fresh developments in the intellectual, moral and social life of man',[47] a conviction he had made plain in

42. *The Incarnation of the Son of God*, pp. 51f.
43. *The Divinity of Our Lord*, 14th ed, p. 474.
44. *The Incarnation of the Son of God*, pp. 265f.
45. *Dissertations on Subjects connected with the Incarnation*, p. 9.
46. See Cheyne's Bampton lectures on *The Origin and Religious Content of the Psalter* (1889), p. 25, and Mason's *The Faith of the Gospel* (1887), pp. 152–9 (1905 edn.).
47. *Dissertations*, p. 213.

Lux Mundi. A turn of phrase Gore was wont to use was that in the incarnation Christ had 'abandoned (or surrendered) his prerogatives', or at any rate the exercise of them. He perhaps was being deliberately imprecise.[48] All he wanted to ensure was that, under the conditions of the mortal incarnate life the divine Son 'did, and as it would appear habitually—doubtless by a voluntary action of his own self-limiting and self-restraining love—cease from the exercise of those functions and powers, including the divine omniscience, which would have been incompatible with a truly human experience'.[49] The Godhead, as he chose to put it, was 'energizing' under the conditions and limitations of manhood. But on the cosmic functions of the Logos Gore continued to maintain what he deemed a proper reserve. Such functions, 'in another sphere', had of course been exercised during the earthly life, but the humiliation and self-limitation of the incarnate state was, it must be supposed, wholly consonant with them. What in fact really concerned Gore was the *moral* force of the kenotic principle. Given this he was, it seems, prepared to let the metaphysical difficulties go unanswered, as constituting a problem essentially unanswerable.

To attempt to deal with the large volume of criticism which Gore's theory provoked during the earlier years of the present century, when kenotist Christianity was still in the forefront of theological discussion, would take us beyond our period.[50] Suffice it to say that much of it was directed against its dubious scriptural basis, particularly the famous passage in Philippians, the language of which, as D. M. Baillie urged, is that of poetry more than metaphysics.[51] Hastings Rashdall considered the theory to demand so complete a break in the consciousness of the Son as to render it ridiculous to say that it is consistent with the Word's being unchanged.[52] Gore's phraseology, with his seemingly reckless use of words like 'abandonment' and 'surrender', was also found to be open to objection. This in particular was William Sanday's point.[53] The difficulties which the kenotic argument presents may well have been lessened by Weston,[54] Forsyth[55] and Mackintosh.[56] But William Temple, in *Christus Veritas* (1924), could still look on kenotic theories as 'intolerable' and reject the principle as involving 'something dangerously close to mythology'.[57] Creed, however, is less ready to condemn, and

---

48. In the original edition of the *Dissertations* Gore had spoken of 'a real abandonment of divine prerogatives *and attributes* by the Eternal Son within a certain sphere' (p. 206, italics ours). His modification of the wording in the second edition evidently indicates his awareness of the metaphysical difficulties it could have raised.
49. *Dissertations*, p. 95.
50. In 1938 J. M. Creed wrote that 'though kenotic doctrine is no longer so much in favour as it was, I should think it probable that a majority today of those among us who have a Christology which they are prepared to state and defend, are still kenoticists' (*The Divinity of Jesus Christ*, p. 75). O. C. Quick, in *Doctrines of the Creed* (1938), stoutly upholds the principle.
51. *God was in Christ* (1948), p. 94.
52. *God and Man*, ed. H. D. A. Major and F. L. Cross (1930), p. 95.
53. *Christologies, Ancient and Modern* (1910), pp. 76f.
54. Frank Weston, *The One Christ* (1907).
55. P. T. Forsyth, *The Person and Place of Christ* (1909).
56. H. R. Mackintosh, *The Person of Jesus Christ* (1912).
57. See especially *op. cit.*, pp. 161ff.

whilst not arguing expressly for kenoticism he nevertheless commits himself to the opinion that 'if we take seriously both the human conditions of the life of Jesus and the theory of His personal identity and continuity with the eternal Word, then a kenotic Christology seems to be indispensable'.[58] What Gore did was to compel theologians to take the human conditions of Jesus's life seriously, and no Christology could nowadays gain attention which, whatever else it might succeed in doing, failed in this.[59]

One other but a signal contribution by Gore to theological debate at the turn of the century remains to be noted: his study of eucharistic doctrine in *The Body of Christ*, published in 1901. On this subject it remains one of the best works by an English divine, and E. L. Mascall was right in deploring the undeserved neglect into which it has fallen.[60] That the eucharist is 'the extension of the incarnation' is an idea, he claims, not only Tractarian but patristic, and he himself willingly adopts it. But it would be truer to the turn of Gore's thought to refer the expression to the Church itself, or at all events to the sacraments in general, with the eucharist as the special medium or focus of the divine presence.[61] The sacramental principle, he holds, is consonant with the entire procedure of God in creation and redemption, as also in the twofold nature of man, compounded as he is of body and spirit (the body being the spirit's organ).[62] Opposition of body and spirit can draw no sanction from the New Testament. Gore further considers that between the incarnation and the sacraments there is an analogy of fundamental principle, even though it may not admit of being carried out in detail. In communion it is the whole Christ who is received, not merely 'the Spirit for our spirits, or the teaching for our intellects'. Touching the eucharistic sacrifice Gore strongly denies any repetition of Calvary. Its true meaning is determined by its relation to the offering of the glorified Christ in heaven.

> The sacrifice of the Son of Man once offered in death has been accepted in glory. In the power of that sacrifice Christ ever lives, our high priest and perpetual intercessor, the continually accepted propitiation of our sins unto the end of time. All that we need to do and can do is to make thankful commemoration, in His way and by His Spirit, of His redemptive sufferings, and to unite ourselves to His perpetual intercession when He presents Himself for us in the heavenly places, or as He makes Himself present among us in our eucharistic worship.[63]

The description of his theological and ecclesiastical standpoint which seems best to have satisfied Gore himself is that of 'liberal Catholicism', an expression he

---

58. *Op. cit.*, p. 136.
59. See K. E. Kirk's Charles Gore Memorial Lecture, *The Coherence of Christian Doctrines* (1950), p. 9.
60. See *Corpus Christi* (1953), p. 138.
61. Cp. *The Incarnation of the Son of God*, p. 218: 'For this primarily the Church exists: to be the Spirit-bearing body, and that is to be the bearer of Christ, the great "Christopher", perpetuating, in a new, but not less real way, the presence of the Son of Man in the world.'
62. *The Body of Christ*, p. 40.
63. *Ibid.*, p. 183.

frequently employed.[64] But by it he meant nothing idiosyncratic or exotic. He was a liberal Catholic simply because he was a member of the Church of England, an Anglican. Anglicanism as he understood it was but a convenient name for liberal Catholicism as it had developed under the historic conditions, political and cultural, of the English people.[65] There was, he judged, no doubt about what the English Church had stood for since the Reformation, when it inherited the ancient faith and order of Christendom, other than a Catholicism reformed and preserved in accordance with the teaching of Scripture. This was his firm conviction throughout life. The spiritual test was necessary as the guarantee of liberty against the pressures of ecclesiastical authority and an inordinate dogmatism. But the Church of England did not attempt to make 'the Bible and the Bible only' the fixed norm of its doctrine. History also plays its part: Catholicism, that is, is identifiable as a historical tradition within which Scripture has been interpreted in terms of a continuing experience under varying circumstances. Of this experience the Catholic creeds and the decisions of the ecumenical councils are at once the embodiment and the safeguard. That Bible, creeds and councils are in essential agreement Gore did not for a moment doubt and any attempt to separate them he steadfastly opposed. On the other hand the claims of reason, of which the best Anglican divinity at all periods has never been oblivious, had also to be met. In the sixteenth century and after the English Church had opened her arms alike to the new learning, to the new appeal to Scripture, to the freedom of historical criticism and to the duty of private judgment.[66] Anglican Catholicism believed in freedom as a principle and thus was bound to repudiate an absolutist authoritarianism of whatever kind. 'True authority does not issue edicts to suppress men's personal judgment or render its action unnecessary, but is like the authority of a parent, which invigorates and encourages, even while it restrains and guides the growth of our individuality.'[67]

To some Anglicans of more ultramontane sympathies—Lord Halifax, for example—Gore seemed indeed too much a Protestant, if not a 'modernist'. Were the charge meant to imply only the exercise of personal responsibility in the matter of faith he would certainly not have rejected it. But to the type of liberalism which

---

64. See J. Carpenter, *Gore: a Study of Liberal Catholic Thought* (1960), Ch. 2. For the use of the term in a Roman Catholic context see Appendix III below.
65. 'I have always maintained that we in the Church of England represent a liberal Catholicism' (*The Basis of Anglican Fellowship in Faith and Organization*, 1914, p. 4. Cp. p. 23).
66. In the earliest of his published works, a paper on 'The Nature of Faith and the Condition of its Exercise', privately printed and circulated in 1878, he had written: 'The Church of England truly adopts a *via media* in that she will side neither with those who, in confidence of the powers of the unaided reason, would have each man his own pope; nor with those who, in despite of their own capacity to find out truth at all for themselves, would submit their reason once and for all, by a single act, to an external, infallible voice. She will not acquiesce in this Manichaean severance of reason and authority' (p. 28).
67. *Roman Catholic Claims* (11th ed.), p. 54. This book was first published in 1884. A second, enlarged edition appeared in 1899.

in his opinion tampered with the Catholic creeds he was implacably hostile.[68] Intransigence towards modernism became in fact increasingly characteristic of his policy as a diocesan bishop. On the substantial historicity of the events in which Christianity originated, as presented in the New Testament, he was ever insistent. Doctrines of an overtly metaphysical or symbolic nature might admit of differing modes of interpretation, but not the historical affirmations; and to the end Gore made the historical claims of Christianity the foundation of his apologetic method. Among such claims were the literal truth of Christ's virgin birth and bodily resurrection, express assent to which he deemed an obligation incumbent at least upon the clergy.[69] For these doctrines, to his mind, could not be taken in any merely figurative sense, although he conceded that the ascension may be placed in a rather different category, the idea of Christ's *upward* motion to his final, heavenly state being necessarily symbolical, since heaven itself is not a locality. But the virgin birth and the resurrection had been actual historical occurrences, fully capable of description in the language of ordinary experience. To object to them on the *a priori* ground of the incredibility of miracle seemed to him totally illegitimate inasmuch as nature is not a closed system excluding all possibility of intrusion from without. Christian philosophy recognizes the reign of law, but law may pertain to a higher or a lower order of things; and in the interest of the higher the divine action may fittingly abrogate the lower. He who imposes law may also suspend or transcend it. In any case 'the point of a divine miracle, as the Bible conceives it, is not to be a mere portent, but a sure indication that the moral will of God is supreme in the world'.[70]

As time went by Gore appeared more and more of a conservative: a Catholic assuredly, although never of the 'Romanizing' kind; but a liberal, at least as measured by the criteria of the Churchmen's (later the Modern Churchmen's) Union, by no means. He even seemed a conservative by the standards of a younger school of High Churchmen more open to the influences of what he himself regarded as a dangerously radical type of New Testament criticism, a school whose religious philosophy, accordingly, was based less upon the assumed authenticity of Christ's historical claims than upon the pragmatic value of the Christian experience itself. However, Gore's influence upon Anglican opinion throughout the first quarter of the present century was greater than that of any other living divine. W. R. Inge, a thinker of a very different mental cast and an always abrasive critic of

68. 'There must', he wrote in 1903, 'be no compromise as regards the Creeds .... If those who live in an atmosphere of intellectual criticism become incapable of such sincere public profession of belief as the Creed contains, the Church must look to recruit her ministry from classes still capable of a more simple and unhesitating faith' (*Report of the Church Congress of 1903*, p.17). Later, when bishop of Birmingham, he declared: 'I have taken occasion before now to make it evident that, as far as I can secure it, I will admit no one into this diocese, or into Holy Orders, to minister for the congregation, who does not *ex animo* believe the Creeds' (*The New Theology and the Old Religion*, 1907, p. 162).
69. 'Our Church leaves lay folk to their own discretion, but it does make specific requirements on the clergy, its officers' (*The Basis of Anglican Fellowship*, p. 7). Cp. *The Clergy and the Creeds* (1887), p. 28.
70. *Belief in God* (1921), p. 238.

Anglo-Catholicism, deemed him 'one of the most powerful spiritual forces in our generation', a view in no way exaggerative.[71] Gore combined a wealth of theological learning with great independence of judgment, intense moral fervour and the strength of a personality never deterred by opposition. He was a teacher, prophet and natural leader of men, and among his successors in the Church of England only William Temple is to be compared with him.

Liberalism, Anglican and Free Church

'A devout Christian', it has been said, 'may be a Liberal Protestant or a Liberal Catholic; he can hardly be a Liberal without any qualification'.[72] Liberalism in western Christianity is bound, that is, to qualify one or the other of its two divergent traditions. Gore and his fellow–contributors to *Lux Mundi* represented a liberalizing of the High Church or 'Catholic' strain in the Church of England; but what of the Low Church or Evangelical? How far did it show itself responsive to the demands of the changed and changing cultural environment? The Evangelical party had never been noted for its interest in or concern for theological learning or the relations between Christian thought and contemporary science and scholarship. On the contrary, its aims were strictly practical and the religious atmosphere it tended to create (and certainly found congenial) was predominantly emotional. Intellectual curiosity in religious matters is eschewed as misleading and purposeless. An old-fashioned orthodoxy, centred on the doctrine of the atonement as a penal substitutionary sacrifice, was all, theologically speaking, that it had to offer. This included a largely Old Testament theism, a naïve supernaturalism, a literalist view of the Bible and an eschatology which admitted heaven and hell but not purgatory. The evangelical idea of salvation was still prevailingly individualist.[73] Such attitudes would not yield readily to new influences from outside the traditional religious sphere.

Nevertheless the party was not quite without its scholars; and of them one of the most learned was Henry Wace (1836–1924), dean of Canterbury, an authority on the sixteenth-century Protestant Reformers and a hard–hitting controversialist.[74] Another was the Church historian, H. M. Gwatkin (1844–1914), whose work on the early Church, and especially the Arian controversy, is still of real value.[75] Yet another respected figure was H. C. G. Moule (1841–1920) a fellow of Trinity College, Cambridge, and a former pupil of Lightfoot's, who after holding the

---

71. *Outspoken Essays: First Series* (1919), p. 134. The essay on 'Bishop Gore and the Church of England' was written in 1908.
72. W. R. Inge, *Vale* (1934), p. 74.
73. Even Queen Victoria disapproved of 'ultra-Evangelicals' as narrow-minded. See W. F. Monypenny and G. E. Buckle, *The Life of Benjamin Disraeli*, p. 45.
74. His editing (with W. Smith) of *The Dictionary of Christian Biography* (1880–86) was carried out with admirable impartiality and complete competence.
75. Notably *Studies of Arianism* (1882), *The Arian Controversy* (1889) and *Early Church History to 313* (1909).

Norrisian professorship of divinity succeeded Westcott as bishop of Durham.[76] But his theological conservatism, seemingly impervious to every current trend, never wavered, and his outlook remained that of a bygone age. The Oxford Evangelical, F. J. Chavasse, afterwards a much–respected bishop of Liverpool, although less of a scholar than Moule, was more open–minded, realizing that critical theories of the Bible's literary history could not be refuted by being ignored and that evolution might after all have some relevance to theology. But the day of Liberal Evangelicalism, as represented by such men as V. F. Storr[77] and, somewhat later, C. E. Raven, had not yet dawned.

It is probable, however, that the real roots of liberal Evangelicalism lay in what had already become known, as far back as the 1850s, as the 'Broad Church', a term first used, it would seem, by W. J. Conybeare in an article in *The Edinburgh Review* for 1853. Maurice, although a man of broad views, sharply repudiated the label when applied to himself. Jowett, on the other hand, could very well have been classed as such, and his friend Stanley would have welcomed the name. 'Broad' too was the standpoint of the Cambridge historian, Sir James Seeley, whose *Ecce Homo*, published anonymously in 1865, aroused a good deal of attention. The book was reviewed by Dean Church in *The Guardian* of 7 February 1866, and was commended as 'a protest against the stiffness of all cast-iron systems, and a warning against trusting what is worn out'.[78] Gladstone too gave it fairly favourable notice. Seeley's aim was to depict the central figure of the gospels in a way that a historian as distinct from a theologian might see it, although the attempt was read by many as intending to reduce Christ to purely human status, despite the fact that the author did not deny Jesus's miraculous powers. Perhaps the common opinion was expressed by Westcott when he complained that 'it is this so-called morality as "the sum of the Gospel" which makes Christianity so powerless now'.[79] A sequel, entitled *Natural Religion*, appeared in 1882, but did not repeat its predecessor's popular success. Its argument is the familiar one that nature provides a truer revelation of God's presence and purpose than does miracle. Another professed liberal was E. A. Abbott, whose *The Kernel and the Husk*, was published (like *Ecce Homo*, anonymously)· in 1886. Abbott defended the practice of clergymen who, whilst personally in doubt on certain doctrines, continued to affirm them in the course of public worship. The priest reciting the offices, he contended, was stating not his private convictions but the formal teaching of the Church.

A distinguished Broad Church bishop was William Boyd Carpenter (1841–1918), whose 1887 Bampton lectures on *The Permanent Elements in Religion* were a plea for the serious study of comparative religion, not least as a means of testing the truth of the Christian faith itself. The ethical criterion in all instances must, he thought, be held supreme, and judged by this the Christian religion had done more than any other to promote morality. Unfortunately in the past, all too often, orthodoxy had been preferred to ethics.

76. He was also first principal of the Evangelical theological college at Cambridge, Ridley Hall, founded in 1881.
77. Author of *The Development of English Theology in the Nineteenth Century*, 1800–1860 (1913).
78. *Occasional Papers,* ii, pp. 133ff.
79. A. Westcott, *op. cit.*, ii, p. 289.

The eager and shallow dogmatist who worshipped not God, but clung vehemently and immorally to his creed, demanded intellectual assent. Heedless of the need of intellectual honesty, or of the ethical significance of the creed, he saw no alternative between the declaration of assent to a theological proposition and the eternal damnation of a human soul. He made it possible for men to say, and to say it with a measure of truth, that orthodoxy was the sin against the Holy Ghost.[80]

In his Donnellan lectures at Dublin on *The Witness of Religious Experience* (1914) he noted in such experience the three stages of dependence, fellowship and progress, each associated, in Christianity, with men's relations with the Father, the Son and the Holy Spirit respectively. In this process the religious consciousness becomes a faculty of spiritual verification. Yet the experience of Christ himself was unique. 'He is outside the religion of those storm centres which sin, self-reproach, remorse, and rooted selfishness occasion in others . . . . He is a pattern after which all may strive, but he is not a type whose counterpart can be found in any human being.'[81] In 1898 Boyd Carpenter founded a clergy training college at Ripon, of which diocese he was bishop, with the express purpose of training ordinands in accordance with liberal ideals. It later moved to Oxford where, however, under the name of Ripon Hall, its record was such as to raise doubts of how far liberalism can be 'institutionalized' without producing the very faults which it decries when visible elsewhere.[82]

The question of free-thinking clerics using traditional formularies was provocatively raised by Henry Sidgwick, although himself a layman, in an article in *The International Journal of Ethics* of April 1896 on 'The Ethics of Conformity'. It was an issue he had had to face in his own career, and one on which for conscience' sake he had many years previously resigned his fellowship at Trinity College, Cambridge.[83] His argument was that a degree of latitude could be

---

80. *The Permanent Elements in Religion*, p. 276.
81. *The Witness of Religious Experience*, pp. 89f.
82. See H. D. A. Major, *The Life and Letters of William Boyd Carpenter* (1925), ch. viii. Ripon Hall has long since merged with Cuddesdon Theological College—an institution with very different theological and ecclesiastical traditions—at Cuddesdon, Oxon.
83. Clerical subscription to the Prayer Book and Articles had been rendered easier by the passing of the Clerical Subscription Act of 1865, which instead of demanding 'unfeigned assent and consent to all and everything' contained in them now permitted clergymen to declare only 'a general assent' thereto, affirming their belief in 'the doctrine of the Church of England as therein set forth to be agreeable to the Word of God'. See Chadwick, *The Victorian Church*, Part ii, pp. 132–5. (A similar relaxation, in the form of a Declaratory Statement, was allowed to Scottish presbyterian ministers, first in the United Presbyterian Church in 1879, and then in the Free Church in 1892, although it was not until 1910 that this concession was granted in the established Church of Scotland. Sidgwick himself, however, was not among those who, like some Broad Churchmen, argued that (in the words of H. B. Wilson), 'the legal obligation is the measure of the moral one'. As he put it (in a private letter to Mrs A. H. Clough) it was his 'painful conviction that the previously lax subscription is not perfectly conscientious in the case of many subscribers'; indeed, that 'those who subscribe laxly from the highest motives are responsible for the degradation of the moral and religious feeling that others suffer'. What strikes the modern reader is the concern then shown for the *ethics* of subscription—maintenance of the subscriber's personal moral integrity—as compared with the relative lack of interest in the actual truth of the matters as to which subscription was required.

permitted to the laity, but in the case of clergymen assent to statements which they do not personally believe is dishonest and to be condemned. Some months later, and in the same journal, an answer was given by Hastings Rashdall, then a tutor of New College, Oxford. This article was a plea for greater freedom of interpretation and in the matter of conformity the right of individual judgment. Some disparity between personal belief and formal profession is, he contended, all but inevitable and is recognized to be so by men of all parties; nor was this to be regretted: reinterpretation of ancient formulae is necessary if the life of the Church is to continue, a principle applying to the creed as well as to the Articles. On the particular problem of the virgin birth, always a test case, he pointed out that it was not in the original creed of Nicea and is not in fact essential to the doctrine of the incarnation.[84]

Rashdall's main publications in philosophy and theology fall outside our period, but he had already gained high reputation as a historian with his impressive volumes on *The Universities of Europe in the Middle Ages* (1895). His position as a theological liberal was made evident in a collection of university sermons published in 1898 with the title *Doctrine and Development*. This he described as an effort at theological reconstruction, while denying that 'liberal' theology meant only 'vague and indefinite' theology. All theology arises, he believes, from the attempt to set the facts of the moral and religious consciousness in due relation to science and history. The place of development must be conceded and with it the obsoleteness of not a little of the teaching of the past. Theories of verbal inspiration are plainly no longer tenable; but also difficult for the modern mind are theories of the atonement which in their day seemed proper to an Anselm or a Luther but which are felt now to be objectionable on moral grounds. Already indeed was Rashdall defending that Abelardian doctrine which was to form the thesis of his subsequent Bampton lectures, *The Idea of Atonement in Christian Theology* (1915), that the death of Christ—'the culminating act of a self-sacrificing *life* '[85]—has its essential meaning in the example which it sets us. He also, in a sermon of 1889, anticipated Gore's discussion of the limitation of Christ's knowledge and indicated the need for a type of kenotic theory which in certain directions went beyond Gore's own. He did not think kenoticism incompatible with Catholic doctrine but stressed that 'we should in all our teaching put the simpler presentations—the moral, the spiritual, the personal aspects—of Christ's divinity foremost'.[86] In an address on the doctrine of the Trinity given in Balliol College chapel on Trinity Sunday 1894 he sketches his characteristic 'Sabellian' view—for which he claims the authority of Augustine and Aquinas—that in the context of trinitarian theology the word 'person' requires a meaning very different from its usual modern acceptation. Those who framed what are still the acknowledged orthodox formulae could have had

---

84. On Sidgwick's own attitude see D. G. James, *Henry Sidgwick: Science and Faith in Victorian England* (1970). On the wider issue of the ethics of religious belief, and in particular of subscription to religious formularies, see J. C. Livingston, *The Ethics of Belief: an Essay on the Victorian Religious Consciousness* (American Academy of Religion publication, 1974).
85. *Doctrine and Development*, p. 129.
86. *Ibid.*, p. 55.

no such idea in mind, whereas most people today, 'at least in their orthodox moments, when they are trying to realize to themselves the doctrine of the Holy Trinity, think of the three Persons as three distinct beings, three consciousnesses, three minds, three wills'.[87] God is not three personalities, but three 'essential' properties or activities, distinguishable as Power, Wisdom and Will (or Love) respectively.[88]

Rashdall was firmly convinced both of the possibility of a natural theology and its necessity if Christian teaching is to have a sound foundation. His position hereon is set out in the essay 'The Ultimate Basis of Theism' which he in 1902 contributed to *Contentio Veritatis*, a volume of composite authorship broadly representative of the liberal standpoint; as too in that on 'Personality Human and Divine' included in a symposium, edited by Henry Stout and entitled *Personal Idealism*, which appeared in the same year.[89] It is a Green-inspired idealism, but one which emphasizes the reality and importance of individual persons or spirits. Rashdall argues the existence of God in a manner reminiscent of Berkeley. The world depends on mind, but not on finite minds. One must assume therefore a *divine* mind, an infinite intelligence creative of both material and spiritual reality. There are, of course, difficulties in the way of ascribing personality to God, yet personality is the highest category we know and if God is mind he must be so *sensu eminentiori*. Also as a Person coexisting with other persons he cannot be identified with the all-inclusive Absolute: consciousnesses are mutually exclusive. Accordingly God is limited to the extent at least of not including his creation. As rational and moral he represents the power of good in the universe and thus gives assurance of the final defeat of evil. Rashdall's theism is therefore ethical to its roots. With mysticism he had no sympathy and any apologetic appeal to 'religious experience'—a type of argument coming into favour among his contemporaries—he distrusted as too subjective and tending to irrationalism.

By the close of the century Rashdall was already prominent as a leader of liberal opinion in the Church of England, and throughout the next two decades his pre-eminence in this respect was unquestionable, his standing indeed among Anglican liberals being analogous to that of Gore among High Churchmen. The place of his lifelong friend, William Ralph Inge (1860–1954), famous later as dean of St Paul's—the 'gloomy dean' of popular journalism—was more equivocal. In many ways Inge was emphatically not a liberal. Politically and socially his attitudes were not only conservative but anti-democratic. Democracy, he was wont to observe, 'dissolves communities into individuals and collects them again into mobs'.[90] Towards socialism his feelings were hostile and he had scant sympathy even with Gore's diluted and Christianized form of it. 'The position of a Church which would sell itself to the Labour party would be truly ignominious.'[91] A

87. *Ibid.*, pp. 23f.
88. Rashdall's interpretation of Augustine's and Aquinas's trinitarianism has since, however, been challenged. See, e.g., E. J. Bicknell in *Essays Catholic and Critical* (3rd ed., 1920), pp. 148–50. Cp. Ramsey, *From Gore to Temple*, pp. 185ff.
89. See also Rashdall's 'open' lectures at Cambridge, *Philosophy and Religion*, published in 1909.
90. *Outspoken Essays: First Series*, p. ii.
91. *Ibid.*, p.131.

thoroughgoing Platonist, he would have favoured the rule of an intellectual *élite*, though one preferably schooled at Eton. Himself of no party ecclesiastically, he did not share the regret of Harnack and other liberal Protestants at the 'intellectualizing' of Christianity by Hellenism. For the Anglo-Catholics with their supposed concern for what he called 'ecclesiastical millinery' he had only contempt. He was a 'modernist' after his fashion, but of modernism as it showed itself in the Roman Catholic Church at the beginning of this century he was altogether censorious. Its treatment of the New Testament, especially at the hands of Loisy, he thought destructive: 'What more, it may well be asked, have rationalist opponents of Christianity ever said, in their efforts to tear up the Christian religion by the roots, than we find here admitted by Catholic apologists?'[92] And to its pragmatist philosophy his reaction was one of distaste and suspicion: 'Any assertion about fact which commends itself to the will and affections and which is proved by experience to furnish nutriment to the spiritual life, may [in Modernist eyes] be adhered to without scruple.' Like Rashdall, Inge was an 'intellectualist' in his religious philosophy, but Rashdall's dislike of mysticism was the opposite of his own thinking, in which mystical experience, rather broadly interpreted, occupied a central place.

At the time (1889) of his appointment as tutor of Hertford College, Oxford, where he at first had Rashdall for a colleague, he had formed no very definite philosophical or theological opinions of his own. He as yet had only slight acquaintance with the literature of mysticism and had read nothing of Plotinus, whose thought was years later to provide the subject of his most considerable work, the Gifford lectures of 1917–18.[93] It was in fact during this Oxford period that he took up the serious study of Neo-Platonism, and in 1896 determined to make a name for himself as an authority on Christian mysticism as well as an essayist and a preacher.[94] The outcome was his Bampton lectures, published in 1899.[95] The treatment adopted is historical and expository and such indications as are given of the author's personal views hardly amount to a philosophy of mysticism. However the pattern of Inge's later thinking is already emerging: a kind of intuitional rationalism for which the mystical experience becomes an expression, not of mere subjective emotion, but of the entire personality, with reason as its controlling principle. It could be said that for Inge mysticism was a philosophy of the spirit, resting on an apprehension of absolute values. As he phrased it in one of his later writings: 'The goal of philosophy is the same as the goal of religion—perfect knowledge of the Perfect'.[96]

Like Rashdall, Inge contributed to *Contentio Veritatis*, with an essay on 'The Person of Christ' and another on 'The Sacraments'. The former is the more satisfactory of the two—of sacramentalism Inge never acquired any real understanding—and is indeed one of the best of his shorter writings, well thought

---

92. *Ibid.*, pp. 152f.
93. *The Philosophy of Plotinus* (2 vols, 1918).
94. See Adam Fox, *Dean Inge* (1960), p. 60.
95. *Christian Mysticism* (reissued 1912).
96. *Contemporary British Philosophy*, Series I (ed. H. J. Muirhead, 1925), p. 191.

out and lucid in statement. It is imbued with his sense of religion as a matter essentially present and practical. Religion, he says, may relate to both history and science, but its interest is in neither.

> Religion, when it confines itself to its own province, never speaks in the past tense. It is concerned only with what is, not with what was. History as history is not its business. And abstract science, which concerns itself with relations which prevail between phenomena, without reference to ultimate truth, is not its business either... Errors in history, or errors in science, do not save or damn. Errors in religion are always due to what Plato calls 'the lie in the soul' ... What is the truth, in the spiritual order, which it is intended to protect by the doctrines of the virgin birth, resurrection and ascension? The answer is plain: it is the identification of the man Christ Jesus with the Word of God.[97]

Inge remains a thinker not easy to place. An individualist, he disliked institutionalism in religion and despised its familiar manifestations. On the other hand, his antipathy for mere emotionalism was if anything even stronger. His orthodox belief in the incarnation was never qualified by immanentist or 'adoptionist' theories, nor severed from its moorings—despite his Platonism—in the historical figure of Jesus of Nazareth. Nor again was the name of modernist very congenial to him except in so far as it stood for liberality of mind and a critical discrimination. He believed, rather, in the age-old values of European civilization and in the virtues of knowledge and the rational understanding whilst holding steadfastly to the conviction that divine truth is ever accessible to the enlightened spirit.[98]

In the Church of England, then, on one side and on another, the traditional positions were being increasingly modified if not abandoned. But what of the Nonconformists, or the Free Churches as they were now coming to be called? How did they welcome the new trends? Evangelical piety had as a rule been distrustful of exposing religion to worldly culture, yet could the immunity any longer be preserved? Apart from the very small Unitarian sect Protestant dissent was throughout the greater part of the century inconspicuous for its contributions to theological or philosophical thought. Its concerns were practical, its spiritual tone more pietistic than intellectual or scholarly. In so far, however, as any real theological interest existed it was to be found among the Congregationalists, and towards the end of our period the Congregational Union counted some distinguished teachers in its membership.

First in seniority was Robert William Dale (1829–1895), a famed preacher and educationalist and pastor of the well-known Carr's Lane Chapel in Birmingham. Dale deplored the persistent lack of interest shown in systematic theology not only among pastoral ministers but, less excusably, in the theological colleges. To this he attributed 'very much of the poverty and confusion of theological thought, very much of the religious uncertainty, and some of the more serious defects in the

97. *Contentio Veritatis,* pp. 90f.
98. See his presidential address to the 1925 annual conference of the Churchmen's Union, published in *The Modern Churchman* in the September of that year. Inge was president of the Union from 1924 until 1934.

practical religious life' of Victorian nonconformity.[99] Dale's own one major undertaking in this field was his volume on *The Atonement*, based on a series of public lectures and published in 1875. Taking his stand on a progressive but fundamentally orthodox evangelicalism, he was concerned to maintain, as against the views of such men as Jowett or the American theologian, Horace Bushnell, the juridical significance of Christ's atoning death while at the same time trying to avoid the all too familiar legalism. Particularly impressive is his handling of the New Testament data.[100] On the axiom that punishment is 'pain and loss inflicted for the violation of a law'[101] Dale concludes that a sound doctrine of atonement will not exclude the penal element. Christ, however, vindicated the law of righteousness, 'not by inflicting suffering on the sinner, but by enduring suffering Himself'.[102] He received the due penalty of sin, that is, by actually submitting to the authority of the *principle* which such penalty expresses.[103] But although Dale insists on the priority of a 'legal' or 'objective' view he allows that it does not represent the whole truth. Christ's death was also a demonstration of God's love by which 'a real change is wrought in us, a change by which we are reconciled to God'. Further, Dale rejects any idea of an imputation of sin to Christ—'a legal fiction'—and dismisses as mere rhetoric the notion of a ransom paid by the divine mercy to the divine justice. Christ's sufferings were not, in the strict sense, the penalties of sin at all, but, as pains freely endured, were accepted by God as the equivalent thereto—a theory suggesting the influence of Grotius.[104]

A more distinctively liberal thinker was Dale's learned Scottish contemporary, Andrew Martin Fairbairn (1838–1912), principal of the Airedale Theological College, Bradford, from 1877 to 1886 and subsequently of Mansfield College, Oxford. As a young man Fairbairn had studied in Germany and had been affected by the teaching of Dorner, Tholuck and Hengstenberg. His chief works are *The Place of Christ in Modern Theology*, published in 1893, and *The Philosophy of the Christian Religion*, dedicated to R. W. Dale, which appeared some nine years later and contained his mature reflexions on the nature and meaning of Christianity. He was also the author of a perceptive if controversial study, *Catholicism, Roman and Anglican* (1899). By theology Fairbairn understood 'the science of the living God and of His work in and for a living world',[105] and its focal theme is the person and achievement of Christ. Christ, he urges, is not to be thought of, in the manner of much contemporary liberal Protestantism, only as an historical individual whose biography has its ready material in the gospels. On the contrary, he is 'even more intellectually real than historically actual', and the Christian dogma concerning him stands for 'a whole order of thought, a way of regarding the universe, of conceiving

99. See A. W. W. Dale, *The Life of R. W. Dale of Birmingham* (1898), p. 573.
100. Cp. R. C. Moberly's comments in *Atonement and Personality*, p. 389.
101. *The Atonement*, p. 61.
102. *Ibid.*, p. 383.
103. *Ibid.*, p. 423.
104. Cp. G. B. Stevens, *The Christian Doctrine of Salvation* (1905). p. 190, where the author calls attention to the resemblances between Dale's teaching and that of Grotius's *Defensio Fidei Catholicae de Satisfactione Christi*.
105. *The Place of Christ in Modern Theology*, p. 403.

God and man in themselves and in their mutual relations'. Thus in its widest aspect it is more symbolical than factual, although it is 'a symbol which owes all its reality to its being a fact transfigured and sublimed'.[106] Christology, that is, covers both historic fact and speculative interpretation, since one who fulfils universal functions cannot be described and dismissed as if he were no more than a particular individual. Whatever may be said in criticism of the classical formularies, doubtless overspeculative and possibly defective in logic, it must be acknowledged that their purpose was to make the person of Christ representative of 'the natures, relations, inter- activities, community and difference in attribute and being, of God and man'. Had they not existed from an early date something very like them, Fairbairn believed, would have had to be devised later to explain the course things have taken. This task of interpreting Christ and the place he holds and the functions he has fulfilled in the life of man collective and individual, is what Christian theology is essentially about. Where, however, the Church has most obviously defaulted has been in its failure to interpret Christ *ethically* with sufficient insight and consistency. There is nothing in all its history more tragic than its persistence in confining heresy to speculative opinion rather than practical morality. 'If Christ be rightly interpreted, the worst sins against God are those most injurious to man.'[107]

Fairbairn's own theory of the incarnation was kenoticist in the manner of the Lutheran Thomasius, drawing a distinction between the metaphysical and the ethical attributes of divinity, the former alone being laid aside (as it were) with the assumption of humanity. Some such doctrine he, like Gore, held to be entirely necessary if the real manhood of Christ is to be grasped by the imagination. And at the purely historical level he was confident—in the light of subsequent developments in New Testament study over-confident—that 'for the Christian theologian, the most significant and assured result of the critical process is, that he can now stand face to face with the historical Christ, and conceive God as He conceived Him'.[108] Fairbairn even believed that such a book as Renan's best-selling *Vie de Jésus*, superficial as it was, had at least served to show that Christianity is to be explained 'not through abstract principles, tendencies, differences, conciliations, but through its creative Personality'.[109] The pity was, of course, that this same creative personality had been as much thwarted as aided by the institutions, often grossly political, in which Christianity has been historically embodied. Nevertheless the Christian religion could not in its development through the ages have avoided the effects of the changing environment. 'In other words, the religion grew because it lived, and it lived because it carried within it an immanent and architechtonic idea, which governed it and yet was essentially its own.'[110]

106. *The Philosophy of the Christian Religion*, p. 16.
107. *Ibid.*, p.565.
108. *The Place of Christ in Modern Theology*, p. viii.
109. *Ibid.*, p. 279.
110. p. 518. Fairbairn distinguished two types of churches, according to whether they are controlled by a 'political' or a 'theological' interest. The former seemed to him to confine the divine action by rules, beyond which it is only 'irregular, illicit or unconvenanted', whereas the Church really is the visible image of Christ, who 'is too large to be confined within the institutions of men, they too hard and narrow to be equal to His penetrative and expansive grace' (*The Place of Christ in Modern Theology*, pp. 154.).

Two other Congregationalist divines whose reputations as theologians were already founded by the close of the century were Peter Taylor Forsyth (1848–1921), who was appointed principal of Hackney College, Hampstead, in 1901, and Alfred Edward Garvie (1862–1945), principal of New College (which had incorporated Hackney) from 1924 to 1933. Forsyth, who always perhaps had more of the preacher in him than the academic scholar, had in early life followed the liberal trend, having been influenced first by Hegelianism and then by Ritschl, whose pupil at Göttingen he was for a time. Later, however, under pressure of a deepening sense of man's need of redemption, his liberalism became less and less obtrusive, and the atonement more than the incarnation occupied the central place in his teaching. 'There is in the Incarnation', he now wrote, 'that which puts us at once at the moral heart of reality—the Son made sin rather than the Son made flesh. The Incarnation has no religious value but as the background of the atonement.'[111] Revelation, he believed, can truly be found only in redemption. But the body of Forsyth's work—and notably *The Person and Place of Jesus Christ* (1909), *The Work of Christ* (1910) and *The Principle of Authority* (1913)—belong properly to the theological history of the present century.[112] The same is true of Garvie, although his study of Ritschlianism, *The Ritschlian Theology*, published in 1899, at once established him as a leading authority on the subject in the English-speaking world. As the lifelong exponent of a solid though wide-minded Protestant orthodoxy he tended in his later years to devote his time and energies increasingly to active church work, becoming in turn chairman of the Congregational Union of England, and Wales (1920), president of the National Free Church Council (1924), vice-chairman of the Lausanne Conference on Faith and Order (1927) and moderator of the Free Church Federal Council (1928).

Thus with our survey concluded we may ask what overall impression of the period remains. 'It is one of the hardest tasks in the world', observed Matthew Arnold, 'to make new intellectual ideas harmonize truly with the religious life, to place them in the right light for that life. The moments in which such a change is accomplished are epochs in religious history.' That the latter half of the nineteenth century was of this kind is hardly to be doubted. At all events immense efforts had been made to effect a harmony. Scientific methods, in the investigation whether of nature or of human history, had been tried and developed with so overwhelming a success in their yield of positive knowledge that if religion were to retain its place in Western culture the concepts traditionally associated with it would have to undergo more or less drastic revision. Beliefs whose forms at least had come down unchanged from the era of the Reformation, from the middle ages or from antiquity itself could no longer retain their grasp upon the modern educated mind without some resolute attempt by churchmen to shape them to the new conditions. What Arnold was fond of calling the *Zeitgeist* had made demands which only those who

---

111. *Positive Preaching and the Modern Mind* (1907), p. 182.
112. Forsyth can hardly be described as a systematic theologian, but his thought had a remarkable consistency. J. K. Mozley said of him that no theologian of the day had 'fewer loose ends' in this respect (*The Doctrine of the Atonement*, 1915, p. 182).

were most obdurately set in the old ways—identifying them with eternal truth—thought it possible to resist. In general the movement towards intellectual reconciliation could be described as liberal, and if it affected the Protestant churches more than Catholicism this was because of Protestantism's inherent nature, which biblicist authoritarianism could not permanently mask. In England indeed, as to only a somewhat lesser degree in Scotland, the feeling now was one of broad optimism. The first shock of the impact of criticism had been severe, but the orthodox teaching had regained confidence. Bishop Mandell Creighton, for instance, writing in 1896, stated that 'for my part I believe the attack on Christianity is intellectually repulsed'.[113] And of those who led the counter-attack Gore himself was not the last to be assured of victory. The vastness of the universe, in space and in time, had become a commonplace; the theory of evolution, with its particular implications for the origin and status of the human race, had apparently been assimilated; the critical approach to history, and especially the sacred history of the Bible, was an assumption which scholarship had no need to defend; and that the religious experience of mankind as a whole, however devious or defective its forms as judged by Christian standards, witnessed to the reality and manifold providence of the one God, was an idea by now willingly affirmed. In short, although the Catholic faith, in its vital centre, still held, orthodoxy had become critical and even non-believers were rarely hostile.[114]

Yet, looking back to that time, the historian of thought can scarcely but feel that the optimism was somewhat too shining and that self-complacency—a fault of orthodoxies in all ages—was already evident. The changes which the preceding half-century had wrought were by no means concluded. Thus the open conflict between religion and science might to some extent have been silenced, but scientific and technological progress has since gone far to create an intellectual and social climate in which religious supernaturalism has not been able to thrive. Again, the compromise between theology and historical criticism which by the beginning of this century had been not only conceded but welcomed by men like Gore and Sanday, proved to be unstable and the attempt to justify tradition on the grounds of history alone quickly ran into difficulties. Yet again, developing study of the varied patterns of human behaviour, individual and social, have tended to weaken the claim of Christianity to a unique character and authority. Instead it has fallen into ever clearer perspective as a phase, limited and determined by time and circumstance, of man's age-old effort to establish his identity and shape his destiny. The fate of metaphysical beliefs is not that they are proved to be untrue but that they gradually forfeit their meaning and relevance. They are valuable and significant so long only as they retain adherents. But their survival, unfortunately, is not decided by the ingenuity of their apologists. At the outset of the nineteenth century the religion of the Christian churches still provided an intellectual and moral frame

---

113. Louise Creighton, *The Life and Letters of Mandell Creighton* (1904), ii, p. 191.
114. Cp. Herbert Spencer's admission: 'Religious creeds, which in one way or another occupy the sphere that material interpretation seeks to occupy and fails the more it seeks, I have come to regard with a sympathy based on community of need' (*Autobiography*, ii, p. 471).

of reference which even the religiously indifferent in the main admitted. At its end this frame of reference had lost credibility. The liberal compromise was of course—and ere long—to receive a sharp challenge from a form of neo-orthodoxy. But the moderate success of that challenge has been in the nature of a reaction, and like all reactions was the product of the very forces it has sought to repel.

Note
Church and Society

The year of the publication of *Lux Mundi*, 1889, was that also of the founding of the Christian Social Union, an event largely brought about by Scott Holland. Brooke Foss Westcott was chosen as the Union's president, and Holland himself as chairman of committee, its headquarters being a mission house run by Canon A. J. Mason at Tower Hill, London. The aims of the organization were stated to be:

(i) To claim for the Christian Law the ultimate authority to rule social practice; (ii) To study in common how to apply the moral truths and principles of Christianity to the social and economic difficulties of the present time; and (iii) To present Christ in practical life as the Living Master and King, the enemy of wrong and selfishness, the power of righteousness and love.

Holland was insistent that its churchly character be made plain from the start: 'Your fervid socialist Nothingarian' was to be excluded. In his view political problems were giving place to those of large-scale industry.

It is [he wrote] the condition of industry which is absorbing all attention and all anxieties. It is the needs and necessities of industry which are the motive powers now at work to mould and direct the fortunes of human society. It is the intolerable situation in which our industrial population now finds itself, that must force upon us a reconsideration of the economic principles and methods which have such disastrous and terrible results.

But how the problem was to be tackled depended on one's conception of humanity itself and of human need. Secular ideals would not suffice; Christ, 'the Man', was the solution of all human problems. 'We look into the face of Jesus Christ as into a mirror in which we can see what manner of thing man originally and actually is intended to be' (*Our Neighbours*, 1911, p. 143). But the difficulty lay in the application of Christian principles to the complex order of human society as it is, a fact which Holland, like William Temple and others since, realized well enough. The Ricardonian idea of the 'autonomy' of economic laws was morally unacceptable, yet Christian opinion wavered between accepting it on scientific and rejecting it on ethical grounds.

We go a certain distance with the science, and then, when things get ugly and squeeze, we suddenly introduce moral considerations, and human kindness, and charity. And then, again, this seems weak, and we pull up short and go back to tough economic principle . . . When our economy is caught in a tangle, we fly off to our morality. When our morality lands us in a social problem, we take refuge in some naked economic law.

So he wrote in a preface he contributed to a book on *Christian Economics* by his friend, Canon Wilfrid Richmond, published in 1890, but went on to commend the way in which the author had resolved this seeming dilemma. 'The ethical principle does not appear as outside the economic, entering on the scene merely as a sentiment to check, and to limit, and to correct it; but it is itself the intelligent and constructive force which builds up, from within, the scientific principles. The economic laws are exhibited, not as arbitrarily limited by moral considerations, but as themselves the issue of moral considerations' (see Stephen Paget, *Henry Scott Holland: Memoir and Letters*, 1921, pp. 172f).

It was to this conviction that the Christian Social Union was dedicated. Particular enterprises and works of charity like those with which Stewart Headlam's Guild of St Matthew (1877) was associated were admirable in themselves but hardly adequate as an expression of Christian social responsibility. (Cp. Maurice Reckitt, *Maurice to Temple: A Century of Social Movement in the Church of England*, 1947, pp. 136f: 'While Headlam strove to vindicate the outcast and to defy their oppressors, Holland sought to interpret the signs of the times and to win men to his own understanding of what that interpretation required.') What was needed was the more radical purpose of Christianizing (or at least moralizing) the social structure itself. Scott Holland was wholehearted in his belief in the Church's social mission, which he preached up and down the country, always with much rhetorical brilliancy. Gore indeed remarked: 'I sometimes was tempted to wonder whether his brilliant oratory and sparkling wit did not so delight his audience with a sort of physical joy as to conceal from them what severe doctrine and what unpalatable conclusions were really being pressed upon them' (Paget, p. 248). But the Union was not concerned only with social theory. It engaged in a good deal of practical activity as well. Yet its real task was to promote a Christian social philosophy as the basis for action. In this Holland's periodical, *The Commonwealth*, the first issue of which came out in January 1896, played a leading role. Much of its content was provided by Holland himself who found the work suited to his temperament and talents. His own political opinions were in a broad sense socialist; at any rate he was dissatisfied with the official Liberalism of the day. He thought it out of touch with 'Labour'. 'The rich Liberal capitalist is not necessarily more in sympathy with the workers than the rich Tory capitalist. Parliament is still made up for the most part of wealthy men.' He was alienated, moreover, by what he and his friends considered the anti-church attitudes of the Liberal party in many matters. What was required was a wider recognition than Liberalism showed of the importance of the corporate life, of the social significance of the masses as such, and of the need for 'socialistic humanitarianism'. Gore, however, emphatically denied that the policy of the Christian Social Union itself was socialist except in the general sense of countering *laisser-faire* individualism. It did not advocate state ownership 'or tie its members to any particular platform of constructive politics' (Paget, p. 242). But Holland himself was probably ahead of Gore in this respect. He certainly believed in state controls, so long as they were freely accepted. He even praised Marxism for challenging 'the political Economists with a social philosophy as scientific as their own'. But a satisfactory doctrine of society could not be devised without liberal recourse to ethical categories, and here secular socialism, in Holland's view, failed. The questions were: 'How far can Socialism claim the sanction of Jesus Christ? Within what limit? When does it overstep that sanction? What would our Lord really say, if it is true that He would not say all that these others put in His mouth? What, in fact, constitutes Christian Citizenship?' (*Our Neighbours*, p. 10). They are questions still awaiting conclusive answer.[115]

115.   For a general survey of the subject see E. R. Norman, *Church and Society in England 1770–1970* (1976), ch. 4 ('The Victorian Church and the Condition of Society').

Appendix I

THE GORHAM JUDGMENT

Whether the Book of Common Prayer does or does not teach that the baptized are as such regenerate was the issue at stake in the famous Gorham case of 1849–1850. In 1847 Bishop Phillpotts of Exeter, a High Churchman, refused to institute the Rev. George Cornelius Gorham, at the time vicar of St Just-in-Penwith in Cornwall, to the Devon living of Bramford Speke on the ground that as a professed Calvinist in theology he denied the doctrine of the Church of England in holding that the grace of regeneration is not, strictly speaking, conferred by the baptismal rite but is given either 'preveniently' or subsequently at conversion. The bishop had himself conducted a lengthy examination of Gorham and had found the answers to the questions he put to him unsatisfactory. Gorham took his case to the Court of Arches, which, however, upheld the bishop's decision. Thereupon he appealed to the Judicial Committee of the Privy Council, which had not before dealt with a doctrinal or indeed ecclesiastical matter and which now found in the appellant's favour. The Committee did not itself claim authority to determine questions of faith or competence to settle what the doctrine of the Church of England ought in any particular instance to be. Its duty, it declared, extended only to the consideration of what is by law established to be the Church's doctrine upon 'the true and legal construction of her Articles and Formularies'. Gorham's argument was that the Church does not expressly teach that—in the words of his chief supporter, the Rev. William Goode—'an adult is not necessarily in a state of spiritual regeneration because he was baptized as an infant';[1] and it was this view that the Judicial Committee endorsed. As to what the teaching of the Church is the Committee relied for information mainly upon the Articles.

> Devotional expressions involving assertions [it maintained] must not as of course be taken to bear an absolute and unconditional sense. There are other points of doctrine respecting the Sacrament of Baptism which we are of opinion are . . . capable of being understood in different senses; and consequently we think that, as to them, the points which were left undetermined by the Articles are not decided by the Rubrics and Formularies, and that upon these points, all ministers of the Church, having duly made the subscriptions required by law (and taking Holy Scripture for their guide) are at liberty honestly to exercise their private judgment without offence or censure.

Gorham's view, the Committee considered, might be contrary to the opinions

---

1. *The Doctrine of the Church of England as to the effects of Baptism in the case of Infants* (1849).

entertained by many learned and pious persons, but if it could not be shown that it is contrary to the doctrine of the Church of England as by law established, then there was no legal ground for refusing him institution to the living to which he was lawfully presented. This verdict, which constituted an obvious piece of 'case law', was a severe blow for the Tractarian party. A largely secular authority had pronounced upon a doctrinal issue that had always been to them a matter of high spiritual and theological concern.

In spite of the prolonged discussions to which the controversy had given rise, and Phillpotts had throughout been aided by the learning of Dr Pusey, much misunderstanding had been caused. The upholders of baptismal regeneration did not deny that a baptized person might not in fact be in a state of grace and thus require, as Pusey phrased it, 'a solid and entire conversion, notwithstanding the gift of God in Baptism';[2] and this would appear to be no less than what Goode had been contending for as 'the great and all-important doctrine'. Moreover, Pusey himself seems never to have supplied any very clear and definite answer as to what precisely should be understood by baptismal regeneration. It was J. B. Mozley, in his book on the Baptismal controversy, who brought to the subject some much-needed light, and his conclusion was that the Judicial Committee's judgment had been the right one, and that there was nothing inconsistent with Church teaching in denying that baptism necessarily and invariably involves regeneration. The difficulty was, as he pointed out, that the practice of infant baptism had arisen in the early Church 'in combination with the idea of an institution primarily for adults'[3] and never since then had any step been taken to remove the infant from the basis of the adult in baptism. The early Church fathers and the medieval schoolmen had both maintained that the infant as such receives the grace of baptism inasmuch as it offers no impediment to it. It was the Reformers who insisted that baptism is conditional and that infants and adults alike receive grace subject to faith and repentance. But the Reformation baptismal theology followed one or other of two different lines: either baptism, in the case of infants, is *anticipatory* of a grace to be given later, when as an adult the recipient actually comes to believe and repent; or else the child himself receives an infused or implanted faith (*fides infusa*) *before* baptism. (St Thomas had taught that justifying faith, necessary for the right reception of the sacrament, is given *in* baptism; in which event, however, it can only be regarded as itself part of baptism instead of its antecedent condition.) But Mozley felt himself bound to admit that Scripture is silent with respect to infants as recipients of baptismal grace. Hence it follows that 'though the doctors of antiquity give one plan of this omitted ground' and the doctors of the Reformation another, neither of them could, 'according to the rule of faith adopted by our Church, compel our acceptance, and that therefore, according to the rule of our Church, the regeneration of infants is not an article of faith', which was simply what the Gorham judgment had stated.

Mozley allowed that according to the Prayer Book all baptized infants are regenerate, but maintained that the term itself had not been free of ambiguity even

2. H. P. Liddon, *The Life of E. B. Pusey*, iii, p. 236.
3. *A Review of the Baptismal Controversy* (1862).

in ancient times. Thus in a 'poetical, rhetorical, or hypothetical' sense the word could be referred, both in the Old Testament and in the New, to the 'People of God' as a whole—to the Jewish nation, that is, or to the Church of Christ, 'by supposition regarded as being what certain individuals of it really are'. In a more 'technical or conventional' sense it could be referred simply to the outward and visible sign, the rite itself. A third, a 'doctrinal' sense, covered the general statement that regeneration is 'the grace of baptism', or that adults are regenerate in baptism upon the conditions of faith and repentance, or that all infants are regenerate in baptism.[4] But it had always to be borne in mind that when the early Church spoke of baptism it did so in language used primarily of a rite for adults. The objection to Pusey's doctrine, Mozley considered, was the combination in it of the requirements at once of full regeneration—i.e. actual goodness—and the extension of the term to include all baptized infants. This, however, was to demand too much, and Pusey had never satisfactorily explained his meaning. So to insist on the inclusive connotation of the word that the sense of actual conversion of heart 'has to be apologized for' Mozley deemed to be a departure from the best traditions of Anglican theology.[5] 'Is it reasonable', he asked, 'to suppose that a moral habit can be imparted to a human being by a particular outward rite?' This might be less startling in the case of infants because the germ and commencement of life is in itself a kind of mystery. But we must feel great difficulty in the idea of a moral habit being formed by an external rite in the grown and mature man. 'Such an effect of the sacrament comes into direct collision with the reasonable modes of thinking of which we find ourselves possessed.'[6] And he adds—in a way, furthermore, very characteristic of the moral emphasis which was always so strong in Tractarian teaching—'*The* acceptable thing in the sight of God is actual holiness and goodness; where this is had, no defect of ritual can possibly interfere with the individual's favour in His sight.'[7]

4. *Ibid.*, p. 177.
5. *Ibid.*, p. 173.
6. *Ibid.*, p. 128.
7. For a succinct account of the Gorham case see Chadwick, *The Victorian Church*, Part i, pp. 250–71. J. C. S. Nias, *Gorham and the Bishop of Exeter* (1951) gives full details.

Appendix II

LIBERAL CATHOLICISM

The nineteenth-century Liberal Catholic movement, in England as on the European continent, was an attempt to bridge what seemed to its adherents to be a disastrously widening gulf between the doctrines of the Roman Catholic Church and the intellectual, social and political attitudes of the modern world. Its leader in this country was Sir John (afterwards Lord) Acton (1843–1902), its literary organ *The Rambler* periodical (in 1862 renamed *The Home and Foreign Review*), started in 1848 by John Moore Capes, a converted Anglican clergyman, and concluding, under Acton's own editorship, in 1864. Indeed the story of English Liberal Catholicism is virtually that of *The Rambler* and its encounters, increasingly serious, with ecclesiastical authority. The periodical's aim was to urge, in the words of Wilfrid Ward, 'the necessity of absolute freedom and candour in scientific, historical, and critical investigation, irrespective of results.'[1] Whether the truth told for or against Catholic polemics, it was not to be withheld. Acton himself, a man of cosmopolitan upbringing and culture,[2] was an hereditary Catholic, his family—Shropshire baronets of ancient lineage—having embraced Catholicism during the preceding century, but his associations and interests were rather with the new generation of converts, of whom Newman was the most illustrious instance, than with the 'old' Catholics, conservative in outlook and socially withdrawn. He had studied for a time under Dupanloup in Paris, then at Oscott, where Nicholas Wiseman, later archbishop of Westminster and a cardinal, was the college's president, and finally in Munich under the eminent German scholar, Johann Ignaz von Döllinger, with whom he established a relation amounting to discipleship. A political career had from the first been open to him (for a while he represented the Irish borough of Carlow at Westminster), but religion, particularly in its intellectual and ethical aspects, was his life. An admirer of Montalembert and the contemporary French liberals—'the men', he said, 'with whom I must agree'—he believed passionately in the liberty of the conscience. A Christian, he held, 'must seek to extend as much as possible the field in which he is responsible only to his conscience'.[3] Freedom,

---

1. *The Life and Times of Cardinal Wiseman* (1897), ii, p. 227.
2. His paternal grandfather had been prime minister of the Kingdom of Naples, his mother, Marie de Dalberg, was heiress of the Dalbergs of Herrnsheim, barons of the Holy Roman Empire. A great-uncle on his mother's side had been the last archbishop-elector of Mainz. He himself married Countess Marie von Arco-Valley. He spoke and wrote German, French and Italian fluently.
3. Cambridge University Library Additional MSS (Acton Papers) 5751 (quoted by Josef L. Altholz, *The Liberal Catholic Movement in England* (1962), p. 56).

354

in truth, was for Acton a basic spiritual principle, demanding expression alike in scientific inquiry and in political action. Thus hostility to Ultramontanism, of which in England such men as Manning and Ward were the self-chosen apostles and which he saw as the enemy of both political and intellectual liberty, became almost an obsession with him and led in the end to an unhappy disagreement even with the trusted Döllinger, himself by no means an Ultramontane. He was bitterly opposed to the promulgation of papal infallibility at the Vatican Council and believed after the event that Rome had slipped into heresy. Yet he never broke with the Church, although the antagonism he displayed towards the policies of Pius IX certainly brought him near to excommunication. In accepting the Vatican decrees he described his decision as 'an act of pure obedience' only, 'not grounded on the removal of my motives of opposition' to them.

With the years Acton's moral rigorism, as reflected in his judgments on history, became extreme. The passage from the Catholicism of the Fathers to that of the modern popes had been accomplished, he declared, by wilful falsehood. 'The whole structure of traditions, laws and doctrines that supports the theory of infallibility, and the practical despotism of the Popes, stands on a basis of fraud.' The notion that the security of religion could be attained by the suppression of truth and the encouragement of error appalled him. Christianity and Catholicism stood for the truth and had nothing to fear from any agency for whom this was the first objective. 'Our Church stands, and our faith should stand, not on the virtues of men, but on the surer ground of an institution and a guidance that are divine. Therefore I rest unshaken in the belief that nothing which the inmost depths of history shall disclose in time can ever bring to the Catholic just cause of shame or fear.'[4] Anyone, like Mandell Creighton in his *History of the Papacy during the Reformation*, who ventured to excuse or pass over the sins of the Church's leaders and responsible representatives, met with violent denunciation: 'In Christendom time and place do not excuse.' The principles of public morality, he insisted, are as definite as those of the morality of private life. In the end Acton felt himself more and more to be alone, understood neither within his church nor without it, and accordingly with little or no influence. He thus tended to turn inward into himself, immersed in study and in the task of planning and editing *The Cambridge Modern History*—he had been appointed to the Regius professorship of history at Cambridge in 1895. His proposed *opus magnum*, a *History of Liberty*, although laboriously prepared, remained unwritten except for the two sketches 'The History of Freedom in Antiquity' and 'The History of Freedom in Christianity', originally (1877) delivered as addresses to members of the Bridgnorth (Shropshire) Institution and printed in his posthumous *History of Freedom and Other Essays* (1907). In fact Acton published no book. The various works under his name which appeared after his death—*Historical Essays and Studies* (1907), *Lectures on Modern History* (1908), *Lectures on the French Revolution* (1910), as well as the volume just mentioned, together with *The Letters of Lord Acton to Mary Gladstone* (1904)—are collections

4. From a letter of Acton's to *The Times* newspaper, 24 November, 1874.

of essays and lectures delivered or written on divers occasions and assembled and edited by other hands.[5]

Acton began his close connection with *The Rambler* in 1858, in response to a felt need to give periodical expression to his views and even to provide him with an incentive to write at all. He was confident that the sort of article he would be able to contribute to it would accord him a position of influence among his fellow Catholics and a platform from which he also could address educated Protestant opinion. When he commenced writing for it the periodical, which had already been running for ten years, assumed a tone both more political and more liberal. Capes, who had been its first editor, had aimed to serve the interests of the new Oxford converts, especially the laymen. The cultural backwardness of the traditionary Catholics distressed him and he believed the new men, of which he himself was one, would bring to the Roman Catholic community in England fresh spiritual and intellectual vitality. To discuss theology as such was not his intention, but on the other hand not to advert to matters having theological implications was scarcely feasible. Among these 'mixed' questions social issues were well to the fore, especially the disparity of wealth, Capes himself contributing the bulk of the 'copy' besides determining the journal's general policy. But as *The Rambler*'s theological bias also became increasingly evident criticism grew, notably when its editor, in July 1849, voiced his opinion that the claims of Rome could be decided not by the certainty of faith but on a balance of probabilities. After 1852, however, Capes's health having deteriorated, the direction of the periodical was mainly in the hands of Richard Simpson, a convert of 1845 and a man of wide-ranging interests as well as a deep though undemonstrative personal piety. Simpson's editorial 'line' soon proved itself more venturesome than his predecessor's. He spoke out openly, for example, on the subject of the Thomist philosophy.

> We think [he wrote] that no greater injury can be done to the cause of those who would promote the study of St Thomas and the schoolmen, as theologians, than any attempt to identify their philosophical speculations with the truth of Catholicism, or to claim for their *modes* of reasoning on religious topics anything more than an historical, as distinguished from a logical and necessary connection.[6]

Again, he disliked the polemical attitude all too frequently adopted by Catholics, as merely alienating to educated Protestants.[7] Above all he sought to advance intellectual freedom among Catholics themselves. 'It is our firm belief that in these days the Catholic cause will be best subserved by the study of facts. . . . Theology is no longer the dominant science that it was during the middle ages; and the authority of the syllogism of Aristotle has received a counterpoise in the inductive method laid down by Bacon.'[8] Catholic historians should make it their business to go back to original authorities and refrain from concealing embarrassing truths.

5. The volumes of essays and lectures by J. N. Figgis and R. V. Laurence, the letters by H. Paul.
6. *The Rambler* (2nd ser.), ii (Nov. 1854), p. 450.
7. *The Rambler* (2nd ser.), iii (April 1855) ('The True Principle of Religious Controversy'), p. 256.
8. *The Rambler* (2nd ser.), viii (July 1857), p. 76.

Indeed the whole practice of circumscribing truth for the sake of piety offended him, and the popular appetite for modern 'miracles' he deplored as morbid.[9] The desire to know and tell the truth was as religious a motive as the concern to give edification.

Simpson and Acton together made *The Rambler* into one of the most intellectually lively periodicals in England, fully justifying Matthew Arnold's remark, after its demise in 1864, that 'perhaps in no organ of criticism in this country was there so much knowledge, so much play of mind'.[10] Simpson preferred to write on historical, philosophical and literary subjects; Acton, who had a high admiration for his colleague's talents, concentrated on politics and reviews of foreign literature. The latter's article, 'Political Thoughts on the Church', provided his readers with a forthright statement of his views as to the Church's role in politics.[11] Freedom again is the keynote. 'The Christian notion of conscience', he wrote, 'imperatively demands a corresponding measure of personal liberty. The feeling of duty and responsibility to God is the only arbiter of a Christian's actions. With this no human authority can be permitted to interfere.' The Church could not rightly tolerate any species of government in which this right was not recognized and was indeed bound to be the 'irreconcilable enemy' of state despotism in whatever form. In regard to Catholic scholarship both he and Simpson could only regret its manifest lack of knowledge of contemporary biblical criticism. 'It is the absence', Acton confessed, 'of scientific method and of original learning in nearly all even of our best writers that makes it impossible for me to be really interested in their writings.'[12] Careful study of the sources, genesis and growth of the Church's doctrines was an essential equipment for the modern theologian. On the theory of biological evolution, then in the forefront of public discussion, Simpson showed exceptional impartiality. The theory, he considered, should not be confounded with the facts: it was a hypothesis only. But Catholics ought to recognize that the theological doctrine of creation and the scientific concept of natural law are not incompatible: 'Creation is not a miraculous interference with the laws of nature, but the very institution of those laws.'[13] Certainly Catholics ought to encourage and not resist free discussion and should eschew any tendency 'to force all thought into the mould of the average mediocrity'. An account of *Essays and Reviews*, a publication of which Acton himself thought rather lightly, was assigned to another

9. *The Rambler* (2nd ser.), viii (Sept. 1857), p. 197. 'He who falsifies history falsifies the express teaching of the Supreme Judge. Nothing can be weaker than the ecclesiastical historian's concealment of ancient corruptions for fear of giving scandal', *The Rambler* (2nd ser.), ix (June 1858), p. 424.
10. 'The Function of Criticism at the Present Time', in *Essays in Criticism* (1865). Max Müller thought it 'one of the best edited of our quarterlys' (see Wilfrid Ward, *The Life of John Henry Cardinal Newman*, i, pp. 538f.).
11. *The Rambler* (2nd ser.), xi (Jan. 1859). 'I would have', he told Simpson, 'a complete body of principles for the conduct of English Catholics in political affairs, and if I live and do well, I will gradually unfold them. The Catholics want political education' (see Abbot [later Cardinal] Gasquet, *Lord Action and his Circle*, 1906, p. 4).
12. Gasquet, *op. cit.*, p. 56.
13. 'Darwin on the Origin of Species', in *The Rambler* (new ser.), ii (March 1860), p. 372.

'liberal' contributor—formerly an Anglican—Henry N. Oxenham, who, however, stressed what he saw as the inevitably erosive effect of biblical criticism on religious belief. In any case scientific study of the Bible must mean re-examination of the idea of revelation itself: 'And we do not regret that it should be so. It will demand from us a firmer grasp of ascertained principles, a wider range of speculation, a nicer discrimination of what is essential and what is accidental, a more generous estimate of an adversary's position, and bolder proclamation of our own.'[14]

The attitude of Newman towards *The Rambler* was equivocal. As to principle he agreed with its policy, but he had clear misgivings about its practical application. Newman was always studiously respectful of authority. That the Ultramontanes detested the periodical did not at all worry him, but the opinion of the bishops was another matter, and this *The Rambler* flouted. 'I have all the pains in the world', Acton wrote to Simpson, 'to keep Newman in good humour. He is so much riled at what he pleasantly calls your habit of pea-shooting at any dignitary who looks out of the window as you pass along the road, that I am afraid he will not stand by us if we are censured'.[15] The bishops for their part looked to Newman to exert a moderating influence on the liberals, somewhat to his own embarrassment. He admired Acton, liked Simpson and feared the consequences of *The Rambler*'s suppression, were it to occur. Reluctantly he himself took over the editorship from Simpson in 1859, but without success. No change of policy was disclosed and he was responsible for only two numbers. Both to satisfy the episcopate and not repudiate his friends was hardly possible, and when his own diocesan, Ullathorne, suggested his giving up the task he at once complied, although again with reluctance in view of his concern for the educated laity and the service which a journal like *The Rambler* could render them. Newman's withdrawal grieved Acton, for whom Newman was the one safe bridge between the liberal position and the Ultramontanes,

Acton's own first issue appeared in September 1859. His intention was to specialize in politics, but Simpson was also to carry on as a principal contributor, and there was to be no question of a theological censor to appease authority. The debate about the temporal power of the papacy received a good deal of attention. That the papal states were ill-governed Acton was well enough aware, but he nevertheless was prepared to defend the Holy See's territorial integrity as necessary for the pope's independence in spiritual matters, although he realized that territorially the latter's position was becoming precarious. As for the state of Catholicism at home Acton confessed himself disturbed by the growth of a dubious sort of 'devotionalism': devotion without intellectual discipline could be dangerous, piety providing 'a respectable cloak for all kinds of errors and false tendencies'. Simpson was no less uneasy over the tendency to confuse supplementary and optional beliefs with the substance of revelation. If Christians felt modern science to be a peril to faith it was because they had always 'fought for more than the Christian dogma, failing to recognize that 'all except the central core of revealed

---

14. *The Rambler* (new series), iv (March 1861) ('The Neo-Protestantism of Oxford'), p. 298f.
15. Gasquet, *op. cit.*, p. 192.

truth is human addition, and therefore fallible, changeable, and obnoxious to decay'. It was a fault to defend 'the accidental and temporary vestment of truth' with as much obstinacy as the truth itself.[16]

A crisis occurred in the affairs of *The Rambler* (by now under its new name of the *Home and Foreign*) when in January 1864 it presented its readers with an enthusiastic account of the recent congress of Catholic scholars which Döllinger had organized in Munich. Döllinger's own paper, on 'The Past and Present of Theology', was hailed by Acton as 'the dawn of a new era' in Catholic theological thinking. However, in a Brief of December 1863 addressed to the archbishop of Munich Pius IX had already severely criticized the congress's aims, the 'liberal' idea of distinguishing between the Church's actual dogma and its transient theological interpretations being specifically censured. Although the language of the Brief was for the most part loftily vague, there could be no mistaking the pope's mind, which very soon became only too plain with the publication of the encyclical *Quanta Cura* and the accompanying 'syllabus of errors'. Liberal Catholicism had in fact received a grave setback, as Acton realized. But as he would neither compromise with his principles nor defy authority he felt he had no option but to bring the review to an end. The last issue appeared in April 1864 and contained his famous article, 'Conflicts with Rome', in which he stated with profound regret that the 'amity and sympathy' which he personally believed to exist between the methods of science and those employed by the Church were by the 'enemies' of the Church denied and by its friends not yet understood. 'Long disowned by a large part of our Episcopate', such amity and sympathy were now rejected by the Holy See, and the issue was one 'vital to a *Review* which, in ceasing to uphold them, would surrender the whole reason for its existence'.[17] With the promulgation in 1870 of the Vatican decree on papal infallibility liberal Catholicism came to an end. Acton had bitterly opposed the Council's decision, even having published an open letter to a German bishop urging the minority party to continue its resistance. 'No layman', it has been said, 'ever played such a part in Church matters, and no Catholic more narrowly missed excommunication.'[18] His eventual submission was but a token of his obedience to a spiritual authority whose ultimate right he never questioned, whatever his conscientious judgment might be as to the human media through which it was exercised. 'Our Church stands, and our faith should stand, not on the virtues of men, but on the surer ground of an institution and a guidance that are divine.'

The extent to which the *Rambler*'s promoters were theologically liberal is open to debate. Upon the rights of historical criticism to investigate tradition they were firm. At the same time they were confident that the Church's dogmatic teaching represents an unshakable truth. The dogmas are infallible and binding, the theological commentary on them not so. Thus as between faith and knowledge a clear line could be drawn, and if each kept to its proper sphere no clash need ever arise. According to Simpson:

16. *The Rambler* (new series), v (July 1861) ('Reason and Faith') p. 182.
17. *The History of Freedom and Other Essays*, p. 489.
18. Shane Leslie, *Henry Edward Manning: His Life and Labours* (1921), p. 220.

A detailed review of the contents of the creeds and definitions would show that their subject matter is all outside the sphere of phenomena, which is the realm of science. The Trinity, the Incarnation, the Fall and the Redemption, Grace, the Sacraments, the authority of the Church, the inspiration of Scripture, the immortality of the soul, the resurrection of the body, heaven and hell, offer no hold for scientific experiments. The philosopher may theorize upon them in a way that offends faith; but it will be only theory, not science. He will have once more proved the venerable truism, that without revelation we have no demonstration of any Christian doctrine, that each dogma becomes a mere guess, and therefore as susceptible of denial as of affirmation.[19]

But can the problems of faith and reason, science and religion, be settled quite so easily? In defence of the liberal Catholics it may be pointed out that they were active at a time when the conflict between traditional religious belief and the new knowledge was still concentrated in a relatively small area, namely the bearing upon Genesis of geology and the theory of evolution. Biblical criticism, especially in regard to the New Testament, had not yet made its full impact, and in truth Acton himself was inclined to underrate the theological significance of criticism altogether. In so far as he and his friends did consider it they took the view that Protestant biblicism would turn out to be in a more precarious position than Catholicism, with its reliance on tradition and Church. It is hardly surprising, therefore, that the Modernists, in the early years of the present century, derived little or nothing from the ideas of the liberal Catholics. The Modernists were faced with an intellectual situation more complex and more urgent than that which had confronted their forerunners. Their problems were such in fact that any real attempt at solving them would have had to do much more than recall the arguments of a half-century before. Moreover, the fate of the liberal Catholic movement was scarcely of encouragement to this new generation of thinkers and scholars and to have appealed openly to the liberals' example would have been to invite the disaster in which, as it was, they themselves were soon to founder. The standpoint of *L'Evangile et L'Église* or *Christianity at the Cross-Roads* was, besides, utterly remote from the liberal position.[20] Simpson's views, with their concern to distinguish a 'central core' of belief from its passing theological embodiments sounded a Modernist note, but Simpson himself, unlike Loisy or Tyrrell, was convinced that this central core included the dogmas of the faith. Indeed it is arguable that the Modernist conception of development was a solvent of all doctrinal fixity. Friedrich von Hügel, it might have been supposed, would have been in general sympathy with the opinions of *The Rambler*, but it appears that he had never read it.[21]

19. *The Rambler* (new series), v (September 1861), p. 327.
20. The Anglo-Irish Jesuit Fr George Tyrrell (1861–1909) himself passed through a 'liberal' stage in his thinking—initially under the impact of Newman's writings—before arriving at his full-blown Modernism. It is best represented by his volumes *Lex Orandi* (1903) and *Lex Credendi* (1907). On the influence of Matthew Arnold's *Literature and Dogma* on Tyrrell's view of the nature of religious doctrine see N. Sagovsky, *Between Two Worlds: George Tyrrell's Relationship to the Thought of Matthew Arnold* (1983).
21. Cp. W. Ward, *W. G. Ward and the Catholic Revival*, p. 363. Von Hügel's main publications—most notably *The Mystical Element of Religion* (1908)—lie outside our period. In the early decades of the present century he occupied a conspicuous place in

Modernism belongs properly to the religious history of the twentieth century, not only as an ecclesiastical movement but in its theological temper and outlook likewise, and it is best to be studied in the light of Vatican II than in that of the liberal Catholicism extinguished by Vatican I.

English religious thought, being especially well-esteemed by Anglicans, although a leader in the Roman Catholic Modernist movement, for his liberal and ecumenical outlook. Archbishop William Temple thought it 'quite arguable' that *The Mystical Element* was 'the most important theological work written in the English language during the last half-century' (i.e. 1875–1925) (M. de la Bedoyère, *The Life of Baron von Hügel*, 1951, p. 223).

GLADSTONE ON CHURCH AND STATE

The most fully articulated contribution to the nineteenth-century discussion of the relations of Church and State was an early work of W. E. Gladstone's, *The State in its Relation with the Church*, first published in 1838 and again, in a much enlarged (fourth) edition, in 1841. Gladstone's book, especially in this latter edition, makes heavy reading, but of the strength of the convictions which lay behind it—and the author at the time was only twenty-nine—there can be no question. They were convictions which had been shaping in his mind for some years previously—he had even at one time contemplated ordination—and it is arguable that he adhered to them, in the form at least of an ideal, to the end of his life. Certainly, as Morley remarks, his intensity of interest in Church affairs never for an instance slackened.[1] A long career in politics meant, of course, a considerable chastening of the rigorism of his views, but, in the words of Sir Philip Magnus, 'the right relationship between two societies—the one eternal and divine, the other mortal and mundane—which has troubled the conscience of Europe for two thousand years, continued to torment Gladstone and to plunge his mind into a seething ferment of restlessness'.[2] Disraeli used to say of his great political opponent that he was 'never a man of the world'.

The author's mode of procedure is analytical, involving an inquiry into the nature of the State itself. The testimony of Scripture he willingly recognizes, but finds it insufficient and inconclusive, since the Old Testament does not distinguish the differing *functions* of Church and State, whilst the New Testament is hardly of relevance since it was written 'at a time when there was no case of a nation of persons professedly Christian'.[3] Other considerations—pragmatic or historical—are likewise indecisive. Our guide, accordingly, must be the light of nature, by which the 'grounds and proofs of the principle of public religion' may be well enough discerned, although not without some help, so far as it allows, from divine revelation. It requires an examination of 'the moral character and capacities of nations and rulers', from which it can be seen that 'the whole idea of their duty' is founded upon 'that will which gave them their existence'.[4] Gladstone begins, however, by asserting the theological doctrine of the fall of man and its consequences. These, he points out, would have been even more disastrous but for

---

1. John Morley, *The Life of William Ewart Gladstone* (1903), ii, p. 158. Cp. *ibid.*, iii, p. 471.
2. *Gladstone* (1954), p. 440.
3. *The State in its Relation with the Church* (ed. 1841), i, p. 40.
4. *Ibid.*, i, p. 45.

God's intermediate provisions for mitigating them—intermediate because only preparatory for his great act of final redemption in Christ. Among them are to be counted the institutions of the common life: family, tribe and nation. Thus an altruistic motive and a scheme of duties are supplied which so far limit human selfishness. Even so, in a sinful world the institutions of men's collective life are themselves productive of evil results, in greed, injustice and aggression, more than would have been committed by 'the feebler means of its members as individuals'.[5] For this reason some agency is needed by which the abuse of collective power, as well as individual wrongdoing, can be rebuked. Hence the role of publicly acknowledged religion not only as a single factor but as 'a consecrating principle' within the nation's life as a whole. For religion teaches that power is held in trust to God and is rightly exercised only in conformity with his laws. This does not mean that all forms of human association ought similarly to make an explicit profession of religion, but only such as are general, natural and permanent, notably the family and the State. For family and State share alike the basic characters of being 'parts of the dispensation into which [man] is providentially born', of being 'parallel to his entire existence', and of being both manifold in their functions and unlimited in their claims upon him. Above all they have a *moral* status in that 'they require in a high degree moral motives and restraints for the right discharge of the obligations subsisting under them' and 'distinctly contemplate moral ends'.[6]

Gladstone proceeds to specify why the State needs religion no less than the family. As an institution which is general, natural and permanent 'there is no limit of quantity to the obligations of the individual towards it'. It is, in other words, a *moral* and not merely an economic entity 'inasmuch as its laws and institutions, and the acts done under them, are intimately connected with the formation of our moral habits, our modes of thought, and that state of our affections, and inasmuch as its influences pervade the whole scheme and system of our being'.[7] The individual indeed is what he is largely through his membership of a nation or state (terms which Gladstone uses for the most part interchangeably). In short, by speaking of the State as moral the author means that of its nature it assumes moral responsibilities under an acknowledged moral law and that it cannot be morally indifferent. It has, of course, responsibilities which are sub-moral and which are 'first in time and necessity', but its concern is not restricted to matters of sheer utility, however pressing and engrossing. Further, from its moral responsibility it has, like the individual, the obligation to profess and promote a religion, providing 'that worship which shall publicly sanctify its acts'.[8] How far and in what manner this public patronage of religion will be extended depends, naturally enough, upon the given circumstances; but the principle itself is unaffected.

By religion Gladstone understands (as he makes clear) one specific religion. The State cannot afford its patronage to two or more, with their diverse and perhaps inconsistent claims. But this implies that the State is capable of recognizing truth

5. *Ibid.*, p. 61.
6. *Ibid.*, p. 94.
7. *Ibid.*, p. 86.
8. *Ibid.*, p. 105.

in the religious sphere, even though unable to attend to the details of theology. On the other hand, although one religion be singled out for express recognition, others are properly to be tolerated. The form which the State's recognition will take indudes the acknowledgement of God by worship and prayer, the avowed submission of its laws and actions to the divine conmandments, and the diffusion of religion throughout the body of the nation.[9] Gladstone sees Christianity, that is, as 'a principle of life intended to govern and pervade the whole of human life'. As itself a principle of common life it should govern and pervade the common life in both family and State.[10] But although the State and the Church thus have common and co-ordinate ends they also importantly differ, as to objectives as well as to means. 'The State and the Church', we read, 'have both of them moral agencies. But the State aims at character through conduct: the Church at conduct through character; in harmony with which, the State forbids more than enjoins, the Church enjoins more than forbids.'[11]

The essentials of Gladstone's theory are set out in the first part of the work, and it is here that the student of nineteenth-century religious thought will focus his attention; the remainder of the book, concerned for the most part with Church-State relations as they existed at the time of its writing, is now of slight interest. The author's other (and also voluminous) work on the subject, *Church Principles considered in their Results*, published in 1840, is likewise subordinate, although more overtly theological in content.[12] It made virtually no impression on public opinion, for not only is Gladstone's literary style ponderous, the book was scouted as the product of a mere theological amateur. Again, although Gladstone sympathized with the religious standpoint of the Tractarians he was not himself identified with a Church party and wrote from an angle of deliberate independence, a fact which, regrettably, was of no help in winning him an audience.

What strikes the modern reader of *The State in its Relations with the Church* is the archaism of its outlook. Indeed it was archaic in its own day. Gladstone was then a strong Tory and the thesis of his book was in total contrast with that enunciated in Arnold's *Principles of Church Reform*. Its affinity, as we have remarked, is much more with Coleridge's doctrine, except that Gladstone works out his theory with greater consistency than does Coleridge, whose own *Church and State* is really no more than a brilliantly suggestive (and provocative) sketch. In the light of Gladstone's later career as leader of the Liberal party his early writings seemed insignificant and came to be forgotten. As touching the relationship of Church and State, however, it does not appear that his convictions ever underwent fundamental change, although he realized increasingly how impracticable they were. At heart, as has frequently been observed by

---

9.   *Ibid.*, pp. 110f. Cp. i, pp. 244f.
10. *Ibid.*, p. 115.
11. *Ibid.*
12. William Palmer's *Treatise on the Church of Christ* (1838) was a major influence on Gladstone's thinking. 'It gave me', he said, 'at once the dear, definite and strong conception of the Church' (*op. cit.* p. 162). He judged it to be the most powerful and least assailable defence of the Anglican position to have been attempted since the sixteenth century (Morley, *op. cit.*, i, p. 168n).

twentieth-century commentators, and despite his own rather sententious references to 'liberal principles', he was himself a traditionalist with very little affection for the type of free-thinking radicalism with which the word liberal was associated in minds more sensitive to the intellectual climate of the times.[13]

13. See A. R. Vidler, *The Orb and the Cross* (1945), ch. vii.

SELECT BIBLIOGRAPHY

General

Chadwick, O., *The Victorian Church* (2 vols, 1966–70)

Cockshut, A. O. J., *The Unbelievers: English Agnostic Thought 1840–1890* (1964)

Crowther, M. A., *The Church Embattled: Religious Controversy in Mid-Victorian England* (1970)

Davies, H., *Worship and Theology in England, vol. 4: Newman to Martineau (1850–1900)* (1962)

Edwards, D. L., *Leaders of the Church of England 1828–1944* (1971)

Elliott-Binns, L. E., *English Thought 1860–1900: The Theological Aspect* (1956)

Helmstadter, R. J., and Lightman, B. (eds), *Victorian Faith in Crisis: Essays on Continuity and Change in Nineteenth Century Religious Belief* (1990)

Hinchliff, P., *God and History: Aspects of British Theology 1875–1914* (1992)

Jasper, D., and Wright, T. R., *The Critical Spirit and the Will to Believe: Essays in Nineteenth Century Religion and Literature* (1989)

Jay, E., *Faith and Doubt in Victorian Britain* (1986)

Parsons, G. (ed.), *Religion in Victorian Britain* (i, Traditions; ii, Controversies; iv, Interpretations) (Manchester University Press in association with the Open University, 1988)

Smart, N., *et al.*, *Nineteenth Century Religious Thought in the West*, vol. ii, chs 1, 3, 7 and 8, and vol. iii, ch.1 (1985)

Tulloch, J., *Movements of Religious Thought in Britain during the Nineteenth Century* (1885; repr. 1971)

Webb, C.C.J., *Religious Thought in England from 1850* (1933)

Willey, B., *Nineteenth Century Studies: Coleridge to Arnold* (1949; repr. 1966)

Willey, B., *More Nineteenth Century Studies* (1956; repr. 1966)

The early decades: Evangelicals, High Churchmen, Liberals

Balleine, G. A., *A History of the Evangelical Party in the Church of England* (1908; repr. 1933)

Brown, F. K., *The Fathers of the Victorians* (1961)

Newsome, D., *The Parting of Friends* (1966)

Storr, V. F., *The Development of English Theology in the Nineteenth Century (1800–1860)* (1913), chs 4–6

Select Bibliography

Williams, E. L., *The Liberalism of Thomas Arnold* (Alabama, 1964)
Wymer, N., *Dr Arnold of Rugby* (1953)

S. T. Coleridge

Barth, J. R., *Coleridge and Christian Doctrine* (1969)
Jasper, D., *Coleridge as Poet and Religious Thinker* (1985)
Perkins, M. A., *Coleridge's Philosophy: the Logos as Unifying Principle* (1994)
Prickett, S., *Romanticism and Religion; The Tradition of Coleridge and Wordsworth in the Victorian Church* (1976)
Sanders, C. A., *Coleridge and the Broad Church Movement: Studies in S. T. Coleridge, Dr Arnold of Rugby, J. C. Hare, Thomas Carlyle and F. D. Maurice* (1942; repr. 1972)

The Oxford Movement

Brilioth, Y., *The Anglican Revival: Studies in the Oxford Movement* (1925)
Chadwick, O. (ed.), *The Mind of the Oxford Movement* (1960)
Church, R. W., *The Oxford Movement: Twelve Years 1833–1845* (1891; repr. 1970)
Faber, G., *The Oxford Apostles* (1933)
Fairweather, E. R. (ed.), *The Oxford Movement* (1964)
Griffin, J. R., *The Oxford Movement: a Revision* (1980)

J. H. Newman

Dessain, C. S., *John Henry Newman* (1966)
Coulson, J., and Allchin, A. M. (eds), *The Rediscovery of Newman* (1967)
Ker, I., *John Henry Newman: a Biography* (1988)
Ker, I., *The Achievement of John Henry Newman* (1991)
Lash, N., *Newman on Development: the Search for an Explanation in History* (1979)
Newman, J. H., *Apologia pro Vita Sua*, ed. M. Svaglic (1967)
Pailin, D. A., *The Way to Faith; an Examination of Newman's Grammar of Assent* (1969)
Thomas, S., *Newman and Heresy: the Anglican Years* (1991)
Walgrave, J. H., *Newman the Theologian* (trans. A. V. Littledale, 1960)

F. D. Maurice

Christiansen, T., *The Divine Order: a Study of F. D. Maurice's Theology* (1973)
McClain, F., *Maurice, Man and Moralist* (1972)
Norman, E. R., *The Victorian Christian Socialists* (1987)
Ramsey, A. M., *F. D. Maurice and the Conflicts of Modern Theology* (1951)
Vidler, A. R., *Maurice and Company: Nineteenth Century Studies* (1966)

Christian Socialism. Church and Society

Christiansen, T., *The Origin and History of Christian Socialism 1848–1854* (Aarhus, 1962)

Clark, G. K., *Churchmen and the Condition of England 1832–1885* (1973)

Gilbert, A. D., *Religion and Society in Industrial England* (1976)

Norman, E. R., *Christianity and Society in England 1770–1970,* chs 4 and 5 (1976)

The Broad Church

Faber, G., *Jowett: a Portrait with a Background* (1957)

Hinchliff, P., *Benjamin Jowett and the Christian Religion* (1987)

Swanston, H. F. G., *Ideas of Order: Anglicans and the Renewal of Theological Method in the Middle Years of the Nineteenth Century* (Assen, 1974)

Matthew Arnold

Collini, S., *Arnold* (1988)

Robbins, W., *The Ethical Idealism of Matthew Arnold: a Study of the Nature and Sources of his Moral Ideals* (Toronto, 1959)

Super, R. H. (ed.), *Matthew Arnold: Dissent and Dogma* (contains the text of *St. Paul and Protestantism* and *Literature and Dogma*) (Ann Arbor, 1968)

Trilling, L., *Matthew Arnold* (1939; repr. 1989)

B. F. Westcott

Barrett, C. K., *Westcott as Commentator* (1958)

Newsome, D., *Bishop Westcott and the Platonic Tradition* (1968) (Bishop Westcott Memorial Lectures, Cambridge)

Westcott, B. F., *Essays in the History of Religious Thought in the West* (1891)

T. H. Green

Vincent, A. (ed.), *The Philosophy of T. H. Green* (1986) (Contains an essay by the present writer on 'T. H. Green as a Theologian')

Gore and the 'Lux Mundi' Group

Avis, P., *Gore: Construction and Conflict* (1988)

Carpenter, J., *Gore: a Study of Liberal Catholic Thought* (1960)

Morgan, R. (ed.), *The Religion of the Incarnation: Anglican Essays in*

Commemoration of Lux Mundi (especially chs by G. Rowell and P. Hinchliff) (1989)

Ramsey, A. M., *From Gore to Temple* (1960)

Roman Catholicism in England

Altholz, J. L., *The Liberal Catholic Movement in England* (1962)

Himmelfarb, G., *Lord Acton: a Study in Conscience and Politics* (1952)

Holmes, J. D., *More Roman than Rome: English Catholicism in the Nineteenth Century* (1978)

Norman, E. R., *The English Catholic Church in the Nineteenth Century* (1984)

English Nonconformity

Binfield, C., *So Down to Prayer: Studies in English Nonconformity 1790–1920* (1977)

Sellers, I., *Nineteenth Century Nonconformity* (1877)

Scottish Presbyterianism

Cheyne, A. C., *The Transforming of the Kirk: Victorian Scotland's Religious Revolution* (1983)

Riesen, R. A., *Criticism and Faith in Late Victorian Scotland: A. B. Davidson, William Robertson Smith and George Adam Smith* (University Press of America, 1985)

INDEX

Abbott, E. A., 338
Aberglaube, 288
Acton, Lord, 112, 354–60
Agnosticism, 218, 220f
Aids to Reflection (Coleridge), 46, 47–9, 52, 56, 295
Allen, W. C., 235
Apologia pro vita sua (Newman), 20, 32n, 40n, 66, 69n, 85, 90, 93n, 94, 102, 105
Apostolic Fathers, The (Lightfoot), 257
apostolical succession, 24, 32, 40, 70f, 131f
Appearance and Reality (Bradley), 229
Aquinas, St Thomas, 138, 323, 352, 356
Arnold, M., 21, 37n, 195, 266, 274–6, 282–92, 346, 357
Arnold, T., 35–42, 43, 64, 66, 67, 75, 82, 181, 192
Articles, the thirty-nine, 39, 72, 84, 118, 123f, 242
Ashley, Lord (Earl of Shaftesbury), 125n, 150, 252
Associationism, *see also* Hartley, D., 45, 201
atonement, the, 18f, 80, 84, 117, 138–40, 178, 246f, 299, 300–2, 312, 315f, 320, 326–8, 340, 344, 346
Atonement, The (Dale), 344
Atonement, The Idea of in Christian Theology (Rashdall), 340
Atonement, The Nature of (Campbell), 300–2
Atonement and Personality (Moberly), 302, 326–8
Augustine, St, 340

Bacon, Francis, 50
Bagehot, W., 21
Baillie, D. M., 317, 333
Baillie, J., 317
Balfour, A. J., 233f
baptism, doctrine of, *see also* Gorham judgment 28, 86, 124f, 129, 163, 351–3
Barth, K., 309
Bauer, F. C., 5, 245
Begg, J., 156n

belief, nature of, 94–8 *see also Essay In Aid of a Grammar of Assent* (Newman)
Belsham, T., 3
Benn, A. W., 44
Benson, Archbishop E. W., 260
Bentham, J., 11, 43, 184, 198, 199n, 231n
Berkeley, Bishop, 165
Bethune-Baker, J. F., 317
Bible and geology, 210–13
Bible, authority of, 59f, 132f, 329
Bible, inspiration of, 58–61, 132–4, 185, 242f, 248, 264, 265, 328f
Bible, Revised Standard Version of, 258, 259
Bible, Revised Version of, 259
Biblical criticism, 5f, 58f, 134, 185, 187, 232, 248–50, 254, 263–5, 304–7, 315, 329f
Binyon, G. C., 150, 154
Biographia Literaria (Coleridge), 45–53nn
Body of Christ, The (Gore), 62
Bosanquet, B., 229n, 230
Boulger, J. D., 51n
Bowden, J. W., 75
Bradley, F.H., 229f, 291n
Bray, C., 184, 186f, 208
Bremond, H., 101
Bridgewater, Earl of, 211
Bridgewater Treatises, 211
British Critic, The, 66n, 76
'Broad Church', 79, 181
Brodie, Sir B., 138n
Brown, T., 293
Browne, E. K., 282
Browning, R., 14, 266, 272–4
Bruce, A. B., 307, 312–15
Bryce, Lord, 224
Buckland, W., 212, 243
Bunsen, Baron, 41, 239f
Burgon, Dean, 259
Bushnell, H., 161, 344
Butler, Bishop, 79, 100, 103, 110, 215
Byron, Lord, 7

Cabanis, G., 11

Caird, E., 227f, 307, 308, 310f
Caird, J., 307–10
Cairns, D. S., 317
Calvinism, 94, 286, 289, 293, 299, 302, 304
Cambridge, G., 23
Campbell, J. McL., 293, 294, 299
Campion. W. J. H., 321, 328
Candlish, R. S., 141
Capes, J. M., 354
Carlyle, A. J., 235n
Carlyle, T., 118, 201, 276–82
Carpenter, Bishop Boyd, 338f
Catholic Apostolic Church ('Irvingites'), 303
Catholic emancipation, 65
Catholic Thoughts on the Bible and Theology (Myers), 159–61
Catholicism, Liberal, *see* Liberal Catholicism (Roman)
Cecil, R., 17
Certitude of faith, 100f, 103f
Chalcedon, Definition of, 316
Chalmers, T., 211, 293, 295, 302
Chambers, R., 213
Channing, W. E., 162n, 233
Chapman, J., 189
Chateaubriand, F.-R. de 7
Chavasse, Bishop F. S., 338
Cheyne, T. K., 264, 332
Christian Ecclesia, The (Hort), 258
Christian Social Union, 262n, 348–50
Christian Socialism, 122, 143n, 148–56
Christianity and Hellenism, 262f
Church, doctrine of the, 32, 39f, 70–2, 127–9
    and State and Society relations of, 39, 61–4 (Coleridge on), 66, 142–8, 328, 348–50, 362–5
    of England, 66, 72, 73, 74, 75, 87, 104, 148, 182, 242
    reform, 39f, 66
    unity, 39
Church, R. W., 33n, 65n, 88, 113n, 136, 217, 250f, 257, 338
churches, national,
    Coleridge on, 62f
    Maurice on, 132
'Clapham Sect', 22
Clarke, A., 5
Clerical subscription, 339
'Clerisy', the 62
Clifford, W. K., 219, 291
Clough, A. H., 184, 195, 196–8, 266, 275, 286
Coburn, K., 53n
Cockburn, W., 212
Colenso, Bishop, W., 13, 134, 181, 251, 254f, 286

Coleridge, S. T., 7, 12, 37, Ch 3 *passim*, 96, 97, 115f, 267, 279, 295, 303
Combe, G., 187
Comte, A., 82, 190, 223, 262
Confessions of an Inquiring Spirit (Coleridge), 58–61
Conscience, 100f
Constitution of Church and State (Coleridge), 61–3
Contentio Veritatis, 341, 342
Conybeave, W. J., 338
Copleston, E., 30
Cours de philosophie positive (Comte), 190f
Creed, J. M, 333
creeds, 80, 130f, 258, 318, 335f, 340
Creighton, Bishop Mandell, 255, 347, 355
Cross, F. L., 69n, 109n
Culture and Anarchy (Arnold), 282f
Curtis, W. A., 317

Dale, R. W., 156n, 327, 343
Darby, J. N., 192
Darwin, C., 106, 207, 212, 214–17, 220
Darwin, E., 213
Daubeny, C., 23, 24
Davenport, C., 72n
Davidson, A. B., 304
Dawson, C., 69n
Dawson, G., 156n
Deists, 244
Deluge, the, and geology, 213
Democracy, 341
Denison, Archdeacon, 319
Denney, J., 315f
Descent of Man, The (Darwin), 215
De Wette, W., 5
Difficulties felt by Anglicans in Catholic Teaching, 4 vols, (Newman), 73f
Disraeli, B., 362
Disruption, The Great (1843), 293, 295
Dissertations on Subjects connected with the Incarnation (Gore), 330, 332
Divine Immanence (Illingworth), 324f
Doctrine and Development (Rashdall), 340
Dodds, M., 307
dogma, 296f, 314
Döllinger, J. I. von, 354
Dowden, E., 272, 273
D'Oyley, Archdeacon, 180
Drew, G. S., 154
Driver, S. R., 264
Drummond, H., 303n

Ecce Homo (Seeley), 338
Eichhorn, J. G., 5, 59

Empiricism, 198–202, 224
Encyclopaedia Biblica, 264, 313, 314
Encyclopaedia Britannica (W. R. Smith's
    contributions to), 305f
Episcopacy, 131f, *see also* Apostolical
    Succession
Erskine, T., of Linlathen, 12, 116, 293–9
Essay in Aid of a Grammar of Assent
    (Newman), 93, 95, 97n, 98–104, 111
Essay on the Development of Doctrine
    (Newman), 105–11
Essays and Reviews, 13, 41, 113, 114, 132,
    182, 216, 237–45, 250f, 252, 265, 305,
    320, 328
Essays on Religion (Mill), 203–8
Essays on Truth and Reality (Bradley), 229
eternal punishment, 138
ethics, naturalistic, 222f
Eucharistic doctrine, 76, 129f, 334
evangelicalism, weaknesses of, 150, 286, 337
Evans, Mary Ann (George Eliot), 13, 14,
    184, 185, 186, 188–90, 208
Evidences of Christianity (Paley), 3
evolution, theory of, 213–20, 220–2, 312,
    314, 323
Ewald, H. G. A., 5
Ewing, Bishop, 159, 295

Fairbairn, A. M., 15, 320n, 344f
Faith, nature of, 321f
Fall, doctrine of the, 126f, 362f
Fellowes, R., 29
Feuerbach, L., 190
Fichte, J. G., 279
Fitzgerald, Bishop W. L., 253
Flint, R., 311f
Forsyth, P. T., 15, 333, 346
Fox, C. J., 11
Frazer, Sir J., 6
French Revolution, 11
Froude, H., 68f, 80, 88, 89f, 195f, 276
Froude, J. A., 184, 195
Fundamental Principles of Christianity, The
    (Caird, J.), 308–10

Galloway, G., 317
Gardner, P., 317
Garvie, A. E., 346
Geological Evidences of the Antiquity of Man
    (Lyell), 213
Gibbon, E., 180
Gladstone, W. E., 362
God and the Bible (Arnold), 289
God's existence, proofs of, 101–4, 206f,
    233–5, 311f, 341

Goethe, J. W. von, 278f
Goode, W., 351
Goodwin, C. W., 238, 243
Gore, Bishop C., 10, 14, 220, 261, 263, 319,
    328–37, 347
Gorham judgment, 113, 351–3
Gosse, P., 212
Graf, K. H., 5, 305
Gray, Bishop R., 254
Green, J. R., 216
Green, T. H., 9, 224–7, 245, 321, 331
Greg, W. R., 187, 191
Grote, G., 199, 200
Grotius, H., 344
Guild of St Matthew, 349
Gwatkin, H. M., 337

'Hackney Phalanx', 22, 24
Halifax, Lord, 335
Hall, R. 4
Hamilton, Sir W., 165–7
Hampden, R. D., 32–5, 116, 252
Hancock, T., 155
Hardy, T., 266
Hare, J. C., 41, 44n, 115–18
Harnack, A. von, 110n, 263, 315, 342
Harrison, F., 251
Hartley, D., 201n
Hatch, E., 262f
Hawkins, E., 30f
Headlam, S., 155, 349
Hebraism, 283
Hegel, G. W. F., 4, 9, 41, 225, 227, 245, 308
Hegelians, neo-, 227–30, 245, 307, 310f
Hennell, C., 184, 185f
Hennell, S., 184
Herder, J. G. von, 4
Heroes and Hero Worship (Carlyle), 277
Heurtley, C. A., 253
'High Church', use of term, 23f
'Higher criticism', *see* Biblical criticism
'higher pantheism', 323f
Hobbes, T., 175n
Holbach, Baron d', 11
holiness, 27f, 77–9
Holland, H. S., 262n, 320, 321, 348, 349
Holy Spirit, doctrine of, 328f
Hooker, R., 75
Horne, T., 20
Horsley, Bishop S., 3, 25
Hort, F. J. A., 137, 157, 175, 216, 256, 257,
    261n
Howley, Archbishop, W., 25, 70
Hügel, Baron, F. von, 360
Hughes, T., 154

Hume, J., 113
Hutton, W. H., 111, 272, 277
Huxley, T. H., 9, 110, 216, 217–19

Idea of a University, The (Newman), 91
idealism, 9f, 227–30
personal, 230–5
Ideal of a Christian Church, The (Ward), 82f, 111
Illative sense, the, 103f
Illingworth, J. R., 320, 323–324f
immanence, divine, 10, 159f, 226, 279–81, 323f, 331
immortality, 194
incarnation, doctrine of the, 320, 325f, 344f
Incarnation of the Son of God, The (Gore), 330, 334n
infallibility, papal, 359
Influence of Greek Ideas on Christianity, The (Hatch), 263
Inge, W. R., 336, 341–3
In Memoriam (Tennyson), 268–71
Inspiration (Sanday), 264
intuitionism (in ethics), 224
Irish Church Bill (1833), 68f
Irving, E., 293, 302

Jackson, Bishop, 252
Jacobi, F. H., 51n
Jebb, Bishop, 24, 27
Jelf, Dr R. W., 138n
Jesus, the historical, 187, 194, 309f, 313, 338, 345
Jevons, F. B., 6
Jowett, B., 119, 237, 241, 245–50, 252, 253, 338
Justification, doctrine of, 84f
Justification, Lectures on (Newman), 52

Kant, I., 5, 8, 49–51, 52, 55, 117, 225, 227, 245
Keble, J., 65, 74, 76, 88f, 91n, 165
kenoticism, 330, 332, 333f, 344
Kierkegaard, S., 64, 92
Kingdom of Christ, The (Maurice), 123–8
Kingsley, C., 75, 138, 157f, 164, 217, 218
King's College, London, 136–8
Knox, A., 22, 23, 24, 26–9, 67, 75
Kuenen, A., 305

Lamarck, J-B de, 212, 213
Lang, A., 6
Laplace, 210, 268
La Saisiaz (Browning), 273f
Last Essays on Church and Religion (Arnold), 284, 291n, 292n

Laurence, R., Archbishop, 20n
Law, W., 295
Lee, Bishop Prince, 253, 256
Leighton, Archbishop, 50
Le Roy, E., 81n
Leslie, Sir J., 293
Lessing, W. G.. 4, 59
Lewes, G. H., 184, 189, 190f, 208
Liberal Catholicism
(Anglican), 334f
(Roman), 354–61
Liberal Protestantism, 344
Liddon, H. P., 16, 217, 318f
Lightfoot, Bishop, J. B., 256f, 326
Limits of Religious Knowledge, The (Mansel), 164
Literature and Dogma (Arnold), 38, 284, 287
liturgy, 131f
Lloyd, Bishop C., 23
Lock, W., 321, 328
Locke, J., 50, 231
Loisy, A., 110, 228, 360
Longley, Archbishop, 254
Lotze, H., 225, 234
Ludlow, J. M., 143, 146, 149n, 151, 152, 153
Lux Mundi, 9, 14, 318–26, 337, 348
Lyell, Sir C., 212f
Lyttleton, A., 320, 327f

M'Dougall, Bishop, 254
Macaulay, Z., 17
Mackay, R. W., 184, 188
Mackintosh, H. R., 317, 333
McTaggart, J. M. E., 236n
Magnus, Sir P., 362
Manning, Cardinal H. E., 78n
Mansel, H. L., 13, 143, 156, 164–79, 257n, 309
Mant, Bishop, 180
Marsh, Bishop H., 23, 25
Martineau, H., 191
Martineau, J., 105, 119, 191, 230–3, 276
Mascall, E. L., 334
Mason, A. J., 332, 348
Materialism, *see* naturalism
Matthews, W. R., 175n
Maurice, F. D., 6, 12, 27, 44, 64 Ch. 5 *passim*, Ch. 6 *passim*, 176–9, 201, 217, 256, 261, 262, 276, 277, 294, 320, 338
Maurice, Sir Frederick, 119
Meredith, G., 266
Methodism, 286
Middleton, Bishop T., 23
Mill, J., 184, 198f, 201
Mill, J. S., 43, 118, 165, 176n, 184, 198–208

Miller, H., 243
Milman, H. H., 179–81
Milner, I., 17, 19, 21
Ministerial Priesthood (Moberly), 326
ministry, the Church's, 131
miracles, 160f, 192f, 240f, 288f, 331
Moberly, R. C., 302, 320, 325–8
Moberly, W. H, 327n
Modern Churchmen's Union, 336, 343n
modernism, Catholic, 81n, 110, 322, 360f
Möhler, J. A., 106
Montalembert, C. de, 354
Moore, A., 320, 322–4
moralism, Tractarian, 77–83
More, Hannah, 17
More, Henry, 50
Morley, J., 214n, 362
Morris, W., 21
Moule, Bishop H. C. G., 256, 337
Mozley, J. B., 113f, 119, 137f, 257n, 352, 353
Muirhead, J. H., 53n
Müller, Max, 6, 181, 220
Myers, F., 159
Myers, F. W. H., 159–61, 189
mysticism, 312, 315, 342

Nation, the, 143–5, *see also* Appendix III
'National Apostasy' (Keble's sermon on), 65f
naturalism, 233–6
Naturalism and Agnosticism (Ward), 234
natural theology, 309, 341
Neale, V., 153
Newman, F. W., 184, 191–5
Newman, Cardinal J. H., 17, 20, 31, 32, 40, 42, 64, 66, 67, 69, 70–4, 77, 78, 79, Ch. 4 *passim*, 296, 358
New Testament, Greek (ed. Westcott and Hort), 257f
Newton, Sir I., 211
Newton, J., 17, 20
Noetics, the, 30, 115
Nolan, F., 211
Norris, H. H., 24
Novalis, 278

Oakeley, F. W., 76
Oliphant, Mrs, 295
Oman, J., 317
Origen, 261
Origin of Species, The (Darwin), 13, 106, 132, 214f, 258, 269
Orr, J., 315, 317n
Ottley, R. L., 321, 328
Overton, J., 18
Owen, R., 211, 214

Oxenham, H. N., 358
Oxford Movement, Ch. 3 *passim*

Paget, Bishop F., 321
Paley, W., 3, 47, 210
Palmer, W., 67, 117n, 364n
pardon, 297
Pascal, 52, 92
passibility, divine, 310
Past and Present (Carlyle), 281
Pater, W., 21
Paterson, W. P., 317
Pattison, M., 13, 74, 92n, 181–3, 238, 243–5, 253, 321
Paul, St, 245f, 256, 285f, 288
Pentateuch, the, 254
Pentateuch and Book of Joshua Critically Examined, The (Colenso), 254
Perceval, A. P., 75
Personal Idealism (ed. Stout), 341
Petavius, D. (Petau, D.), 106n
Pfleiderer, O., 294
Philosophy of the Christian Religion, The (Fairbairn), 344
Phillpotts, Bishop H., 351, 352
piety, Evangelical, 18–20
Pius IX, Pope, 355, 359
Place of Christ in Modern Theology, The (Fairbairn), 344
Platonism, 123, 342
Plotinus, 342
Politics for the People, 151f
Porteus, Bishop B., 3, 16
Positivism, 190f *see also* Comte, A., and Spencer, H.
Powell, Baden, 238, 240f, 252f
Practical View of Christianity, A (Wilberforce), 17, 25
prayer (Coleridge on), 52, 54
Priestly, J., 5, 45, 46n
Principles of Church Reform (Arnold), 39f
Principles of Geology, The (Lyell), 211, 269
Prolegomena to Ethics (Green), 225
Prophetical Office of the Church, The (Newman), 69f, 96
Prophets of Israel, The (Smith), 306
Providentissimus Deus (Leo XIII), 265n
punishment, eternal, 136–8
Pusey, E. B., 25, 67, 74, 78, 84, 86, 90f, 165, 264, 318, 352

Quanta Cura (papal encyclical), 359
Quick, O. C., 333

Rainy, Principal, 305

Rambler, The, 356–61
Rashdall, H., 14, 225n, 233, 235, 316, 327n, 333, 340f, 342
Raven, C. E., 150, 338
Realm of Ends, The (Ward), 234
reason (Coleridge on), 48–52, 58
Reform Bill (1832), 65
Reimarus, H., 59
religion,
  comparative study of, 6, 338
  natural and supernatural, 248
religion and culture, 282–4
  and ethics, 287f
  and science, 9f, 54, Ch. 9 *passim*, 227, 240f, 287
Religion of the Semites, The (Smith), 306
Renan, E., 190, 265, 284, 345
Reserve in Communicating Religious Knowledge, On (Williams), 77
revelation, 121, 167f, 173–5, 177–9, 232, 261
Richmond, Legh, 20
Richmond, W., 349
Richter, Jean-Paul, 278
Rigg, J. H., 123
Ripon Hall, 339
Ritschl, A., 8, 235, 309, 311, 316
Robertson, F. W., 159, 161–4
Robinson, Armitage, 259n
Romanes, J. G., 219f
romanticism, 7, 67
Rose, H. J., 24
Rossetti, D. G., 154
Rousseau, J.-J., 7
Ruskin, J., 154, 210
Russell, G. W. G., 19
Ryder, Bishop H., 16

Sabatier, A., 315
sacrifice, 139–42, 334
Sacrifice, The Doctrine of (Maurice), 138, 140
St. Paul and Protestantism (Arnold), 284–6, 289
Sainte-Beuve, 7
sanctification, 84f
Sanday, W., 262, 263, 333, 347
salvation (T. Erskine on), 297f
Sartor Resartus (Carlyle), 280
Sartorius, E., 330n
Schelling, F. W. von., 53f
Schiller, F. C. S., 235
Schiller, Friedrich, 278
Schleiermacher, F. E. D., 7, 64, 245
scholastic philosophy, 33
Scott, T., 20, 79
Sedgwick, A., 211

Seeley, Sir J., 338
'Septem contra Christum', *see Essays and Reviews*
Senancour, E. P. de, 274
seriousness, Evangelical, 19f
Shaftesbury, Lord, *see* Ashley, Lord
Shairp, J. C., 275n
Sharp, G., 17
Shuttleworth, H. C., 155
Sidgwick, H., 183, 220, 223f, 339, 340n
Sikes, T., 24, 25f
Simeon, C., 17
Simpson, R., 112, 356f
sin, original, doctrine of, 113, 126
Smith, Sir G. A., 307
Smith, John, 50
Smith, J. P., 5
Smith, W. Robertson, 6, 15, 304
Smith, V., 181
Socialism, Christian, *see* Christian Socialism
sociology, 223
Soul, The (F. W. Newman), 193
Spencer, H., 175, 184, 189, 220–3, 230, 347n
Spinoza, 208, 209, 286
Stanley, A. P., 78, 114, 181, 237, 245, 246, 252, 275, 338
Statesman's Manual, The (Coleridge), 49
Stephen, J., 17
Stephen, Sir L., 183, 201, 238
Stephenson, J. A., 138n
Sterling, J., 115, 116, 277, 279
Stevens, G. B., 344n
Stevens, W., 24
Storr, V. F., 338
Story, R., 299
Stout, G. F., 235
Strauss, D. F., 5, 13, 132, 172n, 185, 189
Sumner, Archbishop J. B., 76
Sumner, Bishop C. R., 75
Supernatural Religion (Cassels), 257
Sutton, Archbishop Manners, 23
Swete, H. B., 264
Swinburne, A. C., 276
Synthetic Philosophy, 220, 223
System of Logic, A (Mill), 201f

Tait, Archbishop, A. C., 252, 256, 318n
Talbot, Bishop E. S., 320
Taylor, I., 189
Teignmouth, Lord, 17
Temple, Archbishop F., 216, 238f, 253
Temple, Archbishop, W., 333, 337, 348, 361n
temporal power (of the papacy), 358
Tennyson, Alfred Lord, 14, 215n, 266, 268
Test and Corporation Acts, repeal of, 65

Theological Essays (Maurice), 127, 136–42
Thirlwall, Bishop C., 41, 239, 242, 252, 255
Thomasius G., 330n, 345
Thompson, Archbishop, 252
Thompson, Bishop W., 253
Thomson, Dr A., 295, 299
Thornton, H., 17
Tomline, G., 20n
Tract 90 (Newman), 72f, 77
Tractarianism, *see* Oxford Movement
Tracts by Christian Socialists, 152
Tracts for the Times, 67, 70f, 75, 87, 89, 90
Trendelenburg, F., 232
Trilling, L., 286
Trinity, doctrine of the, 309f
Tulloch, J., 294f
Tylor, E. B., 6
Tyndall, J., 219, 230
Types of Ethical Theory (Martineau), 231
Tyrrell, G., 110, 322, 360

Ullathorne, Bishop, 358
Ultramontanism, 355
understanding, the, Coleridge on, 45–51
University Sermons (Newman), 94, 95
unknowable, the, *see* Agnosticism *and*
    Spencer, H.
utilitarianism, 49, 198–200, 201, 202f
Utilitarianism (Mill), 202f

Van Mildert, Bishop W., 20n, 23, 25, 67, 75
Venn, J., 17
Vestiges of the Natural History of Creation
    (Chambers), 213f, 269
Via Media, theory of the, 69f, 96
Vidler, A. R., 116n, 127n
Vincentian Canon, 107
Voltaire, 278

Wace, Dean, 217, 337
Wallace, A. R., 215
Ward, Mrs Humphrey, 266
Ward, J., 233f
Ward, Wilfrid, 82, 94, 354
Ward, William G., 82f, 111–13
Watson, J. J., 23
Watson, Joshua, 75
Watson, Bishop R., 3, 29
Way, the Truth, the Life, The (Hort), 157
Webb, C. C. J., 230
Wellek, R., 50n
Wellhausen, J., 5, 305
Wesley, J., 26, 27
Westbury, Lord, 252
Westcott, Bishop B. F., 14, 157, 216, 256,
    259–62, 272n, 348
Westminster Confession, 299f
Weston, Bishop F., 333
Whately, Archbishop R., 31f
What is Revelation? (Maurice), 165, 176, 178
Whichcote, B., 261
White, W. H. (Mark Rutherford), 209, 267
Wilberforce, R., 168n
Wilberforce, Bishop S., 216, 237, 251n, 252,
    253
Wilberforce, W., 17, 18, 19, 21, 126n
will, Coleridge on the, 45f
Williams, I., 77, 80, 89
Williams, R., 238, 239f
Wilson, H. B., 238, 242, 251n
Winkelmann, E., 50n
Wiseman, Cardinal N., 354
Wordsworth, Bishop C., 24
Wordsworth, W., 11, 266–8, 278
Working Men's College, 154
Wright, T., 302, 304